The Handbook of Children, Media, and Development

D1308192

Handbooks in Communication and Media

This series aims to provide theoretically ambitious but accessible volumes devoted to the major fields and subfields within communication and media studies. Each volume sets out to ground and orientate the student through a broad range of specially commissioned chapters, while also providing the more experienced scholar and teacher with a convenient and comprehensive overview of the latest trends and critical directions.

The Handbook of Children, Media, and Development, *edited by Sandra L. Calvert and Barbara J. Wilson*

The Handbook of Crisis Communication, *edited by W. Timothy Coombs and Sherry J. Holladay*

The Handbook of Internet Studies, *edited by Mia Consalvo and Charles Ess*

The Handbook of Rhetoric and Public Address, *edited by Shawn J. Parry-Giles and J. Michael Hogan*

The Handbook of Critical Intercultural Communication, *edited by Thomas K. Nakayama and Rona Tamiko Halualani*

The Handbook of Global Communication and Media Ethics, *edited by Robert S. Fortner and P. Mark Fackler*

Forthcoming

The Handbook of Global Research Methods, *edited by Ingrid Volkmer*

The Handbook of International Advertising Research, *edited by Hong Cheng*

The Handbook of Communication and Corporate Social Responsibility, *edited by Oyvind Ihlen, Jennifer Bartlett and Steve May*

The Handbook of Gender and Sexualities in the Media, *edited by Karen Ross*

The Handbook of Global Health Communication and Development, *edited by Rafael Obregon and Silvio Waisbord*

The Handbook of Global Online Journalism, *edited by Eugenia Siapera and Andreas Veglis*

The Handbook of Children, Media, and Development

Edited by

Sandra L. Calvert and Barbara J. Wilson

A John Wiley & Sons, Ltd., Publication

Library of Congress Cataloging-in-Publication Data
The handbook of children, media, and development / edited by Sandra L. Calvert & Barbara J. Wilson.
        p. cm.
   Includes bibliographical references and index.
   ISBN 978-1-4051-4417-9 (hardcover : alk. paper)
   ISBN 978-1-4443-3694-8 (pbk : alk. paper)   1. Mass media and children.
2. Child development.   3. Children's mass media.   I. Calvert, Sandra L.
II. Wilson, Barbara J.

   HQ784.M3H26 2008
   302.23083—dc22

                                                                2008009039

A catalogue record for this book is available from the British Library.

Set in 10/13pt Galliard by Graphicraft Limited, Hong Kong.
Printed and bound in Malaysia by Vivar Printing Sdn Bhd

01   2011

Dedicated to
Cheryl, Lee, and Mary Ann
and
John, Bob, and Joan

Contents

Notes on Editors and Contributors

Sandra L. Calvert is Chair and Professor of the Department of Psychology at Georgetown University and the Director of the Children's Digital Media Center (http://cdmc.georgetown.edu), a multi-site interdisciplinary research center funded by the National Science Foundation (2001–11; BCS-0126014 and BCS-0623871) and the Stuart Family Foundation. Dr Calvert authored *Children's Journeys through the Information Age* (1999), and co-edited *Children in the Digital Age: Influences of Electronic Media on Development* (2002). She has served on two committees for the National Academies, leading to two committee co-authored books: *Food Marketing to Children and Youth: Threat or Opportunity* (2006) and *Youth, Pornography, and the Internet* (2002). Dr Calvert, who received her doctorate in Developmental and Child Psychology from the University of Kansas, is a fellow of the American Psychological Association. She serves on advisory boards for Cable in the Classroom, PBS Kids Next Generation Media, and the Joan Ganz Cooney Center for Educational Media and Research. She provides technical assistance to Congress in the development of the Children and Media Research Advancement Act (CAMRA). She has also consulted for Nickelodeon Online, Sesame Workplace, *Blue's Clues*, and Out of the Blue Enterprises.

Barbara J. Wilson is the Paul C. Friedland Professorial Scholar and Head of the Department of Communication at the University of Illinois at Urbana-Champaign. Her research focuses on the social and psychological effects of the mass media, particularly on youth. She is co-author of *Children, Adolescents, and the Media* (2002; second edition, in press) and three book volumes of the *National Television Violence Study* (1997–8). In addition, she has published more than 60 scholarly articles and chapters on media effects and their implications for media policy. Recent projects focus on preschoolers' attachment to media characters, parents' and children's fright reactions to kidnapping stories in the news, and children's attraction to media violence. She has served as a research consultant for Nickelodeon, the National Association of Television Program Executives, Discovery Channel Pictures, and the Centers for Disease Control and Prevention.

Alison Alexander (PhD, Ohio State University) is Professor and Senior Associate Dean for academic affairs at the Grady College of Journalism and Mass Communication at the University of Georgia. She was editor of the *Journal of Broadcasting and Electronic Media*, and is past President of the Association for Communication Administration, and the Eastern Communication Association. Her work focuses on children and media. She is the author of numerous book chapters and journal articles, and the co-editor of four books. She was named the 1998 Frank Stanton Fellow by the International Radio and Television Society for "outstanding contribution to broadcast education."

Daniel R. Anderson received his PhD from Brown University and is Professor of Psychology at the University of Massachusetts at Amherst. He has published numerous research articles concerning children's use of television and its impact, especially the cognitive aspects (attention and comprehension while watching television, impact on intellectual development and school achievement). His current research concerns the impact of television on infants and toddlers. Professor Anderson has worked extensively with television networks and production companies concerning the development of educational television programs including *Sesame Street, Allegra's Window, Gullah Gullah Island, The Wubbulous World of Dr Seuss, Blue's Clues, Bear in the Big Blue House, Dora the Explorer, The Fimbles* (BBC), *Go, Diego Go, It's a Big Big World*, and *Super Why*. He serves on numerous advisory boards in organizations concerned with children and media.

Rachel Barr, PhD, is an Assistant Professor at Georgetown University. She is currently the Director of the Georgetown Early Learning Project studying how infants learn from television, computers, or books and how the home environment influences such learning. She received her PhD in developmental psychology from the University of Otago, New Zealand, and completed a post-doctoral fellowship at Rutgers University before moving to Georgetown University in 2001.

David S. Bickham, PhD, was trained at the Center for Research on Interactive Technology, Television, and Children at the University of Texas at Austin where he studied with Aletha Huston, John Wright, Ellen Wartella, and Elizabeth Vandewater. His work ranges from an examination of the effects of the television rating system on children's viewing preferences to an exploration of the academic outcomes linked to children's educational and non-educational media use. Currently, he is developing an integrated model of the social effects of exposure to violent and non-violent television and videogames.

Dina L. G. Borzekowski, (EdD, Harvard, 1994), is an internationally recognized expert in the area of children, media, and health. She is a faculty member at the Johns Hopkins Bloomberg School of Public Health in the Department of Health, Behavior and Society. Borzekowski's research involves studying how youth come to use media and how media has an impact on children and adolescents. Besides conducting high-quality research, Borzekowski takes pride in the teaching and advising awards she has received in working with Hopkins students interested in Health Communication.

Amy Branner, PhD, received a BA in Sociology and Interdisciplinary Studies at the University of Missouri-Columbia under the guidance of Mary Jo Neitz and Peter Hall. She then moved to the Annenberg Public Policy Center where she worked with Larry Gross and Amy Jordan. She now serves as the Research Manager for the Children's Media Use Study, a collaborative project between RTI International and the Centers for Disease Control and Prevention which examines how to reduce media use and sedentary behaviors.

Jane D. Brown (PhD, Wisconsin-Madison, 1977), is the James L. Knight Professor in the School of Journalism and Mass Communication at the University of North Carolina at Chapel Hill. Her research focuses on the uses and effects of the media on adolescents' health, including early sexual activity, aggressive behavior, and tobacco and alcohol use. She is the co-author or co-editor of four books about the effects of the media on children and adolescents, including *Sexual Teens, Sexual Media* (2002).

Moniek Buijzen (PhD, 2003) is an Associate Professor in the Amsterdam School of Communications Research, ASCoR, at the University of Amsterdam. Her research interests include adult mediation of children's responses to the media, parent–child communication about consumer decisions, and the intended and unintended effects of advertising on children. In 2003 she received a prestigious three-year Veni award for talented junior researchers from the Dutch National Science Foundation (NWO). Buijzen has received several awards from the International Communication Association.

Alice Cahn is Vice President of Programming and Development for Cartoon Network daytime. Prior to joining Cartoon Network, she served as a Managing Director of the Markle Foundation where she headed the Interactive Media for Children Program. Cahn came to Markle from Children's Television Workshop (now Sesame Workshop) where she served as President of the Television, Film, and Video group. Prior to that, she was Director of Children's Programming at the Public Broadcasting Service (PBS). Cahn did her master's degree work in Educational Technology at San Francisco State University and holds a Bachelor of Science in Education from New York University.

Jennifer L. Chakroff (MA, Michigan State University) is a doctoral candidate in the School of Communication at The Ohio State University. Her research interests include the social and psychological effects of the mass media on children. In particular, she studies how parental mediation may mitigate the negative effects of television including the harmful effects of violent television and the unintended effects of advertising.

Hope M. Cummings is a graduate student in the Department of Communication Studies at the University of Michigan. Her research interest addresses the relationships between media and technology and human development across the lifespan. She is a Rackham Merit Fellow and a member of the Research Center for Group Dynamics at the Institute for Social Research. She is currently working under the supervision of Elizabeth Vandewater at the University of Texas at Austin, L. Rowell Huesmann, and Brad Bushman.

Douglas A. Gentile, PhD, is a developmental psychologist, and is Assistant Professor of Psychology at Iowa State University and the Director of Research for the National Institute on Media and the Family. As the Director of the Media Research Laboratory at Iowa State University, he is one of the country's leading researchers of media's impacts on children and adults (both positive and negative). Dr Gentile has authored numerous studies and is the editor of the book *Media Violence and Children: A Complete Guide for Parents and Professionals* (2003) and co-author of the book *Violent Video Game Effects on Children and Adolescents: Theory, Research, and Public Policy* (2007). His research has been reported widely in outlets such as National Public Radio's *Morning Edition*, NBC's *Today Show*, the *New York Times*, *Washington Post, Los Angeles Times*, and *USA Today*. He received his doctorate in child psychology from the Institute of Child Development at the University of Minnesota.

Bradley S. Greenberg is University Distinguished Professor Emeritus of Communication and Telecommunication, Information Studies, and Media at Michigan State University. Dr Greenberg's research career has centered on the social effects of contemporary mass media on children, adolescents, and adults.

Patricia Greenfield received her PhD from Harvard University and is currently Professor of Psychology at UCLA, where she directs the FPR-UCLA Center for Culture, Brain, and Development and the UCLA site of the Children's Digital Media Center. Her central theoretical and research interest is in the relationship between culture and human development. She is a past recipient of the American Association for the Advancement of Science Award for Behavioral Science Research, and has received teaching awards from UCLA and the American Psychological Association. She has held fellowships at the Bunting Institute, Radcliffe College, the School of American Research, Santa Fe, and the Center for Advanced Study in the Behavioral Sciences, Stanford. Her books include *Mind and Media: The Effects of Television, Video Games, and Computers* (1984), which has been translated into nine languages. In the 1990s she co-edited (with R. R. Cocking) *Interacting with Video* (1996) and *Cross-Cultural Roots of Minority Child Development* (1994). She has done field research on child development, social change, and weaving apprenticeship in Chiapas, Mexico, since 1969. This cumulative work is presented in a book entitled *Weaving Generations Together* (2004). Her research program includes basic and applied cross-cultural projects in Los Angeles, as well as cross-species and neural investigations linking the ontogeny and phylogeny of cultural processes in language and cognition.

Kristen Harrison (PhD, University of Wisconsin-Madison) is Associate Professor in the Department of Communication at the University of Illinois at Urbana-Champaign. She studies mass communication processes and effects, with an emphasis on child and adolescent health. The bulk of her research explores the role of the media in shaping children's self-perceptions, body image, eating behaviors, and conceptions of nutrition.

Veronica Hefner (MA, University of Illinois, Urbana-Champaign) is a doctoral student studying mass communication processes and effects. She is particularly interested in exploring the intersection between media effects and interpersonal communication. She plans to devote her dissertation to the study of romantic-ideal media effects on young adults' romantic expectations and perceptions.

Cynthia Hoffner (PhD, University of Wisconsin-Madison) is an Associate Professor in the Department of Communication, Georgia State University. Her research focuses on media uses and effects. Specific research areas have included children's and adults' emotional reactions to media entertainment and news, parasocial attachments to media characters, and the third-person effect.

Stacey J. T. Hust (PhD. 2005, University of North Carolina at Chapel Hill) is Assistant Professor of Communication in the Edward R. Murrow School of Communication at Washington State University. Her research explores whether the mass media can be used for health promotion through strategies such as entertainment education and media advocacy. As a health communication scholar, Hust studies the media's effects on sexual and reproductive health and adolescents' alcohol, tobacco, and drug use. Her work has been published in *Journal of Health Communication, Health Communication, Journal of International Advertising, Women and Health Journal,* and *Mass Communication and Society.*

Aletha C. Huston is the Pricilla Pond Flawn Regents Professor of Child Development, the Co-Director of the Center for Research on Interactive Technology, Television, and Children (CRITC), and the Associate Director of the Population Research Center at the University of Texas at Austin. She currently specializes in understanding the effects of poverty on children and the impact of childcare and income support policies on children's development. She is a Principal Investigator in the New Hope Project, a study of the effects on children and families of parents' participation in a work-based program to reduce poverty, and collaborator in the Next Generation Project, a cross-study investigation of childcare, income, and employment effects of welfare and employment policies. She is an Investigator for the National Institute of Child Health and Human Development Study of Early Child Care and Youth Development, a longitudinal study following a national sample of children from birth through middle childhood. Her books include *Children in Poverty: Child Development and Public Policy, Big World, Small Screen: The Role of Television in American Society,* and *Developmental Contexts of Middle Childhood: Bridges to Adolescence and Adulthood.* She is past President of the Society for Research in Child Development and has won numerous research awards, including the Urie Bronfenbrenner Award for Lifetime Contributions to Developmental Psychology, the Nicholas Hobbs award for Research and Child Advocacy, and the SRCD award for contributions to Child Development and Public Policy.

Joah G. Iannotta is a Senior Policy Analyst in the US Government Accountability Office (GAO). Her work at GAO has covered a broad range of topics, including child welfare, national adoption policy, and transportation issues such as fuel economy standards. Prior to GAO, she was a Research Associate at the National Academy of Sciences and completed her PhD at the University of Minnesota. Iannotta completed her master's degree at Smith College and received a BA from Wesleyan University.

Terry Kalagian is president of Kalagian Productions, a US-based television and media consulting company. In this role, she assists both US and international entertainment companies in developing, acquiring, and producing new properties for both the children and non-children audience. Prior to this, she spent over 10 years with Cartoon Network US in varying capacities from heading up research to programming, scheduling, acquiring and co-producing for the network. Kalagian came to Cartoon Network with several years of agency and local television affiliate experience. Kalagian earned a Master of Business Administration degree from Fontbonne College and a Bachelor's degree in Business Administration from National University.

Heather L. Kirkorian received her PhD in Developmental Psychology from the University of Massachusetts at Amherst. Her dissertation was the first in a series of studies on children's eye movements during video viewing. Currently she is a post-doctoral fellow at the University of Massachusetts. Her research interests include young children's attention to and comprehension of video and the impact of television on cognitive development and parent–child interaction.

Catherine Lyon is a children's media development consultant in Alexandria, Virginia. Her clients include commercial and public broadcasters in the US and abroad. Previously, she was the Associate Director of Children's Programming at the Public Broadcasting Service. She holds a BA in Theology from Georgetown University and an MA in Applied Developmental Psychology from George Mason University.

Marie-Louise Mares is an Assistant Professor in the Department of Communication Arts at the University of Wisconsin-Madison. Her research interests focus on the interface between media and cognitive and socio-emotional development across the lifespan. With regard to children, she is interested in the role of comprehension in children's responses to prosocial television content.

Dana E. Mastro (PhD, Michigan State University) is an Associate Professor in the Department of Communication at the University of Arizona. Her research documents depictions of race/ethnicity in the media and assesses the extent to which exposure to these images influences stereotyping and racial/ethnic cognitions as well as a variety of intergroup and identity-based outcomes.

Emily J. Moyer-Guse is currently a PhD candidate in the Communication Department at the University of California, Santa Barbara. She received her MA in Communication at Michigan State University. Her research focuses on mass media effects on individuals, with a particular emphasis on youth and the cognitive, emotional, and developmental processes that underlie these effects. More specifically, she is interested in how young people's emotions, attitudes, health-risk behaviors, and well-being can be affected by the mass media.

Amy I. Nathanson (PhD, University of Wisconsin) is an Associate Professor of Communication at The Ohio State University. She studies the uses and effects of television among children. In particular, she investigates the role of parental mediation in mitigating some of the harmful effects of television on children. Her work has appeared in outlets such as *Communication Research, Human Communication Research, Journal of Broadcasting and Electronic Media, Journal of Communication*, and *Media Psychology*.

Edward Palmer is Wayne M. and Carolyn A. Watson Professor of Psychology at Davidson College. He has been a Visiting Scholar at Harvard University's Center for Research in Children's Television, UCLA, the University of North Carolina at Chapel Hill, the University of Exeter (United Kingdom), and the College of Communication at the University of Alabama. His professional works include *Children and the Faces of Television: Teaching, Violence, Selling* (with Aimee Dorr); *Children in the Cradle of Television*; *GRE: Psychology* (with Sharon Thompson-Schill); *Faces of Televisual Media: Teaching, Violence, Selling to Children* (with Brian Young); "Food and beverage marketing to children and youth: Trends and issues" (with Courtney Carpenter); and several other research articles and book chapters in the children's televisual media field. He served on the American Psychological Association's Task Force on Advertising and Children, authoring their report on commercialism in schools. He is a member of Phi Beta Kappa, the American Psychological Association, the American Psychological Society, Southeastern Psychological Association, and the Society for the Psychological Study of Social Issues.

Katherine M. Pieper (MA, University of Southern California) is a PhD candidate at the University of Southern California. Her research interests include the effects of the mass media on children and the use of media for health and social change. She currently works as a Partnership Coordinator for World Relief Cambodia.

Michael Rich, MD, MPH, is founder and Director of the Center on Media and Child Health at the Children's Hospital Boston. The Center pursues research, develops interventions on negative health effects of media, and creates health-positive media. Dr Rich is an Assistant Professor of Pediatrics at Harvard Medical School, Assistant Professor in Society, Human Development, and Health at the Harvard School of Public Health, and practices adolescent medicine at Children's Hospital Boston. As a leading pediatrician addressing the issue of media effects on children's health, he has authored or co-authored four policy statements on that topic for the American Academy of Pediatrics, presented to decision-makers in the fields of media production and healthcare, and testified numerous times before the United States Congress, various state legislatures, and city governments. Dr Rich was honored by the Society for Adolescent Medicine with their New Investigator Award for developing Video Intervention/Prevention Assessment, which explores the illness experience through patient-created visual illness narratives. He also received the prestigious Holroyd-Sherry Award from the American Academy of Pediatrics for his contributions to children, adolescents, and the media.

Ronda Scantlin is an Assistant Professor in the Department of Communication at the University of Dayton, in Dayton, Ohio. Her teaching and scholarship focus on mass media effects, media policy, and family communication. One area of specialization includes examining how children and adolescents use media in their daily lives and how that use influences their development. Prior to holding the position at the University of Dayton, Scantlin completed a post-doctoral fellowship at the Annenberg Public Policy Center at the University of Pennsylvania, during which time she was a member of the research team examining the impact of V-Chip technology on dynamics within the family and on children's viewing. She received her BA in Psychology from Bethany College, MA in Human Development from the University of Kansas, and PhD in Child Development and Family Relationships from the University of Texas at Austin.

Marie Evans Schmidt, PhD, began studying the effects of media on children as an undergraduate at Georgetown University, where she worked with Sandra Calvert. After graduating magna cum laude from Georgetown with a BA in Psychology and English, she received a PhD in Developmental Psychology from the University of Massachusetts at Amherst, under the mentorship of Dan Anderson. She has served as an Assistant Professor of Cognitive Development at Hampshire College and as a consultant to Sesame Workshop. Her research interests include: preschoolers' understanding and use of symbolic media, the effects of television on infants and toddlers' cognitive development, how environmental factors like media exposure influence the development of attention in children, and the development of interventions on unhealthy media use by very young children.

Dorothy G. Singer is Senior Research Scientist, Department of Psychology, Yale University. She is also Co-Director, with Jerome L. Singer, of the Yale University Family Television Research and Consultation Center. An expert on early childhood development, television effects on youth, and parent training in imaginative play, she has written 20 books and over 150 articles. Dr Singer is a Fellow of the American Psychological Association (APA), and received the award for Distinguished Scientific Contributions to the Media by Division 46 of the APA in 2004. She received the Distinguished Alumni Award from Teachers College, Columbia University, in 2006.

Jerome L. Singer received his doctorate in Clinical Psychology from the University of Pennsylvania. He is Professor Emeritus of Psychology at Yale University, where he served for many years as Director of the Graduate Program in Clinical Psychology and also as Director of Graduate Studies in Psychology. Dr Singer has authored more than 270 technical articles on thought processes, imagery, personality, and psychotherapy as well as on children's play and the effects of television. He is a past President of the Eastern Psychological Association. He is also a past President of the APA Division of Personality and Social Psychology and the APA Division of Psychology of Aesthetics, Creativity, and the Arts.

Stacy L. Smith (PhD, University of California, Santa Barbara, 1999) is an Associate Professor of Entertainment at the Annenberg School for Communication at the University of Southern California. Her research interests include examining media content patterns and effects, with a particular focus on children and their understanding of and reactions to different types of messages (i.e., portrayals of violence, hypersexualization). She has published over 40 journal articles and book chapters, with her work appearing in the *Journal of Communication, Communication Research, Media Psychology*, and the *Journal of Broadcasting and Electronic Media*.

Victor C. Strasburger (MD, Harvard Medical School, 1975) is Professor of Pediatrics, Professor of Family and Community Medicine, and Chief of the Division of Adolescent Medicine at the University of New Mexico School of Medicine. He is the author of eight books and more than 120 peer-reviewed articles, reviews, and book chapters on adolescent medicine and effects of media on children and adolescents, including *Children, Adolescents, and the Media* (with Barbara Wilson and Amy Jordan, 2008).

Kaveri Subrahmanyam is a Professor of Psychology at California State University, Los Angeles, and the Associate Director of the Children's Digital Media Center at the UCLA site. She received her PhD in Developmental Psychology from UCLA in 1993. She studies youth and digital media and uses developmental theory to understand the effects of their interactions with these new media forms. She has examined a variety of digital media including computer/videogames and Internet communication forms such as chat rooms, blogs, and social networking sites. She is currently studying adolescent use of blogs and social networking sites such as MySpace and Facebook.

Tia Sullivan graduated from Furman University with a BS in Psychology. She was a recipient of the Furman Advantage Summer Research Fellowship and worked with Edward Palmer to investigate the child-based effects of prosocial media. She is a member of the Psi Chi and Alpha Epsilon Delta National Honor Societies and received a Psi Chi regional research award in May 2006 for her work on self-presentation. She currently works as a research assistant investigating public education in South Carolina for the Riley Institute's Center for Education Policy and Leadership. She also works as a counselor in a residential treatment facility that encourages behavior modification among 6–13-year-old children.

Michael Robb is a doctoral student in Psychology at the University of California, Riverside. His research focuses on the impact of electronic media on very young children.

Patti M. Valkenburg is a Professor in the Amsterdam School of Communications Research, ASCoR, and Director of CAM, the center of research on Children, Adolescents, and the Media at the University of Amsterdam, http://www2.fmg.uva.nl/cam/. Her research interests include children's likes and dislikes of entertainment, their development as consumers, and the cognitive, emotional, and/or social effects of television, advertising, computer games, and the Internet on children and adolescents. In 2003, she received a five-year Vici award for talented senior researchers from the Dutch National Science Foundation (NWO) to form a research group and investigate the social implications of the Internet for children and adolescents.

Elizabeth A. Vandewater is Director of the Children and Media Research Center, Associate Director of the Population Research Center, and Associate Professor of Human Development and Family Sciences at the University of Texas at Austin. Her research interests include the impact of media and technology on children's health outcomes and health behaviors, particularly obesity. She is currently conducting research on the developmental linkages between media use and obesity across childhood and adolescence funded by the William T. Grant Foundation and the National Institute of Child Health and Human Development.

Ellen Wartella is the Executive Vice Chancellor and Provost and Distinguished Professor of Psychology at the University of California Riverside. Dr Wartella earned her PhD in Mass Communication from the University of Minnesota in 1977 and completed her post-doctoral research in development psychology in 1981 at the University of Kansas. Dr Wartella, a leading scholar of the role of media in children's development, was a Co-Principal Investigator on the National TV Violence Study (1995–8) and is currently Co-Principal Investigator of the Children's Digital Media Center project funded by the National Science Foundation (2001–11). She serves on the Kraft Food Global Health and Wellness Advisory Council, the Decade of Behavior National Advisory Board, the Board of Trustees of the Sesame Workshop, the National Educational Advisory Board of the Children's Advertising Review Unit of the Better Business Bureaus, and the National Academy of Sciences Board on Children Youth and Families. She recently served on the Institute of Medicine's Panel Study on Food Marketing and the Diets of Children and Youth (2006). She is a member of the American Psychological Association and the Society for Research in Child Development and she is a past President of the International Communication Association.

Brian Young is an economic psychologist in the School of Psychology at the University of Exeter. He has published extensively in the area of children and advertising with several books such as *Television Advertising and Children* (1990) and, most recently, *The Faces of Televisual Media: Teaching, Violence, Selling to Children* (co-edited with E. L. Palmer; 2nd edn., 2003). He has also published extensively in academic journals. He is the Editor of *Young Consumers* which covers economic and consumer socialization of children, and marketing to children. He teaches courses in developmental and consumer psychology to undergraduate and postgraduate students at the University of Exeter.

Foreword

Aletha C. Huston

Over the past 100 years, as Ellen Wartella and Michael Robb point out in this volume, scholars and social pundits have reacted to every new set of media with a mixture of panic and optimism about potential influences on children. Radio and film each generated some research and social commentary, but the advent of television in the 1950s ushered in a new level of media pervasiveness in children's lives and the first wave of solid, theoretically-based research on the topic. In the 1960s through the 1980s, psychologists and communication scholars forged a field that spanned disciplines as they examined the effects of both the formal features and content of the media that children were using several hours a day. In the last 15 or 20 years, media forms have proliferated, with new technologies transforming how children and adolescents use media as well as blurring the old distinctions among telephones, computers, television sets, radio, and records.

The chapters in this volume represent the state-of-the-art knowledge about young people's media use and the roles that media play in their lives. Despite the dramatic technological changes of the last several years, many of themes are familiar from earlier work. One of the fundamental tensions throughout the years has been form versus content. Some theorists have emphasized the importance of the qualities of the medium itself (e.g., visual versus auditory, interactive versus unidirectional); others have argued that content messages have similar effects across different forms of presentation. These questions about form and content remain central to the research presented in this book.

Many content issues are perennial and familiar, including the effects of violence, sexually explicit material, social stereotypes, and advertising on aggression, fear, imagination, and beliefs about the social world. The potential for positive effects of prosocial and educational content continues to be supported by evidence as well. Health concerns have increased considerably, as indicated by a whole section devoted to research on health effects, much of which is inspired by the obesity epidemic and societal awareness of the role of social influences on young people's health behavior. Chapters on attention and learning, cognitive processing of media symbol systems, and learning from educational media have ancestors in earlier media research. In each case, the new work described here has advanced our understanding of the processes and issues involved, but the continuity with the past is nonetheless striking. These topics represent important, fundamental questions that form the core of efforts to understand young people's uses of media and the ways in which their thinking, behavior, and lives are influenced by those media.

In the past several years, media forms have expanded, proliferated, and morphed at a startling rate, opening up new uses and functions. Some of the most striking changes are the increase in user agency and control and the increasing opportunity for interactivity. Media devices are now small and portable, making them available for filling time while waiting in line, traveling from place to place, or just sitting. When television was the dominant entertainment medium, the viewer was exposed to a world "out there," whether it was fictional stories or real-life events. These functions have not disappeared, as evidenced by young people's devotion to favorite comedy and drama series, but the newer media offer opportunities for developing and expanding one's own internal identities and thoughts, interacting with individual friends or family, and interacting with groups in cyberspace. The chapter on parasocial and online relationships presents what we have learned about these functions. The Internet, cell phones, and text messaging have become integral parts of young people's social interactions, and we are just beginning to understand how such mediated relationships may or may not be similar to face-to-face interactions. The first wave of social commentary about these new media functions was predictable – fears about children being exposed to predators or exploitation through the Internet along with optimism about children being able to find compatible friends and activities across cyberspace, but the chapters in this book indicate that research has begun to move beyond such simplistic formulations.

Media studies of children have always straddled the boundaries between basic research on developmental processes on the one hand and policy and practice on the other. Many of the policy and practice issues have remained stubbornly similar over the years, in part because media are big business, particularly in the United States. The chapter on business models goes beyond the "bad" business image to consider a variety of modes for producing and distributing children's media. Several chapters on policy and interventions, however, remind us of some intractable issues, both old and new. It has long been clear that government regulation can play a minor role at best in protecting children from inappropriate content. Government has more potential to promote high-quality positive media content through requirements imposed on broadcasters (e.g., the Educational Children's Television Act) and through funding production, though neither of these options is used extensively in the United States, largely because of the absence of political will to do so.

Educating viewers in media literacy and related skills is one solution outside government, but our overall progress in maximizing the positive and minimizing the negative effects of media is discouraging. The reasons are undoubtedly complex, but I believe that part of the problem is that, at some level, researchers and the public alike trivialize media. Although there is periodic public outrage about violence, sex, or Internet predators, most adults do not consider television and other media to be sufficiently serious that they are willing to modify their own use (e.g., to limit children's exposure) or to support the use of their tax dollars to alter the menu of content available. Both research and policy on media are in isolated silos. Discussions of poverty and children, for example, invoke a range of social contexts including family environments, neighborhoods, schools, childcare, and after-school programs, but virtually never mention media despite the fact that children in low-income families use television and other media extensively. Similarly, education policies focus on school climate and curriculum, family environments, access to libraries, and the like, but almost never include media – educational or otherwise. Media are important components of children's social ecology; their role could be understood and expanded if scholars and policy makers integrated them into these larger social discussions. Maybe the next handbook will contain some progress on this front.

In summary, this handbook represents the state of our current knowledge about media, demonstrating both how far we have come and how many questions remain. The authors are to be congratulated for a comprehensive and balanced presentation of theory, research, policy, and applied issues. It is an excellent source summarizing scholarship in depth in a readable form.

Acknowledgments

We gratefully thank the following people who gave generously of their time to make this handbook possible. Tiffany Pempek assisted us in organizing, proofing, and providing support in all phases needed to get the final materials completed. Samantha Goodrich, Yevdokiya Yermolayeva, Alexis Lauricella, Mary Katherine Ciccodicola, Lisa Alvy, Natasha Birnbaum, Joanne Hathaway, Catherine Lally, and Amber Hornick also worked on various tasks that assisted us as we completed this handbook.

Sandra L. Calvert
Barbara J. Wilson

Introduction: Media and Children's Development

Sandra L. Calvert and Barbara J. Wilson

From the beginnings of life, children in the twenty-first century typically develop in front of a screen (Wartella & Robb, Chapter 1). Once solely television based, these screen media have now evolved to be digital, interactive, pervasive, and increasingly under the control of those who use them. Media continue to advance rapidly, making it challenging for scholars to keep pace with the rate of adaptation and adoption of technologies in children's lives. This handbook is an effort to address the role of digital media in children's development at this point in time, and to place media in context with what we know from the past as well as what we expect as we look forward to the future.

In this handbook, experts in the interdisciplinary field of children and the media bring their diverse perspectives to bear on the range of topics associated with young people's media experiences. The handbook is divided into six sections. Part I addresses the historical and financial underpinnings of children's media. In Part II, access patterns as a function of viewer qualities and family constellations are considered. Part III focuses on the cognitive influences of media. Social influences of media are examined in Part IV. Media and health issues are the topic of Part V. We end with a discussion of media and policy issues in Part VI. Chapters are designed to be concise overviews of a rapidly changing field. Because so much of the research has strong interdisciplinary roots, our authors come from the fields of psychology, communication, health, and business. Each chapter brings major theoretical paradigms to bear on the literature, including uses and gratifications theory, social cognitive theory, cognitive developmental theory, cultivation theory, and social identity theory. Indeed, many theories can and have been used to understand the role that media play in children's development.

The empirical literature is rich in places, but sparse in others. Although there is a vast literature on how observational screen media affect preschool-aged children, how screen exposure affects the early development of infants and toddlers is a major source of controversy. Organizations such as the American Academy of Pediatrics recommend that very early development should be based solely in experiences with live adults (Evans Schmidt et al., Chapter 22). Others, by contrast, argue that screen media, with their audio-visual representational devices, are ideally suited for how young children think in visual, iconic forms of thought (Subrahmanyam & Greenfield, Chapter 8). Still others find that background media content made for adults is detrimental to development (Kirkorian & Anderson, Chapter 9; Barr, Chapter 7), but that the verdict is still out on foreground programs made for a child audience (Barr, Chapter 7). One point is perfectly clear: screen media are now the normative experience in Western cultures, and there will be no turning back.

As each new cohort has emerged, time spent with media has increased. Indeed, media are now so pervasive that youth multitask as they divide their time and attention across many different windows and media simultaneously (Scantlin, Chapter 3).

Time spent with media, however, is only part of the story. Indeed, the content is the story, beginning with the cultural messages beamed into children's living rooms and learned within the context of the family (Alexander, Chapter 6). Content drives interest and it also drives the types of learning that take place for infants, children, and youth. Although toddlers have difficulty transferring the representations that they view on a screen to real-life situations, under certain circumstances even babies can imitate the behaviors that they see others perform on a screen (Barr, Chapter 7). For children, exposure to violent content involves harmful outcomes such as increased aggression (Wilson, Chapter 11), increased fear (Smith, Pieper, & Moyer-Guse, Chapter 10; Valkenburg & Buijzen, Chapter 15), and reductions in imagination (Singer & Singer, Chapter 13). Exposure to typical media content can also lead to increased stereotypical beliefs and behaviors (Greenberg & Mastro, Chapter 4; Hust & Brown, Chapter 5), increased obesity (Vandewater & Cummings, Chapter 16), and increased materialism (Young, Chapter 18). By contrast, exposure to prosocial content yields constructive outcomes like increased helping and sharing (Mares, Palmer, & Sullivan, Chapter 12), and exposure to educational content yields long-term cognitive benefits (Kirkorian & Anderson, Chapter 9). With development, children increasingly create their own online content through blogs, online diaries, social networks, and other digital forms of expression. Thus, the cultural stories created by others are increasingly displaced by each child's own unique story.

As digital devices become smaller and better integrated, cell phones and future iPods can serve as around-the-clock links to peers and families. As youth walk down the street or drive in their cars, they are connected to, and at home in, a digital world that they use to communicate with others, to explore who they are, and to play with one another in spaces that are not confined to the here and now. Music, television programs, and movies are downloaded and played on demand. Youth construct their own language systems, creating forms of Internet speak that allow them to communicate at the speed of talking while sending text messages or instant messages to one another through abbreviated language codes such as "u" for "you" and "brb" for "be right back" (Subrahmanyam & Greenfield,

Chapter 8). Although documented effects of newer digital media are emerging, much more research remains to be done in this area.

Who children are – that is, their personal and social identity – plays an important role in what they learn from media (Hoffner, Chapter 14). Gender, ethnicity, and age all influence what children take away from media experiences, in part because children tune into the characters they see and the people with whom they interact. Indeed, the very nature of relationships is shifting due to media experiences. For example, if children think they are interacting with a cartoon character, known as a parasocial interaction, does it influence them in the same way that face-to-face interactions do? If an adolescent pretends to be someone else online, even altering his or her own gender, does it change who that adolescent becomes? These are questions yet to be answered, but grappling with such issues is fundamental to our understanding of developmental outcomes in the twenty-first century.

Because media are such a pervasive aspect of children's daily lives, it is not surprising that there are serious health concerns surrounding this topic. The obesity epidemic that currently influences many youth and their families in Western cultures can be partly explained by media use, particularly exposure to advertising (Vandewater & Cummings, Chapter 16). Similarly, eating disorders are explained in part by exposure to very thin media models; in fact, youth can readily find groups to acerbate their eating problems via online websites that support anorexic behaviors (Harrison & Hefner, Chapter 17). Drug, tobacco, and alcohol exposure leads to addictive behaviors that can set a trajectory for lifelong health risks. Although there have been some government efforts to curtail exposure to media portrayals of alcohol, tobacco, and drugs, access to these substances via online websites remains readily available (Borzekowski & Strasburger, Chapter 19).

Government policies in the media area have made some progress in improving the media experiences of youth. The Children's Television Act, for instance, requires commercial broadcasters in the United States to provide educational and informational programming for children and also limits the amount of commercial advertising that can take place during children's television programming (Calvert, Chapter 20). Efforts have been made to control exposure to sexually explicit content, to advertisements of low nutritional foods, to advertisements of alcohol, tobacco, and drugs, and to violent content (Evans Schmidt et al., Chapter 22; Gentile, Chapter 23, Iannotta, Chapter 21). The US government, however, has been reluctant to create restrictive media policies, due to First Amendment issues that guarantee freedom of speech, or to finance children's programs; this reluctance has led to ongoing issues of who is willing to pay for quality content (Cahn, Kalagian, & Lyon, Chapter 2).

In the United States where First Amendment rights are a fundamental marker of our individual and collective freedom as a people, censorship is not a preferred mode for eliminating marginal content. Instead, media ratings systems that identify quality content and that mark problematic content have emerged to try to help parents monitor their children's media experiences (Gentile, Chapter 23).

Media literacy programs and parental mediation efforts also seem to benefit children by encouraging critical thinking skills (Chakroff & Nathanson, Chapter 24; Singer & Singer, Chapter 13). In fact, censorship no longer works in a world that is global and where inappropriate content – such as sexually explicit material – can simply move beyond national borders and be readily available via the Internet (Iannotta, Chapter 21).

Two major themes that permeate this handbook remain to be explored. In a world in which media fill the daily lives of our youth, a world in which media have gone from background to foreground experiences each and every day (Wartella & Robb, Chapter 1), why is there so little empirical research about the long-term effects of these mediated experiences on developmental outcomes? In addition, as we begin to differentiate beneficial content more clearly from that which is potentially harmful, why is there not more prosocial and educational material available for youth in the media landscape? These are the challenges that lay ahead as our children grow up in a "multidevice, multiplatform, multichannel world" (Carr, 2007).

References

Carr, D. (2007). Do they still want their MTV? *New York Times*, February 19. Retrieved April 3, 2007, from http://www.nytimes.com/2007/02/19/business/media/19carr.html?ex=1178683200&en=f925807ad304b5a6&ei=5070.

Part I

Historical, Conceptual, and Financial Underpinnings of Media

1

Historical and Recurring Concerns about Children's Use of the Mass Media

Ellen Wartella and Michael Robb

Promises, Promises. That is what proponents of every new media technology over the past 100 or so years have made. How the movies, or radio, or television, or computers would fundamentally alter the way children learn – making children smarter at younger ages or making learning easier and more accessible to more children – have been recurring claims. Juxtaposed to these are the naysayers who decry children's time spent with media content that is morally questionable – too much sex, too much violence, too commercial. In many places this history of recurring controversies that surround the introduction of each of the mass media of the twentieth century has been recounted (Davis, 1965; Paik, 2001; Rogers, 2003; Wartella & Jennings, 2000; Wartella & Reeves, 1985).

What are the roots of the recurring historical concerns about children's use of media? Apart from the specific medium of concern, has anything about how children use media or are influenced by media changed over the past 100 years? In this chapter, we will examine these issues. Our plan is not to recount a new historical view of the controversies which have recurred. Rather, we hope to provide a slightly different angle on the nature of these recurring controversies and we suggest that some things have changed, especially since the advent of television. The dominance of television and other screen media in children's lives has been sustained longer than the dominant role of earlier technologies and the potential impact may be more powerful as well.

Time

Life events unfold over the course of time (Baltes, Reese, & Nesselroade, 1988). Who children spend time with – be it parents, peers, teachers, clergy, media characters – and the context and content of that time spent provide important parameters of the health and welfare of children. Because the activities of daily life provide the knowledge, skills, and behaviors children acquire as they develop, it is no wonder that so much of parental concern focuses on how children spend their time. Are children spending enough time working on schoolwork? Are they playing too much . . . or too little? Are children spending too much time watching television, playing videogames, or browsing on the computer?

Not only is children's use of time of concern to parents, it is also a public policy concern. How much time should children spend in school? At what age can children spend time unsupervised and not be thought to be neglected by their caregivers?

Since children historically have been early and eager adopters of media technologies, Wartella and Reeves (1985) argued that how much time is taken up with media is at the root of the recurring controversies about children and the media. These controversies are personal and of concern to parents, as well as public topics of recurring public discussion, debate, and regulation.

Historical Influences and Changes in Children's Use of Leisure Time

The cycle of recurring concerns about children spending time with media was set in the late nineteenth and early twentieth centuries, during the Progressive Era from roughly 1880 to 1930. During this period, the rise of the scientific study of children, the establishment of federal social legislation to monitor the health and welfare of children, and the institutionalization of public education for children occurred (Hawes & Hiner, 1985). Clearly, there was acknowledgement that children's needs and interests were now topics to be considered by policymakers as well as parents and caregivers during this period (Cravens, 1985). In addition to attention being focused on children, a new social category of adolescence as a distinct stage in the lifecycle of human development became institutionalized and a topic of public discussion (Hawes & Hiner, 1985). Finally, during this period far-reaching technological and social changes brought about a new concept of leisure time, discretionary time when children and adolescents could choose with whom and with what to spend their free time (Somers, 1971). The automobile, movies, and radio were revolutionizing how children and adults spent their time and marked a distinct break with earlier generations (Lynd & Lynd, 1929).

Exactly how children and adolescents spent their time became a barometer of their health and welfare during this period, and the earliest scientific studies of how children spent their time emerged (Wartella & Mazzarella, 1990). In recounting the historical changes in children's use of time during the twentieth century, Wartella and Mazzarella (1990) observed that as early as the second decade of the twentieth century, there was already concern about children having too much leisure time. Moreover, their leisure time was increasingly being spent with first film, and then radio and films, and later television. The ongoing theme of concern about children's leisure time use masks a fundamental shift that occurred after the introduction of television into American life. In short, television colonized

Americans' leisure time. This phenomenon is most apparent in looking at the differences in how children spent their leisure time before and after the emergence of television.

Perhaps the easiest way of demonstrating the quantitative difference in how children spent their time over the course of the twentieth century is to describe what available evidence we have on time use. An early time use study by M. M. Davis (1911), who surveyed 1,140 children aged 11 to 14 in the 1910s, found that 62 percent of these children reported going to the movies once or twice a week. By the 1930s media time use had increased due to the popularity of radio. For instance, sociologists Lundberg, Komarovsky, and McInerny (1934) conducted extensive fieldwork in Westchester County, New York, and had 795 high-school students keep a diary of their leisure time use during 1932 and early 1933. They found both social-class- and gender-based differences in the amount of leisure time youth reported: those from more economically deprived backgrounds spent more time at paid jobs outside the home and girls spent more time in domestic work than boys. Although there was a considerable amount of leisure time, most of it was not spent on media use. For instance, Lundberg and colleagues found that his suburban adolescents averaged 7 hours and 25 minutes of leisure time on weekdays and about 11 hours on weekend days. Most of this time, however, was spent away from home hanging out with friends, attending club meetings, participating in or watching sports events, going to church-related activities, or motoring. Reports of the amount of this leisure time spent with media were relatively small in that most leisure time was spent away from home. Even when at home, the number one pastime of listening to the radio did not take up vast amounts of time: "two thirds of a sample group of children spent at least one half hour listening in on everything from detective stories to the Lucky Strike Orchestra. This pursuit occupies more of the boys' time than of the girls' and takes up from 17 to 30 percent of all leisure which the children spend at home" (Lundberg, 1934, as cited in Wartella & Mazzarella, p. 181). In total Lundberg and colleagues estimated that their sample of high-school students spent 11 percent of their leisure time, or 4 hours and 40 minutes per week with radio, and another 5.5 hours per week going to movies, concerts, or listening to records for a total of a little over 10 hours *per week* with the mass media.

Now compare that 10 hour weekly media use figure with the amount of media use time Timmer, Eccles, and O'Brien (1985) found 50 years later in a national sample of US children. Using children's self-reports via a similar diary method to that used by Lundberg and his colleagues, Timmer, Eccles, and O'Brien found that their sample of children reported 14 hours and 14 minutes per week of television use alone. By the beginning of the twenty-first century, the proliferation and penetration of media into children's daily lives resulted in yet another quantum leap in the way that children spent their leisure time. For example, current media use studies (e.g., Roberts, Foehr, & Rideout, 2005) report that 8–18-year-old youth spend about 6.5 hours *a day* with various media (e.g., television, computers, and videogames) in the home. Even babies and young children under age 6 spent an average of 2 hours per day with screen media (Rideout & Hamel, 2006).

Put simply, while media have been a part of children's leisure time since the 1910s, there has been an overall shift in the role that screen media, especially television, play during children's leisure time. This shift led not only to a quantitative change in how children spent their leisure time, but also to a qualitative shift as youth increasingly added media activities to their leisure activities that historically had taken place outside the home.

Television's Introduction into Children's Lives and Time Use

As occurred with other mass media including radio and films, the introduction of television into American life was received with ambivalence on the part of the public. Television was seen both as a utopian instrument of egalitarianism and as a destructive device capable of wreaking havoc on family life. In the words of Spigel (1992), television was a "panacea for the broken homes and hearts of wartime life," (p. 2) as well as the object that could destroy family relationships and cause massive disruptions to the smooth functioning of households. Some critics saw an opportunity to use television to keep children off the street and in their homes, strengthening the family unit and promoting education. Others worried about the impact of television on children, fearing they might imitate dangerous or socially undesirable behaviors after viewing antisocial television content, thereby becoming more aggressive or delinquent. Another concern, germane to this discussion, was simply the amount of time children were spending with television. However, these early apprehensions failed to stop television from quickly becoming a common presence in American households.

After a decade of existence as a technological curiosity, television began to catch on with Americans at the end of the Second World War. A postwar economic prosperity saw consumer spending increase by 60 percent in the five years after the end of the war (Spigel, 1992). Much of this spending went to consumer electronic appliances, including brisk sales of televisions. In 1946, televisions occupied a miniscule 0.02 percent of homes. By 1950, this had increased to 9 percent and by 1955, 65 percent of US homes held a set. Spigel (1992) notes that the adoption of television sets coincided with an increasing birth rate, as well as the rise of the middle class in America. A reemerging focus on domesticity gave rise to the notion of the nuclear family as an American ideal, where recreation and family activities were highly valued. Television was the most prominent of these family, recreational activities. Could television actually function as a glue to keep families closer? Not surprisingly, social scientists of the era, who were concerned about television's increasingly important and time-consuming role, questioned the use of this new medium and how it impacted children and families.

Assessments of television use reveal a trend of increased total home television use. Television sets were on for about six hours per day in the 1960s, increased to 7 hours by the end of the 1970s, and jumped yet again to about 8 hours at the end of the 1980s (Comstock, 1989). This should not be confused with viewing. Rather it reflects how often the television is on during the day, even when no one is watching. George Comstock (1989) noted the omnipresence of television in American homes, saying "the large number of hours that the set is on each day in the average household makes it the framework within which human interaction occurs" (p. 253).

The upsurge in television use coincides with a shift from one-set households to multi-set households. According to 2003 Census data, televisions now exist in 98.2 percent of homes. In fact, the Census revealed that there are a staggering 260 million televisions in this country, or about 2.4 televisions per home (US Census Bureau, 2006). Televisions have increasingly become a part of children's bedrooms; 68 percent of children aged 8–18 and 36 percent of children under age 6 have television sets in their own rooms (Rideout & Hamel, 2006; Rideout et al., 2003; Roberts, Foehr, & Rideout, 2005). Not surprisingly, children with television sets in their rooms tend to view more than those who have no sets in their rooms (Roberts, Foehr, & Rideout, 2005).

Did this time in front of a television actually provide a context for family contact and interaction? The answer seems to be no. In the early days of television, one-set households were far more common, leading advocates to propose that television was a unifying factor, physically bringing families together in the home to watch common programming that could be enjoyed by all. But as Spigel (1992) noted, bringing together a family to watch television did not necessarily translate into increased interactions between family members. Indeed, Maccoby (1951) found that although families did watch together, there was increased family togetherness only in the sense of family members being physically in the same room. Television did not promote much interaction in the way of talking to each other while viewing. Maccoby characterizes the viewing experience as follows:

> The viewing atmosphere in most households is one of quiet absorption in the programs on the part of the family members who are present. The nature of the family social life during a program could be described as "parallel" rather than interactive, and the set does seem quite clearly to dominate family life when it is on. (p. 428)

With the increase in multi-set households, the perceived benefit of using television to bring families closer seems to have disappeared. The new household setup allows individuals to view their preferred programming apart from other family members. Rather than serving as a medium that binds people together, the increase in multi-set households may actually serve to segregate youth from their parents (Wartella & Mazzarella, 1990).

With television occupying significant parts of the child's day, what activities are given up for viewing? One study found that television use reduced the amount of time devoted to other leisure activities, including other kinds of media consumption (Riley, Cantwell, & Ruttiger, 1949). Children without access to television listened to the radio for about 30 minutes in the evening. By comparison, children with access to television viewed approximately 2 hours and 20 minutes at night and listened to the radio for about 2 minutes, which is an increase in media use of almost 2 hours. Reading also seemed to decline with the introduction of television in a community in Norwich, Great Britain: 13–14-year-old viewers read about 1.75 hours per week, while non-viewers read about 2.5 hours – a 45 minute difference (Himmelweit, Oppenheim, & Vince, 1958).

The differences in media use patterns support the idea that television is a unique media form in the way that it "colonizes" leisure time, occupying time normally spent with other media or leisure activities (Sahin & Robinson, 1981). In their review of children's use of leisure time, Wartella and Mazzarella (1990) noted the early research evidence pointing to a reorganization of children's time. Rather than simply displacing other leisure-time activities such as outdoor sports, playing musical instruments, going to the movies, or listening to the radio, researchers documented an increase in the overall amount of time devoted to mass media use.

Might new technologies affect children's time in ways similar to television when it was first introduced? Recent studies suggest that new media such as computers, videogame consoles, and the Internet have failed to displace television from its perch of dominance. Roberts, Foehr, and Rideout (2005) found that levels of total media exposure, as measured by the amount of time using any individual medium (screen, audio, or print), had increased from 7 hours and 29 minutes to 8 hours and 33 minutes in the five-year span from 1999 to 2004. The increase was attributed to increased videogame and computer exposure during that time, while television remained static at just over 3 hours a day. However, in terms of media use, which takes into consideration that more than one medium may be used at the same time (e.g., reading while watching television or playing videogames while listening to music), the levels remained almost identical over the same five-year span at about 6 hours, 20 minutes. Rideout and her colleagues suggest this finding indicates a ceiling in the amount of time children can or will dedicate to using media. In other words, not only might there be a limit for time allotted to media use, but new technologies are not displacing television or other media forms in the amount of time they consume. To make room for computers and videogames, children are multitasking more frequently, spending about 26 percent of their media time with more than one medium at the same time. However, Roberts, Foehr, and Rideout (2005) did not measure cell phone or iPod use in their study, media that can be and are used at times in the absence of other media. Moreover, the overall amount of time spent using media has still increased over what was occurring when the newer technologies were not available in most children's homes.

The screen media are now a part of even the very youngest babies' waking hours. This trend raises yet again concerns about children's use of time with media. In the next section we will take up another aspect of the recurring controversies about media and youth: the appropriateness of the media content for child users. While there have been recurring controversies about violent and sexual content in the media, there has also been a growing improvement in youth- or child-oriented content. But is quality age-appropriate content even a good use of a baby's time?

The Rise of Children's Content

Since the earliest days when film was introduced into US society, there has been interest and indeed programming for youth. Over time, and especially since the advent of television, there has also been increasing interest in programming more content for youth and for ever younger children. Today we have media content developed specifically for babies. Moreover, this shift in programming content especially directed to children and youth arises both to attract youthful audiences and to counter concerns about the effects of violent and sexual content of the media on children. One piece of evidence of the ever expanded range of media content for children comes from comparison of the kinds of programming available over the course of the twentieth century. A second piece of evidence involves the growth of concern about youth as an audience for media. For instance, violence and sexuality were once concerns; now even educational content is of concern when directed at infants. In this section, we track this emergence of child-directed content across the dominant media at various historical time periods.

The content and issues of film

In a wide-ranging book on the history of the "American audience," Richard Butsch (2000) notes the changes that occurred in public interest in audiences at the turn of the twentieth century and the rise of the mass media. Whereas theater audiences before the twentieth century were noted for their activity (e.g., shouting at the performers, asking for specific songs, teasing actors on the stage, and generally engaging in rowdy behavior), active audiences were not the concern of the film era. As Butsch notes:

> as movies became popular in the early twentieth century, public debate shifted from a focus on audience behavior to a worry about the movies' content and its effects on audiences, particularly children. Attention shifted from the place to the play, from effects of dangerous people in those places to effects of dangerous media messages on people. Audiences were being redefined through the rest of the twentieth century. (pp. 6–7)

From the beginnings of movie-going at the turn of the twentieth century through the 1920s and 1930s, children and youth were clearly members of movie audiences, but there is little evidence that specific films were created just for them. But that does not mean that producers did not want to attract children to their films. As early as 1929, Walt Disney instituted a series of promotional activities to attract children to his movies; he instituted Mickey Mouse Clubs with weekly meetings at local theaters for Saturday matinee showings (Butsch, 2000).

A number of factors converged in the first third of the twentieth century which raised concerns about youthful audiences' viewing of films. For example, large numbers of unchaperoned children and adolescents (and here the data are more anecdotal than substantive) were reported to be attending movies in the 1910s and the 1920s. The Progressive Era's interest in saving the recent immigrant and poorer children focused on the role of movies in leading to delinquency among boys and sexual immorality among girls. (Child advocates, known then as "child savers," such as Jane Addams claimed that movies were the source of ideas of delinquent behavior among the children she counseled; Butsch, 2000). When combined with the rising interest in adolescence as a distinct period of childhood, youthful movie-going audiences were seen as being in need of protection from the effects of media. Psychologist Hugo Münsterberg (1916) refers to the way in which the audience's "mind is so completely given up to the moving pictures" (p. 221).

Yet, there is no evidence of large-scale children's films being produced, even though enterprising mothers and child savers tried to develop guidelines for what were and were not appropriate films for children. Indeed, as Butsch notes, throughout the 1910s there were a number of women's groups in cities across the country who attempted to organize special Saturday movie matinees that were more appropriate for youthful audiences.

The published commentary surrounding the early days of film, including debates over censorship of films during and right after the First World War, is filled with attempts by the proponents of the film industry to demonstrate the educational benefits to be derived from that medium. For instance, Thomas Edison, a famous inventor and holder of many of the key patents for movies, proclaimed in 1913 that films might do away with schoolbooks (*Holiday Magazine*, 1913). Edison argued that films could educate better than teachers in classrooms because of their ability to use vivid and compelling visuals and sounds of distant places, peoples, and ideas. Consequently, Edison Studios were involved in producing educational films. In 1914 *Nation* magazine commented on the "teaching provided by the motion pictures," and exhorted educators to look on films more positively with the commentary that "within the next decade, the moving pictures will be the indispensable adjunct of every teacher and education lecturer" (p. 154).

Nonetheless, it was difficult to find evidence of the production of educational films that would be appropriate for children during the 1910s and into the 1920s. For instance, according to industry figures from 1911, in the earliest days of the film industry and when the industry was trying to develop a positive image in the public's mind, very few educational films were produced. Of 630 independent and licensed films produced that year, only 5 percent were categorized as educational, 2 percent were current events, and 86 percent were entertainment dramas (Wartella, 1991). This pattern helped to fuel a censorship movement during that time. In 1909, a National Board of Censorship of Motion Pictures was organized and for several years it inspected some 95 percent of the films produced in the United States. This board had the authority to keep films from public screening or to recommend modifications in the films. For several years thereafter there were continued attempts to introduce national legislation to set up a national licensing board for all films. These attempts failed. Meanwhile the film industry continued to promote the idea of socially responsible movies (Jowett, 1976).

Public controversies about the morality and educational potential of films led to increased interest in how movies were impacting youthful audiences. It is with the Payne Fund Studies of the late 1920s and early 1930s that public concerns about media's effects on youth became the topic of social scientific studies. Between 1928 and 1933, The Payne Fund, a private foundation from New York, supported 12 major investigations into films' effects on youth. These studies brought together the finest social scientists of the day to examine the effects of movies on youth's knowledge, attitudes, social behavior, and leisure time pursuits. The focus was clearly on the influence of film's sexual and violent content on young people.

As noted in *Movies and Conduct* (Blumer, 1933) and *Movies, Delinquency and Crime* (Blumer & Hauser, 1933), the movies did indeed "implant" their ideas about social behavior in young people's minds and were powerful in influencing youth's behavior. Just as the arrival of movies set the stage for concerns about the types of content children were being exposed to, the Payne Fund Studies established an "effects paradigm" for studying how media content influences audiences. The Payne Studies also set the stage for recurring concerns about violent and sexual content in influencing youth and adolescent behavior.

The content and issues of radio

The introduction of radio into American life came with similar concerns about the role of this medium in children's lives and about the kinds of content available to children. From the late 1920s through the mid-1930s, radio increased its time devoted to self-designated "children's shows." According to Eisenberg (1936), the total number of children's radio programming hours per year provided by the four leading stations in New York City increased from 34.5 hours total in 1928 (or about 40 minutes per week), to 70.5 hours in 1929 (or about 81 minutes per week) to 304.5 hours in 1930 (or nearly 6 hours per week) to 1093.75 hours in 1933 (or slightly more than 21 hours per week). In short, the amount of time devoted to children's shows substantially expanded in a five-year period. Yet, over this same period, the number of educational stations in the country diminished. In 1927 there were 95 local educational radio stations in the country, typically affiliated with a local school system or college, and 115 non-profit stations typically associated with a religious group. By 1934, only 35 educational radio stations remained along with 30 non-profit stations (McChesney, 1987).

Critics of children's radio shows considered them to be violent, emotionally arousing, and suspenseful – not educational. One group of parents from Scarsdale, New York, created an offshoot of the local Parent Teacher Association to lobby against commercial radio's children's programs. In 1934, the Women's National Radio Committee was formed by representatives of 28 women's organizations around the country. Among their activities was publication of an approved list of radio programs for children. The networks responded. According to Dorothy Gordon (1942), the radio networks in 1938 introduced a number of well-publicized educational programs that won praise from parents' groups as well as professional groups of child advocates, such as the American Library Association and the Child Study Association. There were programs on music appreciation and great literature, current affairs discussion groups for high-school students, and fairy tales for young children. To try to quell criticism, in 1939 the National Association of Broadcasters also adopted a set of standards for all children's programs: content should respect parents and not over-stimulate children (West, 1988). To avoid further controversy, Gordon argued that radio broadcasters gradually replaced their children's programs with adult fare: by 1941, for instance, the Columbia Broadcasting System (CBS) had replaced almost all of its children's shows with soap operas (Gordon, 1942).

The content and issues of television

While in many ways these same concerns recur with the advent of television – too few educational programs, too few programs designed especially with children's concerns in mind, too much violence and other inappropriate content available to children and youth – the television era actually raised concerns to a new level. For example, television has provided children with unprecedented access to violent and sexual content. In addition, over the past nearly 60 years, television more than any other medium has expanded programming to children who are younger and younger, providing them with a wide range of educational and entertainment fare. Starting with the television era, then, the sheer volume of media content available to children today – both good and bad – was qualitatively different from earlier eras. Because of television, children now live in a media-saturated world.

Expansion of children's television and video programs According to Melody (1973), in 1951 there were approximately 27 hours of children's programs available weekly on the four television networks – the American Broadcasting Company (ABC), the Columbia Broadcasting System (CBS), the National Broadcasting Company (NBC), and DuMont – and these were distributed throughout the broadcast week. In 1956 there were 37 hours of children's programs. It was not until the 1960s that "kidvid" – Saturday morning animated fare directed to children – emerged on network television. The interest in consolidating children's programs on Saturday morning was economically feasible because there was no better audience for networks to deliver to advertisers. Over time, heavy amounts of commercials (16 minutes per hour by the late 1960s) coupled with relatively cheap animated programs amortized over multiple showings proved extremely profitable for the networks (Turow, 1981). By the 1960s, the weekly hours of children's television on the broadcast networks had declined, airing between 20 and 22 hours a week in total across the decade. In the 1970s, children's weekly programming increased, peaking in 1970–71, 1972–3, and 1976–7 seasons when 36 hours of children's programs aired weekly; the low of this decade was still 30 hours per week of children's broadcasts across the three major networks in 1978.

With the advent and growth of cable television in the 1980s and 1990s, children's television programming exploded. For example, Wartella, Heintz, Aidman, and Mazzarella (1990) conducted a study of the children's videos, comprised of broadcast television, cable TV and video rentals, which were available in one Mid-Western community in 1987. They found a substantial increase in children's content from that which was available in the 1970s. For four broadcast networks – ABC, NBC, CBS, and the Public Broadcasting Service (PBS) – they found 52 hours of children's programs on weekdays and another 21 hours on weekends. If a family subscribed to cable television in that community, their children had access to 149 hours of additional children's programs on weekdays and 36 hours on weekends. In total, during one week, programming created for and targeted to children under 12 in 1987 amounted to 201 hours on weekdays and 57 hours on weekends. The amount of programming today has proliferated further with several all-children's cable channels available, including Nickelodeon, Disney, ABC Family, Noggin, and Sprout. There is even a cable channel aimed at babies, named BabyFirstTV.

Educational and prosocial media content As in earlier media eras, the television era is marked by public interest in the quality of children's programs. Specifically calls to increase the number of educational programs and reduce violent ones continued. While there had been educational shows before 1969 such as *Ding Dong School, Kukla Fran and Ollie,* and *Mister Rogers' Neighborhood,* it was the advent of *Sesame Street* in 1969 that changed the face of children's educational television forever. *Sesame Street* demonstrated that preschool children could learn their letters, numbers, and other planned educational content from television and that such content can contribute to success in school. For example, The Early Window Project (Wright & Huston, 1995) and the Recontact Study (Anderson et al., 2001) assessed the long-term impact of educational television. The original Early Window Project tracked the effects of educational television viewing for three years on two cohorts of children, initially ages 2–5 and 4–7, from relatively low-income homes. In addition to finding positive relationships between watching educational television and school achievement, the researchers also found that viewing planned educational television shows at ages 2 and 3 predicted higher scores at age 5 on measures of language, math, and school readiness (Wright & Huston, 1995). In a follow-up study in the 1990s when these children were teenagers (between 15 and 19 years old), gender differences favoring boys were found for long-term cognitive effects for those who viewed more educational television programs early in life (Anderson et al., 2001). In addition, both boys and girls who viewed educational television programs early in development were more creative, and positive attitudes toward learning were also found for higher educational television viewers. These findings suggest that viewing educational television programs during the preschool years sets the child on a trajectory for educational success that persists beyond the learning of letters and numbers in the preschool years. Research on prosocial content in television – teaching children to help, share, and cooperate – also emerged during the 1970s as scholars realized that children can learn constructive behaviors from viewing television (Friedrich & Stein, 1973; Mares, Palmer, & Sullivan, this volume, Chapter 12).

With the recent explosion of video products directed at infants and toddlers (Garrison & Christakis, 2005), the value of educational content has been questioned for very young children. Specifically, the American Academy of Pediatrics (1999) calls for no screen exposure for children under age 2. Although evidence is emerging that exposure to programs designed for adults is harmful to the play of children under the age of 2 (e.g., Anderson & Pempek, 2005), there is still little evidence that television content designed specifically for children under age 2 is either helpful or harmful (Barr, this volume, Chapter 7).

Violent and sexual media content   While educational content can teach, so can other types of content. Since early in the last century there has been concern about violent content and its effects on children. From Münsterberg's notion that films can impress themselves on the minds of children, through Blumer's (1933) Payne Fund Studies on the ways in which film content can impress the impressionable youth, to radio concerns about violent children's fare, public concern over media violence and its effects on children and youth has recurred over the course of the twentieth century. But it has been in the past nearly 60 years of television research that media violence issues and recurring studies of violence effects have nearly colonized all studies of media and youth.

Over the past 60 years, a substantial body of research documents the effects of television violence on child viewers in the United States. Three major reviews of the literature support the conclusion that media violence contributes to aggressive behavior and aggressive attitudes as well as to desensitization and fear effects. In particular, the statement from the American Academy of Pediatrics (2000) declared television violence to be a public health hazard. The study of violence in American life from the National Commission on the Causes and Prevention of Violence implicated media along with other social and psychological factors as a contributor to violence (Baker & Ball, 1969). Finally, the American Psychological Association's study (1993) implicated media violence as a cause of aggressive behavior. No study claims that viewing media violence is the *only*, nor even the most important, contributor to violent behavior. Furthermore, it is not every act of violence in the media that raises concern, nor is every child or adult affected. Nevertheless, there is clear evidence that exposure to media violence contributes in significant ways to real-world aggression. The report of the American Psychological Association concluded that, "there is absolutely no doubt that those who are heavy viewers of this violence demonstrate increased acceptance of aggressive attitudes and increased aggressive behavior" (p. 33).

The effects of sexual televised content on children's development, though of ongoing concern, have been far less studied. As Huston, Donnerstein, and Wartella (1998) reported, there are only a handful of studies (at the time fewer than a dozen) on the effects of sexual television content on children and youth. The authors point to the political difficulties in getting funding, and the legal and ethical constraints that arise, when scholars try to study sexual material directed at underage youth.

The content and issues of interactive screen media

By the early 2000s, concern about media violence shifted from television to video-games which can be played on consoles or online. There have been congressional investigations of videogame violence. The findings are similar to those of the television studies: children can and do learn aggression from playing videogames (Anderson & Bushman, 2001; Anderson et al., 2004; Gentile & Anderson, 2006). Concern about sexual content is another recurring theme which reappeared with the introduction of Internet pornography. While sexuality has been a public issue from the early days of the movies (see the Payne Studies), the Internet allows easy access to increasingly explicit sexual content. A National Academies Panel found little research to document the effects of online pornography on youth, in part because this area cannot be studied (Thornburg & Lin, 2002). Moreover, regulatory action is virtually impossible to enforce since online boundaries are so permeable across nations that have different laws about sexually explicit content (Iannotta, this volume, Chapter 21; Thornburg & Linn, 2002).

Summary

Violence, sexuality, and the lack of educational content – and even the use of educational content too early in development – have been recurring and emerging topics of concern over the past century. The rise of television brought these concerns to new levels of interest, and the digital age has exacerbated them. With the expansion of media platforms and the proliferation of media into the homes of children, content designed just for children has increasingly become part of the media landscape. One last recurring area of concern over the past nearly

100 years of mass media, and one that has changed the face of childhood, is the ongoing commercialization of children through the media.

Commercialization of Youth through the Media

It is hard to argue that it is only since the advent of television that children and youth have been the target of advertising and marketing messages. Nonetheless, one can point to changes in advertising and marketing practices over the past 60 years that have led to an unprecedented and nearly inescapable commercialized childhood. From babies in diapers through adolescence, children and youth are constantly marketed to across media for numerous products. To say that childhood is media saturated is to say that childhood is commercialized, for the two go hand in hand in US culture.

Butsch (2000) notes that the rise of films and radio in the 1920s and 1930s was synonymous with the rise of advertising and marketing to media audiences, as well as the segmentation of that audience into groups of interest – women and youth. Starting with college students in the 1920s, the media – in this case films, radio, and magazines – catered to ever younger age cohorts of youth, selling them a distinct set of values that differed from their parent's generation, social behaviors, clothing and hair styles, and distinct media practices (Fass, 1977). Beginning in the 1920s, social activities such as attending the movies, attending football games and other college sports, and driving and drinking at college parties were portrayed in various media. The "flapper" and the "college coed" are the images represented in the advertisements and media of the day. Businesses sold products catering to this age group including cigarettes, movies, and fashions (Wartella & Mazzarella, 1990).

With the advent of *Seventeen* magazine in 1944, a new younger market of high-school students was targeted by advertisers. The importance of high-school teenagers was presaged by several social changes. By the early 1930s, high-school attendance had increased to about 60 percent of high-school-aged students. The high school, like the colleges of the 1920s, offered a place where large groups of youth at specific ages could spend time together in activities to establish their own youth culture. Adolescents of the era were using media – movies, radio, magazines, and books – and these media set about catering to the specific needs of these teens. By the 1940s, high-school students as a group were labeled, identified, and catered to as "teenagers" and the media supported the creation of this subculture. This high-school teen culture is easily described: it is characterized by teen music (first the Bobby Soxers heartthrob Frank Sinatra in the 1940s and then rock and roll music stars like Elvis Presley in the 1950s and 1960s), teen movies (*I Was a Teenage Werewolf*, *Rock Around the Clock*), and teen hangouts (the drive-in movie and listening to top 40 radio in your cars). This teen culture is vividly captured in George Lucas's film *American Graffiti*, which was set in 1962 in Modesto, California.

Starting in the 1960s and through the 1980s, a younger age group of youth became the focus of media and advertisers: grade-school children who were the target of kidvid Saturday morning cartoons with heavy advertising for sugar-coated cereals, snacks, and toys. Into the 1970s and 1980s, this targeting at the under-12 demographic grew substantially. The advent of the "program length commercial" occurred in the 1980s where toys became the focus of cartoon shows such as *Teenage Mutant Ninja Turtles* and *He-Man: Masters of the Universe*. The advent of cable channels, including Nickelodeon and Cartoon Network, resulted in numerous programs created just for this age group. The proliferation of advertising also occurred. New kinds of products were developed and aimed at the under-12 age group; these included more food products, clothing, and travel ads for family vacations (Wartella, 1995).

Aiding and abetting this interest in reaching the under-12 age group was the growth in the spending power of children. According to McNeal (1999), spending increased considerably from an estimated $2.2 billion in 1968 to an estimated $35 billion for 1999. What helped bring this about? A number of social changes in American family life occurred: (1) the decrease in the size of the average American family gave parents more money to spend on each child; (2) the increase in one-parent families led to children sharing shopping duties with their parents; (3) because more women were having babies later in life, their families had more income, and hence, more money to spend on their children; (4) the rise in two-career households where both parents worked outside the home also increased available income to spend on children; and (5) children had larger disposable incomes, making them an increasingly important target of advertisers (Wartella, 1995). By 1999, McNeal was reporting that the median age at which children first visited a retail store was two months.

From 2000 onward, we have seen an explosion of marketing to ever younger preschool children and even babies through ever more media venues and through new kinds of marketing practices. Branded products are now part of many preschools, including their very books (McGinnis, Gootman, & Kraak, 2006). Advertising via cable channels aimed at preschoolers has also expanded. The under-2 age group is no longer left out of media programmers' or advertisers' sights. Marketing to children has reached far beyond television and far beyond the traditional television spots for toys, snack food, and cereal products. Indeed, the proliferation of commercial messages is now everywhere for children to see at virtually any time. The Internet and other interactive technologies are, in part, a reason for this increasingly long arm of marketers.

As the Internet swiftly moved into American homes in the 1990s, the youth marketing enterprise intensified and expanded its efforts (Montgomery, 2007). When the World Wide Web was launched in 1993, children already were positioned in the center of a burgeoning media marketplace, with a full array of brands tailored exclusively to their needs – from specialized television channels to magazines to music. In the ensuing dot-com boom, the value of youth in the new digital marketplace became even greater. As Montgomery (2007) writes:

All the ingredients were in place to create a highly commercial digital-media culture, with unprecedented access to the child consumer. The dramatic crash of the over hyped online market did little to stop the flow of the new media into young people's lives. As a consequence, the Digital Generation has become the most heavily researched demographic group in the history of marketing. (p. 25)

According to a Kaiser Family Foundation study (Moore, 2006) of online marketing to children, advertisers who advertise on television also advertise online. Marketing to children now occurs across an increasingly integrated commercialized media environment including television, radio, Internet, videogame, cell phone, and digital devices such as iPods (McGinnis, Gootman, & Kraak, 2006). Calvert (in press) documents the movement from practices such as the traditional commercial advertisements to newer, increasingly stealth techniques. One of these newer practices is *product placement* where the product is embedded in videogame, television, film, or DVD content. For instance, nearly three quarters of the Internet sites examined in the Kaiser Family Foundation study (Moore, 2006) used "advergaming," online games featuring a company's product or characters such as Tony the Tiger or Barbie dolls. *Viral marketing*, where popular youth spread the word and are often given free products to increase other youths' interest in, and purchases of, that product, is another emerging practice. For example, popular youth are often given branded clothing, such as Nike sports and athletic gear, in exchange for wearing, and thereby promoting, the Nike brand (Calvert, forthcoming). A third emerging approach is *integrated marketing campaigns* where the product occurs across multiple venues, such as free merchandise being given with product purchases at a restaurant that is linked to a current film (McGinnis, Gootman, & Kraak, 2006). For example, the Sponge Bob Square Pants movie was associated with companies such as the Burger King fast food restaurant chain where Sponge Bob Square Pants toys were given for food purchases.

While marketing has reached unprecedented levels to ever younger age groups of children, there is no evidence that children are better able to make sense of these messages today than were earlier generations. Since the 1970s, research conducted on the impact of television advertising on children has yielded consistent findings: children under 8 are less able to understand persuasive intent (i.e., that advertisers want to sell you the product) than are older children and adolescents (Young, this volume, Chapter 18). According to Roberts (1982) the understanding of persuasive intent requires that a child initially recognize the source of the advertising message, and recognize that the advertiser has a perspective and an interest that is different from that of the child. The child must then understand that advertisers want consumers to buy their product, and therefore, the message may be biased in favor of the advertiser. Consequently, making sense of advertising messages, especially on television and perhaps other screen media, requires different and more sophisticated strategies than making sense of other content. The blurry lines between commercial and program content used in the newer stealth marketing practices may make it even more difficult for children to discriminate the commercials from the surrounding content. At present, there has been relatively little research conducted on children's understanding of these emerging marketing practices, particularly in the newer interactive media. Because of these age-based limitations, the American Psychological Association recently recommended that no advertising be directed to children under age 8 (Kunkel et al., 2004).

Exposure to television advertising can lead to harmful outcomes for children. Indeed, television advertising has been implicated as one source of the increased levels of obesity in US culture. In a systematic review of the effects of food advertising on childhood obesity, an Institute of Medicine committee (McGinnis, Gootman, & Kraak, 2006) found television advertising effects on children's food preferences, food choices, and short-term food consumption. Although there was a positive correlation between food advertising and adiposity (i.e., children's body fatness), the committee could not rule out all other alternative explanations. Based on the overall evidence, the report concluded that food marketing practices are implicated in the rise of childhood obesity. One recommendation of the committee was that marketers and media programmers take a more balanced approach about what kinds of foods are advertised and marketed to children as one step in trying to combat the childhood obesity crisis. Put simply, the high caloric and low nutritional value of the foods advertised to children on television are out of balance with a healthy diet and with healthy children.

Conclusion

Over the past 100 or so years during the rise of mass and now digital media, the role of these media in children's lives has been a recurring focus of the media industry, a concerned public, and social science researchers. While one might argue that nothing new has occurred, that does not truly capture the remarkable inroads media have made in influencing the context of how children develop in American life. Most especially, since the advent of television about 60 years ago, American children live and grow from infancy onward in a world dominated by media. The introduction of the Internet and other digital technologies into children's homes has further exacerbated the effects of screen media on the lives of youth. The real import of children living and growing in a media-saturated environment is only rudimentarily understood. We know far too little about the role that media play in developmental outcomes. The knowledge base is particularly lacking in terms of documented long-term consequences of exposure to violent, sexual, and commercialized screen content, or of the still untapped potential of media to foster long-term social and academic success. Plus la même chose, plus ça change!

References

American Academy of Pediatrics. (1999). Media education. *Pediatrics*, 104(2), 341–3.

American Academy of Pediatrics. (2000). Joint statement on the impact of entertainment violence on children. Retrieved April 15, 2007, from http://www.aap.org/advocacy/releases/jstmtevc. htm.

American Psychological Association. (1993). *Violence and youth: America's response*. Vol. 1, *Summary report of the American Psychological Association commission on violence and youth*. Washington, DC: American Psychological Association.

Anderson, C. A., & Bushman, B. J. (2001). Effects of violent video games on aggressive behavior, aggressive cognition, aggressive affect, physiological arousal, and prosocial behavior: A meta-analytic review of the scientific literature. *Psychological Science*, 12, 353–9.

Anderson, C. A., Carnagey, N. L., Flanagan, M., Benjamin, A. J., Eubanks, J., & Valentine, J. C. (2004). Violent video games: Specific effects of violent content on aggressive thoughts and behavior. *Advances in Experimental Social Psychology*, 36, 199–249.

Anderson, D. R., Huston, A. C., Schmitt, K. L., Linebarger, D. L., & Wright, J. C. (2001). Early childhood television viewing and adolescent behavior: The recontact study. *Monographs of the Society for Research in Child Development*, 66(1), vii–147.

Anderson, D. R., & Pempek, T. A. (2005). Television and very young children. *American Behavioral Scientist*, 48(5), 505–22.

Baker, R. K., & Ball, S. J. (1969). *Mass media and violence: A staff report to the national commission on the causes and prevention of violence*. Washington, DC: United States Government Printing Office.

Baltes, P. B., Reese, H. W., & Nesselroade, J. R. (1988). *Life-span developmental psychology: Introduction to research methods*. Hillsdale, NJ: Lawrence Erlbaum Associates.

Blumer, H. (1933). *Movies and conduct*. New York: Macmillan.

Blumer, H., & Hauser, P. M. (1933). *Movies, delinquency, and crime*. New York: Macmillan.

Butsch, R. (2000). *The making of American audiences: From stage to television, 1750–1990*. Cambridge: Cambridge University Press.

Calvert, S. L. (in press). Growing consumers: Advertising and marketing in the electronic media. To appear in J. Brooks-Gunn & E. Donahue (Eds.), *The future of children: Children, media and technology*. Princeton, NJ: Princeton/Brookings.

Comstock, G. (1989). *The evolution of American television*. Newbury Park: Sage.

Cravens, H. (1985). Child-saving in the age of professionalism, 1915–1930. In J. M. Hawes & N. Hiner (Eds.), *American childhood: A research guide and historical handbook* (pp. 415–88). Greenwich, CT: Greenwood.

Davis, M. M. (1911). *The exploitation of pleasure: A study of commercial recreation in New York City*. New York: Department of Child Hygiene of the Russell Sage Foundation.

Davis, R. (1965). Response to innovation: A study of popular arguments about new mass media. Unpublished Ph.D. dissertation, University of Iowa.

Eisenberg, A. L. (1936). *Children and radio programs*. New York: Columbia University Press.

Fass, P. (1977). *The damned and the beautiful: American youth in the 1920s*. New York: Oxford University Press.

Friedrich, L. K., & Stein, A. H. (1973). Aggressive and prosocial television programs and the natural behavior of preschool children. *Monographs of the Society for Research in Child Development*, 38(4), 1–64.

Garrison, M., & Christakis, D. A. (2005). *A teacher in the living room? Educational media for babies, toddlers, and preschoolers*. Menlo Park, CA: Kaiser Family Foundation.

Gentile, D. A., & Anderson, C. A. (2006). Violent video games: Effects on youth and public policy implications. In N. Dowd, D. G. Singer, & R. F. Wilson (Eds.), *Handbook of children, culture, and violence* (pp. 225–46). Thousand Oaks, CA: Sage.

Gordon, D. (1942). *All children listen*. New York: George W. Stewart, Publisher, Inc.

Hawes, J. M., & Hiner, N. R. (Eds.). (1985). *American childhood: A research guide and historical handbook*. Westport, CT: Greenwood Press.

Himmelweit, H., Oppenheim, A. N., & Vince, P. (1958). *Television and the child*. London: Oxford University Press.

Holiday Magazine. (1913). May.

Huston, A. C., Donnerstein, E. I., & Wartella, E. (1998). *Measuring the effects of sexual content in the media: A report to the Kaiser Family Foundation*. Menlo Park, CA: Kaiser Family Foundation.

Jowett, G. (1976). *Film: The democratic art*. Boston: Little, Brown.

Kunkel, D., Wilcox, B. L., Cantor, J., Palmer, E., Linn, S., & Dowrick, P. (2004). *Report of the APA task force on advertising and children*. Washington, DC: American Psychological Association.

Lundberg, G. A., Komarovsky, M., & McInerny, M. A. (1934). *Leisure: A suburban study*. New York: Columbia University Press.

Lynd, R. S., & Lynd, H. M. (1929). *Middletown: A study in contemporary American culture*. New York: Harcourt, Brace.

Maccoby, E. E. (1951). Television: Its impact on school children. *The Public Opinion Quarterly*, 15(3), 421–44.

McChesney, R. (1987). *Enemies of the status quo: The national committee on education by radio and the debate over the control and structure of American broadcasting in the early 1930s*. Paper presented at the Association for Education in Journalism and Mass Communication Convention, August, San Antonio, TX.

McGinnis, J. M., Gootman, J. A., & Kraak, V. I. (Eds.). (2006). *Food marketing to children and youth: Threat or opportunity?* Washington, DC: National Academies Press.

McNeal, J. U. (1999). *The kids market: Myths and realities*. Ithaca, NY: Paramount Market Publishing.

Melody, W. H. (1973). *Children's television: The economics of exploitation*. New Haven, CT: Yale University Press.

Montgomery, K. (2007). *Generation digital: Politics, commerce, and childhood in the age of the internet*. Cambridge, MA: MIT Press.

Moore, E. S. (2006). It's child's play: Advergaming and the online marketing of food to children. Menlo Park, CA: Kaiser Family Foundation.

Münsterberg, H. (1916). *The photoplay: A psychological study*. New York: D. Appleton and Company.

Nation, The. (1914). Editorial, August 6, 154.

Paik, H. (2001). The history of children's use of electronic media. In D. G. Singer & J. L. Singer (Eds.), *Handbook of children and the media* (pp. 7–27). Thousand Oaks, CA: Sage.

Rideout, V. J., & Hamel, E. (2006). *The media family: Electronic media in the lives of infants, toddlers, preschoolers and their parents.* Menlo Park, CA: Kaiser Family Foundation.

Rideout, V. J., Vandewater, E. A., & Wartella, E. A. (2003). *Zero to six: Electronic media in the lives of infants, toddlers and preschoolers.* Menlo Park, CA: Kaiser Family Foundation.

Riley, J. W., Cantwell, F. V., & Ruttiger, K. F. (1949). Some observations on the social effects of television. *Public Opinion Quarterly*, 13, 223–34.

Roberts, D. F. (1982). Children and commercials: Issues, evidence, interventions. *Prevention in Human Services*, 2, 19–35.

Roberts, D. F., Foehr, U. G., & Rideout, V. J. (2005). Generation M: Media in the lives of 8–18-year-olds. Menlo Park, CA: Kaiser Family Foundation.

Rogers, E. M. (2003). *Diffusion of innovations.* New York: Free Press.

Sahin, H., & Robinson, J. P. (1981). Beyond the realm of necessity: Television and the colonization of leisure. *Media, Culture, and Society*, 3(1), 85–95.

Somers, D. A. (1971). The leisure revolution: Recreation in the American city, 1820–1920. *Journal of Popular Culture*, 5(1), 125–47.

Spigel, L. (1992). Make room for TV: Television and the family ideal in postwar America. Chicago: University of Chicago Press.

Thornburg, D., & Lin, H. S. (Eds.). (2002). *Youth, pornography, and the internet.* Washington, DC: National Academy Press.

Timmer, S. G., Eccles, J., & O'Brien, K. (1985). How children use time. In F. Juster & F. P. Stafford (Eds.), *Time, goods, and well-being* (pp. 353–82). Ann Arbor, MI: Institute for Social Research.

Turow, J. (1981). *Entertainment, education, and the hard sell: Three decades of network children's television.* New York: Praeger Publishers.

US Census Bureau. (2006). Statistical abstract of the United States – information and communications. Retrieved October 18, 2006, from http://www.census.gov/prod/2005pubs/06statab/infocomm.pdf.

Wartella, E. A. (1991). *An historical perspective on the children and television policy debates.* Paper presented at the Society for Research in Child Development, April, Seattle, WA.

Wartella, E. A. (1995). The commercialization of youth: Channel One in context. *Phi Delta Kappan*, 76(6), 448–51.

Wartella, E. A., Heintz, K. E., Aidman, A., & Mazzarella, S. R. (1990). Television and beyond: Children's video media in one community. *Communication Research*, 17(1), 45–64.

Wartella, E. A., & Jennings, N. (2000). Children and computers: New technology, old concerns. *The Future of Children*, 10(2), 31–43.

Wartella, E. A., & Mazzarella, S. (1990). A historical comparison of children's use of leisure time. In R. Butsch (Ed.), *For fun and profit: The transformation of leisure into consumption.* Philadelphia: Temple University Press.

Wartella, E. A., & Reeves, B. (1985). Historical trends in research on children and the media: 1900–1960. *Journal of Communication*, 35(2), 118–33.

West, M. I. (1988). *Children, culture, and controversy.* Hamdon, CT: Archon Books.

Wright, J. C., & Huston, A. C. (1995). Effects of educational TV viewing of lower income preschoolers on academic skills, school readiness, and school adjustment one to three years later: A report to Children's Television Workshop. Lawrence, KS: University of Kansas Center for Research on the Influences of Television on Children.

2

Business Models for Children's Media

Alice Cahn, Terry Kalagian, and Catherine Lyon

A significant factor in the development and evolution of children's media is funding. Children's media are a complex business that must be sustained economically within specific public policy parameters in order to provide the educational and entertaining programming the public demands. This chapter will focus upon the ways in which attitudes toward media, market forces, and media public policy affect the financial and business models that fund children's television programs.

Models for funding the production of children's media in the United States have undergone important changes since 1970 in response to many factors, including public policy pressures, technological developments, and reevaluation of audience needs and interests. Children's media have now become a global business. It is, therefore, important to understand how these same factors interact in other countries in order to fully grasp the funding and financial landscape that facilitates children's media production. In this chapter, we also examine those factors that have affected change in the past and are likely to continue to influence children's media's development and financing.

History and Foundation: US Children's Media Environment and Early Public Policy

Television broadcasting began with the three major terrestrial networks – the American Broadcasting Company (ABC), the Columbia Broadcasting System (CBS), and the National Broadcasting Company (NBC) (Paik, 2001). Today, these commercial broadcasters are supported by advertising revenues. The rates that businesses pay for on-air advertising are based upon industry-accepted statistics on audience size and demographic characteristics provided by Nielsen Media Research (Allen, 2001). Programs that garner larger audience are more attractive both to advertisers who want to sell products and to broadcasters who want to attract advertising.

The Federal Communications Commission (FCC) is the governmental agency that manages the electromagnetic spectrum through which stations broadcast television programming (http://www.fcc.gov/). The FCC is made up of five commissioners who are appointed by the President and confirmed by the Senate for five-year terms. They are charged with regulating interstate and international communications by radio, television, wire, satellite, and cable throughout the 50 states, the District of Columbia, and US possessions. Broadcasters are constrained to serve the "public interest, convenience, and necessity" according to Congress's Communications Act of 1934 and must demonstrate that they have so served that interest in order to retain a broadcast license from the FCC (Allen, 2001). The license is a renewable eight-year-contract given free to stations that comply with FCC regulations (FCC, n.d.).

Broadcast licensees have not, historically, enjoyed the same First Amendment rights as other forms of mass media, due to the "scarcity rationale": because the electromagnetic spectrum is a limited resource owned by the public, the government has the right and responsibility to see that it is used for the public good. The constraint to serve the public's interest, convenience, and necessity constitutes the price that stations pay to broadcast (Allen, 2001).

Although the Communications Act of 1934, which first established the FCC, required broadcasters to act in the public interest, it did not define any special obligations to provide programming that was necessarily or distinctly of value to children. Broadcasters were, therefore, at liberty to maximize a children's audience for those advertisers whose products depended upon child loyalty. They did this by broadcasting inexpensively produced cartoons on Saturday mornings when adult audience levels were down and child audience numbers were up. Children tolerated far more program repeats, as well as more advertising, than did an adult audience during prime time (Allen, 2001). Thus, the profitable Saturday morning cartoon tradition was born.

Some attempts were made by the FCC in the 1970s (FCC, 1974, p. 39398) to establish the precedent that providing service to children was a part of each station's public interest obligation. However, at each key point in the ruling, the FCC set minimal standards rather than formal regulations and stations interpreted those standards differently (Kunkel & Wilcox, 2001).

Non-Commercial Television

Many saw in television's potential reach not only a rich source for entertainment, but also a tremendous educational opportunity for society. As part of this vision, President Lyndon B. Johnson signed the Public Broadcasting Act of 1967 in order to set aside a portion of the broadcast spectrum for non-commercial, educational use (CPB, n.d.a). The act also created the Corporation for Public Broadcasting (CPB) to serve as a guardian of the public broadcasting mission and to facilitate the development of high-quality programming (CPB, n.d.b).

Two years later, in 1969, the Public Broadcasting Service (PBS) was created (PBS, n.d.a).

PBS provides its member stations with educational, cultural, news, and children's programs that are produced by local stations and by independent producers worldwide. Production funding is provided primarily by viewers' contributions, state governments, and grants from businesses and private foundations. The US government, through the CPB, supplies about 15 percent of the PBS operating costs and the rest is obtained from foundations, federal grants, and membership fees from stations (Franklin, Rifkin, & Pascual, 2001). Local stations support themselves through funding from the CPB, varying levels of state government funds, grants, corporate support, and member dues. In the earliest days of public television, strict guidelines for "underwriting" credits limited the length and content of the funder credits. However, those guidelines have undergone major revisions in the last 10 years, and underwriting announcements with video, animation, music, and other effects have made them arguably increasingly more similar to commercial advertisements (PBS, n.d.b).

The Cable Revolution

With the advent of cable television service in the 1980s, both the commercial and non-commercial television landscape underwent a major change. Cable television service began as a means for remote areas to obtain a strong, clear broadcast signal (Paik, 2001). Early FCC regulations favored broadcasters' interests over the fledgling cable industry by limiting cable service to local interest programming (Paik, 2001). However, the 1980s found US culture more favorable toward deregulation and minimal government intervention in all industries. This trend was reflected in the FCC's 1984 elimination of its regulations on the amount of commercial minutes permitted during children's programs (Allen, 2001). In fact, the FCC relieved most stations from any obligation to serve the child audience, citing the wide range of media available (cable, satellite, videocassettes, and public television) as justification (Kunkel & Wilcox, 2001).

Passage of the Cable Communications Act of 1984 overturned many, if not most, regulatory restrictions on cable, allowing it the freedom to expand as the market would allow (Cable Communications Act, 1984). However, continued lobbying brought about the Cable Television Consumer Protection and Competition Act of 1992, which re-regulated rates for services and required that the FCC generate a plan by which broadcasters would receive compensation for their channels (FCC, 2000). Technically, cable service was outside of the broadcast spectrum, so both Congress and the FCC moved cautiously as it was not entirely clear that traditional broadcast limitations were applicable to cable rights and responsibilities (Strover, n.d.).

Cable proliferation (60 million homes by 1990) plus a strong wave of videocassette recorder penetration caused a significant drop in audiences for both public television and the major broadcast networks, with a concurrent slump in revenues and funding (Strover, n.d.). Industry executives began to explore international co-venture opportunities to offset the financial losses in the United States and to generate new sources of production funding.

Children's advocates, in the meantime, were growing concerned about the lack of quality children's programming available as well as the amount of advertising to which children were being exposed (Richter, n.d.). Child and health advocacy organizations were also outspoken about the amount of violence found in children's programming (Kunkel & Wilcox, 2001). Academic studies had previously found compelling evidence that high quality programs such as *Sesame Street* and *Mr. Rogers' Neighborhood* had a positive effect on children's academic and social skill development (Jordan, Schmitt, & Woodard, 2002). As a consequence, concerned parents and child advocacy groups began to work together for better public policy that would require network broadcasters to provide programming with minimal advertising and that would better serve the needs of the growing young children's audience. The grassroots organization, Action for Children's Television, founded by Peggy Charren, was particularly instrumental in bringing about legislative reform concerning television broadcasting, leading to the passage of the Children's Television Act of 1990 (Richter, n.d.).

The Children's Television Act required commercial broadcasters to provide educational and informational programs and limited the amount of commercial advertising on children's television programming as a condition for broadcasters to renew their licenses. The 1934 Communications Act was the legal platform for making these requirements because of scarce airwaves that belonged to the public. The FCC enforces these rules. However, cable broadcasters were not obligated to follow these rules since they do not use the public airwaves, and hence, operate in a different regulatory environment than the commercial broadcasters do (Calvert, this volume, Chapter 20). Government obligations to limit advertising and to fulfill public interest requirements make the landscape for the profitable production of children's media a challenging one to navigate for commercial broadcasters.

The FCC has, however, indicated a strong preference to leave the business of defining the terms "educational" and "informational" to media industry experts and to allow the marketplace to drive the development, production, distribution, and funding of educational children's television on commercial media venues. This media public policy reflects a particular set of cultural and legislative mores, particularly the protection of free speech, which is important in the United States. Other countries' media policies also reflect cultural and legal mores that influence their philosophies and priorities for media use by their nations' children. Since the 1970s, the business of children's media has increasingly become a global one, primarily due to financial necessity. These international ventures offer both opportunities and challenges as all parties strive to satisfy their own and other countries' media policies and financial parameters.

Current Environment for Children's Media

Virtually all nations produce some quantity of screen-based programming designed for young people. That said, the United States, Canada, Japan, and western Europe are the major providers of content that is not only screened in their home countries, but sold to other countries (Fry, 2002). While one can make the argument that this does not allow for as diverse a pool of content as one might desire, it does provide the necessary revenue streams and incentives that allow for projects aimed at a wide variety of segments within the children's audience. In addition, it also encourages the businesses necessary to support the production and distribution of children's media worldwide.

In examining media production environments worldwide, it is important to consider the range of businesses that currently both drive and depend on a robust system of children's media. At the most basic level, the talent necessary to produce any screen-based property includes legal and business affairs professionals; writers, artists, and filmmakers; engineers and technicians; network development professionals; marketing and public relations teams; sales professionals; and licensing and merchandising teams. The roles of these team members are as follows. The legal and business affairs professionals create, negotiate, and track the necessary contracts, budgets, and rights issues associated with any screen-based enterprise. The writers, artists, animators, videographers, and filmmakers create the characters, narrative, and look of any project. The engineers and technicians operate the now mostly digital equipment that records, stores, edits, and distributes content. Network development, programming, and acquisitions professionals guide, purchase, and schedule the content. The marketing and public relations teams get the project into the public consciousness. The sales professionals sell corporate underwriting, advertising, and/or sponsorships to support the project's creation and distribution. The merchandising and licensing groups ensure that books, DVDs, games, toys, and other products created in a property's interests/image provide the best possible off-air experience for consumers.

It is unclear how newer technologies will impact this structure. With broadband and digital distribution approaching ubiquity in the West, will the current distribution models continue to prevail? How will services as different as YouTube.com (a video website that allows users to create and upload content to share) and Video on Demand (a service provided by cable companies that allows viewers to request specific programs whenever they choose to watch them) shift parental and young viewer behavior? Will young people's facility with technology and interest in their own and peers' activities lead to the creation and popular use of viewer-created content? We are certainly seeing trends like the proliferation of instant messaging and cell phone ownership and use (AP-AOL, 2006) manifest themselves amongst teens and 18–25-year-olds; how they will translate in the long term for younger viewers is as yet unknown.

What, however, has been a constant and seems as though it will remain true, is the bifurcated nature of the younger viewer audience. Programming for and to young children is not only about children, it is also about their parents. Despite the fact that children are using media more independently at younger ages than they were 20 years ago, parents still play a major role in their children's media behavior and choices (Yankelovich Preschool Study, 2005).

Also worth noting is the relatively new age differentiation in terms of content creation and broadcast/cable/digital distribution. With the exception of state-supported public broadcasting entities such as the British Broadcasting Corporation and Canadian Broadcasting Corporation, the existence of a preschool screen marketplace is a new business. Until the late 1980s, there were few television programs aimed specifically at preschool-aged children, and those involved in the industry across sectors measured the children's audience as a whole. It was not until the massive commercial success in the United States of projects such as *Barney & Friends* and *Shining Time Station* in the early 1990s (followed throughout the 1990s by *Blues Clues, Teletubbies, Dora the Explorer*, and others) that a US media industry aimed specifically at preschoolers arose.

With the success of infant-focused media properties such as *Baby Einstein* and *Baby Genius*, it appears that a generation of media-savvy parents, having grown up on not only television but personal computers, is comfortable allowing children's media use to begin at younger and younger ages. Will we see the current demographic markers shift? Content/media use is now measured by Nielsen Media Research and other research companies in terms of 2–5-year-old children and 6–11-year-old children. Will an infant category be added? Or, will we see the 2–5 category shift to accommodate 1-year-olds and acknowledge that there is a 1–3-year-old audience, a 4–7-year-old audience, and an 8–11-year-old audience? The answers to these questions, as well to those raised earlier about how content is distributed to audiences (i.e., audience's traditional use of cable and broadcast television versus content distribution via broadband channels, YouTube and/or Video On Demand), will directly impact the design, development, and distribution of children's media around the globe.

Four Prototypical Television Financing Models

There are as many different ways now of producing and distributing children's media as there are the technologies to support them. Nevertheless, there are common patterns that can be found throughout the world, depending on a host of factors. Two key issues involve the amount of government financing and the amount of government control. We have identified four major models – *Let's make a deal* (United States), *A question of balance* (Canada), *There's no place like home* (France), and *Marketplace rules* (Japan) – that provide a foundational overview of the business of children's television.

In examining these models and the countries in which they exist, we can detail not only the market forces but the public policies that both encourage, and limit, each region's children's media industry. By exploring the models within each region, we begin to understand how the majority of globally distributed children's television is created and distributed. The models also help to illustrate what consumers/audiences can do to encourage quality content. The information about these models comes from interviews that we conducted with people working in the children's media business, as well as from our own knowledge from working inside the children's media business for many years.

Let's make a deal model

In the United States, capitalism has created a marketplace where being distributed by one of four stations – PBS Kids, Nickelodeon, Cartoon Network, or Playhouse Disney – is key to success in the children's media area throughout the world. The United States is the biggest exporter of media and is involved in numerous financial co-productions and deals with other countries. Distribution in the United States is equivalent to the Holy Grail.

The overall financial picture involves mixed sources of funding, few constraints on the staff, and minimal government constraints on creative practice. Unlike other countries around the world, the US government has no formal treaties, tax credits, or funding programs that support the television business. There are, however, some individual state programs: New Jersey, for instance, provides approximately $10 million a year in tax credits through its Economic Development Authority to production companies who work in the state. The tax credits, amounting to one fifth the amount of money spent on each project in New Jersey, are designed to foster film and television production. Those businesses are credited with bringing $85.5 million into the state's economy in 2005 (McNichol, 2006). *Law and Order*, awarded $4.46 million in tax credits based on the $22.3 million it spent in New Jersey while filming 14 episodes, collected the biggest tax credit. The smallest credit, $35,000, went to a reality show called *The ArchiTECHS*, which was filmed over a period of 4 days (McNichol, 2006).

Despite the lack of any reliable stream of federal funds, the US children's television market is the most sought-after market for producers. Getting a regularly scheduled slot on a major broad/cable caster in the United States is crucial to the economic success of a television series, no matter where the series is created or produced. While airing on Nick Jr., PBS Kids, Playhouse Disney, or Cartoon Network does not guarantee success, it is near to impossible to create an economically viable television series without them. In fact, there has not been a major global success in young children's television in the last 15 years without the support of one of those four venues. The size of the business, and hence its competitive nature, can be gauged by assessing the number of series these distributors air each season. Between them, there are approximately 50 series on the air at any one time. In addition, each network develops, or prepares scripts for, multiple series each season that may or may not be produced as scheduling time and financing becomes available.

That said, the economics of developing and producing a young children's television series within the United States are extremely challenging. Unless financed, and thus wholly owned, by the distributing network, independent producers are faced with the daunting task of finding, or deficit financing, large amounts of money.

Depending on the style of a series, per episode budgets can run from $100,000 to several hundred thousand dollars and most networks order 26 episodes for an initial season's air. Finding series funding, especially for new producers, is difficult. US-based producers face an intensely competitive environment on-screen and off. There are limited marketing and publicity budgets to help audiences learn about a series; the on-air advertising market is shrinking; the home video market, once a staple of series' financing, has shrunk considerably since the advent of digital children's channels; and there is growing competition from video gaming and other screen-based activities.

Despite these odds, each one of the aforementioned networks receives several hundred, or more, pitches for new projects every year. There are several thousand independent production companies in the United States devoted to the development and production of children's television, and over the last 15 years the number of distributors who focus a significant portion of their airtime to younger children's series has increased six fold.

What accounts for this increase? We believe the answer is a combination of commerce, education, and creativity. For some, it is a desire to catch the brass-merchandising ring by using an effective and widely popular medium to influence young children. That is, some broadcasters hope that they will find a way to make a considerable amount of revenue through a hit program and the potential income that it brings along with it. For others, it is a belief that screen-based media are excellent teachers with an unparalleled ability to easily and effectively reach millions of children. And for yet others, creating screen-based narrative is their way of exploring their art and creativity. But no matter what the motivator, the marketplace imperatives are the same. To illustrate the *Let's make a deal* model, we offer two examples: one, WGBH, a public broadcasting station-based production company focused on using television to educate entertainingly; the other, Animation Collective, an independent production company, focused on providing prosocial entertainment. Both want to provide appealing and popular entertainment for children; both struggle with the economics of the business; and both have, over the years, come to understand that partnerships with broadcasters and other related companies are essential to their success.

WGBH, Boston's public television station, has established a reputation over the last 40 years as a production powerhouse across genres. Nowhere has that hallmark been more apparent than in children's programming. Beginning with the original *Zoom* in the 1970s through *Where in the World is Carmen Sandiego?*, *Arthur, Peep and the Big Wide World*, and *Curious George*, producers Kate Taylor and Carol Greenwald have established their unit as one committed to providing educational media that entertains and inspires.

WGBH's Children's Television Department has a staff of 33 and an annual budget of $20 million. In 2006, they had four shows in development and eight in production. It often takes several years to put together the financing for any one of these projects, and they are aided in the fundraising effort by a financial development team also funded by the station. They are also supported by the station's other, more profitable, activities. Financing is accomplished by combining resources and typically includes monies from multiple sources such as PBS, CPB, government agencies such as the Department of Education, and private foundations. Also, a part of the funding mix is corporate sponsors in industries where families are consumers, and merchandising and licensing companies whose products are based on the series' characters. In this model, there is no reliable stream of federal funding. The funding process begins anew for each individual project.

Because of the difficulty these multi-part funding partnerships pose, WGBH has called for increased and sustained public funding for non-commercial media. According to Kate Taylor, Director of Children's Television at WGBH,

> It would be great to have educational programming funded by the government so that it would be done right, with the appropriate research attached before, during and after, and not subject to commercial pressures. It might also allow us to broaden the notion of what is included in educational television. Literacy is important, but so are health education, the environment and citizenship. Sustained government funding might allow us to broaden our subject matter horizons and really prepare our children for a global future. (personal communication, 2006)

WGBH is in the children's media business because it believes in the power and positive impact of educational television. Each of its series is curriculum based and begins with the establishment of a clear instructional design. To date, the series have focused on geography (*Where in the World is Carmen Sandiego*), history (*Time Warp Trio, Where in Time is Carmen Sandiego*), literacy and life-skills (*Arthur, Zoom, Between the Lions*), and science (*Zoom, Peep and the Big Wide World*). Each of the series has also, with varying degrees of commercial success, launched publishing and merchandising programs based on the series' characters and narrative.

Educational goals intact, WGBH acknowledges that children's television is a business – a business that has become more commercially viable, at least potentially, in the last 20 years, and one where commercial partners investing money want to see some return. Of its projects over the last 15 years, *Arthur* has accomplished that in large measure. However that commercial success has been mostly through continued international program sales, not merchandising. The hope is that future projects will succeed more fully in reaching commercial (television sales and merchandise) as well as instructional goals. Even so, the station's primary goal is not to make a profit but to produce effective educational programming that children will want to watch.

As producers for a non-profit educational organization, Taylor and Greenwald believe that a foundation of instructional design is the key difference in developing projects within a non-commercial venue. Although it is imperative to create characters and narrative that children want to watch and spend time with, it is equally important to adhere to the series' curriculum goals. Within the young children's television universe, there are those series that accomplish both – meeting curriculum and commercial goals. Those include _Sesame Street, Blues Clues, Barney & Friends, Bob the Builder_ and _Dora the Explorer_. There are more that garner good ratings but do not succeed fully as off-screen properties such as: _Arthur, Magic School Bus, Where in the World is Carmen Sandiego_, and _Kratts Creatures_. When neither significant merchandising nor advertising revenue is available, it makes it more difficult for producers to fund subsequent seasons and keep the series on the air.

There is no recipe for achieving the combination of ratings and merchandise success. One key component, according to WGBH, is the mandatory inclusion of educational outreach materials with every series it produces. Lesson plans, art activities, games, puzzles, and reading lists are all distributed online and/or via print to community-based organizations, schools, and homes. These materials extend the learning beyond the screen and seek to actively engage young viewers in the educational experience. WGBH's belief is that these materials are an essential component of its work and that they should be developed whether a broadcaster requires them or not.

> "Juicy Juice brand juice was a sponsor for _Arthur_ for many years. One of our storylines a few years back focused on nutrition and a key part of the story was that drinking water was healthier than drinking juice. We ended up losing Juicy Juice as a sponsor a year later, but we did a story that worked for the series, the characters, and most importantly, our audience. The idea that we would consider the whims or thoughts of one of our sponsors didn't enter into the creative process."
>
> Carol Greenwald, _Arthur_ executive producer

Our second exemplar involves Animation Collective, one of the largest animation studios in New York City with multiple original series in production. The company is a leader in creating and producing children's programming for television, the Internet, home video, and other platforms. Larry Schwarz is the creator and executive producer of all of Animation Collective's original television series including _Ellen's Acres_ and _HTDT_ for Cartoon Network and _Kappa Mikey, Thumb Wrestling Federation: TWF, Leader Dog_, and _Tortellini Western_ for Nickelodeon's networks. Schwarz also served as producer of _Wulin Warriors_ for Cartoon Network and the first season of _The Incredible Crash Dummies_ for 4KidsTV.

Animation Collective is also the largest provider of original content for KOL, America Online's kid's channel, and Red, its teen channel. Its first multi-platform success, *Princess Natasha* for America Online, was featured on Cartoon Network and has been released as a book series from Little Brown Books for Young Readers, as an upcoming comic book series from DC Comics, and as licensed consumer products.

Animation Collective is an independent company, owned by President Larry Schwarz. In order to survive, it must raise money for development and production from a variety of sources: US network acquisition fees, presales of unfinished series to networks outside the United States, merchandise advances from companies contracted to create toys, apparel, and paper goods based on the characters and shows, and renting out studio and staff to do animation for other creators' properties. In order to keep working, the company rolls its deficits forward with the goal that future work will continue to pay for current and past projects.

Although there is no federal funding available, Animation Collective is based in New York City so it could avail itself of New York State tax credits. However, this provides limited relief. For example, the company is not able to access manufacturing tax credits destined for New York City businesses. Despite the fact that this company is one of the larger employers in the city's midtown garment district area, it is not eligible for tax relief because it "manufactures" television, not clothing.

To manage finances, Animation Collective continues to consider possible affiliation with Canadian companies, or even the opening of a branch office in Canada to be able to access the more generous tax credits offered to Canadian producers. Even so, Schwartz expressed concerns about government funding of creative enterprises: "I am a total free market person and don't necessarily believe the government should support industry, but the playing field is uneven because other countries' governments support their media industries." Other nations' co-production treaties encourage producers to form alliances and cooperatively produce projects with companies from other treaty-nations. The United States' lack of any co-production treaties makes it more difficult for independent US-based producers to fund and distribute their projects.

With successful projects airing on multiple networks it would seem as though the company could easily continue to develop, produce, and distribute series of its own design. Animation Collective's experience, however, has been that the field constantly, almost spontaneously, changes based on each different network's needs. While networks each have their own distinct brands, once one network finds a hit genre, others follow that trend until a new trend is created or appears. With its openness to exploring new ideas and projects based on network needs, Animation Collective works carefully to design projects that can succeed on-screen and off. Network decisions, called green-lights, are based on potential program ratings and how well the project will translate into merchandise.

Animation Collective prefers to work as partners with networks, rather than allowing a network to fully fund, and thus wholly own, the productions. In this way, it keeps the copyright and a measure of control over both the on-screen creative as well as the off-screen merchandising rights. Network license fees have shrunk over the last 10 years, meaning that producers have to find additional international distribution partners in order to be able to afford to produce their projects. License fees can range from as low as $5,000–$10,000 per episode to multiple tens of thousands; episode production budgets range from $100,000 upwards. Given the disparity between those numbers, it is easy to see why multiple partners across platforms and territories are necessary in order to provide the basis for funding.

It is important to remember that digital and online distribution have easily doubled the number of outlets that networks have at their disposal. Animation Collective, among others, is relying on the fact that networks will need to license more projects in the coming years in order to fill additional channels and technology-driven outlets.

In sum, the *Let's make a deal* model is a challenging approach for funding children's media. Although the potential for new, technology-fueled distribution seems positive in terms of motivating new production, there are essentially very limited financing options. Given the lack of federal funding and the economic disparity between the cost to produce and the prices paid for productions, where does the money come from? Some support can come from state tax benefits, private foundations, and even the CPB. But all of these provide modest sources of revenue. Because of this dilemma, there has been an increasing shift to those projects that are "toyetic," defined as having the ability to inspire off-screen play and generate audience desire for merchandise based on a series' characters and narrative.

"Commercialism in children's television is sometimes treated as a dirty word within the industry. Shows that are a commercial success are perceived, by some, as being of a lower quality than those that win awards but not much else. Let's make it clear that commercialism does not equate with cheap or uncreative programming. From day one we look at the total picture. We look at the strength, appeal and uniqueness of the show and its characters, and just as importantly how the series' premise will translate internationally and commercially. And we make no apology for this. Commercial exploitation is not a necessary bolt-on that will just give us funding but is an integral part of our planning. We do not believe for one moment that looking at the bigger picture at the start of a project makes it a less creative process. Parents expect to see merchandise for their children's favorite shows. In fact, they demand it and often ask when products will be available within weeks of the show transmitting. Merchandising gives an extended dimension to the show, increasing children's relationship with the characters and the pleasure they gain from the program."

Keith Chapman, Chapman Entertainment's creative director and
managing director, and Greg Lynn, executive producer, *Bob the Builder*

A question of balance model

The Canadian government provides a balance between financial support and regulatory constraints in the creation of children's programs. In particular, it provides funding for the creation of children's programs, regulates the staffing of those programs, and provides minimal constraints on creative activities. Beginning in 1983, the Canadian government began aggressively supporting the construction and maintenance of an indigenous children's television industry. These efforts have been enormously successful. Through a series of federal and provincial incentive programs, the Canadian animation and live action media business has grown into a thriving sector of the economy. In brief, both the Canadian federal government and provincial governments offer production companies/distributors incentives in the form of tax credits and subsidies for work done by Canadian/provincial citizens in Canada/specific provinces and sold to a Canadian broadcaster. In addition, provincial subsidies can be piggybacked on top of federal subsidies.

In order for producers to avail themselves of these funds, they must use Canadian talent in front of and behind the screen. Using a point system, producers get specific numbers of points for using Canadian writers, actors, producers, and directors. The more points a producer has, the more tax and/or grant money is potentially available. There are few, if any, restrictions put upon the content. Those parameters are set by Canadian broadcasters and the response of the viewing audiences.

Depending on the combination of federal and provincial subsidies on any given production, producers can cover, at best, up to 50 to 60 percent of a production's costs (CAVCO Guidelines, n.d.). Despite that, the economics of the children's television business also demand that in order for a series to succeed financially, it must also find broadcast homes outside Canada. This has led to animation dominating the children's production business; live action is more culture-bound, and it does not travel as well because it needs to be re-shot in order to appeal to non-Canadian, non-English speaking audiences. For example, while there are multiple language versions of the US program *Sesame Street*, each version is wholly recreated in each country. In contrast, animation needs to be revoiced, but that is an easier, more cost-effective process.

To encourage the production of new media, there is a separate federal program (Ontario Media Development Corporation, n.d.) as well as private funds administered by Canadian cable companies. These private funds are government mandated. The funds are allocated to the cable companies by the Canadian Television Fund (CTF), and the cable companies pass them on to producers in the form of matching grants. Not only do these and other government programs provide production incentives, but whole new supporting industries have grown strong and profitable as a side benefit. As an example, there are now thriving legal, accounting, and business affairs businesses that deal solely with the complex legal and financial matters resulting from the grant and tax credit funds.

Although the upside of these regulations is immediately apparent, so is the potential downside. Limiting all jobs within a given production to one locale could easily limit the resulting products' global appeal. In addition, nationally restrictive regulations could prevent Canadian productions from being aired in other countries with similarly focused protectionist policies. To address these issues, the Canadian government established co-production treaties with global partners. Simply stated, cooperative production treaties (co-productions) stipulate that talent from countries covered by the treaties counts in a producer's favor as he/she adds up points toward tax subsidies. These treaties also allow producers to combine different nations' tax credits (Telefilm Canada, n.d.). As of 2006, Canada had more co-production treaties around the world than any other nation.

Despite the seemingly generous tax subsidies and multiple co-production treaties, the economic landscape is far from rosy. The cost of productions ($225,000 to $350,000 US dollars per half-hour animated program) far outstrips the average license fees from global broadcasters. License fees are those fees paid by a broadcaster to a producer for the right to acquire and distribute a series. As examples, in the United States, fees range from $10,000 to $60,000 per half-hour, in Canada $25,000 to $80,000, and in the United Kingdom in the $10,000 range. Australia and the smaller countries in Europe, Africa, and Asia offer fees commensurate with the size of their market and the popularity of the program. That is, the more popular a program has proven itself to be in territories where it is already airing, the more desirable. This is because the program will, at least theoretically, bring a larger audience to any other broadcaster who purchases it. Even combining multiple license fees does not add up to the cost of production, and it is not common for every series to be bought by every country.

This disparity between the production costs and broadcaster's fees has led to the need to find other sources of revenue to support production. Because in the case of Canada, the government has already provided support, the emphasis then shifts to the commercial marketplace: advertising and merchandising. Advertising is not a major source of revenue in Canada because government regulations prohibit advertising directly to young children. Therefore, licensed merchandise is an alternative that Canadian producers are increasingly exploring.

In summary, the *Question of balance* model that exists in Canada has allowed a video production industry to flourish. Much of the animation young children watch in the United States is produced or co-produced by Canadian animation companies, and there is a thriving broadcast business. That is not to say there are not serious challenges, but Canadian producers have reliable access to federal money, a plethora of international co-production treaties, and few, if any, government restrictions on content.

"Merchandise is the pot of gold at the end of the rainbow, the elusive ring on the carousel. It is an inexact business; it is as much about timing as it is about the popularity of a series. Retailers are fickle; if merchandise doesn't sell immediately it gets pulled off the shelves. Because of this, producers are looking at every other distribution possibility in order to piece together the money needed to make a show. New media production and distribution possibilities are going to play a larger and larger role. While TV's economic model is not easy to figure out at this point, there hasn't yet emerged a model for new media. Will it be advertising? Will it be immersive content/ads? Will it be sponsored content? There are inherently negative issues regarding these options in terms of programming for younger children, but it seems as though there might be some new options for older kid's content."

Annette Frymer, chief operating officer, Cambium Catalyst International

There's no place like home model

The French government subsidizes an entirely in-house model that relies on French talent for the creation of children's programs. To do so, the government finances these programs, regulates staffing to French citizens, and provides an atmosphere that encourages unconstrained creative activities.

There are about 23 million homes in France, most with at least one television set. Unlike in the United States, where cable penetration is about 90 percent, only about 25 percent of French homes buy cable services. Instead, the roll-out of interactive satellite channels drove satellite penetration to much higher numbers.

There are about 31 television networks that carry children's programming in France. Although it is tempting to try to compare this number of networks with other countries, such parallels are somewhat difficult to draw because of the plethora of distribution platforms in countries such as the United States and Canada (with combination of broadcast, cable, digital, and Video on Demand platforms) or Japan where content is not so discretely defined as being targeted to children or adults.

Of the free over-the-air, what we call "broadcast" networks, six air some children's programming while about 25 of the 200–300 cable/satellite channels provide children's programming. Three of the free networks, France 2, France 3, and France 5 are public television stations that are owned by the government. They tend to air more hours of children's television whereas the privately owned networks, TF1, Canal Plus, and M6, air only a few hours per week.

Many of the cable/satellite networks are French branches of US cable networks (Cartoon Network, Disney, Nickelodeon, and Jetix). Unlike the United States where the local channels are required to air three hours of educational content per week, French networks must commit to an amount of money they contribute to the production of children's programming. In other words, it is a production commitment rather than a content or broadcast commitment. The amount of money, which is a percentage of a television network's revenue for the year, is negotiated with the Conseil Supérieur de l'Audiovisuel, the French version of the FCC. As with the educational and informational (E/I) children's programming requirement in the US, the monetary contribution in France is mandatory in obtaining and maintaining a broadcast license. The way that these minimums are administered, then, has a direct impact on production costs.

In the spectrum of children's programming funding, hardly any country matches the assistance that the French government offers its creative and production communities. No one will be surprised that art, literature, and entertainment are highly valued vocations in French culture and this has translated into government policy that provides tremendous economic subsidies to creators, producers, and broadcasters. Additionally, this policy is utilized specifically to keep the French economy going, so the maximum use of these subsidies occurs when all of the work, effort, and consumption stay in France. These subsidies are accessible at both the national (federal subsidies) and local (cities and townships) levels as well. Unlike other countries, so much funding comes from the French government that there is no need for producers to tap into other commercial sources (i.e., toy companies, fast food companies) to help fund production.

Similar to Canada, there is a point system and a producer receives the maximum subsidies if he/she meets the maximum number of points allowed (14). For example, if certain elements of the process originate from a French citizen, a producer receives points accordingly. The point breakdown is as follows: concept story (one point); scripts (two points); character designs (two points); music (one point); director (two points); storyboard creation (two points); other production elements (four points).

The subsidies are generated and administered via government "accounts." A producer has a government subsidy "account" that is started when he/she produces and sells a show to a French broadcaster. When this happens, the producer gets a certain amount of credit that can be applied to the next project, thereby reducing the production cost. Each new show that is produced and sold/licensed in France generates these subsidies, establishing a closed loop with each project funding the next.

For the purpose of this chapter, we will limit the discussion to the production of television programming, but these subsidies exist for film and many other art, literary, and entertainment endeavors as well. Recently, subsidies have become available for new media creation, production, and display. It is a broad and expansive economic policy that has resulted in France becoming the biggest producer of European theatrical movies. France has outpaced both the United Kingdom and Italy such that it is now third in animation production, just after the United States and Japan.

Despite the government influence on generating media income and keeping that income in France, there are no content mandates or educational guidelines for children's programming. Each broadcaster sets goals and requirements for its channel, and producers create content to fit those targets. For example, the three national broadcasters each air a significant amount of children's programming; but rather than compete with each for the same audience, they collaborate and segregate their demographic targets. France 3 targets teens, France 2 targets children aged 6–11, and France 5 targets preschoolers. Each of these networks has crafted specific content guidelines, usually reflecting public sentiment, and producers create series that meet those guidelines.

More recently, the French government has recognized that there is a limit to how much production its economy can support and has opened the door to co-production treaties with other countries. Producers do not receive the maximum credits but receive an economic boost that, when combined with international financing, makes co-productions financially possible if not lucrative. In addition, co-production treaties provide a welcome opportunity to learn about and work with new talent as well as gain exposure for French productions in other countries. Because of these new government guidelines, French co-productions are proliferating.

> "If we didn't have these subsidies, we couldn't have this much production. The one drawback is that you can't go outside of France for some of the creative elements [i.e., writers, storyboard artists, etc.]. But you do what's best for the show and because you have to play by the rules it increases the cost [of the show]. There are also different funds that help with international [business]. Funds that are set aside to assist distributors in the production of tapes, dubbing of tapes into foreign languages, and in the promotion and selling of their shows in other countries. A lot of people are talking about new media and VOD [Video on Demand] but it will probably not affect us [as producers] as we are still [about] making shows. It will affect the production budget because it will increase what you produce like shorts and [creative for] other platforms and currently we don't make money [at that] so [it] must be used for marketing the brand and launching the brand. Broadcasters are starting to ask for this content, however, so there might be money there in the future."
>
> Nicolas Atlan, partner, Moonscoop Entertainment

Marketplace rules model

In Japan, few constraints are available in financing or creating children's programs. The industry finances itself primarily through commercial activities, and the government provides no interference, allowing unfettered opportunities for creative activity and commercialization. As in the United States, there are no government subsidies that assist in funding the cost of television production or children's programming. However, in contrast to the United States, most of the program funding comes from non-television commercial interests, such as toy companies, packaged goods companies, fast food companies, video gaming companies, and trading-card companies. The one exception is Japan's public broadcaster, NHK; it is funded through government taxes and has fairly stringent programming sponsorship requirements.

There are roughly 40 million homes in Japan and, as in most of the world, only about 20–25 percent of homes have access to cable or satellite. The main free, over-the-air networks are NHK (the public station), TV Tokyo, Fuji TV, TV Asahi, TBS (Tokyo Broadcasting System), YTV (Yomiuri TV), and NTV (Nippon TV), and they all air animation at least once per week. Like in the other countries, there are hundreds of cable/satellite channels. It is difficult to designate the number of hours of programming that are dedicated to children's television on either the free, over-the-air format or cable/satellite as animation is produced for every demographic, including teens and adults, in Japan and most of it is watched by the family.

Not unlike France, it was the introduction of satellite into the marketplace that initiated the proliferation of channels in Japan. Because Japan tends to be a fairly isolated culture, it has been difficult for non-Japanese companies to enter the market. Up until recently, non-Japanese companies had to form joint ventures with Japanese companies in order to find distribution on Japanese television. Recently, regulations have opened a bit, and two US companies have been able to start US-owned channels (Disney and Nickelodeon), but they have fairly low numbers of viewers.

There are no government-mandated requirements on content or number of hours of programming for children. Each network sets its own guidelines and buys or co-produces programming that meets those goals. Japanese standards for children and family television are less conservative than in the United States in terms of language, nudity, subject matter, and violence. Some of the program-ming that airs during children's and family hours in Japan is considered adult or late-night viewing in the United States (i.e., *Inuyasha, Lupin, Full Metal Alchemist*).

Japanese children's television series ideas can come from any sector. A children's show production partner can just as easily be a packager of frozen foods as it can be a publisher. In fact, any popular item (food, videogames, stuffed animals, books, comics) is likely to be made into a cartoon. For example, one of the longest-running shows in Japan is *Anpanman*, starring a piece of toast, a favorite breakfast food in Japanese households. *Anpanman* literally means "toast man." Another example is the ubiquitous Pokemon which originated as a trading-card game and then expanded into both manga (comic books) and anime (Japanese animation).

The largest percentage of animation or anime is drawn from Japanese comic books called manga; in fact, the manga functions as the television series' pilot or first episode. For the sake of this discussion, we will focus specifically on children's programming, but the reality is that neither manga nor anime are restricted to the children's audience. There are manga and anime for every age from children to seniors, males and females, and on almost any topic, from samurai to Pokemon battles to fairies to fishing to chess. How successful a manga is determines whether a television show will be produced.

Children's programming is generally funded by a "production committee" made up of a publisher, television network, advertising agency, production company (which bears the largest percentage of the cost), and, very often, an advertiser. The rights and associated revenue to the program are shared by all committee members. As a side note, this is one of the reasons that international exploitation of Japanese properties is often unwieldy at best. Trying to get approvals from multiple committee members in Japan about a simple marketing tagline will often take weeks or months. Trying to unravel rights for international licensees is often impossible.

Why are all these players in a typical production committee? The publisher (e.g., Shueisha, Shogakukan, Kodansha) sees the opportunity to sell more manga and receive revenue through the brand extensions of licensed merchandise and home video. The television station (e.g., TV Tokyo, Fuji TV, Nippon TV, TV Asahi, TBS, NHK, YTV) sees the potential in high ratings and has already "sold" the time-slot to an advertising agency. The advertising agency (e.g., Dentsu, ADK) sees the potential of high ratings for its already bought time-slot and, therefore, more exposure for its client. The production company (e.g., Toei, Pierrot, Bandai) gets some work and a guaranteed broadcast commitment for its show. And if advertisers (e.g., trading-card game company Konami, toy company Tomy, videogame company Bandai) get in on the production, they very often will be able to have their product actually be the basis of the show or, at the very least, in the show.

Because of all the links between on-screen and off-screen play, this economic model is more often used for children's programming in Japan than for those targeted at other audiences. It is obviously a model that is commercially driven rather than one dictated by any educational or government mandate. However, as Japan's population has started to change (birth rate down, senior population expanding) and, as in the rest of the world, kids' media usage has fragmented, revenue from this model has started to decline. Producers have been looking for other ways to continue producing children's programming. The Japanese government, unaccustomed to subsidizing or investing in animation, has become more interested in increasing trade and opening the door to other countries. Regulations have relaxed, and Japan is beginning to allow wholly-owned foreign businesses to exist. The government also has outreach programs to entice foreign partners/buyers to come to Japan to meet potential production/business partners, and the production committees themselves are opening doors to sharing rights and revenue with foreign partners.

"The Japanese production model is changing and there is more international investment in productions. The reason why the Japanese have started going out of the
country is because many projects are starting to lose money. Media [consump-
tion] is fragmenting, like the rest of the world, and advertisers are losing money
on their products at retail. This means these companies have to grow globally.
Also, new platforms are getting exploited in Japan [i.e., the broadband Bandai Channel]
but there is still a real fear of piracy and problems with international separation
of [content] rights. And while Japan's distribution methods are more developed
than in other countries [fiber optic broadband], animation rights are not. We
recognize the world is changing though and are on the front edge of meeting
that change."

John Easum, president / VIZ Media USA (the first Japanese media
company to partner with a US broadcaster, Cartoon Network,
to bring Japanese shows to American viewers via broadband)

Summary

The prototypical models presented here vary in how much the government subsidizes children's television programs, ranging from virtually nothing in Japan, to
some funding (PBS) in the United States, to considerable funding in Canada, to
heavy funding in France. With those subsidies come government policies that favor
or require hiring people from within those countries and even within local areas
of those countries to create the programs. This practice, in turn, yields jobs and
economic success for those who work in the children's media business, as well as
the production of numerous children's television programs. Even then, however,
the cost of creating children's programs is extremely expensive. Producers who
are not subsidized turn to marketing, in the form of advertising or having toy
tie-ins with the characters in their programs, or by selling their programs internationally. The less programs are subsidized, the more producers must rely on
marketing and co-productions to finance the creation of their children's programs.

Conclusion

Television has dominated the global entertainment culture for the last 50 years.
Despite recent and continuing challenges from interactive technologies, linear screen-
based storytelling continues as a robust creative and business opportunity.
Television is our children's window and mirror, showing them a world beyond
their own backyards and offering them a reflection of the lives they lead. The economics of the children's television business are challenging at best; the politics
and policies are as yet unfinished, and the research on television's impact incomplete. Yet the enterprise persists and will continue to do so because a good story,

well told and easily accessed, is undeniably compelling. The challenges in addressing both the creative and business issues are the historical and ongoing tensions between art and commerce, and between education and entertainment.

All authors contributed equally to the chapter.

References

Alexander, A. (2001). Broadcast networks and the children's television business. In D. Singer & J. Singer (Eds.), *Handbook of children and the media* (pp. 495–506). Thousand Oaks, CA: Sage.

Allen, C. (2001). The economic structure of the commercial electronic children's media industries. In D. Singer & J. Singer (Eds.), *Handbook of children and the media* (pp. 477–94). Thousand Oaks, CA: Sage.

AP-AOL. (2006). Instant messaging trends survey, April 3. Retrieved May 2007, from http://press.aol.com/article_print.cfm?article_id=964.

Cable communications act of 1984. (1984). Retrieved September 2006, from http://www.publicaccess.org/cableact.html.

Canadian Audio-Visual Certification Office (CAVCO) guidelines. (n.d.). Retrieved September 2006, from http://www.pch.gc.ca/pc-ch/pubs/2002/02_e.htm.

Corporation for Public Broadcasting (CPB). (n.d.a). *Remarks of President Lyndon B. Johnson upon signing the public broadcasting act of 1967.* Retrieved September 2006, from http://www.cpb.org/aboutpb/act/remarks.html.

Corporation for Public Broadcasting (CPB). (n.d.b). *Public broadcasting act of 1967* (47 U.S.C. 296, Section 396). Retrieved September 2006, from http://www.cpb.org/aboutpb/act/text.html.

Federal Communications Commission (FCC). (1974). Children's television programs: Report and policy statement. *Federal Register, 39,* 39396–409.

Federal Communications Commission (FCC). (2000). *Fact sheet.* Retrieved September 2006, from http://www.fcc.gov/mb/facts/ csgen.html.

Federal Communications Commission (FCC). (n.d.). *About the FCC.* Retrieved September 2006, from http://www.fcc.gov/aboutus.html.

Franklin, J., Rifkin, L., & Pascual, P. (2001). Serving the very young and the restless: Children's programming on public television. In D. Singer & J. Singer (Eds.), *Handbook of children and the media* (pp. 307–520). Thousand Oaks, CA: Sage.

Fry, A. (2002). Getting the green. *Kidscreen, 7*(9), 105.

Jordan, A., Schmitt, K., & Woodard, E. (2002). Developmental implications of commercial broadcasters' educational offerings. In S. Calvert, A. Jordan, R. Cocking (Eds.), *Children in the digital age* (pp. 145–64). Westport, CT: Praeger.

Kunkel, D., & Wilcox, B. (2001). Children and media policy. In D. Singer & J. Singer (Eds.), *Handbook of children and the media* (pp. 589–604). Thousand Oaks, CA: Sage.

McNichol, D. (2006, October 8). State tax credits say thanks for the films. *The Star Ledger,* p. 18.

Ontario Media Development Corporation. (n.d.). *Ontario computer animation and special effects tax credit.* Retrieved September 2006, from http://64.34.131.47/PageFactory.aspx?PageID=3402.

Paik, H. (2001). The history of children's use of electronic media. In D. Singer & J. Singer (Eds.), *Handbook of children and the media* (pp. 7–28). Thousand Oaks, CA: Sage.

Public Broadcasting Service. (n.d.a). *About PBS: Editorial standards.* Retrieved September 2006, from http://www.pbs.org/aboutpbs/aboutpbs_standards.html.

Public Broadcasting Service. (n.d.b). *PBS red book: Underwriting.* Retrieved September 2006, from http://www.pbs.org/producers/redbook/specs/underwriting.html.

Richter, W. (n.d.). *Action for children's television.* Retrieved September 2006, from http://www.museum.tv/archives/etv/A/htmlA/actionforch actionforch.htm/.

Roberts, D. F., Foehr, U. G., & Rideout, V. J. (2005). *Generation M: Media in the lives of 8–18 year-olds.* Menlo Park, CA: Kaiser Family Foundation.

Strover, S. (n.d.). *United States: Cable television.* Retrieved September 2006, from http://www.museum.tv/archives/etv/U/htmlU/unitedstatesc/unitedstatesc.htm.

Telefilm Canada. (n.d.). Retrieved November 2006, from http://www.telefilm.gc.ca/04/48.asp.

Yankelovitch Preschool Study. (2005). *"Pop" go the parents: Taking back parenting on the horizon.* Chapel Hill, NC: Yankelovitch Preschool Study.

Part II
Media Access and Differential Use Patterns

3

Media Use Across Childhood: Access, Time, and Content

Ronda Scantlin

Children and adolescents now live in complex, media-saturated environments – ones filled with televisions, videocassette recorders, DVD players, digital video recorders, TiVos, computers, the Internet, videogame consoles, CD players, iPods, print media, and other portable electronic devices. Media are a ubiquitous force in children's daily lives, and they clearly play integral roles in children's education, communication, entertainment, and leisure as well as influence their daily routines. Moreover, childhood is characterized by early and frequent media use, preparing youth for life-long relationships with communication technologies. This chapter examines these diverse media experiences at different points in children's lives – from infancy through adolescence – as well as explores the ways in which boys and girls and children from different racial and socioeconomic groups use media.

The chapter is organized around three primary aspects of media use: access and use, time spent with different technologies, and content preferences. The first section addresses access to media, which is a precursor to message exposure and media effects. Because children's access is often determined by parents (e.g., making the decision to purchase a computer for the family), the focus of the discussion will be availability and use of various media within the home. The second section of the chapter examines children's time use. How much time do children and adolescents spend in front of screens? How do they manage their time with so many media choices? Research indicates that time commitment is substantial and time itself is more flexible than once thought. Studying this generation of media users moves us away from a simple displacement model to one characterized by multitasking. Finally, the third section of the chapter explores genre or content preferences. Children's media choices – from *SimCity* to *Grand Theft Auto* – can have a profound positive or negative impact on their development.

Children's Access to and Use of Media

Children and adolescents have unprecedented access to a diverse range of media activities. According to a recent national survey of 2,032 children aged 8 to 18 years, the typical American child lives in a household with three televisions, three videocassette recorders (VCRs), three radios, three CD or tape players, two videogame consoles, and one personal computer (Roberts, Foehr, & Rideout, 2005). These devices are ubiquitous in young peoples' lives and can be found in their living rooms, bedrooms, family vehicles, and backpacks. They can even be found outside the home in school classrooms and childcare centers.

Media use has an impact on concurrent social interactions and is itself conditioned by the social context in which it is used. The home environment is clearly an important context as parents make technology available and play a role in socializing children to use media in specific ways. It is also within this environment that parents have the opportunity to establish boundaries that influence their children's media use – how much time they spend in front of the screen, the specific content they watch or use, and what messages they take away from those media-use choices (e.g., Jordan, 1992; Lull, 1980; Nathanson, 2001). Media access in children's homes, then, becomes the focus of the data discussed in this chapter.

Access and use as a function of age

Even young children – infants, toddlers, and preschoolers – are growing up in homes where media are a central part of their daily experiences. With the exception of the family, television reaches children at a younger age and for more time than any other socializing institution (Huston & Wright, 1996). This highlights television's potential to influence children from a very early age.

In a nationally representative study, Rideout and Hamel (2006) conducted a telephone survey of 1,051 parents (81 percent of whom were mothers) of children ages 6 months to 6 years. To augment the survey data, eight focus groups were also conducted in four locations across the United States. The study revealed that nearly all children (99 percent) live in homes with at least one television set and 84 percent live in homes with two or more sets; 80 percent have access to cable or satellite television; nearly all (93 percent) have a VCR or DVD player in the home; and 33 percent have a portable DVD player.

One consequence of families purchasing newer television sets is that the older ones tend to migrate to children's bedrooms, providing additional opportunities to watch with little to no adult supervision. Thus, even at an early age, many children have television sets in their bedrooms. In fact, a third of children between the ages 6 months to 6 years have their own set in their room. The percentage increases with age (19 percent for children 6 months to 1 year, 29 percent for those 2–3 years, and 43 percent for those 4–6 years).

These very young viewers have also recently become a sought-after market for video products. *Baby Einstein* videos and DVDs, which were launched in 1997 (e.g., *Baby Einstein: Baby Van Gogh, Baby Beethoven, World Animals, A Day on the Farm*), have gained popularity with parents because of their alleged educational benefits. In 2005, Disney followed the *Baby Einstein* brand success with a new television program for preschoolers: *Little Einsteins*. The newest addition to the media family is *BabyFirstTV*, the nation's first channel for babies which was launched via satellite television in May of 2006. The mission of *BabyFirstTV* is to provide engaging and educational experiences for babies during the first years of learning and to provide opportunities for parents to interact and play with their infants. Despite this trend in newer media content for the youngest viewers, the American Academy of Pediatrics (1999) has recommended that television viewing should be discouraged for children under the age of 2. There is clearly a disconnect between the goals of media industries (i.e., attract audiences and increase profits) and the goals of the medical community (i.e., advocate for the health and well-being of children). At present, scientific evidence is lacking on the potential effects of these visual media made especially for babies on infants' and toddlers' development (Barr, this volume, Chapter 7).

Interactive technologies are commonplace as well for the 6 month to 6 year age group, although generally older children have more access to these technologies than younger children do. According to the Rideout and Hamel (2006) national study, 78 percent of 6-month- to 6-year-old children live in homes with a computer, 69 percent have Internet access, and 50 percent have a console videogame player. Similar findings were reported by Calvert, Rideout, Woolard, Barr, and Strouse (2005) in their analyses of data collected in the spring of 2003 from the first Zero to Six study. In this nationally representative telephone survey of 1,065 parents of children ages 6 months through 6 years, Calvert and colleagues (2005) found that 75 percent of families reported owning a computer and 88 percent of those who owned a computer reported having Internet access. Older children were more likely to have used a computer than younger children were, and "the acquisition of specific computer skills demonstrates linear trends with age for using a mouse to point and click, using a computer without sitting on a parent's lap, loading a CD-ROM by themselves, and turning on the computer by themselves" (Calvert et al., 2005, p. 597). These data indicate that toddlers begin to use computers with the help of their parents, but very quickly gain autonomy and acquire skills necessary to use technology on their own.

Finally, it is not surprising that very young children have significant access to print media and music. Results from the first Zero to Six survey indicated that among children younger than 2 years, 81 percent listened to music and 71 percent read or were read to in a typical day; nearly all children aged 6 months to 6 years read or were read to (95 percent) and listened to music (97 percent) (Rideout, Vandewater, & Wartella, 2003).

Middle-school age children and adolescents have more access to, and experience with, a diverse range of media activities when compared to their younger counterparts. Roberts, Foehr, and Rideout (2005) found that the television, VCR, radio, and CD/tape player had reached close to 100 percent penetration in the homes of 8- to 18-year-olds. Yet the sheer number of these four basic technologies in a given home does seem to increase with age. In particular, 15- to 18-year-olds are more likely to live in homes with three or more of each of these media staples than are 8- to 14-year-olds (Roberts, Foehr, & Rideout, 2005). There are also significant age differences associated with access to communication technologies. Eighty percent of 15- to 18-year-olds live in homes with Internet connections and 70 percent live in homes with instant messaging (IM) programs; in contrast, 63 percent of 8- to 10-year-olds live in homes with Internet connections and 42 percent live in homes with instant messenger (Roberts, Foehr, & Rideout, 2005).

In addition to living in homes with a diverse array of media options, youth also possess personal media (i.e., media in their bedrooms or portable devices that they own). Having access to personal televisions and VCRs/DVDs is not related to age; however, access to personal music media (e.g., radios, CD players, MP3 players) is more common for 11- to 18-year-olds than for 8- to 10-year-olds. In contrast, 8- to 10-year-olds are more likely to have a video gaming device in their bedrooms or own a handheld gaming device than are 15- to 18-year-olds (Roberts, Foehr, & Rideout, 2005). These findings illustrate the changing gratifications sought by young people as they mature, with adolescents choosing media activities that potentially shape personal identity and facilitate social connectedness (e.g., Huntemann & Morgan, 2001).

Access and use by gender

When considering availability of media in the home, girls and boys tend to experience similar levels of access to almost all media activities. The videogame is one exception; boys are more likely to live in homes with videogame consoles than girls are, and boys are more likely to use them. Roberts and colleagues found this to be the case in both the 1999 and 2004 national surveys of media use (Roberts et al., 1999; Roberts, Foehr, & Rideout, 2005). Roberts and colleagues (2005) also found that boys were more likely than girls to own several different personal media. The largest difference existed for videogames, but differences were also present for computers and Internet connections. Boys were twice as likely as girls to have a videogame console in their bedrooms (63 percent versus 33 percent) with similar differences found for handheld gaming devices (63 percent versus 48 percent).

Access and use by race

The research efforts focusing on media-use patterns of very young children are relatively recent and thus studies exploring the differential experiences of Caucasian, African American, and Hispanic children are lacking for this age group.

Calvert and colleagues (2005) did find that Latino parents of children ages 6 months to 6 years were less likely to report owning a computer, and African American and Latino parents were less likely than Caucasian parents to have Internet access on their home computer. For 8- to 18-year olds, a young person's race is not associated with differences in the likelihood of living in a household with at least one television set, VCR, radio, CD/tape player, and videogame console (Roberts, Foehr, & Rideout, 2005). Similar to the findings reported for younger children, however, there are racial differences with regard to computer and Internet access. Ninety percent of Caucasian children, 80 percent of Hispanic children, and 78 percent of African American children live in homes with a computer; with regard to Internet access the percentages are 80 percent, 67 percent, and 61 percent respectively; the percentage of children living in homes with IM programs are 63 percent, 55 percent, 47 percent respectively (Roberts, Foehr, & Rideout, 2005). In contrast, African American children (39 percent) and Hispanic children (40 percent) are slightly more likely to have digital video recorders in their homes than Caucasian children are (30 percent). While ethnicity and race do play a role in differential access to computers and the Internet, a family's income or socioeconomic status, which is associated with ethnicity and race, has historically been the variable driving inequities surrounding ownership of new technologies (e.g., Civille, 1995).

Access and use by income and socioeconomic status

The term socioeconomic status (SES) has been used to describe a composite of variables including one's income, education, and occupation. These factors appear to be good predictors of computer ownership and use, such that those with high incomes, advanced educations, and professional positions tend to purchase new technologies first and utilize them more frequently (e.g., Civille, 1995; Steinfield, Dutton, & Kovaric, 1989; Vitalari & Venkatesh, 1987). SES can directly influence the use of computer technologies in the home by reducing or increasing economic constraints on access to that technology.

Unequal access to computer technology across specific groups of people has been labeled the "digital divide." The research evidence suggests that while the digital divide has narrowed, it continues to persist (e.g., Calvert et al., 2005; Fairlie, 2005; Fox, 2005; Roberts, Foehr, & Rideout, 2005). Consistent with their 1999 survey, Roberts and colleagues (2005) found that 54 percent of 8- to 18-year-olds in communities where the median income is less than $35,000 per year go online in a typical day, 57 percent in the income range of $35,000 to $50,000 do so, and 71 percent of those from communities where the median income is greater than $50,000 a year go online in a typical day. A greater percentage of youth from lower income brackets go online most often from school or other non-home locations when compared to youth from higher income brackets (35 percent of those earning less than $35,000, 25 percent in the $35,000 to $50,000 bracket, and 12 percent of those earning greater than

$50,000). Further evidence of this divide is provided by Lenhart, Madden, and Hitlin (2005). They found that teenagers from households earning less than $30,000 were less likely than teens from any other income group to report Internet use.

The underlying concern is whether children without access to computers and Internet connections in their *homes* will be disadvantaged in the increasingly wired schools and in the workplace. Users who have computers and online access in their homes encounter fewer constraints (e.g., time limits on use, "one-size-fits-all" filters on content) than do those using technology in public places such as libraries, schools, and recreation centers. Moreover, it is a widely held belief that children with access to computers from an early age develop skills and attitudes that give them a substantial advantage in education and skills that facilitate achievement. The research literature exploring the effects of home computer use on educational outcomes, however, is sparse. One notable study is Fairlie's (2005) analysis of approximately 4,239 16- to 18-year-olds from the Computer and Internet Usage Supplement to the September 2001 Current Population Survey. Access to home computers increased the likelihood of school enrollment and high-school graduation among teenagers, after controlling for family income, parental education, and parental occupation.

Another "digital division" pertains to access speeds (i.e., dial-up versus broadband). Connection speed has become an important predictor of online use, perhaps even more important than experience; users with fast connections tend to be those who go online every day and engage in a wider variety of online activities (e.g., accessing news, purchasing products, utilizing online banking services, and playing online games). Time is valuable and limited; connection speeds (translating into various levels of success versus frustration) may partially determine how we choose to spend our time with media. In a recent nationally representative survey of 2,001 adults from the Pew Internet & American Life Project, Fox (2005) reported that Internet users living in the highest-income households ($75,000 or higher) are most likely to go online (93 percent have access) and most likely to have a fast connection (71 percent of these users had broadband connections in their homes). In contrast, those online users in the lowest income households ($30,000 or less) are half as likely to go online (49 percent have access) and less likely to have fast connections (42 percent of these users have broadband connections) (Fox, 2005).

Although the Pew study involved adults, connection speeds likely have important consequences for children's and adolescents' online activities as well. Lenhart and Madden (2005) estimate that half of all American teenagers, which would be about 12 million youth, create content for the Internet and World Wide Web. Popular activities include sharing self-authored content, working on webpages for others, creating blogs, sharing artwork or photos, and creating personal webpages. Half of teens report downloading music files and one third report downloading video files (Lenhart & Madden, 2005). These digital publishing and downloading activities require bandwidth, and while there are few demographic differences between those who create content and those who do not, teen content creators are more likely to have broadband Internet access at home (Lenhart & Madden, 2005).

While there are no easy solutions to bridging the divide, new interactive technologies provide intriguing possibilities. For instance, the new generation of videogame consoles (such as the Xbox 360) allow for Internet access. Research indicates that videogame consoles (which can be less expensive than computers) are as common in households of lower-income families as they are in households of higher-income families (Roberts et al., 1999; Roberts, Foehr, & Rideout, 2005; Woodard, 2000). Cell phones are becoming the new personal computers (PCs), and access to these mobile devices is widespread. These new digital media may enable underserved groups to gain access to the networked world of the Internet, bypassing PC ownership completely.

Time Spent with Media

How children spend their time – from reading books to playing with friends – can influence numerous developmental outcomes and provide opportunities for learning. Similarly, time spent with media activities can affect children's cognitive, social, emotional, and health-related development in positive ways (e.g., Friedrich & Stein, 1975; Subrahmanyam & Greenfield, 1996; Wright, Huston, Murphy, et al., 2001). Yet television, in particular, has long been criticized for taking children away from or "displacing" other worthy endeavors such as reading and socializing with family. Time displacement refers to the idea that time spent participating in one activity will displace time spent in another activity (e.g., Huston & Wright, 1998). Research findings, however, do not support a simple hypothesis that television displaces other valuable activities (e.g., Huston et al., 1999). Similar concerns have been voiced about children's use of the Internet and other interactive media activities, based on the assumption that there is only a limited amount of time and energy available to devote to social and non-social activities (Orleans & Laney, 2000).

In contrast to this static model of time displacement, children and adolescents no longer use only one medium to the exclusion of others, but rather often engage in multitasking in which they experience several activities simultaneously. For instance, anecdotal conversations with teens indicate they now listen to music, surf the web, and contact their friends via IM, all while doing homework. Hence, it is important to reconceptualize our traditional perceptions of how young people use time. Roberts and colleagues (2005, p. 35) distinguish between *media exposure* and *media use*, with media exposure defined as "the sum of the amount of time youth spend with each medium to obtain an estimate of total exposure" and media use defined as the number of "person hours" devoted to media. Therefore, hours of total exposure may be higher than hours of use, because it is commonplace for children and adolescents to engage in two, three, or even four activities at the same time. Multitasking, as opposed to displacement, appears to provide a more realistic conception of how young people currently use their time.

Measures of children's media use patterns

Measuring the amount of time children participate in media-related activities is among the most basic steps in understanding the potential effects of each medium on children's development (Kubey & Larson, 1990). The following section will provide a brief overview of methods that have been commonly used to measure time in front of the screen, content preferences, or media-use experiences, followed by a discussion of how children's time-use patterns change as a function of age, gender, and race.

Time-use diaries   Time-use diaries require individuals to describe their activities, or the activities of their child, sequentially for a 24-hour period (Juster & Stafford, 1985). Diaries are more accurate than the self-reported time estimates that are often used in surveys, particularly if collected relatively soon after the time period being described (Anderson & Field, 1991). Time-use diaries have the advantages of (1) increasing accuracy, as systematic reporting of daily activities is easier for participants than recollection of general time estimates; (2) capturing all of the child's activities, permitting examination of a diverse range of activities from personal care to social and recreational behaviors; and (3) being less subject to distortions of social desirability than are survey questions about frequency of use (Huston et al., 1999). Time-use diaries have been used successfully in media research, including a longitudinal investigation of children's media use (Wright, Huston, Murphy, et al., 2001) and in national surveys of media use (e.g., Wright, Huston, Vandewater, et al., 2001). Collection of such diaries, however, does require substantial persistence and effort.

Respondents' reports or self-estimates   Respondents' reports or self-estimates of media use are the most frequently used indicator of media-use behaviors and can be assessed in a questionnaire or interview. Not surprisingly, more specific questions yield more accurate responses. For example, a question asking for an estimate of weekly television viewing time provides less accurate information than does a question about a specific time period (e.g., How much time did you spend watching television yesterday?). One advantage to using this method is convenience – large amounts of data can be collected quickly and inexpensively for large numbers of respondents. Time estimates of media use, however, tend to be less accurate than diaries, although the two measures are correlated with one another (Anderson et al., 1985).

It is important to note that when assessing children's media-use habits (via questionnaires, interviews, and time-use diaries), it is often the parents who are providing information about their children. Few studies report conversations with children themselves (for an exception see Calvert & Kotler, 2003). Parents' reports of children's media experiences, therefore, should be viewed with some care as parents are not always aware of what their children are watching, playing, or surfing. Rideout and Hamel (2006) acknowledged this possibility in their most recent national survey with parents of infants, toddlers, and preschoolers; only 50 percent of parents interviewed said they spent all or most of the day with their child and therefore their knowledge of media use was potentially limited. Similarly, researchers have demonstrated that parents are often not aware of their children's videogame habits and cannot accurately describe the content of the games their children are playing (Funk et al., 1999; Funk, Hagan, & Schimming, 1999). Two methods that can be used to improve accuracy of reported information include asking parents and children to complete diaries/questionnaires together, and questioning childcare providers or other caregivers about children's activities.

Experience sampling method The *beeper or pager method*, also called the *experience sampling method*, can offer rich data regarding the context of media use (e.g., is the person alone or with friends or family, in his/her bedroom or family living room) and can be documented at the time those experiences occur. Kubey and Larson (1990) had 483 children and adolescents (aged 9–15) carry electronic pagers; they filled out self-reports of their activities and experiences when they were signaled. The participants recorded the name of the activity, where they were located, who they were with, a description of their affective state, as well as the amount of time they engaged in the activity. Disadvantages to using this method include availability (throughout the day) of the recording diary forms and disruption of the participants' daily activities.

Home video observation Home video observation uses video equipment to record what is on the television, who is in the room, and what is happening when the set is turned on. Daniel Anderson and his colleagues (Anderson & Field, 1991; Anderson et al., 1985) used this method to examine children's and families' attention to television programs. The researchers placed video cameras and other equipment in families' homes – one camera to record what programs were on the television and one camera to record what was happening in the room. Videotapes of home viewing indicate no correlation between amount of exposure and percentage of attention (Anderson & Field, 1983), highlighting the fact that children often participate in other activities while the television set is on.

Clear disadvantages of this method are the intrusive nature and substantial financial costs associated with home video observation techniques. Advantages include capturing actual viewing patterns (which can be correlated with changing action on the television set), assessing activities concurrent with television viewing, and having an archive to address subsequent research questions. For example, when Schmitt, Woolf, and Anderson (2003) re-analyzed home video recordings from the early 1980s, they were able to quantify the types of behaviors (e.g., socializing, playing, vigorous activity) that occurred *while* young children watched television.

Time spent with media as a function of age

Despite the myriad of media choices, television viewing continues to consume more of children's time than any other media activity. Television viewing among 8- to 18-year-olds, for instance, averages 3 hours per day, and when television, videos/DVDs, and movies are combined that number increases to 4 hours and 15 minutes per day (Roberts, Foehr, & Rideout, 2005). Researchers have consistently found in both cross-sectional and longitudinal studies that children's television viewing time increases steadily from infancy through age 6, slightly declines once children enter school and then tends to increase through late childhood, peaking around age 11 or 12 (e.g., Bianchi & Robinson, 1997; Comstock, 1991; Huston et al., 1999; Timmer, Eccles, & O'Brien, 1985). The decline in viewing time during adolescence is presumably due to increased time spent in extra-curricular or school activities, time developing social relationships outside the family, and perhaps time spent with other types of media activities.

Infants and toddlers   Infants and toddlers are spending substantial amounts of time with a variety of media. In a typical day, children younger than 2 years spend an average of 2 hours and 5 minutes in front of a screen (Rideout, Vandewater, & Wartella, 2003). Time spent watching television steadily increases from 6 months to 4 years of age, and then declines from 5 years to 6 years; a similar pattern is found for watching videos and DVDs, with an increase in viewership through 3 years and a decline thereafter (Anand & Krosnick, 2005).

The Panel Study of Income Dynamics (PSID), a longitudinal survey of a nationally representative sample of US families that has been conducted annually since 1968, provides another source of information about the media-use habits of children from birth through age 12. As part of this assessment, the primary caregiver was asked to complete a 24-hour time-use diary for one weekend day and one weekday for each child in the study. The time-use diary data of 2,902 children provides additional evidence that from birth through age 2, very young children are spending time in front of the screen, watching on average 67 minutes on the weekend (Wright, Huston, Vandewater, et al., 2001).

In a typical day, the vast majority of younger children spend some time with media. For example, 88 percent of infants (aged 1 and under) listen to music, 77 percent read or are read to, 56 percent watch television, and 24 percent watch a video or DVD (Rideout & Hamel, 2006). In contrast, few infants use a computer (2 percent) or play a video game (1 percent). These figures increase slightly for 2- to 3-year-olds: 84 percent listen to music, 81 percent read or are read to, 81 percent watch television, 41 percent watch a video/DVD, 12 percent use a computer, and 8 percent play a videogame in a typical day. Many younger children are just as likely to spend time with media as to spend time in social play. For example, 55 percent of infants and 80 percent of toddlers play outside in a typical day, which is roughly comparable to the proportion of very young children who watch television in an average day.

While one can debate whether it is or is not healthy for infants and toddlers to spend time with media, an examination of parents' personal media-use habits and perceptions provides insight into reasons why very young children spend time in front of screens. Parents influence children's viewing by setting an example of media use and habits, by co-viewing with their children, by discussing their values and attitudes about television, and by regulating or encouraging viewing of particular types of content (Austin, 1993; Schmitt, 2000; Wright, St Peters, & Huston, 1990). Many parents watch significant amounts of television themselves, leave the television on during meals, and use television as background throughout the day. Rideout and Hamel's (2006) findings revealed that parents (the sample consisting of primarily mothers) not only encouraged their children to use media for educational reasons, but encouraged media use to keep their children occupied; this then provided parents with uninterrupted time to do chores and tasks within the home. Parents also discussed their need for personal time or time away from their children, a need easily satisfied by turning on the television. Younger children clearly have less control over their media choices. While they may not be able to comprehend or articulate their motivations for watching, they nevertheless are gratified or entertained by the experience of watching their favorite television program or DVD.

Preschool and school-age children Recent survey data suggest that children under the age of 6 are using screen media about 2 hours per day (Rideout & Hamel, 2006; Rideout, Vandewater, & Wartella, 2003). Because the kinds of media (e.g., DVDs) and content (e.g., videos designed for babies) have varied over time, it is also useful to examine cohort differences.

The Early Window Project, a study of more than 250 families, provides rich time-use data for two cohorts of children ages 2–5 and ages 4–7 (Wright, Huston, Murphy, et al., 2001). Time-use diaries were collected over a three-year period (1) during office and home visits with parents and (2) in telephone interviews during the intervening time periods. Although content preferences are discussed in a subsequent section of this chapter, cohort differences are nicely illustrated by comparing the types of programming children watch on weekdays and weekends. In particular, children spent more time watching child-informative, child-animated, and general audience programming on a typical weekday than on a weekend day. Up until approximately 4 years of age, children watched child-informative programs for about 2 hours per week. This dropped to about 1 hour per week at ages 5 through 7 years. Children watched cartoons for about 7.5 hours per week until age 5, with a decrease by age 7 to about 5 hours per week; children also spent about 16 hours per week watching general-audience programs at ages 2 and 3, with a decrease to around 10 hours per week by ages 6 and 7 (Wright, Huston, Murphy, et al., 2001). The decline in general audience viewing was due to a decline in secondary viewing (as opposed to a decline in primary viewing). Secondary viewing refers to viewing accompanied by another activity. Secondary viewing for young children often means playing nearby while their parents are watching general audience programming (Wright & Huston, 1995).

The Panel Study of Income Dynamics diary data also reveal differences between weekday and weekend viewing for this age group. Weekday viewing peaked at 3–5 years (111 minutes) with 6- to 8- and 9- to 12-year-olds watching 92 minutes and 98 minutes, respectively; in contrast, weekend viewing peaked at 6–8 years (160 minutes) with 3- to 5-year-olds and 9- to 12-year-olds watching 131 minutes and 157 minutes, respectively (Wright, Huston, Vandewater, et al., 2001). School attendance reduces weekday television viewing for 6- to 12-year-olds; in contrast, more discretionary time is available on the weekends and children's bedtime routines often change, allowing for more time with media.

Computer and videogames remain a popular leisure activity during middle childhood, with use declining as children grow older. Buchman and Funk (1996) surveyed children 9–12 years and found that total time playing interactive games steadily decreased as a function of age (from 5.6 hours per week to 2.5 hours per week for fourth- to eighth-grade girls, and from 9.4 hours per week to 5 hours per week for fourth- to eighth-grade boys).

Adolescents   During the adolescent years, teens assert their independence and are given more freedom of choice by their parents in both non-media and media-related activities. As such, they are more likely to have media in their bedrooms and engage in media activities with less adult supervision. Moreover, they are using media in increasingly diverse ways. Roberts and colleagues (2005) found that youth ages 8–18 years spend approximately 6.5 hours per day with media, and if one also considers multitasking behaviors, that 6.5 hours translates into 8.5 hours of total media exposure each day. Adolescents spend almost 4 hours watching television (television, videos, DVDs), 1.75 hours listening to music (radio, CDs, tapes, MP3s), 1 hour using the computer (online and offline), 49 minutes playing videogames (console and handheld), 43 minutes reading (books, magazines, and newspapers), and 25 minutes watching movies (in a theatre); in comparison, youth spend 2.25 hours with parents, 1.5 hours in physical activity, 1 hour participating in hobbies or other activities, and 50 minutes doing homework in a typical day (Roberts, Foehr, & Ridout, 2005).

When examining multiple categories of interactive media – from video gaming to IM – it is apparent that time spent with these activities also changes from the preteen years through late adolescence. Total time playing videogames tends to steadily decrease during this period of time (e.g., Buchman & Funk, 1996). Roberts and colleagues (2005) reaffirmed this pattern indicating that 8- to 10-year-olds spend about 1 hour, 11- to 14-year-olds spend 52 minutes, and 15- to 18-year-olds spend 33 minutes per day playing videogames. In contrast, overall time spent on computers increases with age (37 minutes, 1 hour, and 1 hour 22 minutes, respectively.) Consistent with earlier data, (Roberts et al., 1999), gaming accounted for more minutes than other activities for 8- to 18-year-olds. Communicating with peers via IM, however, significantly increases as a function of age; 8- to 10-year-olds spend 3 minutes per day with IM, 11- to 14-year-olds spend 18 minutes, and 15- to 18-year-olds spend 27 minutes per day (Roberts, Foehr, & Rideout, 2005). A similar pattern emerges for visiting websites.

Youth aged 11–18 years spend 2.25 hours with friends and 53 minutes talking on the phone daily (Roberts, Foehr, & Rideout, 2005). Cell phones are now a widely used communicative device with 32 percent of teens aged 12–14 and 57 percent of teens aged 15–17 owning one (Lenhart, Madden, & Hitlin, 2005). Teens, however, are not the only consumers of this mobile technology. Firefly Mobile and Disney Mobile now manufacture cell phones for children and preteens, with the marketing strategy focusing on safety and connectedness.

For school age and teenage media consumers, electronic media are clearly a more attractive option than is using print. Research consistently demonstrates that youth do not spend significant amounts of time reading for leisure, and as they mature they tend to spend less and less time engaged in reading. Eight- to eighteen-year-olds spend an average of only 23 minutes reading books, 14 minutes reading magazines, and 6 minutes reading newspapers per day (Roberts, Foehr, & Rideout, 2005).

Time spent with media by gender and race

There do not appear to be notable differences in how much time boys and girls spend using media at the youngest ages. Boys and girls spend similar amounts of time watching television, reading, listening to music, and using the computer (Rideout, Vandewater, & Wartella, 2003).

While boys and girls also devote similar amounts of time to computer use during middle childhood and the teen years, the specific activities of young males and females differ. In general, boys spend more time playing interactive games, and girls spend more time visiting websites, sending emails, and using IM (Roberts, Foehr, & Rideout, 2005). Historically, boys have consistently reported significantly higher preference for and time commitment to playing computer games and videogames than do girls in both home and arcade settings (e.g., Funk, Germann, & Buchman, 1997; Huston et al., 1999; Kubey & Larson, 1990; Roberts et al., 1999). Similarly, studies of online gaming indicate that males are overwhelmingly the most frequent participants (Griffiths, Davies, & Chappell, 2004). These findings highlight evidence that gender differences are significant for particular interests and preferences of young media consumers.

Race is associated with differences in time spent in front of screen media (i.e., television, videos/DVDs, and movies). In general, African Americans spend more time watching television than do European Americans. African American children use all screen media almost 6 hours per day, compared to 3.75 hours for Caucasian children and 4.5 hours for Hispanic children (Roberts, Foehr, & Rideout, 2005). This pattern remains even when considering level of parent education and income.

The Uses and Gratifications of Media

That children and adolescents choose to spend significant amounts of time in a typical day engaged in media-related activities is readily apparent. Why do they devotedly watch their favorite television programs, play the newest videogames, or download their favorite music? The simple answer is entertainment; however, uses and gratifications theory can be used to further understand selective exposure to media. The uses and gratifications approach focuses on users' motivations and needs, their media preferences, the ways in which they make use of the media, and their patterns of use (Van Evra, 2004).

Three overarching categories of motivation have emerged from uses and gratifications research: (1) *Diversion/escape* (i.e., to achieve stimulation, relaxation, emotional release); (2) *Personal identity/social utility* (i.e., to strengthen contact with others, to overcome loneliness, to form one's identity); and (3) *Information seeking/cognition* (i.e., to obtain useful information such as factual or sociocultural knowledge) (Rubin, 2002). Children and adolescents use media to satisfy their needs and wants, particularly social and emotional needs. In a recent analysis of home video recordings from 1980 and 1981, Schmitt, Woolf, and Anderson (2003) found that 2-year-olds spent significant time socializing, playing, and being physically active while watching television. In contrast, older children spent more time focused on the television screen and less time engaging in other activities. The authors suggest that the uses and gratifications of television for very young viewers may be to provide a context for social activity and play.

Media-use behaviors can also be characterized as instrumental (e.g., seeking out a particular television program) or ritualistic (e.g., surfing channels until finding something of interest). Instrumental use is seeking certain media *content* for informational reasons, and suggests purposive, intentional, or selective behavior (Rubin, 2002). Ritualistic use refers to engaging with a *medium* more habitually to consume time or for diversion (Rubin, 2002). This distinction between instrumental and ritualized use is associated with the amount of time individuals spend with media and the types of content they prefer to view or use. Heavy overall media use, for example, generally reflects a ritualized approach. Different media may also lend themselves to ritualistic or instrumental orientations. For example, Metzger and Flanagin (2002) found that "traditional" media – specifically television – tended to be used more ritualistically; in contrast, talking on the telephone and reading the newspaper tended to be used instrumentally.

Uses and gratifications theory provides a useful framework when examining how individuals use interactive communication technologies such as the Internet. Computers and their accompanying software, by nature, require active engagement initiated and sustained by the individual. Use of the World Wide Web in particular requires active searching for the information of interest, and can satisfy diverse needs for diverse users. Metzger and Flanagin (2002) noted, however, that use of the conversational aspects of the Internet and the Web was more ritualistic in nature. These findings are intriguing when considering the communicative behaviors of young people, particularly their use of cell phones. Some cell phone behaviors are clearly instrumental, yet constant chatter on cell phones suggests their use also includes a ritualistic component. The next section explores how users approach media to fulfill their needs, with content being the main organizer of media choice.

Media-Use Patterns – Content Preferences

To understand the role of media in the lives of children, it is essential to gather data about time spent using *particular types* of content or genre, not just an index of total use. Media effects are partially dependent on which programs children watch, what kind of music they listen to, or which videogames they play. For instance, there is a substantial body of evidence demonstrating that watching educational television programs can teach academic and prosocial lessons, while watching general entertainment programming is associated with lower levels of school readiness and academic performance (e.g., Anderson et al., 2001; Huston & Wright, 1998; Wright, Huston, Murphy, et al., 2001). Similarly, interactive games offer a diverse range of experiences – from those that provide challenging, skill-building environments like *The Sims* series to those prominently featuring violent themes such as *Grand Theft Auto*. The lessons learned depend on the games played. These games have tremendous capacity to encourage exploration and facilitate sustained engagement, yet they can also teach violent methods of resolving conflicts and expose youth to other negative social messages.

Television programs and videogames can readily be coded by content types or genres and have been a focus for researchers examining children's media-use habits. These two media will also take center stage in the subsequent discussion of children's content preferences. While researchers may slightly differ in how they categorize television programs, there are commonalities across studies. For instance, Wright, Huston, Vandewater, and colleagues (2001) created a coding system that included children's educational, children's non-educational, action, comedy, reality, relationship drama, fantasy, and sports; similarly, Roberts, Foehr, and Rideout (2005) utilized a system that included children's educational, comedy, movie, reality, entertainment/variety, drama, sports, documentary, music videos, and news. Coding systems for interactive games have been designed to reflect the cognitive and physical demands of the game (i.e., types of mental and sensorimotor activity required) as well as content features. Wright, Huston, Vandewater, and colleagues (2001) utilized a system that captured educational/informational, sports, sensorimotor (action/arcade, fighting/shooting, driving/racing, other vehicular simulations), and strategy (adventure/role playing, war, strategic simulations, puzzles/games). Researchers have also interviewed children about their preference for particular types of content including fantasy violence and realistic human violence (Buchman & Funk, 1996; Funk, Germann, & Buchman, 1997). We turn now to genre categories for which there are statistically significant preference differences found among children of different ages, between boys and girls, or among children of different racial groups.

Preferences as a function of age

Children's media choices and preferences change as they mature. Media-use habits appear to result from changes in use opportunities, in cognitive abilities, and in one's social environment (Huston et al., 1992). Parents and caregivers play an influential role in their children's habits, encouraging some programming and limiting others. Moreover, media industries influence availability of content from which children and adolescents must select.

Educational content is designed to teach academic skills taught in school (e.g., vocabulary, math, science, and geography) or teach prosocial behaviors (e.g., altruism, self-control, and positive social interactions). This type of media content – whether it is *Sesame Street* on the television screen or *Reader Rabbit* on the computer – is most popular with the youngest media users; children are entertained as well as educated and parents encourage time spent with such material. Educational television viewing peaks around age 4 or 5 (e.g., Huston et al., 1999). Wright, Huston, Vandewater, and colleagues (2001) found that 0- to 2-year-olds watched 199 minutes of educational programming per week, 3- to 5-year-olds watched 240 minutes, 6- to 8-year-olds watched 114 minutes, and 9- to 12-year-olds watched 96 minutes per week. Roberts, Foehr, and Rideout (2005) noted similar declines through the late adolescent years; 47 percent of 8- to 10-year-olds, 21 percent of 11- to 14-year-olds, and 8 percent of 15- to 18-year-olds watched educational programming. Children's preference for educational computer games also decreases as a function of age for both girls and boys, with younger children more likely to prefer them than older children (Buchman & Funk, 1996; Roberts et al., 1999). In their analyses of the 730 children aged 0–12 years from the PSID who reported computer game use, Wright, Huston, Vandewater, and colleagues (2001) found that the youngest children (0–5 years) spent significantly more time per week playing games with educational content than older children did (84 minutes versus 22 minutes, respectively). Clearly, parents have more influence and control over children's choices during their earliest years and this impact is reflected in developmental shifts regarding the use of educational media.

Watching cartoons is also a staple of childhood, and interestingly time use follows a pattern similar to that of educational programming: viewing time increases through age 5 (Huston et al., 1999; Huston et al., 1990; Wright, Huston, Vandewater, et al., 2001). The presence of family members may influence these viewing choices as well. Children with older siblings tend to watch more cartoons with their siblings but without adults present, while those who have younger siblings continue to watch educational programs past the age of 4 (Wright, St Peters, & Huston, 1990).

Comedy programs consistently attract young viewers beginning in middle childhood (Condry, 1989). This pattern holds true regardless of age, gender, race or SES (Roberts, Foehr, & Rideout, 2005). For instance, of children who reported watching television the previous day, 39 percent of 8- to 10-year-olds reported watching comedy, 36 percent of 11- to 14-year-olds did so, and 34 percent of 15- to 18-year-olds reported watching comedies (Roberts, Foehr, & Rideout, 2005). In the PSID sample, 9- to 12-year-olds watched 200 minutes of comedy programming per week, which is significantly more time than their younger counterparts (i.e., 131 minutes for 6- to 8-year-olds, 67 minutes for 3- to 5-year-olds, and 26 minutes for 0- to 2-year-olds) (Wright, Huston, Vandewater, et al., 2001).

Adolescents are clearly developing media habits and preferences that diverge from their earlier years, perhaps because they are in the midst of searching for self or identity. Huntemann and Morgan (2001) suggest that media play a multi-faceted role in the ongoing process of identity development among young people by providing media models, encouraging media consumption, and promoting media choices. *Media models* include characters in favorite television programs, who provide information about style, outlook, and physical appearance that can be incorporated into one's identity (Huntemann & Morgan, 2001). Therefore, uses and gratifications theory suggests that one's motivation for viewing a particular television program and its associated characters may be related to personal identity or self-evaluation. *Media consumption* refers to advertising images that tell young audiences what (or who) is cool, attractive, or valued in youth culture. *Media choices* include behaviors that can be personal expressions of adolescent identity. For instance, choosing a certain type of music or watching *The O.C.* or *Veronica Mars* with friends can signal group membership. Correspondingly, 9- to 12-year-old girls are attracted to relationship dramas, with girls spending twice as much time (62 minutes per week) watching such programs as boys do (35 minutes per week) (Wright, Huston, Vandewater, et al., 2001). These examples illustrate the applicability of the uses and gratifications paradigm when examining media choices and preferences – whether young people gather to watch a specific television program for social utility (i.e., to strengthen contact with others) or watch particular characters as guides in the development of their personal identity.

Preferences as a function of gender

Differences between boys and girls are of theoretical interest because young children are thought to develop sex-typed attitudes, preferences, and behaviors through observations of the world around them, including exposure to media messages (Serbin, Powlishta, & Gulko, 1993). The development of sex typing occurs very early, as children 3 years of age can make gender classifications and are aware of many social expectations (Huston, 1983). Uses and gratifications theory would suggest that boys and girls select media content for purposes of self-evaluation, comparing themselves to persons of the same gender. Adolescent girls' increasing interest in relationship dramas (Wright, Huston, Vandewater, et al., 2001) provides one example of watching television for this purpose. Frequent television viewing in general is associated with stereotypical assumptions about male and female activities, traits, and occupations (Jacobson, 2005). Consequently, continued exposure to gender stereotyped media portrayals can have powerful effects on learning what it means to be male or female (Hurst & Brown, this volume, Chapter 5).

The body of research exploring gender differences indicates that boys and girls prefer different types of media content, with those differences especially prominent for computer games and videogames. When it comes to educational media, girls tend to watch educational television programming more (e.g., Wright, Huston, Vandewater, et al., 2001) and maintain an interest in this genre longer than boys do (Anderson et al., 2001; Wright, Huston, Vandewater, et al., 2001). In a survey of 900 children grades four through eight, Funk and colleagues (1997) also found that girls were more likely than boys to list educational computer games as favorites. Moreover, girls report a preference for puzzle or spatial-relation computer games (such as Tetris) and fantasy-adventure genres (Barnett et al., 1997; Gailey, 1996; Griffiths, 1997).

Girls' preferences are in stark contrast to those of boys. The research evidence overwhelmingly demonstrates that boys prefer sports-related content more than girls do. They spend more time per week watching sports on television and playing interactive sports games (Wright, Huston, Vandewater, et al., 2001). They also report stronger preferences for and enjoyment of interactive sports games (e.g., Barnett et al., 1997; Funk, Germann, & Buchman, 1997; Gailey, 1996; Griffiths, 1997; Roberts et al., 1999). Similarly, Roberts and colleagues (1999) and others have reported that boys have a much stronger preference for action or action/adventure games than girls do. When boys and girls are specifically asked about playing interactive games containing violence, boys more often prefer games categorized as realistic human violence whereas girls express a stronger preference for games containing cartoon fantasy violence (Buchman & Funk, 1996; Funk, Germann, & Buchman, 1997).

Uses and gratifications theory provides a useful framework for explaining these sex differences. Watching a sporting event on television or playing *Madden 2007* on the Xbox involves experiencing the theme of competition. Numerous observers have suggested the predominant masculine themes (e.g., fighting, war, aggressive competition) within computer games and videogames in particular likely account for the differential appeal of these games to boys and girls (e.g., Kafai, 1996; Subrahmanyam & Greenfield, 1998). Such behaviors are generally considered undesirable for females. The interactive game "culture" is also a prominent part of boys' socialization experiences. It is a collective leisure activity for boys, and their tendency to incorporate computing or gaming into friendship networks – a social utility function – may influence use at home and at school. Roberts and colleagues (1999) reported that 36 percent of the adolescents who played videogames reported playing them with peers or siblings.

Preferences as a function of race

Media images and messages can influence the development of racial and ethnic identity. *Sesame Street*, a program set in an inner-city neighborhood, is one of the best examples of a children's television program that appeals to preschoolers of all racial and ethnic groups. Similarly, LeVar Burton, the African American host of *Reading Rainbow*, introduces children to new books and the importance of storytelling. Children who see characters similar to themselves on television are learning basic lessons about the significance of their group in society. Potential consequences of not having such role models may be greater self-consciousness or looking to other groups or cultures for constructing one's own social identity (Huntemann & Morgan, 2001). Preference for certain types of media content, then, is partly influenced by whom a child sees or hears in the role of actor, singer, host, reporter, or performer.

Race is a strong predictor of particular tastes in music. Interestingly, Roberts and colleagues (2005) found that all 8- to 18-year-olds, regardless of race, preferred listening to Rap/Hip Hop over all other genres (81 percent of African Americans, 70 percent of Hispanics, and 60 percent of Caucasians). In addition to Rap/Hip Hop, African American youth tend to choose music genres that focus on African American performers, including Rhythm & Blues/Soul, Reggae, and Gospel/Christian. In contrast, Caucasian youth tend to listen to a broad range of music including Alternative Rock, Hard Rock/Heavy Metal, Punk, Country and Western, and Classic Rock (Roberts, Foehr, & Rideout, 2005).

Researchers have also documented that African American children spend less of their media time with educational content – either television programming or computer gaming – when compared to Caucasian children (Bickham et al., 2003). Hispanic children's preferences for educational content fall in between those of Caucasians and African Americans. However, African American children in higher income brackets spend more time with educational content than do those in lower income brackets (Bickham et al., 2003). One possible explanation for why African American children spend less time with educational computer games in particular may be due to differential access to computers in homes (and therefore fewer opportunities to use the corresponding software). But it also may be that there are too few educational games of interest to African American children – in terms of characters, contexts, or storylines. For instance, 9- to 12-year-old African American boys spend time playing sports games and this genre often contains African American male characters who provide models to whom boys can relate.

Conclusion

The research literature reviewed in this chapter highlights the complexities of the media environments in which children now grow up. It is clear that children and adolescents have extraordinary access to media, devote significant amounts of time to media activities, and select content that gratifies their needs. Young children are socialized at early ages as they watch their favorite *Sesame Street* episode or learn to navigate with a computer mouse. Maturity brings with it a more sophisticated set of technological skills and interest in a diverse range of media content. Multitasking is now the norm. Media can be a positive or negative force in shaping children's development as each new media activity provides opportunities for learning. Although the ongoing introduction of newer technologies makes understanding children's media-use habits a moving target, the developmental needs that children bring to the media context remain a constant for understanding their use.

References

American Academy of Pediatrics. (1999). Media education. *Pediatrics*, 104(2), 341–2.

Anand, S., & Krosnick, J. A. (2005). Demographic predictors of media use among infants, toddlers, and preschoolers. *American Behavioral Scientist*, 48, 539–61.

Anderson, D. R., & Field, D. E. (1983). Children's attention to television: Implications for production. In M. Meyer (Ed.), *Children and the formal features of television* (pp. 56–96). Munich, Germany: Saur.

Anderson, D. R., & Field, D. E. (1991). Online and offline assessment of the television audience. In J. Bryant & D. Zillman (Eds.), *Responding to the screen: Reception and reaction processes* (pp. 199–216). Hillsdale, NJ: Lawrence Erlbaum.

Anderson, D. R., Field, D. E., Collins, P. A., Lorch, E. P., & Nathan, J. G. (1985). Estimates of young children's time with television: A methodological comparison of parent reports with time-lapse video home observation. *Child Development*, 56, 1343–57.

Anderson, D. R., Huston, A. C., Schmitt, K. L., Linebarger, D. L., & Wright, J. C. (2001). Early childhood television viewing and adolescent behavior: The recontact study. *Monographs of the Society for Research in Child Development*, 66(1), vii–147.

Austin, E. W. (1993). Exploring the effects of active parental mediation of television content. *Journal of Broadcasting and Electronic Media*, 37, 147–58.

Barnett, M. A., Vitaglione, G. D., Harper, K. K. G., Quackenbush, S. W., Steadman, L. A., & Valdez, B. S. (1997). Late adolescents' experiences with and attitudes toward videogames. *Journal of Applied Social Psychology*, 27, 1316–34.

Bianchi, S. M., & Robinson, J. (1997). What did you do today? Children's use of time, family composition, and acquisition of social capital. *Journal of Marriage and the Family*, 59, 332–44.

Bickham, D. S., Vandewater, E. A., Huston, A. C., Lee, J. H., Caplovitz, A. G., & Wright, J. C. (2003). Predictors of children's electronic media use: An examination of three ethnic groups. *Media Psychology*, 5, 107–37.

Buchman, D. D., & Funk, J. B. (1996). Video and computer games in the '90s: Children's time commitment and game preference. *Children Today*, 24, 12–15.

Calvert, S. L., & Kotler, J. A. (2003). The Children's Television Act: Can media policy make a difference? Special issue of the *Journal of Applied Developmental Psychology*, 24, 375–80.

Calvert, S. L., Rideout, V. J., Woolard, J. L., Barr, R. F., & Strouse, G. A. (2005). Age, ethnicity, and socioeconomic patterns in early computer use. *American Behavioral Scientist*, 48, 590–607.

Civille, R. (1995). The Internet and the poor. In B. Kahin & J. Keller (Eds.), *Public access to the Internet* (pp. 175–207). Cambridge, MA: MIT Press.

Comstock, G. (1991). *Television and the American child*. Orlando, FL: Academic Press.

Condry, J. C. (1989). *The Psychology of Television*. Hillsdale, NJ: Lawrence Erlbaum.

Fairlie, R. W. (2005). The effects of home computers on school enrollment. *Economics of Education Review*, 24, 533–47.

Fox, S. (2005). *Digital divisions*. Washington, DC: Pew Internet & American Life Project.

Friedrich, L. K., & Stein, A. H. (1975). Prosocial television and young children's behavior: The effect of verbal labeling and role playing training. *Child Development*, 46, 27–38.

Funk, J. B., Flores, G., Buchman, D. D., & Germann, J. N. (1999). Rating electronic games: Violence is in the eye of the beholder. *Youth and Society*, 30, 283–312.

Funk, J. B., Germann, J. N., & Buchman, D. D. (1997). Children and electronic games in the United States. *Trends in Communication*, 2, 111–26.

Funk, J. B., Hagan, J. D., & Schimming, J. L. (1999). Children and electronic games: A comparison of parent and child perceptions of children's habits and preferences in a United States sample. *Psychological Reports*, 85, 883–8.

Gailey, C. W. (1996). Mediated messages: Gender, class, and cosmos in home video games. In I. E. Sigel (Series Ed.) & P. M. Greenfield & R. R. Cocking (Vol. Eds.), *Interacting with video*. Vol. 11, *Advances in applied developmental psychology* (pp. 9–23). Norwood, NJ: Ablex.

Griffiths, M. (1997). Computer game playing in early adolescence. *Youth and Society*, 29, 223–37.

Griffiths, M. D., Davies, M. N. O., & Chappell, D. (2004). Online computer gaming: A comparison of adolescent and adult gamers. *Journal of Adolescence*, 27, 87–96.

Huntemann, N., & Morgan, M. (2001). Mass media and identity development. In D. Singer & J. Singer (Eds.), *Handbook of children and the media* (pp. 309–22). Thousand Oaks, CA: Sage.

Huston, A. C. (1983). Sex-typing. In E. M. Hetherington (Ed.), *Handbook of child psychology* (pp. 402–7). New York: Wiley.

Huston, A. C., Donnerstein, E., Fairchild, H., Feshbach, N., Katz, P., Murray, J., Rubinstein, E., Wilcox, B., & Zuckerman, D. (1992). *Big world, small screen: The role of television in American society*. Lincoln, NE: University of Nebraska Press.

Huston, A. C., & Wright, J. C. (1996). Television and socialization of young children. In T. M. MacBeth (Ed.), *Tuning into to young viewers: Social science perspectives on television*. Thousand Oaks, CA: Sage.

Huston, A. C., & Wright, J. C. (1998). Mass media and children's development. In W. Damon, I. Sigel, & A. Renniger (Eds.), *Handbook of child psychology* (5th edn., vol. 4, pp. 999–1058). New York: Wiley.

Huston, A. C., Wright, J. C., Marquis, J., & Green, S. (1999). How young children spend their time: Television and other activities. *Developmental Psychology*, 35, 912–25.

Huston, A. C., Wright, J. C., Rice, M. L., Kerkman, D., & St Peters, M. (1990). Development of television viewing patterns in early childhood: A longitudinal investigation. *Developmental Psychology*, 26, 409–20.

Jacobson, M. (2005). *Young people and gendered media messages*. The International Clearinghouse on Children, Youth and Media. Nordicom: Goteborg University.

Jordan, A. B. (1992). Social class, temporal orientation, and mass media use within the family system. *Critical Studies in Mass Communication*, 9, 374–86.

Juster, F. T., & Stafford, F. P. (Eds.). (1985). *Time, goods, and well-being*. Ann Arbor, MI: Survey Research Center, University of Michigan.

Kafai, Y. B. (1996). Gender differences in children's constructions of video games. In P. M. Greenfield & R. R. Cocking, *Interacting with video*. Vol. 11, *Advances in applied developmental psychology* (pp. 39–66). Norwood, NJ: Ablex.

Kubey, R., & Larson, R. (1990). The use and experience of the new video media among children and young adolescents. *Communication Research*, 17, 107–30.

Lenhart, A., & Madden, M. (2005). *Teen content creators and consumers*. Washington, DC: Pew Internet & American Life Project.

Lenhart, A., Madden, M., & Hitlin, P. (2005). *Teens and technology*. Washington, DC: Pew Internet & American Life Project.

Lull, J. (1980). The social uses of television. *Human Communication Research*, 6, 197–209.

Metzger, M. J., & Flanagin, A. (2002). Audience orientation toward new media. *Communication Research Reports*, 19, 338–51.

Nathanson, A. (2001). Mediation of children's television viewing: Working toward conceptual clarity and common understanding. *Communication yearbook*, vol. 25 (pp. 115–51).

Orleans, M., & Laney, M. C. (2000). Children's computer use in the home: Isolation or sociation? *Social Science Computer Review*, 18, 56–72.

Rideout, V. J., & Hamel, E. (2006). *The media family: Electronic media in the lives of infants, toddlers, preschoolers and their parents*. Menlo Park, CA: Kaiser Family Foundation.

Rideout, V. J., Vandewater, E. A., & Wartella, E. A. (2003). *Zero to six: Electronic media in the lives of infants, toddlers and preschoolers*. Menlo Park, CA: Kaiser Family Foundation.

Roberts, D. F., Foehr, U. G., & Rideout, V. (2005). *Generation M: Media in the lives of 8–18-year-olds*. Menlo Park, CA: Kaiser Family Foundation.

Roberts, D. F., Foehr, U. G., Rideout, V. J., & Brodie, M. (1999). *Kids and media @ the new millenium*. Menlo Park, CA: Kaiser Family Foundation.

Rubin, A. M. (2002). The uses-and-gratifications perspective on media effects. In J. Bryant & D. Zillmann (Eds.), *Media effects: Advances in theory and research* (2nd edn., pp. 525–48). Mahwah, NJ: Lawrence Erlbaum.

Schmitt, K. (2000). *Public policy, family rules and children's media use in the home* (Report Series No. 35). Philadelphia: University of Pennsylvania, Annenberg Public Policy Center.

Schmitt, K. L., Woolf, K. D., & Anderson, D. R. (2003). Viewing the viewers: Viewing behaviors by children and adults during television programs and commercials. *Journal of Communication*, 53, 265–81.

Serbin, L. A., Powlishta, K. K., & Gulko, J. (1993). The development of sex typing in middle childhood. *Monographs of the Society for Research in Child Development*, 58(2, Serial No. 232).

Steinfield, C. W., Dutton, W. H., & Kovaric, P. (1989). A framework and agenda for research on computing in the home. In J. L. Salvaggio & J. Bryant (Eds.), *Media use in the information age: Emerging patterns of adoption and consumer use* (pp. 61–85). Hillsdale, NJ: Lawrence Erlbaum.

Subrahmanyam, K., & Greenfield, P. M. (1996). Effect of video game practice on spatial skills in girls and boys. In I. E. Sigel (Series Ed.) & P. M. Greenfield & R. R. Cocking (Vol. Eds.), *Interacting with video.* Vol. 11, *Advances in applied developmental psychology* (pp. 94–114). Norwood, NJ: Ablex.

Subrahmanyam, K., & Greenfield, P. M. (1998). Computer games for girls: What makes them play? In J. Cassell & H. Jenkins (Eds.), *From Barbie to Mortal Kombat: Gender and computer games* (pp. 46–71). Cambridge, MA: MIT Press.

Timmer, S. G., Eccles, J., & O'Brien, K. (1985). How children use time. In F. T. Juster & F. P. Stafford (Eds.), *Time, goods, and well-being* (pp. 353–82). Ann Arbor, MI: Survey Research Center, Institute for Social Research.

Van Evra, J. (2004). *Television and child development* (3rd edn.). Mahwah, NJ: Lawrence Erlbaum.

Vitalari, N. P., & Venkatesh, A. (1987). In-home computing and information services: A twenty-year analysis of the technology and its impacts. *Telecommunications Policy,* 11, 65–81.

Woodard, E. (2000). *Media in the home 2000: The fifth annual survey of parents and children* (Survey Series No. 7). Philadelphia: University of Pennsylvania, Annenberg Public Policy Center.

Wright, J. C., & Huston, A. C. (1995). *Effects of educational TV viewing of lower income preschoolers on academic skills, school readiness, and school adjustment one to three years later.* Report of Children's Television Workshop, Center for Research on the Influences of Television on Children, University of Kansas, Lawrence, KS, June.

Wright, J. C., Huston, A. C., Murphy, K. C., St Peters, M., Pinon, M., Scantlin, R. M., & Kotler, J. A. (2001). The relations of early television viewing to school readiness and vocabulary of children from low-income families: The Early Window Project. *Child Development,* 72, 1347–66.

Wright, J. C., Huston, A. C., Vandewater, E., Bickham, D. S., Scantlin, R. M., Kotler, J. A., Caplovitz, A. G., Lee, J., Hofferth, S., & Finkelstein, J. (2001). American children's use of electronic media in 1997: A national survey. *Journal of Applied Developmental Psychology,* 22, 31–47.

Wright, J. C., St Peters, M., & Huston, A. C. (1990). Family television use and its relation to children's cognitive skills and social behavior. In J. Bryant (Ed.), *Television and the American family* (pp. 227–51). Hillsdale, NJ: Lawrence Erlbaum.

4

Children, Race, Ethnicity, and Media

Bradley S. Greenberg and Dana E. Mastro

Mass media portrayals of racial and ethnic groups may influence children's attitudes, beliefs, and behaviors toward their own and other races. This proposition can be derived from theories of mass communication and intergroup processes that identify the role of media in children's acquisitions and applications of racial cognitions (Bandura, 2001; Gerbner et al., 2002; Harwood & Roy, 2005).

However, research that examines the effects of such exposure on racial and ethnic minority and majority children is limited. To advance this critical issue, our chapter reviews the social scientific research assessing the intersection of children, media, and race and ethnicity. We document (1) the manner in which race and ethnicity affects media characterizations, (2) the extent to which children's media usage and preferences vary based on race and ethnicity, and (3) the degree to which perceptions of media content and the subsequent effects of exposure are influenced by children's race and ethnicity. Particular attention goes to studies examining African Americans, Asian Americans, Caucasians, Latinos, and Native Americans, the largest racial and ethnic groups in the United States (US Census Bureau, 2000). We begin with an overview of the primary theoretical frameworks used in assessing media effects.

Theoretical Approaches to Media Effects

Pertinent theories of media effects and intergroup processes propose that information acquired from mass media can teach and reinforce ideas about the social world (Bandura, 2001; Gerbner et al., 2002), including perceptions about race and ethnicity (Berry & Mitchell-Kernan, 1982). These theories have value in understanding outcomes associated with children, as research on the recognition of racial categories indicates that awareness of race is acquired early in a child's development (Brown & Bigler, 2005). Children are able to distinguish visually among racial groups near their first birthday (Brown & Bigler, 2005). Between ages 3 and 4, they develop an awareness of race and ethnicity and can sort them-selves and others based on those categories (Lovelace et al., 1994; McKown & Weinstein, 2003). By 5 years, they are knowledgeable about the concrete features of racial stereotypes, including observable, visual features such as body type, skin color, and attire (Brown & Bigler, 2005). By 6, they are able to differentiate between their own and other racial groups. Although these early cognitive advancements focus primarily on discriminating among physical features, 10-year-olds typically have developed an awareness of more abstract and non-observable qualities asso-ciated with race, such as inferred characteristics, traits, and attributes associated with different groups (Brown & Bigler, 2005). They also are likely to be able to derive conclusions and implications, make social comparisons between ingroup and outgroup race members, and recognize racial discrimination. We shall describe three theoretical approaches that can be used to understand linkages between the media and children's development of ideas about race.

Social cognitive theory

Bandura's social cognitive theory proposes that the mass media contribute to acquir-ing value systems and rules of conduct for society by providing models from which children can learn (Bandura, 2001). Because mass media messages are pervasive in society, observing media images is expected to play a central role in the selection of role models and in the construction of social reality. As a result, interactions with media models have the potential to create and alter beliefs and expectations about racial and ethnic groups. Based on their exposure to potential role models, children may learn what they perceive to be normative behaviors for their own group as well as their perceptions of members from other groups. If ingroup media models are less available, as is more likely the case with minorities, then less information is available to inform and guide perceptions and behaviors.

Four sub-processes – attention, retention, production, and motivation – govern observational learning (Bandura, 2001). First, attention guides the selection of what is seen. It is influenced by such factors as the availability and complexity of messages as well as observer-based attributes including preferences and cog-nitive capability. Further, the more that characters are perceived to be similar to one's self in terms of physical features and social perspectives, the greater the likelihood of attention and identification (Bandura, 2001; Eyal & Rubin, 2003). Research indicates that viewers favor content featuring models of their own race and ethnicity (Greenberg & Atkin, 1982; Jose & Brewer, 1984). Audience data show that African Americans are more likely to select programs featuring African American characters (Nielsen Media Research, 1998).

The next steps in learning from the media are retention and production. Viewers must retain the behavior for use at a later time and possess the physical and intellectual capability to replicate the action. Therefore, these messages also provide a conceptual guide for race-based attitudes and actions under varying con-ditions. Research has shown that such deductive processes are likely to begin around the ages of 5 to 6 (Brown & Bigler, 2005; McKown & Weinstein, 2003). By this age children move beyond merely replicating behaviors and begin to develop the ability to create generative rules that can be applied across contexts and modified for appropriateness.

Cognitive storage, recall, and motor reproduction are influenced by such factors as age and developmental sophistication (Bandura, 2001). Faulty conception and motor deficits, for instance, impede reproducing an observed event. Similarity with the media model also is likely to facilitate these processes, especially among minority viewers. Research finds that recall of a stored event is significantly enhanced among minorities when viewing media figures of the same racial and ethnic background; no such effect emerges for racial majority viewers (Appiah, 2002).

The final step in this paradigm involves motivation. According to Bandura (2001), the motivation to perform a behavior is influenced by three potential reinforcers – external, vicarious, and self. External reinforcements include direct rewards and valued outcomes, such as parental approval or tangible compensations. Vicarious reinforcements emphasize the important role of similarity with the media model, noting that people are motivated by the success of similar others and are discouraged by their failures. Self-reinforcement suggests that personal standards and morals provide a source of motivation. Unlike external and vicarious reinforcers, self-incentives may require more mature cognitive reasoning skills. Children begin to develop moral reasoning skills with concepts of equality (i.e., parity) between the ages of 4 and 7 and concepts of equity (e.g., recognition of ability, effort) between 8 and 12 (Brown & Bigler, 2005). After 10, children recognize racial stereotypes as grounds for evaluating others (McKown & Weinstein, 2003). These abilities allow for detection and interpretation of differential treatment of racial and ethnic groups as well as subtle and more blatant forms of prejudice. Overall, this framework suggests that media messages may constitute a form of social instruction for children, imparting information regarding how to think about, act around, and treat others in society.

Cultivation theory

From a more macro-level perspective, Gerbner's cultivation framework proposes that over time, exposure to the themes in television content shifts viewer's social perceptions toward the television version of reality, regardless of the accuracy or precision of that content (Gerbner et al., 2002). Critical in this perspective are the amount of television consumption and the consistency of media messages, such that heavy viewers are more likely than light viewers to conceptualize reality in a manner consistent with a repetitious television world. Through recurring dominant themes, media messages act as a socializing force, providing knowledge about the world (Shrum & Bischak, 2001) and contributing to cultural constructions (Gerbner et al., 2002) including racial and ethnic stereotypes (Mastro, Behm-Morawitz, & Ortiz, 2007). With this conception, Latin lovers, Asian whiz kids, and African American criminals, for example, would be accepted as normative if they were dominant minority portrayals.

The cultivation perspective posits that first order and second order learning-based outcomes are derived from the level of abstraction of the information (Hawkins & Pingree, 1982). First order outcomes are those associated with the concrete features of content, such as the acquisition of demographic information, e.g., if there are few Asian men in sitcoms, there may be fewer Asian men in the real world. Second order outcomes represent learning derived from content implied in the pattern of television messages, for example, racial and ethnic stereotypes that must be inferred from the content by individual viewers (Shrum, 2004). In this sense, the lack of Asian men in sitcoms could also imply that they lack humor and are not good at telling jokes.

In terms of race-based outcomes, children begin to make reference to surface-level stereotypes associated with race and ethnicity between the ages of 6 and 8 (McKown & Weinstein, 2003). Research suggests that racial and ethnic minority children may report earlier awareness of stereotypes than Whites because these cognitions are more salient in their daily lives. Thus, media messages may have an early influence on children's perceptions of the observable features of the social world (first order effects). Moreover, their perceptions regarding the implicit characteristics of the social environment (second order effects) are likely to be affected as cognitive abilities progress.

Cultivation theory looks for consistency across messages and the dominance of specific themes. Therefore, it does not traditionally account for individual differences in character portrayals – all Blacks count the same. As an alternative the "drench hypothesis" proposes that an intense, dynamic portrayal of an individual or a theme could outweigh weaker characterizations for the viewer, especially where portrayals are infrequent, as with race and ethnicity (Greenberg, 1988). For example, a generation of children who matured with the Bill Cosby television family, featuring an African American doctor father and a lawyer mother, may have different beliefs about the possible economic and professional status of Blacks than children not exposed to that success story, or children exposed to a host of more minor black portrayals. As another example, the 2006 primetime television season features one Latino female in a starring role, "Ugly Betty," a compassionate and competent, but very un-cool young woman. The significance and salience of this major character may serve to override the effects of exposure to the handful of less consequential Latino characters who appear in primetime. From this perspective, the reactions of young viewers, Latinos and others, to this highly individual portrayal warrant study.

Social identity theory

Tajfel's social identity theory posits that individuals seek to create and maintain a positive identity by comparing the favorable characteristics of their ingroup with corresponding and unfavorable characteristics of a pertinent outgroup (Tajfel, 1978; Turner, 1982). Individuals perceived to be similar to the self along contextually salient dimensions, such as race and ethnicity or age, are considered ingroup members and those deemed dissimilar are identified as outgroup members. Once categorizations have been made, comparison strategies are used to help protect self-concept and esteem by maximizing intergroup differences to ensure the advantage for the ingroup (Abrams & Hogg, 1990). In this framework, individuals must preserve their ingroup's favorable distinctiveness from other groups by constantly exploiting differences across categories (Turner, 1982). Media characterizations may facilitate that comparison process.

Even children as young as preschool age appear to recognize the value of their race in the larger society and attempt to maintain a positive self-concept by attaching favorable evaluations to ingroup members (Corenblum & Annis, 1993). These comparative features may not be rooted in the real world, but could instead be derived from such sources as media messages (Hogg, Terry, & White, 1995). Consequently, the potential for media content to influence intergroup comparisons is highly likely, as these images may provide a comparative basis to maintain and enhance self-concept. In particular, research has found that exposure to media depictions of race and ethnicity plays a role in such processes as stereotype acquisition and use (Mastro, Behm-Morawitz, & Ortiz, 2007).

Media messages also can be integrated into consumers' ideas about racial and ethnic group characteristics, their understanding of treatment norms, and their perceptions about appropriate power relationships (Harwood & Roy, 2005; Mastro & Kopacz, 2006). In other words, media images become part of the constant negotiation of identity and social standing in relation to others by constructing and sustaining race-based characterizations for use in later evaluations.

From a social identity approach, both the frequency and nature of racial and ethnic media representations are meaningful. The sheer number of racial and ethnic minority depictions can be seen as an indication of the value and status of these groups in society (Harwood & Roy, 2005). Thus, viewers may use the information gleaned from mass media to make generalizations about both ingroup and outgroup members, with the goal of applying these characterizations to benefit their ingroup. If the quality of the characterization of race and ethnicity in the media is unfavorable, it may negatively influence evaluations of self and ingroup identity (Fryberg, 2003). It may do the same if the total number of representations is distinctively small. Here, the primary difficulty for the minority child may be the inability to find positive role models in the media.

Taken together, these theoretical perspectives emphasize content, context, and social comparisons as the bases for the outcomes they propose. How children will learn about and respond to different races then, will rely, in part, on what media messages are made available.

Portrayals of Race and Ethnicity in the Media

Cultivation theory documents how children come to construct a world view based on media exposure. First viewers must identify the overall number and kind of messages portrayed, in this instance messages about racial and ethnic groups (e.g.,

Children Now, 2001, 2004). The US Census (2000) reports that among adults (with youths in parentheses), Whites comprise approximately 69 (65) percent of the US population, Latinos 13 (16) percent, African Americans 12 (15) percent, Asian Americans 4 (4) percent, and Native Americans 1 (1) percent. When comparing the racial and ethnic breakdown of media characters with that of the US population, disparities become apparent in terms of the sheer number of adult and youth depictions by race. Although it is essential to understand *how* different groups are presented in the media as a determinant of the potential effects of exposure, the sheer *rate* of media representation also is important because numeric representations are associated with a variety of social learning, socialization, and group-based outcomes. Who and what, then, are children likely to encounter when they make their media choices?

Prime-time television

Most studies have examined the content of primetime television, whose first hour of programming is watched regularly by 10 million US children (Children Now, 2002). In primetime, the major broadcast television networks offer few opportunities for children to see images of their own age groups, as only 3 percent of the characters depicted are children and only 8 percent are adolescents (Children Now, 2001). Among these young characters, between 77 and 78 percent are white, 15–16 percent are African American, 2–4 percent are Latino, 1–3 percent are Asian American, and 0.0–0.4 percent are Native American (Children Now, 2001, 2004). In terms of adult representations – with whom children may identify based on similarities in such characteristics as race (Greenberg & Atkin, 1982) and gender (Cohen, 2001) – the pattern is not much different. Studies report that the range of African American representation is between 14 and 17 percent of characters appearing on primetime television (Children Now, 2001, 2004; Mastro & Behm-Morawitz, 2005; Mastro & Greenberg, 2000), a rate that exceeds their proportion of the US population. On the other hand, Latinos are substantially underrepresented when compared with real-world demographics, comprising between 2 and 6.5 percent of the television population. Much the same is true for portrayals of Asian Americans, who make up between 1 and 3 percent of primetime characters, and even more absent are Native Americans, representing between 0 and 0.4 percent of the characters appearing on primetime television (Children Now, 2004; Mastro & Behm-Morawitz, 2005).

When considering the ways in which minority groups are represented on primetime television, the nature of these portrayals varies according to the race and ethnicity of the model. For nearly a decade, African Americans have been found almost exclusively in sitcoms or crime dramas (Mastro & Behm-Morawitz, 2005; Mastro & Greenberg, 2000; Matabane & Merritt, 1996; Stroman, Merritt, & Matabane, 1989–90). On dramas, they are most often in mixed-race casts (Children Now, 2004) whereas on sitcoms (the most popular genre among young viewers), they are most often in a cast that is almost exclusively African

American. A composite sketch of the typical African American on primetime television depicts a recurring cast member, a middle-class male law enforcer or professional, in his 30s, discussing work-related topics (Children Now, 2001, 2004; Mastro & Behm-Morawitz, 2005; Mastro & Greenberg, 2000). With moderate levels of both job and social authority (Mastro & Behm-Morawitz, 2005), these characters are among the least physically aggressive (Mastro & Greenberg, 2000). African Americans also are rated more hot-tempered and more provocatively and less professionally dressed than white characters (Mastro & Greenberg, 2000).

Like African Americans, Latino characters are confined largely to sitcoms and crime dramas (Children Now, 2004; Mastro & Behm-Morawitz, 2005). Their primary roles are as family members, talking most often about crime (Mastro & Behm-Morawitz, 2005). In general, Latinos are portrayed as younger, lower in job authority, more provocatively dressed, lazier, less articulate, and less intelligent than other races. They also are the most hot-tempered. Latino women on television have the lowest work ethic and the highest level of verbal aggression.

Although rarely depicted, Asian Americans appear primarily in minor and non-recurring roles (Children Now, 2004). Notably, Asian American characters are often (37 percent) in high-status, professional positions. No study finds enough Native Americans to yield a quantitative analysis.

Children's programming

In commercial television shows for children, content changes over the past three decades are due in part to a larger number of network and cable channels (Children Now, 2002; Woodard, 1999). Despite changes, both Whites and males continue to dominate children's commercial television (Dobrow & Gidney, 1998; Graves, 1996; Greenberg & Brand, 1993; Weigel & Howes, 1982). Eighty-five percent of Saturday morning programs for children contain casts of main characters that are exclusively white (Greenberg & Brand, 1993).

In contrast, public television offerings provide a richer racial and ethnic environment with attention specifically paid to issues of diversity, both in terms of character composition and dialogue (Greenberg & Brand, 1993). Among shows most watched by preschool children, primarily Public Broadcasting Service (PBS) offerings, approximately 55 percent of characters are white, 32 percent are African American, 3 percent are Asian American, and 3 percent are Latino (Borzekowski & Poussaint, 1998). Woodard (1999) found that 55 percent of PBS children's programs contained a cast in which at least 33 percent of characters were racial and ethnic minorities. But even the PBS shows focus on African American character portrayals as the hallmark of diversity.

General advertising

In television advertisements, minority groups have been underrepresented compared with US population figures (Greenberg, Mastro, & Brand, 2002; Stern, 1999).

In the last decade, the rate of minority presence in television commercials has remained relatively stable. White actors dominate the commercial landscape, comprising 83–86 percent of the characters depicted (Coltrane & Messineo, 2000; Mastro & Stern, 2003). African Americans are 11–12 percent of the commercial population, with Asian Americans (2 percent) and Latinos (1 percent) lagging (Coltrane & Messineo, 2000; Mastro & Stern, 2003), and with Native Americans at 0.4 percent (Mastro & Stern, 2003). Signorielli, McLeod, and Healy's (1994) analysis of characters appearing in advertisements on MTV yielded even less diversity – 9 of 10 characters were white, with scarce images of African Americans (2.3 percent), Asian Americans (2.1 percent), or Latinos (0.6 percent).

Minorities fare somewhat better when the commercial, rather than the individual, is the unit of analysis. White characters are seen in nearly all television advertisements (Taylor & Stern, 1997), African Americans appear in from 25 to 35 percent of the advertisements (Licata & Biswas, 1993; Taylor & Stern, 1997; Wilkes & Valencia, 1989), Latinos are seen in 6–9 percent (Taylor & Stern, 1997; Wilkes & Valencia, 1989), and Asian Americans are present in 8 percent (Taylor & Stern, 1997).

Minority characters in advertising also differ in their product associations and in the physical locations in which they appear. Advertisers link some products more strongly with certain racial and ethnic groups based on purchase behavior. Generally speaking, product associations are seen as an indication of the interests, values, and competencies of the groups with which they are associated. Similarly, settings can be viewed as a reflection of the social positioning of the group, possibly reinforcing a group's status in society.

African Americans appear most often in advertisements for food/beverages (Mastro & Stern, 2003; Taylor & Stern, 1997; Wilkes & Valencia, 1989) as well as financial services (Mastro & Stern, 2003). Whites are seen more often in cosmetics (Taylor & Stern, 1997), technology, and food commercials (Mastro & Stern, 2003). Asian Americans are found most frequently in advertisements for retailers (Taylor & Stern, 1997) and technology (Mastro & Stern, 2003). Latinos are found with a variety of products including banking/finance advertisements (Taylor & Stern, 1997), food commercials, entertainment commercials (Wilkes & Valencia, 1989), and advertisements for soaps/deodorants (Mastro & Stern, 2003).

Race differences by physical location also have been documented. Asian men appear most often at work (Mastro & Stern, 2003; Taylor & Stern, 1997) and Asian women are ordinarily outdoors (Taylor & Stern, 1997). Latino men are evenly split between the workplace and outdoors, with Latino women mainly shown outdoors. Both African American men and women are most often seen at work. By contrast, white men and women are found more frequently at home (Mastro & Stern, 2003; Taylor & Stern, 1997), perhaps signifying stronger family ties for them.

Racial and ethnic minorities more commonly appear in minor or background roles in these advertisements as well as in larger, non-family groups (Taylor & Stern, 1997; Wilkes & Valencia, 1989) and are less often depicted as parents or spouses (Coltrane & Messineo, 2000), supporting the suggestion that minority families are weaker. Whites also are more likely to give orders than minorities (Coltrane & Messineo, 2000; Mastro & Stern, 2003). Yet African American characters, particularly males, are more likely than Whites to behave aggressively (Coltrane & Messineo, 2000). Mastro and Stern (2003) reported that African American female characters were less friendly and more hostile than their on-air female counterparts. They also report that Latinos are associated more often with sexuality than other characters – they give more sexual glances, use more alluring behavior, and dress more provocatively.

Advertisements targeted at children

A few content analyses have examined contemporary portrayals of race and ethnicity in children's television commercials. Findings reveal both quantitative and qualitative differences in depicting race and ethnicity in commercials and in the types of advertisements likely to feature diverse casts (Bang & Reece, 2003; Larson, 2002; Li-Vollmer, 2002). Taken together, Whites are ubiquitous in children's commercials (appearing in 99 percent); African Americans are in 51 percent; and both Latinos and Asian Americans are portrayed in 9 percent (Bang & Reece, 2003). Moreover, roughly half the commercials targeted to children feature only white characters (Bang & Reece, 2003; Larson, 2002). In contrast, merely 1 percent of such advertisements portray only African Americans, and no advertisements exclusively feature Asian Americans or Latinos (Bang & Reece, 2003).

At the character level, 74 percent of actors seen in commercials are white, 19 percent are African American, 2 percent are Latino, 2 percent are Asian American, and 0.2 percent are Native American (Li-Vollmer, 2002). These findings identify the locus of diversity in children's commercials primarily as the presence of African Americans (Greenberg & Brand, 1993).

Studies of children's advertisements further show that the race and ethnicity of the actor is significantly related to the number of models in the advertisements and the status of the actor (Li-Vollmer, 2002). When commercials feature only one or two characters, there are no minorities 78 percent of the time. Instead, racial and ethnic minority actors are found most frequently in advertisements with larger casts. In advertisements containing majority and minority characters, Whites dominate the roles and the amount of time speaking. As for the advertised products, more Whites (37 percent), African Americans (51 percent), and Asian Americans (49 percent) are found in commercials for cereal than for any other single product, whereas Latinos are nearly exclusively depicted in advertisements for restaurants (97 percent; Bang & Reece, 2003). Notably, 36 percent of all Asian Americans are found in commercials for technology, whereas only 3 percent of white characters, 0.4 percent of African Americans, and no Latinos appeared in these product advertisements – possibly strengthening the characterization of Asian Americans as the "model minority." Further, white children are significantly more likely to be found in the home than racial and ethnic minority children, particularly in advertisements with only white children (Larson, 2002). This pattern continues the greater emphasis on family ties for white adult and child characters in commercials.

In terms of specific roles, Whites are more frequently identified as "go-getters" and problem-solvers than are other minorities (Li-Vollmer, 2002). White characters also are more likely than others to be found in major roles (Bang & Reece, 2003).

Television news

Audiences look to the news for accurate information and knowledge about the social world (Gilens, 1996). Moreover, roughly 40 percent of children report watching television news/news magazines on almost a daily basis (Children Now, 2002). Consequently, the images of racial and ethnic minorities highlighted in a news context are meaningful to examine as young viewers may use these messages expressly to learn.

News coverage depicting racial and ethnic minorities has been largely unfavorable and unrepresentative of real-world indicators – particularly for African Americans (Entman, 1992). In non-crime stories, Blacks and Whites receive proportional representation, but minorities are nearly twice as prominent as Whites when the news topic is crime (Romer, Jamieson, & DeCoteau, 1998). In crime stories, African Americans are more often unnamed, menacing, disheveled, and in restraints than are Whites (Entman, 1992). Dixon and Linz (2002) found that reporting prejudicial information (e.g., mentioning prior arrests) was significantly more likely to occur with African American and Latino defendants than with Whites.

African Americans and Latinos are depicted as crime perpetrators on television news more frequently than are Whites (Dixon & Linz, 2000a). These rates of representation are inconsistent with real-world arrest reports. Compared to crime statistics, African American adults are overrepresented as perpetrators on television news, Latinos are underrepresented, and Whites are presented either at a rate comparable to that in the real world (Dixon & Linz, 2000b) or are underrepresented (Dixon & Linz, 2000a). In terms of youth depictions on the news, Dixon and Azocar (2006) found that African American and Latino youth appear as perpetrators more frequently than Whites. Among all juvenile perpetrators depicted, 39 percent were African American (18 percent in Department of Justice statistics), 29 percent were Latino (53 percent in Department of Justice statistics), and 24 percent were white (22 percent in Department of Justice statistics).

Compared with Whites, African Americans and Latinos also are portrayed less often as victims (Dixon & Linz, 2000b). Contrasting television crime figures with real-world crime reports shows that Whites are more likely to be seen as homicide victims on television than in the real world, Latinos are less likely to be depicted as television victims than in the real world, and the rate of African American television news victims is nearly equivalent to their real-world rate (Dixon & Linz, 2000b).

On the news, 91 percent of police officers shown are white, and 3 percent are African American (Dixon, Azocar, & Casas, 2003). US Department of Labor statistics identify 80 percent of officers in the United States to be white and 17 percent to be African American.

Movies and videogames

Children also are avid movie-viewers and videogame enthusiasts (Roberts, Foehr, & Rideout, 2005). In analyzing 101 top-grossing G-rated films (i.e., those made for a General audience) over a 14-year period from 1990 to 2004, Kelly and Smith (2006) found that 86 percent of male characters were white, 5 percent were African American, 3 percent were Asian, 2 percent were Latino, and 1 percent were Native American. The researchers examined males separately due to their dispropor-tionately high degree of gender representation – 72 percent of speaking characters were male. Among these male models, minorities were far more likely (62 percent) than Whites (38 percent) to be physically aggressive and violent.

One study assessed the representation of Native Americans in the 5,868 US motion pictures released between 1990 and 2000 (Fryberg, 2003). Only 13 (0.2 percent) included Native Americans in speaking roles. All were characterized by their spiritual nature. This image was coupled with that of Native Americans as warriors (85 percent) and people with social problems (85 percent). Only two films featured Native Americans in professional roles.

A content analysis of videogames finds that diversity varies greatly based on the gender of the character. In top-selling videogames for home gaming consoles and personal computers, 52 percent of player-controlled male characters are white, 37 percent African American, 5 percent Latino, and 3 percent Asian. Among female characters, 78 percent are white, 10 percent African American, 7 percent Asian, 1 percent Native American, and none are Latina. In games designed specifically for children, *only* white characters appear (Glaubke et al., 2001).

Among the videogame characters' roles, the vast majority of protagonists or heroes are white (87 percent). The few Latino protagonists appear in sports-based games. Similarly, 83 percent of African American protagonists are cast in sports games. Most Asian characters are portrayed as fighters or wrestlers (69 percent) and are seen more often as antagonists than other ethnicities. In these games, more African American females are victimized by violence than are females from any other racial group. Both male and female African American characters are least likely to experience realistic responses to violence, such as pain and physical harm, perhaps indicative of greater desensitization to the outcomes of violence.

Children's Media Use and Identification

In this section, we identify racial and ethnic differences in children's media habits. We will focus on how children spend their time, what motives they have for media use, and content preferences they have as a function of race.

Television

On average, children between 8 and 18 years of age watch over 4 hours of television per day (Roberts, Foehr, & Rideout, 2005). This amount varies by the child's race and ethnicity (Children Now, 2002; Roberts, Foehr, & Rideout, 2005), with white children watching among the lowest levels of television (Anand & Krosnick, 2005; Roberts, Foehr, & Rideout, 2005). Specifically, the total screen viewing time (i.e., television, videos and DVDs, and movies) for African American children amounts to nearly 6 hours of exposure a day, for Latino children about 4.5, and for white children approximately 3.75 hours (Roberts, Foehr, & Rideout, 2005).

Television sets can be found in the bedrooms of a majority of American children between the ages of 8 and 18 (Roberts, Foehr, & Rideout, 2005). However, this practice is more common among minority children. In particular, 82 percent of African American children, 74 percent of Latino children, and 65 percent of white children report having televisions in their bedrooms. Research indicates that children who have televisions in their rooms spend more time watching television and less time reading than do children with no set in their rooms (Roberts, Foehr, & Rideout, 2005).

Both white children (Greenberg, 1972; Greenberg & Reeves, 1976) and racial and ethnic minority children (Greenberg & Atkin, 1982) report using television to learn about other racial and ethnic groups in society and believe in the importance of seeing their own racial and ethnic group in media presentations (Children Now, 2002). Such portrayals, say children, signify the value and inclusion of their race and ethnicity in society as well as offer meaningful role models (Children Now, 2002). Most often, children of all races and ethnicities are viewing comedies when watching television. No genre preference differences emerge based on the child's race.

Consistent with social cognitive theory, minority children are more likely to report wanting to be like media models of their own race and ethnicity (Greenberg, 1972; Greenberg & Atkin, 1982) and generally prefer both shows (Stroman, 1986) and characters of their same race when selecting media content (Eastman & Liss, 1980; Stroman, 1986). When asked to name the television character they would most like to emulate, 75 percent of African American fourth and fifth graders chose an African American model (Greenberg, 1972). African American youngsters are three times more likely than Whites to identify with African American television figures (Greenberg & Atkin, 1982), and this discrepancy increases as the strength of their ethnic identity increases (Whittler, 1991). In other words, the greater the importance of children's race and ethnicity to their self-concept, the more they look for and look to same-race media models. Moreover, African American adolescents are significantly more likely to perceive themselves to be similar to African American than to white models (Appiah, 2001). African American children also report an elevated belief in the veracity of television programs (Poindexter & Stroman, 1981) and commercials (Donohue, Meyer, & Henke, 1978), find television more pleasurable (Albarran & Umphrey, 1993), and express more positive attitudes about television (Huston et al., 1992).

In research with Latino youngsters, fifth and tenth graders expressed stronger beliefs in the reality of television portrayals than Whites, especially the fifth-grade Latinos (Greenberg et al., 1983). Further, both Latino and Asian American adolescents perceived themselves to be more similar to African American than to white characters (Appiah, 2001). Differences such as these should predispose racial and ethnic minority children to be more accepting of television's messages, particularly those depicting minority groups.

Gender may compete with ethnicity as a characteristic that predicts role model selections. In studying four-year-old Latino and Caucasian children, Calvert, Strong, Jacobs, and Conger (2007) found gender to better predict similarity and identification with the popular children's television character, Dora the Explorer, than ethnicity. In particular, Caucasian children were more likely than Latinos to perceive themselves to be similar to this Latina television model, primarily because of Latino boys' perceptions of her. Moreover, Latino children were no more likely than Caucasians to identify with the character. The authors reason that these antithetical results may reflect greater pressure on Latino boys to abide by traditional gender stereotyped roles, an assertion that is consistent with social-identity-based assumptions regarding variability in the salience of important group memberships.

Latino children are more likely than Whites to say they use television to learn new behaviors (Greenberg et al., 1983). Similar results occur among adults. In examining Latina media viewing, Johnson (1996) found that women with low levels of acculturation used television to learn about social norms in the US and to improve English-speaking skills. Her findings provide modest support for the proposition that viewing mainstream television offerings and identifying with certain programs is associated with higher levels of acculturation. Additional support emerges from Stilling's (1997) study of the influence of television on Latino adults' acculturation, revealing that English-language television exposure increases acculturation among Latinos with shorter residency in the US. The opposite holds for exposure to ethnic media.

Music

The amount of time spent listening to music each day does not vary based on the race and ethnicity of the child, averaging about 1.75 hours per day. However, there are major differences in genre preferences (Roberts, Foehr, & Rideout, 2005). The most preferred genre for white, African American, and Latino children is Rap/Hip Hop, but the two minority groups are significantly more likely than white children to listen to Rap/Hip Hop and Rhythm & Blues/Soul. On the other hand, white children are significantly more likely to indicate a fondness for Alternative, Classic, Hard Rock, Country and Western, and Ska/Punk. Latino children listen to significantly more Latin/Salsa music. Genre differences may be of interest if there are substantial differences in their content. Although the subject matter found in different music genres has yet to receive systematic attention, Rap/Hip Hop music has been linked to themes of sex and violence in music videos, particularly as related to African Americans (Ward, Hansbrough, & Walker, 2005).

Print media

Youth spend less time with print media compared to other types, and there are no major differences in these habits as a function of race. Total time devoted to reading print media is 42 minutes a day for white children, 38 minutes for African American children, and 47 minutes for Latino children (Roberts, Foehr, & Rideout, 2005). For all three groups, this time is primarily spent with books, followed by magazines, and last with newspapers.

Videogames and computers

African American children not only spend more time watching television, but also playing videogames compared to other groups. On an average day, African American youth play videogames (i.e., computer- and console-based games) for nearly 1.5 hours, whereas white and Latino children spend about an hour in such activities (Roberts, Foehr, & Rideout, 2005). Although educational games are not very popular with youth in general, both Latino and African American children are less likely to play those games than are white children (Bickham et al., 2003).

In terms of computers, the major difference is access to such technologies in the home. White children are far more likely to have at least one computer at home (90 percent) than are African American (78 percent) or Latino (80 percent) children (Roberts, Foehr, & Rideout, 2005). Similarly, white youth (80 percent) are more likely to have access to the Internet at home, compared to African Americans (61 percent) and Latino youth (67 percent). However, average daily time spent on the computer does not differ among these groups. There also are few race-based differences in the specific computer activities in which they engage (Roberts, Foehr, & Rideout, 2005). They all spend comparable amounts of time chatting, emailing, using graphics, and surfing websites. However, significantly fewer African Americans play online videogames or create instant messages.

When online, what can be said about the race-related experiences of young users? Tynes, Reynolds, and Greenfield (2004) analyzed racial and ethnic discourse in monitored and unmonitored popular adolescent chat rooms. They found that 97 percent of adolescents' online discussions contained at least one racial expression. Overall, positive racial statements were found in 87 percent of conversations, neutral utterances in 76 percent, and negative statements in 47 percent. The presence of an adult monitor significantly reduced the amount of negative racial comments. Specifically, adolescents "had a 19% chance of being exposed to negative remarks about a racial group (potentially their own) in monitored chat rooms and a 59% chance in unmonitored chat" (Tynes, Reynolds, and Greenfield, 2004, p. 673). The researchers argue that such high levels of race-related discourse indicate the importance of race in adolescents' social identities and in their media experiences.

Media Effects

Too little research exists that explores the impact of exposure to racial stereotypes in the media on consumers. Further, most studies focus on adults rather than children, and nearly all the studies look only at short-term effects. We have no longitudinal research on the effects of repeated exposure to media images about race. While social cognitive theory has been studied, it is difficult to assess a number of the theoretical assertions rooted in cultivation theory and those related to group perceptions in social identity theory with the evidence at hand. Our knowledge base is further restricted by the limited number of studies about developmental outcomes.

This section is organized around the types of effects that have been examined. Given that most research focuses on white, adult media users, we will look first at the influence of racial stereotypes on majority adult attitudes. These findings offer insights into outcomes that may be anticipated among children. Next, we review research on the effects of racial portrayals on such policy issues as affirmative action. Third, we explore the small body of research that examines the impact of the media on minority children's attitudes, identity, and self-esteem.

Impact on adult viewer attitudes about race

Bodenhausen, Schwarz, Bless, and Wänke (1995) examined the effects of viewing black media exemplars (e.g., Oprah Winfrey, Spike Lee) on whites' racial attitudes. They found that the priming of well-liked, positive media exemplars directly predicts more favorable attitudes about minorities and more sympathetic responses towards discrimination as a problem. Similarly, Power, Murphy, and Coover (1996) investigated how negative stereotypes and positive counter-stereotypes of Blacks in the news impacted white adults' subsequent judgments of Blacks. Their data suggest that exposure to black stereotypic representations results in more negative judgments of Blacks in unrelated news events, whereas exposure to constructive counter-stereotypes results in more positive evaluations.

Studies investigating the intersection of race and crime in the news have comparable results. White viewers' responses to crime news reports vary based on the perpetrator's race (Gilliam & Iyengar, 2000; Johnson et al., 1997; Mendelberg, 1997; Peffley, Shields, & Williams, 1996). Whites give higher scores on culpability, personal responsibility, and length of punishment when exposed to African American suspects versus white ones.

Impact on adult viewer attitudes about social policies

Research links news depictions of race and crime with white adults' decision making about policy issues. Viewers of news about a furloughed African American convict were more likely than those who did not watch the story to be resistant to government actions aimed at reducing racial inequality and to report elevated perceptions of racial conflict in the United States (Mendelberg, 1997). Similarly, Valentino (1999) found less support for Democratic and more support for Republican candidates when voters were exposed to minority perpetrators in crime news stories. Valentino maintains that these news stories activated existing perceptions of Democrats as sympathetic to minorities and soft on crime, resulting in negative evaluations of their candidates.

In addition to news, white adult positions on race-based policies are influenced by exposure to a variety of media offerings, including entertainment television. Mastro and Kopacz (2006) and Tan, Fujioka, and Tan (2000) found that exposure to undesirable media portrayals of minorities led whites to make more stereotypic evaluations of real-life minorities. These latter evaluations, then, were negatively related to support for policies like affirmative action.

Impact on intergroup processes among adults

Effects studies further involve media portrayals of race in such identity-based outcomes as intergroup comparisons and esteem maintenance. In particular, viewing a single stereotypical portrayal of outgroup members on television (e.g., Latinos) can initiate race-based social comparisons favoring ingroup members (Mastro, 2003). Moreover, this comparison process appears to enhance self-esteem. Alternatively, consuming unfavorable images of one's ingroup (e.g., Native Americans) is associated with depressed self-esteem and lowered ingroup efficacy (Fryberg, 2003).

Impact on children

Given that children are less able and less likely to critically evaluate media content, its influence is potentially of greater consequence for them than it is for adults. Survey research establishes a small but significant relationship between white children's exposure to television and real-world perceptions about racial and ethnic minorities, including how they talk, how they behave, and how they interact (Atkin, Greenberg, & McDermott, 1983; Zuckerman, Singer, & Singer, 1980). Zuckerman and colleagues (1980) found that viewing violent television among white children was associated with perceptions of Blacks as less competent and less obedient than Whites. Further, their results indicated that children who watched programs with more black characters (and whose mothers watched fewer violent shows) characterized Blacks as more athletic than Whites. Moreover, exposure to same-race characters has been linked to minority children's positive self-esteem. For example, McDermott and Greenberg (1984) found that both talking about television with their parents and viewing programs with African American characters were positively related with self-esteem among African American fourth and fifth graders.

Impact on children's intergroup relations

After viewing scenes from *Sesame Street* with minority children as major characters, children report an increased willingness to choose minority playmates (Gorn, Goldberg, & Kanungo, 1976). However, research also shows that African American and white children believe their mothers would be displeased with their decision to befriend a child of another race, despite their own interest in doing so (Lovelace et al., 1994). Vignettes were created and broadcast by *Sesame Street* to address this issue. Exposure to one vignette in which a white child visits the home of her African American friend resulted in 70 percent of the child viewers (African American and white) reporting that they wanted to play with a black Barbie doll (Fisch, Truglio, & Cole, 1999).

Discussion and Research Agenda

Research on the social effects of exposure to minority characters on television or any other medium is scarce with regard to all audiences, especially children, let alone minority children. This review is flush with content analyses of program content and advertising that point out continuing disparities in how often minorities appear and how they are characterized. There is ample evidence of media underrepresentation of Latinos. Native Americans are invisible. African Americans achieved parity in proportional representation with Whites in fictional television series a quarter century ago, but continue to be overrepresented as criminals on television news shows. Yet this area is remarkably barren of systematic research that examines whether and what kind of difference these disparities make. Why has the systematic research that is necessary to test the merits of key theoretical frameworks been so incomplete within the context of minority portrayals? For one, issues related to minority portrayals may not be of sufficient political and/or economic import to merit the external funding that drives the social research agenda. Violence, promiscuity, drinking, and drug use are all issues that are universally unacceptable; all have been well-funded areas for communication and media research. To probe into the origins and consequences of the biased portrayal or non-portrayal of racial and ethnic minorities, and how minority and majority audiences respond to them, appears to lack any particular institution's imprimatur.

In addition to funding issues, the challenges inherent to conducting research aimed at uncovering media effects among children regarding race and ethnicity are considerable. Isolating media effects can be an arduous task given the comparatively small (but meaningful) influence of the media relative to other social influences (see Morgan & Shanahan, 1997, for a meta-analysis of cultivation effects).

Then, there are difficulties associated with measuring race-related outcomes – such as participants' attempts to avoid making real or perceived racially driven responses (see Dovidio & Gaertner, 2000, and Wegener & Petty, 1995, for reviews). Another difficulty is obtaining access to large samples of minority children for research, as well as the special efforts required in working with children. All of these factors contribute to a complex undertaking.

Serious gaps exist in empirical research documenting the effects of exposure on majority and minority youth. A research agenda should focus initially on media usage and content preferences among ethnic minority children. Research by Roberts and colleagues (2005) begins to address this need by providing a comprehensive catalog of the media-use behaviors of minority and majority youngsters. The next step is a systematic study that uncovers the combinations of media activities that differentiate among age, gender, and racial and ethnic groups. We can see what an "average" media day looks like, but those averages can mask considerable variability in usage and patterns of exposure.

Data also are lacking that indicate the particular content features of media preferred by minority youth. Each of our primary theories focuses attention on the role of media content in determining responses. To assess any outcomes associated with exposure, a better understanding of the media content experienced by minority children is needed. For example, what television characters are preferred, what videogame characters are selected for play and which are chosen as opponents, what magazine stories are examined, and which music videos are played? The answers to these questions would help identify a myriad of potential cultivation, social cognitive, and/or social-identity-based outcomes. They would be additionally beneficial in planning media-based interventions focusing on health, education, and related social issues.

Added to the mix of traditional media is the wealth of research opportunities to study newer media such as videogames, MP3s, and the Internet. Are there differences in videogame preferences and consequences? What are the genders and ages of preferred videogame characters? What gaming characters do majority and minority children identify with? Those are old questions applied to newer media. There also are new questions: Who do majority and minority children "morph" onto when given such opportunities? In creating avatars, what attributes are favored by majority and minority children? If their Internet site visits were tracked, what differences would we find and why?

Conclusion

US culture is becoming increasingly diverse, with ethnic minorities becoming more prevalent and Caucasians becoming less prevalent in the coming decades; this trend is foreshadowed by the prevalence of minority youth in the US population (US Census Bureau, 2000). With the exception of African American portrayals, the number of ethnic minority media presentations is out of step with the changes in US demographics. Moreover, we know precious little about how these portrayals (or lack thereof) influence ethnic minority children. Having adequate portrayals of minority children and understanding the effects of both older and newer media on youth development is a research area that requires immediate attention.

References

Abrams, D., & Hogg, M. (1990). An introduction to the social identity approach. In D. Abrams & M. Hogg (Eds.), *Social identity theory: Constructive and critical advances* (pp. 1–9). Hertfordshire, UK: Harvester Wheatsheaf.

Albarran, A., & Umphrey, D. (1993). An examination of television motivations and program preferences by Hispanics, Blacks, and Whites. *Journal of Broadcasting and Electronic Media*, 37, 95–103.

Anand, S., & Krosnick, J. (2005). Demographic predictors of media use among infants, toddlers, and preschoolers. *American Behavioral Scientist*, 48, 539–61.

Appiah, O. (2001). Ethnic identification on adolescents' evaluations of advertisements, *Journal of Advertising Research*, 41, 7–22.

Appiah, O. (2002). Black and white viewers' perception and recall of occupational characters on television. *Journal of Communication*, 52, 776–93.

Atkin, C., Greenberg, B., & McDermott, S. (1983). Television and race role socialization. *Journalism Quarterly*, 60, 407–14.

Bandura, A. (2001). Social cognitive theory of mass communication. *Media Psychology*, 3, 265–99.

Bang, H., & Reece, B. (2003). Minorities in children's television commercials: New, improved, and stereotyped. *The Journal of Consumer Affairs*, 37, 42–67.

Berry, G., & Mitchell-Kernan, C. (1982). *Television and the socialization of the minority child*. New York: Academic Press.

Bickham, D., Vandewater, E., Huston, A., Lee, J., Caplovitz, A., & Wright, J. (2003). Predictors of children's electronic media use: An examination of three ethnic groups. *Media Psychology*, 5, 107–37.

Bodenhausen, G., Schwarz, N., Bless, H., & Wänke, M. (1995). Effects of atypical exemplars on racial beliefs: Enlightened racism or generalized appraisals? *Journal of Experimental Social Psychology*, 31, 48–63.

Borzekowski, D., & Poussaint, A. (1998). *Latino American preschoolers and the media*. University of Pennsylvania, The Annenberg Public Policy Center Report Series.

Brown, C., & Bigler, R. (2005). Children's perceptions of discrimination: A developmental model. *Child Development*, 76, 533–53.

Calvert, S. L., Strong, B. L., Jacobs, E. L., & Conger, E. E. (2007). Interaction and participation for young Hispanic and Caucasian children's learning of media content. *Media Psychology*, 9, 431–45.

Children Now. (2001). *Fall colors, 2000–2001: Prime time diversity report*. Oakland, CA: Children Now.

Children Now. (2002). *Why it matters . . . Diversity on television*. Children Now Newsletter, Summer. Retrieved September 14, 2005, from http://www.childrennow.org/assets/pdf/issues_media_medianow_2002.pdf.

Children Now. (2004). *Fall colors, 2003–2004: Prime time diversity report*. Oakland, CA: Children Now.

Cohen, J. (2001). Defining identification: A theoretical look at the identification of audiences with media characters. *Mass Communication and Society*, 4, 245–64.

Coltrane, S., & Messineo, M. (2000). The perpetuation of subtle prejudice: Race and gender imagery in 1990s television advertising. *Sex Roles*, 42, 363–9.

Corenblum, B., & Annis, R. (1993). Development of racial identity in minority and majority children: An affect discrepancy model. *Canadian Journal of Behavioral Science*, 25, 499–521.

Dixon, T., & Azocar, C. (2006). The representation of juvenile offenders by race on Los Angeles area television news. *Howard Journal of Communications*, 17, 143–61.

Dixon, T., Azocar, C., & Casas, M. (2003). The portrayal of race and crime on television network news. *Journal of Broadcasting and Electronic Media*, 47, 498–523.

Dixon, T., & Linz, D. (2000a). Overrepresentation and underrepresentation of African Americans and Latinos as lawbreakers on television news. *Journal of Communication*, 50, 131–54.

Dixon, T., & Linz, D. (2000b). Race and the misrepresentation of victimization on local television news. *Communication Research*, 27, 547–73.

Dixon, T., & Linz, D. (2002). Television news, prejudicial pretrial publicity, and the depiction of race. *Journal of Broadcasting and Electronic Media*, 46, 112–36.

Dobrow, J., & Gidney, C. (1998). The good, the bad, and the foreign: The use of dialect in children's animated television. In A. Jordan & K. Hall Jamieson (Eds.), *The annals of the American academy of political and social science: Children and television* (pp. 105–19). Thousand Oaks, CA: Sage.

Donohue, T., Meyer, T., & Henke, L. (1978). Black and white children: Perceptions of television commercials. *Journal of Marketing*, 42, 34–40.

Dovidio, J. F., & Gaertner, S. L. (2000). Aversive racism and selection decisions: 1989 and 1999. *Psychological Science*, 11, 315–19.

Eastman, H., & Liss, M. (1980). Ethnicity and children's television preferences. *Journalism Quarterly*, 57, 277–80.

Entman, R. (1992). Blacks in the news: Television, modern racism and cultural change. *Journalism Quarterly*, 69, 341–61.

Eyal, K., & Rubin, A. (2003). Viewer aggression and homophily, identification, and parasocial relationships with television characters. *Journal of Broadcasting and Electronic Media*, 47, 77–98.

Fisch, S., Truglio, R., & Cole, C. (1999). The impact of *Sesame Street* on preschool children: A review and synthesis of 30 years' research. *Media Psychology*, 1, 165–90.

Fryberg, S. (2003). Really? You don't look like an American Indian: Social representations and social group identities. *Dissertation Abstracts International*.

Gerbner, G., Gross, L., Morgan, M., Signorielli, N., & Shanahan, J. (2002). Growing up with television: Cultivation processes. In J. Bryant & D. Zillmann (Eds.), *Media effects: Advances in theory and research* (2nd edn., pp. 43–67). Mahwah, NJ: Lawrence Erlbaum.

Gilens, M. (1996). Race and poverty in America: Public misperceptions and the American news media. *Public Opinion Quarterly*, 60, 515–41.

Gilliam, F., & Iyengar, S. (2000). Prime suspects: The influence of local television news on the viewing public. *American Journal of Political Science*, 44, 560–73.

Glaubke, C., Miller, P., Parker, M., & Espejo, E. (2001). *Fair Play? Violence, gender, and race in video games*. Oakland, CA: Children Now.

Gorn, G., Goldberg, M., & Kanungo, R. (1976). The role of educational television in changing the intergroup attitudes of children. *Child Development*, 47, 277–80.

Graves, S. (1996). Diversity on television. In T. Macbeth (Ed.), *Tuning in to young viewers: Social science perspectives on television* (pp. 61–86). Thousand Oaks, CA: Sage.

Greenberg, B. (1972). Children's reactions to TV Blacks. *Journalism Quarterly*, 49, 5–14.

Greenberg, B. (1988). Some uncommon television images and the drench hypothesis. In S. Oskamp (Ed.), *Applied social psychology annual*. Vol. 8, *Television as a social issue* (pp. 88–102). Newbury Park, CA: Sage.

Greenberg, B., & Atkin, C. (1982). Learning about minorities from television: A research agenda. In G. L. Berry & C. Mitchell-Kernan (Eds.), *Television and the socialization of the minority child* (pp. 215–43). New York: Academic Press.

Greenberg, B., & Brand, J. (1993). Cultural diversity on Saturday morning television. In G. Berry & J. Asamen (Eds.), *Children and television: Images in a changing sociocultural world* (pp. 132–42). Newbury Park, CA: Sage.

Greenberg, B., Heeter, C., Burgoon, M., Burgoon, J., & Korzenny, F. (1983). Mass media use, preferences, and attitudes among young people. In B. Greenberg, M. Burgoon, J. Burgoon, & F. Korzenny (Eds.), *Mexican Americans and the mass media* (pp. 147–201). Norwood, NJ: Ablex.

Greenberg, B., Mastro, D., & Brand, J. (2002). Minorities and the mass media: Television into the twenty-first century. In J. Bryant & D. Zillmann (Eds.), *Media effects: Advances in theory and research* (pp. 333–51). Hillsdale, NJ: Lawrence Erlbaum.

Greenberg, B., & Reeves, B. (1976). Children and the perceived reality of television. *Journal of Social Issues*, 32, 86–97.

Harwood, J., & Roy, A. (2005). Social identity theory and mass communication research. In J. Harwood & H. Giles (Eds.), *Intergroup communication* (pp. 189–211). New York: Peter Lang.

Hawkins, R., and Pingree, S. (1982). Television's influence on constructions of social reality. In D. Pearl, L. Bouthilet, & J. Lazar (Eds.), Television and behavior: Ten years of scientific progress and implications for the eighties, vol. 2 (pp. 224–47). Washington, DC: US Government Printing Office.

Hawkins, R., & Pingree, S. (1990). Divergent psychological processes in constructing social reality from mass media content. In N. Signorielli & M. Morgan (Eds.), *Cultivation analysis: New directions in media effects research* (pp. 35–50). Newbury Park, CA: Sage.

Hogg, M., Terry, D., & White, K. (1995). A tale of two theories: A critical comparison of identity theory with social identity theory. *Social Psychology Quarterly*, 58, 255–69.

Huston, A., Donnerstein, E., Fairchild, H., Feshbach, N., Katz, P., & Murray, J. (1992). *Big world, small screen: The role of television in American society*. Lincoln, NE: University of Nebraska Press.

Johnson, M. (1996). Latinas and television in the United States: Relationships among genre identification, acculturation, and acculturation stress. *Howard Journal of Communications*, 7, 289–313.

Johnson, J. D., Adams, M. S., Hall, W., & Ashburn, L. (1997). Race, media, and violence: Differential racial effects of exposure to violent news stories. *Basic and Applied Social Psychology*, 19, 81–90.

Jose, P., & Brewer, W. (1984). Development of story liking: Character identification, suspense, and outcome resolution. *Developmental Psychology*, 20, 911–24.

Kelly, J., & Smith, S. (2006). *G movies give boys a D: Portraying males as dominant, disconnected, and dangerous*. See Jane Program at Dad's and Daughters: SeeJane.org.

Larson, M. (2002). Race and interracial relationships in children's television commercials. *Howard Journal of Communications*, 13, 223–35.

Licata, J., & Biswas, A. (1993). Representation, roles, and occupational status of black models in television advertisements. *Journalism Quarterly*, 70, 868–82.

Li-Vollmer, M. (2002). Race representation in child-targeted television commercials. *Mass Communication and Society*, 5, 207–28.

Lovelace, V., Scheiner, S., Dollberg, S., Segui, I., & Black, T. (1994). Making a neighborhood the *Sesame Street* way: Developing a methodology to evaluate children's understanding of race. *Journal of Educational Television*, 20, 69–78.

Mastro, D. (2003). A social identity approach to understanding the impact of television messages. *Communication Monographs*, 70, 98–113.

Mastro, D., & Behm–Morawitz, E. (2005). Latino representation on primetime television. *Journalism and Mass Communication Quarterly*, 82, 110–30.

Mastro, D., Behm–Morawitz, E., & Ortiz, M. (2007). The cultivation of race-based social perceptions of Latinos: A mental models approach. *Media Psychology*, 9, 1–19.

Mastro, D., & Kopacz, M. (2006). Media representations of race, prototypicality, and policy reasoning: An application of self-categorization theory. *Journal of Broadcasting and Electronic Media*, 50, 305–22.

Mastro, D., & Greenberg, B. (2000). The portrayal of racial minorities on prime time television. *Journal of Broadcasting and Electronic Media*, 44, 690–703.

Mastro, D., & Stern, S. (2003). Representations of race in television commercials: A content analysis of primetime advertising. *Journal of Broadcasting and Electronic Media*, 47, 638–47.

Matabane, P., & Merritt, B. (1996). African Americans on television: Twenty-five years after Kerner. *Howard Journal of Communications*, 7, 329–37.

McDermott, S., & Greenberg, B. (1984). Parents, peers and television as determinants of black children's esteem. In R. Bostrom (Ed.), *Communication yearbook*, vol. 8 (pp. 164–77). Beverly Hills, CA: Sage.

McKown, C., & Weinstein, R. (2003). The development and consequences of stereotype consciousness in middle childhood. *Child Development*, 74, 498–515.

Mendelberg, T. (1997). Executing Hortons. Racial crime in the 1988 presidential campaign. *Public Opinion Quarterly*, 61, 134–57.

Morgan, M., & Shanahan, J. (1997). Two decades of cultivation analysis: An appraisal and meta-analysis. In B. Burleson (Ed.), *Communication yearbook*, vol. 20 (pp. 1–45). Thousand Oaks, CA. Sage.

Nielsen Media Research. (1998). *1998 Report on Television*. New York: Nielsen Media Research.

Peffley, M., Shields, T., & Williams, B. (1996). The intersection of race and crime in television news stories: An experimental study. *Political Communication*, 13, 309–27.

Poindexter, P.M., & Stroman, C. (1981). Blacks and television: A review of the research literature. *Journal of Broadcasting*, 25, 103–22.

Power, J., Murphy, S., & Coover, G. (1996). Priming prejudice: How stereotypes and counterstereotypes influence attribution of responsibility and credibility among ingroups and outgroups. *Human Communication Research*, 23, 36–58.

Roberts, D. F., Foehr, U. G., & Rideout, V. J. (2005). *Generation M: Media in the lives of 8–18-year-olds.* Menlo Park, CA: Kaiser Family Foundation.

Romer, D., Jamieson, K., & DeCoteau, N. (1998). The treatment of persons of color in local television news: Ethnic blame discourse or realistic group conflict. *Communication Research*, 25, 286–305.

Shrum, L. (2004). The cognitive processes underlying cultivation effects are a function of whether judgments are on-line or memory based. *Communications*, 29, 327–44.

Shrum, L., & Bischak, V. (2001). Mainstreaming, resonance, and impersonal impact: Testing moderators of the cultivation effect. *Human Communication Research*, 27, 187–215.

Signorielli, N., McLeod, D., & Healy, E. (1994). Gender stereotypes in MTV Commercials: The beat goes on. *Journal of Broadcasting and Electronic Media*, 38, 91–102.

Stern, B. (1999). Gender and multicultural issues in advertising: Stages on the research highway. *Journal of Advertising*, 28, 1–9.

Stilling, E. (1997). The electronic melting pot hypothesis: The cultivation of acculturation among Hispanics through television viewing. *Howard Journal of Communication*, 8, 77–100.

Stroman, C. (1986). Television viewing and self-concept among black children. *Journal of Broadcasting and Electronic Media*, 30, 87–93.

Stroman, C., Merritt, B., & Matabane, P. (1989–1990). Twenty years after Kerner: The portrayals of African Americans on prime-time television. *Howard Journal of Communications*, 2, 44–56.

Tajfel, H. (1978). *Differentiation between social groups: Studies in the social psychology of intergroup relations.* London: Academic Press.

Tan, A., Fujioka, Y., & Tan, G. (2000). Television use, stereotypes of African Americans and opinions on affirmative action: An effective model of policy reasoning. *Communication Monographs*, 67, 362–71.

Taylor, C., & Stern, B. (1997). Asian-Americans: Television advertising and the "Model Minority" stereotype. *Journal of Advertising*, 26, 47–60.

Turner, J. (1982). Towards a cognitive redefinition of the social group. In H. Tajfel (Ed.), *Social identity and intergroup relations.* Cambridge: Cambridge University Press.

Tynes, B., Reynolds, L., & Greenfield, P. (2004). Adolescence, race and ethnicity on the Internet: A comparison of discourse in monitored vs. unmonitored chat rooms. *Journal of Applied Developmental Psychology*, 25, 667–84.

US Census Bureau. (2000). *All across the USA: Population distribution and composition, 2000.* Retrieved August 25, 2005, from http://www.census.gov/population/pop-profile/2000/chap02.pdf.

Valentino, N. A. (1999). Crime news and the priming of racial attitudes during evaluations of the president. *Public Opinion Quarterly*, 63, 293–320.

Ward, L. M., Hansbrough, E., & Walker, E. (2005). Contributions of music videos to black adolescents' gender and sexual schema. *Journal of Adolescent Research*, 20, 143–66.

Wegener, D., & Petty, R. (1995). Flexible correction processes in social judgment: The role of naïve theories in corrections for perceived bias. *Journal of Personality and Social Psychology*, 68, 36–51.

Weigel, R., & Howes, P. (1982). Race relations on children's television. *Journal of Psychology*, 111, 109–12.

Wilkes, R., & Valencia, H. (1989). Hispanics and Blacks in television commercials. *Journal of Advertising*, 18, 19–25.

Whittler, T. (1991). The effects of actors' race in commercial advertising: Review and extension. *Journal of Advertising*, 20, 54–60.

Woodard, E. (1999). *The 1999 state of children's television report: Programming for children over broadcast and cable television*. The Annenberg Public Policy Center of the University of Pennsylvania. Retrieved August 25, 2005, from http://appcpenn.org.

Zuckerman, D., Singer, C., & Singer, J. (1980). Children's television viewing, racial and sex role attitudes. *Journal of Applied Social Psychology*, 10, 281–94.

5

Gender, Media Use, and Effects

Stacey J. T. Hust and Jane D. Brown

Gender socialization is the process by which children learn the norms and expectations for males and females in their culture (Ward, 2003). Traditionally, children learned gender roles through observation of males and females in their families, and later from their friends and at school. In recent decades, the media provide children with an "early window" on the larger world almost as soon as they are old enough to be propped up in front of a screen (e.g., Rideout, Vandewater, & Wartella, 2003). Through this window, children can see girls and boys and men and women who may or may not be like the men and women in their own families or neighborhoods.

Research during the past 50 years has asked to what extent the media are an accurate reflection of both the proportion of men and women in the society as well as the extent to which the activities and values portrayed are diverse. The underlying concern is that the media's worldview is a distortion of reality and rarely depicts the wide variety of roles and attributes of women and men in the real world. This narrow reflection of reality may limit the aspirations and expectations of girls and boys who are looking to see what is expected of people of their gender.

In this chapter, we first define what is meant by gender and gender socialization and then summarize current research on media selection that finds that preference for different kinds of media starts early for boys and girls. We identify common gender stereotypes in different kinds of media content, and then briefly introduce key theories that help explain how the media affect gender. We then look at what social scientific studies have found about the effects of media portrayals on children's and adolescents' understanding of themselves and others as males and females. Finally, we offer some suggestions for future research on the role of the media in gender socialization in a culture that is increasingly defined and known through the media. Throughout the chapter we consider the array of media now readily available to young people, often in the privacy of their own bedrooms (Scantlin, this volume, Chapter 3), including not only television, but also music, movies, magazines, Internet sites, video and computer games, and the advertising that permeates all these media.

Sex and Gender

Biological sex characteristics (differences based on chromosomes and genitalia) typically identify individuals as male or female. Early research, particularly from an evolutionary psychology tradition, considered sex a binary variable, male and female, but these categories did not cover some important anomalous situations, such as when a person born with female biological characteristics chooses to live as a male. To address such possibilities, the idea of "sex category" was developed. Membership in a sex category is clear when individuals use "identificatory displays that proclaim one's membership to one or the other category" (West & Zimmerman, 1987, p. 27). Gender can then be defined as the socially constructed conduct that is perceived as acceptable for the members of a sex category, regardless of how one was born. In this chapter we use the term "gender" rather than "sex" or "sex category" to suggest that what it means to be male or female depends on what the culture makes of it (Zinn, Hondagneu-Sotelo, & Messner, 2001).

Typically, between 2 and 7 years old most children come to understand that their biological sex is constant and does not change over time (Kohlberg, 1966). Young children also begin to establish patterns, or schemas, of beliefs and behaviors typically associated with biological sex differences prevalent in their culture. They then use these gender schemas to process and understand gender-oriented behavior (Martin & Halverson, 1981). These schemas also influence memory and problem solving as well as guide the development of self-concepts and self-esteem (Bem, 1987; Calvert, 1999). Gender schemas lead to gender stereotypes because behavior that conforms to the established schema is more easily processed, understood, and remembered. Children, for example, who have adopted traditional gender schemas will report having seen a female nurse and a male doctor even though the video they just watched featured a male nurse and a female doctor (Cordua, McGraw, & Drabman, 1979). Such misperceptions may influence what girls and boys consider appropriate or possible in their own lives as well as how they relate to others.

Individuals in a culture typically learn about gender roles and expectations in at least three ways. First, cultural expectations about gender are conceived of and distributed through *gendered institutions* such as the family, schools, workplaces, and the media. These gendered institutions reflect the idea that "gender is present in the processes, practices, images and ideologies, and distributions of power in the various sectors of social life" (Acker, 1992, p. 567). The family, for example, is traditionally organized with different roles for the father and the mother, and schools and workplaces tend to be run by men and have different expectations of what can be achieved by boys and girls and men and women. As gendered institutions, the media are organized in a gendered way (e.g., the

decision-makers are more likely to be male than female), and the media disseminate images and information that reflect the gendered ideology of the culture
(e.g., women are passive and submissive, males are active and dominant) (Acker,
1992).

The culture's gender ideologies as reflected in these institutions are then repro-
duced through interactions between individuals and groups in a process sometimes referred to as *doing gender* (West & Zimmerman, 1987, p. 135). Males and
females reproduce the power relations and gendered expectations they see in their
families, the media, and other institutions as they interact with each other. Finally,
individuals construct *gender identities*, typically made up of various attributes
and schemas of socially sanctioned norms that are displayed in various social
settings. This process is ongoing and cyclical in that gender identities influence
which social settings, including media, are chosen, how the media representations
of gender are interpreted, and thus, which norms are reinforced and incorporated
into everyday behavior and the developing gender schema and identity (Steele &
Brown, 1995).

Gendered Media Selection

Up until about 6 years old, boys and girls tend to use media in similar ways –
spending about the same amount of time with the same kind of content (Anand
& Krosnick, 2005). The major exception is videogame playing, which seems to
be a male domain right from the start (Anand & Krosnick, 2005). But as gender
schemas differentiate more in early and middle childhood, patterns of media use
also begin to vary dramatically. By adolescence it is as if boys and girls are living
in different media worlds (Roberts, Foehr, & Rideout, 2005). Such gendered
media selection is increasingly easy as advertisers have recognized the spending potential of young audiences and the media have responded by producing
content that appeals primarily to one gender or the other (Zollo, 2004).

Television

Although there is little difference in the amount of *time* boys and girls in the
United States spend watching television per day (in 2004, 3 to 4 hours a day),
gender differences in *content* are clear by middle childhood, and sometimes even
earlier (Brown & Pardun, 2004). Some recent studies, however, have found that
girls as young as 4 years old prefer shows such as *Dora the Explorer* more
than boys do (Calvert, Strong, Jacobs, & Conger, 2007). From surveys of nationally representative samples of 8- to 18-year-olds conducted in 1999 and 2004,
Roberts and his colleagues concluded that gender was the main motivation
behind television show choices (Roberts & Foehr, 2004; Roberts, Foehr, &
Rideout, 2005). Boys preferred sports and action programs on television; girls
chose child- and family-oriented content, romance, and comedy. In another

study of early adolescents (12- to 14-year-olds), only four shows on a list of 150 were watched by a sizeable proportion of both males and females (Brown & Pardun, 2004). In 2002, for example, the television show with the largest number of teen girl viewers was *American Idol* – a show that chose a new singing star from amateur contenders. Teen boys, meanwhile, were watching *World Wrestling Entertainment* and National Football League games (*Teen Media Monitor*, 2003).

Researchers consistently have found, however, that males are more likely to choose male-oriented content than girls are to choose only female-oriented content, especially after they achieve gender constancy (Luecke-Aleska et al., 1995; Slaby & Frey, 1975), the knowledge that their biological sex is a fixed and immutable characteristic (Kohlberg, 1966). In a large national survey of more than 1,000 adolescents, girls identified both male and female television actors as their favorite television stars, but boys identified only male stars (Heintz-Knowles et al., 1999). Boys said they chose their favorite stars because they were humorous, while girls chose stars based on their physical appearance. Hoffner (1996) found similar patterns with children ages 7–12. Such a cross-over effect for females may be because it is less culturally sanctioned for males to exhibit feminine characteristics than it is for females to exhibit masculine attributes. Females also identify with male characters because the portrayals of televised males often involve more interesting and challenging tasks than are found in the portrayals of televised females (Signoreilli & Bascue, 1999). Teen girls also tend to mature faster than their male peers so some of the girls' selections may also be based on sexual attraction rather than a desire to emulate.

Movies

Both characteristics of the film and the gender identities of viewers affect preferences for and emotional responses to the movie genre. In a study of emotional reactions to sad films, such as *Beaches* and *Brian's Song*, researchers found that both boys and girls who had a more communal or feminine gender role identity were more likely than boys and girls who had a more agentic or masculine gender identity to enjoy a sad film, especially if it featured a relational theme (Oliver, Weaver, & Sargent, 2000).

Other research on reactions to graphic horror or "slasher" films, such as *Friday the Thirteenth* and *Nightmare on Elm Street*, found that adolescent viewers with less empathy for the victim and those with more interest in seeing gore enjoyed the movie more than did those who identified with the victim (usually a female) (Sparks, 1991). Some viewers, typically the males, liked such movies because they felt a sense of mastery in not remaining frightened after the end of the movie (Johnston, 1995). Similar emotional preference patterns have been found for adolescent males who play violent videogames (Jansz, 2005).

Some scholars have proposed that violent or graphic movies and videogames provide opportunities for young men to engage in modern-day rituals of fearlessness. In one study, women enjoyed the horror film more if they were in the company of a fear-mastering man than when they were with a distressed man, and men preferred being with a distressed female (Zillmann et al., 1986).

Emotional expectations are learned early as part of gender role socialization. Parents and other cultural agents tend to discourage boys from crying and expressing sadness and fear, and girls are encouraged not to display anger and aggression (Brody, 1993). Such expectations affect which media genre males and females prefer as well as how they respond emotionally.

Music

As anyone who has spent hours singing "Old McDonald's Farm" or "Ring Around the Rosie" with a toddler knows, even young children love music. Girls spend more time listening to music than do boys from early on. By middle childhood (8–10 years old), girls are listening to music on the radio and on CDs and tapes more than 1 hour a day on average while boys are listening about 15 minutes less. Early adolescent girls (11–14 years old) spend almost one third (30 percent) of their media time each day listening to music (more than 2 hours a day); boys are more likely to be watching television and playing videogames. By later adolescence (15–18 years old), boys' music listening has increased, too, but girls still are bigger music fans than boys are, spending almost 3 hours a day listening to music, even more time than they spend watching television (Roberts & Foehr, 2004).

In the early part of the new century, Rap and Hip Hop music were the preferred genres for adolescents from all racial and ethnic groups (Pardun, L'Engle, & Brown, 2005). However, girls continued to prefer softer, more ballad-type music, whereas boys preferred harder rock and edgier Rap and Hip Hop music (Heintz-Knowles et al., 1999; Hoffner, 1996; Roberts & Foehr, 2004). In 2001, for example, adolescent girls' favorite music artists were female Rhythm and Blues groups and pop singers such as Destiny's Child and Jennifer Lopez. Two of the boys' favorites were Ja Rule and Jay Z, both rappers who sang about sex, violence, and growing up black in urban America (Pardun, L'Engle, & Brown, 2005).

Magazines

Magazines were one of the first media to differentiate themselves by the gender of their intended audience, and they are increasingly differentiated by age and interests. So today, American adolescent girls read teen girl fashion magazines such as *Seventeen* and *Cosmo Girl* and soon graduate to the grown-up versions (*Cosmopolitan*, *Glamour*, and *Vogue*). Boys are more likely to be reading sports and recreation magazines (Taveras et al., 2004). In one study involving a large sample of early adolescents (12 to 14 years old), more than three quarters of the girls said they read a teen girl fashion magazine. Similar proportions of boys were reading magazines such as *Sports Illustrated*, *Computer Gaming World* and/or *Motor*

Trend. Girls said they primarily read magazines to monitor trends in fashion and hairstyles and to follow the lives of famous people; boys read primarily to follow sports (Pardun, L'Engle, & Brown, 2005).

Computers, videogames, and the Internet

Among young children, the small gender differences in time spent with screen media are due primarily to boys' greater interest in video and computer games. In 2003, a national survey of the parents of young children found that more than half (56 percent) of 4- to 6-year-old boys but only about one third (36 percent) of girls had played videogames. In a typical day, about one quarter (24 percent) of the boys played while fewer than one in ten (8 percent) of the girls played (Rideout, Vandewater, & Wartella, 2003). The girls on average spent about 2 hours a day with screen media (television and computer) while the boys spent about 20 minutes more per day, primarily because they were more likely to be playing videogames.

Boys and girls continue to use computers differently as they age. In a survey of older children (8 to 18 years old), boys were two times more likely than girls to have a videogame player in their bedrooms (63 percent to 33 percent) and to own a handheld game player, such as a Gameboy (Roberts, Foehr, & Rideout, 2005). Teen girls spend more time than boys on girl-oriented websites such as gURL.com and seventeen.com. Boys, in contrast, are more likely than girls to be looking for better ways to play their videogames (e.g., Cheat Planet, GameWinners), playing games online, or downloading music (*Teen Media Monitor*, 2003; Roberts, Foehr, & Rideout, 2005).

Studies have shown that boys and girls gain greater social acceptance if they play video and computer games that are considered appropriate for their gender (Lucas & Sherry, 2004). Young males are more likely to play games that focus on physical enactment (i.e., fighting games) with more "realistic" human violence and imagination (i.e., role playing games). Adolescent females are more likely to play more traditional kinds of games (i.e., puzzles or electronic board games) and games with animated "fantasy" violence (Funk & Buchman, 1996a, 1996b). Although it appeared initially that girls were spending more time than boys in contact with their friends online, a survey in 2004 found that computer-mediated communication such as instant messaging was the primary online activity for both male and female adolescents, averaging about 40 minutes a day (Roberts, Foehr, & Rideout, 2005).

In sum, the new media environment provides more opportunity than ever before for boys and girls to use media to satisfy developing gender differences in preferences and expectations. But even in the more traditional media forms, gender-consistent preferences emerge in early childhood and persist through adolescence. Boys spend more time than girls playing violent videogames and girls spend more time listening to music than boys do. Across the media, males tend to prefer more competitive and active content and girls choose content that is more about who they are in relation to others.

Dominant Themes in Children's and Adolescents' Media

Many studies of the representation of males and females across the range of media have been conducted over the past half century. These studies have looked not only at how frequently men and women are portrayed but also at their physical and socio-emotional characteristics and occupational roles. Six broad themes characterize much of what these content analyses have found. From the media's perspective: (1) It's a man's world; (2) Men are strong and muscular; women are thin and sexy; (3) Men are serious and powerful; women are emotional and passive; (4) Heterosexuality prevails; (5) Boys will be boys and girls better be prepared; and (6) A woman's place is still in the home.

It's a man's world

In most of the media attended to by children and adolescents, men appear twice as frequently as women, even though in real life women outnumber men (Signorielli & Bacue, 1999). Prime-time television, movies, and music videos feature two times as many men as women (Signorielli & McLeod, 1994; Signorielli, 1997). Males appear up to four times more frequently than females in children's Saturday morning programs (Calvert, 1999).

Domestic comedies, which appeal primarily to female audiences, are the only kind of prime-time entertainment programs in which women outnumber men (62 percent female characters) (Steenland, 1995). Although women appear as frequently as men on soap operas, studies in the 1970s and 1980s found that minority women were significantly underrepresented and women in traditional roles had easier lives than "liberated" or more modern women (Cantor & Pingree, 1983).

In the late 1990s, female characters were included in only 30 percent of the videogames studied (Dietz, 1998). In 1997, the year the country music industry dubbed the "Year of the Woman," male artists appeared on the Country Music Television channel three times more frequently than female artists (Andsager & Roe, 1999).

In early analyses of the lack of women in the news media, sociologist Gaye Tuchman and colleagues (1978) called the relative absence of women in the media "symbolic annihilation." She argued that simply by disproportionately excluding women from media roles, women are marginalized and appear less important and/or powerful than the men who appear more frequently in the media than in real life.

Men are strong and muscular; women are thin and sexy

Stereotypes of men as physically strong and women as sex objects still prevail in the media. In magazine advertisements, women are as likely to be shown in suggestive clothing (30 percent), partially clad (13 percent) or nude (6 percent) as they are to be fully clothed (Reichert & Carpenter, 2004). Although research on the sexual objectification of men is scarce, male bodies are increasingly being portrayed in more sexually explicit ways, essentially becoming "more masculin-ized" by revealing muscled "buff" bodies (Reichert et al., 1999, p. 15).

The majority of women pictured in teen fashion magazines are dispropor-tionately thin, and particularly in advertising most women exhibit the "thin ideal" body (Thompson & Heinberg, 1999). When women with heavier body types are portrayed on television or in the movies, their weight is often part of the storyline or their character is mocked and ridiculed (e.g., Kirstie Alley's *Fat Actress*).

Men are serious and powerful; women are emotional and passive

In television programs, cartoons, music videos and in commercials, males typically are depicted as more adventurous, aggressive, violent, and dominant in interactions; females are more subservient, nurturing, affectionate, and frequently the object of implicit, explicit, and aggressive sexual advances (Glascock, 2001; Signorielli & McLeod, 1994).

On television, women routinely exhibit less agency in their relationships than their male counterparts do (Glascock, 2001). In an analysis of 50 popular movies, Hedley (1994) found that female characters typically lose in emotional and physical conflict with male characters. Romance articles, advice columns, and fictional stories in magazines promote girls' subordination to males in sexual and relationship decisions (Duke & Kreshel, 1998). Movies watched mostly by adolescent girls, such as *Princess Diaries* and *Legally Blonde*, may be the one genre in which female characters are portrayed as more independent and direct in dealing with other characters, but even in these movies, the female lead's primary goal often is to get the guy (Signorielli, 1997).

In music videos and videogames, females are disproportionately the victims of violence. When included in videogames, females are most often damsels in distress rather than heroines – one content analysis found that one in five (21 per-cent) of popular videogames included violence against female characters (Dietz, 1998). Even children's cartoons have been identified as emphasizing masculine violence. A majority of children (4–9 years old) who were interviewed about the television cartoons they watched reported that male cartoon characters were likely to act violently (Thompson & Zerbinos, 1997).

Heterosexuality prevails

Homosexuality is still rarely portrayed in mainstream media, and is even less likely in media targeted to children and adolescents. Although more frequent portrayals of gays and lesbians have appeared in adult television programming (e.g., *Will and Grace* and *Queer as Folk*), such characters are rarely included in children's or adolescents' television programming. In situation comedies in 2000, fewer than

2 percent of the characters were homosexual, and all of the homosexual characters were between the ages of 20 and 35 (Fouts & Inch, 2005).

When gay youth have been included on such popular teen shows as *Dawson's Creek*, they typically are shown solely in interactions with their heterosexual peers, allowing the audience to "safely" see homosexuality outside of a context of sexual desire (Meyer, 2003). Even the news media's scarce coverage of sexual minorities rarely discusses their daily lives, instead focusing primarily on popular gay characters in entertainment media (Gibson, 2004).

Further complicating the image of gays and lesbians is the media's connection of homosexual sexual behavior to AIDS. Although reality programming characters living with AIDS, such as the *Real World's* Pablo, may have increased awareness about the transmission of the disease, the entertainment media's depiction of white, gay males with AIDS may leave viewers with an inaccurate perception that AIDS is primarily a homosexual disease (Hart, 2002).

Viewing audiences typically do not endorse the portrayal of homosexuality in programming targeted toward children or adolescents (Sprafkin, Silverman, & Rubenstein, 1980). In 2005, an episode of the children's public television show *Postcards from Buster* featured the title character, an animated bunny named Buster, on a trip to Vermont to visit maple sugar farms run by a lesbian couple. The episode was not aired after the US Secretary of Education said many parents would not want children exposed to such "lifestyles" (MSNBC, 2005). Scholars concerned about the few portrayals of homosexuals in the media have suggested that such lack of representation can result in further stigmatization as well as young people's reluctance to acknowledge their own sexual orientations (Gross, 2001; Fejes & Petrich, 1993).

Boys will be boys and girls better be prepared

The typical American adolescent encounters approximately 10,000–15,000 sexual references, jokes, and innuendoes in the media each year (Strasburger, 2005). Content analyses of television have shown that sexual content has become increasingly prevalent and more explicit since the mid-1990s, so that by 2005 more than 70 percent of television shows included some sexual content (Kunkel et al., 2005). Sexual content on television is typically more verbal than visually graphic; occurs outside marital relationships; rarely includes discussion or depiction of sexual planning or negative consequences; and emphasizes women's physical beauty and men's strength and physical prowess. Sexual behavior is also different for men and women on television, with men portrayed as seeing sex as recreation while women are looking for love and enduring relationships (Ward, Gorvine, & Cytron, 2002).

Across four media important to young people (television, music, magazines, and movies), Hust, Brown, and L'Engle (in press) found very little content that could be characterized as promoting sexual health. Qualitative content analysis of the rare instances of sexual health identified consistent gender-related sexual themes that could be summarized as "boys will be boys and girls better be prepared." The few mentions of condoms and contraceptives were almost always addressed to girls as the sexual gatekeepers, assuming that they would be the ones to decide whether the substantial sexual appetites of the young men would be satisfied.

A woman's place is still in the home

The majority of men in the media are depicted as professionals (i.e., doctors, lawyers, law enforcement officials). Women, in contrast, are most often depicted as staying at home and/or not in professional occupations (Glascock, 2001; Signorielli & Bacue, 1999; Signorielli & McLeod, 1994). Even if portrayed in professional roles, women's status is diluted by a focus on their appearance and prospects for romance. One study of the depiction of female scientists and engineers in popular films found that in interactions with male colleagues, overt and subtle forms of stereotyping undermined the women's authority (Steinke, 2005).

In sum, the media world in which girls and boys are growing up continues to portray males and females in stereotypical ways that may constrain children's expectations about what is valued and/or possible as a male or female in this culture. Women simply are less likely to appear in the media world than they are in real life; when they do appear, women are emotional and passive while men are in control, violent, and interested primarily in sex rather than love and relationships.

Theoretical Perspectives

Four key theories, cultivation, cognitive information processing, gender schema theory, and social cognitive theory, help explain how these patterns of exposure and content contribute to young people's gender socialization and developing gender schemas, identities, and behaviors.

Cultivation theory assumes that television is the primary storyteller in the culture and that televised stories are consistent across programming and time (Gerbner et al., 1994). Given this consistency of content, the primary hypothesis is that frequent viewers will be more likely than those who view less frequently to believe the worldview presented on television. In applying the hypothesis to gender, studies have found, for example, that heavier viewers of television are more likely to underestimate the proportion of working women in the society, and more likely to hold traditional views of women's work (Signorielli, 2001).

In a series of experiments, Shrum (2004) has applied cognitive information processing theory to help explain how the cultivation process works. Gender stereotypes frequently appearing on television may become chronically accessible to television viewers because they see the same images so frequently. So, for example, when asked to make estimates of how frequently men are doctors or women are housewives, the heavy television viewer overestimates because the image of the male doctor and the female at home are the most accessible mental constructs available.

Cultivation theory originally was conceived and tested primarily with television because television had been such a dominant and compelling medium and representations had been so consistent over time. However, the same principles should apply across different media. The effect is most likely when a young person chooses a media diet that includes frequent and consistent images of gender, which is likely given the tendency of girls and boys to choose stereotypically gendered media fare.

Gender schema theory builds on the idea that children develop cognitive constructs from exposure to experiences in the real world as well as in the media (Bem, 1981). Gender stereotypes are a simple type of gender schema (Calvert & Huston, 1987). Research has shown that gender schemas influence individuals' perceptions, memory, and inferences about content (Bem, 1981). Individuals who hold stronger gender stereotypes are most likely to perceive and remember media portrayals in a stereotypical way (Calvert & Huston, 1987).

Social cognitive theory predicts that children will imitate the behavior of people they observe in real life and in the media who are rewarded and/or not punished for their behavior. The theory also predicts that identification with, or the desire to be like a real or media model, will increase the likelihood of imitating what the model looks like, says, or does (Bussey & Bandura, 1999). Research shows that children identify strongly with same-sex characters (Hoffner, 1996). Studies also have established that identification and modeling are enhanced when characters appear frequently, are familiar, and are portrayed as attractive (Tan, 1986). Children and adolescents who see media content as realistic, desirable, entertaining, and/or familiar, are more likely to be affected by the media portrayals (Bussey & Bandura, 1999). Ward and colleagues (2005), for example, found in experimental studies that young adults who identified with the stereotypically portrayed characters they watched were more likely to endorse the traditional gender stereotypes portrayed than were those who did not identify with the characters.

The Media's Role in Gender Socialization

Each theory suggests that frequent exposure to consistent themes about gender can affect a young person's developing sense of what is expected in the culture for males and females. In this section, we will review the empirical evidence for such effects.

Differential selection, attention, and memory patterns

Boys' and girls' content preferences clearly are guided by their developing gender schemas (Calvert & Huston, 1987). As we have discussed, boys and girls tend to choose very different media genres in keeping with their traditional gender roles (e.g., boys view more cartoon and action-adventure programs and play more realistic violent videogames than girls do; see Funk & Buchman, 1996a, 1996b; Huston et al., 1990).

Gender schemas also influence comprehension and memory of content. For instance, when boys and girls were shown a television program about a male nurse and a female doctor, they typically remembered a male nurse and a female doctor, roles that reflect gender stereotypes (Cordua, McGraw, & Drabman, 1979). Children who scored higher on gender stereotypical personality measures also remembered more gender stereotyped content about women's roles (e.g., being a wife), whereas androgynous children remembered women's traditional and non-traditional roles equally well (e.g., being a surgeon) (List, Collins, & Westby, 1983). Taken together, the research indicates that gender schemas influence what children select for processing, their attention to content, and what they remember, even leading to distorted memories of events at times.

Gender role beliefs

A number of studies, most often focused on television, have investigated the cultivation hypothesis that increased exposure to the gender-stereotyped media world affects children and adolescents' general attitudes about appropriate gender roles and behavior. The findings for overall television viewing have been inconsistent, with some studies finding no correlation between exposure to television and belief in traditional gender roles (e.g., Ex, Janssens, & Korzilius, 2002; Kalof, 1999; McCauley, Thangavelu, & Rozin, 1988; Meyer, 1980), and others finding small to modest relationships (Morgan, 1982, 1987).

To sort through the evidence more systematically, Herrett-Skjellum and Allen (1996) conducted a meta-analysis of the large array of studies that existed at the time (19 non-experimental and 11 experimental studies). They found a moderate but significant relationship (effect size of .10) between television viewing in general and the endorsement of gender stereotypes.

In general, however, the effects of television on gender beliefs are stronger for specific genres. More frequent viewing of music videos, talk shows, and soap operas tends to be highly correlated with traditional gender role attitudes (Buerkel-Rothfuss & Mayes, 1981; Ward, Hansbrough, & Walker, 2005).

One of the challenges in this arena is the difficulty of isolating the effects of media use from the effects of other gendered institutions and gendered interactions, such as with parents and peers. These other socialization agents contribute to young people's gendered expectations and may affect both what kind of media and content is chosen as well as how it is interpreted (Durkin & Nugent, 1998). However, because the media also influence parents' and peers' conceptions of gender, the media's role in perpetuating societal stereotypes about femininity and masculinity has likely been underestimated (Ward, 2003). Studies of more specific gender-related outcomes support the idea that the media do play an important role.

Beliefs about activities and occupations

Even young children are aware of the media's stereotypical depictions of male and female activities and occupations. In a test of the cultivation hypothesis, Signorielli and Lears (1991) found that elementary-school-aged children who viewed television most frequently were most likely to identify household chores with traditional gender stereotypes (e.g., men mow the lawn and women wash the dishes). More than one third of teens in a national survey said television males do not perform household chores (Heintz-Knowles et al., 1999). In the media, occupations are assigned gender, status, and class attributes (i.e., attorneys are men and nurses are women), and children exposed to these stereotypes are more likely to rank real world occupations similarly (DeFleur & DeFleur, 1967). These limited occupational choices available to women in the media may lead to a lack of awareness among female viewers of the much wider array of career options (Peterson et al., 1982).

Beliefs about dominance and aggression

Viewing violent media, which typically depicts males as perpetrators of aggression, can increase behavioral aggression by males and females (Wilson, this volume, Chapter 11). Although the empirical evidence is scarce, media can also influence children's beliefs about dominance and assertiveness. In one study, Duke and Kreshel (1998) found that young teen girls believed in the authority that magazines bestowed on boys' opinions regarding male perceptions of what is attractive for young girls.

Beliefs about physical beauty and thinness

More than 50 studies have explored the possible linkage between frequent exposure to body ideals in the media and young women's (mostly college students) satisfaction with their own bodies, weight concerns, and eating behaviors (Harrison & Hefner, this volume, Chapter 17). In general, both correlational and experimental studies find that the greater the exposure to the media's unrealistically thin body ideals, the more likely young women are to be dissatisfied with their own bodies, to be self-conscious and concerned about their weight, and to be engaged in dieting, exercising, and disordered eating (i.e., binging and purging) (Harrison & Hefner, this volume, Chapter 17).

A related area concerns beliefs about physical beauty as it relates to gender. In one experiment, Tan (1979) exposed high-school girls to a series of commercials that focused on beauty products or on other types of products. Girls who saw the beauty advertisements were significantly more likely than those who saw the neutral advertisements to rate physical attraction as a desirable quality and one that is important for being popular with men. Cultivation theory would have difficulty explaining such an effect for a single exposure to advertising, but the addition of Shrum's information processing principles can shed light here. In this case, the beauty advertisements presumably made gender schemas about physical attractiveness more accessible and hence more influential in the subsequent task of rating different qualities as important.

Sexual beliefs and behaviors

Early correlational studies, and a few experimental studies in which exposure to sexual content was varied, found that more frequent exposure to sexually oriented television genres, such as soap operas and music videos, was associated with more permissive attitudes about premarital sex among adolescents (for review, see Strasburger, 2005). Two recent longitudinal studies also have shown that more frequent exposure to sexual content in the media is related to subsequent sexual behavior among adolescents. For example, Collins and colleagues (2004) conducted a telephone survey of a representative sample of 12–17-year-olds and found that exposure to sexual content on television increased the likelihood of a teen having sexual intercourse within the following year. Even after controlling for many other factors that might predict early sexual behavior (e.g., pubertal status, closeness to parents, religiosity, perceptions of peers' sexual behavior), Brown and colleagues (2006) found that the greater the exposure to a diet of sexual content across four media (television, movies, music, magazines) for both boys and girls in early adolescence (12 to 14 years old), the greater the likelihood of initiation of sexual intercourse two years later. The pattern was stronger for white than for black teens. One possible reason for this difference is that there are more white characters in the media and hence a wider range of sexual role models available for Caucasian youth, an idea that is congruent with social cognitive theory.

Although most concern has focused on the idea that the media *cause* young people to have sex earlier than they might otherwise, it is likely that young people also seek sexual information in the media as they enter puberty and sexual feelings and relationships become more relevant. The media may serve as a kind of super-peer about sexual behavior since young people have few other sources of information. Brown, Halpern, and L'Engle (2005) found that girls who matured sexually earlier than their age mates were more interested in sexual content in the media than those who had not yet entered puberty. Turning to the media for information and norms can be a compelling and less embarrassing way to learn about taboo topics for young people when the other socialization agents in their lives are either reticent or not aware that the young person is interested in the information. Borzekowski and Rickert (2001) found that half of a sample of suburban New York tenth graders had used the Internet to get information on a range of sensitive health information such as sexually transmitted diseases, diet, fitness, and exercise.

Interventions

Given the existing evidence of effects and the likelihood that the media will continue to present men and women in stereotypical ways, we might ask if anything can be done to help decrease the potentially negative effects on children's gender-related self-concepts, expectations, and relationships. Media interventions designed to reduce gender role stereotyping and media literacy education are two promising possibilities.

In the 1970s when the women's liberation movement was a dominant force in the United States, a number of initiatives designed to present less stereotypical roles for males and females on television were tested. In a test of alternative programming, Johnston and Ettema (1982) found significant reductions in gender stereotypes among 9–12-year-olds after children watched 26 episodes of *Freestyle* – an educational television series that included episodes in which girls and boys were depicted in non-stereotypical activities (e.g., girls climbed mountains, fixed broken toys) and men and women were shown in non-traditional roles (e.g., nurturing man, male nurse, women executives). Evaluation showed that the effects were strongest when viewing was combined with follow-up classroom discussions among viewers and their teachers.

Extensive evaluations of the benefits of preschool children's television programming, such as *Sesame Street*, however, have found that it is more difficult to change social beliefs and behaviors such as gender schemas, than it is to increase school readiness (Fisch, 2005). Educational television producers now have a great deal of experience developing programming with non-stereotypical messages, however, and their expertise should be drawn on to encourage more content that might promote less gender-stereotypical behavior.

Media literacy

In the future, children will be even more able than they are now to choose what media they will attend to based on their in-the-moment needs and desires. Whole television cable channels already are dedicated to women (e.g., Lifetime, Lifetime Movie) and children (e.g., Nickelodeon, Disney) and special interests that have gendered appeal (e.g., sports on ESPN, shopping on The Shopping Channel). Most of what we now know as different media (e.g., television, radio, magazines, movies) will soon all be available on the Internet, probably readily accessible on cell phones or other handheld devices that children will be able to use whenever they want to, wherever they are.

The new media environment brings both opportunity and threat to the potential for more equitable and more flexible gender roles for children and adolescents. So, while girls now have personal webpages in which they can explore and express who they are as young women, they also have access to websites that share tips on how to be a more effective bulimic (Stern, 2002).

With such unprecedented access and personal choice, children need to be taught how to make wise choices about their media diets (Brown, 2000). Media literacy education (Chakroff & Nathanson, this volume, Chapter 24) becomes vitally important in such a media environment. Children need to know that some kinds of content are more appropriate than others and that excessive use of the media can distort their perceptions of the real world and themselves.

Parents may need guidance about how to help their children make good media choices because the media world in which their children are growing up is very different from the media world in which they grew up. Research has shown that active adult mediation (e.g., "The show is wrong. Lots of girls do things besides paint their nails and put on make-up.") can reduce the negative effects of stereotypically gendered media depictions (Nathanson et al., 2002, p. 937).

Future Research Needs

Although we now know a great deal about the role the media play in gender socialization, a number of questions remain, especially as increasingly accessible media make it easier for children and teens to make individualized media choices.

Pornography

Young people's greater access to sexually explicit images on the Internet may increase gender differences in perceptions of what men and women do sexually and may affect perceptions of appropriate and inappropriate sexual behavior. We currently know very little about young people's use of sexually explicit material on the Internet. One study of Dutch adolescents (13 to 18 years old) found that 71 percent of the males and 40 percent of the females had been exposed to some kind of online sexually explicit material in the prior six months (Peter & Valkenburg, 2006). Studies of adults suggest that young males will be more interested in such content, and exposure will result in distorted perceptions of women's willingness to have sex, and may increase acceptance of rape myths – the illusion that women like sexual aggression (Zillmann, 2000). In a series of correlational studies with college student males and older men, Frable, Johnson, and Kellman (1997) found that those who saw more pornography either in magazines or in films were more likely to think that most men perform masculine behaviors and to describe women in sexual terms. We need to know more about the effect of early exposure to explicit sexual content on adolescents' gender and sexual expectations.

Occupational opportunities

The selection of different kinds of media and genres may affect occupational opportunities. Some scholars have speculated, for example, that early and persistent gender differences in uses of the computer and interactive media such as videogames will affect later interest in and aptitude for careers in computer-based occupations. It may be that boys' greater use of and familiarity with the interactive components of computer technology will give them an advantage in working with computers and females will continue to lag behind (Rideout, Vandewater, & Wartella, 2003). Such patterns should be monitored and interventions developed to ensure that girls have equal opportunity for occupations that will increasingly depend on high-tech skills.

Racial and ethnic differences

Only a few studies have investigated how these patterns of gendered media selection and effects play out for children and teens who are not white. In one of the few studies of Latino youth, Rivadeneyra and Ward (2005) found a relationship between frequency of television viewing and stereotypical gender role attitudes for girls but not for boys. The researchers speculated that the reduced effect for boys was because boys were already "quite traditional in their ideas about gender" (p. 471). Other studies have found that exposure to music videos is highly correlated with gender stereotyping for black adolescents, but exposure to prime-time television programs and movies is not (Ward, Hansbrough, & Walker, 2005). The effects of the thin body ideal may be stronger for white girls than for black girls (Botta, 2000).

In the Brown and colleagues (2006) study, the linkage between sexual media diet and sexual behavior was stronger for the white adolescents than it was for the black youth. Surprisingly, given the consistent finding that black youth spend more time with media than any other racial/ethnic group in the United States, the black teens were more influenced by perceptions of their parents' expectations and their friends' sexual behavior than by what they saw or heard in the media. The authors speculated that the media's effects on black youths' sexual beliefs and behavior may occur earlier than for white youth because Blacks mature physically earlier than Whites, and the media they attend to include more sexual content than the media white youth are choosing. More work is needed to understand how racial and ethnic differences influence both media selection and effects on gender-related attitudes and behaviors.

Conclusions

The media clearly are an important part of gender role socialization for children and adolescents. From early on in their development, girls and boys choose very different media content that speaks to their emerging sense of themselves as males and females in the culture. Even as young children, boys play more videogames than girls do and girls listen to more music than boys do. By adolescence, boys and girls are selecting such different content that it is as if they are living in different worlds. The world of males is action-packed, public, and violent.

Women are still in their homes, caring for children, and invested in social relationships. In these media worlds, there are more men than women, and men are dominant, fearless, and in powerful jobs. Despite great strides by women in the real world over the past decades, women in the media are still typically portrayed as weaker, dependent on men, and more focused on physical attractiveness. Children and adolescents learn these stereotypes and integrate them into their own developing gender schemas and identities, as girls obsess about their bodies and boys suppress their emotions.

These patterns of gendered choice, content, and effects are somewhat surprising in this increasingly differentiated media world. We might think that the dramatic increase in channels and content would open up gender possibilities. Instead, it looks like the variety is providing opportunity for even more focused emphasis on gendered pursuits. It will be important to follow these trends as the media become increasingly under the control of younger and younger consumers. Media literacy programs can provide information about how to negotiate this world of ubiquitous and gendered information so conceptions of gender are expanded rather than only reinforcing traditional, more restricted ideas about how to be a boy or a girl, and ultimately a man or woman.

References

Acker, J. (1992). From sex roles to gendered institutions. *Contemporary Society*, 21(5), 565–69.

Anand, S., & Krosnick, J. A. (2005). Demographic predictors of media use among infants, toddlers, and preschoolers. *American Behavioral Scientist*, 48, 539–61.

Andsager, J. L., & Roe, K. (1999). Country music video in the country's Year of the Woman. *Journal of Communication*, 49, 69–82.

Bem, S. L. (1981). Gender schema theory: A cognitive account of sex typing. *Psychological Review*, 88, 352–64.

Bem, S. L. (1987). Probing the promise of androgyny, In M. R. Walsh (Ed.), *The psychology of women: Ongoing debates* (pp. 206–25). New Haven, CT: Yale University Press.

Botta, R. A. (2000). The mirror of television: A comparison of black and white adolescents' body image. *Journal of Communication*, 50, 144–59.

Borzekowski, D., & Rickert, V. L. (2001). Adolescent cybersurfing for health information. *Archives of Pediatrics and Adolescent Medicine*, 155, 813–17.

Brody, L. (1993). On understanding gender differences in the expression of emotion: Gender roles, socialization and language. In S. L. Ablon, D. Brown, E. J. Khantzian, & J. E. Mack (Eds.), *Human feelings: Explorations in affect development and meaning*. Hillsdale, NJ: Analytic Press.

Brown, J. D. (2000). Adolescents' sexual media diets. *Journal of Adolescent Health*, 27(2) (Supplement), 35–40.

Brown, J. D., Halpern, C., & L'Engle, K. (2005). Mass media as a sexual super peer for early maturing girls. *Journal of Adolescent Health*, 36(5), 420–27.

Brown, J. D., & Pardun, C. (2004). Little in common: Racial and gender differences in adolescents' television diets. *Journal of Broadcasting and Electronic Media*, 48(2), 266–78.

Brown, J., L'Engle, K., Pardun, C., Guo, G., Kenneavy, K., & Jackson, C. (2006). Sexy media matter: Exposure to sexual content in music, movies, television and magazines predicts black and white adolescents' sexual behavior. *Pediatrics*, 117, 1018–27.

Buerkel-Rothfuss, N. L., & Mayes, S. (1981). Soap opera viewing: The cultivation effect. *Journal of Communication*, 31(3), 109–15.

Bussey, K., & Bandura, A. (1999). Social cognitive theory of gender development and differentiation. *Psychological Review*, 106(4), 676–713.

Calvert, S. L. (1999). *Children's journeys through the information age*. Boston, MA: McGraw Hill.

Calvert, S. L., & Huston, A. C. (1987). Television and children's gender schemata. In L. Liben & M. Signorella (Eds.), *Children's gender schemata: Origins and Implications. New Directions in Child Development*, 38, San Francisco: Jossey-Bass.

Calvert, S. L., Strong, B. L., Jacobs, E. L., & Conger, E. E. (2007). Interaction and participation for young Hispanic and Caucasian children's learning of media content. *Media Psychology*, 9(2), 431–45.

Cantor, M. B., & Pingree, S. (1983). *The Soap Opera*. Sage COMMTEXT Series, vol. 12. London: Sage.

Collins, R., Elliott, M., Berry, S., Kanouse, D., Kunkel, D., Hunter, S., & Miu, A. (2004). Watching sex on television predicts adolescent initiation of sexual behavior. *Pediatrics*, 114(3), E280–E289.

Cordua, G., McGraw, K., & Drabman, R. (1979). Doctor or nurse: Children's perceptions of sex-typed occupations. *Child Development*, 50, 590–93.

DeFleur, M. L., & DeFleur, L. B. (1967). The relative contribution of television as a learning source for children's occupational knowledge. *American Sociological Review*, 32(5), 777–89.

Dietz, T. L. (1998). An examination of violence and gender role portrayals in video games: Implications for gender socialization and aggressive behavior. *Sex Roles*, 38(5/6), 425–42.

Duke, L. L., & Kreshel, P. J. (1998). Negotiating femininity: Girls in early adolescence read teen magazines. *Journal of Communication Inquiry*, 22(1), 48–72.

Durkin, K., & Nugent, B. (1998). Kindergarten children's gender role expectations for television actors. *Sex Roles*, 38(5/6), 387–402.

MSNBC. (2005). Education chief rips PBS for gay character: Network won't distribute episode with animated "Buster" visiting Vt. January 26. Retrieved January 21, 2006, from http://www.msnbc.msn.com/id/6869976/.

Ex, C. T. G. M., Janssens, J. M. A. M., & Korzilius, H. P. L. M. (2002). Young females' images of motherhood in relation to television viewing. *Journal of Communication*, 52(4), 955–71.

Fejes, F., & Petrich, K. (1993). Invisibility, homophobia and heterosexism – Lesbians, gays and the media. *Critical Studies in Mass Communication*, 10(4), 396–422.

Fisch, S. (2005). Children's learning from television. *Televizion*, 18E, 10–14.

Fouts, G., & Inch, R. (2005). Homosexuality in TV situation comedies: Characters and verbal comments. *Journal of Homosexuality*, 49(1), 35.

Frable, D. E. S., Johnson, A. E., & Kellman, H. (1997). Seeing masculine men, sexy women, and gender differences: exposure to pornography and cognitive constructions of gender. *Journal of Personality*, 65(2), 311–55.

Funk, J. B., & Buchman, D. D. (1996a). Children's perceptions of gender differences in social approval for playing electronic games. *Sex Roles*, 35(3–4), 219–31.

Funk, J. B., & Buchman, D. D. (1996b). Playing violent video and computer games and adolescent self-concept. *Journal of Communication*, 46(2), 19–32.

Gerbner, G., Gross, L., Morgan, M., & Signorielli, N. (1994). Growing up with television: The cultivation perspective. In J. Bryant & D. Zillman (Eds.), *Media effects: Advances in theory and research* (pp. 17–41). Hillsdale, NJ: Lawrence Erlbaum.

Gibson, R. (2004). Coverage of gay males, lesbians in newspaper lifestyle sections. *Newspaper Research Journal*, 25(3), 90.

Glascock, J. (2001). Gender roles on prime-time network television: Demographics and behaviors. *Journal of Broadcasting and Electronic Media*, 45, 656–69.

Gross, L. (2001). *Up from invisibility: Lesbians, gay men, and the media in America*. New York: Columbia University Press.

Hart, K-P. (2002). Representing men with HIV/AIDS in American movies. *Journal of Men's Studies*, 11(1), 77.

Hedley, M. (1994). The presentation of gendered conflict in popular movies: Affective stereotypes, cultural sentiments, and men's motivation. *Sex Roles: A Journal of Research*, 31(11–12), 721–41.

Heintz-Knowles, K., Li-Vollmer, M., Chen, P., Harris, T., Haufler, A., Lapp, J., & Miller, P. (1999). *Messages about masculinity: A national poll of children, focus groups, and content analysis of entertainment media*. Oakland, CA: Children Now.

Herrett-Skjellum, J., & Allen, M. (1996). Television programming and sex stereotyping: A meta-analysis. *Communication yearbook*, vol. 19 (pp. 157–85).

Hoffner, C. (1996). Children's wishful identification and parasocial interaction with favorite television characters. *Journal of Broadcasting and Electronic Media*, 40, 389–402.

Hust, S. J. T., Brown, J. D., & L'Engle, K. L. (in press). Boys will be boys and girls better be prepared: An analysis of the rare sexual health messages in young adolescents' media. *Mass Communication and Society*.

Huston, A. C., Wright, J. C., Rice, M., Kerkman, D., & St Peters, M. (1990). The development of television viewing patterns during early childhood: A longitudinal investigation. *Developmental Psychology*, 26, 409–20.

Jansz, J. (2005). The emotional appeal of violent video games for adolescent males. *Communication Theory*, 15, 219–41.

Johnston, D. (1995). Adolescents' motivations for viewing graphic horror. *Human Communication Research*, 21(4), 522–52.

Johnston, J., & Ettema, J. S. (1982). *Positive images: Breaking stereotypes with children's television*. Beverly Hills, CA: Sage.

Kalof, L. (1999). The effects of gender and music video imagery on sexual attitudes. *The Journal of Social Psychology*, 139(3), 378–85.

Kohlberg, L. (1966). A cognitive-developmental analysis of children's sex-role concepts and attitudes. In E. E. Maccoby (Ed.), *The development of sex differences* (pp. 82–172). Stanford, CA: Stanford University Press.

Kunkel, D., Eyal, K., Finnerty, K., Biely, E., & Donnerstein, E. (2005). *Sex on TV (4): A biennial report to the Kaiser Family Foundation*. Menlo Park, CA: Kaiser Family Foundation.

List, J., Collins, W. A., & Westby, S. (1983). Comprehension and inferences from traditional and nontraditional sex-role portrayals on television. *Child Development*, 54, 1579–87.

Lucas, K., & Sherry, J. L. (2004). Sex differences in video game play: A communication-based explanation. *Communication Research*, 31(5), 499–523.

Luecke-Aleska, D., Anderson, D. R., Collins, P., & Schmitt, K. (1995). Gender constancy and television viewing. *Developmental Psychology*, 31, 773–80.

Martin, C. L., & Halverson, C. F., Jr. (1981). A schematic processing model of sextyping and stereotyping in children. *Child Development*, 52, 1119–34.

McCauley, C., Thangavelu, K., & Rozin, P. (1988). Sex stereotyping of occupations in relation to television representations and census facts. *Basic and Applied Social Psychology*, 9(3), 197–212.

Meyer, B. (1980). The development of girls' sex-role attitudes. *Child Development*, 51, 508–14.

Meyer, M. D. E. (2003). "It's me. I'm it.": Defining adolescent sexual identity through relational dialectics in Dawson's Creek. *Communication Quarterly*, 51, 262–76.

Morgan, M. (1982). Television and adolescents' sex-role stereotypes: A longitudinal study. *Journal of Personality and Social Psychology*, 43(5), 947–55.

Morgan, M. (1987). Television, sex-role attitudes, and sex-role behavior. *Journal of Early Adolescence*, 7(3), 269–82.

Nathanson, A. I., Wilson, B. J., McGee, J., & Sebastian, M. (2002). Counteracting the effects of female stereotypes on television via active mediation. *Journal of Communication*, 52(4): 922–37.

Oliver, M. B., Weaver, J. B., & Sargent, S. L. (2000). An examination of factors related to sex differences in enjoyment of sad films. *Journal of Broadcast and Electronic Media*, 44(2), 282–300.

Pardun, C. J., L'Engle, K. L., & Brown, J. D. (2005). Linking exposure to outcomes: Early adolescents' consumption of sexual content in six media. *Mass Communication and Society*, 8, 75–91.

Peter, J., & Valkenberg, P. (2006). Adolescents' exposure to sexually explicit material on the Internet. *Communication Research*, 33(2), 178–204.

Peterson, G. W., Rollins, B. C., Thomas, D. L., & Heaps, K. (1982). Social placement of adolescents: Sex-role influences on family decisions regarding the careers of youth. *Journal of Marriage and the Family*, 44(3), 647–58.

Reichert, T., & Carpenter, C. (2004). An update on sex in magazine advertising: 1983 to 2003. *Journalism and Mass Communication Quarterly*, 81(4), 823–37.

Reichert, T., Lambiase, J., Morgan, S., Carstarphen, M., & Zavoina, S. (1999). Cheesecake and beefcake: No matter how you slice it, sexual explicitness in advertising continues to increase. *Journalism and Mass Communication Quarterly*, 76(1), 7–20.

Rideout, V. J., Vandewater, E. A., & Wartella, E. A. (2003). *Zero to six: Electronic media in the lives of infants, toddlers, and preschoolers*. Menlo Park, CA: Kaiser Family Foundation.

Rivadeneyra, R., & Ward, L. M. (2005). From *Ally McBeal* to *Sabado Gigante*: Contributions of television viewing to the gender role attitudes of Latino adolescents. *Journal of Adolescent Research*, 20, 453–75.

Roberts, D. F., & Foehr, U. G. (2004). *Kids and media in America*. New York: Cambridge University Press.

Roberts, D. F., Foehr, U. G., & Rideout, V. J. (2005). *Generation M: Media in the lives of 8–18-year-olds*. Menlo Park, CA: Kaiser Family Foundation.

Shrum, L. J. (2004). The cognitive processes underlying cultivation effects are a function of whether the judgments are on-line or memory-based. *Communications*, 29, 327–44.

Signorielli, N. (1997). *Reflections of girls in the media: A content analysis.* Menlo Park, CA: Kaiser Family Foundation.

Signorielli, N. (2001). Television's gender role images and contribution to stereotyping: Past, present, future. In D. G. Singer & J. L. Singer (Eds.), *Handbook of children and the media* (pp. 341–58). Thousand Oaks, CA: Sage.

Signorielli, N., & Bacue, A. (1999). Recognition and respect: A content analysis of prime-time television characters across three decades. *Sex Roles*, 40(7–8), 527–44.

Signorielli, N., & Lears, M. (1991). Children, television, and conceptions about chores: Attitudes and behaviors. *Sex Roles*, 27(3–4), 157–70.

Signorielli, N., & McLeod, D. (1994). Gender stereotypes in MTV commercials: The beat goes on. *Journal of Broadcasting and Electronic Media*, 38(1), 91–102.

Slaby, R., & Frey, K. (1975). Development of gender constancy and selective attention to same-sex models. *Child Development*, 46, 849–56.

Sparks, G. (1991). The relationship between distress and delight in males' and females' reactions to frightening films. *Human Communication Research*, 17(4), 625–37.

Sprafkin, J. N., Silverman, T., & Rubinstein, E. A. (1980). Reactions to sex on television: An exploratory study. *The Public Opinion Quarterly*, 44(3), 303–15.

Steele, J. R., & Brown, J. D. (1995). Adolescent room culture: Studying media in the context of everyday life. *Journal of Youth and Adolescence*, 24(5), 551–76.

Steenland, S. (1995). Content analysis of the image of women on television. In C. M. Lont (Ed.), *Women and media: Content/ careers/ and criticism* (pp. 179–89). Belmont, CA: Wadsworth.

Steinke, J. (2005). Cultural representations of gender and science: Portrayals of female scientists and engineers in popular films. *Science Communication*, 27(1), 27–63.

Stern, S. R. (2002). Virtually speaking: Girls' self-disclosure on the www. *Women's Studies in Communication*, 25(2), 223–53.

Strasburger, V. (2005). Adolescents, sex, and the media: Ooooo, baby, baby – a Q & A. *Adolescent Medicine Clinics*, 16(2), 269–88.

Tan, A. S. (1979). TV beauty ads and role expectations of adolescent female viewers. *Journalism Quarterly*, 56, 283–8.

Tan, A. S. (1986). Social learning of aggression from television. In J. Bryant & D. Zillmann (Eds.), *Perspectives on media effects* (pp. 41–56). Hillsdale, NJ: Lawrence Erlbaum.

Taveras, E. M., Rifas-Shiman, S. L., Field, A. E., Frazier, A. L., Colditz, G. A., & Gillman, M. W. (2004). The influence of wanting to look like media figures on adolescent physical activity. *Journal of Adolescent Health*, 35(1), 41–50.

Teen Media Monitor, The. (2003). February. Menlo Park, CA: Kaiser Family Foundation.

Thompson, J. K., & Heinberg, L. J. (1999). The media's influence on body image disturbance and eating disorders: We've reviled them, now can we rehabilitate them? *Journal of Social Issues*, 55, 339–53.

Thompson, T. L., & Zerbinos, E. (1997). Television cartoons: Do children notice it's a boy's world? *Sex Roles*, 37(5–6), 415–32.

Tuchman, G., Daniels, A. K., & Benét, J. (Eds.). (1978). *Hearth and home: Images of women in the mass media.* New York: Oxford University Press.

Ward, L. M. (2003). Understanding the role of entertainment media in the sexual socialization of American youth: A review of empirical research. *Developmental Review*, 23(3),
347–88.

Ward, L. M., Gorvine, B., & Cytron, A. (2002). Would that really happen? Adolescents'
perceptions of sexual relationships according to prime-time television. In J. D. Brown,
J. R. Steele, & K. Walsh-Childers (Eds.), *Sexual teens, sexual media: Investigating
media's influence on adolescent sexuality* (pp. 95–121). Mahwah, NJ: Lawrence
Erlbaum.

Ward, L. M., Hansbrough, E., & Walker, E. (2005). Contributions of music video
exposure to black adolescents' gender and sexual schemas. *Journal of Adolescent Research*,
20(2), 143–66.

West, C., & Zimmerman, D. H. (1987). Doing gender. *Gender and Society*, 1(2), 125–51.

Zillmann, D. (2000). Influence of unrestrained access to erotica on adolescents' and young
adults' dispositions toward sexuality. *Journal of Adolescent Health*, 27(2 Supplement),
41–4.

Zillmann, D., Weaver, J. B., Mundorf, N., & Aust, C. F. (1986). Effects of an opposite-
gender companion's affect to horror on distress, delight, and attraction. *Journal of
Personality and Social Psychology*, 51(3), 586–94.

Zinn, M. B., Hondagneu-Sotelo, P., & Messner, M. A. (Eds.). (2001). *Through the prism
of difference: Readings on sex and gender*. Boston: Allyn and Bacon.

Zollo, P. (2004). *Getting wiser to teens: More insights into marketing to teenagers*. Ithaca,
NY: New Strategist Publications.

6

Media and the Family

Alison Alexander

The average television set is turned on for over 8 hours a day in the typical American home (Nielsen Media Research, 2005). Families eat their meals while watching television, arrange furniture around big-screen televisions, and even schedule their evenings around favorite programs. But television is not the only medium that is intertwined in family life. Siblings use email and text messaging to communicate with one another, even when they are in the same physical location; teens use the Web to download music and to look up health information; and parents buy CD players, music, and books to help their children fall asleep at night. Indeed, media transform family space and change family schedules.

At the same time that families bring new technologies into the home, they are often uneasy about them. Digital cable and wireless Internet make certain types of content, such as violence and sex, readily available to young children. By bringing two-way communication into the home, the Internet allows the outside world into the family space. Parents, for example, worry that children might give out personal information over the Internet (Turow, 2003). Thus, though media are an integral part of the home environment, they often seem like uninvited strangers.

This chapter will explore the changing nature of family and the media. The first section will attempt to define what constitutes a family, focusing on how that definition is changing. The second section will discuss how families use the media. The third section will focus on how the media portray families and family life. The fourth section will provide an overview of various theoretical perspectives that have been used to understand relationships between the family and media. The fifth and sixth sections will look at these relationships more closely: how do the media influence families, and in turn, how do families influence the media experiences of individual members in that unit?

The Changing Nature of the Family

Census data indicate that the nuclear family is no longer the norm in the United States. For the first time, married couples, with or without children, have slipped below 50 percent of American households. In 2005 they comprised only 49.7 percent of the nation's 111.1 million households (US Census Bureau, 2005). Also for the first time, there are more non-family households (33.1 percent), which is defined as people living alone or with non-related individuals, than people living in traditional nuclear families (31.6 percent) (US Census Bureau, 2005). Family households now involve complex kinship patterns because of divorce, remarriage, multi-generational living arrangements, adoption, and foster care. Women are having fewer children and are delaying childbirth until later years (Wetzel, 1990). Economic roles have changed as well with women more likely to work outside the home than to work solely as a homemaker (Wetzel, 1990).

With all these changes, trying to define what comprises a family is a complicated endeavor. Family communication scholars tend to focus on families as constituted through communication (Floyd, Judd, & Mikkelson, 2006). Fitzpatrick and Caughlin (2002) argued that family relationships are defined by the way people act and interact – a transactional process definition. Such an approach highlights family process at the expense of structural or legal definitions. However, the Census Bureau defines family households as a householder plus one or more people living in the same dwelling who are related to the householder by marriage, blood, or adoption (US Census Bureau, 2005). Andreason offers a broader definition: "Families are systems bound by ties of blood, law, or affection and, like all systems, they require cohesiveness and adaptability for their survival" (Andreason, 2001, p. 10).

In the context of the media, how should we define family? If we limit it to shared households, then families separated by divorce may not be included. Yet such arrangements can affect media use, as children of divorce often spend time in two households where there may be different "rules" about media use. If we only examine current familial structure, we may ignore crucial relationships that influence members even in the absence of regular interaction, such as non-custodial parents. The challenge for scholars is to develop a definition that permits the study of the rich and varied ways that individuals with familial connections use and are influenced by mediated communication.

How Families Use the Media

Most families are immersed in media technologies. In 2000, Woodard and Grindina reported that almost half of American families owned four "media staples": television, a videocassette recorder (VCR), a videogame console, and a computer. In 2005, Roberts, Foehr, and Rideout found that 95 percent of

American households with children 8 to 18 owned four devices: television, CD/tape player, radio, and VCR/DVD player. These households also had an average of 2.1 videogame consoles and 1.5 computers, with 74 percent of households having Internet access. One third of these homes had a digital video recorder (DVR), and 82 percent had cable or satellite television.

Young people spend an average of 6.5 hours a day with some form of media, but television still dominates their time (Roberts, Foehr, & Rideout, 2005). When adding together all the "screen" time (television, DVDs, DVRs, VCRs), total viewing averages 3 hours and 51 minutes a day. Listening to music is a distant second with an average of 1 hour and 44 minutes daily. Yet these high levels of media use do not isolate young people from family and peer interaction. Children between the ages of 8 and 18 report spending 2 hours and 17 minutes a day with parents and 2 hours and 16 minutes a day hanging out with friends. Physical activity, pursing hobbies, and talking on the phone all hovered around 1 hour, beating out the reported 50 minutes allocated for doing homework.

Computer use is another facet of screen time. Roughly three out of four homes today have Internet access (Roberts, Foehr, & Rideout, 2005), but concern about the digital divide remains. Gaps based on ethnicity, parent education, and income persist. For example, while 80 percent of white youth have Internet access at home, only 61 percent of African American youth do. Only 68 percent of parents with a high-school education or less have Internet access at home, but 82 percent of college-educated parents do. In communities where the median income is less than $35,000, only 54 percent of students access the Internet on a daily basis; in communities with incomes above $50,000, 71 percent are online daily (Roberts, Foehr, & Rideout, 2005). Thus, the family unit, particularly its financial status, affects the media-use patterns of children living in those homes.

The prevalence and portability of media in the home have inevitably led to increased availability of technologies in children's bedrooms. Today, there is a television set in the bedrooms of 68 percent of American children between the ages of 8 and 18 (Roberts, Foehr, & Rideout, 2005). Children watch substantially more television when there is a television set in their bedroom (3 hours and 31 minutes with television in the bedroom versus 2 hours and 4 minutes without). Videogames are in the bedrooms of 49 percent of youth, and although the amount of time spent with this medium is small, those with consoles in their bedroom play three times as much as those without (45 versus 15 minutes a day) (Roberts, Foehr, & Rideout, 2005). Because children with easy access to media spend more time using those media, some experts are concerned that heavy media exposure in the home may isolate these youth from important family interactions (Turow & Nir, 2003). However, media provide one venue where family interaction occurs.

One way to understand family use of media is to focus on how central or important certain technologies are to family life. Comstock and Paik (1991) created the term "household centrality" to reflect this idea. High centrality refers to families who keep the television turned on most of the time and have few rules governing its use. In their national US survey of over 2000 children, Roberts and his colleagues (2005) used a similar concept that they called "household TV orientation." These authors found that 63 percent of youth reportedly live in homes where the television is on at meals, 53 percent live in homes where there are no rules about television watching, and 51 percent live in homes where television is on "most of the time." To qualify as having a household television orientation, all three of these patterns needed to be present; 25 percent of youth live in such homes. In households with a high television orientation, children are likely to watch television daily, watch it for longer periods of time, and read less (Roberts, Foehr, & Rideout, 2005).

Even when the television is on most of the time, individuals in the family vary in their responses to it. Family members often engage in concurrent activities while viewing, relegating television to a background activity. Family members within the same room may allocate different levels of attentiveness to the screen. Individuals vary considerably in how they experience viewing, depending on mood and social situation. The history of uses and gratifications research points to the multiplicity of gratifications that can be obtained from the same content. For example, some family members may watch television for escape or information, while others may watch because it brings the family together to view.

The experience sampling method of Kubey and Csikszentmihalyi (1990) sheds light on the quality of life for families, and thus provides a hint about the meaning of television within the family. The researchers measured self-reports of perceived activity, involvement, mood, and physical state in situations where the individual was with the family when the television was off, watching television with the family, and watching television alone. Watching television with the family was reportedly a relaxing and cheerful experience. Watching alone was also relaxing, though less cheerful and challenging than viewing with the family. Family viewing was both significantly less activating (i.e., feeling alert, strong, active) and less challenging than was family time spent in other activities.

Increasingly, however, the media experience in the home is a solitary activity. Although expensive big-screen televisions may dominate the family room, the viewing options have increased so dramatically that family members' content preferences may rarely coincide. Multiple sets mean that each family member can view privately. The plethora of other media options can further diminish shared media experiences, as family members choose video games, Internet surfing and instant messaging, or listening to music in their room or on headphones in the car. As Andreason (2001) notes, much of the newer media to which youth are exposed is unfamiliar to parents, ranging from currently popular YouTube website video clips to the mechanics of instant messaging.

Media Portrayals of Families and Family Life

Families can look to the media as a source of information about norms and values. As it turns out, television has developed a genre, the family sitcom, that focuses on family life. Early shows of the 1950s displayed limited, but some, diversity in family portrayals. According to Spigel (2001), these portrayals included the suburban, white, nuclear family of *The Adventures of Ozzie and Harriet* to the urban, Jewish family of *The Goldbergs*. As Hollywood studios began to dominate network production in the mid-1950s, programs became more standardized with classic family portrayals such as *Leave it to Beaver* and *Father Knows Best*. In the 1960s, television portrayals began to feature single parents such as *My Three Sons and Julia* and fantasy families such as *The Addams Family*. Change continued in the 1970s as popular programs explored class politics in programs like *All in the Family*, black success in *The Jeffersons*, and divorced and working women in *One Day at a Time*. Nostalgic portrayals still abounded in shows like *The Waltons, Little House on the Prairie*, and the perfect blended family, *The Brady Bunch*. The 1980s will be remembered as the decade of *The Cosby Show*. Since the 1980s, it has become increasingly difficult to characterize the family as portrayed on television because cable has generated innumerable shows featuring families and returned many programs from the past to the screen as reruns, for example in Nick at Night.

Several content analyses have systematically documented how families are portrayed on television. Robinson and Skill (2001), for example, examined television series featuring a family from 1950 through 1995. They found that television tends to reinforce conservative to moderate portrayals of American families, although depictions are becoming more complex and diverse in recent years. Family structure on television, interestingly, has always differed from real-world demographics. In particular, the researchers found that the average size of television families has grown across the decades, increasing from 1.8 children in the 1950s to 2.45 in the 1990s, in contrast to the actual shrinkage of US family household size during that time frame. As another example of the discrepancy between television and the real world, single fathers headed 16.8 percent of television families, compared to census figures from the 45-year span of their study that ranged between 1 and 3 percent of US households headed by single fathers (Robinson & Skill, 2001). Unmarried and divorced family heads, though exceedingly common demographically, are not represented proportionally on television. Reconstituted families on television have grown steadily since the 1950s. Finally, diversity is lacking – 97 percent of families in the 1950s and 1960s were white. The 1970s brought an increase in the number of black families featured on television, though this number fell in the 1980s (14 percent in the 1970s versus 6 percent in the 1980s). Nevertheless, other minority families have been virtually invisible.

Studies have looked beyond demographics to determine how families interact and get along on television. Research from the 1970s demonstrated that relationships in television families were predominantly positive in nature, exhibiting more interactions that were affiliative rather than conflictual in nature (Greenberg et al., 1980). A more recent analysis finds that this affiliative pattern continues (Douglas, 2003). Sibling interaction over time has also been positive (Larson, 2001), with nearly two thirds of the interactions described as informative, supportive, direct, and social. The other one third, however, was conflictual, focusing on opposing and attacking. Although conflict does occur in televised family interactions, Comstock and Strzyzewski (1990) found that conflictual interactions were often short, and the conflict strategies used were generally prosocial in nature.

Mazur and Kalbfleisch (2003) examined lying in televised situation comedy families, and found that this type of behavior was generally used to spare feelings. Fathers lied most often; children were most honest. Most lies were not detected, a finding that Mazur and Kalbfleisch (2003) suggest mirrors real families with respect to the ability to detect deception.

A few analyses of content have asked viewers to evaluate portrayals. Elementary school children find portrayals of families on television to be appealing, and they rate portrayals of feelings within families as realistic (Weiss & Wilson, 1996). Douglas (2001, 2003) asked viewers to evaluate multiple dimensions of television family portrayals. From these viewer evaluations, he concluded that parent–child and sibling interactions are more distressed in contemporary portrayals, with parents having less authority and being less effective in the socialization of their children than in older programming. Sibling relations are also more conflictual and less supportive and stable than in the past.

In general, however, portrayals of television families are positive and traditional. Despite the uproar over shows such as *Roseanne* or *Married with Children*, the normative portrayal is of a close-knit white family whose members are generally supportive. When arguments in television families occur, they are resolved relatively easily (Douglas, 2003). Two parents head most television families, and single-parent portrayals significantly overrepresent households headed by a single father. In one study, television families of the 1990s were described as cohesive, democratic, flexible, and able to communicate fluidly with other family members (Bryant, Bryant, Aust, & Venugopalan, 2001). Dramatic conventions require conflicts to be resolved within the confines of the program. Family series portray families using predominantly affiliative interactions to do so.

Theoretical Approaches for Studying the Family and Media

As research into family and the media has evolved, so too have the theoretical approaches used to guide the design and analysis of research. Scholars from mass communication have tended to approach the intersection of family and media from four theoretical traditions: social cognitive theory, cultivation theory, systems theory, and sociocultural perspectives. Each of these theoretical perspectives is discussed in this section.

Social cognitive theory

Social cognitive theory suggests that children can learn behaviors and attitudes from observing television models, particularly when the models are attractive and similar to the child (Bandura, 1994). This idea emerged from social learning theory, which was one of the first theoretical perspectives used to explain television's impact on children (Bandura, 1977). Bandura's (1977) social cognitive theory shifted the focus from behavioral imitation to include the viewer's cognitive representations of what is seen on television. Learning results from cognitive activities such as attending to televised depictions, storing the portrayals in memory, and understanding the consequences of the model's behavior in relation to the world of family and friends.

In the media and family literature, two separate bodies of work are informed by social cognitive theory. First, analyses of media portrayals of families are predicated on the notion that through observational learning, portrayals can influence the viewers' perceptions of families. Content analyses of media portrayals have examined household structure and demographics as well as interactional patterns and rewards and punishments, the latter of which should make a difference in children's social learning. Second, family context has been conceptualized as a mediating variable between media content and its effect on children. Studies of the influence of family norms and attitudes on children's learning from the media often reference social cognitive theory.

Cultivation theory

Cultivation theory examines long-term consequences of exposure to consistent television messages. Repeated exposure to messages over time cultivates views of the world that are consonant with television content (cf., Gerbner et al., 1994). Thus, according to cultivation theory, if families are portrayed in consistent ways in the media, repeated exposure to these depictions can alter children's views about what families are like. If families are heavy viewers of television, cultivation effects are more likely to occur. The central argument is that "television cultivates or creates a world view that, although possibly inaccurate, becomes the reality simply because we, as a people, believe it to be the reality and base our judgments about our own everyday worlds on that reality" (Baran & Davis, 2006, p. 330).

Cultivation methods require detailed content analysis to demonstrate recurring and persistent images, themes, values, and portrayals. Once those messages are discovered, one can compare television and social reality to formulate questions that will allow researchers to explore the differences in perception between heavy and light viewers. Heavy viewers are expected to be more likely to possess a "television world view" because of assumptions that they are not selective in their viewing, do not view critically, and are exposed to homogeneous messages.

Family and media researchers have examined the messages of television about families, as well as the cultivation of images about families over time. Again, content analytic studies of portrayals of family are used, but with the additional requirement that they address the consistency of patterns over time and across channels or programs, rather than focus on a single media message. The cultivation prediction is that heavier viewers will be more likely to adopt the television view of the world. In support of this idea, children who are heavy viewers of television report more homogeneous viewpoints about families that are consistent with what is portrayed on the screen than do light viewers (Buerkel-Rothfuss & Mayes, 1981; Greenberg et al., 1980).

Family systems theory

Social cognitive theory and cultivation theory both tend to focus on the effects of media on individuals. In contrast, a family systems perspective argues that the family should be the primary unit of analysis in research. Classically, a system is a set of parts that are interlinked so that changes in one part induce changes in other parts (Baran & Davis, 2006). Such an approach allows the researcher to examine the complex interactions with the family system, and to examine family process, including "family boundaries, rules, decision making, independence, control, roles and communication among the components" (Goodman, 1983, p. 409).

Jordan (2002) argued that the media are major factors in family structure and social dimensions of family functioning. According to Jordan, "The interactions of family members subtly create patterned ways of thinking about and using the media. These patterns become habits, and the habits become the stuff of everyday experience" (p. 231). Indeed, traditional as well as newer media have become part of the way in which our households interact, develop, and adapt (Bryant & Bryant, 2001).

Bryant and colleagues (2001) used the circumplex model, an approach based on systems analysis, to examine the psychological health of family portrayals on television during 1991, 1996, and 1999. This circumplex model (Olson, Russell, & Sprenkle, 1989) focuses on three dimensions of analysis: family cohesion (i.e., family bonding), family adaptability (i.e., ability to change), and family communication (i.e., behaviors such as listening, speaking for self or others, self-disclosure). The authors concluded that American's prime-time television families were shown as psychologically healthy; that is they were portrayed as cohesive, adaptive, and highly communicative.

In another example of family and media systems research, Jordan (2005) used Urie Bronfenbrenner's ecological systems theory to examine two contexts – home and school – for the use of educational television by low-income, minority preschoolers. Jordan identified differences in how reading and educational television were used in the preschools. Teachers read to children; media were used at transitional times. Teachers expressed disdain for television, even when it was useful in the curriculum and in the management of the day. In contrast, parents revealed the many stresses in their homes, discussed their guilt over not reading more to their children and noted how useful television was in managing the environment.

Sociocultural perspectives

Family systems paradigms are criticized for ignoring larger cultural patterns that also shape family interactions. Carey argued that, "Communication is a symbolic process whereby reality is produced, maintained, repaired, and transformed" (1989, p. 23). Craig (1999) identified this as a "socio-cultural tradition" in which communication is theorized as the reproduction of social order. Society exists in an environment that is constituted and maintained by symbolic codes, both mediated and interpersonal. Family and media research in this tradition focuses on describing communicative processes that are created and negotiated within the family. The focus of this research is not on individual outcomes, but on descriptions – usually qualitative – of the everyday interactions that largely reproduce the social order. For example, Morley (1986) argued that patterns of television viewing can only be understood in the overall context of family leisure activity. His in-depth interviews investigated how class and gender differences are expressed in control of media choices, with particular attention to gendered patterns of selections, preference, enjoyment, and integration into everyday life.

Buckingham's (1993, 1998) work on the meaning of television in families found that children are exposed to extensive information about television, including the views of parents. Yet, he described how children are able to construct and create their own interpretations of events and formulate their own opinions, which may be different from their parents. Nonetheless, interaction with parents was important as a "reality test" and fulfilled several functions for children, including asserting their own power, defining their position, entering adult conversations about issues, and affiliating with others (Buckingham, 1993, 1998). Other studies also focus on the patterns created by families in the media environment. For example, Lull (1980) described the social functions of media within the family. Research in this tradition also describes how mothers use child programming to help teach language skills (Lemish, 1987); how mediated reality is learned through mother–child interaction (Messaris, 1987); and how siblings interact while viewing television (Alexander, Ryan, & Munoz, 1984).

Summary

To summarize, research has conceptualized the family as an aggregate of individuals, as a system, or as part of a larger negotiation of social order. Both social cognitive theory and cultivation view the family as an aggregate of individuals; their attention is focused on individual consequences. On the other hand, a system is seen as *more than* the sum of its parts. Systems research is not concerned with individuals effects, but with how change influences all parts of the family system in total. Within the sociocultural tradition, family is one of many social institutions that exist to re-create the social order. Family is, following the tenets of Carey, a communicative construction.

The outcomes of interest in the preceding perspectives range from individual learning from media messages, to family cohesiveness and adaptability, to the creation of patterns that support – or at times resist – the social order. The effects of family portrayals on perceptions of families, for example, is an outcome of interest to both social cognitive theory and cultivation. Cultivation research examines the long-term influence of homogeneous television messages on distorted perceptions about the nature of families among heavier viewers. Social cognitive theory is also concerned about learning from media messages, but theorizes that the effect of messages on an individual is a process of integrating information and attitudes into cognitive representations that will influence later attitudes, perceptions, and behaviors. Systems theory explores the inter-linkages of a family to see how changes in one member or part induce changes in all members, or how certain states are maintained within the family system (e.g., balance, adaptation). Within the sociocultural tradition, researchers examine the rituals and practices of families and link them to the larger social order. Issues in applying these perspectives to the intersection of media and family communication are discussed in the remaining sections of this chapter.

The Media's Influence on Families

This section will explore how the media impact families. First, I will examine the influence of media portrayals of family. Second, I will explore the power of media to create a place for family interaction, both within and outside of the media exposure context. Third, I will provide an overview of issues regarding control of media within the family, including ways that conflict is both managed and avoided through media. Finally, I will explore how new technologies are influencing families. Most of the research on the impact of media on family interaction has focused on television, the dominant medium of the child and often a shared family activity.

Learning about families from media portrayals

The importance of family portrayals lies in the belief that they may influence perceptions of families, and thus families themselves. Research indicates that portrayals of families, particularly on television, are perceived as highly realistic by children (Weiss & Wilson, 1998). Douglas (2003) argued that this perception of reality is particularly likely to influence cognitive representations of families. Cultivation theorists note that the powerful storytelling ability of television creates a social reality for heavy viewers that can be at odds with the real world (Gerbner et al., 1994). In support of this idea, there is extensive literature to suggest that heavy viewers believe the world to be more violent than light viewers do (Gerbner et al., 1994), which is consistent with the extreme amounts of violence on television. Views about families can be similarly influenced. Heavy teen viewers of soap operas overestimate the proportion of spouses who have extramarital affairs, get divorced, and have illegitimate children (Buerkel-Rothfuss & Mayes, 1981). Greenberg et al. (1980) found that children who are regular viewers of family sitcoms are more likely than infrequent viewers to believe that families are affiliative and supportive.

Heintz (1992) surveyed children about their perceptions of family. Elementary school children reported learning most of what they knew about families from television. They also perceived both television and real-world families as happy, cheerful, and nice. In an experimental study, Weiss and Wilson (1998) found that elementary school children exposed to a negative emotional event in a family sitcom, and who perceived that event as realistic, altered their perceptions of comparable real-world emotional events to fit the sitcom depiction.

Overall, then, this small body of literature suggests that media portrayals can influence learning and cultivation of social reality about families. These effects seem to occur most often among those who perceive media portrayals as realistic, and who are the heaviest viewers. Additional research is needed on how those perceptions influence real-world families to help us better understand the social influence of media on families.

Creating a media viewing context within the family

A number of qualitative, sociocultural investigations of how media are used in everyday life emerged in the 1980s as researchers began to observe the functions of television-related interaction in the home (cf., Lindlof, 1987, 1991; Lull, 1980). Because family members spend time together in the presence of television, television at least partially defines the context within which family interaction occurs and therefore helps determine the meaning of that interaction. From this perspective, family themes, roles, or issues are carried out in a variety of contexts, and television viewing becomes one of those contexts in which it is useful to study patterns of family interaction. As such, media are involved in the accomplishment of numerous family functions, including facilitating communication, demonstrating competence, and avoiding interpersonal contact (Lull, 1980).

Television can influence family interaction even when family members are not watching. Indeed, the influence of media does not always occur within the primary exposure context but can be observed in numerous ongoing and communicative contexts (Fry, Alexander, & Fry, 1990). Contexts could range from family discussions over the dinner table as to what movie to rent for family viewing night, to heated debates over what content children should be allowed to view, to delicate discussions with children about topics encountered in the media. These contexts are separated spatially and temporally from the primary exposure context, but are, nonetheless, important for understanding media influence. Such a focus takes a sociocultural approach and acknowledges the range and complexity of different ways in which media texts and individuals can come together, to create the meaning of media content and of the medium itself.

Media experiences are often structured by the family. Television viewing with family members, for example, is common. Roberts and his colleagues (2005) reported that children 8–18 years of age spend over 50 percent of their viewing time with parents. However, children generally watch more often with siblings than with parents (Lawrence & Wozniak, 1989). This amount of co-viewing decreases with age and with the presence of television sets in the bedroom (Roberts, Foehr, & Rideout, 2005). Unfortunately, co-viewing does not equal interaction. In some homes, co-viewing simply means that parents and children share similar tastes. If not actively involved in the child's viewing, the parent is simply modeling television viewing behavior (Van Evra, 2004). If parents watch extensively and uncritically, their children are likely to do the same (Van Evra, 2004).

Television can provide material for interaction within the family and can be used as a platform to teach children information. Lemish (1987), for example, documented the ways that mothers use television to teach language. She observed the home television-viewing behavior of 16 children between 6 and 30 months of age. Amount of talk was related to the program being watched, with *Sesame Street* eliciting the most verbal interaction, including such activities as naming or identifying familiar objects, repeating labels, asking questions, and relating television content to the child's experience. Vocabulary teaching appeared to be a major focus of these interactions, and Lemish speculated that those interactions might enrich vocabulary learning from television.

Parents are not the only family members to converse with children in media contexts. Alexander, Ryan, and Munoz (1984) observed siblings in the viewing situation. Approximately 40 percent of the interaction was about television. The majority of that interaction was interpretive in function, and geared to informing younger siblings. For example, younger children asked older siblings about characters' identities, problematic visual devices, and narrative conventions.

Parents are often called upon to interpret media content. McLeod, Fitzpatrick, Glynn, and Fallis (1982), for example, noted that a majority of mothers report frequent use of interpretive or evaluate statements when interacting with their children about television. Messaris (1986) interviewed over 100 mothers about their responses to questions concerning television realism. Mothers described a variety of interactions in which they told elementary-age children about things that could not happen in real life, including some complex distinctions between the improbable and the impossible and explaining certain disturbing images such as immoral actions and poverty. Messaris argued that audience members are creative, and one consequence of these interactions between mother and child is the "interpersonal calibration of interpretations among members of a social network" (p. 104).

There is perhaps no better demonstration of the power of media to generate family communication than the creation of family narratives. Constructing narratives about the family is recognized as an important bonding activity within family communication research (Langellier & Peterson, 2006). Media can provide the context: songs to sing together, dialogue to quote, stories to tell about how Mom screams every time a certain scene comes on, or how a brother cannot reach the next level in his newest videogame. Whether jokes or tales, family narratives create family meaning (Galvin, 2006).

Media in the creation and avoidance of family conflict

In many families, television gives rise to issues involving control of how much and what is viewed (Gantz, 2001). The allocation of time, the selection of content, and the use of media resources can cause family conflict over media. Families adopt strategies or enact ritual practices to control the effect of the medium (Morley, 1986). Television viewing *per se* can create conflict within the home as parents voice concern about the amount of time spent with television and the other activities that television displaces. Television content can create similar conflicts when members argue over program choices, or parents are concerned about the effects of content (Alexander, 2001).

The remote control can be a family battleground. Fathers are generally perceived as having the most power in terms of controlling the remote, and thus the programming viewed (Lull, 1978; Morley, 1986). Gantz (2001) documented complaints about too much grazing (i.e., changing the channel during programs) by husbands who control the remote and are inattentive to interpersonal communication with other family members. In this multi-stage, multi-measure study, Gantz combined data from existing Internet newsgroups, face-to-face interviews, focus groups, and telephone interviews with 145 adults (2001). Because of these struggles, children and the "non-remote" parent (most often the wife) frequently choose to leave the room. With the proliferation of televisions in the home, family conflict over control of the remote can result in increased solitary viewing.

One way families control conflict is to establish formal or informal rules (Wilson, 2004). Rules are typically viewed as a type of mediating variable: attempts by parents to moderate the potential impact of television on children through control of viewing. Rules are also, however, constructions. They are the account offered by children or parents to describe the explicit practices about television viewing that operate within that family system. As such, studies that simply ask parents or children about the rules that operate within their family tend to uncover the explicit rules and inevitably underestimate the power that existing structures impose on media consumption. At the family level, it is easy for researchers to miss the implicit rules that govern viewing. For example, in one family the television may never be on during weekend days because children have learned that if parents find them "goofing off too much" they will be assigned chores. Although it is doubtful that anyone would describe this as a family rule, such practices have the force of limiting viewing contexts (Alexander, 2001).

What do we observe about power relations in families by looking at conflict over media choices? One major conclusion from this line of research is that television may serve an almost limitless range of diverse uses and functions. Family members can watch television to be together or to get away from each other; as a basis for talk or to avoid interaction; as a source of conflict, or an escape from it. Rosenblatt and Cunningham (1976) found that television viewing and tension were positively correlated. They also found that television viewing was a means to avoid tense interaction in crowded homes where avoiding conflict through physical separation is impossible. Over 30 years later, Bickham and colleagues (2003) conducted a national study of over 1000 children between the ages of 2 and 12 and found heavy television viewing correlated with a cluster of negative family characteristics, including low parental self-esteem, depression, and a lack of educational materials in the environment. The researchers suggested that these problems motivate higher levels of viewing to escape from family problems. Vandewater, Lee, and Shim (2005) found family conflict correlated with higher uses of moderately violent media in both television and videogames. Family conflicts, thus, predicted types of use rather than amount. The researchers reasoned that the conflict modeled in the family environment increased children's interest in conflict portrayed in the media.

The influence of new technologies on families

New technologies provide another set of challenges for the family system. The Internet erodes the boundaries between family and the outside world (Turow & Nir, 2003). Families with Internet access can experience negative outcomes as its use reduces the time families and children spend together, exposes children to commercial messages, and raises privacy and safety issues (Turow & Nir, 2003).

Early research on the Internet suggested that it had negative consequences for the family. Kraut and colleagues (1998) found that first and second year Internet users showed declines in communication with family members, as well as a smaller number of people in their social circle. A follow-up study (Kraut et al., 2002) reinvestigated respondents from the initial study as well as a new sample. In contrast to the earlier study, Kraut and colleagues (2002) found that people who used the Internet more often showed *increased* family communication and larger social circles. The authors suggested that the larger numbers of users attracted by increased Web content and services formed a different population from earlier users, which partly accounted for the change. Nonetheless, research is divided on whether or not families experience negative effects of the Internet. Mesch (2006) interviewed nearly 400 Israeli adolescents about whether Internet use eroded family cohesiveness. In his structural model, Internet use was negatively related to family time (i.e., time spent together as a family). Moreover, the social use of the Internet (as opposed to informational use) was positively related to family conflict. Thus, he concluded that Internet use indirectly and negatively influenced family cohesiveness.

Parents may be losing their influence over children in the realm of videogames. Bickham and colleagues (2003) found that videogame use was predicted by child-level variables (i.e., interest, availability), rather than family variables. They suggested that while television viewing may be influenced by modeling of parental behavior, videogame playing did not seem to show the same influence.

But parents too can utilize technology, and that use may be prompting a new form of family conflict. The *Wall Street Journal* (Rosman, 2006) reported a new generation of kids trying to get their parents to disengage from their Blackberry and reconnect to family life. Children reported parents sneaking away from family gatherings to read and send emails. Some youth worry that their parent may be distracted by technology while driving. Others cringe as parents misbehave in public by sending emails or playing games on their Blackberries during school events or at the movies.

Family Influence on Children's Media Experiences

What are the ways in which the family influences the use and understanding of media? In social science terms, the family is the independent variable; changes in media use and understanding are the dependent variables. There are two primary ways in which family influences on children's media experience have been studied. First is the family communication pattern perspective advanced by McLeod and Chaffee (1973). Second is the extensive literature on mediation, which is explored in the last chapter of this volume (Chakroff & Nathanson, Chapter 24).

In early research, McLeod and Chaffee (1973) identified two different patterns in family communication: socio and concept orientation patterns. Parents who use a socio orientation stress harmony, getting along with others, and obedience in their children. Parents who use a concept orientation encourage their children to openly express ideas, engage in critical thinking, and be self-reliant (McLeod & Chaffee, 1973). These dimensions are not mutually exclusive – parents can be low on both or even high on both of these dimensions. Based on the two communicative dimensions, the researchers developed a four-quadrant conceptualization of family communication.

The two dimensions have been used extensively by other researchers to examine media experiences. In studies on media and the family, the family communication pattern typically has been studied as a variable that influences media habits (Fitzpatrick & Ritchie, 1994). For instance, families high on the socio orientation tend to watch more television, but less news, than concept-oriented families do (Chaffee, McLeod, & Atkin, 1971). Families high in socio orientation also are more likely to use television for social purposes, including children watching more with their parents. Concept-oriented families tend to watch more news and information programming, and are higher in political knowledge (Chaffee & Tims, 1976).

This type of macro-measure of family communication has been criticized. Ritchie and Fitzpatrick (1990) reconceptualized the dimensions as conformity orientation and conversation orientation, based on concern over the face validity of several items in the original measure. Conformity orientation, they argued, is a better label than socio orientation for parental messages that emphasize parental power or authority to create conformity. Conversational orientation is a better term for parental messages that encourage expression of ideas. Using this reconceptualized measure, Krcmar and Vieira (2005) found that conversational orientation in the family was negatively related to children's exposure to television violence; in contrast, conformity orientation patterns in the family were positively related to violence exposure.

Another criticism of the family communication dimensions is that individual members of a family can vary considerably in the patterns they perceive as existing in their home (Ritchie & Fitzpatrick, 1990). This type of family disagreement suggests that the pattern of family communication is more complex than what is tapped by these two dimensions. Furthermore, aspects of family interaction such as conflict, avoidance strategies, power strategies, or affiliative behaviors are not included in this measure.

Future Directions

Most of the theories informing research on media and the family focus on individuals within a family context, examining who uses technology, how much, where, and with whom. Few examine the dynamic interactions that create and maintain family systems. Similarly, the examined outcomes of communication are quite varied, ranging from cohesiveness and adaptability to individual learning from media messages. One of the most crucial methodological debates in the arena of media and family is how to best theorize and operationalize these concepts and relationships. Evolving work in systems theory highlights efforts to capture the synergy of the family interacting with media. Yet most of our research to date is cross-sectional and often correlational (Wilson, 2004). We need longitudinal studies, as well as studies that systematically examine the confluence of media technologies, rather than individual media in isolation.

Both the institution of the family and the face of the media are changing. Our knowledge of family communication and media also needs to expand. Family communication theory needs to be applied more specifically to media in the home. Media scholars need to collaborate with family scholars to enhance their understanding of ways to fruitfully observe family communication.

New technologies particularly demand our attention. What influence will newer technologies have on families? Under what circumstances will newer technologies isolate individuals in the family unit, and under what circumstances will they integrate them? Who will lead in the adoption and use of technologies within the family? Robertson (1971) offered the idea that innovations are technologically continuous (VCRs added to television viewing) or technologically discontinuous (newspaper to Internet). Technologically continuous innovations require little adaptation; discontinuous innovations can be disruptive. We may not be able to predict the next innovation or its consequence, but we can continue to describe the process and consequences of these changes as previously unimagined digital developments challenge the boundaries of the home.

Family communication and media operate at the juncture of two contexts of communication: interpersonal and mediated. Traditionally, scholars of communication have conceived of these processes as separate: people talk to others in a face-to-face context, or people use mediated technologies that influence them. When these processes meet, the "ideal" forms no longer work. Today, people are not simply interacting with others face-to-face, and media consumers are not simply using or being influenced by technologies in a vacuum. Our ability to understand these intersections is still evolving and in need of further study.

Conclusion

Families integrate media within the family system. These patterns can be an important stabilizing force in the face of changing media systems. Media also shape the family, creating patterns of interaction and conflict and offering messages about the nature of families. How will families change in the face of rapidly evolving media? Only time and additional research will allow us to answer this question.

References

Alexander, A. (2001). The meaning of television in the American family. In J. Bryant & J. A. Bryant (Eds.), *Television and the American family* (2nd edn., pp. 273–87). Mahwah, NJ: Lawrence Erlbaum.

Alexander, A., Ryan, M. S., & Munoz, P. (1984). Creating a learning context: Investigations on the interaction of siblings during television viewing. *Critical Studies in Mass Communication*, 1, 345–64.

Andreason, M. (2001). Evolution in the family's use of television: An overview. In J. Bryant & J. A. Bryant (Eds.), *Television and the American family* (2nd edn., pp. 3–30). Mahwah, NJ: Lawrence Erlbaum.

Bandura, A. (1977). *Social learning theory*. Englewood Cliffs, NJ: Prentice Hall.

Bandura, A. (1994). Social cognitive theory of mass communication. In J. Bryant & D. Zillman (Eds.), *Media effects: Advances in theory and research* (pp. 61–90). Mahwah, NJ: Lawrence Erlbaum.

Baran, S., & Davis, D. (2006). *Mass communication theory: Foundations, ferment, and future* (4th edn.). Belmont, CA: Wadsworth.

Bickham, D. S., Vandewater, E. A., Huston, A. C., Lee, J. H., Caplovita, G. A., & Wright, J. C. (2003). Predictors of children's electronic media use: An examination of three ethnic groups. *Media Psychology*, 5, 107–37.

Bryant, J., & Bryant, J. A. (Eds.). (2001). *Television and the American family* (2nd edn.). Mahwah, NJ: Lawrence Erlbaum.

Bryant, J., Bryant, J. A., Aust, C. F., & Venugopalan, G. (2001). How psychologically healthy are America's prime-time television families? In J. Bryant & J. A. Bryant (Eds.), *Television and the American family* (2nd edn., pp. 247–70). Mahwah, NJ: Lawrence Erlbaum.

Buckingham, D. (1993). *Reading audiences: Young people and the media*. Manchester, UK: Manchester University Press.

Buckingham, D. (1998). Media education in the UK: Moving beyond protectionism. *Journal of Communication*, 48(1), 33–41.

Buerkel-Rothfuss, N. L., & Mayes, S. (1981). Soap opera viewing: The cultivation effect. *Journal of Communication*, 31(3), 108–15.

Carey, J. W. (1989). Communication and culture: Essays on media and society. Boston: Unwin Hyman.

Chaffee, S. H., McLeod, J. M., & Atkin, C. K. (1971). Parental influences on adolescent media use. *American Behavioral Scientist*, 14, 323–40.

Chaffee, S. H., & Tims, A. R. (1976). Interpersonal factors in adolescent television use. *Journal of Social Issues*, 32, 98–115.

Comstock, G., & Paik, H. (1991). *Television and the American child*. San Diego, CA: Academic Press.

Comstock, J., & Strzyzewski, K. (1990). Interpersonal interaction on television: Family conflict and jealousy on prime time. *Journal of Broadcasting and Electronic Media*, 34, 263–82.

Craig, R. T. (1999). Communication theory as a field. *Communication Theory*, 9, 119–61.

Douglas, W. (2001). Subversion of American television family. In J. Bryant & J. A. Bryant (Eds.), *Television and the American family* (2nd edn., pp. 273–87). Mahawah, NJ: Lawrence Erlbaum.

Douglas, W. (2003). *Television families: Is something wrong in suburbia?* Mahwah, NJ: Lawrence Erlbaum.

Fitzpatrick, M. A., & Caughlin, J. P. (2002). Interpersonal communication in family relationships. In M. L. Knapp & J. A. Daly (Eds.), *Handbook of family relationships* (2nd edn., pp. 726–78). Thousand Oaks, CA: Sage.

Fitzpatrick, M. A., & Ritchie, L. D. (1994). Communication schemata within the family: Multiple perspectives on family interaction. *Human Communication Research*, 20, 275–301.

Floyd, K., Judd, J., & Mikkelson, A. C. (2006). Defining and interpreting the family. *The Family Communication Sourcebook*, 2, 21–39.

Fry, V., Alexander, A., & Fry, D. (1990). Textual status, the stigmatized self, and media consumption. In J. Anderson (Ed.), *Communication yearbook*, vol. 13 (pp. 519–44). Newbury Park, CA: Sage.

Galvin, K. M. (2006). Joined by hearts and words: Adoptive family relationships. In K. Floyd & M. T. Morman (Eds.), *Widening the family circle: New research on family relationships* (pp. 137–52). Thousand Oaks, CA: Sage.

Gantz, W. (2001). Conflicts and resolution strategies associated with television in marital life. In J. Bryant & J. A. Bryant (Eds.), *Television and the American family* (2nd edn., pp. 289–316). Mahwah, NJ: Lawrence Erlbaum.

Gerbner, G., Gross, L., Morgan, M., & Signorielli, N. (1994). Growing up with television: The cultivation perspective. In J. Bryant & D. Zillman (Eds.), *Media effects: Advances in theory and research* (pp. 17–41). Mahwah, NJ: Lawrence Erlbaum.

Goodman, I. F. (1983). Television's role in family interactions: A family systems perspective. *Journal of Family Issues*, 4, 405–24.

Greenberg, B. S., Hines, M., Buerkel-Rothfuss, N., & Atkin, C. K. (1980). Family role structures and interactions on commercial television. In B. S. Greenberg (Ed.), *Life on television: Content analyses of U.S. television drama* (pp. 149–60). Norwood, NJ: Ablex.

Heintz, K. E. (1992). Children's favorite television families: A descriptive analysis of role interactions. *Journal of Broadcasting and Electronic Media*, 31, 153–68.

Jennings, N., & Wartella, E. A. (2004). Technology and the family. In A. L. Vangelisti (Ed.), *Handbook of family communication* (pp. 593–608). Mahwah, NJ: Lawrence Erlbaum.

Jordan, A. B. (2002). A family systems approach to examining the role of the Internet in the home. In S. Calvert, A. Jordan, & R. Cocking (Eds.), *Children the digital age: Influences of electronic media on development* (pp. 231–47). Westport, CT: Praeger.

Jordan, A. B. (2005). Learning to use books and television: An exploratory study in the ecological perspective. *American Behavioral Scientist*, 48, 523–38.

Katz, J. E., & Rice, R. (2002). *Social consequences of Internet use: Access, involvement and interaction*. Cambridge, MA: MIT Press.

Kraut, R., Kiesler, S., Boneva, B., Cummings, J., Helgeson, V., & Crawford, A. (2002). Internet paradox revisited. *Journal of Social Issues*, 58, 49–74.

Kraut, R., Patterson, M., Lundmark, V., Kiesler, S., Mukopadhyay, T., & Scherlis, W. (1998). Internet paradox: A social technology that reduces social involvement and psychological well-being? *American Psychologist*, 53(9), 1017–31.

Krcmar, M., & Vieira, E. T. (2005). Imitating life, imitating television: The effects of family and television models on children's moral reasoning. *Communication Research*, 32(3), 267–94.

Kubey, R., & Csikszentmihalyi, M. (1990). *Television and the quality of life: How viewing Shapes everyday experience*. Hillsdale, NJ: Lawrence Erlbaum.

Langellier, K. M., & Peterson, E. E. (2006). Narrative performance theory: Telling stories, doing family. In D. O. Braithwaite & L. A. Baxter (Eds.), *Family communication theories* (pp. 99–114). Thousand Oaks, CA: Sage.

Larson, M. S. (2001). Sibling interaction in situation comedies over the years. In J. Bryant & J. Bryant (Eds.), *Television and the American family* (2nd edn., pp. 163–76). Mahwah, NJ: Lawrence Erlbaum.

Lawrence, F. C., & Wozniak, P. H. (1989). Children's television viewing with family members. *Psychological Reports*, 65, 395–400.

Lemish, D. (1987). Viewers in diapers. In T. Lindlof (Ed.), *Natural audiences: Qualitative research of media uses and effects* (pp. 33–57). Norwood, NJ: Ablex.

Lindlof, T. (Ed.). (1987). *Natural audiences: Qualitative research of media uses and effects*. Norwood, NJ: Ablex.

Lindlof, T. (1991). The qualitative study of media audiences. *Journal of Broadcasting and Electronic Media*, 35, 15–30.

Lull, J. (1978). Choosing television programs by family vote. *Communication Quarterly*, 26, 53–7.

Lull, J. (1980). The social uses of television. *Human Communication Research*, 6, 197–209.

Mazur, & Kalbfleisch, M. (2003). Pamela. *Communication Research Reports*, 20(3), 200–207.

McLeod, J. M., & Chaffee, S. (1973). Interpersonal approaches to communication research. *American Behavioral Scientist*, 16, 469–99.

McLeod, J. M., Fitzpatrick, M. A., Glynn, C. J., & Fallis, S. F. (1982). Television and social relations: Family influences and consequences for interpersonal behavior. In D. Pearl, L. Bouthilet, & J. Lazar (Eds.), *Television and behavior: Ten years of scientific progress and implications for the eighties*, vol. 2 (pp. 272–86). Washington, DC: US Government Printing Office.

Mesch, G. S. (2006). Family relations and the internet: Exploring a family boundaries approach. *Journal of Family Communication*, 6(2), 119–38.

Messaris, P. (1987). Mothers' comments to their children about the relationship between television and reality. In T. Lindlof (Ed.), *Natural audiences: Qualitative research of media uses and effects* (pp. 33–57). Norwood, NJ: Ablex.

Morley, D. (1986). *Family television: Cultural power and domestic leisure.* London: Comedia.

Nie, N. H. (2001). Sociability, interpersonal relations and the Internet: Reconciling conflicting findings. *American Behavioral Scientist*, 45, 420–35.

Nielsen Media Research. (2005). *Nielsen reports Americans watch television at record levels*, September 29. Retrieved November 14, 2006, from www.nielsenmedia.com/newsreleases/2005/AvgHoursMinutes92905.pdf.

Olson, D. H., Russell, C. S., & Sprenkle, D. H. (Eds.). (1989). *Circumplex model: Systemic assessment and treatment of families.* New York: Haworth.

Ritchie, L. D., & Fitzpatrick, M. A. (1990). Family communication patterns: Measuring intrapersonal per captions of interpersonal relationships. *Communication Research*, 17, 523–44.

Roberts, D., Foehr, U. G., & Rideout, V. J. (2005). *Generation M: Media in the lives of 8–18-year-olds.* Menlo Park, CA: Kaiser Family Foundation.

Robertson, T. (1971). *Innovative behavior and communication*, New York: Holt.

Robinson, J. D., & Skill, T. (2001). Five decades of families on telelvison: From the 1950s through the 1990s. In J. Bryant & J. A. Bryant (Eds.), *Television and the American family* (2nd edn., pp. 139–62). Mahwah, NJ: Lawrence Erlbaum.

Rosenblatt, P. C., & Cunningham, M. R. (1976). Television watching and family tensions. *Journal of Marriage and the Family*, 37, 308–26.

Rosman, K. (2006). Blackberry orphans. *Wall Street Journal*, December 8, p. W1.

Spigel, L. (2001). *Welcome to the dreamhouse: Popular media and postwar suburbs.* Durham, NC. Duke University Press.

Turow, J. (2003). *Americans and online privacy: The system is broken.* Philadelphia: Annenberg Public Policy Center of the University of Pennsylvania.

Turow, J., & Nir, A. (Eds.). (2003). *The wired homestead: An MIT Press sourcebook on the Internet and the family.* Cambridge, MA: MIT Press.

US Census Bureau. (2005). American community survey. Retrieved May 19, 2007, from http://www.census.gov/acs/www/Area percent20Sheets/Area percent20Sheet percent20US.doc.

Vandewater, E. A., Lee, J. H., & Shim, M. (2005). Family conflict and violent electronic media use in school-aged children. *Media Psychology*, 7, 73–86.

Van Evra, J. (2004). Television and child development (3rd edn.). Mahwah, NJ: Lawrence Erlbaum.

Weiss, A. J., & Wilson, B. J. (1996). Emotional portrayals in family television series that are popular among children. *Journal of Broadcasting and Electronic Media*, 40, 1–29.

Weiss, A. J., & Wilson, B. J. (1998). Children's cognitive and emotional responses to the portrayal of negative emotions in family-formatted situation comedies. *Human Communication Research*, 24, 584–609.

Wetzel, J. (1990). American families: 75 years of change. *Monthly Labor Review*, 113(3), 4–13.

Wilson, B. J. (2004). The mass media and family communication. In A. L. Vangelisti (Ed.), *Handbook of family communication* (pp. 563–92). Mahwah, NJ: Lawrence Erlbaum.

Woodard, E. H., & Grindina, N. (2000). *Media in the home 2000: The fifth annual survey of parents and children.* Philadelphia: Annenberg Public Policy Center of the University of Pennsylvania.

Part III

Cognitive Effects of Media: How and What Children Learn

7

Attention and Learning from Media during Infancy and Early Childhood

Rachel Barr

Media products directed at very young children have exploded into the marketplace (Garrison & Christakis, 2005). At the same time, parent surveys reveal that very young children are being exposed to high levels of screen-based media (Rideout & Hamel, 2006; Rideout, Vandewater, & Wartella, 2003; Zimmerman, Christakis, & Meltzoff, 2007). Although the American Academy of Pediatrics (AAP) (1999) recommended no screen exposure before age 2, the empirical research about the effects of early media exposure on developmental outcomes is still in its infancy.

This chapter will focus on empirical studies that have measured the influence of media on attention, imitation, object search, and language learning. In a final section, these converging data will provide a conceptual framework to examine the potential impacts of early media exposure on cognitive and social development in the context of the AAP recommendation.

Very Early Media Exposure

US children are born into and develop in a world in which media pervade their daily experiences (for review, see Calvert, 2006). Recent nationally representative surveys of homes with children aged 6 months to 6 years found that 99 percent of homes contain a television set, 95 percent have a DVD player or videocassette recorder, 50 percent have three or more televisions, and 73 percent have a computer. Moreover, one third of these young children have televisions in their bedrooms (Rideout & Hamel, 2006; Rideout, Vandewater, & Wartella, 2003).

Access to media content directed at infants and young children is also changing, resulting in much earlier exposure to infant-directed programming. During the 1970s, children were first exposed to television on a regular basis at approximately 2.5 years of age (Anderson & Levin, 1976; Anderson et al., 1986). During the 1990s, television programs such as *Teletubbies* and videos/DVDs such as *Baby Einstein* started to be produced specifically for infants (Garrison & Christakis, 2005).

Over the past five years, the media landscape for infants has changed dramatically; in 2004, media products directed at very young children produced sales of approximately $100 million in the US alone (Garrison & Christakis, 2005). Because there are media products designed just for them, many infants now begin consistently viewing videos and DVDs at 6 to 9 months of age; 74–90 percent are exposed to television before age 2 (Rideout, Vandewater, & Wartella, 2003; Zimmerman, Christakis, & Meltzoff, 2007).

Children below the age of 2 years spend approximately 1 to 2 hours per day with screen media, predominantly viewing television and prerecorded videos and DVDs, but only about 40 minutes reading books or being read to (Rideout & Hamel, 2006; Zimmerman, Christakis, & Meltzoff, 2007). Many parents view screen media favorably; for instance, 58 percent of parents in a nationally representative sample believe that early exposure to educational television programming is "very important" (Rideout, Vandewater, & Wartella, 2003). Computer experience and videogame play is still relatively rare prior to age two, but computers tend to be viewed very favorably by parents of preschool-aged children (Calvert et al., 2005) and that pattern may also hold true for those with even younger children as products become available that infants and toddlers can use.

Patterns of television use differ for children from different ethnic groups. In particular, African American and Latino children spend more time watching television than Caucasian children do (Rideout & Hamel, 2006). Similarly, patterns of viewing differ across socioeconomic groups. Families with lower incomes report higher levels of daily media use (Rideout & Hamel, 2006; Zimmerman, Christakis, & Meltzoff, 2007).

Availability also influences levels of television exposure. When children have television in their own rooms, they are exposed to higher levels of television content (Rideout & Hamel, 2006). When the television is on most or all of the time, children have higher levels of television exposure, they begin watching at an earlier age, are more likely to watch television every day, and watch it for longer periods of time (Vandewater et al., 2005). These children are also significantly less likely to be read to every day. Daily book reading is positively associated with language and cognitive development (Raikes et al., 2006). Birth order also impacts the amount of exposure and the type of exposure for children under 2. Specifically, infants with older siblings are exposed to more television and more non-educational content than first-born infants are (Zimmerman, Christakis, & Meltzoff, 2007).

In households with strict rules regarding the amount of television exposure, children watch less television (Vandewater et al., 2005). In households with strict rules about content, parents are significantly more likely to co-view with their children (Vandewater et al., 2005), which provides potential opportunities for parent-child interactions that can foster learning.

Taken together, the findings suggest that there is a complex interplay of factors involved surrounding household media patterns. These patterns are influenced by race and ethnicity, income, family composition, and parental beliefs about whether media has the potential to be a positive or a negative influence on their child's development.

American Academy of Pediatrics Recommendation: No Screen Exposure before Age Two

Partly in response to rapid changes in the media landscape, the AAP (1999) recommended that parents should limit television exposure during early childhood. Specifically, children under the age of 2 should not be exposed to any type of screen media, and for children over 2, screen time (including television and computers) should be limited to 1 to 2 hours per day. This recommendation was based on two major concerns.

First, numerous studies have shown negative effects of media on preschoolers' behavior, particularly in the arena of media violence (Paik & Comstock, 1994), and the AAP predicted that such negative effects would also occur when exposure occurred at a younger age. After the recommendation was released, reports have emerged that heavy exposure to television during early childhood is associated with poor school performance, increased bullying, attention problems, and sleep problems (Christakis et al., 2004; Thakkar, Garrison, & Christakis, 2006; Thompson & Christakis, 2005; Zimmerman et al., 2005). For example, in one study an association was found between heavy television exposure during the first three years of life and parental reports of attention problems in first graders, as indexed by the Behavior Problems Index (Christakis et al., 2004). The study included a large sample and statistically controlled for multiple potential risk factors including differences in socioeconomic status, maternal risk factors such as maternal depression, and child risk factors such as prematurity or prenatal drug exposure.

Although it is possible that early television viewing causes later attention disorders, it is also possible that children with attention disorders are motivated to watch more television and/or are encouraged to do so by parents who are finding it difficult to cope with young children who are hyperactive and have poor attentional control (Calvert, 2006). Furthermore, the data were collected when there was no infant-directed programming available, suggesting that these findings may largely be due to exposure to incomprehensible content that is designed for an older audience, known as *background television* (Calvert, 2006). In fact, two recent studies in which data were collected since 2000 have failed to replicate the findings (Acevedo-Polakovich et al., 2006; Stevens & Muslow, 2006).

A second concern of the AAP is that time spent with screen media may be displacing other activities that are more important for children's development, such as face-to-face time with parents and caregivers. The AAP reasoned that during television viewing, parental attention would be directed to program content, thereby reducing the quality of parent-child interactions. Several studies have supported this supposition and cited negative associations between television viewing and time spent with parents engaging in other activities when programs were being directed at the adult viewers (e.g., Kirkorian & Anderson, this volume, Chapter 9; Vandewater, Bickham, & Lee, 2006). In the study by Vandewater and colleagues (2006), television viewing also was negatively related to creative play among children under age 5. No relationship was found between time spent watching television and time spent reading (or being read to) or time spent in active play (Vandewater, Bickham, & Lee, 2006).

Despite the AAP concerns, other research has indicated that there are beneficial effects of screen media that is specifically designed for children who are ages 2 years and older. For example, exposure to high-quality children's educational programs such as *Sesame Street* and *Mister Rogers' Neighborhood* during the preschool years has enhanced cognitive development, language development, and prosocial skills and has a long-lasting positive impact on school readiness and academic performance (Anderson et al., 2001). In light of mixed findings of both positive and negative impacts of media content on behavior, current data on attention and learning from television during early childhood will be reviewed and implications for the AAP recommendation will be discussed.

Attention

It has been difficult to find the most appropriate means to index and quantify attention during early childhood. On the one hand, eye movements are one of the most practiced motor behaviors of infancy and also, with regard to any other system, most closely approximate that of adults (Haith, Hazan, & Goodman, 1988). On the other hand, although researchers using this measure often assume that attention implies encoding, it cannot be directly known what information the infant is encoding in the course of a visual fixation or the rate at which the infant is encoding it.

Media researchers have therefore adopted a number of different measures of attention, examining overall looking time and patterns of looking time, as well as verbal and non-verbal imitative behavior, pointing, vocalizations, and physiological correlates of heart rate and event-related potentials that take place during viewing (Anderson et al., 2001; Barr & Hayne, 1999; Carver, Meltzoff, & Dawson, 2006; Crawley et al., 1999; Richards & Casey, 1992; Richards & Turner, 2001; Rolandelli et al., 1991). The use of a variety of methods has resulted in the emergence of converging data and provides a more precise index of information processing of media during early childhood.

Selective attention

The grammar and syntax or "representational codes" of television that are thought to guide infant and young children's attention to and information processing of television are called formal features (Calvert & Scott, 1989; Huston & Wright, 1983; Rice, Huston, & Wright, 1982; Schmitt, Anderson, & Collins, 1999).

Formal features are the auditory and visual production and editing techniques characterizing the medium, such as action, sound effects, and pacing (the rate of scene and character changes). Some features, such as sound effects and rapid action are perceptually salient and likely to elicit attention and interest, whereas other features such as dialogue are not salient but important in processing the narrative (Huston & Wright, 1983).

There are a number of salient formal features that consistently increase toddlers' and preschoolers' selective attention to television content. In particular, attention to televised content increases and remains high in the presence of female adults, character action, children, puppets, animation, active movement (including dancing and repetition), singing and lively music, peculiar voices, and sound effects (Anderson & Levin, 1976; Calvert et al., 1982; Huston & Wright, 1983; Schmitt et al., 1999). Attention decreases as the length of a segment increases, during low-action sequences, and during periods of adult narration or abstract adult dialogue (Anderson & Levin, 1976; Calvert et al., 1982; Huston & Wright, 1983; Schmitt et al., 1999). Research has also shown that formal visual effects such as cuts, zooms, and pans, known as montage, enhance the attention of preschoolers (Calvert et al., 1982; Schmitt et al., 1999; Smith, Anderson, & Fischer, 1985) but not as effectively as formal auditory features, including sound effects (Huston-Stein & Wright, 1979; Rice, Huston, & Wright, 1982).

Development of sustained attention to comprehensible media content

Studies examining children aged 2 months to 5 years (e.g., Alwitt et al., 1980; Crawley et al., 1999; Richards & Cronise, 2000; Richards & Gibson, 1997) and even adults (Anderson & Burns, 1991) show similar looking patterns, suggesting that an attentional mechanism for processing dynamic media content emerges very early in development. The looking patterns are characterized by large numbers of 2 to 3 second looks but fewer looks of longer duration (Richards & Anderson, 2004). Rapid looks toward and away from the screen indicate that participants are responding to the formal features. The looks that last longer than 15 seconds are termed *sustained attention*. During periods of sustained attention active cognitive processing of material is occurring. While looking patterns to media are similar across development, sustained attention to media increases systematically as a function of age (Anderson & Levin, 1976; Anderson et al., 1986; Lemish, 1987).

Measuring sustained attention   Studies have demonstrated that during periods of sustained attention to television presentations, infants and toddlers are less distractible than they are during periods when attention is more variable (for review, see Lorch, 1994). Richards and Turner (2001), for example, showed 6- to 24-month-olds a *Sesame Street* movie. At random intervals, 5 second distracters of another *Sesame Street* movie were presented on a second television monitor. Across age, infants were significantly less likely to turn toward the distracter if the distracter was presented during a look that lasted longer than 15 seconds. If infants did turn their heads, they were significantly slower in doing so than during shorter looks. These findings imply that sustained attention involves focused information processing such that other stimuli are less likely to distract selective attention to media content. Sustained attention in turn allows the media content to be processed.

Sustained attention is typically accompanied by heart rate (HR) deceleration. Sustained lowered HR, in turn, is thought to allow for optimal and active information processing as HR variability, respiration, body movement, and distractibility decrease (Clifton & Nelson, 1976). During sustained attention, HR decelerates as the duration of the look continues and accelerates back to baseline levels immediately before the offset of the look (Richards & Cronise, 2000). In contrast, HR acceleration is thought to reflect a rejecting or defensive response (Clifton & Nelson, 1976). HR patterns have been used to index 2- to 24-month-olds sustained attention during media presentations and correlate strongly with looking patterns (Richards & Anderson, 2004).

Age-related changes in sustained attention   Both the amount of sustained attention and when sustained attention is allocated changes as a function of age. The amount of sustained attention gradually increases during infancy (Richards & Gibson, 1997; Richards & Chronise, 2000) and continues to increase through the preschool years and into adulthood (Richards & Anderson, 2004).

Infants do not begin to discriminate between content until late in the first year of life. During the first year of life infants allocate the same amount of sustained attention to a comprehensible narrative sequence and to incomprehensible sequences of randomly generated patterns. In contrast, older 18- and 24-month-olds differentiate between comprehensible and incomprehensible sequences, allocating more sustained attention to comprehensible sequences (Richards & Chronise, 2000). Taken together, these findings indicate that information processing of media content changes gradually across infancy and toddlerhood because of an increasing ability to understand the content.

Processing two-dimensional stimuli during early childhood

Very early in development, both the auditory and the visual components of television are processed in a rudimentary way (see also Hollenbeck & Slaby, 1979; Lemish, 1987). Four-month-olds, for example, will preferentially attend to audiovisual tracks where the speech matches the visual track over comparable mismatched auditory and visual tracks (Kuhl & Meltzoff, 1982).

Processing of televised information is, however, cognitively demanding. Recently researchers using event-related potentials (ERPs), that provide a precise measure of the speed of processing of information, have shown that 18-month-old infants require more time to process two-dimensional (2D) images than they require to process real three-dimensional (3D) objects. To document this, Carver, Meltzoff, and Dawson (2006) paired the infants' favorite familiar toy with an unfamiliar toy matched on shape, color, and size. For the 3D condition, toys were placed in a display box. For the 2D condition, digital photos of the familiar and unfamiliar toys were presented on a computer monitor. Although ERPs showed that 18-month-olds differentiated between familiar and novel toys in both the 2D and 3D conditions, toddlers were much slower at differentiating the 2D pictures of novel and familiar objects than the real 3D objects.

The relationship between attention, media content, and comprehension

Both overall duration of looking and looking at specific times predict children's comprehension of content during early childhood. Perceptually salient production techniques such as sound effects can facilitate attention to specific program points, thereby increasing young children's processing of the content that immediately follows that feature (Calvert et al., 1982; Rice, Huston, & Wright, 1982). The sound effect initially creates an attentional orienting response, which later becomes a learned signal or marker that important content will follow, thereby disrupting any habituation process (Calvert et al., 1982). Through this process, children learn to use sound effects as guides for their selective attention to important plot-relevant content.

The comprehensibility of the content also leads to increased attentional interest by young children (Anderson et al., 1981; Field & Anderson, 1985; Lorch, Anderson, & Levin, 1979; Lorch & Castle, 1997). Anderson and colleagues (1981), for example, found that 3- and 5-year-olds attended significantly more to the correctly sequenced version of a *Sesame Street* episode than to any distorted versions, such as foreign or backwards dialogue or randomly ordered shots. Using the same kind of methodology, Anderson and colleagues presented 6- to 24-month-olds with either correct or distorted versions of *Teletubbies*, a program that is designed for 1-year-olds (Anderson & Pempek, 2005; Kirkorian et al., 2005). The 18- and 24-month-olds paid significantly less attention to the distorted sequences of the program (either random sequence or backwards dialogue) than the correctly sequenced program. However, the 6- and 12-month-olds in the study paid equal amounts of attention to the correct and distorted versions of the program. These findings suggest that children begin to understand very simple television programs sometime between 12 and 18 months of age.

Repeated presentations of the same television program also help to maintain attention, in part because comprehension increases across exposures until it finally reaches ceiling levels (Anderson & Levin, 1976; Anderson et al., 1981; Barr et al., 2007; Crawley et al., 1999). Crawley and colleagues (1999), for example, showed 3-, 4-, and 5-year-olds an episode of *Blues Clues*, once per day for five days. Although there were significant age-related differences in comprehension scores, comprehension at all ages increased with repeated exposure to the program.

Child interaction with media content is thought to increase information processing because of higher levels of active cognitive engagement. In particular, verbal and non-verbal imitative behavior, pointing, and vocalizations during viewing have all been associated with increased comprehension. For example, levels of verbal responding increased across five successive exposures to an episode of *Blues Clues* (Crawley et al., 1999).

Individual differences in attention to media   Habituation is the ability to attenuate looking at familiar stimuli after repeated presentations. It is thought to reflect the speed of encoding; the more rapidly habituation occurs, the more rapidly the information is processed (Thompson & Spencer, 1966). Individual differences in infants' visual attention during habituation studies are reliable; for instance, infants with shorter looking times typically habituate faster than infants with longer looking times and subsequently have higher IQs (e.g., Colombo et al., 1991).

Similarly, during the processing of dynamic media, there are individual differences in discriminating non-meaningful screensavers and more meaningful content (Courage, Reynolds, & Richards, 2006; Richards & Casey, 1992). For example, Courage and colleagues (2006) measured HR variability and looking time to complex stimuli (faces and Sesame Street vignettes) and simple stimuli (geometric patterns) in 3- to 12-month-olds. HR variability reflects the ability to rapidly adapt to and process novel information and higher HR variability is associated with higher IQ. Older infants with higher HR variability were increasingly likely to attend to more complex stimuli and less to random geometric patterns. That is, infants who are better information processors are faster at deriving meaningful content from media.

Attention seems to be consistent across various tasks, including television viewing. Ruff, Capozzoli, and Weissberg (1998), for instance, observed 2.5-, 3.5-, and 4.5-year-old children as they viewed television, played with toys, and participated in structured repetitive tasks. Those children who were classified as attentive demonstrated that same pattern across all tasks. Thus, attentional patterns seem to be an individual style that children bring to many different tasks, and television viewing is subject to that same general style.

Role of co-viewing   Attention to television also reflects joint attention patterns between the child and the parent (for review, see Butterworth, 2001), which provide a platform for learning. Both book-reading and television studies have shown differences in the ways that parents provide scaffolds, i.e., links between what the child knows and the content to be learned (Barr et al., in press; DeLoache & DeMendoza, 1987; Fletcher & Reese, 2005; Lemish & Rice, 1986).

In a recent semi-naturalistic study conducted in infants' homes, we examined 120 parents' and their 12-, 15-, or 18-month-olds' viewing of one of two popular infant-directed programs, *Baby Mozart* and *Kids Favorite Songs 2* (Barr et al., in press). Half of the infants in our sample had prior exposure to the video content, half did not. Infants who had previously seen the content looked for significantly longer periods of time. Infant's looking times and interactions were also influenced by parental scaffolding. In particular, the more questions, descriptions, and labels about program content that parents provided, the more infants looked at and interacted with the infant-directed program content. These findings suggest that both prior experience and parent-child interactions during early viewing experiences influence how well the infant will understand the content.

The role of background television   Children are often inadvertently exposed to programming designed for adults simply because they are in a particular room when the television is on. This "background television" is typically incomprehensible to younger ages (Anderson & Pempek, 2005). Because play is critical for subsequent social and cognitive development (Singer & Singer, this volume, Chapter 13), Evans-Schmidt, Pempek, Kirkorian, Frankenfield, and Anderson (submitted) have recently examined the impact of background television on children's play behavior. Children aged 1, 2, and 3 years were observed during a 1 hour play session in a laboratory playroom. For 30 minutes an adult television show played in the background; for the other half of the time, no television show played. Although parents were in the room, they were asked to complete study forms and to limit interaction with their children. Children only attended to the background television 5 percent of the time, but play episodes were shorter, less complex, and included less focused attention than when the television was not on.

Subsequently, Kirkorian and colleagues (2005) conducted the same experiment but asked parents to interact with their children. Parents engaged in significantly less toy play, and were less actively involved with their young children when the adult television program was on than when it was off. Overall, the authors argue that background television may be acting as a distracter and may have long-term negative consequences for social and cognitive development. Specifically, it may interfere with learning on two fronts: by decreasing parent-child interaction and by disrupting the focus on play via incidental sounds that attract infant attention to the television. Reorienting to play is difficult, and it is more difficult because there is no parental support to do so.

Summary and theoretical implications   Overall, studies of attentional processing of television during early childhood have demonstrated a number of important principles. First, the similarity of looking patterns of 2- to 24-month-olds suggests that an attentional mechanism for processing 2D dynamic stimuli emerges very early in development. Second, processing of televised information is cognitively demanding. Physiological measures indicate that sustained attention increases across infancy, and that infants require additional time to process 2D images relative to processing real 3D objects. Third, although the underlying process does not change as a function of age, content strongly influences processing of information. That is, looking patterns begin to show discrimination between comprehensible and incomprehensible content during infancy. Fourth, looking time measures also reflect the role of parental mediation and interaction during viewing. When parents and their young children attend to the television together and parents make direct reference to the television content, looking time increases. Similarly, when adult-directed television is on in the background, parents interact less with their young children and do not actively engage their babies and toddlers with program content, and thus looking time decreases.

There are competing theories of the development of attention to television during early childhood. Aspects of each of these theories account for some but not all of the findings described above. According to the comprehensibility theory, attention to media is guided by the comprehensibility of the content and by similar principles to those that guide selective attention more generally. Consistent with this theory, comprehensibility begins to guide attention to media during early infancy and attentional mechanisms, such as sustained attention, develop gradually across early childhood (Richards & Anderson, 2004).

As proposed in the "sampling model of attention," toddlers and preschoolers begin to decide when to view and when to play with toys based on their knowledge of formal features (Huston & Wright, 1983). That is, attention can be divided between toy play and television viewing because children learn that formal features signal and mark specific media content. There is also a developmental component to this theory. In terms of television specific features, attention to television is initially directed by perceptually driven processes, but with development and experience, children come to learn that different perceptually salient features serve to mark content for further processing as well as provide visual and verbal modes that children can use to represent content (Anderson et al., 1981; Calvert et al., 1982; Huston & Wright, 1983).

Mediation of viewing by adults is a third perspective that influences attention and learning. According to Vygotskian theory, all cognitive functions develop through social experiences (Vygotsky, 1978). Specifically, once a child has mastered a skill in a supportive social context, the skill will be internalized which enables the child to apply this skill in new contexts. Consistent with Vygotskian theory, parents mediate looking patterns toward television stimuli during infancy, either positively by directing their child's attention to programs made for babies during co-viewing, or negatively by reducing interaction patterns with their infant when absorbed in watching an adult program (Barr et al., in press).

The theories share two important principles: (1) that attention to media content follows a gradual developmental trajectory, and (2) that attention is mediated. The theories differ, however, in the ways in which attention is mediated. Based on the current literature, a comprehensive theory of the development of attention to 2D dynamic stimuli during early childhood will have to consider how the processes interact. In particular, a comprehensive theory must take into consideration features unique to television, the content of the program, and the role of parent mediation.

Imitation

Historically, researchers chose imitation to investigate the potential impact of television exposure. At the time, policy makers were concerned about the impact of violent media content on children's aggressive behavior outside of the media context. As such, imitation provided a direct measure of information transfer from the media context to the real world (Bandura, 1965; Bandura, Ross, & Ross, 1963). While the initial focus was on the imitation of aggressive actions (for review, see Paik & Comstock, 1994), subsequent research focused on imitation of prosocial behavior (Stein & Friedrich, 1972).

The fact that imitation paradigms are non-verbal, a characteristic of very early development, allows researchers to directly examine learning from media by the youngest audiences. For these reasons, the ability of infants and toddlers to learn from televised presentations has also been examined using imitation paradigms (Barr & Hayne, 1999; Hayne, Herbert, & Simcock, 2003; Huang & Charman, 2005; Hudson & Sheffield, 1999; McCall, Parke, & Kavanaugh, 1977; Meltzoff, 1988).

Imitation paradigms allow the manipulation of a number of important media variables. First, people do not typically encounter actual television actors. In imitation studies, this can be simulated by having one experimenter demonstrate the target actions on television and another experimenter interact with the child in the real world. Second, infants would only infrequently have immediate access to what they see on television. To more closely simulate these real-world conditions, researchers therefore use a deferred imitation procedure. The experimenter demonstrates the target actions on television, and infants are tested after a delay. From a theoretical perspective, deferred imitation from television is a complex representational task (e.g., Barr & Hayne, 2000; Meltzoff, 1988). Successful completion of the imitation task from a videotaped model requires participants to form a memory of the event on television, and, only after a delay, participants must transfer that memory to 3D objects in the real world and reproduce the target actions. That is, examining deferred imitation from television also examines memory development, a key component of cognitive development.

Studies have shown that infants as young as 6 months can imitate limited actions demonstrated by videotaped models after a 24-hour delay (Barr, Garcia, & Muentener, in press). A videotaped demonstration has also been shown to be an effective reminder for 18-month-olds for events they learned 10 weeks earlier. In a study by Hudson and Sheffield (1999), infants learned 6 or 8 novel event sequences in a laboratory playroom. After a 10-week delay, 18-month-olds were presented with a videotaped demonstration of the activities that they had previously learned. Infants who watched the video performed significantly more target actions than did infants who did not see the video.

Video Deficit Effect

Infants learn better from a live adult than they do from a video presentation, a phenomenon known as the video deficit effect (Anderson & Pempek, 2005; Barr & Hayne, 1999; Hayne, Herbert, & Simcock, 2003; Hudson & Sheffield, 1999). In Barr and Hayne (1999), for example, infants were shown a demonstration either live or on video. On one imitation task the 12-, 15-, and 18-month-olds imitated the live model after a 24-hour delay. In contrast, only 18-month-olds imitated the televised model, and their performance was inferior to that of the group who had seen the live model. On a different imitation task, 15-, 18-, 24-, and 30-month-old infants who saw a video model imitated significantly fewer actions than did infants who saw a live model when tested either immediately or after a 24-hour delay (Barr & Hayne, 1999; Hayne, Herbert, & Simcock, 2003). Imitation tasks reveal evidence of the video deficit until children are 3 years of age (Hayne, Herbert, & Simcock, 2003; Hudson & Sheffield, 1999; McCall, Parke, & Kavanaugh, 1977).

The *video deficit effect* is not task specific. The video deficit effect is also seen during emotion processing tasks. In a study by Mumme and Fernald (2003), infants were given unfamiliar objects (e.g., plastic valve) to explore. Next, they watched a videotape in which an actor responded in either a positive or negative manner to each of these objects. When given a second opportunity to play with the object, 12-month-olds avoided the object if they had seen the televised adult react negatively, and they showed increased exploration if they had seen the televised adult react positively. In contrast, 10-month-olds' behavior showed no impact of the televised adult's emotional reaction. The authors concluded that babies as young as 12 months old are capable of responding to emotional cues shown on television but 10-month-olds are not. It is important to note that 10-months-olds can use emotional cues from analogous live demonstrations.

The video deficit is also exhibited when children search for objects (Deocampo & Hudson, 2005; Schmitt & Anderson, 2002; Troseth, 2003; Troseth & DeLoache, 1998; Troseth, Pierroutsakos, & Deloache, 2004). Using a standardized paradigm, children are given an extensive orientation where they are shown the correspondence between a video representation of a room and an actual room. Then the experimenter goes into the room and hides a toy. The child views the toy being hidden on a television monitor in an adjacent room. Immediately after the toy is hidden, the child goes into the room and is asked to retrieve the hidden toy. Two-year-olds are unable to find the hidden toy, but 2.5-year-olds are successful (Troseth & DeLoache, 1998).

One explanation for these findings is that the sheer magnitude of change in size between the television monitor and the room where the object was hidden as well as the change in dimension from a 2D screen to a 3D real-world experience might be causing the poor performance. To test this hypothesis, Evans, Crawley, and Anderson (submitted) built a felt-board that was the same size as the television screen. Two-year-olds saw either a live model hide a sticker behind a felt object on the felt-board or saw a video model hide the same object on a television screen. Toddlers who viewed the live model found the sticker behind the felt object, but toddlers who saw the video model did not find the sticker.

Overall, the video deficit effect is exhibited across multiple different experimental paradigms by infants ranging from one year to three years of age. The ability of infants and toddlers to learn from media is reduced by the video deficit. Recently, however, researchers have investigated whether the video deficit effect can be ameliorated, and in so doing have uncovered potential mechanisms to explain the effect.

Reducing memory demands

Infants often see material repeatedly because of television programming content and video technology. Indeed, parents report that preschoolers frequently ask to view the same program repeatedly (Mares, 1998). Because comprehension of television content is cognitively demanding during early childhood, repetition allows for additional processing time which enhances comprehension of material. More specifically, repeated presentation of the same television episode maintains attention and increases comprehension of television content by preschoolers (Abelman, 1990; Anderson et al., 1981; Crawley et al., 1999; Sell, Ray, & Lovelace, 1995). For this reason, the same episodes of programs such as *Blues Clues* are aired multiple times per week.

Similar beneficial effects of repetition take place for infants. For example, vocabulary gains occur when infants repeatedly viewed *Sesame Street* videos or educational DVDs, but not when they viewed television programs only once (Linebarger, 2005). Barr and her colleagues (2007) found that repetition enhanced deferred imitation for 12- to 21-month-olds. In this study, infants exhibited the same level of deferred imitation after observing a live and a televised model if the number of demonstrations of the target actions presented on television was doubled. If the number of demonstrations of the target actions presented on video was not doubled, however, 21-month-olds continued to exhibit a video deficit effect (Barr et al., 2007).

When memory demands are decreased, 2-year-olds are also often successful in searching for objects. For example, if 2-year-olds thought that they were viewing the event through a window rather than on a television screen, the cognitive demands of transferring information from a 2D image to a 3D object were reduced and they were able to find a hidden toy (Troseth & DeLoache, 1998). If given extensive experience of seeing themselves on television, toddlers were able to find a hidden toy; presumably seeing themselves on a screen increased their understanding that information presented on a television could represent real-world events (Troseth, 2003).

Toddlers may also exhibit a video deficit if a toy is hidden in more than one location, presumably because they are unable to change their representation of where the toy is hidden initially, a working memory limitation. That is, 2-year-olds find a toy on trial one and this is very memorable to them. They view a second hiding location, but when they return to the room they perseverate and look again in the original hiding place because the memory representation formed from finding a real object is stronger than that formed when viewing a 2D hiding demonstration. They fail to update their memory representations. Suddendorf (2003) tested this working memory hypothesis. He predicted that if the memory demands were reduced such that memory updating was not necessary, then 2-year-olds would be able to find a toy after viewing it hidden on television. Consistent with his hypothesis, performance remained high if toddlers were tested in four different rooms rather than being tested repeatedly in the same room (Suddendorf, 2003).

Formal features

During early childhood, attention increases in the presence of a perceptually salient formal feature such as a sound effect because it elicits a primitive orienting response, thereby improving comprehension of contiguously presented content (Calvert, et al., 1982; Huston & Wright, 1983). Such formal features could be used to provide an entry point for very young children's viewing. That is, features like sound effects could be used to assist very young children's attention to, and imitation of, targeted content.

Initial studies of imitation from television (Barr & Hayne, 1999; Hayne, Herbert, & Simcock, 2003; Hudson & Sheffield, 1999; McCall, Parke, & Kavanaugh, 1977; Meltzoff, 1988) failed to incorporate common attention-capturing features into their televised segments. Recently, however, Somanader, Garcia, Miller, and Barr (2005) examined whether adding sound effects would enhance imitation from television by 6- and 12-month-old infants. Infants were assigned to one of three conditions: matched sound effects (salient sound effects timed to each target action), mismatched sound effects (deliberately mismatched to the target actions), or no salient formal features. We hypothesized that infants may initially orient to salient formal features but with experience may learn to use these features as markers of important content (Calvert et al., 1982; Huston & Wright, 1983). Consistent with this prediction, young 6-month-olds exhibited deferred imitation of the target actions regardless of whether the sound effects were matched or mismatched to the target actions. In contrast, 1-year-olds imitated target actions from television when the sound effects were matched to the target actions but performed at baseline when the target actions and sound effects were deliberately out of synch with the target actions. That is, mismatching sound effects that commonly convey informational content interfered with performance by 12-month-olds, presumably because they expected the sound to match up with an important visual event; such expectations did not seem to exist for the younger 6-month-old infants. There are a number of formal features, including zooms, cuts, music, and pacing, that are part of infant-directed programming that have received no empirical research at this point.

Social contingency

During live interactions, social partners engage in contingent ongoing behaviors with one another. For example, when one partner asks a question, he/she pauses and waits until the other social partner responds. It has been argued that the lack of such social contingency is the critical factor missing from televised information. Consistent with that argument, research with older toddlers and preschoolers has demonstrated that the lack of contingency and control reduces interactivity and comprehension of video material (Calvert, Strong, & Gallagher, 2005; Crawley et al., 1999; Troseth, 2003; Troseth, Saylor, & Archer, 2006).

Troseth and colleagues (2006) hypothesized that increasing social contingency would improve learning from television. Toddlers in a contingent condition interacted with an experimenter across a close-circuit television screen for 5 minutes. At the end of the interaction, the experimenter told children where they could find the hidden toy in the room next door and asked them to go and find it. Toddlers in the non-contingent control group watched pre-taped social interactions that were not contingent upon their behavior. The 2-year-olds who received contingent feedback were significantly more likely to find the hidden toy than were the toddlers who had seen a pre-taped non-contingent interaction. Troseth, Saylor, and Archer (2006) concluded that during the second year of life, toddlers increasingly expect to obtain relevant information from a contingent social partner. Lack of contingency during the televised demonstration disrupts the transfer of information from television to real-life activities.

Language: grammar and vocabulary

Live social interaction is necessary for processing complex grammatical structures of a language (Kuhl, Tsao, & Liu, 2003; Naigles & Mayeux, 2001). Kuhl and colleagues (2003) tested 9-month-olds for learning of a phonetic discrimination present only in Mandarin after the infants had interacted with a native Mandarin speaker for a total of 4 hours over 12 sessions. Typically native English speakers at 9 months of age and even as adults cannot make the distinction between the two sounds, but native Mandarin speakers at both ages can. After brief exposure to live interactions, the 9-month-olds were able to make the distinction, but if the information was presented on television, they were not.

Vocabulary learning is also more effective from a live interaction than from a video demonstration for 15- to 24-month-olds (Grela, Krcmar, & Lin, 2004). Other language studies have indicated, however, that vocabulary learning can be facilitated by specific content during infancy and preschool (Barr, 2006; Linebarger & Walker, 2005; Rice et al., 1990). Linebarger and Walker (2005) followed infants longitudinally from 6 to 30 months and recorded television exposure and vocabulary acquisition growth curves as a function of specific media exposure. The researchers found that positive vocabulary growth was associated with content that had strong narratives (e.g., *Clifford, Arthur*) and interactive components (e.g., *Blues Clues*). In a recent experimental study, Barr (2006) examined whether infants would apply novel labels to objects if the labels were presented on television or if they were presented by parents. Two-year-olds were randomly assigned to a voiceover video group, a parent-mediated video group, a parent-mediated live group, or a baseline condition. Infants in all three experimental conditions imitated significantly more target actions than did those in the baseline control condition and there were no differences between the experimental conditions. That is, 2-year-olds were able to apply novel labels regardless of whether the television or a parent provided the label. Whether such labeling is similarly effective at younger ages is not known (Hayne & Herbert, 2004).

Theoretical explanations

There are two primary, but not mutually exclusive, theories to account for the video deficit effect. The first is termed the perceptual impoverishment hypothesis, and the second is the dual representation hypothesis. The perceptual impoverishment hypothesis accounts for the video deficit in the following way: because the 2D perceptual input is impoverished relative to a real 3D presentation, learning is impaired (Barr & Hayne, 1999; Schmitt & Anderson, 2002; Suddendorf, 2003). Johnson (e.g., Johnson & Aslin, 1996; Johnson, 1997) has proposed that the perceptual system requires a minimum amount of information for perception regardless of its source (e.g., 2D or 3D stimuli). Studies using 2D stimuli have demonstrated that younger infants require information from more sources to form an object percept than older infants do (Johnson, 1997, 2000). Similarly, a 2D presentation may not match its 3D counterpart until a sufficient number of attributes are available to match from 2D to 3D (see Smith, 2000, for a similar argument regarding language acquisition).

Data collected from imitation studies is consistent with the perceptual impoverishment hypothesis. Between 1 and 2.5 years of age, infants exhibit a video deficit effect, but by 3 years it disappears. Furthermore, some situations can increase performance; these include additional information provided by repetition (Barr et al., 2007), the signaling of crucial information through formal features (Somander et al., 2005), a change in rooms to reduce memory load (Suddendorf, 2003), the inclusion of social contingency (Troseth, Saylor, & Archer, 2006) and the addition of language cues (Barr, 2006).

According to the dual representation hypothesis, the video deficit effect may be due to an emerging ability to use symbols and to treat televised images differently than real objects (Barr & Hayne, 1999; DeLoache, 1995; Pierroutsakos & Troseth, 2003; Troseth, Pierroutsakos, & DeLoache, 2004). DeLoache and colleagues have investigated children's ability to perceive and understand the nature of pictures (both moving and static images) and to act upon that knowledge by exploring infants' manual responses to 2D images (for review, see Troseth, Pierroutsakos, & DeLoache, 2004). Pierroutsakos and Troseth (2003) found that 9-month-olds treated the high-resolution video images as if they were real objects, manually exploring the toys presented on video, rubbing them and attempting to pick them up. By 19 months of age, the reaching behavior had been replaced by pointing; 15-month-olds were intermediate between the two.

DeLoache and colleagues argue that the change between 9- and 19-months is due to experience exploring 2D and 3D objects. Beginning around 5 months of age, when reaching develops and independent manual exploration begins, infants treat images and objects in very similar ways, attempting to explore both as physical objects to determine their properties. Over time, infants come to recognize the different functional properties of 2D and 3D objects. For example, a ball can bounce but a picture of a ball does not. Based on this acquired knowledge, 1- to 2.5-year-olds fail to use 2D information presented by the image to inform behavior in the 3D world. In other words, children learn to disregard the possible informational content of pictures and television. Some time during the third year of life, children master dual representation and can understand that a picture provides meaningful information that can be acted upon in the real world. The video deficit effect disappears. At this stage, children can represent the image of the picture both as an object and as a symbol for the real object and thus transfer of information can occur.

Taken together, these findings suggest that understanding the symbolic nature of media develops slowly across early childhood. Clearly perceptual processing and memory demands, as well as social contingency and symbolic processing limitations, contribute to reduced ability to learn from television during early childhood. Neither perceptual impoverishment theory nor dual representation theory accounts for all the current findings, suggesting a need for the integration of the two major competing theories.

Conclusions and Implications: The AAP Recommendation

The long-term effects of early media exposure on social and cognitive development are largely unknown. Although the American Academy of Pediatrics recommended that infants and toddlers have limited exposure to television, the amount of programming targeted to very young children has increased dramatically, and television exposure during infancy has increased accordingly. As parents are being told to avoid exposing their infants to screen media, they may also feel pressures to ensure that their children are media literate.

The negative effects of background television exposure on play and the fact that infants learn less from television than from live demonstrations underscore the limitations on what infants can gain from media exposure. Even so, the fact that repeated exposure to televised segments enhances imitation and language learning, and the growing evidence of the beneficial effects of television on older children suggest that television has potential to provide positive and cost-effective benefits during early childhood.

Based on our limited state of knowledge about the costs and potential benefits of very early television exposure, the current AAP recommendation of no television for children under 2 remains premature. Yet there is no doubt that infant development now occurs, in part, in the company of screen media. The types of early screen exposure that are potentially beneficial or harmful remain important questions to be unraveled by future research.

References

Abelman, R. (1990). You can't get there from here: Children's understanding of time-leaps on television. *Journal of Broadcasting and Electronic Media*, 34, 469–76.

Acevedo-Polakovich, I., Lorch, E. P., Milich, R., & Ashby, R. D. (2006). Disentangling the relation between television viewing and cognitive processes in children with attention-deficit/hyperactivity disorder and comparison children. *Archives of Pediatric Adolescent Medicine*, 160, 354–60.

Alwitt, L. F., Anderson, D. R., Lorch, E. P., & Levin, S. R. (1980). Preschool children's visual attention to attributes of television. *Human Communications Research*, 7, 52–67.

American Academy of Pediatrics (AAP). (1999). Media Education. *Pediatrics*, 104(2), 341–3.

Anderson, D. R., & Burns, J. J. (1991). Paying attention to television. In J. Bryant & D. Zillmann (Eds.), *Responding to the screen: Perception and reaction processes* (pp. 3–26). Hillsdale, NJ: Lawrence Erlbaum.

Anderson, D. R., Huston, A. C., Schmitt, K. L., Linebarger, D. L., & Wright, J. C. (2001). Early childhood television viewing and adolescent behavior: The recontact study. *Monographs of the Society for Research in Child Development*, 66(1).

Anderson, D. R., & Levin, S. R. (1976). Young children's attention to "Sesame Street." *Child Development*, 47, 806–11.

Anderson, D. R., Lorch, E. P., Field, D. E., Collins, P. A., & Nathan, J. G. (1986). Television viewing at home: Age trends in visual attention and time with TV. *Child Development*, 57, 1024–33.

Anderson, D. R., Lorch, E. P., Field, D. E., & Sanders, J. (1981). The effects of TV program comprehensibility on preschool children's visual attention to television. *Child Development*, 52(1), 151–7.

Anderson, D. R., & Pempek, T. (2005). Television and very young children. *American Behavioral Scientist*, 48, 505–22.

Bandura, A. (1965). Influence of models' reinforcement contingencies on the acquisition and performance of imitative responses. *Journal of Personality and Social Psychology*, 1(6), 589–95.

Bandura, A., Ross, D., & Ross, S. A. (1963). Imitation of film-mediated aggressive models. *Journal of Abnormal and Social Psychology*, 66, 3–11.

Barr, R. (2006). *Toddlers apply language learned from television: Reenactment of televised content by 2-year-olds.* Paper presented at the International Society for the Study of Behavioral Development, Melbourne, Australia.

Barr, R., Garcia, A., & Muentener, P. (in press). Age-related changes in deferred imitation from television by 6- to 18-month-olds. *Developmental Science*.

Barr, R., & Hayne, H. (1999). Developmental changes in imitation from television during infancy. *Child Development*, 70(5), 1067–81.

Barr, R., & Hayne, H. (2000). Age-related changes in imitation: Implications for memory development. In C. Rovee-Collier, L. P. Lipsitt, & H. Hayne (Eds.), *Progress in infancy research*, vol. 1 (pp. 21–67). Hillsdale, NJ: Lawrence Erlbaum.

Barr, R., Muentener, P., Garcia, A., Chávez, V., & Fujimoto, M. (2007). The effect of repetition on imitation from television during infancy. *Developmental Psychobiology*, 49, 196–207.

Barr, R., Zack, E., Garcia, A., & Muentener, P. (in press). Infant attention to television is influenced by prior exposure and parent scaffolding. *Infancy*.

Butterworth, G. (2001). Joint visual attention in infancy. In G. B. A. Fogel (Ed.), *Blackwell handbook of infant development* (pp. 213–40). Madden, MA: Blackwell Publishers.

Calvert, S. (2006). Media and early development. In K. McCartney & D. Phillips (Eds.), *Blackwell handbook of early childhood development* (pp. 508–30). Madden, MA: Blackwell Publishing.

Calvert, S. L., Huston, A. C., Watkins, B. A., & Wright, J. C. (1982). The relation between selective attention to television forms and children's comprehension of content. *Child Development*, 53, 601–10.

Calvert, S. L., Rideout, V., Woolard, J., Barr, R., & Strouse, G. (2005). Age, ethnicity, and socioeconomic patterns in early computer use: A national survey. *American Behavioral Scientist*, 48, 590–607.

Calvert, S. L., & Scott, M. C. (1989). Sound effects for children's temporal integration of fast-paced television content. *Journal of Broadcasting and Electronic Media*, 33, 233–46.

Calvert, S. L., Strong, B., & Gallagher, L. (2005). Control as an engagement feature for young children's attention to and learning of computer content. *American Behavioral Scientist*, 48, 578–89.

Carver, L. J., Meltzoff, A. N., & Dawson, G. (2006). Event-related potential (ERP) indices of infants' recognition of familiar and unfamiliar objects in two and three dimensions. *Developmental Science*, 9(1), 51–62.

Christakis, D. A., Zimmerman, F. J., DiGiuseppe, D. L., & McCarty, C. A. (2004). Early television exposure and subsequent attentional problems in children. *Pediatrics*, 113, 708–13.

Clifton, R. K., & Nelson, M. N. (1976). Developmental study of habituation in infants: The importance of paradigm, response system, and state. In T. R. N. Leaton (Ed.), *Habituation* (pp. 159–205). Hillsdale, NJ: Lawrence Erlbaum.

Colombo, J., Mitchell, D., Coldren, J. T., & Freeseman, L. J. (1991). Individual differences in infant visual attention: Are short lookers faster processors or feature processors? *Child Development*, 62, 1247–57.

Courage, M. L., Reynolds, G. D., & Richards, J. E. (2006). Infants' attention to patterned stimuli: Developmental change from 3 to 12 months of age. *Child Development*, 77, 680–95.

Crawley, A. M., Anderson, D. R., Wilder, A., Williams, M., & Santomero, A. (1999). Effects of repeated exposures to a single episode of the television program *Blue's Clues* on the viewing behaviors and comprehension of preschool children. *Journal of Educational Psychology*, 91, 630–37.

DeLoache, J. S. (1995). Early understanding and use of symbols: The model model. *Current Directions in Psychological Science*, 4(4), 109–13.

DeLoache, J. S., & DeMendoza, O. A. (1987). Joint picturebook interactions of mothers and 1-year-old children. *British Journal of Developmental Psychology*, 5(2), 111–23.

Deocampo, J. A., & Hudson, J. A. (2005). When seeing is not believing: Two-year-olds' use of video representations to find a hidden toy. *Journal of Cognition and Development*, 6, 229–58.

Evans, M. K., Crawley, A. M., & Anderson, D. R. (submitted). Two year olds' object retrieval based on television: Testing a perceptual account. *Submitted for publication.*

Evans-Schmidt, M., Pempek, T. A., Kirkorian, H. L., Frankenfield, L. A., & Anderson, D. R. (submitted). The effects of background television on the toy play behavior of very young children. *Submitted for publication.*

Field, D. E., & Anderson, D. R. (1985). Instruction and modality effects on children's attention and comprehension. *Child Development*, 77, 91–100.

Fletcher, K. L., & Reese, E. (2005). Picture book reading with young children: A conceptual framework. *Developmental Review*, 25, 64–103.

Garrison, M., & Christakis, D. A. (2005). *A teacher in the living room: Educational media for babies, toddlers, and preschoolers.* Menlo Park, CA: Kaiser Family Foundation.

Grela, B. G., Krcmar, M., & Lin, Y. J. (2004). Can television help toddlers acquire new words? Retrieved from http://www.speechpathology.com/articles/article_detail.asp?article_id=72.

Haith, M. M., Hazan, C., & Goodman, G. S. (1988). Expectation and anticipation of dynamic visual events by 3.5-month-old babies. *Child Development*, 59, 467–79.

Hayne, H., & Herbert, J. (2004). Verbal cues facilitate memory retrieval during infancy. *Journal of Experimental Child Psychology*, 89, 127–39.

Hayne, H., Herbert, J., & Simcock, G. (2003). Imitation from television by 24- and 30-month-olds. *Developmental Science*, 6, 254–61.

Hollenbeck, A. R., & Slaby, R. G. (1979). Infant visual and vocal responses to television. *Child Development*, 50, 41–5.

Huang, C., & Charman, T. (2005). Gradations of emulation learning in infants' imitation of actions and objects. *Journal of Experimental Child Psychology*, 92(3), 276–302.

Hudson, J. A., & Sheffield, E. G. (1999). The role of reminders in young children's memory development. In C. S. Tamis-LeMonda & L. Balter (Eds.), *Child psychology: A handbook of contemporary issues* (pp. 193–214). New York: Psychology Press.

Huston, A. C., & Wright, J. C. (1983). Children's processing of television: The informative functions of formal features. In J. Bryant & D. R. Anderson (Eds.), *Children's understanding of television: Research on attention and comprehension* (pp. 35–68). New York: Academic Press.

Huston-Stein, A. C., & Wright, J. C. (1979). Children and television: Effects of the medium, its content, and its form. *Journal of Research and Development in Education*, 13, 20–31.

Johnson, S. P. (1997). Young infants' perception of object unity: Implications for development of attentional and cognitive skills. *Current Directions in Psychological Science*, 6, 5–11.

Johnson, S. P. (2000). The development of visual surface perception: Insights into the ontogeny of knowledge. In C. Rovee-Collier, L. P. Lipsitt, & H. Hayne (Eds.), *Progress in Infancy Research*, vol. 1 (pp. 113–54). Mahwah, NJ: Lawrence Erlbaum.

Johnson, S. P., & Aslin, R. (1996). Perception of object unity in young infants: the roles of motion, depth, and orientation. *Cognitive Development*, 11, 161–80.

Kirkorian, H. L., Anderson, D. R., Evans-Schmidt, M., & Pempek, T. A. (2005). *TV and Toddlers.* Paper presented at the Society for Research on Child Development, Atlanta, GA.

Kuhl, P. K., & Meltzoff, A. N. (1982). The bimodal perception of speech in infancy. *Science*, 218, 1138–41.

Kuhl, P. K., Tsao, F., & Liu, H. (2003). Foreign language experience in infancy: Effects of short term exposure and interaction on phonetic learning. *Proceedings of the National Academy of Sciences*, 100, 9096–101.

Lemish, D. (1987). Viewers in diapers: The early development of television viewing. In T. R. Lindlof (Ed.), *Natural audiences: Qualitative research of media uses and its effects* (pp. 33–57). Norwood, NJ: Ablex.

Lemish, D., & Rice, M. L. (1986). Television as a talking picture book: a prop for language acquisition. *Journal of Child Language*, 13, 251–74.

Linebarger, D. L. (2005). *Infants' and toddlers' video and on-air viewing and language development*. Paper presented at the Society for Research on Child Development, Atlanta, GA.

Linebarger, D. L., & Walker, D. (2005). Infants' and toddlers' television viewing and language outcomes. *American Behavioral Scientist*, 48, 624–45.

Lorch, E. P. (1994). Measuring children's cognitive processing of television. In A. Lang (Ed.), *Measuring psychological responses to media messages* (pp. 209–26). Hillsdale, NJ: Lawrence Erlbaum.

Lorch, E. P., Anderson, D. R., & Levin, S. R. (1979). The relationship between visual attention and children's comprehension of television. *Child Development*, 50, 722–7.

Lorch, E. P., & Castle, V. J. (1997). Preschool children's attention to television: Visual attention and probe response times. *Journal of Experimental Child Psychology*, 66, 111–27.

Mares, M. L. (1998). Children's use of VCRs. *Annals of the American Academy of Political and Social Science*, 557, 120–31.

McCall, R. B., Parke, R. D., & Kavanaugh, R. D. (1977). Imitation of live and televised models by children one to three years of age. *Monographs of the Society for Research in Child Development*, 42(5).

Meltzoff, A. N. (1988). Imitation of televised models by infants. *Child Development*, 59, 1221–9.

Mumme, D. L., & Fernald, A. (2003). The infant as onlooker: learning from emotional reactions observed in a television scenario. *Child Development*, 74, 221–37.

Naigles, L. R., & Mayeux, L. (2001). Television as an incidental language teacher. In D. G. Singer & J. L. Singer (Ed.), *Handbook of children and the media* (pp. 135–52). Thousand Oaks, CA: Sage.

Paik, H., & Comstock, G. (1994). The effects of television violence on antisocial behavior: A meta-analysis. *Communication Research*, 21, 516–46.

Pierroutsakos, S. L., & Troseth, G. L. (2003). Video verite: Infants' manual investigation of objects on video. *Infant Behavior and Development*, 26, 183–99.

Raikes, H., Pan, B. A., Luze, G., Tamis-LeMonda, C. S., Brooks-Gunn, J., Constantine, J., et al. (2006). Mother-child bookreading in low income families: Correlates and outcomes during the first three years of life. *Child Development*, 77(4), 925–53.

Rice, M. L., Huston, A. C., Truglio, R., & Wright, J. C. (1990). Words from *Sesame Street* – learning vocabulary while viewing. *Developmental Psychology*, 26, 421–8.

Rice, M. L., Huston, A. C., & Wright, J. C. (1982). The forms of television: Effects on children's attention, comprehension, and social behavior. In L. B. D. Pearl & J. Lazar (Eds.), *Television and behavior: Ten years of scientific progress and implications for the eighties*. Washington, DC: US Government Printing Office.

Richards, J. E., & Anderson, D. R. (2004). Attentional inertia in children's extended looking at television. In R. V. Kail (Ed.), *Advances in child development and behavior*, vol. 32 (pp. 163–212). San Diego, CA: Elsevier Academic Press.

Richards, J. E., & Casey, B. J. (1992). Development of sustained visual attention in the human infant. In B. A. Campbell, H. Hayne, & R. Richardson (Eds.), *Attention and information processing in infants and adults: Perspectives from human and animal research* (pp. 30–60). New York: Lawrence Erlbaum.

Richards, J. E., & Cronise, K. (2000). Extended visual fixation in the early preschool years: Look duration, heart rate changes, and attentional inertia. *Child Development*, 71, 602–20.

Richards, J. E., & Gibson, T. L. (1997). Extended visual fixation in young infants: Look distributions, heart rate changes, and attention. *Child Development*, 68, 1041–56.

Richards, J. E., & Turner, E. D. (2001). Extended visual attention and distractibility in children from six to twenty-four months of age. *Child Development*, 72, 963–72.

Rideout, V., & Hamel, E. (2006). *The media family: Electronic media in the lives of infants, toddlers, preschoolers and their parents*. Menlo Park, CA: Kaiser Family Foundation.

Rideout, V., Vandewater, E., & Wartella, E. A. (2003). *Zero to six: Electronic media in the lives of infants, toddlers, and preschoolers*. Menlo Park, CA: Kaiser Family Foundation.

Rolandelli, D. R., Wright, J. C., Huston, A. C., & Eakins, D. (1991). Children's auditory and visual processing of narrated and nonnarrated television programming. *Journal of Experimental Child Psychology*, 51, 90–122.

Ruff, H., Capozzoli, M., & Weissberg, R. (1998). Age, individuality, and context as factors in sustained visual attention during the preschool years. *Developmental Psychology*, 34, 454–64.

Schmitt, K. L., & Anderson, D. R. (2002). Television and reality: Toddlers' use of visual information from video to guide behavior. *Media Psychology*, 4, 51–76.

Schmitt, K. L., Anderson, D. R., & Collins, P. A. (1999). Form and content: Looking at visual features of television. *Developmental Psychology*, 35, 1156–67.

Sell, M. A., Ray, G. E., & Lovelace, L. (1995). Preschool children's comprehension of a *Sesame Street* video tape: The effects of repeated viewing and previewing instructions. *Educational Technology Research and Development*, 43, 49–60.

Smith, L. B. (2000). From knowledge to knowing: Real progress in the study of infant categorization. *Infancy*, 1, 91–7.

Smith, R., Anderson, D. R., & Fischer, C. (1985). Young children's comprehension of montage. *Child Development*, 56, 962–71.

Somanader, M., Garcia, A., Miller, N., & Barr, R. (2005). *Effects of sound effects and music on imitation from television during infancy*. Paper presented at the Society for Research on Child Development, Atlanta, GA.

Stein, A. H., & Friedrich, L. K. (1972). Television content and young children's behavior. In J. P. Murray, E. A. Rubenstein, & G. A. Comstock (Eds.), *Television and social learning*, vol. 2 (pp. 202–317). Washington, DC: US Government Printing Office.

Stevens, T., & Muslow, M. (2006). There is no meaningful relationship between television exposure and symptoms of attention-deficit/hyperactivity disorder. *Pediatrics*, 117, 665–72.

Suddendorf, T. (2003). Early representational insight: Twenty-four-month-olds can use a photo to find an object in the world. *Child Development*, 74, 896–904.

Thakkar, R. R., Garrison, M., & Christakis, D. A. (2006). A systematic review for the effects of television viewing by infants and preschoolers. *Pediatrics*, 118, 2025–31.

Thompson, D. A., & Christakis, D. A. (2005). The association between television viewing and irregular sleep schedules among children less than 3 years of age. *Pediatrics*, 116, 851–6.

Thompson, R. F., & Spencer, W. A. (1966). A model phenomenon for the study of neuronal substrates of behavior. *Psychological Review*, 73, 16–43.

Troseth, G. L. (2003). TV guide: two-year-old children learn to use video as a source of information. *Developmental Psychology*, 39, 140–50.

Troseth, G. L., & DeLoache, J. S. (1998). The medium can obscure the message: Young children's understanding of video. *Child Development*, 69, 950–65.

Troseth, G. L., Pierroutsakos, S. L., & Deloache, J. S. (2004). From the innocent to the intelligent eye: The early development of pictorial competence. In R. V. Kail (Ed.), *Advances in child development and behavior*, vol. 32 (pp. 1–35). San Diego, CA: Elsevier Academic Press.

Troseth, G. L., Saylor, M. M., & Archer, A. H. (2006). Young children's use of video as a source of socially relevant information. *Child Development*, 77, 786–99.

Vandewater, E. A., Bickham, D. S., & Lee, J. H. (2006). Time well spent? Relating television use to children's free-time activities. *Pediatrics*, 117, 181–91.

Vandewater, E. A., Park, S. E., Huang, X., & Wartella, E. A. (2005). "No – You Can't Watch That": Parental rules and young children's media use. *American Behavioral Scientist*, 48, 608–23.

Vygotsky, L. S. (1978). *Mind and society: The development of higher mental processes*. Cambridge, MA: Harvard University Press.

Zimmerman, F. J., Christakis, D. A., & Meltzoff, A. (2007). Television and DVD/video viewing by children 2 years and younger. *Archives of Pediatric and Adolescent Medicine*, 161, 1–7.

Zimmerman, F. J., Glew, G. M., Christakis, D. A., & Katon, W. (2005). Early cognitive stimulation, emotional support, and television watching as predictors of subsequent bullying among grade-school children. *Archives of Pediatric Adolescent Medicine*, 159, 384–8.

8

Media Symbol Systems and Cognitive Processes

Kaveri Subrahmanyam and Patricia Greenfield

Tools have played a central role in human evolution. The stone tools of pre-historic man, the machine tools of the industrial revolution, and recent computerized and digital tools, have all driven changes in human behavior in the era in which they appeared. Tools, particularly mental ones, have played an important role in developmental theory – on the Vygotskian view, psychological tools (i.e., language, mathematics) provided by the culture lead to the emergence of higher mental functions. Elsewhere we have argued (Maynard, Subrahmanyam, & Greenfield, 2005) that the particular tools provided by the culture – be they the back strap loom or the computer – elicit and develop particular sets of cognitive skills.

Media, which are the focus of this book, are first and foremost tools provided by the culture, and our central concern is their influence on our thinking and learning. When considering media as tools, it is important to distinguish between the physical platform or hardware (i.e., the television set, computer, or videogame system), formal features (i.e., audiovisual production features that characterize a medium), and the content (i.e., the topic or focus of a television program or software program) within it (Calvert et al., 1982; Wright & Huston, 1983). The hardware aspects are akin to physical tools and are not the focus of this chapter. The formal features are independent of content and are akin to a language, which is a psychological tool and a symbol system. Just as the words of a language are symbols that a listener has to decode, the formal features of media consist of symbol systems that the user has to decode to understand the message. The content is the material or message conveyed by the formal features, for example, a particular story, as well as the words and actions of the characters in the story. We start by presenting the theoretical framework of our analysis and then examine the formal features of each medium to understand their influence on cognitive processes.

Theoretical Framework

According to Olson and Bruner, "each form of experience, including the various symbolic systems tied to the media, produces a unique pattern of skills for dealing with or thinking about the world. It is the skills in these systems that we call intelligence" (Olson & Bruner, 1974, p. 149). We draw on this line of reasoning as we focus on the symbol systems of older media such as print, radio, and television, as well as the newer media forms such as videogames and Internet interfaces; we will show how the symbolic systems used in different media forms influence cognitive skills.

The theoretical premise of this chapter is that using a particular tool set develops the cognitive skills that are part of a group's implicit definition of intelligence (Greenfield, 1998). Different cultural or ecological niches provide different tools and these different tools not only utilize, but also develop particular sets of cognitive skills. Most importantly, from the perspective of this paper, is the idea that tools evolve and change over time. These changes in cultural tools are accompanied by changes in the cognitive skills and valued forms of intelligence within that ecological niche (Maynard, Subrahmanyam, & Greenfield, 2005). In this view, we should expect changes in cognitive processes and skills as media forms have evolved and changed – from print to radio, television, and, more recently, the Internet. This is the heart of our developmental idea – that different media forms develop different cognitive skills.

Here we examine cognition at two different levels – attention and representation. Almost a hundred years ago, William James defined attention as the focusing of the mind on some aspects of the sensory input over others (James, 1890), a concept known as selective attention. Representation concerns the internal mental encoding of objects and events (e.g., Piaget, 1951). Information about the world can be encoded in many different ways such as auditory, linguistic, visual/iconic, and motor/enactive representations. For example, a simple object such as a ball can be represented by a verbal description of what it is and what one can do with it, a visual/iconic representation of what it looks like, a motor/enactive representation of the action/s one can perform with it, or an auditory representation of what it sounds like when it bounces.

Bruner (1965) has distinguished three different kinds of representation which appear in a developmental order: enactive – representation through action; iconic – representation through images that resemble their referent; and symbolic – representation through symbols that bear no resemblance to their referent, are arbitrary, and are therefore established by social agreement or convention. Because Bruner was referring to the child's ways of representing the world, it can be difficult to apply the developmental ordering to media. However, the general ideas that different modes of representation can be used to symbolize the same content and that different kinds of representations can be at different developmental levels are important for understanding the role of representation in mediated experience and cognitive development. These ideas are central to our developmental theory, to which we now turn.

A new developmental theory of media understanding and use

We propose that the more real-world perceptual and cognitive cues a media representation makes available, the less mental transformation it will require and the earlier it will become accessible and usable to a child. This is really an extension of Piaget's emphasis on mental transformation as a hallmark of cognitive development. In line with this basic idea, prior research (e.g., Wright & Huston, 1983) suggests that the information delivered in different media forms may become accessible at different developmental periods depending on the particular representational systems they employ and the user's level of representational development. Taken together this means that there likely will be developmental trends in the internalization of the symbol form presented in a medium. In this view, television, which preserves the static and dynamic cues of the real world as well as its sounds, may be more appropriate for the very youngest children; picture books, which contain less realistic iconic representations in mainly static forms and, in their pure form, no sound, may be more appropriate for slightly older preschool and school-aged children; and books with only printed text – an arbitrary symbolic representational form bearing no physical relation to the real world – may be most appropriate for older children and adolescents. These developmental ideas can apply not just to chronological age ordering, but can also predict the degree of effort involved in using a particular medium. In particular, the more real-world cues and the less mental transformation involved in using and processing a mediated representation, the less effort to use and the more "natural" the use will seem.

Individual differences In addition to developmental trends, we also speculate that there will be individual differences in preferences for different media forms given the evidence that there are individual differences in processing style (e.g., Childers, Houston, & Heckler, 1985). Of relevance to us is Richardson's (1977) visualizer/verbalizer distinction, which captures individual preferences for processing words versus pictures and images. Accordingly we expect that individuals or groups of individuals who prefer to process certain symbol forms (e.g., verbal versus visual) will prefer media that incorporate those representations.

Representational competence The recognition that different modes of representation can be used to symbolize a common referent constitutes the skill of representational competence as defined by Sigel and Cocking (1977). Simply put, representational competence is involved when we grasp that stick figures and photographs are both two-dimensional representations of three-dimensional individuals. However, the idea that meaning is conserved across transformations of medium (Sigel, 1993) is only partially true. While reference may remain constant, meaning changes in the translation of content from one medium to another (Greenfield, 1993). A dramatic play broadcast over radio might draw attention to a character's words and the emotions conveyed in those words; in contrast, the same play broadcast over television might draw attention to the very same character's physical appearance and actions, leading to different meanings or interpretations (Greenfield & Beagles-Roos, 1988).

Sigel also introduces the notion of psychological distancing as one dimension of representational competence. He uses the term to refer to "a class of cognitive demands that serve to activate a separation of self cognitively from the here and now" (Sigel, 1993, p. 142). He continues, "Irrespective of the context in which it is used, the meaning of distancing is similar, namely, the interposing of physical and/or psychological space between the person and the event" (Sigel, 1993, p. 142). This notion of psychological distance between the self and the here-and-now event is very relevant to developing human beings operating in interactive virtual environments and is illustrated in the distance between users and their virtual representations such as nicknames and avatars. We will come back to this concept in relation to online multiplayer games.

Internalization of media forms   Another theoretical piece is Salomon's (1979) idea that the symbol forms found in media, such as a computer, can become internalized mental representations for the user. A related theoretical idea comes from Bandura's (2001) social cognitive theory. According to Bandura, observational learning from mass communication is governed by cognitive representational processes; retention of modeled information occurs when the observer symbolically transforms modeled information into memory codes, and when recall involves the reconstruction of the coded information.

Greenfield (1993) coined the term cognitive socialization to refer to the internalization process by which cultural tools influence the development of processing skills; in this view media are important tools of cognitive socialization. It is important to remember that media differ in the symbol systems that they utilize and thus each medium has its own strengths and weaknesses in terms of the information that it presents (Greenfield, 1984). These differences result in subtle transformations of meaning. That is, when content is transferred from one medium to another, meaning is only partially conserved. For instance, television utilizes both auditory and visual symbol systems whereas print uses text and pictures. What do these different theoretical ideas predict about media symbol systems and their influence on cognitive skills? Salomon's work (1979) leads us to expect that the way a particular medium represents information will provide opportunities for different kinds of representational processes and skills.

Relation between Medium, Attentional Skills, and Representational Competence

In the next sections, we analyze the particular representational processes utilized by a medium and then provide evidence that the medium enables the construction of those kinds of representational skills. Note that we are talking about internalization of symbol systems rather than the learning of content. Where available, we present evidence that bolsters our claims about the developmental appropriateness of different media forms and individual differences.

We start with the oldest medium, print, then turn to radio, television/movies, and finally computers and the Internet. For our purposes, it is not necessary to distinguish different physical platforms (for example, we consider the DVD to be a particular platform for delivering movies); a movie utilizes the same representational codes and content whether it is delivered via a DVD or on a computer or seen in a movie theater. On the other hand, each medium is not totally separate either, but relates historically and representationally to other media. Thus, radio utilized the verbal aspect of print, but replaced the symbolic medium of print with that of spoken language. Television encompassed the verbal and sound environment of radio, but added moving images. Computers encompassed all of these prior media and added interactivity. In terms of Bruner's modes of representation, print and radio are similar in being mainly symbolic media. However, radio adds non-verbal sound elements such as music, sound effects, and intonation, while print can add pictures and diagrams.

Print

While print is older as a medium than electronic media, its lack of resemblance to the real-world stimuli – people, objects, and events – it is used to represent, makes it appear much later in development. Children typically learn to read around age 6, years after they can process the representations of television or even a simple videogame. But print itself also occurs in different formats. According to Kozma (1991), books employ the symbol systems of text and pictures; importantly the orthographic symbols that are used for text are stable – in English, text is placed horizontally from left to right and goes top to bottom. The stability of the symbols used in books is an important feature that distinguishes it from other technologies that also use these orthographic symbols; for instance the moving ticker tape on the television screen or on the Internet allows both text and pictures/images to be either static or dynamic. Kozma points out that the stability of books contrasts with other media such as lectures or audiotapes, which provide the same linguistic information but use different symbol systems in a transient, dynamic format.

Because books have been around human life for at least the past thousand years, they are taken for granted. Therefore, one does not see research examining the effect of its symbol systems on verbal representational skills in the same way that we have seen research on the effects of television and the computer. So we draw on research from other relevant areas to speculate about their influence on representational competence. Firstly, we know from research on early childhood education (Teale & Suzby, 1986) that the suite of skills referred to as emergent literacy skills comprise knowledge of the symbol systems and its conventions (e.g., that text goes from left to right, a book has a front and a back) among very young children. Research suggests that these emergent literacy skills are critical for the development of reading and require practice with the medium of books to develop (Scarborough & Dobrich, 1994).

Research also suggests that reading skill and vocabulary knowledge are related (Chall, Jacobs, & Baldwin, 1990) and that the size of a child's vocabulary can be predicted from the amount that he or she reads (Cunningham & Stanovich, 1991). Hence, there is feedback from the representational medium of print to that of speech. We also know that, when the amount of education is held constant, vocabulary has declined between 1974 and 1990 (Glenn, 1994). Similarly, there has been a corresponding decline in reading newspapers and other print sources as well as a decline in verbal Scholastic Achievement Test (SAT) scores (Greenfield, 1998). Hayes, Wolfer, and Wolfe (1996) argue that the 50+ point decline in mean SAT-verbal scores between 1963 and 1979 may be linked to the simplification of school textbooks published between 1919 and 1991. It could also be linked to the simplified vocabulary utilized on television, a medium that was developed and became popular within this period of time. It is too soon to tell how performance on the new SAT, particularly the writing section, may be linked to these reading patterns. Although there is consensus that reading of traditional print sources such as books has declined, the Internet has opened new avenues for reading and writing text; the relation of Internet use to writing skills is a fertile area for future research. We will discuss the Internet in relation to writing and representation in a later section.

Although books primarily use text, they also contain pictures and diagrams. According to Kozma (1991), the research suggests that recall is increased by the use of pictures with text particularly when the pictures are related to central themes, new ideas, or structural relationships that are addressed in the text. This increase in recall is especially true for poor readers. What is relevant to us is that pictures seem to aid learners as they construct mental models of the concept in question – Kozma suggests that this may be because pictorial symbol systems are more similar to objects and events compared to linguistic symbol systems. In other words, they are visual iconic forms of representation. The particular symbol system utilized by a medium helps users construct representations of that kind. We therefore expect that books with text alone will aid the construction of verbal/linguistic representations and books with text and pictures will aid the construction of verbal and pictorial representations.

Radio and television

Next we turn to the effects of radio and television on children's representational processes. Radio is an audio medium and television is a largely audiovisual medium. From our developmental theory, we would predict that the dearth of visual cues would make radio more difficult for young children to use to process action information, and this is what the research shows (Greenfield & Beagles-Roos, 1988). We would also predict that radio would be more effortful to process than television and therefore less popular as a vehicle for drama for adults; the history of television replacing radio for fictional entertainment, and even to a great extent for news, provides evidence on this point. In addition, the processing of televised action by infants as young as 14 months in Meltzoff's (1988) research also provides evidence that the large number of real-world cues provided by television makes its processing possible extremely early in development.

Wright and Huston (1983) classified the formal features of television to include action, pace, visual techniques such as camera zooms, cuts, and visual special effects, and auditory features such as music, dialogue, and sound effects. They group fast action and rapid pace, high levels of auditory features such as sound effects and loud music, and high levels of visual effects such as rapid cuts and visual special effects as perceptually salient features. These features, they argued, were more likely to attract attention and interest from young children. By contrast, features such as dialogue and narration, which provide a verbal linguistic mode to represent content, are non-salient.

In addition to audio and visual features, television also uses other symbol systems such as text, pictures, and diagrams, both stationary and in motion (Kozma, 1991). Although both radio and television are transient, coming and going in a dynamic and changing fashion on the screen (Kozma, 1991), they can be recorded on audio- and videotapes as well as CDs and DVDs. When used with such hardware, their symbol systems can be played, stopped, rewound, and fast forwarded, thereby coming under the control of the user.

Cognitive implications   Greenfield and colleagues explored the effects of adding moving visual imagery to an audio narrative of a story on children's (grades 1–2 versus 3–4) imaginal representation (defined as children's representational construction of elements that were not in the original narrative) and memory representation (defined as children's representational construction of elements that were present in the narrative) (Greenfield & Beagles-Roos, 1988; Greenfield, Farrar, & Beagles-Roos, 1986). In both studies, the stimuli consisted of a video version and an audio version of children's stories using the same soundtrack. Children were exposed to one story in the audio version and the other in the video version. Imaginal representation was assessed by stopping the story a bit before its ending and asking the participants to continue the story orally. The results showed that children who heard the audio version created endings with greater representation of novel events, characters, and words whereas children who heard the video version constructed endings with greater repetition of material from the story they heard. The findings support the following hypothesis: because television provides richer information in an explicit external representation, it is less stimulating to the children's internal imaginal representation.

To test memory representation, children saw and heard the stories until the end and were then given a free recall task (retell the story to another adult, who had never heard or seen the story), a cued recall task, and inference questions. In this instance, television led to significantly better performance – better recall of information, greater focus on action representation, and greater use of audio-visual detail both in direct recall and as a source of inferences. In contrast, radio led to a greater focus on material presented only in the auditory channel, such as dialogue. When asked to retell the story using pictures (picture sequencing), television yielded better performance than a radio presentation, highlighting the fact that television stimulates visual representational processes. Similarly, school-aged children performed better on a picture sequencing task following an audio-visual compared to an audio-only presentation (Calvert, 2001). Visually presented information has also been found to lead to greater recall compared to the same information presented aurally for preschool-aged children (Hayes & Birnbaum, 1980). Overall, the research points to the superiority of visual/action representations over verbal/audio representations for a variety of cognitive processes, at least from preschool through middle childhood. However, transfer effects are strongest when the modality of presentation matches the modality of retrieval (Calvert, 2001; Greenfield, Farrar, & Beagles-Roos, 1986).

In their review of television formal features, Wright and Huston (1983) concluded that the perceptually salient features of television productions (e.g., fast action and pace) are effective at attracting and holding attention irrespective of the program content. In fact, they report that when studies separated violent content from perceptually salient formal features, it was form, not content, that directed and sustained attention (Wright & Huston, 1983). Even so, the interface of form with content has implications for what children learn. For example, Calvert and colleagues (1982) found that perceptually salient features such as character vocalizations elicited attention and facilitated learning of central verbal content that was presented immediately after that feature. Features such as moderate action levels facilitated comprehension of verbal content by providing dual visual and verbal modes that children could use to represent content. These effects occurred for preschool-aged children, but also for children as old as 9 and 10.

Other aspects of television grammar that have been studied include zoom-in and zoom-outs, fragmented spaces, logical gaps, and close-ups. In particular, Salomon and Cohen (1977) showed children four versions of the same television program – the content was the same, but the versions varied in the use of formal features. Children who viewed the version that emphasized close-ups did better on knowledge concerning the relation between parts and whole. In contrast, children who viewed the version with logical gaps were better at comprehending the logical structure and continuity of the plot. According to Salomon (1976), any single medium, such as television, utilizes a wide variety of symbolic codes, and the particular combinations of the codes have very different effects on cognitive skills and processes, which in turn influence the way information is processed and learned.

Motor implications Another aspect of representational competence that may be influenced by television is that of motor or enactive representational skills, particularly among young pre-linguistic infants. Meltzoff (1988) has pointed out that television presents a two-dimensional representation of reality and asked whether young infants are capable of incorporating such two-dimensional representations into their own motoric behavior involving real objects in three-dimensional space. He studied 14- and 24-month-old infants' ability to imitate television models immediately after exposure and after a 24-hour delay. Infants in his study either saw the experimenter disassemble and reassemble a toy (imitation condition), saw the experimenter manipulate the toy without displaying the target action (adult manipulation control), or saw the experimenter but not the toy or the target action (baseline condition). Even the 14-month-olds remembered the actions of a televised model over a 24-hour delay and produced those actions in their motor behavior when given access to that three-dimensional object. This study suggests that motor actions represented as moving iconic imagery on television can be internalized by very young pre-verbal infants. In other words, infants have representational competence to equate an iconic image with a motoric act. They can translate from an iconic medium of representation to a real-world action.

The research reviewed above is also relevant to questions about developmental patterns in the accessibility of different symbol systems. Meltzoff's (1988) study showed that children as young as 14 months were able to represent enactive or motoric representations on television; recall that enactive representations are the first kinds of representations to emerge in Bruner's (1965) developmental progression of representational kind. The finding is that representations organized around visual/action-based information generally lead to better cognitive processing. This finding is consistent with the hypothesis that television may be more effective among young children as it incorporates representations that are available early in development.

Videogames and computer games

The best-known and earliest videogames and computer games are even more complex than television when it comes to presenting two-dimensional representations of three-dimensional space, but more recently very simple games have been developed for young children. Using a mouse involves creating an action representation on the part of the user, so it makes developmental sense, in terms of Bruner's representational theory, that children who are quite young should be able to master the basics of this technology. The 2003 Kaiser Report, Zero to Six, found that 64 percent of children between 4 and 6 years of age know how to use a computer mouse to point and click. In doing so, they are integrating their own enactive representations using the mouse with the icons and iconic representations they find on the screen (Rideout, Vandewater, & Wartella, 2003).

But screen representations in games are typically very complex and require much more than simple point-and-click skills with a mouse. Most action video/computer games, which are spatial, iconic, and dynamic, have multiple, often simultaneous things happening at different locations and require a variety of attentional, spatial, and iconic representational skills compared to earlier media forms such as print, radio, and television.

Given such complexity, one would expect action games to utilize and develop a different profile of cognitive processes compared to earlier media forms such as print (e.g., Greenfield, 1984). There is now a solid body of work that has shown that computer game playing does have an impact on the specific cognitive skills that are utilized in the game, such as attention and representation (iconic and spatial). In the next sections we review this research to demonstrate how the symbol systems used in a medium are internalized, thus affecting users' cognition and learning.

Computer games and attentional skills   One basic skill involved in playing most computer games and videogames is that of divided visual attention, which is the ability to keep track of multiple events occurring simultaneously at different locations of the screen. Greenfield, deWinstanley, and colleagues (1994) explored the effect of videogame expertise and experience on strategies for dividing visual attention among college students who were expert and novice game players. Skill in dividing attention was assessed by measuring participants' response time to two events of varying probabilities at two locations on a computer screen. For participants in the unequal probability condition, the target appeared more often at one location than another. For participants in the equal probability condition, the target appeared with equal probability at both locations.

Expert players had faster response times than novices at both the high and low probability positions of the icon in the unequal probability condition, whereas there was no difference between the groups in the equiprobable condition. Based on attention research (Posner, Snyder, & Davidson, 1980), which shows that people generally allocate more attention to high probability targets compared to equiprobable targets, Greenfield, deWinstanley, and colleagues (1994) suggest that expert players did better when the probability of the targets was unequal because they were better able to deploy attentional resources strategically. This use of attentional strategies to monitor multiple screen locations can be thought of as a precursor to the multitasking required by simultaneously monitoring multiple computer windows, an increasingly common experience on the Internet.

In a second experiment, Greenfield, deWinstanley, and colleagues (1994) found a causal relationship between playing an action game and improving strategies for monitoring events at multiple locations. College students were randomly assigned to either play the action game *Robotron* (experimental group) or to not play any game (control group). *Robotron* consisted of multiple entities acting simultaneously. Participants in the experimental group received 5 hours of practice playing *Robotron* between the pretest and the posttest. On the pretest, more and less experienced players differed only at the higher probability target, where the more experienced players again had significantly faster response times; there was no difference at the low probability target. However after 5 hours of playing *Robotron*, members of the experimental group responded significantly faster to the target at the low probability position on the screen; in contrast, members of the control group did not show this improvement. Participants in the control condition showed selective improvement with the equiprobable targets, presumably because of practice on the test. The equiprobable targets require less strategic skill, and there was no difference between expert and novice players for such targets in the first study.

Subsequent research by Green and Bavelier (2003), using both a correlational and a training study, has confirmed that videogame playing does improve attentional skill and importantly this effect was found to transfer to very different attentional tasks. In the correlational study, participants who had consistently played videogames in the six months prior to the study had better attentional capacity, compared to participants who had little videogame usage in the six months prior to the study. In the training study comparing the action game *Medal of Honor* and the puzzle game *Tetris*, Green and Bavelier found that the action game led to greater improvements on all the attentional tests compared to *Tetris*. In contrast to *Tetris*, which is a dynamic puzzle game in which only one event takes place at a time, *Medal of Honor* is a battle game in which multiple entities are simultaneously engaged in various actions.

Together the studies suggest that videogame experts are better than novices at monitoring two or more locations on a game screen and that practice improves strategies for monitoring low probability targets. They show that videogame training can have immediate short-term effects on the development of divided attention strategies and that expert game players also had better-developed attention skills than novices. Finally, they suggest that transfer effects can also occur.

Computer games and spatial representational skills   Spatial representational skills are comprised of several sub-skills (Pellegrino & Kail, 1982), including the ability to judge speeds and distances, the ability to mentally rotate objects, the ability to visualize spatially, and the ability to deal with two-dimensional images of a hypothetical two- or three-dimensional space. Researchers have suggested that these skills are utilized in all kinds of computer applications, from word processing and programming to action videogames (Greenfield, 1983, 1984, 1990). Research demonstrates that repeated practice with games enhances selected spatial skills.

In a training study of 10- to 11-year-old children, Subrahmanyam and Greenfield (1994) compared the effects of two computer games, *Marble Madness* and *Conjecture*, on spatial skills such as anticipating targets and extrapolating spatial paths. *Marble Madness* involved guiding a marble along a three-dimensional grid using a joystick – the player had to keep the marble on the path and prevent it from falling off or being attacked by intruders. *Conjecture* was a word game with no action. As predicted, playing *Marble Madness* improved children's spatial skills including the ability to anticipate targets and visualize paths. Interestingly the effects were obtained after just 2.25 hours of training and were limited to participants who started out with weaker spatial skills, typically girls. Even so, participants with better initial spatial skills – typically the boys – also showed better results: their videogame performance improved at the end of the training period. Thus, it would appear that skill in understanding dynamic spatial representations in a videogame is both required for videogame playing and developed with repeated game play.

A different kind of spatial skill is required in the mental paper-folding tasks in which one has to visualize three-dimensional movement from a two-dimensional display. This skill was utilized in an arcade game from the 1980s called *The Empire Strikes Back*. Researchers (Greenfield, Brannon, & Lohr, 1994) found that better players of this game also performed better on a classical mental paper-folding task. In a follow-up study, no effect was obtained from playing this game in an experimental setting; however structural equation modeling revealed that accumulated skill in playing *The Empire Strikes Back* played a causal role in spatial representational skill development, as measured by the mental paper-folding task (Greenfield, 1993).

Okagai and Frensch (1994) examined the effect of practice with the videogame *Tetris*, which requires the rapid rotation and placement of differently shaped rectangular falling blocks, on spatial representation skills of older adolescents. Mental rotation and visualization skills were assessed by using paper-and-pencil tests in the first experiment and a computerized test in the second experiment. In experiment one, transfer effects on the paper-and-pencil tests were found only for males. In experiment two, game practice led to quicker mental rotation and visualization times for both males and females. Subsequently, De Lisi and Wolford (2002) demonstrated that playing *Tetris* improved the mental rotation skills even among third graders and the effects were especially pronounced for girls. In sum, the research indicates that videogame play enhances visual spatial skills. Effects are often most pronounced for those who initially have weaker visual spatial skills. Transfer effects are also most likely to occur in a same or similar medium and on tasks that utilize the same skills as the game.

Computer games and iconic representational skills Most videogames and computer games use iconic or analog representation – that is they require the user to "read" and interpret visual and iconic images such as pictures and diagrams. Although games today also utilize verbal and auditory representations (and activate neural regions involved in both visual and auditory processing; Murray 2001), more important information is typically conveyed via iconic images. Research suggests that exposure to iconicity in videogames does transfer to iconic representational skills.

In a cross-cultural study, Greenfield, Camaioni, Ercolani, Weiss, Lauber, and Perucchini (1994) found that playing a computer game shifted representational styles from verbal to iconic. College students played the game, *Concentration*, either on a computer or on a board. The player has to open either virtual or real doors to identify the location of pairs of numerals. In the computer version, icons were used – a virtual door and cursor in the shape of a hand – to perform the task. The board version had no icons, but involved direct action on an object: the participant used his or her hand to lift a solid door in order to reveal a numeral.

Iconic representational skills were assessed using a pretest and posttest that included several dynamic video displays from *Rocky's Boots*, an educational computer simulation designed to teach the logic of computer circuitry. Participants were given no information as to the content or operation of the displays and were asked questions about the displays (e.g., what does a particular game element represent?). Those who had played the game on the computer provided more iconic drawings in their answers, whereas those who had played the game on a board provided more verbal descriptions. Playing a computer game that utilized icons, then, influenced participants to use icons in their representations.

Not only did the experimental manipulation lead to more iconic representations, prior videogame exposure seemed to be related to participants' understanding of iconic representations as well. Experienced players, Americans, and males showed better understanding of the dynamic iconic simulations of computer circuitry in *Rocky's Boots*, compared to inexperienced videogame players, Italians (computer technology was less diffuse in Italy at that time in history), or females. The results suggest that exposure to videogames is related to both the comprehension and production of iconic representation.

Representational implications of new game technologies   The technology is moving so fast that research cannot keep pace with it. Consider the representational issues brought up by new games – for example, the genre of sports games, including games such as EA Sports' football and basketball games. The images are very realistic and appear to be almost three-dimensional. How will these games influence representational skill development? Another genre is the music videogames such as the *Dance Dance Revolution* series. A dance pad with four arrow panels (left, right, up, and down) is connected to the computer and the player has to press the panels with his/her feet in response to the arrows that appear on the screen in front of him/her. The visual information provided via the arrows on the screen is synchronized to the beat of a song that is played simultaneously. Success on the game requires intermodal integration – the player has to see the arrows that have to be pressed and then press the correct ones with his/her feet. Additional research is needed to understand how these newer games influence the cognitive skills of youth.

Internet

In terms of the symbol systems that it uses, the Internet is unlike every other medium preceding it and actually seems to incorporate all the symbolic features of its predecessors. For instance, like books, the Internet contains text; like the radio, the Internet contains audio; like television, the Internet contains audiovisual representations; and like computer games and videogames, the Internet contains interactive audio and video.

Potential cognitive effects   There has been surprisingly little systematic research on the effects of the Internet's symbol systems on the development of cognitive skills. We think that Internet use is most likely to have an impact on verbal and spatial representational skills.

While the information applications of the Internet largely require comprehension of text, the communication applications (e.g., email, instant messaging) require both the comprehension and production of text. However, as Greenfield and Subrahmanyam (2003) point out, online text has features of both oral and written representation – for instance chat conversations consist of incomplete, grammatically simple, and often incorrect sentences (Herring, 1996). Novel abbreviations, such as the ubiquitous "a/s/l" (asking others to give their age, sex, and location) are also rife in Internet communication (Greenfield & Subrahmanyam, 2003; Calvert et al., 2003). One wonders at the cumulative impact of such online reading and writing on verbal representational skills. On the one hand, online reading affords previously unavailable opportunities to read and write text; on the other hand, will online forms of written discourse transfer to more formal writing contexts such as tests and papers? Our experience grading papers suggests that students have considerable difficulty with the idea that oral forms of language are not appropriate in written contexts; these observations suggest that transfer effects would involve the use of informal writing modes in formal written contexts.

The other area of transfer is likely to be spatial representation skills, particularly with regard to two-dimensional representations of three-dimensional space. We consider a couple of different ways that the symbol systems used on the Internet may be internalized. First, unlike books, in which pages are arranged in a linear fashion, the Internet allows much more complex forms of linking across several websites and pages within websites. For example, Suzuki and Beale (2006) report that the personal web home pages of adolescent cancer patients contained hyperlinks to a variety of other sites. Navigating around a website requires users to create mental maps of the site organization. Thus, we would predict that users with more Internet surfing experience may have better spatial visualization skills.

A second example is the use of online map routing sites as well as global positioning systems (GPS). The current generation of navigation sites (e.g., www.maps.google.com) provide maps with detailed information about streets and landmarks; they are user-friendly, can be zoomed to the level of detail required, and allow one to use the mouse to navigate around the map in any direction. Even less cognitive processing is required with the GPS units that are available now – all one has to do is enter in the destination address, and follow the directions that are provided aurally by the system. What are the likely effects of such tools on users' spatial representation skills?

Perhaps the most distinctive feature of computer and Internet symbol systems is the phenomenon of multiple windows, each one representing a different activity. This system of representation leads to multitasking (Gross, 2004), which is the phenomenon of using multiple computer applications (e.g., Internet and word processing applications) or multiple windows of the same application (e.g., multiple instant message windows) at the same time; this is different from media-multitasking which is the practice of using different media at the same time, such as the telephone, computer, and television.

Knowledge is just starting to accumulate about the cognitive and neural effects of processing multiple representations and tasks, all present at once. Foerde, Knowlton, and Poldrack (2006) have found that dual-task conditions (i.e., multitasking) decreased the acquisition of meta-knowledge about a weather-prediction task (learning what cues were associated with what weather outcomes). Relative to a single-task condition, multitasking shifted the neural processing of the task from the medial temporal lobe, which supports flexibly accessible knowledge and meta-knowledge, to the striatum, which supports habit learning. Although the neural processing differed, the basic task performance (being able to use cues to predict the weather) did not differ under single- or dual-task conditions.

Calvert and Wells (2007) examined the cognitive cost of multitasking. Although college students who were heavy multitaskers took twice as long to write a critique, there was no difference between heavy and light multitaskers with regard to the quality of the critiques. While the tasks are different in each study, both of these studies suggest that multitasking produces a decrement in higher-level or executive processing skills, and the study by Foerde and colleagues (2006) suggests a neural basis for this decrement.

Another kind of Internet forum is the "massively multiplayer role-playing game," that combines the visual qualities of stand-alone games with the virtuality not only of the game but of many other players. What are the effects of how the self and others are represented on the screen, both as physical beings and as agents of action? Ethnographic research suggests that, in one of these games, *The Sims Online*, the absence of a first-person player viewpoint in favor of an all-seeing "godlike" perspective was one factor in the dissociation of the all-seeing self from the embodied avatar (Steen et al., 2006). In other words, players do not see the scene from their avatar's visual perspective; instead they see the whole scene from above, including a view of their own avatar. Clearly it is difficult to identify with an entity that you are viewing from the outside. Another barrier to avatar identification in this game was the mode of avatar control, which had very specific representational characteristics. In direct avatar control, which is typical in stand-alone action videogames, one's actions with the joystick represent avatar or cursor movement. In *The Sims Online*, however, the representational link between hand action and avatar action is much more distant. In particular, Sims avatars are controlled robotically through giving them instructions to move in various directions; that is, they had to be programmed to move. In other words, there is psychological distance, to use Sigel's term, between player and avatar. Cognitively, this distance is undoubtedly challenging, but socially it is a disaster. The study of *The Sims Online* revealed that the time and operational lag caused by the use of robotic control disrupted social interaction (Steen et al., 2006).

On the one hand, we can see direct avatar or cursor control as a representational situation in which there is an iconic relationship between hand movement and cursor or avatar movement. On the other hand, we can see robotic control as a representational situation in which there is a symbolic relationship between player action and cursor or avatar movement. In Bruner's (1965) scheme, symbolic representation constitutes a higher level of cognitive development than iconic representation. However, in a multiplayer game, robotic control seems to contribute so much distance that virtual social interaction moves so far away from direct social interaction that it is no longer interesting or motivating (Steen et al., 2006). Players had to program instructions to their robots as to how to act; they could not simply act or react using a joystick or cursor that would move in parallel to the action desired by the player for his or her avatar. Social interaction in the game – that is, interaction among players from different locations – was represented as interaction among avatars controlled by the different players; this mode of controlling one's avatar through programmed instructions rather than "direct" action removed all spontaneity from the interaction among avatars. In this way, robotic control removed all spontaneity from the social interaction the game could provide, and players quit playing.

Advances in hardware

Recent advances in hardware have set the stage for new lines of research questions. There is now an incredible variety and complexity of television screens that are available – high-definition television, wide-screen television, projection television – that have sophisticated digital and surround sound systems. Will the dominance of visual information continue in the newer generations of enhanced televisions? Or will the visual track receive competition from the better audio systems of today?

The merging of hardware platforms is another technological advance – television shows are available on videos and DVDs, and these make possible very different viewing experiences. Similarly books are now available on CD and iPods. IPods are really mini-computers that allow one to play audio and audiovisual information. Music can now be played on cell phones and movies on handheld game systems such as the Sony PSP. Earlier distinctions between media are getting very blurry and raise interesting questions for research. For instance, consider books and their use of verbal representational skills. Will the effects of conventional book reading on vocabulary continue to hold if books are heard on tape, CD, or iPod? Does one have to "see" the text in order for reading to impact verbal representational skills? These are but a sampling of the cognitive questions raised by the symbol systems of newer digital media.

Implications of the Research for a New Developmental Theory of Media

Having examined a variety of research studies on the symbols systems of media and their relation to cognitive processes, it is important to consider the larger implications of this body of work. Greenfield (1998) has argued that the change from print to visual media has contributed to the Flynn effect – the well-documented gains in visual and spatial IQ compared to verbal IQ. The research discussed in the previous sections fits well with her proposal. Consider some of the key findings: (1) the decline in reading over the past couple of decades has been accompanied by a decline in vocabulary as well as a decline in SAT English scores; (2) television exposure, an audiovisual experience, facilitates learning of visual/action information over verbal/audio information; and (3) playing with visual symbols facilitates the development of iconic and spatial representational skills. All of these findings are indications of the theoretical points of Olson & Bruner (1974), Salomon (1979), and Greenfield (1984): the representational systems of media become internalized and become intellectual tools, developing the valued skills of a particular culture, be they visual or verbal in form.

Developmental issues

The developmental framework that we have expanded to media, based on Bruner's theory of modes of representation, seems to predict approximate lower bounds of age when a particular medium can be understood and will contribute to learning. Developmentally, we expect very young children to be facile in understanding and therefore to be able to be influenced by and learn from television, which involves action stimuli, iconic representations, and so many real-world cues. Meltzoff and colleagues' finding that 14-month-olds imitate televised actions confirms this idea (see also Barr, this volume, Chapter 7). The Kaiser report indicates that this kind of imitative learning from a televised representation often transfers to the real world (Rideout, Vandewater, & Wartella, 2003). Seventy percent of parents had seen their 6-month- to three-year-old children imitate positive behavior and 27 percent had seen their children imitate negative behaviors from television. These percentages rise dramatically between ages 4 and 6.

With the recent development of computer graphics that equal the realism and three-dimensionality of television graphics, we also expect the age of videogame and computer use to decline. Indeed, the Kaiser Report (Rideout, Vandewater, & Wartella, 2003) indicates that the age for using computers and videogames is declining rapidly. Parents report that 14 percent of their 6- month to 3-year-olds and 50 percent of their 4- to 6-year-old children have played a videogame. For computers, the findings are even more dramatic: 31 percent of 6-month- to 3-year-olds and 70 percent of 4- to 6-year-olds have used a computer.

Because of its arbitrary symbolic nature, we would not expect the age of learning to read to decline, and it has not. The minimal age for reading is clearly constrained by cognitive development. However, parents do make use of the iconic nature of most children's books, which are profusely illustrated and sometimes even have sounds and actions built in (e.g., pop-up books, electronic books). Seventy-six percent of parents report reading to their 6-month- to 3-year-olds on a typical day, and 83 percent report reading to their 4- to 6-year-olds (Rideout,

Vandewater, & Wartella, 2003). Even so, the picture/action/sound books of today can be as much socialization for visual media and mixed media as for print-only media. As the Internet is such a medley of media, age and developmental considerations are more complex. A historical movement towards increasingly young access has begun. No children who were 6 in 2003 had visited a children's website before age 2. However, in the cohort that was 2 years old in 2003, 10 percent had already visited websites for children.

Nevertheless, the use of the Internet for social communication presents cognitive challenges not present in visiting a website. Recall our theoretical proposal that the more real-world perceptual and cognitive cues a media representation makes available, the less mental transformation it will require and the earlier it will become accessible to a child. Social networks linked by the Internet provide virtually no real-world perceptual cues that other members of an Internet network are present, whether it is a question of email, chat, or a social networking program such as MySpace. Yet understanding that the Internet links you to other people in a network is basic to using the Internet as a means of maintaining or establishing social relationships. In line with Piaget's stage definitions, one might place email in concrete operations because the user is manipulating representations of real objects, that is, representations of (and by) known others. However, in the case of an Internet application like chat, where the social network consists of people one does not know in the real world, our developmental theory would predict that an understanding of the social network would appear later, in Piaget's stage of formal operations, which involves the mental manipulation of purely symbolic representations in the absence of real-world referents.

A systematic test of this hypothesis remains for future research. However, existing facts concerning both use and comprehension are encouraging. Let us begin with comprehension. Assessing children from age 5 to age 12, plus a group of adults, Yan (2005) found that understanding of the Internet as a network was virtually absent through age 10. Indeed, even the majority of 11- and 12-year-olds did not have an understanding of the Internet as a network, while the majority of adults did have such understanding. Although Yan did not survey adolescents, these facts concerning cognitive understanding are in line with the facts about use: communication uses of the Internet do not reach their zenith of popularity before adolescence, a time period when the abstract thinking of formal operations can also be well developed. Our theory would of course also predict that email would be used at an earlier age than are applications that connect the user to a network of never-seen strangers.

Conclusion

The historical development of representational systems in media corresponds to trends in information processing skills. Print stimuli were linear; television and videogames could have multiple events happening simultaneously in one screen – the greater socialization of parallel processing had begun (Greenfield, deWinstanley, et al., 1994). The effects of visual media on cognition became greater as the graphics became more highly developed and as games became increasingly popular (Green & Bavelier, 2003). Then simultaneous processing took a new leap as multiple locations on a screen were transformed into multiple tasks in each location – the dawn of computer and Internet multitasking. We are just starting to know some of the costs and benefits of this new mode of action and cognition.

As children are increasingly growing up in a virtual world that reaches its epitome in the Internet, they are spending less and less time in face-to-face interaction, in physical activity, and in interactions with solid objects. Put another way, distancing is one of the outcomes of the increasing "screen" time that developing individuals are experiencing over historical time. To use Sigel's terminology, media serve to activate a separation of the self both cognitively and socially from the here and now.

Societies provide experience to develop what they consider to be the most important skills. Technology skills have become important survival skills in our environment, and the lowering of the age of introduction reflects this belief. As online representations become an increasingly larger part of life, that is, as life becomes increasingly virtual, what will be the developmental costs and benefits?

References

Bandura, A. (2001). Social cognitive theory of mass communication. *Media Psychology*, 3, 265–9.

Bruner, J. S. (1965). The growth of mind. *American Psychologist*, 20, 1007–17.

Bruner, J. S., Olver, R. R., & Greenfield, P. M. (1968). *Studies in cognitive growth*. New York: McGraw Hill.

Calvert, S. L. (2001). Impact of televised songs on children's and young adults' memory of educational content. *Media Psychology*, 3, 325–42.

Calvert, S. L., Huston, A. C., Watkins, B. A., & Wright, J. C. (1982). The relation between selective attention to television forms and children's comprehension of content. *Child Development*, 53, 601–10.

Calvert, S. L., Mahler, B. A., Zehnder, S. M., Jenkins, A., & Lee, M. S. (2003). Gender differences in preadolescent children's online interactions: Symbolic modes of self-presentation and self-expression. *Journal of Applied Developmental Psychology*, 24, 627–44.

Calvert, S. L., & Wells, J. (2007). Age and gender effects of multitasking on academic performance. Poster presented at the Hawaii International Conference on Education, January, Honolulu, Hawaii.

Chall, J. S., Jacobs, V. A., & Baldwin, L. E. (1990). The *reading crisis: Why poor children fall behind*. Cambridge, MA: Harvard University Press.

Childers, T. L., Houston, M. J., & Heckler, S. E. (1985). Measurement of individual differences in visual versus verbal information processing. *Journal of Consumer Research*, 12, 125–34.

Cunningham, A. E., & Stanovich, K. E. (1991). Tracking the unique effects of print exposure in children: Associations with vocabulary, general knowledge, and spelling. *Journal of Educational Psychology*, 83, 264–74.

De Lisi, R., & Wolford, J. (2002). Improving children's mental rotation accuracy with computer game playing. *Journal of Genetic Psychology*, 163, 272–82.

Foerde, K., Knowlton, B., & Poldrack, R. (2006). Modulation of competing memory systems by distraction. *Proceedings of the National Academy of Sciences*, 103, 11778–83.

Glenn, N. D. (1994). Television watching, newspaper reading, and cohort differences in verbal ability. *Sociology of Education*, 67, 216–30.

Green, C. S., & Bavelier, D. (2003). Action video game modifies visual selective attention. *Nature*, 423, 534–7.

Greenfield, P. M. (1983). Video games and cognitive skills. In *Video games and human development: Research agenda for the '80s* (pp. 19–24). Cambridge, MA: Monroe C. Gutman Library, Graduate School of Education.

Greenfield, P. M. (1984). *Mind and media: The effects of television, video games and computers.* Cambridge, MA: Harvard University Press.

Greenfield, P. M. (1990). Video games as tools of cognitive socialization. *Psicologia Italiana*, 10, 38–48.

Greenfield, P. M. (1993). Representational competence in shared symbol systems: Electronic media from radio to video games. In R. R. Cocking & K. A. Renninger (Eds.), *The development and meaning of psychological distance* (pp. 161–83). Hillsdale, NJ: Lawrence Erlbaum.

Greenfield, P. M. (1998). The cultural evolution of IQ. In U. Neisser (Ed.), *The rising curve: Long-term gains in IQ and related measures* (pp. 81–123). Washington, DC: American Psychological Association. Reprinted in a German journal, *Leisure Spectrum*, 2000.

Greenfield, P. M., & Beagles-Roos, J. (1988). Radio vs. television: Their cognitive impact on different socio-economic groups. *Journal of Communication*, 38, 71–92.

Greenfield, P. M., Brannon, C., & Lohr, D. (1994). Two-dimensional representation of movement through three-dimensional space: The role of video game expertise. *Journal of Applied Developmental Psychology*, 15, 87–103.

Greenfield, P. M., Camaioni, L., Ercolani, P., Weiss, L., Lauber, B., & Perucchini, P. (1994). Cognitive socialization by computer games in two cultures: Inductive discovery or mastery of an iconic code? *Journal of Applied Developmental Psychology*, 15, 59–85.

Greenfield, P. M., deWinstanley, P., Kilpatrick, H., & Kaye, D. (1994). Action video games and informal education: Effects on strategies for dividing visual attention. *Journal of Applied Developmental Psychology*, 15, 105–23.

Greenfield, P. M., Farrar, D., & Beagles-Roos, J. (1986). Is the medium the message? An experimental comparison of the effects of radio and television on imagination. *Journal of Applied Developmental Psychology*, 7, 201–18.

Greenfield, P. M., & Subrahmanyam, K. (2003). Online discourse in a teen chat room: New codes and new modes of coherence in a visual medium. *Journal of Applied Developmental Psychology*, 24, 713–38.

Gross, E. (2004). Adolescent Internet use: What we expect, what teens report. *Journal of Applied Developmental Psychology*, 25, 633–49.

Hayes, D. S., & Birnbaum, D. W. (1980). Preschoolers' retention of televised events: Is a picture worth a thousand words? *Developmental Psychology*, 16, 410–16.

Hayes, D. P., Wolfer, L. T., & Wolfe, M. F. (1996). Schoolbook simplification and its relation to the decline in SAT-verbal scores. *American Educational Research Journal*, 33, 489–508.

Herring, S. C. (1996). Introduction. In S. Herring (Ed.), *Computer-mediated communication: Linguistic, social, and cross-cultural perspectives* (pp. 1–12). Philadelphia, PA: John Benjamins Publishing Company.

James, W. (1890). *Principles of Psychology*. New York, NY: Holt.

Kozma, R. B. (1991). Learning with media. *Review of Educational Research*, 61, 179–211.

Maynard, A. E., Subrahmanyam, K., & Greenfield, P. M. (2005). Technology and the development of intelligence. In R. J. Sternberg & D. Preiss (Eds.), *Intelligence and technology*. Mahwah, NJ: Lawrence Erlbaum.

Meltzoff, A. N. (1988). Imitation of televised models by infants. *Child Development*, 59, 1221–9.

Murray, J. (2001). TV violence and brainmapping in children. *Psychiatric Times*, October, 70–71.

Okagaki, L., & Frensch, P. A. (1994). Effects of video game playing on measures of spatial performance: Gender effects in late adolescence. *Journal of Applied Developmental Psychology*, 15, 33–58.

Olson, D. R., & Bruner, J. S. (1974). Learning through experience and learning through media. In D. R. Olson (Ed.), *Media and symbols: The forms of expression, communication, and education*. Chicago, IL: University of Chicago Press

Pellegrino, J. W., & Kail, R. (1982). Process analyses of spatial aptitude. In R. J. Sternberg (Ed.), *Advances in the Psychology of Human Intelligence*, vol. 1 (pp. 311–65). Hillsdale, NJ: Lawrence Erlbaum.

Piaget, J. (1951). Play, dreams, and imitation in childhood. New York: Norton.

Posner, M., Snyder, C., & Davidson, B. (1980). Attention and the detection of signals. *Journal of Experimental Child Psychology*, 109, 160–74.

Richardson, A. (1977). Verbalizer–visualizer: A cognitive style dimension. *Journal of Mental Imagery*, 1, 109–26.

Rideout, V. J., Vandewater, E. A., & Wartella, E. A. (2003). *Zero to six: Electronic media in the lives of infants, toddlers and preschoolers*. Menlo Park, CA: Kaiser Family Foundation. Also available at www.kff.org.

Salomon, G. (1976). A cognitive approach to media. *Educational Technology*, 16, 25–8.

Salomon, G. (1979). *Interaction of media, cognition, and learning*. San Francisco: Jossey-Bass.

Salomon, G., & Cohen, A. A. (1977). Television formats, mastery of mental skills and the acquisition of knowledge. *Journal of Educational Psychology*, 69, 612–19.

Scarborough, H. S., & Dobrich, W. (1994). On the efficacy of reading to preschoolers. *Developmental Review*, 14, 245–302.

Sigel, I. E. (1993). The centrality of a distancing model for the development of representational competence. In R. R. Cocking & K. A. Renninger (Eds.), *The development and meaning of psychological distance* (pp. 141–58). Hillsdale, NJ: Lawrence Erlbaum.

Sigel, I. E., & Cocking, R. R. (1977). Cognition and communication: A dialectic paradigm for development. In M. Lewis & L. A. Rosenblum (Eds.), Interaction, conversation, and the development of language: The origins of behavior, vol. 5 (pp. 207–26). New York: Wiley.

Steen, F. F., Greenfield, P. M., Davies, M. S., & Tynes, B. (2006). What went wrong with *The Sims Online?* Cultural learning and barriers to identification in a massively multi-player online role-playing game. In P. Vorderer & J. Bryant (Eds.), *Playing computer games – motives, responses, and consequences* (pp. 307–23). Mahwah, NJ: Lawrence Erlbaum.

Subrahmanyam, K., & Greenfield, P. M. (1994). Effect of video game practice on spatial skills in girls and boys. *Journal of Applied Developmental Psychology,* 15, 13–32.

Suzuki, L. K., & Beale, I. L. (2006). Personal web home pages of adolescents with cancer: Self-presentation, information dissemination, and interpersonal connection. *Journal of Pediatric Oncology Nursing,* 23, 152–61.

Teale, W. H., & Suzby, E. (Eds). (1986). *Emergent literacy: Writing and reading* (pp. vii–xxv). Norwood, NJ: Ablex.

Wright, J. C., & Huston, A. C. (1983). A matter of form.: Potentials of television for young viewers. *American Psychologist,* 38, 835–43.

Yan, Z. (2005). Age differences in children's understanding of the complexity of the Internet. *Journal of Applied Developmental Psychology,* 26, 385–96.

9

Learning from Educational Media

Heather L. Kirkorian and Daniel R. Anderson

Much contemporary media content designed for children claims to be educational, but do children actually learn? If so, how extensive is the learning? How long lasting are the effects? What factors determine whether children transfer what they learn from educational media to real-world problems? This chapter approaches these questions by reviewing research on the impact of educational media on knowledge and academic achievement. We start with a summary of relevant theories. Next we provide examples of specific knowledge gained from particular media products and review literature on the impact on academic achievement more generally. We then highlight some known moderators of the educational value of media. Finally, we describe factors that influence transfer from media content to real-world problems.

Defining Educational Media

The Children's Television Act of 1990 broadly defines educational and informative programming as containing content that will "further the positive development of the child in any respect, including the child's cognitive/intellectual or emotional/social needs" (FCC, 1991). With respect to other media, including videogames and Internet websites, there are as yet no formal definitions or federally backed guidelines regarding educational content. In the context of this chapter, we define all educational media as curriculum-driven products developed around a deliberate plan to teach. Short of detailed content analyses, it is impossible to determine whether any programs that are not working from a stated curriculum actually have educational content. Although many programs may be unintentionally educational, and others may teach messages not normally endorsed by a curriculum (e.g., glorifying violence), these should not be considered "educational." We consider television programs such as *Sesame Street, Blue's*

Clues, and *Dora the Explorer* to be educational because these programs not only have educational advisors but also work from a written, formal curriculum and from educational theory. Conversely, purely entertainment programs such as *Tom and Jerry* may teach children certain information, but were not developed with any intent other than entertainment.

Although educational media are produced for use within schools, this chapter will not address material designed for formal education. Rather, we will focus on modes of informal education such as television programs, videogames, and computer use outside of school that is not part of the school curriculum. An important distinction between these two types of educational media is that informal education is usually produced to be perceived by the child as entertainment and not necessarily educational, a pattern begun by *Sesame Street* (e.g., Lesser, 1972). The producers of informal educational programming, moreover, cannot be assured a captive audience. Nonetheless, it has been known for some time that children spontaneously learn facts and other information simply from watching an entertainment program and without specific instructions to learn (e.g., Field & Anderson, 1985; Noble, 1983).

Media Platforms for Communicating Educational Content

There is more research on television than on relatively new, interactive media. In some cases these different types of media may be thought of as conceptually similar, but, particularly in the case of educational content, there may be substantial differences between television and interactive screen media. As such, this chapter will generally discuss them separately. Many of the studies of computer and Internet use do not distinguish between different types of uses (e.g., homework, information seeking, gaming, messaging). In addition, we do not yet know if the interactive platform itself (computer, videogame console) has any unique effect on learning. For purposes of this chapter, all interactive media will be discussed collectively, noting differences between platforms where appropriate.

Despite our conceptual organization, we do not claim greater effectiveness of one medium over another. Although media may differ in their effectiveness (e.g., interactive games may be more educationally valuable than television programs because the user is more actively involved), little convincing research exists to investigate this systematically. Rather, we agree with previous authors (e.g., Clark, 1983) in positing that such cross-medium comparisons are difficult to control in practice and of little value theoretically; differences between media may be due to content, novelty of the medium, and a host of other possible confounds. Nevertheless, we maintain the distinction between interactive media and television because the degree to which findings from television research can be generalized to other media is as yet unclear.

Theories that Inform
the Design of Educational Media

Until the 1980s, there was only an implicit theory of how viewers pay attention to television and that was the notion that television viewing, particularly by young children, was reactive and passively controlled by salient attention-eliciting features of the program (e.g., sound effects). Singer (1980) formalized this theory and proposed that television uniformly elicits orienting responses in children. According to Singer, the "busyness" of television leads to a sensory bombardment that interferes with cognition and reflection thereby preventing children from processing content. Only programs that were not designed to capture attention, such as *Mister Rogers' Neighborhood*, were deemed suitable for young children's learning. Others proposed similar views, arguing that television in the form of programs such as *Sesame Street* provided nothing that could be truly educational (e.g., Healy, 1990).

Huston and Wright (1983) characterized formal features by their perceptually salient versus informative functions. Perceptually salient features embodied stimulus qualities like movement, contrast, surprise, and incongruity. Applied to television productions, features like action, sound effects, non-speech vocalization, and rapid pacing were considered perceptually salient whereas informative features included dialogue and narration. With age and experience, children were expected to habituate to formal features that were perceptually salient and attend to informative ones. However, empirical research documented that salient features could also be informative. For example, non-speech character vocalizations initially created an attentional orienting response that recruited younger children's attention to content, and that feature later became a learned marker whereby older children deliberately attended to content that was meaningful (Calvert et al., 1982). Moreover, perceptually salient features also improved plot comprehension when non-verbal features like vocalizations were contiguously presented with important program content or when moderate action was paired with dialogue (Calvert et al., 1982). Thus, the judicious use of formal features could enhance the effectiveness of educational programs by helping children understand the important content. Perceptually salient formal features like sound effects may also enhance learning from interactive media by maximizing attention and interest in educational content, resulting in beneficial outcomes such as improved vocabulary for children with autism (Moore & Calvert, 2000).

Anderson and Lorch (1983) created a model consistent with accumulating evidence that television viewing is based on active cognition. In their conception, attention to television is under active control by viewers, even children, and is largely driven by comprehension schemes that reflect viewers' knowledge base and experience with television. This theory incorporates individual characteristics of viewers, including prior knowledge, form and content of programs, and the nature of viewing environments as predictors of attention.

Research supports the hypothesis that attention is primarily guided by comprehension activities. At least by 2 years of age, children are selective in what they watch and are cognitively active while viewing. When they watch with siblings, peers, or parents, children make comments and predictions about the show and often ask questions about the content (e.g., Alexander, Ryan, & Munoz, 1984). Children learn strategies for viewing television that allow them to divide attention between the program and a concurrent activity (e.g., toy play; Lorch, Anderson, & Levin, 1979). Preschool children pay less attention to television when the program is incomprehensible as compared to comprehensible programs containing exactly the same features that are hypothesized to produce orienting responses (Anderson et al., 1981; Pingree, 1986). Preschoolers also pay more attention to children's programs than to commercials despite the fact that commercials have a greater density of salient formal features (Schmitt, Woolf, & Anderson, 2003). Moreover, child viewers use their knowledge of formal features to deploy attention strategically to content that is interesting and understandable (Campbell, Wright, & Huston, 1987; Lorch, Anderson, & Levine, 1979), and, by at least age 5, children are capable of actively considering perceived difficulty of the material and task demands when assessing how much mental effort to invest in watching the program (e.g., Field & Anderson, 1985; Salomon, 1983; Salomon & Leigh, 1984). Lastly, children engage in a variety of inferential activities in order to process and understand video employing standard video montage such as cuts, pans, and zooms (Smith, Anderson, & Fischer, 1985).

Although attention and comprehension do not necessarily lead to learning, they are clearly prerequisites: in terms of academically relevant knowledge, children cannot learn from content they never initially attended to and understood. Current thinking in this area assumes that children are cognitively active during television viewing and can learn from what they watch. Recent theory emphasizes attention and comprehension as ways to maximize the value of educational media. For example, Fisch (2000) outlined a model of comprehension of educational television based on the notion that our capacity for processing information within working memory at any given time is limited (Baddeley, 1986). By decreasing the cognitive load the program places on the viewer, producers can maximize the cognitive resources available to the viewer to attend to, comprehend, and elaborate on the material.

An important part of Fisch's (2000, 2004) capacity model with respect to educational television is the distinction between narrative and educational content. The narrative is the ongoing story or plot, whereas educational content refers to the specific curriculum-based lessons. For example, consider a program or videogame in which the hero is trying to rescue his friend who has been locked in a dungeon; the only way to unlock the door is to identify a pattern and determine which symbol comes next (e.g., red circle, blue square, yellow triangle, red circle, blue square, and so on). In this example, the mathematical concept of series is the educational content, whereas the rest of the story constitutes narrative content.

The capacity model assumes that processing of narrative and educational content will compete for resources in working memory as a function of *distance* between them. Distance is defined as the degree to which the educational content is integrated into the narrative. Low distance occurs when the educational content is embedded in the primary chain of events with many causal connections and placed at higher levels in the hierarchy of story structure. The example provided above has relatively low distance; that is, the educational lesson is integral to the narrative because the hero is required to solve the problem in order to rescue his friend. As distance increases, so does the competition for cognitive resources between narrative and educational content. Increased distance, therefore, reduces the likelihood of the viewer actually learning the material. Conversely, the more integrated the narrative and curriculum, the more easily the viewer can use the same cognitive resources to process both. Importantly, when the narrative and educational content are in competition for resources, Fisch (2000, 2004) suggests that there is a narrative dominance. Indeed, some research has actually documented low levels of recall for educational content relative to recall for narrative content (Friedlander, Wetstone, & Scott, 1974).

According to Fisch's (2000, 2004) model, both narrative and educational processing are affected by characteristics of the viewer and of the program. Relevant characteristics include the viewer's cognitive abilities and prior knowledge of content, story structure, and formal features of television. For example, a viewer with greater cognitive ability and specific domain knowledge will require fewer cognitive resources to process the program. Relevant context features that influence processing include program complexity, the degree to which the narrative matches a typical story structure, the need for inferences, the viewer's relative interest, and developmental appropriateness of content. For example, a complex program that requires many inferences on the part of the viewer will be more cognitively taxing. Overall the capacity model highlights the importance of a well-developed curriculum that is age-appropriate in determining the effectiveness of educational content.

With respect to interactive electronic media, there has never been a theory that cognition is passive. This is presumably because, unlike television, these media usually require active decision-making and overt responses from the users. Although Fisch's (2000, 2004) capacity model was originally designed to address educational television, it could easily be applied to educational videogames or other media.

Developmental Considerations

Since the late 1990s, there has been an increase in the availability of videos and programs for infants and toddlers. Many of these make explicit claims about their educational value or implicit claims with titles such as *Baby Einstein*. Despite these claims, little is known about the extent to which children 2 years and younger understand or learn from television programs. Experiments on learning from video have repeatedly found that infants and toddlers show better performance following exposure to live rather than video information on tasks such as imitation (e.g., Barr & Hayne, 1999) and object retrieval (e.g., Evans, Crawley, & Anderson, 2004; Troseth & DeLoache, 1998). This difference has come to be called the "video deficit" (Anderson & Pempek, 2005), and is a topic covered in detail elsewhere in this volume (Barr, Chapter 7).

There is as yet no published research regarding computer and interactive game use in infants and toddlers although these products are currently being produced for children as young as 6 months of age and many parents report that their infants and toddlers use them regularly (Rideout & Hamel, 2006). Given a relative dearth of empirical research on infants and toddlers and disputes over whether such young children even comprehend screen media, the remainder of this chapter will focus on educational media designed for older children. Because most of the relevant research has been conducted with preschoolers, we put particular emphasis on this age group. Research is greatly needed, however, to determine the impact of video and interactive media on infants and toddlers.

Impact of Educational Content

Television

It is clear that television programs designed to educate do so. Most of the research assessing the effectiveness of educational children's programs comes from summative evaluations that are not published in archival sources and so are difficult to obtain. Fortunately there are some reviews of this research that demonstrate the potential of specific shows designed to be educational. In a review of children's learning from educational television, Bryant, Alexander, and Brown (1983) reported that children can and do learn what educational programs intend to teach. Some of the findings involve comprehension of specific facts presented in individual episodes, such as reading and math skills, vocabulary, and knowledge of health and human anatomy, whereas others reflect positive associations between regular viewing and subsequent cognitive and social skills as well as children's attitudes toward entering school. In a recent review, Fisch (2004) reported both short- and long-term benefits of educational programs on specific knowledge and general skills in a range of topics including literacy, mathematics and problem solving, science and technology, civics and social studies, and prosocial behavior. A selection of published studies will be presented here as examples of the types of research and findings.

A substantial amount of research has been conducted on the program *Blue's Clues*, a preschool program emphasizing problem-solving skills. In an evaluation of the first two years of the program, Bryant and colleagues (1999) followed preschoolers who were regular viewers of *Blue's Clues* and preschoolers who did not watch the program because it was not available in their place of residence. Although the two groups in this quasi-experiment did not differ at pretest on many of the measures used, viewers outperformed non-viewers during posttests on several measures of problem-solving skills and flexible thinking. Furthermore, these effects increased over the 2-year period such that group differences were accentuated during the second season. Although every attempt was made to equate the two groups in this longitudinal study, it is important to note that subjects were not randomly assigned to groups. Nonetheless, true experimental studies have since demonstrated a positive impact of viewing *Blue's Clues* on problem-solving skills (e.g., Crawley et al., 1999).

Sesame Street has been by far the most studied children's program, probably due to Sesame Workshop's commitment to research and education, the program's longevity and popularity, and its long history of both criticism and praise. Studies by several external research groups have found short- and long-term benefits of viewing *Sesame Street*. Educational Testing Service conducted the earliest assessment of *Sesame Street* after the first and second seasons of the program (Ball & Bogatz, 1970; Bogatz & Ball, 1971). In these studies, some families with preschoolers were encouraged to view *Sesame Street* while others were not explicitly encouraged to view the program. Results indicated that children who watched the program more showed greater gains in a variety of domains with the strongest effects found for content emphasized most heavily in the programs (e.g., letters of the alphabet). It should be noted that this research was criticized because many children in the non-encouraged families became regular viewers, eliminating the intended control group of children and thus rendering the evaluation a correlational rather than an experimental study. In addition, a re-analysis of the data led to suggestions that the program primarily benefited middle-class children (Cook et al., 1975). Later research, however, indicates that the program benefits lower-class children as well (e.g., Wright, Huston, Scantlin, et al., 2001; Zill, 2001).

Exposure to educational television programs early in development also predicts long-term academic success. Anderson, Huston, Schmitt, Linebarger, and Wright (2001) reported that after controlling for several possible confounds such as parent education and sex of the child, viewing *Sesame Street* as a preschooler significantly predicted high school-grades in science, math, and English as well as amount of leisure book reading, participation in extracurricular activities, and positive attitudes toward education. The authors proposed that early educational television viewing might help create early success in school as well as foster an interest in learning and academics. Although information learned from *Sesame Street* probably has little immediate value in high school, early school readiness likely sets children on positive trajectories that endure over time.

It should be noted that not all educational television programs are beneficial to all children all of the time. For example, some research on the impact of *Sesame Street* found benefits of the show only for its target age range (i.e., between 2 and 5 years; Rice et al., 1990; Wright, Huston, Scantlin, et al., 2001), demostrating the importance of developmental appropriateness in assessing the impact of educational television. Furthermore, a study reported by Linebarger and Walker (2005) provides evidence for the importance of content in mediating the very early impact of television viewing. These authors followed children from 6 months to 30 months of age, recording television exposure and language development periodically throughout the study. They reported that the relationship between early television exposure (during the first three years of life) and subsequent language development (at 30 months) varied across programs. For example, watching shows such as *Blue's Clues* and *Dora the Explorer* was positively associated with vocabulary and expressive language whereas *Teletubbies* viewing was negatively associated with these measures of language ability at 30 months of age. These findings held true after controlling for several possible confounds such as parents' education, income, and involvement. It should be noted, however, that this study was correlational and tracked viewing as it normally occurred at home. It is possible that faster language learners were more attracted to programs such as *Blue's Clues*.

Interactive screen media

Although there are professionally produced, curriculum-based Internet websites designed for children, often associated with television shows (e.g., *Sesame Street*), there is as yet no substantial amount of research on the impact of these websites on children. Furthermore, there is relatively little educational software developed for use at home compared to the amount of entertainment television and entertainment software available. Some studies on interactive media have been published, however, and we will review the extant research here.

In a relatively early study, Hess and McGarvey (1987) investigated the potential academic advantage of educational software by comparing pretest and posttest scores for kindergarteners randomly assigned as a class to have computers in the classroom, computers both at home and in the classroom, or no access to computers. Children used a total of 11 educational and age-appropriate programs that largely focused on pre-reading skills during the 6-month study period. Results indicated that the benefits varied from classroom to classroom, perhaps as a function of the extent to which the program material was integrated into the regular class routine. Generally, gains between pretest and posttest were greatest for students with computer access both at home and in school, followed by the school-only group, and lastly the no-computer group. The additional benefit for students with computer exposure at home may be due to additional time with the program content, utilization of information in a different context, or some other factor. Similar benefits of educational software have been reported by others (e.g., Din & Calao, 2001; Haugland, 1992; Shute & Miksad, 1997).

It should be noted that there have been no extensive studies of the impact of educational software used solely at home. The studies cited above typically include experience with the software both at school and at home. Overall, the evidence indicates that educational media can be effective teachers when children at home use them, presumably in competition with entertainment media for the children's time. As indicated in the controversy over whether social class is a moderator of *Sesame Street's* effects, however, it is likely that not all children are equally benefited all of the time by all educational titles. Later in this chapter we review research on moderators of the impact of educational media. Moderators, in the present context, are considered to be variables that modify the outcome effect of an educational treatment.

Relationships between Media Use and Academic Achievement

In the previous section we demonstrated that children can learn specific knowledge from educational media. In this section, we will examine general associations between the amount of media exposure and measures of overall academic achievement. Although there are some claims of overarching negative effects of media use (with some support, as described below), most studies suggest that content is more important than overall amount of time spent with media in determining effects on academic achievement.

Displacement

One of the most common hypotheses about children's media use is that it displaces other more beneficial activities such as outdoor play, homework, and leisure reading. On the whole, however, research suggests that media use actually displaces other media use. Historically, television viewing, for the most part, displaced use of other entertainment media such as reading comic books, listening to radio, and attending the movie theater (e.g., Himmelweit, Oppenheim, & Vince, 1958; Murray & Kippax, 1978; Mutz, Roberts, & van Vuuren, 1993; Neuman, 1991; Schramm, Lyle, & Parker, 1961). Displacement effects of relatively new, interactive media, however, are somewhat more complex. Although one might predict that new media such as computers and videogames are displacing their predecessors (e.g., television), this does not appear to be the case. These entertainment media appear to interact rather than compete with each other (e.g., Coffey & Stipp, 1997). For example, computer time may not always displace television time insofar as one can engage in both activities concurrently.

With respect to cognitive development and academic achievement, it is not clear that screen time displaces activities that are intrinsically more valuable than watching television or playing computer games. The relationships of screen time to reading time are not clear and may depend on age. It is possible that reading displacement is important during the crucial period when children are learning to read, typically in first and second grade. During this time, reading is difficult, and television and computer games may provide attractive alternatives, thus slowing reading acquisition (e.g., Corteen & Williams, 1986; Koolstra & van der Voort,

1996). Another exception may be for children with unusually high levels of television exposure (e.g., Vandewater et al., 2005). Nonetheless, as noted above, most research suggests that media use typically displaces functionally similar activities rather than activities that are more educationally valuable. The remainder of this section reviews research on associations between media use and academic achievement.

Television

The typical investigation of television's impact on education simply examines the relationship of some measure of television exposure with some contemporaneous measure of achievement (e.g., Williams et al., 1982). The correlations are often negative (i.e., achievement is lower with high levels of viewing), but the relationships are also usually quite small. Interpreting such simple correlations is problematic. It could be that television viewing causes lower achievement but it also could be that children who are low achievers are drawn to watch television. Alternatively, some third factor could cause both. For example, children from low-income homes watch more television than do children from middle- or upper-class homes, and poor children also tend to have lower achievement (for review, see Comstock & Paik, 1991). In this case, it may be that poverty causes both outcomes. When studies incorporate extensive statistical controls to take such factors into account, they often fail to find a significant relationship between television viewing and academic achievement in either children (e.g., Gortmaker et al., 1990; Ritchie, Price, & Roberts, 1987) or adolescents (Anderson et al., 2001; Gaddy, 1986).

Other investigations suggest that the relationship between television viewing and academic achievement is more complex. In a review of 23 studies with a total of 277 correlations, Williams and colleagues (1982) reported that the average correlation between total television viewing and academic achievement was only −.05. Moreover, a more accurate description of the relationship was curvilinear such that television viewing in moderation (i.e., up to 10 hours per week) was positively associated with academic achievement after which additional viewing had an increasingly negative relationship with measures of achievement. Similar findings have been reported by others (e.g., Fetler, 1984; Neuman, 1991).

In a more recent meta-analysis, Razel (2001) reported a curvilinear relationship between television viewing and academic achievement but also noted that the optimal amount of television viewing may decrease with age. For example, in this analysis the estimated optimal exposure was 3, 2, and 1 hours of television viewing per day for 4-, 9-, and 15-year-olds, respectively. The author noted that this may be due to the educational quality of the programs available to different age groups, but content was not measured in any of the studies included in this analysis.

In one of the few studies to examine the relationship between television viewing and achievement in very young children, Zimmerman and Christakis (2005) reported that viewing before age 3 years is a negative predictor of later achievement test scores whereas viewing at 3 years and older is a positive predictor of later achievement test scores. Importantly, these researchers did not distinguish between types of television content. Other research suggests that viewing educational programming at young ages can be beneficial (Linebarger & Walker, 2005; Wright, Huston, Murphy, et al., 2001).

The lack of a straightforward relationship between television use and achievement may be at least partially a function of the content of the programs viewed. For instance, although Fetler (1984) reported that light viewers had generally higher achievement test scores than heavy viewers, light viewers in this study were more likely to report watching informational programming whereas heavy viewers were more likely to report entertainment viewing. Huston, Wright, Marquis, and Green (1999) followed 2- and 4-year-old children for three years during which parents completed diaries of children's activities (e.g., reading, outdoor play, television viewing). The researchers assessed variations in other activities as a function of television viewing and concluded that displacement effects of television vary with content. Specifically, entertainment viewing was negatively associated with reading and social and outdoor activities whereas informative viewing was positively related to these activities. Furthermore, Potter (1987) reported that some entertainment viewing categories were negatively associated with achievement whereas viewing informational programs positively predicted scores in adolescents.

To summarize, after accounting for important confounding variables such as income and parent education, there appears to be no systematic relationship between overall television viewing and achievement. Rather, the impact of television viewing is likely mediated by the content viewed, except in cases of extremely heavy exposure. Additional research is needed, however, to determine the impact of television exposure during the first few years of life.

Interactive screen media

Although studies on interactive media are less common than those for television, there have been a few relevant investigations. For example, Harris and Williams (1985) surveyed high-school students regarding their videogame use and current grades in English. They found that self-reported game time per week was negatively correlated with English grades. It is important to note that game time was not associated with time spent studying, suggesting that a simple displacement of studying does not explain this relationship. There was no information to distinguish between various types of content, although it is unlikely that the types of videogames played by high-school students in this sample would be considered educational given the relative lack of such content.

Other studies of interactive media suggest a more positive association with academic achievement. Attewell and Battle (1999) re-analyzed data from the National Educational Longitudinal Study of 1988, which consisted of a nationally representative sample of eighth graders and their parents. Computer ownership was measured as a dichotomous variable without a measure of amount of exposure or the kind of content. After controlling for several relevant variables, these authors found that having a home computer was associated with higher standardized reading and math scores. It should be noted, of course, that computer owners in that era were a fairly select group of early adopters of technology. This early adoption may have been reflected in home environments that fostered achievement.

In a recent longitudinal study of school-aged children and adolescents from low-income homes, Jackson and colleagues (2006) assessed the relationship between Internet use and academic achievement. They provided computers and Internet access to low-income families who reported never having home Internet access in the past. Children's Internet use was recorded continuously for a 16-month period and measures of academic achievement were obtained directly from the school district. Results indicated that the amount of time children spent using the Internet positively predicted subsequent grade point averages and standardized test scores in reading. Although these data are correlational, the reverse relationship (i.e., achievement predicting subsequent Internet use) was not significant, providing stronger support for a causal relationship in the direction of Internet use increasing grades and reading skills. The authors proposed that the positive impact of Internet use may be due to additional reading that comes from surfing websites even if the content of the sites is non-academic.

Taken together, there is no consistent evidence that amount of television or interactive technology strongly influences academic achievement. Although the few studies cited above may suggest differential effects of interactive platforms (i.e., videogames versus computer and Internet), further research is needed to investigate this potential difference systematically. There is some evidence that television viewing during the early years of elementary school may interfere with early reading and that Internet use may enhance reading. As is clear above, however, the evidence becomes more consistent when the content of media use is considered.

Moderators of the Effectiveness of Educational Media

One moderator of the effectiveness of educational media is comprehension: obviously children cannot learn lessons from content that they do not understand. This topic was discussed in detail earlier in this chapter as it related to Fisch's (2000, 2004) capacity model. We now discuss four more moderators.

Invested mental effort

Salomon (1983) argued that media users make judgments about the amount of invested mental effort (AIME) demanded by media and different classes of content. He hypothesized that AIME is directly proportional to media users' judgments about the amount of mental effort required to comprehend the content.

He described research comparing Israeli and American children in assessing the impact of educational television. Israeli children learned more from the same programs because, he suggested, television at that time was a novel medium and these viewers invested more mental effort. In an experiment, Field and Anderson (1985) told 5- and 9-year-old children that they would be tested on information from a television program while other children were simply asked to watch the program. These authors found that when both older and younger children expected to be tested on the show, they increased visual attention to the program and had greater recall of content. They also rated themselves as expending more mental effort than did control children.

Similar findings have been reported with respect to videogame play. Blumberg (2000) instructed students in second and fifth grade to play *Sonic the Hedgehog 2* for 10 minutes following different sets of instructions. The instructions were designed to encourage the children to use different goal foci (e.g., judging appeal of the game versus their own performance in the game). Results indicated that a player's goals upon approaching a game are predictive of performance. For example, experienced gamers who were instructed in advance to pay particular attention to their performance in the game outperformed experienced gamers without specific instructions.

Although this chapter has focused on informal education from entertainment media, children may be more likely to perceive computers and the Internet, as compared to television and videogame consoles, as requiring mental effort (Carey, Tryee, & Alexander, 2002). Children may thus be more likely to invest effort in learning educational content presented in computer programs and Internet websites than in games played on videogame consoles. As yet, no empirical research has directly addressed this possibility.

Repetition

Literal repetition is something that is relatively simple with modern electronic media and is an inexpensive way to enhance learning of program content. For example, in an investigation of the effects of program repetition on children's attention and comprehension, Crawley and colleagues (1999) compared groups of preschoolers who viewed an episode of *Blue's Clues* once or on five consecutive days and a control group of preschoolers who viewed an episode of another program once. Not surprisingly, children who viewed the *Blue's Clues* episode demonstrated greater comprehension of and memory for the material presented in that episode than did the control group, and recall was higher for repeat viewers than for one-time viewers. Overall visual attention did not decrease as the children watched the same episode repeatedly; in fact, overt audience participation (shouting out answers to questions, pointing at the screen, laughing) greatly increased. Similar benefits of repeated viewing have been reported for other preschool-aged children (e.g., Skouteris & Kelly, 2006). Moreover, Crawley and colleagues reported that children who viewed the episode five times outperformed one-time viewers on problem-solving tasks identical to those presented in the episode as well as transfer problems only moderately similar to those modeled in the program. Transfer of learning from video will be addressed in greater detail later in this chapter.

Adult co-viewing and mediation

Adults may enhance the effectiveness of educational television for children by answering questions, drawing attention to important parts of the program, and extending lessons presented in the program. Although somewhat limited, there is some evidence to suggest that co-viewing with a parent or other adult may increase learning from television programs, particularly when co-viewing is accompanied by mediation (e.g., actively drawing attention to important aspects of the program, answering and asking questions).

In a study on parent co-viewing, Salomon (1977) gave half of the mothers in his study instructions to co-view during their kindergarteners' regular viewing of *Sesame Street* at home while the other half of the mothers received no special instructions. Unfortunately no direct observations were taken of the mothers' co-viewing behavior so it is impossible to determine the extent to which mediation took place. Nonetheless, lower-income children recalled significantly more from the program when their mothers were instructed to co-view. Moreover, co-viewing had a particularly positive effect on low-income children's reported enjoyment of the program, which may have mediated the impact of co-viewing on comprehension. This effect was not found for children from high-income homes.

Other research has directly compared passive co-viewing with more active mediation during television viewing. Valkenburg, Krcmar, and de Roos (1998) compared fourth and sixth graders' comprehension of and responses to a program in the presence of either a co-viewing adult or a mediating adult. The co-viewing adult provided no comments about the program, divided her attention between the program and other activities, and demonstrated neutral affect toward the program. The mediating adult, on the other hand, provided commentary about the program and demonstrated positive affect toward the program. Although children in both conditions learned at least some of the target information from the program, comprehension scores following the program were significantly higher for the mediation group than the co-viewing group.

Other research has examined the effectiveness of explicit direction regarding educational program content. Friedrich and Stein (1975) compared comprehension for prosocial messages from *Mister Rogers' Neighborhood* for kindergarteners who viewed it or another program with or without follow-up sessions in which an adult provided instruction designed to highlight and extend lessons from the episodes. Not only did exposure to the prosocial program increase knowledge and transfer of the material but these effects were particularly true for children who viewed the prosocial program with follow-up training sessions. Role playing in which adults helped children reenact the key content with puppets was particularly beneficial for boys' performance of the important content whereas verbal labeling in which adults described key program points to children was particularly useful for girls' learning of the content. Thus, the kind of rehearsal used influenced program effects. Although some studies fail to find a significant positive effect of adult co-viewing and mediation (e.g., Skouteris & Kelly, 2006), to our knowledge no research exists suggesting that parent involvement during children's television viewing has a negative impact on learning.

With respect to interactive media, Kafai and Sutton (1999) found that computer use by children between 4 and 12 years of age consisted largely of games and educational software but that games are relatively more frequent. The authors proposed that parent mediation might be necessary to realize the potential benefits of educational interactive media. Research by Calvert, Strong, and Gallagher (2005), however, suggests that children should still be free to control the interactive media experience to maintain interest in and attention to the activity. Specifically, co-viewing adults who allowed children control of educational activities fostered more attentional involvement by preschoolers over repetitions than when the adult took charge of the interactive experience and children could only watch. Other studies report enhanced beneficial effects of educational software when adults provide feedback or demonstrations regarding the educational messages (Haugland, 1992; Shute & Miksad, 1997).

Demographics, gender, and prior knowledge

Results from some studies suggest that the impact of media on academic achievement varies as a function of viewer characteristics such as intelligence, socioeconomic status (SES), or gender. The review by Williams and colleagues (1982) reported that any negative impact of overall television viewing on achievement was more detrimental for girls and for individuals with higher IQ. The interaction with IQ has been replicated in subsequent research (e.g., Keith et al., 1986). In a re-analysis of California educational achievement test data, Comstock and Paik (1991) concluded that whereas television viewing impedes upper-middle-class children's achievement, lower-class children's achievement is enhanced. A similar pattern of results was found by Fetler (1984) in that time spent watching television during the week negatively predicted achievement for high-SES high-school students (also those with overall highest achievement scores) whereas television viewing had a neutral to positive association with achievement for lower-SES students.

None of the above studies took into account the differential effects of educational versus entertainment content. On the other hand, the study conducted by Anderson and colleagues (2001), which reported positive associations between early exposure to educational programming and subsequent high-school academic achievement, found stronger effects for boys than for girls. The authors' interpretation of this finding related to the socialization of boys and girls with respect to school. Socialization of girls generally places greater emphasis on academics. As a result, early exposure to educational programs such as *Sesame Street* may help boys become relatively more prepared for school. Girls are less in need of such exposure.

Other research suggests that prior knowledge can mediate the impact of educational television. Linebarger, Kosanic, Greenwood, and Doku (2004) investigated the effectiveness of the educational television program *Between the Lions* for increasing literacy skills in kindergarteners and first graders identified as at-risk, moderately at-risk, and not at-risk based on emergent literacy pretest scores. This television program is designed to enhance the literacy skills of early readers and is normally viewed at home. Twelve classrooms were randomly assigned to a control group or an experimental group. Children in the experimental group watched 17 episodes of the program over several weeks. Teachers were explicitly instructed not to address any of the program content in class. The results indicated that emergent literacy skills increased with viewing but these effects were moderated by reading risk status. Moderately at-risk and not at-risk children benefited more than at-risk children from watching the program. The authors proposed that a lack of prior exposure to the ideas presented in the program might have rendered the material incomprehensible to the at-risk children. As previously discussed, comprehension failure has serious implications for any beneficial impact of educational media.

Similar moderators have also been identified in the use of interactive media. In Attewell and Battle's (1999) analysis, the positive effect of computer ownership on academic achievement increased with higher SES, potentially widening a pre-existing gap. Furthermore, the effect was stronger for males than for females and for Caucasians than for minorities. The interaction may be a product of social environment in that higher-SES families may know more about effective interaction and computer use. In Okagaki and Frensch's (1996) study of videogame experience and adults' spatial skills, stronger and more general effects were found for men than for women. In their similar study with children, Subrahmanyam and Greenfield (1996) reported that improvements in spatial skills following videogame use were most dramatic for those with relatively low pretest scores.

Although no broad generalizations can be made about moderators of the effects of educational media, it is clear that moderating effects are common. In both producing and evaluating the impact of media, it should be realized that some subgroups of users benefit more than others. To the extent that these moderating effects can be taken into account in program design, impact may be enhanced.

Transfer of Learning

Although direct factual learning from educational media is certainly beneficial, a goal of most (if not all) educational initiatives is to allow children to apply what they have learned to real-life situations. Relatively little is known about transfer of learning from educational media. Some evidence and theory for transfer from media are summarized below. For a more detailed review of research and theory, see Fisch, Kirkorian, and Anderson (2005).

Evidence for transfer from television

In an early study on transfer from video, Hodapp (1977) observed eye movements while children (5.5–6.5 years) watched a video segment depicting either a problem solution (i.e., using a tool to get an out-of-reach toy) or an unrelated event. Children were then tested using the problem presented in the experimental video to determine the extent to which children in the experimental condition would transfer the solution to the real-life problem. Although children in the experimental group did not have an overall higher success rate (i.e., obtaining the out-of-reach toy), successes were more likely to be due to the use of the modeled strategy than for the control group, and those who saw the video with the problem-solving strategy demonstrated faster problem-solving times. Moreover, problem-solving times for the experimental group were predicted by the frequency and overall amount of visual fixation on the essential tool during the video segment.

Other research demonstrates transfer in older children from professionally produced, educational programs. In an evaluation of *Square One TV*, a program with a math curriculum targeting 8- to 12-year-olds, Hall, Esty, and Fisch (1990) compared fifth graders who viewed 30-minute episodes each weekday for six weeks with peers who did not see the program. There were no differences between the two groups' pretest scores but subjects in the experimental group demonstrated better performance on all levels of assessment at the end of the six-week period. In particular, "new" problem-solving strategies (i.e., those not used by that same individual during pretest) constituted significantly more of the strategies used by subjects in the experimental group. More recently, Fisch (2005) found similar effects for another math-based program, *Cyberchase*. Third and fourth graders viewed an episode of either *Cyberchase* or *Liberty's Kids* (a show about American history) each weekday for four weeks. *Cyberchase* viewers were the only group to improve in math skills between the pretest and the posttest and outperformed the control group on measures of direct learning (i.e., concepts explicitly presented in the episodes) and on transfer tasks with varying degrees of similarity to the examples in the program. Importantly, performance was better on tests of direct learning than transfer, and the likelihood of transfer increased as a function of similarity between test problems and those presented in the programs.

Crawley and colleagues (1999) demonstrated that even preschoolers are able to transfer specific strategies from television to real-life problems. Again, transfer was less common than general comprehension of facts, particularly for problems less similar to those used in the episode. Importantly, performance on the transfer problems increased with age and repeat viewing. In a study of transfer more generally, Brown, Kane, and Long (1989) performed a series of studies to investigate analogical problem-solving in children. Even 3-year-olds were capable of transferring a simple solution but spontaneous transfer increased with age.

Together these findings suggest that even preschoolers are capable of transfer from educational television. The findings also suggest several important moderators including attention to the important aspects of the problem, similarity between source and transfer problems, repetition, and age of the learner.

Conditions for transfer from television

Fisch (2004) drew upon theory and research about transfer of learning and analogical reasoning as a first attempt at a theory of transfer from educational television. Again, although the theory was originally intended for educational television, Fisch's theory of transfer can be applied relatively easily to other forms of electronic media. Fisch proposed that there are three possible areas for transfer failure: poor initial comprehension and learning, inadequate mental representation of the problem solution, and failure to apply the solution to the transfer situation. Comprehension is an obvious prerequisite. Children cannot transfer what they never understood. Because comprehension was discussed above, the current section will be devoted to the other two steps in the transfer process.

Representation To be transferred, a mental representation of the content must be abstracted beyond the initial context in which it was learned. Overly contextual representations of the educational content can actually impede transfer (e.g., Bransford & Schwartz, 1999; Eich, 1985; Gott et al., 1993). Recall, however, that according to the capacity model, producers should embed educational content within narrative content to decrease distance between the two and minimize the load on working memory (Fisch, 2000, 2004). The notion of context-independent learning may appear contradictory to this earlier discussion of the capacity model. Fisch (2004) provides a resolution by suggesting that educational content should be presented many times in different contexts within the program. Salomon and Perkins (1989) proposed that *varied practice*, or practice in a variety of somewhat related contexts, forces the representation of the strategy to adapt thereby rendering it increasingly detached from its original context and more evocable in others.

Research on transfer of learning in other contexts suggests that the use of several dissimilar training examples may increase the difficulty of initially learning the concept but, once learned, enhances flexibility of the solution strategy. Chen and Mo (2004) assessed transfer of a problem-solving strategy embedded in a written narrative as a function of different levels of similarity between multiple examples. Using four training problems, participants with variable source solutions were slower to learn the strategy but demonstrated better performance on subsequent transfer than did those with a constant solution. The authors concluded that variable practice leads to slower abstraction, thus requiring multiple examples, but increases transfer due to a more general schema for the problem solution.

Application   The ability to select an appropriate solution procedure is at least partly mediated by perceived similarity between the source and transfer problems (e.g., Salomon & Perkins, 1989). Generally speaking, *near transfer* occurs when the source and target problems are highly similar whereas *far transfer* occurs when there are relatively few similarities between the two. For example, if the educational message is multiplying height and width to measure the area of a rectangle on a piece of paper, a near transfer problem might be calculating the area of a paper rectangle with different dimensions while a far transfer problem might be measuring the area of a bedroom floor. In an assessment of the use of near and far transfer, however, Barnett and Ceci (2002) point out that the terms are used quite differently from study to study. For present purposes, transfer from educational media focuses on the distinction between surface-structure similarity (i.e., the surrounding story or context in which the problem is embedded) and deep-structure similarity (i.e., the underlying principles or problem solutions; Novick, 1988). This is analogous to Fisch's (2000, 2004) distinction between narrative and educational content in a television program.

An important consideration in the present discussion is that television and other electronic media can increase distance in many ways. Not only is the actual format of screen media different from real-life situations (e.g., the two-dimensional nature of screens) but the characters, settings, format (e.g., animation), and stories presented in television programs and videogames may be quite different from what most children are likely to encounter in their everyday experience. To the extent that the mediated lesson is different from the viewer's own experience, transfer is less likely to occur. This fact makes it even more important for producers to consider other ways to enhance transfer such as ensuring initial comprehension of the material and capitalizing on varied repetition.

Future Research Directions

Although we can draw general conclusions from research to date, there are many areas still in need of scientific investigation. Research is still needed to determine the impact of relatively new interactive media as well as television as it evolves in technology and content. Although we have limited the current discussion to television, computer, and videogame use, many toy products for children are digital and may have screens. There is little research on the impact of these electronic toys and games.

Research is also greatly needed to determine the impact of digital media on infants and toddlers. Very young children have become an audience for baby videos. Despite names like *Baby Einstein* that foster implicit beliefs in early learning, there is little evidence to date that babies learn anything of value from educational media.

Although research in other areas of psychology support Fisch's (2000, 2004) capacity model and theory of transfer from television, empirical investigation with electronic media remains scarce. Relatively new and innovative research methods involving neuroscience have recently been applied to the study of electronic media and may shed new light on questions in the field such as how the capacity model operates at the neuronal level (see Anderson, 2007).

The media world in which children live is constantly changing. Almost 40 years ago, *Sesame Street* introduced a new way of thinking about television for children. A similar revolution occurred in the 1990s with programs such as *Blue's Clues* and *Dora the Explorer* that encouraged active participation on the part of the audience. What will be the revolutions to come in the digital age, and how will they affect children's learning?

Conclusion

Children are cognitively active during television viewing and the effects of television on knowledge and academic achievement are primarily mediated by content. Educational media have a positive impact on achievement whereas negative effects are associated with exposure to purely entertainment-driven content. Children often learn the intended curriculum of educational television programs although there are many factors that may moderate this learning. Of particular importance is the need for well-designed content that effectively intertwines educational and narrative material while presenting the key messages in a variety of contexts to maximize transfer of learning.

By the time children graduate from high school, they will have spent more cumulative time using electronic media than they will have spent in a formal school setting (e.g., Roberts, Foehr, & Rideout, 2005). Electronic media have the potential to influence and enhance the academic achievement of all children. They can also be detrimental. It is clear that the broad range of knowledge from child development and education research can be applied to the development of entertaining and effective educational media (for examples see Anderson, 2004; Fisch & Truglio, 2001). Given the positive impact of these media, it is surprising that there is not more of it available to children.

References

Alexander, A., Ryan, M., & Munoz, P. (1984). Creating a learning context: Investigations on the interactions of siblings during television viewing. *Critical Studies in Mass Communication*, 1, 345–64.

Anderson, D. R. (2004). Watching children watch television and the creation of *Blue's Clues*. In H. Hendershot (Ed.), *Nickelodeon nation: The history, politics, and economics of America's only TV channel for kids* (pp. 241–68). New York: New York University Press.

Anderson, D. R. (2007). A neuroscience of children and media? *Journal of Children and Media*, 1, 77–85.

Anderson, D. R., Huston, A. C., Schmitt, K. L., Linebarger, D. L., & Wright, J. C. (2001). Early childhood television viewing and adolescent behavior. *Monographs of the Society for Research in Child Development*, 68(1, Serial No. 264), 1–143.

Anderson, D. R., & Lorch, E. P. (1983). Looking at television: Action or reaction? In J. Bryant & D. R. Anderson (Eds.), *Children's understanding of television: Research on attention and comprehension* (pp. 1–34). New York: Academic Press.

Anderson, D. R., Lorch, E. P., Field, D. E., & Sanders, J. (1981). The effects of television program comprehensibility on preschool children's visual attention to television. *Child Development*, 52, 151–7.

Anderson, D. R., & Pempek, T. A. (2005). Television and very young children. *American Behavioral Scientist*, 48, 505–22.

Attewell, P., & Battle, J. (1999). Home computers and school performance. *The Information Society*, 15, 1–10.

Baddeley, A. D. (1986). *Working memory*. Oxford: Clarendon Press.

Ball, S., & Bogatz, G. A. (1970). *The first year of "Sesame Street:" An evaluation*. Princeton, NJ: Educational Testing Service.

Barnett, S. M., & Ceci, S. J. (2002). When and where do we apply what we learn? A taxonomy for far transfer. *Psychological Bulletin*, 128, 612–37.

Barr, R., & Hayne, H. (1999). Developmental changes in imitation from television during infancy. *Child Development*, 70, 1067–81.

Blumberg, F. C. (2000). The effects of children's goals for learning on video game performance. *Journal of Applied Developmental Psychology*, 21, 641–53.

Bogatz, G. A., & Ball, S. (1971). *The second year of "Sesame Street:" A continuing evaluation*. Princeton, NJ: Educational Testing Service.

Bransford, J. D., & Schwartz, D. L. (1999). Rethinking transfer: A simple proposal with multiple implications. *Review of Research in Education*, 24, 61–100.

Brown, A. L., Kane, M. I., & Long, C. (1989). Analogical transfer in young children: Analogies as tools for communication and exposition. *Applied Cognitive Psychology*, 3, 275–93.

Bryant, J., Alexander, A. F., & Brown, D. (1983). Learning from educational television programs. In. M. J. A. Howe (Ed.), *Learning from television: Psychological and educational research* (pp. 1–30). London: Academic Press.

Bryant, J., Mulliken, L., Maxwell, M., Mundorf, N., Mundorf, J., Wilson, B., et al. (1999). *Effects of two years' viewing of "Blue's Clues."* Tuscaloosa, AL: Institute for Communication Research, University of Alabama.

Calvert, S. L., Huston, A. C., Watkins, B. A., & Wright, J. C. (1982). The relation between selective attention to television forms and children's comprehension of content. *Child Development*, 53, 601–10.

Calvert, S. L., Strong, B., & Gallagher, L. (2005). Control as an engagement feature for young children's attention to and learning of computer content. *American Behavioral Scientist*, 48, 578–89.

Campbell, T. A., Wright, J. C., & Huston, A. C. (1987). Form cues and content difficulty as determinants of children's cognitive processing of televised educational messages. *Journal of Experimental Child Psychology*, 43, 311–27.

Carey, G., Tryee, W., & Alexander, K. (2002). *An Environmental Scan of Children's Interactive Media from 2000–2002*. Retrieved May 26, 2006, from http://www. markle.org/downloadable_assets/imc_environmentalscan.pdf.

Chen, Z., & Mo, L. (2004). Schema induction in problem-solving: A multidimensional analysis. *Journal of Experimental Psychology: Learning, Memory, and Cognition*, 30, 583–600.

Clark, R. E. (1983). Reconsidering research on learning from media. *Review of Educational Research*, 53, 445–59.

Coffey, S., & Stipp, H. (1997). The interactions between computer and television usage. *Journal of Advertising Research*, 37, 61–7.

Comstock, G., & Paik, H. (1991). *Television and the American child*. Orlando, FL: Academic.

Cook, T. D., Appleton, H., Conner, R. F., Shaffer, A., Tamkin, G., & Weber, S. J. (1975). *"Sesame Street" revisited: A study in evaluation research*. New York: Russell Sage.

Corteen, R. S., & Williams, T. M. (1986). Television and reading skills. In T. M. Williams (Ed.), *The impact of television: A natural experiment in three communities*. Orlando, Florida: Academic Press.

Crawley, A. M., Anderson, D. R., Wilder, A., Williams, M., & Santomero, A. (1999). Effects of repeated exposures to a single episode of the television program *Blue's Clues* on the viewing behaviors and comprehension of preschool children. *Journal of Educational Psychology*, 91, 630–37.

Din, F. S., & Calao, J. (2001). The effects of playing educational video games on kindergarten achievement. *Child Study Journal*, 31(2), 95–102.

Eich, E. (1985). Context, memory, and integrated item/context imagery. *Journal of Experimental Psychology: Learning, Memory, and Cognition*, 11, 764–70.

Evans, M. K., Crawley, A. M., & Anderson, D. R. (2004). *Two-year-olds' object retrieval based on television: Testing a perceptual account*. Unpublished manuscript, University of Massachusetts at Amherst.

Federal Communications Commission (FCC). (1991). Report and order: In the matter of policies and rules concerning children's television programming. *FCC Record*, 6 (April), 2111–27.

Fetler, M. (1984). Television viewing and school achievement. *Journal of Communication*, 34(2), 104–18.

Field, D. E., & Anderson, D. R. (1985). Instruction and modality effects on children's television attention and comprehension. *Journal of Educational Psychology*, 77, 91–100.

Fisch, S. M. (2000). A capacity model of children's comprehension of educational content on television. *Media Psychology*, 2, 63–91.

Fisch, S. M. (2004). *Children's learning from educational television: "Sesame Street" and beyond*. Mahwah, NJ: Lawrence Erlbaum.

Fisch, S. M. (2005). *Transfer of learning from educational television: Near and far transfer from "Cyberchase."* Poster presented at the biennial meeting of the Society for Research in Child Development, April, Atlanta, GA.

Fisch, S., Kirkorian, H. L., & Anderson, D. R. (2005). Transfer of learning in informal education: The case of television. In J. Mestre (Ed.), *Transfer of Learning from a Modern Multidisciplinary Perspective* (pp. 371–93). Greenwich, CT: Information Age Publishing.

Fisch, S. M., & Truglio, R. T. (2001). Why children learn from *Sesame Street*. In S. M. Fisch & R. T. Truglio (Eds.), *"G" is for growing: Thirty years of research on children and "Sesame Street"* (pp. 233–44). Mahwah, NJ: Lawrence Erlbaum.

Friedlander, B., Wetstone, H. S., & Scott, C. (1974). Suburban preschool children's comprehension of an age-appropriate informal television program. *Child Development*, 45, 561–5.

Friedrich, L. K., & Stein, A. H. (1975). Prosocial television and young children: The effects of verbal labeling and role playing on learning and behavior. *Child Development*, 46, 27–38.

Gaddy, G. D. (1986). Television's impact on high school achievement. *Public Opinion Quarterly*, 50, 340–59.

Gortmaker, S. L., Salter, C. A., Walker, D. K., & Dietz, W. H. (1990). The impact of television viewing on mental aptitude and achievement: A longitudinal study. *Public Opinion Quarterly*, 54, 594–604.

Gott, S. P., Hall, E. P., Pokorny, R. A., Dibble, E., & Glaser, R. (1993). A naturalistic study of transfer: Adaptive expertise in technical domains. In D. K. Detterman & R. J. Sternberg (Eds.), *Transfer on trial: Intelligence, cognition, and instruction* (pp. 258–88). Norwood, NJ: Ablex.

Hall, E. R., Esty, E. T., & Fisch, S. M. (1990). Television and children's problem-solving behavior: A synopsis of an evaluation of the effects of *Square One TV*. *Journal of Mathematical Behavior*, 9, 161–74.

Harris, M. B., & Williams, R. (1985). Video games and school performance. *Education*, 105, 306–9.

Haugland, S. W. (1992). The effect of computer software on preschool children's developmental gains. *Journal of Computing in Childhood Education*, 3, 15–30.

Healy, J. (1990). *Endangered minds: Why our children don't think*. New York: Simon & Schuster.

Hess, R. D., & McGarvey, L. J. (1987). School-relevant effects of educational uses of microcomputers in kindergarten classrooms and homes. *Journal of Educational Computing Research*, 3, 269–87.

Himmelweit, H., Oppenheim, A., & Vince, P. (1958). *Television and the child*. London: Oxford.

Hodapp, T. V. (1977). Children's ability to learn problem-solving strategies from television. *Alberta Journal of Educational Research*, 23, 171–7.

Huston, A. C., & Wright, J. C. (1983). Children's processing of television: The informative functions of formal features. In J. Bryant & D. R. Anderson (Eds.), *Children's understanding of television: Research on attention and comprehension* (pp. 35–68). New York: Academic Press.

Huston, A. C., Wright, J. C., Marquis, J., & Green, S. B. (1999). How young children spend their time: Television and other activities. *Developmental Psychology*, 35, 912–25.

Jackson, L. A., von Ey, A., Biocca, F. A., Barbatsis, G., Zhao, Y., & Fitzgerald, H. E. (2006). Does home internet use influence the academic performance of low-income children? *Developmental Psychology*, 42, 429–35.

Kafai, Y. B., & Sutton, S. (1999). Elementary school students' computer and internet use at home: Current trends and issues. *Journal of Educational Computing Research*, 21, 345–62.

Keith, T. Z., Reimers, T. M., Fehrmann, P. G., Pottebaum, S. M., & Aubey, L. W. (1986). Parental involvement, homework, and television time: Direct and indirect effects on high school achievement. *Journal of Educational Psychology*, 78, 373–80.

Koolstra, C. M., & van der Voort, T. H. A. (1996). Longitudinal effects of television on children's leisure-time reading: A test of three explanatory models. *Human Communication Research*, 23, 4–35.

Lesser, G. G. (1972). Learning, teaching, and television production for children: The experience of *Sesame Street. Harvard Educational Review*, 42, 232–72.

Linebarger, D. L., Kosanic, A. Z., Greenwood, C. R., & Doku, N. S. (2004). Effects of viewing the television program *Between the Lions* on the emergent literacy skills of young children. *Journal of Educational Psychology*, 96, 297–8.

Linebarger, D. L., & Walker, D. (2005). Infants' and toddlers' television viewing and language outcomes. *American Behavioral Scientist*, 48, 624–5.

Lorch, E. P., Anderson, D. R., & Levin, S. R. (1979). The relationship of visual attention to children's comprehension of television. *Child Development*, 58, 453–563.

Moore, M., & Calvert, S. L. (2000). Vocabulary acquisition for children with autism: Teacher or computer instruction. *Journal of Autism and Developmental Disorders*, 30, 359–62.

Murray, J., & Kippax, S. (1978). Children's social behavior in three towns with differing television experience. *Journal of Communication*, 28, 19–29.

Mutz, D. C., Roberts, D. F., & van Vuuren, D. P. (1993). Reconsidering the displacement hypothesis: Television's influence on children's time use. *Communication Research*, 20, 51–75.

Neuman, S. B. (1991). *Literacy in the television age: The myth of the television effect.* Norwood, NJ: Ablex.

Noble, G. (1983). Social learning from everyday television. In M. J. Howe (Ed.), *Learning from television: Psychological and educational research* (pp. 1–30). London: Academic Press.

Novick, L. R. (1988). Analogical transfer, problem similarity, and expertise. *Journal of Experimental Psychology: Learning, Memory, and Cognition*, 14, 510–20.

Okagaki, L., & Frensch, P. A. (1996). Effects of video game playing on measures of spatial performance: Gender effects in late adolescence. In P. M. Greenfield & R. R. Cocking (Eds.), *Interacting with video* (pp. 95–115). Norwood, NJ: Ablex. Reprinted from Special Issue: Effects of interactive entertainment technologies on development (1994), *Journal of Applied Developmental Psychology*, 15, 33–58.

Pingree, S. (1986). Children's activity and television comprehensibility. *Communication Research*, 12, 239–56.

Potter, W. J. (1987). Does television viewing hinder academic achievement among adolescents? *Human Communication Research*, 14, 27–46.

Razel, M. (2001). The complex model of television viewing and educational achievement. *Journal of Educational Research*, 94, 371–9.

Rice, M. L., Huston, A. C., Truglio, R. T., & Wright, J. C. (1990). Words from *Sesame Street*: Learning vocabulary while viewing. *Developmental Psychology*, 26, 421–8.

Rideout, V. J., & Hamel, E. (2006). *The media family: Electronic media in the lives of infants, toddlers, preschoolers, and their parents.* Menlo Park, CA: Kaiser Family Foundation.

Ritchie, D., Price, V., & Roberts, D. F. (1987). Television, reading, and reading achievement: A reappraisal. *Communication Research*, 14, 292–315.

Roberts, D. F., Foehr, U. G., & Rideout, V. J. (2005). *Generation M: Media in the lives of 8–18-year-olds.* Menlo Park, CA: Kaiser Family Foundation.

Salomon, G. (1977). Effects of encouraging Israeli mothers to co-observe *Sesame Street* with their five-year-olds. *Child Development*, 48, 1146–51.

Salomon, G. (1983). Television watching and mental effort: A social psychological view. In J. Bryant & D. R. Anderson (Eds.), *Children's understanding of television: Research on attention and comprehension* (pp. 35–68). New York: Academic Press.

Salomon, G., & Leigh, T. (1984). Predispositions about learning from television and print. *Journal of Communication*, 34, 119–35.

Salomon, G., & Perkins, D. N. (1989). Rocky roads to transfer: Rethinking mechanisms of a neglected phenomenon. *Educational Psychologist*, 24, 113–42.

Schmitt, K. L., Woolf, K. D., & Anderson, D. R. (2003). Viewing the viewers: Viewing behaviors by children and adults during television programs and commercials. *Journal of Communication*, 53, 265–81.

Schramm, W., Lyle, J., & Parker, E. (1961). *Television in the lives of our children*. Stanford, CA: Stanford University Press.

Shute, R., & Miksad, J. (1997). Computer assisted instruction and cognitive development in preschoolers. *Child Study Journal*, 27, 237–53.

Singer, J. L. (1980). The power and limits of television: A cognitive-affective analysis. In P. Tannenbaum (Ed.), *The entertainment function of television* (pp. 312–60). Hillsdale, NJ: Lawrence Erlbaum.

Skouteris, H., & Kelly, L. (2006). Repeated-viewing and co-viewing of an animated video: An examination of factors that impact on young children's comprehension of video content. *Australian Journal of Early Childhood*, 31, 22–30.

Smith, R., Anderson, D. R., & Fischer, C. (1985). Young children's comprehension of montage. *Child Development*, 56, 962–71.

Subrahmanyam, K., & Greenfield, P. M. (1996). Effect of video game practice on spatial skills in girls and boys. In P. M. Greenfield & R. R. Cocking (Eds.), *Interacting with video* (pp. 115–40). Norwood, NJ: Ablex. Reprinted from Special Issue: Effects of interactive entertainment technologies on development (1994), *Journal of Applied Developmental Psychology*, 15, 13–32.

Troseth, G., & DeLoache, J. (1998). The medium can obscure the message: Understanding the relation between video and reality. *Child Development*, 69, 950–65.

Vandewater, E. A., Bickham, D. S., Lee, J. H., Cummings, H. E., Wartella, E. A., & Rideout, V. J. (2005). When the television is always on: Heavy television exposure and young children's development. *American Behavioral Scientist*, 48, 562–77.

Valkenburg, P. M., Krcmar, M., & de Roos, S. (1998). The impact of a cultural children's program and adult mediation on children's knowledge of and attitudes towards opera. *Journal of Broadcasting and Electronic Media*, 42, 315–26.

Williams, P. A., Haertel, E. H., Walberg, H. J., & Haertel, G. D. (1982). The impact of leisure-time television on school learning: A research synthesis. *American Educational Research Journal*, 19, 19–50.

Wright, J. C., Huston, A. C., Murphy, K. C., St Peters, M., Pinon, M., & Scantlin, R. (2001). The relations of early television viewing to school readiness and vocabulary of children from low-income families: The Early Window Project. *Child Development*, 72, 1347–66.

Wright, J. C., Huston, A. C., Scantlin, R., & Kotler, J. (2001). The Early Window Project: *Sesame Street* prepares children for school. In S. M. Fisch & R. T. Truglio (Eds.), *"G" is for "growing:" Thirty years of research on children and "Sesame Street"* (pp. 97–114). Mahwah, NJ: Lawrence Erlbaum.

Zill, N. (2001). Does *Sesame Street* enhance school readiness?: Evidence from a national survey of children. In S. M. Fisch & R. T. Truglio (Eds.), *"G" is for "growing:" Thirty years of research on children and "Sesame Street"* (pp. 115–30). Mahwah, NJ: Lawrence Erlbaum.

Zimmerman, F. J., & Christakis, D. A. (2005). Children's television viewing and cognitive outcomes: A longitudinal analysis of national data. *Archives of Pediatrics and Adolescent Medicine*, 159, 619–25.

10

News, Reality Shows, and Children's Fears: Examining Content Patterns, Theories, and Negative Effects

Stacy L. Smith, Katherine M. Pieper, and Emily J. Moyer-Guse

Many criticize the news media for emphasizing the negative (Purpura, 1999). A look at today's headlines suggests that such social censure may be warranted: "Russian Jet Crash Kills 170," "Next stop Colorado for JonBenet Suspect," "Iraqis Launch Mahmoudiya Killings Probe," and "Congo Factions Agree to Stop Gunfire" (CNN, 2006). In fact, stories about fatal accidents, child abductions, and violent crime seem to be the bricks and mortar used to build news content.

What impact does exposure to these types of news stories have on children? The purpose of this chapter is to answer that question. Anecdotally, we know that many parents, child advocates, and medical practitioners in the United States are arguing that viewing television news may have detrimental effects on young viewers (Landau, 2006; Purpura, 1999). As psychiatrist Michael Brody stated, "In TV shows, the bad guys generally get hurt . . . but on the news, innocent people are often the victims, which kids find overwhelming" (Landau, 2006, p. 14). Given this potential outcome, many have advocated that children should be shielded from news programming. According to behavioral psychologist Dr Stephen Garber, "If there's anything we need to protect our kids from, it's the evening news" (Rayworth, 2006, p. 10).

The goal of this chapter is to assess whether these concerns are warranted by reviewing empirical research examining the effects of television news on children's fears. The chapter is divided into five major sections. The first section delineates news content patterns, with a particular focus on television, to establish what children may see and hear in a typical broadcast. The second section overviews what is known about children's exposure to news in various media. Despite what many adults believe, research reveals that children and adolescents are routinely exposed to news stories in the media. Third, we discuss theoretical mechanisms for children's news comprehension and fear responses, focusing on developmental differences. Fourth, we explore negative emotional reactions to news viewing both for catastrophic and normative events. Ultimately, the research in this area will reveal the potentially problematic socializing influence news media may have on the lives of youth. Given the growing popularity of reality shows, the final section describes what we know about children's exposure to and understanding of programs that blur the boundaries between news and entertainment.

Content Patterns

Each year, the Center for Media and Public Affairs (CMPA) monitors every story aired during the evening news on ABC, NBC, and CBS, providing comprehensive data over time. The top 10 news topics across a five-year span are displayed in Table 10.1 (CMPA, 2001, 2002, 2003, 2004a, 2005). At least three interesting trends can be observed from this table. The first is that the most heavily covered topics are about national and international conflicts. Across four of the five years evaluated, the top stories revolved around the terrorists' attacks in the United States on September 11, 2001, and the war in Iraq.

The second trend is that crime reporting seems to be a staple of the news, a finding consistent with other content studies (Johnson, 1996). It should be noted that the crime findings in Table 10.1 are lower than trends that CMPA observed in the 1990s, when crime reporting reached its peak, presumably due to high-profile stories such as the O. J. Simpson trial, the Heavens Gate mass suicide, and the Polly Klaas fatal abduction. The most frequently featured type of crime in the news is homicide, despite the fact that murder rates have continued to decline in the United States since the early 1990s (US Department of Justice, 2006).

Third, coverage of political stories and events seems to be contingent upon election year. Even in 2004, stories about Operation Iraqi Freedom appeared more often than stories about the Presidential election. Election coverage has varied over the years with some presidential races receiving substantially more attention than others. CMPA's (2004b) analysis of the national network news coverage of the 2004 presidential race revealed a total of 504 election stories between September and early November, an average of nine election stories each day (CMPA, 2004b). This represents an increase from the year 2000, but still follows an overall decline starting in 1988 and 1992 when an average of 10.5 and 11.5 stories aired per day, respectively.

While the CMPA studies highlight what has received the most intense coverage over the last few years, they do very little to answer the question of whether television news has become more sensationalized with time. To answer this query, Slattery and Hakanen (1994) assessed a random sample of 96 Pennsylvania local evening newscasts from late summer 1976 and 1992. Each story was coded for type with sensational events including both negative content as well as human interest topics. Between 1976 and 1992, coverage of governmental stories *decreased* dramatically in early evening news shows (63 versus 19 percent, respectively) whereas sensationalized/human interest stories *increased* considerably (12 versus 41 percent, respectively). If embedded content is taken into account, the total number of stories with any sensationalism increased from 41 to

Table 10.1 Top 10 Story Topics on Broadcast Evening News Programs Over a Five-Year Period

2000		2001		2002		2003		2004	
Presidential election (n = 2,420)	19.0%	Terrorism (n = 2,228)	17.1%	Terrorism (n = 1,945)	16.0%	Iraq (n = 3,433)	29.1%	Iraq (n = 2,567)	22.2%
Business (n = 1,456)	11.4%	Business (n = 1,320)	10.1%	Crime (n = 1,318)	10.8%	Crime (n = 1,002)	8.5%	Presidential election (n = 1,688)	14.6%
Crime (n = 986)	7.7%	Crime (n = 1,244)	9.6%	Business (n = 1,221)	10.0%	Health (n = 877)	7.4%	Business (n = 1,108)	9.6%
Health (n = 766)	6.0%	Health (n = 1,024)	7.9%	Israel (n = 913)	7.5%	Business (n = 865)	7.3%	Terrorism (n = 917)	7.9%
Disasters (n = 634)	5.0%	Israel (n = 523)	4.0%	Health (n = 770)	6.3%	Terrorism (n = 515)	4.4%	Crime (n = 691)	6.0%
Cuba (n = 432)	3.4%	Weather/disasters (n = 475)	3.7%	Iraq (n = 628)	5.2%	Weather/disasters (n = 508)	4.3%	Weather/disasters (n = 679)	5.9%
Israel (n = 365)	2.9%	Accidents (n = 381)	2.9%	Weather/disasters (n = 549)	4.5%	Israel (n = 344)	2.9%	Health (n = 677)	5.8%
Sports (n = 303)	2.4%	Energy policy (n = 354)	2.7%	Sports (n = 357)	2.9%	Space (n = 213)	1.8%	Sports (n = 331)	2.9%
Accidents (n = 259)	2.0%	Sports (n = 301)	2.3%	Mid-term election (n = 276)	2.3%	Sports (n = 212)	1.8%	Israel (n = 232)	2.0%
Russia (n = 233)	1.8%	China (n = 297)	2.3%	Accidents (n = 236)	1.9%	State elections (n = 201)	1.7%	Entertainment (n = 172)	1.5%
N = 12,752		N = 13,007		N = 12,179		N = 11,834		N = 11,567	

Source: Table numbers are derived from the Media Monitor studies conducted by the Center for Media and Public Affairs.

52 percent in 1992. Among lead stories, this change was more pronounced (11 percent in 1976 versus 58 percent in 1992).

In a follow up study, Slattery, Doremus, and Marcus (2001) examined 60 randomly sampled newscasts airing between September 15 and Election Day in 1968, 1980, and 1996. Sensational content was defined more narrowly in this analysis to include *only* violence, crime, accidents, disasters, sex, and misconduct. The most frequent stories were about government (51 percent), war (21 percent), community (18 percent), and sensational (4 percent) topics. Stories about the government decreased (57 percent in 1968 to 48 percent in 1996) whereas stories about sensational events increased (less than 1 percent in 1968 to 6 percent in 1996). Embedded sensational content increased from 1968 (15 percent) to 1996 (44 percent), particularly in government stories (11 versus 30 percent). Clearly, negative content has become more prevalent across the last three decades.

Perhaps an even more interesting question concerns how children are featured in the news. Social cognitive theory suggests (Bandura, 1986) and research supports that children are attentive to (Schmitt, Anderson, & Collins, 1999) and involved with (Hoffner, 1996; Jose & Brewer, 1984) media characters that are similar to the self on a variety of demographic traits (e.g., age, gender). Consequently, young viewers should be quite responsive to news stories featuring other children. Recent content analyses of local news programming reveal that young people (e.g., 0–18 years) appear in 10 percent of all news stories, though they represent about a quarter of the population (Parker et al., 2001). Children are even less likely to appear on national news, surfacing in only 4 percent of these broadcasts (CMPA, 2000).

When news stories do focus on youth, they tend to emphasize the negative. Nearly half (45 percent) of all local stories involving children revolve around crime (Parker et al., 2001). Interestingly, these crime stories are more likely to be framed episodically (distinct, isolated events) rather than thematically (larger context surrounding problem and its root causes). Most crime stories involve violence (Dorfman et al., 1997), with a particular emphasis on murder (Parker et al., 2001).

Overall, then, these trends emerge in television news. News content is often filled with negative stories involving crime, terror, and war. The amount of government-related stories has decreased whereas sensationalized news content has increased over the last few decades. Much of the recent salacious coverage is embedded in stories covering topics such as the government or community affairs. Finally, children appear infrequently on the news. When they do, it is often in a crime-filled, violent context.

Outside of normative or hard-breaking news, informational content designed specifically for children is becoming increasingly common. Channels such as ABC and Nickelodeon offer news programming (i.e., *Nick News, Teen Kids News*) uniquely tailored to a younger audience by featuring child and adolescent anchors and age-appropriate stories. Similar shows are offered in other countries such as in the United Kingdom (*Newsround*), Germany (*logo!*), and Australia (*Confetti News*). In the educational arena, Channel One and CNN Classroom both produce 10- to

15-minute daily news spots for middle- and high-school aged students (Bachen, 1998). Finally, the Internet offers a number of news sites specifically for youth. Many websites are partnered with newspapers (e.g., *Atlantic Journal Constitution*), news magazines (e.g., *Time*, *Sports Illustrated*), and children's publishers (e.g., *Scholastic*). Researchers will need to examine this type of content in the future to determine what children might be seeing and learning from these informational sources.

Exposure to the News

Studies reveal that a good number of children report watching some news content throughout the week (Roberts, Foehr, & Rideout, 2005; Smith, 1999). Simon and Merrill (1997) found that 27 percent of Kindergartners to third graders, just under a third of fourth to sixth graders, and roughly a quarter of seven to twelfth graders watch news "frequently." Klein (2003) found that a majority of seventh (54 percent) and eighth (58 percent) graders watched news one to three days per week whereas a majority of ninth graders (68 percent) watched news four or more days per week.

Most children do not watch this type of content alone, however (Atkin, 1978). Smith (1999) examined patterns of news exposure among elementary-school aged children. She found that many of the children (86 percent) reported co-viewing the news with a parent or sibling. Not surprisingly, Smith (1999) found that a majority of children report watching television news around dinner (53 percent) or before they go to bed (30 percent).

Although a majority of children are exposed to some form of news content during the week, specific viewer variables influence their patterns of television exposure. Grade in school and children's exposure to television news are positively related (Atkin, 1978; Egan, 1978), such that older children tend to view more than their younger counterparts do (Walma van der Molen, Valkenburg, & Peeters, 2002). More recent data also supports this trend. Rideout and colleagues (2005) demonstrated that 15- to 18- year-olds were significantly more likely to say they view television news on a typical day than were 8- to 10-year-olds and 11- to 14-year-olds.

Children who engage in news-based discussions with their parents and/or peers tend to watch more frequently (Atkin, 1978; Egan, 1978), even after controlling for grade in school, gender, and general television exposure (Smith & Wilson, 2002). These correlational findings may be misleading. It could be the case that watching news content spurs lively discussion about local, national, and/or international events. It is also possible that talking about the news fosters a child's desire to watch and learn about the world in which s/he lives. Atkin and Gantz (1978) used a cross-lagged survey to determine that the relationship between early discussion of the news and later news exposure was stronger than the reverse, even after controlling for grade, sex, race, social status, and academic achievement.

Interpersonal, school-based, or familial discussion about the news may motivate or enhance children's desire to consume such content, whereas simply watching television news contributes little to later interpersonal discussion.

Enjoyment also influences exposure. Some research has documented a positive relationship between viewing and liking news programming (Atkin, 1978; Smith, 1999). Hoffner and Haefner (1994) found that nearly a third of children in their sample reported viewing television news for entertainment, and these youth also reported more interest in overall news viewing. Children with entertainment motives (i.e., watch for enjoyment) tended to prefer neutral or background stories (i.e., how the war began, types of strategies) over those about war coverage (i.e., casualties, injuries). Feeling vulnerable and upset was associated with greater interest in neutral stories and news avoidance. These findings seem to suggest that children's viewing intentions are intertwined with their emotional reactions to content.

Environmental factors also have been found to influence children's patterns of exposure. One important influence may be parents' news viewing. Even if children do not select the news themselves, they may still see or hear news stories because caregivers are watching. Indeed, much of children's news exposure seems to be a function of their parents' viewing habits (Egan, 1978). Atkin (1978) found that children tend to watch for a longer stretch of time when co-viewing than when watching alone.

Viewing may also be impacted by current breaking events or other newsworthy activity. During times of national or international crises, children and adults tend to watch more news coverage than normal (Morrison & MacGregor, 1993). One national poll conducted on the days following September 11, 2001, revealed that 92 percent of the 5- to 18-year-olds surveyed had some exposure to the news coverage on the day of the attacks (Schuster et al., 2001). The researchers also found that the average child consumed roughly 3 hours of news content on that day. This exposure finding is quite high, given that the typical child in this country watches roughly 3 hours of television content per day (Nielsen Media Research, 2000).

Children report exposure to other news media as well. Almost half (43 percent) of the 850 11- to 16-year-olds surveyed in a nationwide poll indicated that they had listened to radio news the day before being interviewed (Children Now, 1994). More recent findings suggest that children may be spending less time with radio news. Among 12- to 17-year-olds, 95 percent of females and 89 percent of males have access to radio news (Project for Excellence in Journalism, 2005), but only a small percentage report listening to radio news per day (Project for Excellence in Journalism, 2006a).

Research reveals that children also are reading the newspaper (Children Now, 1994). Rideout and colleagues' nationwide poll (2005) showed that just over a third (34 percent) of the 8- to 18-year-olds surveyed stated that they spent at least 5 minutes reading the newspaper the day before being interviewed. The Internet is fast becoming a means for children and teens to obtain information. Though data on child users is sparse, teens seem to be adept at news acquisition. According to the Pew Internet and American Life Project (Lenhart, Madden, & Hitlin, 2005), 76 percent of teens (ages 12 to 17) who use the Internet are reading the news, an increase of 38 percent from 2000, and comparable to the 73 percent of adult Internet users who report relying on online news sources. This surge of readers to the Internet has prompted at least one media mogul to refer to children and teens as "digital natives" (Project for Excellence in Journalism, 2006b) who must be considered in terms of news industry relevance and content delivery.

In summary, most children are regularly exposed to news content. As such, many children are being shown information about crime, wars, and other sensationalized actions. Several variables influence how much children watch television news such as age, liking, interpersonal discussion, and parents' level of exposure. Although television still seems to be the preferred media children turn to for news and information, some youth are exposed to news content on the radio or in print, and increasingly on the Internet.

Theories Relevant to News Processing and Effects

It is clear that children are frequently exposed to negative news content. What are the underlying mechanisms that young people use to make sense of informational content and what are the ensuing emotional effects? In this section, we summarize relevant mass media theories to explain the short- and long-term fright responses that may result from exposure. We use developmental theory and research to shed light on age-related differences in how children process and react to dangers depicted in the news.

Stimulus generalization

One complaint leveled against television news is that it is filled with stories about violence, crime, and tragedy. As a consequence, exposure to video footage of destruction and devastation may be frightening to viewers. Some researchers have argued that this is an example of stimulus generalization (Smith & Wilson, 2000). According to Cantor (2002), stimuli that evoke fear in the real world should elicit a similar, less intense response when depicted on screen. Research reveals that many of the real-world dangers children report worrying about are shown routinely on television news (Muris et al., 2000; Silverman, La Greca, & Wasserstein, 1995). For instance, physical injury and death are commonly held fears or worries that start during the preschool years and continue throughout elementary school. Gray (1971) argued that these reactions are probably innate and developed in response to danger over an evolutionary span of time. Thus, news stories featuring these types of threats are likely to be potential sources of fright.

There are many types of dangers shown on the news that could lead to bodily harm. To illustrate, dangers associated with natural disasters (e.g., Hurricane

Katrina), international conflict (e.g., war in Iraq), or contracting an infectious disease (e.g., HIV/AIDS) are all possible sources of fright, and, as mentioned earlier, appear with some regularity on the news. Such examples underscore that not all threats to physical injury shown on the news are the same. And, developmental theory suggests that age may play a significant role in how children interpret and immediately respond to different types of dangers featured in informational programming.

Developmental theory

Theories of child development reveal that younger and older children rely on distinct mechanisms to make sense of the world in which they live. Although there are no definitive age demarcations, research generally shows that 3- to 8-year-olds use different cognitive skills than do 9- to 12-year-olds to comprehend television programming. Further, adolescents often use more sophisticated processing strategies to interpret media content than do older elementary-school aged children. As a result, children's age may moderate their comprehension of dangers depicted in the news.

At least four skills are needed to understand threatening news content. First, a child must attend to relevant information in a story. Research suggests that younger children may be swayed by striking visual presentations. Indeed, categorization studies (e.g., Melkman & Deutsch, 1977; Melkman, Tversky, & Baratz, 1981) reveal that young children are more likely than older children to classify objects based on their perceptual properties. During middle elementary school, children group items more often based on their conceptual attributes. Similar results have been found with audiovisual stories (Hoffner & Cantor, 1985), revealing that younger children are more easily misled than older children by characters' visual appearances. This shift from perceptual to conceptual processing affects the types of news stories younger and older children perceive as scary.

Next, a child must make sense of the news. Television news targets an adult audience and features stories about complex threats such as E. coli bacteria and nuclear testing in North Korea. To further complicate matters, information is presented verbally by anchors or field reporters and is not always in sync with video footage. Studies show that younger children have more difficulty than older children in comprehending abstract topics (Cantor, Wilson, & Hoffner, 1986), drawing inferences from verbal passages (Thompson & Myers, 1985), and inferring implied associations among story components (Collins, 1983). Thus, a great deal of informational content about dangers in the news may be inaccessible to young viewers.

Children's ability to distinguish fantasy from reality should also affect their responses to television content (Cantor, 2002). Wright, Huston, Reitz, and Piemyat (1994) argued that perceptions of reality are multidimensional in nature and studies show that "what is real" changes over the course of a child's development (Morison, Kelly, & Gardner, 1981). Preschoolers' reality judgments are often based on a magic window (Hawkins, 1977), suggesting that objects and events that exist on television also exist in the real world. By mid-elementary school, the reality status of characters, settings, and events is evaluated based on notions of possibility or plausibility (Dorr, 1983). With age and maturity, judgments are based on probability of occurrence (Dorr, 1983). These shifts impact the intensity of younger and older children's fear responses to the news.

Finally, children must also understand notions of geographic distance, which develop over the course of early elementary school (Axia, Bremner, Deluca, & Andreasen, 1998), and correspond to the spatial proximity rule. By age 7, children can usually name their own country, but younger children have more difficulty than older children in accurately identifying neighboring countries (Barrett & Farroni, 1996). As a consequence, younger children should be able to recognize the name of their own city, and understand when threats occur close to home. However, youngsters may evidence less comprehension than older children of distant locations and remote threats.

Using theory and research, we predict the following age differences in children's fear reactions to the news. First, the intensity of youngsters' fear reactions to the news should be moderated by age. Because older children are more likely than younger children to comprehend story content in the news (Smith & Wilson, 2000; Smith & Wilson, 2002), older children should respond with more fear to dangers and threats on the news than their younger counterparts will. Studies also show that with age, realistic and/or possible media dangers increase in their fear-evoking potential whereas fantastic and/or impossible ones decrease (Cantor & Sparks, 1984).

Second, the types of stories children perceive to be frightening will vary with age. Given their perceptual dependence, younger children are likely to be scared by stories with disturbing or graphic visual images even if they do not present any real-world threat of harm. When events are coupled with an impaired ability to draw inferences from location cues about victimization, this may make a young child susceptible to an array of unrealistic fears. To illustrate, a boy living in Los Angeles may see explicit video footage of a tornado ravaging a small Midwestern town and experience heightened concern for his own personal safety.

Older children, by contrast, are more likely than younger children to be frightened of stories featuring threats that could actually cause real-world harm. Stories about crime and violence are often presented verbally on the news, since aggressive acts are rarely caught live on videotape. For example, a story about a local car-jacking may first show video footage at the scene of the crime after a robbery occurred and then depict a photo of the alleged suspect. In this case, an older child must infer that a brutal or violent crime has taken place based on scenes of the aftermath and that the perpetrator may still be at large in his/her local environment. Thus, it is those harmful, local actions that are likely to affect children in later elementary school and adolescence. Overall, children's ability to use these four skills governs both the types of stories that are likely to evoke fear and the immediate intensity of those fright reactions to news.

Schematic processing

Over time, one possible consequence of exposure to television news may be that viewing contributes to children's schemas for fear. A schema is "a cognitive structure that represents knowledge about a concept or type of stimulus, including its attributes and the relations among those attributes" (Fiske & Taylor, 1991, p. 98). For example, children have schemas for concepts such as aggression (Huesmann, 1988), gender (Calvert, 1999), and even emotions like fear.

Schemas can also be regarded as a kind of "mental muscle" that children must exercise regularly during viewing. Children use these structures to selectively attend to content, create meaning, organize information, and draw inferences about what they have seen (Calvert, 1999). Activating schemas can strengthen them, and over time, may influence subsequent memories. Moreover, youngsters' social reality may be altered as schematic content is reinforced in memory. When youngsters spend time with news media, which tells true stories about these very topics, this exposure can activate such schemas, reinforce them, and "fill in the gaps" between imagination and reality.

Televised threats may contribute to unrealistic fears by introducing them into a child's cognitive structure, or by linking them with pre-existing fears. Repeated exposure to news coverage featuring dangerous events may lead to cognitive rehearsal (Calvert, 1999), thereby increasing the strength and chronic accessibility of fear schemas in memory. A type of cultivation effect may result (Gerbner et al., 1994), whereby heavy news viewers show more fear of victimization when responding to the environment than do light news viewers (O'Keefe & Reid-Nash, 1987). This effect should be most pronounced when children lack direct experience with or knowledge of the danger depicted on the news or when threats resonate very closely with events in a child's life course (Gerbner et al., 1994).

News viewing may also impact children's assessment of physical or societal risk of harm. For estimates of social reality, Shrum (2002) argued that individuals rely on the availability heuristic. Estimates of violence or "set size" judgments are a function of the ease with which relevant information is available in memory (Tversky & Kahneman, 1973). The more easily information about a particular construct is recalled, the higher individuals' frequency estimates of a given class of events will be. Therefore, heavy viewers of television news content should have more numerous – and thus readily accessible – instances pertaining to danger or threat in memory. This explains their increased or distorted estimates of dangers and threats in the real world.

Developmentally, news exposure may be an explanation for unique manifestations of fear among younger and older children. At young ages, children who view a great deal of news coverage may selectively attend to and overestimate the amount of natural disasters, graphic crime, or catastrophic events that occur in the real world. Additionally, focusing on such content may provoke a greater degree of unrealistic or exaggerated fear among young viewers. Older children with high exposure may demonstrate traditional cultivation type effects as these viewers are likely to pay greater attention to stories featuring crime and violence. Awareness of these stories may heighten estimations of personal risk, and even increase fears about victimization or vulnerability to such threats.

Throughout childhood, schemas play an important role in the manifestation of fear and approximation of risk. As cultivation theory would suggest, judgments of social reality and estimations of crime are likely to be impacted by the viewing habits and schema formation taking place in the child's mind. We now turn our attention to studies that have quantified children's reactions to frightening news stories in both short- and long-term investigations.

Effects of Exposure to the News

To date, 26 studies have examined children's responses to news. The research can be bifurcated into two groups: those focusing on reactions to catastrophic news events versus those focusing on reactions to normative news events. Research on content patterns of news reviewed earlier suggests that the catastrophic has become the normative, however. Thus, it seems prudent to review all this research as one body of work. Most of the research that has been conducted is cross-sectional in nature, thereby making it impossible to establish causal linkages. Yet a clear pattern of effects seems to emerge across multiple investigations. This section details what is known about children's fear reactions to television news and potential moderators of such effects.

Most of the studies document that television news is a source of fear. Cantor and Nathanson (1996) found that 37 percent of parents of elementary schoolers reported that their child had experienced fright or upset over something they had seen or heard in the news. Interviewing children directly, Smith and Wilson (2002) found that over 75 percent of the 125 kindergartners to sixth graders in their sample rated television news as at least "a little bit" scary.

The emotions experienced after viewing the news range from mild to extreme. For instance, Cantor, Mares, and Oliver (1993) examined fear, worry, and distress surrounding exposure to the Gulf War. More recently, scholars studying the impact of the September 11 terrorist attacks found symptoms of post-traumatic stress disorder among children who watched a great deal of news coverage (Phillips, Prince, & Schiebelhut, 2004; Saylor et al., 2003). Though instances of psychological distress may be rare after viewing a single local evening news broadcast, children may feel anxious or worried because of what they see on television.

Individual difference variables can affect children's fear responses, with age serving as an important moderator. Studies typically show that older children are more likely to be frightened by television news than their younger counterparts are (Cantor & Nathanson, 1996; Smith et al., 2002; Smith & Moyer-Guse, 2006; Smith & Wilson, 2002), presumably due to their increased comprehension of the real-world dangers and threats presented. In addition, a child's age may influence the types of stories that induce fright. Research shows that younger children are more likely to report natural disasters and accidents as specific sources of news-induced fright whereas older children are more likely to report crimes and violent activity as scary (Cantor & Nathanson, 1996; Smith & Wilson, 2002).

Gender also affects children's responses to the news. Many studies show that girls are more likely to report being frightened by television news than boys are (Hoffner & Haefner, 1993; Smith et al., 2002; Wright et al., 1989). These differences may be due to sex-role socialization. When compared to boys, girls are more likely to be taught that expressing their emotions is socially appropriate (Kuebli, Butler, & Fivush, 1995). Thus, girls may be more willing than boys to admit or discuss their fear reactions to the news.

The degree to which a child personalizes a news story also influences his/her emotional responses. Personalization may be a function of identifying with a specific person, place, or group depicted in the news. Studies show that personalizing a story can have a significant impact on children's fear reactions as well as behavioral manifestations of distress (Hoffner & Haefner, 1993; Saylor et al., 2003). Among fourth- through twelfth-grade children, Siegel (1965) found that Democrats and Blacks tended to express more distress over news coverage of the Kennedy assassination than did Republicans or Caucasians. Wright et al. (1989) found that identifying with the *Challenger* space-shuttle crew and their families was a significant positive predictor of negative affect and distress following the shuttle explosion among fourth- through sixth graders.

Children's fright reactions may also be a function of their frequency of exposure to television news. Repeated exposure may function as cognitive rehearsal, thereby increasing the likelihood that fear schemas are chronically accessible when making social reality judgments. Studies show that heavy viewing of the news is a significant positive predictor of youngsters' fear responses as well as safety concerns (Hoffner & Haefner, 1993; Kennedy, Charlesworth, & Chen, 2004; Phillips, Prince, & Schiebelhut, 2004; Smith et al., 2002; van der Voort, van Lil, & Vooijs, 1993). However, the direction between news viewing and fear is impossible to ascertain in cross-sectional surveys. Only one longitudinal study has looked at the effects of news exposure on fear over time. Smith and colleagues (2004) found that early news exposure to the terrorists' attacks was a significant and positive predictor of heightened safety concerns a year later, but only for 5- to 8-year-olds and not for 9- to 17-year-olds. These findings suggest that for young viewers, exposure to graphic images in the news can contribute to lingering concerns long after the viewing situation.

Parents are crucial to the etiology and manifestation of their child's fears. Caregivers may model what to fear through affective expressions and verbal responses to dangers and threats. Muris and colleagues (2000) found that 25 percent of the 4- to 12-year-olds in their sample reported learning what to fear through modeling experiences. Moreover, studies show that parents' fear responses are positively associated with their children's fears (Cantor, Mares, & Oliver, 1993; Kennedy, Charlesworth, & Chen, 2004; Phillips, Prince, & Schiebelhut, 2004;

Smith et al., 2002; Smith & Moyer-Guse, 2006; van der Voort, van Lil, & Vooijs, 1993).

Particular message features also influence children's fear responses. Stories with strong graphic visual images (Smith et al., 2002; Smith & Wilson, 2001) and with child victims (Cantor & Nathanson, 1996; Smith et al., 2002) can elevate youngsters' fear responses. The location of the news story also matters (Heath, 1984), with local dangers instantiating more fear and personal vulnerability than non-local ones do. However, age moderates this effect (Smith & Wilson, 2000), as younger children have more difficulty than older children in drawing the inference that they themselves are especially susceptible to geographically close dangers depicted on the news.

Taken together, the research reveals that a majority of children report being scared by television news. Fear responses are moderated by a variety of individual and environmental factors. Finally, the types of stories depicted in the news influence youngsters' affective responses.

Reality-Based Programming

Another genre of television content saturated with crime and violent activity is reality programming. Shows such as *Cops* or *Unsolved Mysteries* focus on the search for and arrest of criminals. Unlike news, stylistic devices such as music, dramatic reenactments, and police/expert interviews heighten the suspense of crime- and emergency-based rescue shows (e.g., *Missing Persons*). This may be especially true when programs depict violent crimes committed by fugitives that are still on the loose.

With development, children become increasingly able to distinguish fantastical from realistic content. Yet reenactments, scary music, and dramatic effects may make fantasy-reality distinctions more difficult. Moreover, crime-based reality programs offer yet another chance to mentally rehearse fear schemas. Children may see similar threats depicted in shows such as *America's Most Wanted* and these may become salient examples of crime and danger. In addition, to attract a national audience, reality shows may minimize the role of geographic location and portray the risk of harm to citizens in multiple locales. Such depictions may be particularly frightening to children who are only beginning to grasp the role of location in understanding crime threats.

We currently know very little about children's comprehension of, and fear reactions to, reality-based television programs. In "*Mommy, I'm Scared*," Cantor (1998) documents an adolescent's recollection of being frightened by an abduction story on *Unsolved Mysteries*. As the girl states,

> On the show they did a reenactment of what may have happened to her and this is the part I remember most vividly. They showed the girl leaving her house and telling her parents that she is going to the car wash. She drives there; the car wash is one

of those self-clean ones and it looks as though it was in the middle of nowhere. It is in a rural area and there are no other people around. So, she begins to wash her car, and another car pulls up, a bearded, middle-aged man gets out, grabs her, they struggle, and she is taken. Her car door's left open, radio on, with her money and identification left in the car. Her parents were the last people to see her. I think I remember this because I live in a rural area and when I go there I drive past a car wash similar to that one. I never questioned my safety there at any time until this story. (Cantor, 1998, pp. 120–21)

Consistent with this story, a nationwide poll of 8- to 12-year-olds revealed that almost two thirds (64 percent) of youngsters reported being scared or frightened by shows such as *America's Most Wanted* or *Cops* (Stacey, 1994).

Only a few studies have examined the effects of reality shows on viewers. Exposure to crime-based shows is a significant and positive predictor of fear of crime among adults (Holbert, Shah, & Kwak, 2004), which is consistent with a cultivation explanation. Oliver and Armstrong (1999) found that repeated exposure to reality shows is positively correlated with adults' estimates of criminal activity (c.f., Curry, 2001). Wilson, Martins, and Marske (2005) interviewed parents of 5- to 17-year-olds about their youngsters' responses to kidnapping stories in the media. The results revealed that viewing reality-based or drama series about abductions was a significant positive predictor of parents' fears and safety concerns about child kidnapping occurring in their local area. Because parents' fright responses to news programming are positively correlated with their children's (Smith et al., 2002; Smith & Moyer-Guse, 2006), dangers and threats on reality-based police and rescue shows may contribute to the development and/or reinforcement of children's fears.

Overall, then, programming that approximates news coverage but adds dramatic elements may blur the boundary between information and entertainment and challenge the nascent cognitive skills that children rely on to process stories. Such programs may have far-reaching and long-term effects on child viewers based on their age, exposure patterns, and the topics presented. It falls to researchers, child advocates, and parents to continue to ask about the precise consequences of viewing reality-based programs and how best to help children understand and process the content they see.

Future Research

Although news clearly affects children's development, there are precious few studies in this area, particularly about reality-based programs or the newer online venues where children spend a considerable amount of time. A few areas are ripe for investigation.

Methods and measures must be honed to capture the effects of viewing news. Some scholars have conceived of anxiety as "a multicomplex response system, with affective, behavioral, physiological, and cognitive components" (Silverman, La Greca,

& Wasserstein, 1995, p. 671). The cognitive component is worry, which pertains to intrusive thoughts about possible future danger. Fear, the affective component, involves the biological response system and equips individuals to flee in the face of an actual danger or threat. The behavioral component includes physical manifestations of distress. While these dimensions are often correlated (Smith & Wilson, 2000), each may manifest itself differently based on a child's age. Developing definitions and sensitive measures of fear is crucial to understanding the impact of news on children.

Parents are often surveyed in news studies rather than the children themselves (Cantor, Mares, & Oliver, 1993; Smith et al., 2002; Smith & Moyer-Guse, 2006; Wilson, Mares, & Marske, 2005). Studies show that parents tend to underestimate their child's fear responses to mass media programming (Cantor & Reilly, 1982). Thus, some of the documented fear effects of the news on children that are based on parents' reports may reflect underestimations of the phenomena. Though concerns over human subject procedures must be balanced with the rigor of investigation, more accurate assessments of viewing effects require that child participants be studied directly.

Research needs to better pinpoint explanatory mechanisms for children's reactions to news, particularly regarding message features and individual differences. Framing of news stories may impact how children perceive dangers and threats. For example, national news outlets may be more likely to report events in a thematic format, contextualizing the topic within a larger story. Local broadcasts, by contrast, may focus on the individuals and events involved in a story. Research with adults has demonstrated that the type of story frame can impact blame for societal problems such as poverty (Iyengar, 1990), but this finding has not been extended to children. Other individual and environmental differences should also be taken into account (i.e., empathy, attachment, socioeconomic status, parental mediation).

The changing structure of news may be important to consider in light of the known effects on children's fear. Advocates, parents, researchers, and policy makers should pay attention to the evolution of news in the next few years. As the line between entertainment and news continues to blur, particularly in reality-based programming, it will be important to document youth reception and emotional effects. Research on children's enjoyment of and reaction to reality shows is noticeably absent. Given the lifespan and heterogeneity of most reality shows, it is impractical to consider the effects of one show as indicative of all. The next step is to consider how reality programs are shaping the lives of youngsters, what role they play in educating or informing – even entertaining – youth and how this might affect the longevity of this genre.

Finally, the impact of new technology on viewer reception of content should be investigated. The Internet, cell phones, handheld organizers, and other digital devices have emerged as sources of information for many individuals, and these will likely remain or grow in popularity for some time. Scholars should try to understand how young people use these technologies to learn about world events and how youth navigate a more complex news delivery system. Shorter, less developed stories may allow more chances for cognitive elaboration to occur, and might even elicit fear. Children are likely to surpass adults in the use of the Internet. Researchers should capitalize on opportunities to investigate just how children respond to and understand online news.

Conclusion

Television news contains coverage of conflict and crime, and is becoming more sensationalized, a fact augmented by the increased popularity of reality-based television programs. It is also clear that children are viewing news, and consumption increases with age. Particularly during times of crisis, however, children of all ages turn to news for information. Theoretical perspectives concerning media effects and cognitive development can help to explain how youth make sense of the threats presented in news. Viewing news coverage impacts children's affective reactions to troubling news content, and specific story features, as well as developmental and individual differences, may exacerbate their fright.

Television news, then, is an important contributor to a child's development. Repeated exposure to frightening content is likely to strengthen the accessibility and availability of cognitive structures that govern how children react to threats and dangers in real life. Newer online venues have received virtually no research at present, yet it is highly likely that the Internet is becoming a major source of information for youth. Parents, child advocates, researchers, and policy makers have a stake in understanding how the news shapes children's growing understanding of the world, particularly as the genre and its delivery across media platforms evolve.

References

Atkin, C. K. (1978). Broadcast news programming and the child audience. *Journal of Broadcasting*, 22(1), 47–61.

Atkin, C. K., & Gantz, W. (1978). Television news and political socialization. *Public Opinion Quarterly*, 42(2), 183–98.

Axia, G., Bremner, J. G., Deluca, P., & Andreasen, G. (1998). Children drawing Europe: The effects of nationality, age and teaching. *British Journal of Developmental Psychology*, 16, 423–37.

Bachen, C. M. (1998). Channel One and the education of American youths. In A. B. Jordan & K. H. Jamieson (Eds.), *The annals of the American academy of political and social science*, vol. 557 (pp. 132–47). Thousand Oaks, CA: Sage.

Bandura, A. (1986). *Social foundations of thought and action: A social cognitive theory*. Englewood Cliffs, NJ: Prentice-Hall.

Barrett, M., & Farroni, T. (1996). English and Italian children's knowledge of European geography. *British Journal of Developmental Psychology*, 14, 257–73.

Cable Network News (CNN). (2006). August 22, 2006. Retrieved August 22, 2006, from http://www.CNN.com.

Calvert, S. (1999). *Children's journey through the information age*. Boston, MA: McGraw Hill.

Cantor, J. (1998). *"Mommy, I'm scared." How TV and movies frighten children and what we can do to protect them*. San Diego, CA: Harcourt Brace.

Cantor, J. (2002). Fright reactions to mass media. In J. Bryant & D. Zillmann (Eds.), *Media effects* (pp. 287–306). Hillsdale, NJ: Lawrence Erlbaum.

Cantor, J., Mares, M. J., & Oliver, M. B. (1993). Parents' and children's emotional reactions to TV coverage of the Gulf War. In B. S. Greenberg & W. Gantz (Eds.), *Desert Storm and the mass media* (pp. 325–40). Cresskill, NJ: Hampton Press.

Cantor, J., & Nathanson, A. I. (1996). Children's fright reactions to television news. *Journal of Communication, 46*, 139–52.

Cantor, J., & Reilly, S. (1982). Adolescents' fright reactions to television and films. *Journal of Communication, 32*(1), 87–99.

Cantor, J., & Sparks, G. (1984). Children's fear responses to mass media: Testing some Piagetian predictions. *Journal of Communication, 34*(2), 90–103.

Cantor, J., Wilson, B. J., & Hoffner, C. (1986). Emotional responses to a televised nuclear holocaust film. *Communication Research, 13*, 257–77.

Center for Media and Public Affairs (CMPA). (2000). What's the matter with kids today? Images of teenagers on local and national TV news. *Media Monitor, 14*(5), 1–5.

Center for Media and Public Affairs (CMPA). (2001). 2000 year in review: TV's leading news topics, reporters, and political jokes. *Media Monitor, 15*(1), 1–6.

Center for Media and Public Affairs (CMPA). (2002). 2001 year in review: TV's leading news topics, reporters, and political jokes. *Media Monitor, 16*(1), 1–6.

Center for Media and Public Affairs (CMPA). (2003). 2002 year in review: TV's leading news topics, reporters, and political jokes. *Media Monitor, 17*(1), 1–6.

Center for Media and Public Affairs (CMPA). (2004a). 2003 year in review: TV's leading news topics, reporters, and political jokes. *Media Monitor, 18*(1), 1–6.

Center for Media and Public Affairs (CMPA). (2004b). Campaign 2004 final: How TV news covered the general election campaign. *Media Monitor, 18*(6), 1–10.

Center for Media and Public Affairs (CMPA). (2005). 2004 year in review: TV's leading news topics, reporters, and political jokes. *Media Monitor, 19*(1), 1–7.

Children Now. (1994). *Tuned in or tuned out? America's children speak out on the news media*. Available E-mail: Children@dnai.com.

Children Now. (2001, October). *The local television news media's picture of children*. Retrieved May 11, 2007, from http://publications.childrennow.org/assets/pdf/cmp/newsmedia/news-media-pic-01.pdf.

Collins, A. (1983). Interpretation and inference in children's television viewing. In J. Bryant & D. R. Anderson (Eds.), *Children's understanding of television* (pp. 125–50). New York: Academic Press.

Curry, K. (2001). Mediating Cops: An analysis of viewer reaction to reality TV. *Journal of Criminal Justice and Popular Culture, 8*(3), 169–85.

Dorfman, L., Woodruff, K., Chávez, V., & Wallack, L. (1997). Youth and violence on local television news in California. *American Journal of Public Health, 87*(8), 1311–16.

Dorr, A. (1983). No shortcuts to judging reality. In J. Bryant & D. R. Anderson (Eds.), *Children's understanding of television* (pp. 199–220). New York: Academic Press.

Egan, L. M. (1978). Children's viewing patterns for television news. *Journalism Quarterly*, 55, 337–42.

Fiske, S. T., & Taylor, S. E. (1991). *Social cognition*. New York: McGraw Hill.

Gerbner, G., Gross, L., Morgan, M., & Signorielli, N. (1994). Growing up with television: The cultivation perspective. In J. Bryant & D. Zillmann (Eds.), *Media effects* (pp. 17–41). Hillsdale, NJ: Lawrence Erlbaum.

Gray, J. A. (1971). *The psychology of fear and stress* (2nd edn.). New York: Cambridge University Press.

Hawkins, R. P. (1977). The dimensional structure of children's perceptions of television reality. *Communication Research*, 7, 193–226.

Heath, L. (1984). Impact of newspaper crime reports on fear of crime: Multime-thodological investigation. *Journal of Personality and Social Psychology*, 47(2), 263–76.

Hoffner, C. (1996). Children's wishful identification and parasocial interaction with favorite television characters. *Journal of Broadcasting and Electronic Media*, 40(3), 389–402.

Hoffner, C., & Cantor, J. (1985). Developmental differences in responses to a television character's appearance and behavior. *Developmental Psychology*, 21(6), 1065–74.

Hoffner, C., & Haefner, M. J. (1993). Children's responses to news coverage of the war. In B. S. Greenberg & W. Gantz (Eds.), *Desert Storm and the mass media* (pp. 364–80). Cresskill, NJ: Hampton Press.

Hoffner, C., & Haefner, M. J. (1994). Children's news interest during the Gulf War: The role of negative affect. *Journal of Broadcasting and Electronic Media*, 38(2), 193–204.

Holbert, R. L., Shah, D. V., & Kwak, N. (2004). Fear, authority, and justice: Crime related TV viewing and endorsements of capital punishment and gun ownership. *Journalism and Mass Communication Quarterly*, 81, 343–63.

Huesmann, L. R. (1988). An information processing model for the development of aggression. *Aggressive Behavior*, 14, 13–24.

Iyengar, S. (1990). Framing responsibility for political issues: The case of poverty. *Political Behavior*, 12(1), 19–40.

Johnson, R. N. (1996). Bad news revisited: The portrayal of violence, conflict, and suffering on television news. *Peace and Conflict: Journal of Peace Psychology*, 2(3), 201–16.

Jose, P. E., & Brewer, W. F. (1984). Development of story liking: Character identification, suspense, and outcome resolution. *Developmental Psychology*, 20(5), 911–24.

Kennedy, C., Charlesworth, A., & Chen, J. (2004). Disaster at a distance: Impact of 9.11.01 televised news coverage on mothers' and children's health. *Journal of Pediatric Nursing*, 19, 329–39.

Klein, R. D. (2003). Audience reactions to local TV news. *American Behavioral Scientist*, 46, 1661–72.

Kuebli, J., Butler, S., & Fivush, R. (1995). Mother-child talk about past emotions: Relations of maternal language and child gender over time. In J. Dunn (Ed.), *Connections between emotion and understanding in development* (pp. 265–84). Hove, United Kingdom: Lawrence Erlbaum.

Landau, M. D. (2006). Are we overscaring our kids? *Redbook*, 206(3), 170–72.

Lenhart, A., Madden, M., & Hitlin, P. (2005). *Teens and technology: Youth are leading the transition to a fully wired and mobile nation*. Retrieved November 12, 2006, from http://207.21.232.103/PPF/r/162/report_display.asp.

Melkman, R., & Deutsch, H. (1977). Memory functioning as related to developmental changes in bases of organization. *Journal of Experimental Child Psychology*, 23, 84–97.

Melkman, R., Tversky, B., & Baratz, D. (1981). Developmental trends in the use of perceptual and conceptual attributes in grouping, clustering, and retrieval. *Journal of Experimental Child Psychology*, 31, 470–86.

Morison, P., Kelly, H., & Gardner, H. (1981). Reasoning about the realities on television: A developmental study. *Journal of Broadcasting*, 25, 229–41.

Morrison, D., & MacGregor, B. (1993). Anxiety, war and children: The role of television. In B. S. Greenberg & W. Gantz (Eds.), *Desert Storm and the mass media* (pp. 353–63). Cresskill, NJ: Hampton Press.

Muris, P., Merckelbach, H., Gadet, B., & Moulaert, V. (2000). Fears, worries, and scary dreams in 4- to 12-year-old children: Their content, developmental pattern and origins. *Journal of Clinical Child Psychology*, 29, 43–52.

Nielsen Media Research. (2000). *2000 report on television: The first 50 years.* New York: Nielsen Media Research.

O'Keefe, G. J., & Reid-Nash, K. (1987). Crime news and real-world blues: The effects of the media on social reality. *Communication Research*, 14(2), 147–63.

Oliver, M. B., & Armstrong, G. B. (1999). The color of crime: Perceptions of Caucasians and African Americans' involvement with crime. In M. Fishman & G. Cavender (Eds.), *Entertaining crime: Television reality programs.* New York: Aldine de Gruyter.

Parker, M. A., Miller, P., Donegan, K., & Gilliam, F. D. (2001). *The local television new media's picture of children.* Oakland, CA: Children Now.

Phillips, D., Prince, S., & Schiebelhut, L. (2004). Elementary school children's responses 3 months after the September 11 terrorists' attacks: A study of Washington, DC. *American Journal of Orthopsychiatry*, 74, 509–28.

Project for Excellence in Journalism. (2005). *State of the news media 2005: Radio reach by age and gender.* Retrieved November 12, 2006, from http://journalism.org/node/1606.

Project for Excellence in Journalism. (13 March, 2006a). *State of the news media 2006: Radio audience trends.* Retrieved November 12, 2006, from http://journalism.org/node/840.

Project for Excellence in Journalism. (13 March, 2006b). *Online audience – 2006 Report: The youngest of the young.* Retrieved November 12, 2006, from http://journalism.org/node/1259.

Purpura, M. (1999). Should TV news be rated? *Parents*, pp. 91–5.

Rayworth, M. (2006). Many new ways to help children fight fear. Retrieved October 25, 2006, from http://www.dailysouthtown.com/lifestyles/109384,1LIF1-25.article.

Roberts, D. F., Foehr, U. G., & Rideout, V. J. (2005). *Generation M: Media in the lives of 8–18-year-olds.* Menlo Park, CA: Kaiser Family Foundation.

Saylor, C. F., Cowart, B. L., Lipovsky, J. A., Jackson, C., & Finch, A. J. (2003). Media exposure to September 11: Elementary school students' experiences and posttraumatic symptoms. *American Behavioral Scientist*, 46, 1622–42.

Schmitt, K. L., Anderson, D. R., & Collins, P. A. (1999). Form and content: Looking at visual features of television. *Developmental Psychology*, 4, 1156–67.

Schuster, M. A., Stein, B. D., Jaycox, L. H., Collins, R. L., Marshall, G. N., Elliott, et al. (2001). A national survey of stress reactions after the September 11, 2001, terrorist attacks. *New England Journal of Medicine*, 345(20), 1507–12.

Shrum, L. J. (2002). Media consumption and perceptions of social reality: Effects and underlying processes. In J. Bryant & D. Zillmann (Eds.), *Media effects* (pp. 69–96). Hillsdale, NJ: Lawrence Erlbaum.

Siegel, R. S. (1965). Television and the reactions of school children to the assassination. In B. S. Greenberg & E. B. Parker (Eds.), *The Kennedy assassination and the American public* (pp. 199–219). Stanford, CA: Stanford University Press.

Silverman, W. K., La Greca, A. M., & Wasserstein, S. (1995). What do children worry about? Worries and their relation to anxiety. *Child Development*, 66, 671–86.

Simon, J., & Merrill, B. D. (1997). The next generation of news consumers: Children's news media choices in an election campaign. *Political Communication*, 14, 307–21.

Slattery, K., Doremus, M., & Marcus, L. (2001). Shifts in public affairs reporting on the network evening news: A move toward the sensational. *Journal of Broadcasting and Electronic Media*, 45(2), 290–302.

Slattery, L. L., & Hakanen, E. A. (1994). Sensationalism versus public affairs content of local TV news: Pennsylvania revisited. *Journal of Broadcasting and Electronic Media*, 30, 309–23.

Smith, S. L. (1999). Children's comprehension of and fear reactions to television news. Unpublished PhD dissertation, University of California, Santa Barbara.

Smith, S. L., Boyson, A. R., Moyer, E., & Wilson, B. J. (2002). *The impact of victim age and viewer gender on children's fear reactions to a violent news story*. Paper presented at the annual conference of the National Communication Association, November, New Orleans, LA.

Smith, S. L., & Moyer-Guse, E. (2006). Children's fear responses to the war in Iraq. *Media Psychology*, 8(3), 213–37.

Smith, S. L., Moyer, E. J., Boyson, A. R., & Pieper, K. M. (2002). Parent's perceptions of their child's fear reactions to TV news coverage of the terrorists' attacks. In B. S. Greenberg (Ed.), *Communication and terrorism: Public and media responses to 9/11* (pp. 193–209). Cresskill, NJ: Hampton Press.

Smith, S. L., Smith, R. A., Boyson, A. R., Moyer-Guse, E., Chakroff, J., & Crook, S. F. (2004). *A longitudinal investigation of children's safety concerns surrounding the terrorists attacks*. Paper presented at the annual conference of the International Communication Association, May, New Orleans, LA.

Smith, S. L., & Wilson, B. J. (2000). Children's responses to a television news story: The impact of video footage and proximity of the crime. *Communication Research*, 27, 641–73.

Smith, S. L., & Wilson, B. J. (2001). *Children and television news: Features of crime stories that cause fear*. Paper presented to the Society for Research on Child Development Biennial Meeting, April, Minneapolis, MN.

Smith, S. L., & Wilson, B. J. (2002). Children's exposure to, comprehension of, and fear reactions to television news. *Media Psychology*, 4, 1–26.

Stacey, J. (1994). Reality based violence hits harder. *USA Today*, May 10, p. 3D.

Thompson, J. G., & Myers, N. A. (1985). Inferences and recall at ages four and seven. *Child Development*, 56, 1134–44.

Tversky, A., & Kahneman, D. (1973). Availability: A heuristic for judging frequency and probability. *Cognitive Psychology*, 5, 207–32.

US Department of Justice. (2006). *Crime in the United States 2005*. Retrieved September 30, 2007, from http://www.fbi.gov/ucr/05cius/data/table_01.html.

Van der Voort, T. H. A., van Lil, J. E., & Vooijs, M. W. (1993). Parent and child emotional involvement in the Netherlands. In B. S. Greenberg & W. Gantz (Eds.), *Desert Storm and the mass media* (pp. 341–52). Cresskill, NJ: Hampton Press.

Walma van der Molen, J., Valkenburg, P., & Peeters, A. (2002). Television news and fear: A child survey. *Communications, 27,* 303–17.

Wilson, B. J., Martins, N., & Marske, A. (2005). Children's and parents' fright reactions to kidnapping stories in the news. *Communication Monographs, 72*(1), 46–70.

Wright, J. C., Huston, A. C., Reitz, A. L., & Piemyat, S. (1994). Young children's perceptions of television reality: Determinants and developmental differences. *Developmental Psychology, 30*(2), 229–39.

Wright, J. C., Kunkel, D., Pinon, M., & Huston, A. C. (1989). How children reacted to televised coverage of the space shuttle disaster. *Journal of Communication, 39*(2), 27–45.

Part IV
Social Effects of Media

11

Media Violence and Aggression in Youth

Barbara J. Wilson

Violence has long been a staple of entertainment media. In the earliest days of television, slapstick cartoons featured anthropomorphized characters that chased and hit one another. Today, Japanese-inspired anime cartoons portray evil characters attacking heroes with razors, videogames reward young players for attacking law enforcement characters, and popular rap songs contain lyrics that condone aggression against women. One journalist described watching evening television in the following way, "*CSI This* and *CSI That* and *CSI The Other Thing* and *Criminal Minds* and so on and so on, and every one – each and every one – flashed scenes more violent than the last. Not just violent. Off-the-charts violent because, after awhile, routine violence isn't enough. We become hardened. So the fictional violence is escalated, day after day, program after program" (Merzer, 2006).

Public concern over media violence has waxed and waned over the years, often ignited by incidents of youth aggression. In the late 1980s, a 12-year-old boy stomped on and killed a 6-year-old girl while purportedly showing her moves he had learned from professional wrestling on television. In the late 1990s, the Columbine High School massacre stirred debate about the media because the two teen perpetrators of that crime were obsessed with heavy metal music, violent films, and violent videogames. After the shooting, police found a videotape of one of the killers with a sawed-off shotgun he called "Arlene," named after a character in the videogame *Doom*. Countless other examples of youth violence, often enacted by increasingly younger-aged perpetrators, have caused controversy regarding the role that the media may play in encouraging aggressive behavior.

This chapter focuses on the relationship between entertainment violence and youth aggression. Violence can also be found in news media as well but that topic is covered in another chapter in this volume (Smith, Moyer-Guse, & Pieper, Chapter 10). Focusing here on entertainment messages, I begin by reviewing research that documents the amount and nature of violence in various media, particularly those directed at children and adolescents. I then describe the major theoretical perspectives that have been used to account for the relationship between violent media and youth aggression. Next, I overview the empirical evidence pertaining to this linkage, which can be divided into studies that have tested the short-term effects of exposure to media violence and those that have tested more long-term effects. Then I describe a number of moderator variables that have been shown to influence whether young people will learn from and imitate violent messages in the media. Media messages differ in their strength or potency for encouraging youth aggression. In addition, children and teens differ in their susceptibility to these messages as a function of their own cognitive functioning, personality, and environmental situation. I conclude with a discussion of recent issues that have emerged regarding media violence and needed directions for future research.

Violent Messages in the Media

Children in the United States spend an average of 6 hours a day with the media (Roberts, Foehr, & Rideout, 2005). No other activity occupies such a large proportion of their time except sleep. How much of this media exposure involves violence? To answer this question, researchers have conducted numerous content analyses of media, most of which have focused on television. One of the challenges in this research is to determine what constitutes an act of violence on the screen. Should slapstick aggression be included? Should verbal threats of violence be counted? Should accidents be counted, particularly those that occur in the midst of intentional aggression targeted at someone else? There are no universally accepted answers to these questions and the varying definitions of violence that have been used across studies can greatly influence the results. A goal for researchers is to move toward more scientific uniformity on what constitutes violence so that better comparisons can be made across time and across different media.

In this section, I review major content analyses regarding the amount of violence in television, movies, music, and videogames. I also provide a brief discussion of what we know about young people's exposure to the violent messages in each medium.

Television

Early content analyses of television were conducted by George Gerbner and his colleagues (e.g., Gerbner & Gross, 1976). The researchers analyzed an intact week of television each year beginning in 1967 and continuing to the mid-1980s. They focused on prime-time and early morning weekend programs (i.e., cartoons) that aired on the three major broadcast networks in existence at the time (NBC, CBS, ABC). Violence was defined broadly in this project to include any act or threat of physical force against the self or other. The definition included accidents and even natural disasters, which became somewhat controversial over the years, because Gerbner reasoned that such content still conveyed the lessons of violence and power. Based on their definition of violence, Gerbner and his colleagues published annual reports on the status of television and their findings were remarkably consistent over time (Signorielli, 1990). Roughly 70 percent of prime-time programs contained some violence, with an average of five acts of violence per hour. The statistics for cartoons were much higher: 94 percent of these children's shows contained violence with about 20 acts of violence per hour. In other words, programs targeted to young viewers were the most violent content in the sample.

Employing a more comprehensive sample, the National Television Violence Study (NTVS) assessed violence on television across the entire day and on 23 channels, including the broadcast networks, basic cable, independent broadcast, PBS, and premium cable (Smith et al., 1998; Wilson et al., 1997, 1998). Violence in this three-year project was defined as an act or threat of physical force *intended* to cause physical harm against an animate being. The study revealed that a steady 60 percent of programs contained some violence between 1994 and 1997. The lower figure than the 70 percent reported by Gerbner and his colleagues is undoubtedly due to (1) a slightly narrower definition of violence that focused on intention, thereby excluding most accidents, (2) a wider range of hours examined throughout the day (6 a.m. to 11 p.m.), and (3) the inclusion of PBS. Only 18 percent of PBS programming contained violent content compared to 84 percent of premium cable shows, 51 percent of broadcast network shows, and 63 percent of basic cable shows. Thus, the proportion of programs containing violent content varied widely on the different channels.

The NTVS data set is the largest sample ever examined in a single study – it included nearly 10,000 hours of programming over the three-year period. Subsequent analyses focused more closely on children's programming (Wilson et al., 2002) and on how youth are portrayed on television as perpetrators of violence (Wilson, Colvin, & Smith, 2002). Like Gerbner, NTVS documented that children's programs were significantly more likely to contain violence (69 percent) than were non-children's programs (57 percent). Again, the figure is lower than that found by Gerbner because the NTVS sample included PBS programs. Children's shows also had more violent interactions per hour (14) than did non-children's shows (6). When children's programming was divided in subgenres, there were marked differences in the extent of violence. A full 100 percent of slapstick programs (e.g., *Bugs Bunny, Road Runner*) contained violence and nearly all (97 percent) of superhero programs (e.g., *Power Rangers, Captain Planet*) did as well. In contrast, less than half of social relationship programs (e.g., *Care Bears, Rugrats*) contained violence and fewer than 20 percent of magazine programs did (e.g., *Sesame Street, Bill Nye the Science Guy*).

Children pay close attention to programming when it features younger characters that are similar or slightly older in age (Schmitt, Anderson, & Collins, 1999). As it turns out, most of the perpetrators of violence on television are adults (89 percent) rather than teens (7 percent) or children (4 percent) (Wilson, Colvin, & Smith, 2002). Yet these percentages mask the sheer number of portrayals of youth violence – in a typical week of American television, over 1,600 acts of violence are committed by characters under the age of 20. Furthermore, the very programs that are designed for youth are the ones most likely to feature younger perpetrators; in children's programs, child perpetrators (56 percent) were proportionately more likely to be featured than were teen (7 percent) or adult perpetrators (28 percent). In music videos, teen perpetrators (13 percent) were proportionately more likely to be featured than were child (1 percent) or adult perpetrators (4 percent).

In the most recent assessment of television programming, Signorielli (2003) focused on week-long samples of prime-time programming airing on the major broadcast networks (ABC, NBC, CBS, FOX, UPN, and WB) between 1993 and 2001. Using Gerbner's definition of violence, she found that approximately 60 percent of programs contained some violence, which is identical to the figure reported by NTVS. On average, violence occurred at a rate of 4.5 acts per hour, again quite comparable to that found by NTVS.

Most content analyses of television violence have concentrated on programming, but one recent study analyzed the commercial messages aired during children's shows (Larson, 2003). Of the 588 commercials featuring at least one child character, 37 percent contained violence. The definition of violence in this study included both physical and verbal aggression (i.e., insults) so it is difficult to compare the findings to the programming content analyses, which have looked only at physical aggression.

To summarize, the landscape of television is full of violence and it has not changed much since the early 1970s. At least six out of ten programs feature physical aggression in the plot, and a young person will witness roughly six different violent exchanges in a typical hour of viewing. Given that the average American child watches 3 hours of television a day (Roberts, Foehr, & Rideout, 2005), he or she will be exposed to over 5,000 violent acts a year. Those figures rise considerably if a child watches certain genres of programming, particularly slapstick and superhero cartoons, that are targeted to viewers under age 12. A fan of superhero cartoons could witness as many as 31,000 acts of aggression per year on television. Moreover, one out of three advertisements during children's shows contains violence. To be sure, there are pockets of non-violence in the television environment. PBS is one place to go, and children's programs that focus on relationships and those that are in magazine format (i.e., short segments that contain skits, stories, or demonstrations) are also typically nonviolent.

Films/DVDs

Several of the content analyses in the previous section have included movies because they are a genre of programming that airs on television. Compared to other types of content, movies are quite violent. According to the NTVS, roughly 90 percent of movies on television contained violence whereas 70 percent of drama series, 35 percent of comedy series, and 35 percent of reality series did (Smith et al., 1998). Although movies are longer in duration than other types of shows, they are also more likely than other genres to be saturated with violence. Not controlling for length, 60 percent of movies featured nine or more violent interactions whereas only 40 percent of drama series did.

Two recent studies looked specifically at films targeted to children. Yokota and Thompson (2000) examined G-rated animated films (i.e., those made for a General audience) released between 1937 and 1999. All 74 movies in the sample contained at least one act of violence, defined as an act intended to inflict physical harm. Furthermore, there was a significant increase over time in the duration of violence in the films. A common theme in many of the movies was that good guys triumph over bad guys by using physical force. A subsequent study by the same authors revealed that G-rated films that are animated contain more violence than do those that are not animated (Thompson & Yokota, 2004). As with television, then, cartoon movies are some of the most violent fare in the children's market.

Violence is pervasive not only in movies, but also in movie previews. Oliver and Kalyanaraman (2002) analyzed previews appearing on the video releases of 47 movies from 1996. They found that 76 percent of the previews contained at least one scene of physical aggression and 46 percent contained at least one gun scene. Previews for R-rated movies (Restricted, so that a viewer under 17 requires accompanying parent or guardian) were more likely to contain violence than were previews for movies rated PG-13 (Parent Strongly Cautioned because some material may be inappropriate for children under age 13) or movies rated G/PG (General Audiences/Parental Guidance Suggested). The previews of R-rated movies also contained higher rates of aggression per minute. The researchers then coded the actual movies, and found a high positive correlation between the content of the previews and the actual violence in the movies. In other words, the previews are valid indicators of what to expect in a film.

Clearly, movies frequently feature aggression, and there is some evidence that they are becoming more violent over time. For example, a study of top-grossing comedy films released in the United States between 1951 and 2000 found that violence increased sharply around 1970 and has been consistent since then (McIntosh et al., 2003). Showing a similar trend but for different years, a study of American war movies from 1970 to 2002 found that films released since 1990 contained more violence than did those from previous years (Monk-Turner et al., 2004). Moreover, the graphic intensity of gore (i.e., bloody wounds) in these films had increased over time.

To summarize, movies on average feature more violence than television programs do. As with the medium of television, animated movies are some of the most violent content targeted to children under 12. But even comedy films and horror films popular with older viewers contain violence. Many theatrically released films in this country target male adolescents in particular and, therefore, are highly likely to contain action, adventure, and violence.

To influence children's behaviors, children must actually see violent content. How often do young people watch violent movies? Sargent and his colleagues surveyed a sample of over 4,000 10- to 14-year-olds and asked about their exposure to 50 box office hits, some of which were rated as extremely violent (Sargent et al., 2002). On average, extremely violent movies were seen by 28 percent of the students. The most popular violent movie, *Scream*, was seen by 66 percent of the students despite the fact that it is rated Restricted by the Motion Picture Association of America (MPAA) for "strong graphic horror violence and gore." Exposure to extremely violent movies was associated with age, sex (i.e., higher among males), lower parental education, poor school performance, and having cable or satellite television or any movie channel in the home.

Music

Despite the public controversy over the explicit content featured in rap and hip-hop music, very few studies have examined the amount of violence in such songs. This area represents a large gap in our knowledge about violent media. The few content analyses that exist have focused almost exclusively on music videos rather than on the lyrics themselves. In fact, only one published study could be found that coded song lyrics for violence. Armstrong (2001) analyzed 490 gangsta rap songs produced between 1987 and 1993 and found that 22 percent contained violent and misogynistic (i.e., expressing hatred of women) lyrics. The author noted that the sample represents an early period in the genre's development when lyrics were presumably less explicit. To provide some sense of trends, Armstrong analyzed a single top-selling rap album released in 2000: *Marshall Mathers LP* by Eminem. Using the same coding scheme, he found that 11 of the album's 14 songs (78 percent) contained violent lyrics. Admittedly, this represents a single artist who may be an extreme case, but the popularity of this CD means that exposure is high. Overall, the figure of 22 percent is likely to be an underestimate of the amount of violence in rap lyrics today.

The research on music videos has focused on the visual images rather than the lyrics. In the most comprehensive study to date, Smith and Boyson (2002) analyzed a sample of 1,962 videos drawn randomly from three channels: BET, MTV, and VH-1. Only 15 percent of the videos featured a portrayal of intentional physical aggression. However, rap (29 percent) and heavy metal (27 percent) were more likely than other genres (rock, 12 percent; rhythm and blues, 9 percent; adult contemporary, 7 percent) to contain violence. The violence in rap videos was also more likely to involve repeated acts of aggression against the same target, which may increase the chance that the aggression will be learned.

Other studies have replicated the finding that roughly 15 percent or one in six music videos contain some violence (Martin & Collins, 2002). This figure is obviously lower than that found for television programming or for movies. Yet a number of music videos do not contain a story or a concept but instead simply focus on the performers, who are rarely violent in nature. Content analyses of music videos have not yet analyzed the lyrics and the visual content simultaneously. In most cases violent visuals reinforce violent lyrics, but occasionally there are differences. Guns, for example, are shown in only 17 percent of violent rap videos

(Smith & Boyson, 2002), but guns are *talked about* in almost 50 percent of rap videos (Jones, 1997).

The point to underscore here is that rap/hip hop is consistently more violent than other music genres are. We do not have good data on how violent rap lyrics are, but nearly one in three videos of rap music contains violence. As it turns out, rap/hip hop is by far the most popular music for preteens and teens, regardless of race or gender. In a national study by Roberts and his colleagues (2005), for example, 65 percent of 8- to 18-year-olds had listened to rap/hip-hop on the previous day, over twice the proportion that had listened to any other genre. The next most popular categories were alternative rock (32 percent) and heavy metal (27 percent).

It is tempting to conclude that violent music is only an issue for teens. Yet even young children report listening to music. Those under 6 years of age spend almost an hour a day listening to audio media (Rideout & Hamel, 2006). Exposure to audio media more than doubles between the preteen and teen years, so that by age 15 the average adolescent spends 2.5 hours a day listening to music (Roberts, Foehr, & Rideout, 2005).

Videogames

There are a small number of studies that have coded videogames for violence. Thompson and Haninger (2001) assessed 55 E-rated (for Everyone) games released between 1985 and 2000. They found that 64 percent of the games included intentional physical aggression and that on average, 31 percent of the duration of game playing involved violence. In addition, 60 percent of the games required that the player injure characters in order to advance to the next level. In a subsequent study, the same researchers analyzed a sample of T-rated (Teen) games released by 2001. They found that a full 98 percent contained violence, with an average of 36 percent of playing time being violent (Haninger & Thompson, 2004). Nearly all of these teen games (90 percent) offered the player incentives or requirements to commit acts of violence against other characters.

Based on sales figures for the 1999 season, Smith, Lachlan, and Tamborini (2003) content-analyzed 60 of the most popular videogames (i.e., the games that consumers spend most of their time playing). Using the NTVS definition of violence, the researchers found that a full 68 percent of the games contained some physical aggression. On average, there were 2.3 violent interactions *per minute* of game playing. Violence differed greatly by game rating, however. Roughly 9 out of 10 Teen- and Mature-rated games contained violence compared to 6 out of 10 Everyone-rated games. Furthermore, Teen- and Mature-rated games featured almost four times as many violent interactions per minute (4.6) than did Everyone-rated games (1.2).

Instead of looking at videogames *per se*, Scharrer (2004) analyzed advertisements for games appearing in three large-circulation videogame magazines. In all, 56 percent of the 1,054 advertisements contained violence, with an average of 2.5 weapons, 1.5 violent acts, and 2.2 violent words per advertisement.

Overall, then, roughly two out of three videogames marketed for general audiences contain violence, and nearly all games marketed for older players do. But who is actually playing these games? Videogames are more popular with older children than with younger ones, yet playing tapers off during late adolescence. On a given day, only about 11 percent of children under the age of 6 report playing a videogame (Rideout & Hamel, 2006), whereas nearly 60 percent of 8- to 14-year-olds and 40 percent of 15- to 18-year-olds do (Roberts, Foehr, & Rideout, 2005). The amount of time spent playing with games follows a similar pattern with age. Nevertheless, videogame playing is a gender-typed activity. More boys than girls play videogames, and boys spend about three times as much time playing games in a given day (1 hour and 12 minutes) compared to girls (25 minutes) (Roberts, Foehr, & Rideout, 2005). Boys are also more likely to play violent games than girls are (Gentile et al., 2004).

Violence across different media

To summarize across media, violence is slightly more pervasive in videogames (68 percent) than on television (60 percent), it is quite commonly found in movies (90 percent), and rarely seen in music videos (15 percent). However, certain genres within each medium are more typically aggressive in nature. These include: children's cartoons, animated movies, rap/hip hop music, and Teen- and Mature-rated videogames. Many of these genres are targeted to youth. Lastly, the density of violence varies greatly across media. An American child watching an hour of violent television, for example, will experience an average of 6 aggressive exchanges (Smith et al., 1998). That same child who plays an hour of a violent videogame will experience an average of 138 aggressive exchanges (Smith, Lachlan, & Tamborini, 2003). I turn now to major theories that pertain to the relationship between media violence and youth aggression.

Theoretical Approaches Regarding Media Violence and Youth Aggression

Many different theoretical paradigms have been used to explain how exposure to violent media content affects youth aggression. Only one theory, which comes from a psychoanalytic tradition, uses the idea of catharsis to predict reductions in aggression after viewing violent content. The vast majority of theories, by contrast, predict increases in aggression following exposure to media aggression through social learning, priming, information processing, and arousal.

Catharsis

During early Greek times, Aristotle suggested that theatergoers could vicariously release their feelings of grief, fear, or pity by watching drama. The Greek word *katharsis* literally means cleansing or purging. Sigmund Freud believed that negative emotions could build up in a person and cause unhealthy psychological symptoms if such feelings were not released (Breuer & Freud, 1956). This idea has been extended in modern days to media violence. According to catharsis theory, a person's violent impulses can be released directly or they can be "purged" through exposure to fantasy violence (Feshbach, 1955). In other words, exposure to media violence can have a positive, therapeutic effect by reducing aggressive behavior. A few early studies seemed to support this idea. In one field experiment, Feshbach and Singer (1971) found that boys living in institutionalized settings who watched a steady diet of violent television shows for six weeks were less aggressive than were those who watched nonviolent programs during the same time-frame. However, the study was plagued with methodological problems, including the fact that boys in the nonviolent condition were allowed to watch one of their favorite violent shows after vigorously complaining about their restricted television diet. Recent scientific evidence, which is reviewed in subsequent sections, reveals that media violence has quite the opposite effect from what is predicted by catharsis. Yet this notion of therapeutic benefit is still frequently touted by creators and producers in the media industry as a justification for violent entertainment products (Eleison, 1994).

Social cognitive theory

Social learning theory is arguably the most often cited theoretical explanation of the link between media violence and childhood aggression. According to Bandura (1977), children can learn new behaviors through direct experience or by observing others in their social environment. Social learning is a more efficient way to acquire novel ideas because it does not rely on personal trial and error. As it happens, children can imitate people in their immediate surroundings, or they can imitate models in the media. Recent research indicates that infants as young as 12 months old are capable of imitating simple behaviors shown on television (Barr et al., 2007). According to social learning theory, imitation is more likely to occur when the observed behaviors are rewarded than when they are punished (Bandura, Ross, & Ross, 1963b). Children will also imitate behaviors that receive no consequences because, particularly in the case of antisocial actions, the lack of punishment can serve as a tacit reward (Bandura, 1965).

Bandura (1965) also distinguished between the acquisition of a new behavior and the performance of it. In one study, he found that children who had seen a punished model did not immediately imitate that model's aggression, but were able to do so later when they were offered rewards if they could enact what they had seen on television (Bandura, 1965). In other words, the children had mentally acquired or stored the behavior and could perform it later under the right circumstances.

Not all children imitate rewarded characters and not all observed behaviors are immediately performed, which led Bandura to incorporate cognitive variables into his largely behavioristic theory. This newer perspective, social cognitive theory, acknowledges that mental processes such as attention and retention are involved in social learning (Bandura, 1986). To learn a new behavior, the child must be capable of paying attention to the model, storing what is seen in memory, and subsequently recalling that information for performance. Thus, children's skills related to perception and memory will influence how capable they are of social learning. In addition, some models are more salient than others are. For instance, children pay more attention to models that are attractive and similar to the self (Bandura, 1986).

Social cognitive theory continues to influence our thinking by highlighting the importance of attractive role models in children's lives. It is particularly relevant in explaining how children might first acquire novel aggressive attitudes and behaviors from the media that they then imitate.

Priming theory

Once aggressive behaviors are learned, cognitive priming theory explains how the media can prompt their enactment in certain situations. According to priming theory (Berkowitz, 1990), violent stimuli in the media can activate aggressive thoughts, feelings, and even motor tendencies stored in a person's memory. For a short time after exposure, a person is in a "primed" state and can be triggered into aggressive action. Several conditions can encourage these thoughts and feelings to unfold into aggressive behavior, including intense feelings of negative affect or anger (Berkowitz, 1990), justification for aggressive behavior (Jo & Berkowitz, 1994), and cues in the environment that relate to the violent media just experienced (Jo & Berkowitz, 1994). For example, Berkowitz and Rawlings (1963) found that college students were more likely to act aggressively against a confederate when he shared the same name as the protagonist in a violent movie they had just seen than when the confederate had a different name. In other words, there was a "cue" in the environment (i.e., name of the target) that resembled the violent movie.

It is difficult to test priming because the theory does not elucidate the precise nature or strength of the environmental cue that is needed to trigger aggression. The theory is also vague about how long a person will continue to be in a "primed" state after media exposure. Nevertheless, the theory is useful for explaining how particular movies or music can instigate violence in real-life situations that closely resemble the media messages.

Information processing theories

Huesmann (1998) developed an information-processing model that helps to account for the long-term effects of media violence. The model focuses on the learning and reinforcement of scripts, which are mental routines for familiar events that are stored in memory. Well-rehearsed scripts are rich packages of information that contain linkages between causes, goals, and action plans (Abelson, 1981). According to Huesmann, a child who is exposed to a great deal of violence, either in real life or through the media, is likely to acquire scripts that promote aggression as a way of solving problems. Once learned, these scripts can be retrieved from memory at any time, depending on the similarity between the real situation at hand and features of the script, which are influenced by the circumstances in which the script was first encoded (Huesmann, 1998). When an aggressive script is retrieved, it is reinforced and generalized to a new set of circumstances. Thus, children who are repeatedly exposed to media violence will develop a stable set of scripts that are easy to retrieve and that emphasize aggression as an appropriate response to social situations.

Huesmann's script theory incorporates aspects of social learning and priming but takes a broader view of the cumulative effects of exposure to media violence on aggression. It also sheds light on why well-learned aggressive habits are so difficult to change. Moreover, the theory can account for individual differences in aggressive behavior as a function of the range of a child's environmental experiences, both in the real world and those that are mediated through technologies.

Huesmann's theory is largely cognitive in nature and has been criticized for not adequately addressing how emotions play into aggressive responding. To fill this void, Anderson and Bushman (2002) proposed a variant of informational processing called the General Aggression Model (GAM). Their model posits that there are three routes to aggressive responding: (1) aggressive cognitions or scripts can be activated, similar to Huesmann's theory; (2) aggressive affect can be produced, which refers to hostile or angry emotional states; or (3) physiological arousal can be heightened. Any or all of these paths can be triggered by either personal variables (e.g., traits) or situational variables (e.g., exposure to media violence). According to GAM, once an input variable (personal or situational) enhances aggressive cognitions, affect, and/or arousal, a person engages in an appraisal process before responding. Appraisals can be immediate and automatic (similar to priming), which may produce impulsive aggression. Alternatively, appraisals can be more thoughtful in nature, which may result in a decision to not respond aggressively in a given situation. GAM is a broad framework that incorporates components from most of the other theories, yet is difficult to test the GAM theory, or more importantly to falsify it, because it encompasses all possible pathways and outcomes in explaining aggressive behavior.

A developmental perspective

Theoretical accounts of the influence of media violence have focused on properties of the message (social cognitive, priming), on how people process violence and store it in memory (script theory), and on how exposure can prompt imitation and/or aggressive behavior (priming, social cognitive). No theory to date, however, takes into account developmental issues as central to its framework (Kirsh, 2006). Yet there are shifts in cognitive processing during childhood that have important implications for how young people will respond to media violence.

Three developmental differences that distinguish preschoolers and early elementary schoolers (roughly 3–7 years of age) from older elementary schoolers (roughly 8–12 years of age) will be described: perceptual to conceptual processing, comprehending reality and fantasy, and concrete to inferential processing. Two additional features of adolescent cognition have implications for how adolescents will react to media violence compared to their younger counterparts: metacognitive thinking and adolescent egocentrism.

Perceptual to conceptual processing   Preschoolers pay close attention to how stimuli look and sound, a characteristic that has been labeled *perceptual boundedness* (Springer, 2001). For example, children below the age of 6 or 7 typically group objects by color or shape, whereas older children focus more on conceptual properties such as the functions that objects share (Tversky, 1985). Applying this idea to media violence, younger children are likely to pay close attention to the physical appearance of a character as well as to the character's actions. Older children become increasingly selective in their attention, searching for cues that are meaningful to the plot such as the goals and motives of a character. In support of this idea, Cooke and Krcmar (2001) found that younger children focused more on whether a character was punished in judging whether an aggressive behavior was wrong or right, whereas older children focused more on the character's reasons for violence. Thus, an attractive perpetrator who goes unpunished for violence can be a potent role model for younger children, whereas older children are more likely to discount that character if his or her motives are selfish.

Comprehending reality and fantasy   Another cognitive skill that develops during childhood is the ability to discriminate fantasy from reality. Very young children often attribute life to inanimate objects, have imaginary friends, and talk to characters on the television screen (Jaglom & Gardner, 1981). By age 4 or 5, children better understand that what is on television is a representation of real life, and they tend to rely on striking violations of physical reality to make judgments about content (Dorr, 1983). Cartoons are often cited as unreal simply because the characters are animated (Wright et al., 1994). Yet fantasy characters can still be attractive role models for young children (Cobb, Stevens-Long, & Goldstein, 1982), reflecting how tenuous these early reality judgments are. By age 7 or 8, children begin to use multiple cues for judging reality in the media. They are able to consider production techniques, the genre of the content, and even the source of the message (Wright et al., 1994). Older children are likely to pronounce a program, a movie, or even a videogame as realistic if it depicts characters and events that are *possible* in the real world (Dorr, 1983). As children move into the teenage years, they increasingly judge media content in terms of how *plausible* the events are in the real world (Dorr, 1983).

Concrete to inferential processing   Younger children focus on information that is fairly explicit and tangible. Yet full comprehension of most media messages requires an ability to extract information that is implied but not explicitly presented. Television series, for example, require viewers to track and connect multiple storylines in an episode, and even videogames convey implicit information about space and time.

In entertainment media, violence is often separated in time from the goals that motivated this behavior as well as the consequences that ensue because of it. The timing (i.e., temporal contiguity) and the explicitness of plot information affect younger children's plot comprehension. By age 9 or 10, children show dramatic improvements in their ability to link scenes and subplots together and to infer causal and time-ordered connections from media content (Collins, 1983). For example, Collins (1973) showed third, sixth, and eighth graders a television program in which a violent perpetrator was punished immediately or after a 4-minute commercial break. Third graders were more likely to behave aggressively if they had seen the violence separated from the consequence than if they had seen the contingent consequence. By contrast, the separation manipulation had no impact on the older children's behavior. Similarly, plot information that is vague or only suggested will be challenging for younger children because they have difficulty drawing inferences. Often a viewer must infer a character's motives, for example, from dialogue or a seemingly unrelated story event to understand the plot.

Metacognitive thinking   Metacognition refers to the ability to comprehend, monitor, and adjust one's own thought processes during tasks (Metcalfe & Shimamura, 1994). Younger and even older children have difficulty considering their own thoughts, in part because it requires tremendous mental energy just to track the environment (Flavell, Miller, & Miller, 2002). As they move toward adolescence, cognitive skills become routinized, thereby freeing up mental resources for higher-order thinking. Preteens and teens are often able to contemplate their own feelings and reactions to a situation, for example, at the same time that they are also processing what is happening in the environment. Preadolescents and adolescents are also increasingly aware of the mental demands of different tasks (Lovett & Flavell, 1990). When applied to media violence, teens should be able to recognize that intricate movie plots and multiplayer videogames require more concentration, and the depth of processing they employ will, in turn, increase their comprehension of complex material. In addition, preteens and teens should be capable of contemplating their own cognitive scripts for violence and of considering how the media might influence their thoughts and behavior.

Adolescent egocentrism   Adolescence is a time of seeking and experimenting with personal identity. Teens increasingly gravitate away from parents and toward their peers during this exploration, and often confront decisions that involve risk (Jessor, 1992). According to the 2005 National Youth Risk Behavior Survey (Eaton et al., 2006), nearly 20 percent of ninth through twelfth graders reported that they had carried a weapon in the preceding month and 5 percent reported that they had carried a gun. A full 36 percent had been in a physical fight in the preceding year. Some of this risk taking may be a function of what has been called "adolescent egocentrism" (Elkind, 1985). Egocentrism is the inability to distinguish one's own perspective from another's and this tendency is characteristic of early childhood (Flavell, Miller, & Miller, 2002). During the adolescent years, egocentrism is manifested in a preoccupation with one's own thoughts and experiences. This view of the self as exceptional can lead to a feeling of invulnerability to negative consequences (Greene et al., 2002). Indeed, research shows that teens routinely underestimate their own personal risk in situations that they readily perceive as dangerous for others (Finn & Bragg, 1986). Other scholars have linked this tendency to brain functioning, which reveals less activation of frontal cortex regions responsible for rational, higher-order thinking during early adolescence than later adolescence (Kirsh, 2003). Regardless of the mechanism, younger adolescents who are repeatedly exposed to entertainment violence may show poorer executive functioning (Kronenberger et al., 2005) and thus feel even more immune to the dangers associated with weapons and physical aggression.

Summary of developmental issues pertaining to media violence   To recap, preschoolers and younger children are likely to focus on the most striking features of a violent show or videogame, such as how the characters look and act. Violent actions will be highly salient, regardless of whether they are animated or fantasy in nature. Older children, in contrast, can appreciate more conceptual aspects of a violent storyline such as the characters' motives, feelings, and goals. Older children also are able to track the main plot as well as subplots, even when crucial events are temporally separated in a violent story. Older children also will discount the content as unrealistic if the events are impossible in real life. By adolescence, youth will comprehend violent content even if it is complex and intricate and they are capable of analyzing media messages for potential impact on themselves and on society. Nevertheless, teens' tendency toward egocentric thinking may undermine their resilience when repeatedly exposed to violent entertainment media.

Empirical Evidence for a Link Between Media Violence and Aggression

Various methods have been used to assess whether media violence contributes to the learning of aggressive attitudes and behaviors in youth. Experiments provide a strong test of causality but are often conducted in artificial conditions and can only measure immediate, short-term responses to media stimuli. Surveys assess more naturalistic exposure and behavior patterns in youth but do not permit strong causal conclusions. Longitudinal studies address the long-term effects of media violence and can provide a test of the direction of causality – does media violence lead to aggressive behavior or is being aggressive associated with selective exposure to violent content? However, longitudinal research is expensive and, unlike experiments, can only provide control over the extraneous variables that are actually measured in a given study.

Irrespective of method, the vast majority of studies have focused on television rather than other media. Only recently have researchers begun to explore the impact of violence in music and in videogames. I will organize the evidence around two categories that are relevant to the theories: short-term versus long-term effects of media violence on aggression. The short-term effects have been documented most persuasively through experiments, whereas the long-term effects are best illustrated with longitudinal studies. Within each of these categories, three forms of violent media – television, music, and videogames – will be reviewed. This section will conclude with a discussion of the meta-analyses that have been conducted in this arena.

Short-term effects on aggressive attitudes and behaviors

The earliest evidence of short-term effects after exposure to media violence comes from Bandura's classic Bobo doll experiments (e.g., Bandura, Ross, & Ross, 1963b). This research demonstrated that preschoolers would imitate a televised model that aggressed against a plastic inflatable doll, particularly if the model was rewarded for such behavior. Subsequent experiments showed that young children would imitate a cartoon character as readily as a human model (Bandura, Ross, & Ross, 1963a), that they could reproduce aggressive behaviors they had seen on television up to 8 months later (Hicks, 1965), and that they would aggress against a human clown as easily as against a plastic doll (Hanratty, O'Neal, & Sulzer, 1972). Much of this work supported social learning theory.

These early experiments were often criticized for employing artificial measures of aggression, for setting up situations in which adult models seem to condone aggression, and for using video clips created by experimenters (e.g., Freedman, 1986). Since then, field experiments have been conducted in more naturalistic settings and have found that watching television violence can increase children's real-life aggression against peers in social situations like playgrounds (e.g., Friedrich & Stein, 1973). Congruent with social cognitive theory, field experiments demonstrate that children do pay attention to characters engaging in aggression on the screen and that children can store these behaviors in memory and enact them in unconstrained social exchanges with peers. Research also shows that cartoons as well as non-animated programs can encourage youth aggression immediately after viewing, and that this effect can occur after exposure to a single episode of violent television (Boyatzis, Matillo, & Nesbitt, 1995). Furthermore, environmental cues that are associated with a previously viewed violent television show can instigate aggressive behavior in youth (Josephson, 1987), in support of priming theory.

There is far less research on violent music's impact on short-term aggression, and most of it involves undergraduates. In one of the most extensive investigations, five experiments were conducted on college students to assess the impact of violent lyrics on a variety of aggressive outcomes (e.g., Anderson, Carnagey, & Eubanks, 2003). When compared to listening to nonviolent lyrics, listening to violent lyrics increased feelings of hostility and led to more aggressive cognitions. These findings were documented across multiple experiments. In other research, sexually violent lyrics in heavy metal music (St Lawrence & Joyner, 1991) and in rap music (Wester et al., 1997) have been found to produce short-term increases in aggression against women by male undergraduates.

Only two experimental studies could be found that test the short-term effects of violent music on youth. Both involve teen exposure to music videos. In one study, seventh and tenth graders watched either a randomly compiled group of videos from MTV or a pre-selected group of high-impact MTV videos containing sex, violence, and antiestablishment overtones (Greeson & Williams, 1986). The high-impact videos increased tenth graders' self-reported acceptance of the use of interpersonal violence. In contrast, the videos had no significant effect on seventh graders who generally showed high acceptance of such violence regardless of experimental condition. Unfortunately, the high-impact videos contained themes other than aggression, and some of the low-impact videos actually contained violence, so the manipulation was not clean in this study.

In the second study (Johnson, Jackson, & Gatto, 1995), African American males between the ages of 11 and 16 were exposed to eight violent rap videos, to eight nonviolent rap videos, or to no music videos. The teens then read vignettes, one of which involved a jealous boyfriend who assaulted his girlfriend as well as another man who vied for her attention. Teens who had watched the violent videos expressed greater acceptance of the use of violence against the man than did those in the nonviolent and control groups. Compared to the control group, participants in the violent video group also reported a greater acceptance of the use of violence against the girlfriend and a greater likelihood of personally engaging in similar violence.

In contrast to the near absence of research on violent music, there has been a flurry of studies on the effects of videogame violence, especially as this medium has grown in popularity. However, most of the evidence pertains to young adults. Several experiments have found that compared to nonviolent games, playing a violent videogame can lead to short-term increases in aggressive thoughts (Anderson & Dill, 2000), hostile mood (Anderson & Ford, 1986), and aggressive behavior (Bartholow, Sestir, & Davis, 2005) among undergraduates. The fact that media violence can increase negative or hostile emotions is consistent with GAM.

Turning to children, a few early experiments showed no effects of videogame play on younger players' aggression (Cooper & Mackie, 1986; Graybill et al., 1987). However, the games used in the violent conditions in these studies were very mild compared to what is available today.

The more recent experimental evidence is generally in line with studies of violent television. For example, Irwin and Gross (1995) found that second-grade boys who played a violent martial arts videogame exhibited more physical and verbal aggression in free play than did those who played a nonaggressive racing game. Similarly, Kirsh (1998) found that third- and fourth-grade children who played *Mortal Kombat II*, a widely criticized violent game, were more likely than those who played a nonviolent game to attribute negative intent to others in hypothetical stories, reflecting a hostile attribution bias; however, aggressive behavior was not actually measured. In contrast to these two studies, another recent experiment found no effects on aggression. In this study (Funk et al., 2003), 5- to 12-year-olds played either a violent or a nonviolent game for 15 minutes and then responded to 10 hypothetical stories by predicting what would happen next and what they would do in similar situations. There was no difference in children's aggressive responses to the stories as a function of videogame condition.

In the largest and most recent experiment to date (Anderson, Gentile, & Buckley 2007), 161 9- to 12-year-olds were randomly assigned to play either a violent or a nonviolent video game for 20 minutes. Two different E-rated (for Everyone) games were used in the violent condition – both involved cartoon-like characters engaging in continuous violence against nonhuman enemies. Afterward, children played another computer game that allowed them to select the punishment levels (i.e., noxious noise blasts) to be delivered to an opponent, whom they believed was their competitor in the game. Children in the violent game condition delivered significantly more high-intensity noise blasts than did those in the non-violent game condition. Although boys were generally more punitive (i.e., aggressive), violent videogame playing increased short-term aggression for both girls and boys.

To summarize, there are dozens of experiments that demonstrate that exposure to violent television programs can lead to short-term increases in aggressive behavior in children of all ages. The research on violent music and violent videogames is more limited. The impact of music on children under 12 has not really been tested, nor have any of the studies of teens focused on violent lyrics as opposed to violent videos. The studies of violent videogames have focused on children rather than teens. Early studies showed no effects but recent evidence involving more violent games has generally documented increases in short-term aggression. One major limitation is that the studies of music and videogames, for the most part, have employed self-report measures of aggressive tendencies. Unlike the studies of television, few music or videogame studies have looked at actual aggressive behavior in social situations, such as classrooms or playgrounds.

Long-term effects on aggression

Survey research has linked violent television (Kuntsche et al., 2006), violent music (Chen et al., 2006), and even violent videogames (e.g., Gentile et al., 2004) to aggression in youth. However, the only way to ascertain the causal direction of this link is to collect measures of exposure and behavior over time. Huesmann and his colleagues have conducted several longitudinal studies of television violence. In one of the early studies (Eron et al., 1972), the researchers found that heavy viewing of television violence at age 8 predicted a significant increase in aggressive behavior at age 19 for boys but not for girls. This pattern held true even after controlling for initial aggressiveness, social class, and IQ. However, the reverse was not true – aggressive behavior at age 8 did not predict higher exposure to television violence at age 19. This same cohort of participants was tracked down 10 years later (age 30). Once again, exposure to television violence in early childhood predicted subsequent adult aggression in men (Huesmann, 1986). In this case, heavy viewing of violent television at age 8 actually predicted the severity of adult criminal behavior, even after controlling for a variety of other variables.

The researchers conducted another longitudinal study in the late 1990s to explore the issue of gender differences (Huesmann et al., 2003). They interviewed over 500 elementary-school children and then surveyed them again 15 years later. In support of the earlier research, heavy exposure to television violence in childhood predicted increased aggressive behavior in adulthood. This time the pattern held true for both boys and girls. The researchers speculated that the shift in findings pertaining to girls might be a result of increased societal acceptance of assertiveness among females as well as a possible increase in aggressive female characters on television.

Cross-cultural longitudinal work generally finds the same link between childhood exposure to television violence and subsequent aggression that has been found in the United States (Huesmann & Eron, 1986). Furthermore, exposure to television during the teen years has been associated with an increased risk of adult aggression, even after controlling for family income, childhood neglect, psychiatric disorders, neighborhood violence, and parental education (Johnson et al., 2002). However, this latter study found that the relationship was generally stronger for boys than for girls, and it assessed overall television viewing instead of violent viewing habits. Even so, those who watch a great deal of television are often heavily exposed to violence because of the substantial amount of aggressive content in television programs (e.g., Smith et al., 1998).

Once again, the evidence for effects is sparse outside the television arena. Only one longitudinal study of exposure to violent music could be found in the extant literature. Wingwood and her colleagues (2003) surveyed 522 African American girls (ages 14 to 18) twice over the course of a year and assessed their exposure to rap music videos as well as their sexual activity, drug use, and aggressive behavior. Early exposure to rap music videos was a significant predictor of several risk-taking behaviors 12 months later, after controlling for parental monitoring as well as teen employment, age, involvement in extracurricular activities, and participation in religious events. Of particular interest here, girls who reported greater exposure to rap music at baseline were three times more likely to have hit a teacher by the follow-up than were those who reported light exposure to rap. Rap music exposure at baseline was not predictive, however, of getting in a fight or being arrested one year later. Unfortunately, the researchers did not assess the reverse causal relationship – whether risk taking at baseline led to more rap music listening 12 months later.

There is only one published study to date on the long-term effects of playing violent videogames on youth. In the longitudinal study, Anderson and his colleagues (2007) tested a total of 430 third through fifth graders at two points in time, roughly five months apart. Self-reports of violent media exposure, physical aggression, and hostile attribution bias were assessed. In addition, teacher reports and peer ratings of aggression were obtained for the children. The researchers found that violent videogame playing early in the school year predicted a subsequent increase five months later in (1) physical aggression (based on a composite measure), (2) verbal aggression, and (3) hostile attributions, or the tendency to perceive ambiguous situations in a hostile fashion. These patterns held up even after controlling for sex, race, initial levels of aggression, total time spent with screen media, and parental involvement.

Clearly, there is a need for more longitudinal research, especially on the effects of exposure to violent music and videogames. The work on television violence is impressive in scope and length, yet studies that span shorter time intervals could also be helpful, especially if we want to pinpoint media effects during particular developmental periods. Instead of looking at each medium in isolation, we might also profit from assessing media habits more broadly. As an illustration, Ostrov, Gentile, and Crick (2006) asked 60 parents about their preschoolers' exposure to television programs, movies, and videogames over a two-year period. The researchers also observed the children's aggressive behaviors during play and collected teacher reports of aggression. For boys, exposure to violent media predicted an increase in observed physical, verbal, and relational aggression four months later. For girls, violent media exposure was associated with a subsequent increase in verbal aggression only. The authors did not control for other variables that might predict aggression nor did they try to isolate the impact of various media, but the patterns are intriguing nonetheless.

In another study that focused on media diets, Slater (2003) surveyed 2,550 middle-school children over the course of two years regarding their exposure to violent media (i.e., action films, violent videogames, and violent Internet sites) as well as their aggressive attitudes and behaviors. Exposure to violent media predicted subsequent increases in aggression in these teens, even after controlling for age, gender, sensation seeking, and general Internet use. Conversely, being aggressive did not predict increased selective exposure to violent media over time.

Meta-analyses

Meta-analytic techniques allow us to combine individual studies to test hypotheses across different investigations and methodologies. The result is a numerical effect size of the aggregate of research findings. According to scientific convention, an effect size of 0.10 is considered small, 0.30 is medium, and 0.50 is large (Cohen, 1988). There have been several meta-analyses of the research on television violence and aggression and all have found positive effects (Andison, 1977; Hearold, 1986; Wood, Wong, & Chachere, 1991). In one of the most extensive

meta-analyses, Paik and Comstock (1994) analyzed 217 studies and found an overall effect size of 0.31, which is considered medium in size. Effect sizes for experiments were larger than those for surveys or longitudinal studies, presumably because
there is more error in naturalistic measures of aggression, but all were significant
and positive in direction.

To provide some context, Bushman and Anderson (2001) compared the television violence-aggression link to other well-established connections in medical
research. They found that the effect of television violence on aggression is stronger,
for example, than the effect of exposure to lead on IQ scores in children, and
also larger than the effect of calcium intake on increases in bone mass. In fact,
the effect of television violence on aggression is only slightly smaller than the documented effect of smoking on lung cancer. Bushman and Anderson (2001) also
found that the effects of television violence on aggression have been increasing
over time since 1975. They speculated that growing consumption of violent media
as well as increasing levels of violence in entertainment content could be responsible for this trend.

There is simply not enough research on violent music and its relationship to
aggression to permit a meta-analysis. However, two have been conducted on the
violent videogame literature. Sherry (2001) analyzed 25 studies and found an overall effect size of 0.15, which is considerably smaller than that documented for
television. Surprisingly, the effect size was negatively related to playing time, but
this finding was largely due to two studies involving *Mortal Kombat*. A study in
which participants played the game for 10 minutes showed a greater effect on
aggression than a study in which participants played the game for 75 minutes.
Clearly, more research is needed on game playing time.

Anderson (2004) conducted a more recent meta-analysis involving 32 independent
samples of participants and found an overall effect size of 0.20. When studies that
had serious methodological shortcomings were removed (e.g., violence manipulation not clean in an experiment, exposure not focused on violent games in a
survey), the effect size rose to 0.25, which is closer to the effect size for television violence. Thus, the meta-analyses to date do not support the argument made
by some scholars that videogames should produce stronger effects than television
because they require more active involvement and typically reward players for
role playing as violent perpetrators. However, two recent studies by Anderson
and his colleagues (2007) directly compared exposure to violent videogames with
exposure to television and movie violence and found some evidence that gaming
produced more robust effects on aggressive behavior in youth (Anderson, Gentile,
& Buckley, 2007). Clearly, more research is needed on this issue.

In the most comprehensive meta-analysis to date, Bushman and Huesmann (2006)
combined 431 studies that examined the effects of all types of violent media (i.e.,
television, film, videogames, music, and even a few on comic books) on various
indices of aggression. The relationship between violent media and aggressive
behavior was 0.19, a small-to-medium effect. The researchers then separated
studies that looked at short-term effects (lab experiments) from those that looked

at long-term effects (longitudinal studies). They found that effect sizes in lab studies were stronger for adults than for children, whereas effects sizes in longitudinal studies were stronger for children than for adults.

Bushman and Huesmann (2006) argued that this pattern conforms with theoretical accounts of aggression in the following way: Short-term effects should be more pronounced for adults because they possess more elaborated aggressive scripts in memory that can be readily triggered by a single violent message. Long-term effects should be more pronounced for children because they are more susceptible to developing new scripts from violent media; adults already possess established scripts that are more difficult to modify, even with repeated exposure to media. On the other hand, the observed age patterns could be due in part to methodological issues. For example, researchers are likely to use more intensely violent material in laboratory studies with adults than in studies with children because of ethical reasons, hence obtaining stronger effects in the former. Clearly, more research is needed on the magnitude of different types of media violence effects over the course of childhood.

Collectively, then, all eight of the meta-analyses reported here found a significant, positive relationship between exposure to media violence and subsequent aggression. The evidence is stronger for television than for videogames or for music, the latter of which has not received enough empirical attention for a meta-analysis. Unlike television, the conclusions one can draw for videogames and music are hampered by a lack of longitudinal studies. Yet when exposure to violent content is assessed across multiple media, both short-term and long-term effects on aggression exist.

Moderating Variables

No researcher would argue that media violence affects all young people in the same way. Indeed, the small-to-medium effect sizes in meta-analyses suggest that there is a great deal of variation in outcomes among samples of children and teens. The impact of violent programming, music, or even videogames depends upon a host of factors, including the nature of the content, personal characteristics of the individual, and the environment in which media are experienced.

Nature of the violent message

Violence in entertainment media varies considerably. Aggressive behaviors are perpetrated by different types of characters, they occur for different reasons, and they result in different kinds of consequences. As it turns out, the way in which violence is presented has implications for how much risk is posed to young people. In support of social cognitive theory and priming, violence is more likely to be learned and imitated when it is enacted by an attractive character (Paik & Comstock, 1994), when it appears to be justified (Hogben, 1998), when it is realistic (e.g., Atkin, 1983), when it is rewarded (e.g., Carnagey & Anderson, 2005), and when it results in minimal consequences to the victim (Hogben, 1998). The caveat about realism is that it depends upon both cues in the program and the cognitive skills of the viewer; cartoons might be discounted by older children but can be potent sources of social learning for younger children who are still developing their understanding about fantasy-reality distinctions.

In contrast to these high-risk factors, the depiction of punishments (Carnagey & Anderson, 2005) as well as pain and harm to the victim (Wotring & Greenberg, 1973) can actually inhibit the learning of aggression. Unfortunately, much of the violence on television is perpetrated by good characters who use violence to solve problems and whose behavior results in unrealistically low levels of harm to the victim and to society (Wilson et al., 2002). This glorification and sanitization of violence dominates entertainment television. Only 4 percent of all violent programs actually present aggression as a serious problem (Smith et al., 1998). Similar high-risk portrayals have been documented in music videos (Smith & Boyson, 2002) and violent videogames (Smith, Lachlan, & Tamborini, 2003).

Personal characteristics of the child

Media violence influences both males and females, although some research suggests that effects may be slightly stronger for males (Paik & Comstock, 1994). This pattern could be because males prefer violent media content more than females do (Funk, Buchman, & Germann, 2000; Sargent et al., 2002). It also could be due to the fact that the vast majority of aggressive role models in the media are still male (Wilson et al., 2002).

The research on the moderating effect of age is currently unclear. The meta-analysis by Paik and Comstock (1994) found the strongest effects of television violence among preschoolers, supporting the idea that younger children are highly responsive to imitation and have yet to develop norms and scripts that would inhibit antisocial behavior. There has not been enough research to systematically test age in meta-analyses of videogame studies (Anderson, 2004). Yet the meta-analysis by Bushman and Huesmann (2006) on all types of media violence found that both children and adults were influenced, but that children showed stronger long-term effects while adults showed stronger short-term effects. To sort out some of these ambiguities, scholars need to examine how developmental processes interact with violent message characteristics and type of medium.

Research indicates that highly aggressive individuals are more susceptible to the effects of exposure to media violence than less aggressive individuals are (e.g., Bushman, 1995; Josephson, 1987). However, even relatively nonaggressive children can be influenced by violent messages (Gentile et al., 2004). Because youth who are high in trait aggression are often attracted to violent television and videogames (Kronenberger et al., 2005), some have argued that a spiral or cycle of influence is at work (Huesmann & Taylor, 2006). That is, children and teens with aggressive predispositions may seek out violent content because it helps them to justify their behaviors. In turn, repeated exposure to violent role models in the media serves to reinforce and stabilize well-developed aggressive scripts in these youth. In this way, trait aggression is a heightened risk factor. Put another way, the relationship between exposure to violent media and aggression appears to be bi-directional.

Finally, research suggests that children, especially boys, who strongly identify with violent characters in the media are more susceptible to the long-term effects of media violence (Huesmann et al., 2003). Perceiving television and other media as highly realistic also puts a child at risk for learning aggression from entertainment content (Huesmann et al., 2003).

Environmental factors

Children from households of a lower socioeconomic status (SES) watch more violent programming than do those from middle-to-upper SES families (Eron et al., 1972). However, statistically controlling the effects of family background does not eliminate the relationship between media violence and physical aggression in youth (Huesmann et al., 2003). Within every social stratum, the more television violence a person watches, the more likely that person will become aggressive.

Parental behaviors may be more crucial than SES. Theoretically, parents who are violent in the home are themselves encouraging the learning of aggressive scripts and modeling aggressive behaviors for their children. Yet there is still a statistically significant relationship between early violent viewing and subsequent aggression even when parental aggression and parental punishment of the child are controlled (Huesmann et al., 2003). Nevertheless, violence in the home can certainly heighten the risk of a child behaving aggressively (Bauer et al., 2006). Moreover, a national study of over 1,000 children aged 6 to 12 found that family conflict was positively associated with violent television viewing and violent electronic game playing (Vandewater, Lee, & Shim, 2005). There was no overall increase in media use as a function of family conflict, suggesting that attraction to violence rather than escape was motivating the media habits of these children.

It should be noted that parents can actually reduce the risks associated with media violence in several ways. Simply reducing overall exposure to television and videogames has been shown to decrease aggressive behavior in children, perhaps because most screen-based content is violent (Robinson et al., 2001). Moreover, parents who engage in mediation techniques that help children to think critically about media violence can decrease the likelihood that they will enjoy and learn from such content (Nathanson, 2004).

Concluding Issues and Directions for Future Research

Media violence is certainly not the sole cause or even the most important contributor to youth aggression. Nonetheless, the research reviewed in this chapter documents that exposure to violent entertainment can cause children to imitate novel aggressive behaviors and can even prime children and teens to act aggressively immediately after the media encounter. The research also indicates that repeated exposure to a steady diet of media violence is predictive of long-term increases in aggressive behavior even into adulthood. At present, there is far more evidence to implicate violent television than violent music or videogames. Furthermore, there is a shortage of longitudinal evidence in this arena, and much of it that exists pertains to repeated exposure to television.

Several other issues are ripe for further investigation. There is a small but growing body of work now looking at social or relational aggression, especially because it is more common than physical aggression among girls. Social aggression involves harming others' feelings through exclusion, gossip, or social manipulation. In one study, this type of behavior was found in 92 percent of programs popular with teens (Coyne & Archer, 2004). Preliminary research suggests that social aggression on television may be linked to such behavior in teens (Coyne, Archer, & Eslea, 2004), but far more research is needed on this alternative form of youth aggression.

Another issue concerns desensitization. Desensitization has typically been defined as reduced responsiveness to a stimulus after repeated exposure, a phenomenon that has been observed in the context of media violence (Drabman & Thomas, 1974). But what is the relationship between desensitization and aggression? On the one hand, repeated exposure may produce less empathy and more tolerance for violence (Funk, 2005), which in turn could make a child *more* willing to behave aggressively. On the other hand, desensitization means that a child will be *less* aroused by mediated violence, and arousal is an important generator of aggression according to theories such as GAM and priming. Part of the confusion is in how researchers are conceptualizing desensitization – does it pertain to physiological arousal, emotional empathy, tolerance, or some combination of these? Is there a distinction between short-term and long-term desensitization?

A third issue that needs more attention is the content of the violent messages. As demonstrated in this chapter, not all entertainment violence produces the same effects. If violent rap music is of concern, for example, experiments need to examine the impact of the lyrics as well as the visual images in music videos. Experiments should also be conducted to assess the impact of song lyrics that are explicit versus ambiguous, lyrics that reward versus punish violence, and lyrics that seem to justify aggression. Some violent messages can actually be educational and may diminish the likelihood of aggression in youth. We also need more research examining the impact of different media diets among children. Does the combination of violence gaming and violent television pose more risk than violent music? Do violent television shows have more impact if they are watched in the absence of educational programming?

A fourth issue concerns young people's attraction to media violence. We need better empirical evidence concerning whether violence actually draws children to particular television shows, videogames, and music. Or do other features such as action contribute more to children's enjoyment of media (Alverez et al., 1988)? If violence does heighten a media product's appeal, what theoretical mechanisms can explain this attraction and are certain children more susceptible than others? Studies suggest that boys as well as children who are high sensation seekers are likely to have more violence in their media diets (Slater, 2003), but our understanding of selective exposure is inadequate at best.

Finally, we need to take a stronger developmental approach in our research on media violence. Are there age periods that are particularly vulnerable to certain types of violent messages in the media? How do children of different ages interpret pain cues from the victim in a videogame? Do violent lyrics affect older children and teens more strongly because they understand their meaning? Developmental issues need to be incorporated more regularly into our theorizing about the effects of media violence on aggression.

There is little doubt that violence will continue to be a mainstay in entertainment media. Many of the violent games, music, and movies in today's media environment are being marketed directly to children (Federal Trade Commission, 2000). As newer technologies are developed, the images and themes will become even more realistic and potentially involving. Research on the short-term and long-term effects of violent content on youth of different ages and backgrounds is crucial in our understanding of the role that entertainment media play in developmental outcomes.

References

Abelson, R. P. (1981). The psychological status of the script concept. *American Psychologist*, 36, 715–29.

Alverez, M. M., Huston, A. C., Wright, J. C., & Kerkman, D. D. (1988). Gender differences in visual attention to television form and content. *Journal of Applied Developmental Psychology*, 9, 459–75.

Anderson, C. A. (2004). An update on the effects of playing violent video games. *Journal of Adolescence*, 27, 113–22.

Anderson, C. A., & Bushman, B. J. (2002). Human aggression. *Annual Review of Psychology*, 53, 27–51.

Anderson, C. A., Carnagey, N. L., & Eubanks, J. (2003). Exposure to violent media: The effects of songs with violent lyrics on aggressive thoughts and feelings. *Journal of Personality and Social Psychology*, 84, 960–71.

Anderson, C. A., & Dill, K. E. (2000). Video games and aggressive thoughts, feelings, and behavior in the laboratory and in life. *Journal of Personality and Social Psychology*, 78, 772–90.

Anderson, C. A., & Ford, C. M. (1986). Affect of the game player: Short-term effects of highly and mildly aggressive video games. *Personality and Social Psychology Bulletin*, 12, 390–402.

Anderson, C. A., Gentile, D. A., & Buckley, K. E. (2007). *Violent video game effects on children and adolescents: Theory, research, and public policy*. New York: Oxford University Press.

Andison, F. S. (1977). TV violence and viewer aggression: A cumulation of study results 1956–1976. *Public Opinion Quarterly*, 41, 314–31.

Armstrong, E. G. (2001). Gangsta misogyny: A content analysis of the portrayals of violence against women in rap music, 1987–1993. *Journal of Criminal Justice and Popular Culture*, 8(2), 96–126.

Atkin, C. (1983). Effects of realistic TV violence vs. fictional violence on aggression. *Journalism Quarterly*, 60, 615–21.

Bandura, A. (1965). Influence of models' reinforcement contingencies on the acquisition of imitative responses. *Journal of Personality and Social Psychology*, 1, 589–95.

Bandura, A. (1977). *Social learning theory*. Englewood Cliffs, NJ: Prentice Hall.

Bandura, A. (1986). *Social foundations of thought and action: A social cognitive theory*. Englewood Cliffs, NJ: Prentice Hall.

Bandura, A., Ross, D., & Ross, S. A. (1963a). Imitation of film-mediated aggressive models. *Journal of Abnormal and Social Psychology*, 66, 3–11.

Bandura, A., Ross, D., & Ross, S. A. (1963b). Vicarious reinforcement and imitative learning. *Journal of Abnormal and Social Psychology*, 67, 601–7.

Barr, R., Muentener, P., Garcia, A., Fujimoto, M., & Chávez, V. (2007). The effect of repetition on imitation from television during infancy. *Developmental Psychobiology*, 49, 196–207.

Bartholow, B. D., Sestir, M. A., & Davis, E. B. (2005). Correlates and consequences of exposure to video game violence: Hostile personality, empathy, and aggressive behavior. *Personality and Social Psychology Bulletin*, 31, 1573–86.

Bauer, N. S., Herrenkohl, T. I., Lozano, P., Rivara, F. P., Hill, K. G., & Hawkins, J. D. (2006). Childhood bullying involvement and exposure to intimate partner violence. *Pediatrics*, 188(2), 234–44.

Berkowitz, L. (1990). On the formation and regulation of anger and aggression: A cognitive neoassociationistic analysis. *American Psychologist*, 45, 494–503.

Berkowitz, L., & Rawlings, E. (1963). Effects of film violence on inhibitions against subsequent aggression. *Journal of Abnormal and Social Psychology*, 66(5), 405–12.

Boyatzis, C. J., Matillo, G. M., & Nesbitt, K. M. (1995). Effects of the "Mighty Morphin Power Rangers" on children's aggression with peers. *Child Study Journal*, 25, 45–55.

Breuer, J., & Freud, S. (1956). *Studies on hysteria*. London: Hogarth Press.

Bushman, B. J. (1995). Moderating role of trait aggressiveness in the effects of violent media on aggression. *Journal of Personality and Social Psychology*, 69, 950–60.

Bushman, B. J., & Anderson, C. A. (2001). Media violence and the American public: Scientific facts versus media misinformation. *American Psychologist*, 56, 477–89.

Bushman, B. J., & Huesmann, L. R. (2006). Short-term and long-term effects of violent media on aggression in children and adults. *Archives of Pediatrics and Adolescent Medicine*, 160(4), 348–52.

Carnagey, N. L., & Anderson, C. A. (2005). The effects of reward and punishment in violent video games on aggressive affect, cognition, and behavior. *Psychological Science*, 16(11), 882–9.

Chen, M. J., Miller, B. A., Grube, J. W., & Waiters, E. D. (2006). Music, substance use, and aggression. *Journal of Studies on Alcohol*, 67, 373–81.

Cobb, N. J., Stevens-Long, J., & Goldstein, S. (1982). The influence of televised models on toy preference in children. *Sex Roles*, 8, 1075–80.

Cohen, J. (1988). *Statistical power analysis for the behavioral sciences* (2nd edn.). Hillsdale, NJ: Lawrence Erlbaum.

Collins, W. A. (1973). Effect of temporal separation between motivation, aggression, and consequences: A developmental study. *Developmental Psychology*, 8, 215–22.

Collins, W. A. (1983). Interpretation and inference in children's television viewing. In J. Bryant & D. Anderson (Eds.), *Children's understanding of television: Research on attention and comprehension* (pp. 125–50). New York: Academic Press.

Cooke, M. C., & Krcmar, M. (2001). Children's moral reasoning and their perceptions of television violence. *Journal of Communication*, 51(2), 300–16.

Cooper, J., & Mackie, D. (1986). Video games and aggression in children. *Journal of Applied Social Psychology*, 16, 726–44.

Coyne, S. M., & Archer, J. (2004). Indirect aggression in the media: A content analysis of British television programs. *Aggressive Behavior*, 30, 254–71.

Coyne, S. M., Archer, J., & Eslea, M. (2004). Cruel intentions on television and real life: Can viewing indirect aggression increase viewers' subsequent indirect aggression? *Journal of Experimental Child Psychology*, 88, 234–53.

Dorr, A. (1983). No shortcuts to judging reality. In J. Bryant & D. R. Anderson (Eds.), *Children's understanding of television: Research on attention and comprehension* (pp. 199–220). New York: Academic Press.

Drabman, R. S., & Thomas, M. H. (1974). Does media violence increase children's toleration of real-life aggression? *Developmental Psychology*, 10, 418–21.

Eaton, D., Kann, L., Kinchen, S., Ross, J., Hawkins, J., Harris, W. A., et al. (2006). *Youth Risk Behavior Surveillance – United States, 2005*. Atlanta, GA: Centers for Disease Control and Prevention.

Eleison, M. (1994, January). *Scapegoat: Hollywood*. Retrieved April 3, 2007, from http://www.moviemaker.com/magazine/editorial.php?id=160.

Elkind, D. (1985). Egocentrism redux. *Developmental Review*, 5, 218–26.

Eron, L. D., Huesmann, L. R., Lefkowitz, M. M., & Walder, L. O. (1972). Does television cause aggression? *American Psychologist*, 27, 253–63.

Federal Trade Commission. (2000). *Marketing violent entertainment to children: A review of self-regulation and industry practices in the motion picture, music recording & electronic game industries*. Washington, DC: Federal Trade Commission.

Feshbach, S. (1955). The drive-reducing function of fantasy behavior. *Journal of Abnormal and Social Psychology*, 50, 3–11.

Feshbach, S., & Singer, R. D. (1971). *Television and aggression: An experimental field study*. San Francisco: Jossey-Bass.

Finn, P., & Bragg, B. W. E. (1986). Perception of risk of an accident by young and older drivers. *Accident Analysis and Prevention*, 18, 289–98.

Flavell, J. H., Miller, P. H., & Miller, S. A. (2002). *Cognitive development* (4th edn.). Upper Saddle River, NJ: Prentice Hall.

Freedman, J. L. (1986). Television violence and aggression: A rejoinder. *Psychological Bulletin*, 100, 372–8.

Friedrich, L. K., & Stein, A. H. (1973). Aggressive and prosocial television programs and the natural behavior of preschool children. *Monographs of the Society for Research in Child Development*, 38(4, Serial No. 151), 1–63.

Funk, J. B. (2005). Children's exposure to violent video games and desensitization to violence. *Child & Adolescent Psychiatric Clinics of North America*, 14, 387–404.

Funk, J. B., Buchman, D. D., & Germann, J. N. (2000). Preference for violent electronic games, self-concept, and gender differences in young children. *American Journal of Orthopsychiatry*, 70(2), 233–41.

Funk, J. B., Buchman, D. D., Jenks, J., & Bechtoldt, H. (2003). Playing violent video games, desensitization, and moral evaluation in children. *Applied Developmental Psychology*, 24, 413–36.

Gentile, D. A., Lynch, P. J., Linder, J. R., & Walsh, D. A. (2004). The effects of violent video game habits on adolescent hostility, aggressive behaviors, and school performance. *Journal of Adolescence*, 27(1), 5–22.

Gerbner, G., & Gross, L. (1976). Living with television: The violence profile. *Journal of Communication*, 26, 172–94.

Graybill, D., Strawniak, M., Hunter, T., & O'Leary, M. (1987). Effects of playing versus observing violent versus nonviolent video games on children's aggression. *Psychology: A Quarterly Journal of Human Behavior*, 24, 1–8.

Greene, J. O., Krcmar, M., Rubin, D. L., Walters, L. H., & Hale, J. L. (2002). Elaboration in processing adolescent health messages: The impact of egocentrism and sensation seeking on message processing. *Journal of Communication*, 52, 812–31.

Greeson, L. E., & Williams, R. A. (1986). Social implications of music videos for youth: An analysis of the content and effects of MTV. *Youth and Society*, 18, 177–89.

Haninger, K., & Thompson, K. M. (2004). Content and ratings of teen-rated video games. *Journal of the American Medical Association*, 291, 856–65.

Hanratty, M. A., O'Neal, E., & Sulzer, J. L. (1972). Effect of frustration on imitation of aggression. *Journal of Personality and Social Psychology*, 21, 30–34.

Hearold, S. (1986). A synthesis of 1043 effects of television on social behavior. In G. Comstock (Ed.), *Public communication and behavior* (pp. 65–133). New York: Academic Press.

Hicks, D. J. (1965). Imitation and retention of film-mediated aggressive peer and adult models. *Journal of Personality and Social Psychology*, 2, 97–100.

Hogben, M. (1998). Factors moderating the effect of televised aggression on viewer behavior. *Communication Research*, 25, 220–47.

Huesmann, L. R. (1986). Psychological processes promoting the relation between exposure to media violence and aggressive behavior by the viewer. *Journal of Social Issues*, 42, 125–39.

Huesmann, L. R. (1998). The role of social information processing and cognitive schema in the acquisition and maintenance of habitual aggressive behavior. In R. G. Green & E. Donnerstein (Eds.), *Human aggression: Theories, research, and implications for social policy* (pp. 73–103). San Diego, CA: Academic Press.

Huesmann, L. R., & Eron, L. D. (1986). *Television and the aggressive child: A cross-national comparison*. Hillsdale, NJ: Lawrence Erlbaum.

Huesmann, L. R., Moise-Titus, J., Podolski, C., & Eron, L. D. (2003). Longitudinal relations between children's exposure to TV violence and their aggressive and violent behavior in young adulthood: 1977–1992. *Developmental Psychology*, 39, 201–21.

Huesmann, L. R., & Taylor, L. D. (2006). The role of media violence in violent behavior. *Annual Review of Public Health*, 27, 393–415.

Irwin, A. R., & Gross, A. M. (1995). Cognitive tempo, violent video games, and aggressive behavior in young boys. *Journal of Family Violence*, 10, 337–50.

Jaglom, L. M., & Gardner, H. (1981). The preschool viewer as anthropologist. In H. Kelly & H. Gardner (Eds.), *Viewing children through television. New Directions in Child Development*, vol. 13 (pp. 9–29). San Francisco, CA: Jossey-Bass.

Jessor, R. (1992). Risk behavior in adolescence: A psychosocial framework for understanding and action. In D. E. Rogers & E. Ginzburg (Eds.), *Adolescents at Risk: Medical and social perspectives* (pp. 19–34). Boulder, CO: Westview Press.

Jo, E., & Berkowitz, L. (1994). A priming effect analysis of media influence: An update. In J. Bryant & D. Zillmann (Eds.), *Media effects: Advances in theory and research* (pp. 43–60). Hillsdale, NJ: Lawrence Erlbaum.

Johnson, J. D., Jackson, L. A., & Gatto, L. (1995). Violent attitudes and deferred academic aspirations: Deleterious effects of exposure to rap music. *Basic and Applied Social Psychology*, 16, 27–41.

Johnson, J. G., Cohen, P., Smailes, E. M., Kasen, S., & Brook, J. S. (2002). Television viewing and aggressive behavior during adolescence and adulthood. *Science*, 295, 2468–71.

Jones, K. (1997). Are rap videos more violent? *Howard Journal of Communication*, 8, 343–56.

Josephson, W. L. (1987). Television violence and children's aggression: Testing the priming, social script, and disinhibition predictions. *Journal of Personality and Social Psychology*, 53, 882–90.

Kirsh, S. J. (1998). Seeing the world through *Mortal Kombat*-colored glasses: Violent video games and the development of a short-term hostile attribution bias. *Childhood*, 5, 177–84.

Kirsh, S. J. (2003). The effects of violent video games on adolescents: The overlooked influence of development. *Aggression and Violent Behavior*, 8, 377–89.

Kirsh, S. J. (2006). *Children, adolescents and media violence: A critical look at the research.* Thousand Oaks, CA: Sage.

Kronenberger, W. G., Mathews, V. P., Dunn, D. W., Wang, Y., Wood, E. A., Larsen, J. J., et al. (2005). Media violence exposure in aggressive and control adolescents: Differences in self- and parent-reported exposure to violence on television and in video games. *Aggressive Behavior*, 31, 201–16.

Kuntsche, E., Pickett, W., Overpeck, M., Craig, W., Boyce, W., & de Matos, G. M. (2006). Television viewing and forms of bullying among adolescents from eight countries. *Journal of Adolescent Health*, 39, 908–15.

Larson, M. S. (2003). Gender, race, and aggression in television commercials that feature children. *Sex Roles*, 48, 67–75.

Lovett, S. B., & Flavell, J. H. (1990). Understanding and remembering: Children's knowledge about the differential effects of strategy and task variables on comprehension and memorization. *Child Development*, 61, 1842–58.

Martin, B. A. S., & Collins, B. A. (2002). Violence and consumption imagery in music videos. *European Journal of Marketing*, 36, 855–73.

McIntosh, W. D., Murray, J. D., Murray, R. M., & Manian, S. (2003). What's so funny about a poke in the eye? The prevalence of violence in comedy films and its relation to social and economic threat in the United States, 1951–2000. *Mass Communication and Society*, 6(4), 345–60.

Merzer, M. (2006). We in the media share blame for violence in society. *The Miami Herald*, December 10. Retrieved January 4, 2007, from www.miami.com/mld/miamiherald.

Metcalf, J., & Shimamura, A. P. (Eds.). (1994). *Metacognition: Knowing about knowing.* Cambridge, MA: MIT Press.

Monk-Turner, E., Ciba, P., Cunningham, M., McIntire, P. G., Pollard, M., & Turner, R. (2004). A content analysis of violence in American war movies. *Analyses of Social Issues and Public Policy*, 4(1), 1–11.

Nathanson, A. I. (2004). Factual and evaluative approaches to modifying children's responses to violent television. *Journal of Communication*, 54, 321–36.

Oliver, M. B., & Kalyanaraman, S. (2002). Appropriate for all viewing audiences? An examination of violent and sexual portrayals in movie previews featured on video rentals. *Journal of Broadcasting and Electronic Media*, 46, 283–99.

Ostrov, J. M., Gentile, D. A., & Crick, N. R. (2006). Media exposure, aggression and prosocial behavior during early childhood: A longitudinal study. *Social Development*, 15, 612–27.

Paik, H., & Comstock, G. (1994). The effects of television violence on antisocial behavior: A meta-analysis. *Communication Research*, 21, 516–46.

Rideout, V., & Hamel, E. (2006). *The media family: Electronic media in the lives of infants, toddlers, preschoolers and their parents*. Palo Alto, CA: Kaiser Family Foundation.

Roberts, D. F., Foehr, E. G., & Rideout, V. (2005). *Generation M: Media in the lives of 8–18-year-olds*. Menlo Park, CA: Kaiser Family Foundation.

Robinson, T. H., Wilde, M. L., Navracruz, L. C., Haydel, K. F., & Varady, A., (2001). Effects of reducing children's television and video game use on aggressive behavior: A randomized controlled trial. *Archives of Pediatrics and Adolescent Medicine*, 155, 17–23.

Sargent, J. D., Heatherton, T. F., Ahrens, M. B., Dalton, M. A., Tickle, J. J., & Beach, M. L. (2002). Adolescent exposure to extremely violent movies. *Journal of Adolescent Health*, 31, 449–54.

Scharrer, E. (2004). Virtual violence: gender and aggression in video game advertisements. *Mass Communication and Society*, 7, 392–412.

Schmitt, K. L., Anderson, D. R., & Collins, P. A. (1999). Form and content: Looking at visual features of television. *Developmental Psychology*, 35, 1156–67.

Sherry, J. L. (2001). The effects of violent video games on aggression: A meta-analysis. *Human Communication Research*, 27, 409–31.

Signorielli, N. (1990). *Cultivation analysis: New directions in media effects research*. Newbury Park, CA: Sage.

Signorielli, N. (2003). Prime-time violence 1993–2001: Has the picture really changed? *Journal of Broadcasting and Electronic Media*, 47, 36–57.

Slater, M. (2003). Violent media content and aggressiveness in adolescents: A downward spiral. *Communication Research*, 30, 713–36.

Smith, S. L., & Boyson, A. R. (2002). Violence in music videos: Examining the prevalence and context of physical aggression. *Journal of Communication*, 52(1), 61–83.

Smith, S. L., Lachlan, K., & Tamborini, R. (2003). Popular videogames: Quantifying the presentation of violence and its context. *Journal of Broadcasting and Electronic Media*, 47, 58–76.

Smith, S. L., Wilson, B. J., Kunkel, D., Linz, D., Potter, W. J., Colvin, C., & Donnerstein, E. (1998). Violence in television programming overall: University of California, Santa Barbara study. In *National television violence study*, vol. 3 (pp. 5–220). Newbury Park, CA: Sage.

Springer, K. (2001). Perceptual boundedness and perceptual support in conceptual development. *Psychological Review*, 108, 691–708.

St Lawrence, J. S., & Joyner, D. J. (1991). The effects of sexually violent rock music on males' acceptance of violence against women. *Psychology of Women Quarterly*, 15, 49–63.

Thompson, K. M., & Haninger, K. (2001). Violence in E-rated video games. *Journal of the American Medical Association*, 286, 591–8.

Thompson, K. M., & Yokota, F. (2004). Violence, sex, and profanity in films: Correlation of movie ratings with context. *Medscape General Medicine*, 6, 3.

Tversky, B. (1985). The development of taxonomic organization in named and pictured categories. *Developmental Psychology*, 21, 1111–19.

Vandewater, E. A., Lee, J. H., & Shim, M. (2005). Family conflict and violent electronic media use in school-aged children. *Media Psychology*, 7, 73–86.

Wester, S. R., Crown, C. L., Quatman, G. L., & Heesaker, M. (1997). The influence of sexually violent rap music on attitudes of men with little prior exposure. *Psychology of Women Quarterly*, 21, 497–508.

Wilson, B. J., Colvin, C. M., & Smith, S. L. (2002). Engaging in violence on American television: A comparison of child, teen, and adult perpetrators. *Journal of Communication*, 52(1), 36–60.

Wilson, B. J., Kunkel, D., Linz, D., Potter, W. J., Donnerstein, E., Smith, S. L., et al. (1997). Violence in television programming overall: University of California, Santa Barbara study. In *National television violence study*, vol. 1 (pp. 3–268). Thousand Oaks, CA: Sage.

Wilson, B. J., Kunkel, D., Linz, D., Potter, W. J., Donnerstein, E., Smith, S. L., et al. (1998). Violence in television programming overall: University of California, Santa Barbara study. In *National television violence study*, vol. 2 (pp. 3–204). Thousand Oaks, CA: Sage.

Wilson, B. J., Smith, S. L., Potter, W. J., Kunkel, D., Linz, D., Colvin, C. M., & Donnerstein, E. (2002). Violence in children's television programming: Assessing the risks. *Journal of Communication*, 52(1), 5–35.

Wingwood, G. M., DiClemente, R. J., Bernhardt, J. M., Harrington, K., Davies, S. L., Robillard, A., & Hook, E. W. (2003). A prospective study of exposure to rap music videos and African American female adolescents' health. *American Journal of Public Health*, 93(3), 437–9.

Wood, W., Wong, F. Y., & Chachere, J. C. (1991). Effects of media violence on viewers' aggression in unstrained social interaction. *Psychological Bulletin*, 109(3), 371–83.

Wotring, C. E., & Greenberg, B. S. (1973). Experiments in televised violence and verbal aggression: Two exploratory studies. *Journal of Communication*, 23, 446–60.

Wright, J. C., Huston, A. C., Reitz, A. L., & Piemyat, S. (1994). Young children's perceptions of television reality: Determinants and developmental differences. *Developmental Psychology*, 30(2), 229–39.

Yokota, F., & Thompson, K. M. (2000). Violence in G-rated animated films. *Journal of the American Medical Association*, 283, 2716–20.

12

Prosocial Effects of Media Exposure

Marie-Louise Mares, Edward Palmer, and Tia Sullivan

In our increasingly complex technological media environment, children are exposed to a sweeping array of role models and messages. Some of these portrayals and messages are positive ones, teaching children to become more helpful, more curious, and even more tolerant. Other messages are potentially harmful, teaching children stereotypes and antisocial behavior. Media researchers have tended historically to focus on the latter type of effect, in part because of heightened public fear about negative effects of the media (Wartella & Reeves, 1985). There are literally hundreds of studies, for example, on the impact of media violence on children's aggression (Wilson, this volume, Chapter 11). Far less is known about the positive potential of the media.

The focus of this chapter is on whether and how the media can teach children prosocial lessons and behavior. We begin with a discussion of what constitutes prosocial behavior, discuss several theories that can be used to explain the impact of prosocial media, and then turn to the empirical research to summarize what types of effects can occur, which types of children are most affected, and what types of environmental situations can enhance those effects. We also explore how much prosocial content exists in various media and how exposure varies by age.

Defining Prosocial Behavior

What constitutes "prosocial behavior" is somewhat controversial. By some definitions, (e.g., Huber, 2004) an act is only considered prosocial if it is beneficial for the recipient *and* there are no obvious benefits for the actor. Thus, friendly play would not be considered prosocial because all participants benefit, but altruism, generosity, and sympathy (which involve some sacrifice on the part of the actor) would be considered prosocial. There is debate, however, about whether even acts of altruism or generosity have some benefits for the actor, e.g., by enhancing self-esteem (Batson, 1994). For this reason, other definitions of prosocial behavior often focus on outcomes rather than intentions of actions. In their meta-analysis, Mares and Woodard (2005) included (1) positive interactions (friendly play or peaceful conflict resolution), (2) aggression reduction (both physical and verbal), (3) altruistic actions (sharing, donating, offering help, comforting), and (4) stereotype reduction (attitudes, beliefs, and resulting behaviors countering stereotypical portrayals of gender, ethnicity, and sexual orientation).

The focus in the current chapter is on the conditions under which media exposure teaches and encourages positive interpersonal attitudes and behaviors such as sharing, turn taking and helpfulness. Stereotype reduction is considered elsewhere in this volume (Greenberg & Mastro, Chapter 4; Hust & Brown, Chapter 5; Chakroff & Nathanson, Chapter 24).

Theoretical perspectives and underpinnings

Both social learning theory and theories of cognitive development are useful in understanding the potential impact of media on children's prosocial learning and behavior. Social learning theory generates predictions that can explain both the acquisition of prosocial lessons and the imitation of prosocial behavior. Cognitive theories, such as those advanced by Piaget and later by information processing theorists, are more useful in explaining developmental differences in how children interpret and acquire prosocial lessons.

Social learning and social cognitive theory   Social learning theory (Bandura, 1977), later called social cognitive theory (Bandura, 1986), suggests that one way children and adults learn is by watching others. We can observe behaviors, and we can observe the consequences of their actions; then we can make judgments about whether we should perform the behavior too. Our decision to try to imitate a behavior typically depends on a number of things: how successfully we can perform the behavior, whether we are in a relevant similar situation, and whether we have some reason to think it would be good to imitate it (i.e., motivation). These models can be live, or they can be presented symbolically in media like television and films.

Social cognitive theory is a major paradigm that has been used to explore and to explain children's imitations of prosocial actions modeled by television characters (e.g., Friedrich & Stein, 1973). Children are more likely to imitate the behaviors modeled by an attractive (rather than an unattractive) character and to imitate models that are rewarded (rather than punished) for their actions. For accurate translation of observational processes to behavioral matching, attention to the model's actions and memory of the central content must occur. Features of the content being observed (i.e., what the models do and whether they are rewarded or punished) interact with characteristics of the viewer to determine what content is learned and how likely it is to be imitated.

Social cognitive theory, then, suggests not only that prosocial content should present attractive models performing positive, rewarded actions, but also that it is important to investigate how children interpret and remember such content. Much of the emphasis in research to date has been on verifying that prosocial content can, in fact, encourage imitation. Rather less research has focused on investigating the features of the content that would maximize imitation, and relatively little research has investigated individual or group differences in interpretations and responses.

Cognitive developmental and information processing theories   Cognitive developmental theory focuses on age-based changes in children's representations and understanding of information. For example, Piaget (1926) argued that there are qualitative differences in children's interpretations of the world, as they progress from early stages (i.e., sensorimotor during the first two years, and preoperational during ages 2 to 7) to later stages such as concrete operational (approximately ages 7–11) and formal operational (approximately age 11 and older).

Although subsequent research (e.g., Donaldson & Elliott, 1990) has suggested that cognitive development is more gradual and less stage-like than Piaget proposed, many of the developmental characteristics of childhood thinking described by Piaget are very relevant to the possible impact of prosocial messages. One such characteristic concerns children's ability to engage in perspective taking and to respond empathically. Although research suggests that even young children (e.g., those under 7) can experience empathic emotional responses, the tendency to do so increases with age (Radke-Yarrow, Scott, & Zahn-Waxler, 1973). Furthermore, early empathy is often based on emotional contagion or mimicry, whereas empathy in later childhood is typically based on perspective taking, or the ability to imagine the self in another's situation (Eisenberg & Strayer, 1990).

Younger viewers also tend to focus on concrete, perceptually salient features of an event or object. This tendency has a number of implications. One is that young children tend to focus on characters' actions rather than their intentions when making moral judgments. For instance, preoperational children may reason that someone who accidentally breaks many cups when trying to help should be punished more heavily than someone who breaks only one cup while trying to steal a cookie. The tendency to focus on perceptually salient features (known as centration) also explains why preoperational children are more influenced than older children by a character's appearance relative to the character's actions or motives (e.g., Hoffner & Cantor, 1985).

With age, children become better able to engage in abstract reasoning and to understand abstract concepts (Ginsberg & Opper, 1979). Put another way, younger children tend to be more concrete in their processing of information. It is generally only in adolescence that individuals are likely to be swayed by appeals to abstract principles (e.g., justice for all) or to respond to nonvisual, more abstract threats or dangers.

The implication of Piaget's theory is that prosocial messages designed for young viewers should be presented differently from those aimed at older viewers. For example, younger viewers are less likely to be moved by appeals to the emotional consequences of positive or negative behaviors for others or by abstract principles. They are less likely than older children to be able to grasp that a physically unattractive model may have "a heart of gold" and be morally superior to an attractive model. They are more prone to evaluate characters based on how much visible harm they produced or how much punishment they received, and ignore information about their motives or goals.

Piaget as well as Kohlberg (1971) suggested that there are distinct stages in children's moral reasoning. In both accounts, children's beliefs and thoughts about moral dilemmas, which are a central foundation of children's media, move from early egocentrism, to a focus on rules, to more flexible and principled judgments. Focusing on the development of moral schemas, a concept originally advanced by Piaget, Narvaez examined how children of different ages comprehend and extract moral themes from written stories. She found that moral themes were seldom extracted as intended by the author because children interpreted the message in line with their own moral schemas (Narvaez, 2001, 2002). More specifically, children showed a progression from an emphasis on possible punishment (you should be nice to people or you might get into trouble) to a focus on personal gain or loss (you should be nice to people or they might be mean back to you) to a focus on the approval of others (you should be nice to people or your parents won't be proud of you). In her studies, even 10- and 12-year-old children showed signs of distorting the moral messages in line with their schemas. These studies highlight the importance of developing prosocial media content that is congruent with children's current moral schemas.

Information processing theories, which built on Piagetian research, focused less on identifying and describing stages of cognitive development than on describing the amount of information that can be processed successfully at different ages, the speed with which it can be processed, and age-related strategies that children bring to bear on information (Thomas, 2000). For example, research has described developmental increases in visual and auditory attention to stimuli, changes in the amount of information that can be held in working memory, and increases in the speed with which children can process information. As outlined below, research on children's comprehension of television content underscores the importance of these developmental changes in speed and capacity as well as the importance of Bandura's and Piaget's seminal work.

Developmental changes relevant to processing prosocial media messages

Consistent with information processing research, most studies of television comprehension suggest that children aged 7 or younger remember less than older children do, even of the most central, basic events of a televised story. For example, van den Broek, Lorch, and Thurlow (1996) showed 4- and 6-year-old children and college students four short stories embedded in a 25-minute tape of *Sesame Street* and asked them to retell the stories. All three age groups were more likely to mention events with multiple causal connections than less connected events, but 4-year-olds mentioned only 30 percent of the events with the most causal connections, compared to 40 percent for 6-year-olds and nearly 80 percent for college students.

Not only do younger children tend to remember fewer events than older children, but they are less able to remember the order of events (Lowe & Durkin, 1999) and to make inferences connecting parts of the story together (Sheppard, 1994). The more intervening material there is between the parts of the story (e.g., motives, actions, and consequences) or the more complicated the narrative structure (e.g., using flashbacks), the harder it is for young children to understand and remember. These findings are typically explained in terms of the constraints that young viewers' limited processing capacity place on their ability to manipulate and elaborate on material in working memory.

Beyond differences in amount of content recalled, viewers of different ages focus on different parts of a story. A character's goals, motives, and emotional responses are all important components for programs modeling prosocial interactions. However, consistent with Piaget's discussion of young children's tendency to focus on concrete features, research suggests that information about goals, motives, and emotions is easily forgotten by children under 10. For example, Hayes and Casey (1992) reported that 3- to 5-year-old children could recognize emotions displayed by television characters if asked immediately after the emotional display, but that they tended to forget this information by the end of the (5- or 11-minute) episodes, particularly if the characters were Muppets rather than humans. Trabasso, Secco, and van den Broek (1984) found that 6-year-olds were less likely than 10-year-olds to mention characters' emotional reactions when recalling a story they had heard a week earlier. Van den Broek (1989) reported that 8-year-old children thought actions were most important in understanding a story, compared to 11-year-olds who rated protagonists' goals as most important.

Qualities of viewers also impact their understanding of central content. For instance, Calvert, Strouse, and Murray (2006) showed adolescents and college students a film about a tragic love story. Prior to viewing, students answered questions about how much they typically empathized with media characters, a measure of fantasy empathy. Students who generally felt more empathy for media characters reported more empathy for the characters in the film, were more likely to perceive those characters as role models, and, most importantly, understood the story content best. Those who understood the story best also were more likely to report feeling sad and depressed after the film ended (one of the main characters dies).

What does all of this imply for attempts to model prosocial interactions and discourage antisocial interactions? It suggests that, for young viewers, the most exciting, concrete elements of a story will be remembered best (conflict is often exciting and concrete) and that motives or emotional consequences that carry the prosocial message (e.g., conflict makes people feel sad) are less likely to be remembered. Relying on depictions of emotional consequences may be an in-effective way to influence young viewers. However, for adolescents, a tendency to become involved in fictional portrayals leads to empathic engagement and enhanced story comprehension, suggesting that the most effective kinds of por-trayals vary by developmental level and the personal qualities of viewers.

Another potentially difficult feature of prosocial programming for young viewers is the use of a story to teach a moral theme. As an example, in one episode of *Clifford the Big Red Dog*, Clifford accidentally breaks a present that he was sup-posed to deliver to his friend, Emily. At first he conceals the accident but then, as the PBS website puts it, "he learns that it's best to be honest, right from the start." Presumably, the goal is that the 4- and 5-year-old viewers learn that honesty is the best policy, just as Clifford did. However, the moral is not expli-citly stated within the episode, and research suggests that extracting a theme from a story is difficult for children even as old as 10 (McKenna & Ossoff, 1998; Williams, 1993). Moreover, Narvaez (2002) has argued that extracting *moral* themes is particularly difficult because of developmental changes in moral reasoning.

Mares (2006) showed 6- to 8-year-old children the Disney animated film *The Sword in the Stone*. Children were asked whether they thought there was a lesson or moral in the film, and then to say what they thought it was. As would be predicted from Piaget's observations that young children have difficulty with relatively abstract concepts, children did not perform well on this task. When asked, 79 percent of children said that they thought there was a moral, but of those, 14 percent said they could not say what it was, 32 percent repeated some part of the story (e.g., "there was this sword in this stone, and this boy, he pulled it out"), and 53 percent gave a general moral principle that was not specific to the story ("You have to be nice to people").

Of course, children do not necessarily need to be able to articulate or even recognize a moral in order to imitate prosocial actions. However, if children do *not* extract underlying prosocial themes, then it seems even more critical to have models explicitly demonstrate prosocial acts (1) that are easy enough for chil-dren to imitate (2) that are relevant to children's interactions and (3) that seem attractive to child viewers.

Research Findings about Effects of Prosocial Media Content

As with most research on media effects, the majority of studies on prosocial effects have been either correlational or experimental, and very few have used longitud-inal designs to assess long-term impacts of prosocial viewing. This section describes exemplars of different research strategies with a variety of dependent prosocial outcomes, followed by a discussion of the results of a meta-analysis.

Correlational research

Correlational studies are typically surveys that assess the effects of self-selected viewing at home. There are both benefits and limits to this type of research. On the one hand, surveys can report on what we most care about – the effects of children watching programs at home under normal conditions. That is, this research comes closest to capturing the "real world" consequences of having prosocial programming available on television. On the other hand, the question of whether prosocial programming causes prosocial outcomes is plagued by issues of causal direction and spuriousness (as it is in all correlational work). Perhaps children who are already friendly, caring people are attracted to prosocial programming. In addition, prosocial behavior and prosocial viewing may both be influenced by other variables such as parental style and gender.

Sprafkin and Rubinstein (1979) asked 500 children (aged 7–9) from middle-class communities how often they watched each of 55 television series (later coded for frequency of prosocial and antisocial acts). Two weeks later, the children and teachers filled out a roster rating measure of which children in their classroom engaged in specific prosocial behaviors such as helping, sharing, or trying to make others feel good. The strongest predictors of prosocial behavior were background variables. Girls, high academic achievers, and those whose parents were well educated received more nominations. Prosocial television viewing was only weakly related to the number of nominations after controlling for background variables (partial $r = .12$). Total television viewing was negatively related to prosocial behavior, so that heavy viewers received fewer nominations than did light viewers.

More recently, Rosenkoetter (1999) asked first and third graders how often they watched 30 adult situation comedies (rated for level of prosocial content), and asked mothers how often their child engaged in positive behaviors such as sharing and helping others. In one study, Rosenkoetter found a fairly strong positive correlation ($r = .57$) between prosocial situation comedy viewing and prosocial behavior, but only among first graders and without any controls for background variables except gender. In another study reported in the same paper, Rosenkoetter (1999) found a small, marginally significant correlation between viewing adult prosocial situation comedies and mothers' reports, but only among children who were able to identify the moral lesson in a sample episode of *Full House*. There was no relationship between prosocial viewing and behavior among the children who did not perform well on this task.

One explanation for the relatively weak effects in these studies is that young viewers, consistent with all the theory and research discussed earlier, tend to misunderstand, misinterpret, or misremember substantial portions of the prosocial content. Rosenkoetter's finding that the ability to identify the moral of a story predicted the effects of more habitual viewing supports this explanation.

Another explanation is that self-selected viewing at home seldom consists solely of prosocial content. In a large, longitudinal study of children in the Netherlands, Wiegman, Kuttschreuter, and Baarda (1992) found tiny, non-significant correlations between home viewing of prosocial content and teacher and peer ratings of pro-social behavior. The authors noted that watching prosocial behavior on television was highly associated with watching antisocial content as well ($r = .90$), so that those who saw more prosocial models were heavy television viewers who were also exposed to considerable levels of violence.

Experimental research

In one of the earliest experiments in this area, Poulos, Rubinstein, and Liebert (1975) randomly assigned 30 first-grade children to one of three viewing condi-tions: a prosocial episode of *Lassie* in which Jeff risked his life to save a puppy; a neutral episode of *Lassie*; or a neutral episode of *The Brady Bunch*. Afterwards, the children were shown how to play a "game" in which they could accumulate points by pressing a button. The more points they earned, the larger the prize they would win. At the same time, they were asked to listen to puppies in a dis-tant kennel and to push a help button if the puppies seemed distressed. As chil-dren played the game, the recorded puppy sounds grew increasingly loud and intense. The researchers measured the average number of seconds children spent pushing the help button (thereby sacrificing points in the game). Children who saw the prosocial episode pushed the help button nearly twice as long as did children in the other two conditions.

Most of the other experiments on prosocial effects were also conducted dur-ing the 1970s. They typically involved showing children a short film in which a child model behaved in a positive or negative way. Afterwards, children were placed in a similar situation and their behaviors were observed. For example, Elliott and Vasta (1970) showed 5- to 7-year-old children a film about "Johnny the birth-day boy" who got candy for his birthday from his parents, but who chose to put some of his candy in an envelope and mail it to another little boy who had a birthday but whose parents were too poor to buy candy. Some of the children saw Johnny perform the action without being rewarded, some saw Johnny be rewarded with a teddy bear, and some saw Johnny get the teddy bear and be praised as "a good boy." (There was no true control group.) Afterwards the children were asked to pretend that it was their birthday and were given a large bag of candies and the opportunity to put some in an envelope for a little boy "who has no candy and no money" (Elliot & Vasta, 1970, p. 10). They were then given a pile of pennies and allowed to decide whether to put some in a box for the unfortunate little boy. Elliott and Vasta found no significant difference between the no-reward and the teddy-bear-reward conditions in terms of num-ber of candies or pennies donated, but the combination of reward and praise led to more items being donated. They also noted that older children donated more than younger children did.

Unfortunately, few other studies have explored these issues further. For example, no studies have investigated whether there are age differences in the effectiveness of different appeals to altruism. Are young viewers affected by different types of appeals than older children (e.g., to fairness or rules rather than empathy)? Do they require shorter, more explicit messages? Is it more critical for young viewers that the model be physically attractive or rewarded? Experimental research has established that imitation of prosocial actions can occur, but it has not systematically examined the interactions between qualities of the content and features of the viewers that make it most likely to occur.

Field experiments

The most rigorous work on prosocial effects is found in various field experiments. In most of these studies, children were exposed repeatedly (over the course of several days or weeks) to prosocial content, often under quite natural viewing conditions in childcare programs or as part of the school day. Often the researchers took numerous measures of children's attitudes or playground behaviors. All of these studies provided tests of social learning theory, moving beyond merely examining immediate modeling of actions to investigating whether children could generalize learned behaviors to other contexts and whether the effects would endure over time.

Friedrich and Stein (1973) conducted a series of studies on the prosocial effects of watching *Mister Rogers' Neighborhood*. In the first study, 93 preschool children were assigned to a prosocial condition (*Mister Rogers' Neighborhood*), an aggressive condition (*Batman* and *Superman*), or a control group (films about farms and animals). They watched 12 episodes over a four-week period. Observers rated the children's aggressive and prosocial behavior during free play for three weeks before the experimental exposure period, during the four-week exposure period, and then for two weeks afterward.

Friedrich and Stein found no correlation between the frequency of watching *Mister Rogers' Neighborhood* at home and children's baseline measures of prosocial behavior. However, children who watched *Mister Rogers' Neighborhood* in preschool showed several positive changes. They persisted longer at tasks, were more likely to obey rules, and were more likely to delay gratification without protest. The effects on children's playground interactions varied by family background. Children from higher socioeconomic backgrounds were initially more prosocial than were those from low socioeconomic backgrounds, and they did not change significantly after prosocial exposure. Children from families with lower socioeconomic status who saw *Mister Rogers' Neighborhood* showed more cooperation and friendliness in playground interactions, though these effects gradually declined throughout the two-week post-exposure period.

In a second study, Friedrich and Stein (1975) assigned 75 kindergarten children either to a control condition or to watch four episodes of *Mister Rogers' Neighborhood* and receive one of two types of training: verbal labeling (children were taught to describe how characters had felt and behaved) or role playing (children used hand puppets to reenact scenes from the episodes). Over the next few days, the children had opportunities to engage in helping behaviors, either related to the program (helping a puppet from the program during a reenactment of one of the scenes) or in unrelated contexts (helping fix a torn collage). There were slightly higher levels of helping behaviors among the children who had watched *Mister Rogers Neighborhood* than among those in the control group. For boys, however, the effects varied by type of training. Role-play training strengthened the effects of the program, but verbal labeling was associated with some decreases in helping relative to the control group. Girls, by contrast, learned the content best in the verbal labeling condition.

In their third study, Friedrich-Cofer and colleagues (1979) compared the effects of (1) 20 episodes of *Mister Rogers* over eight weeks without any additional pro-social materials; (2) 20 episodes of *Mister Rogers* and access to prosocial books and games; (3) 20 episodes of *Mister Rogers*, access to prosocial materials, and follow-up activities such as verbal labeling and role playing; and (4) neutral films. The researchers found that *Mister Rogers' Neighborhood* alone produced relatively few behavioral changes. Children in the second group (viewing plus materials) displayed more positive *and* more negative behaviors. Only children in the third group (viewing and materials and activities) displayed more positive behaviors without any increases in aggression.

This line of research established that it was possible to use television program-ming in school to produce real-world, positive, enduring changes in children's behaviors. Moreover, rather than merely reinforcing positive behavior among chil-dren who were already predisposed to act prosocially, the effects were strongest among children from low socioeconomic backgrounds who were initially less prosocial. However, producing these positive changes was not easy. Overall, it appeared that prosocial media content was more effective if presented in the con-text of extra material and rehearsal of the program lessons. Similar research on *Barney and Friends* (Singer & Singer, 1998) and *Sesame Street* (Zielinska & Chambers, 1995) also found that these programs produced most positive behavioral changes when watched in school in the context of discussion and other materials. It remains a significant limitation of this research that none of it is developmental: the major-ity of field experiments have been conducted with programming that is primarily targeted toward preschool audiences.

Longitudinal studies

An obvious question is whether early exposure to prosocial media content has any long-term consequences for prosocial attitudes and behavior. There has been only one longitudinal study that tracked the effects of prosocial television on viewers. That study was conducted over a three-year period by Wiegman and colleagues (1992) in the Netherlands. For all three years, viewing of prosocial television con-tent was unrelated to either concurrent or future prosocial behavior as reported by peers and teachers.

Meta-analyses

Meta-analyses involve averaging statistical information across studies on a particular topic in order to estimate the size (or strength) of an effect. In experiments on prosocial effects, the effect size is often the difference between a control group and a group exposed to prosocial content, or between a group that sees some negative content and a group that sees some positive content. In surveys, the effect size is often the relationship between how much prosocial television content children watch and how positively they behave.

In an early meta-analysis of 230 studies published before 1978, Hearold (1986) compared prosocial and antisocial effects of television exposure. Her estimate of positive effects included a wide range of variables such as friendly interactions and altruism, being imaginative, buying books, and being a conversation "activist." Her estimate of antisocial effects combined a variety of outcomes such as aggression, criminal behavior, and stereotyping. Hearold concluded that positive effects of viewing ($r = .34$) were twice as strong as and more enduring than antisocial effects ($r = .15$), both in experimental and home-viewing conditions.

Mares and Woodard (2005) conducted a more narrowly focused meta-analysis of 34 studies that measured the effects of viewing prosocial content on interpersonal interactions. They included studies that contained at least one of four broad sets of dependent measures: positive interactions (e.g., "friendly play" and "positive conflict resolution"), aggression reduction (both physical and verbal), altruism (including sharing, helping, donating, and offering comfort), and reduction of gender and ethnic/racial stereotypes. They reported a weak-to-moderate overall effect size ($r = .27$) that was quite similar to Hearold's more broad-based estimates of positive effects.

Mares and Woodard (2005) also documented conditions under which prosocial learning is most likely to occur. They found stronger effects in experimental contexts ($r = .31$) than in home-viewing situations ($r = .19$ for prosocial). Prosocial effects did not vary by gender but were strongest for children around age 7. Mares and Woodard also reported that effects were stronger for some prosocial outcomes than for others. They found that effect sizes were largest in studies where children watched a model engaging in altruistic behavior (such as donating tokens to a hypothetical poor child) and were immediately given the opportunity to imitate this behavior (for studies of altruism, $r = .37$). Research on stereotype reduction ($r = .20$) or aggression reduction ($r = .16$) or prosocial interactions ($r = .24$) found smaller effects.

What Factors Promote Prosocial Effects of Media Exposure?

While some studies support the idea that prolonged exposure to models brings about an increase in prosocial interactions, others find only weak or nonexistent effects, and even occasional negative outcomes. Some studies support the idea that short-term exposure to explicit modeling of a very specific behavior may, at least momentarily, encourage children to imitate the behavior, but others find no effects. The question, then, is whether there are particular features of program content, viewing context, or of the child's background that make prosocial outcomes more likely to occur. Conversely, are there particular situations in which prosocial effects are less likely to occur?

Specificity

Mares and Woodard (2005) speculated that studies of altruism generally found stronger effects because such studies were more likely to include explicit modeling of very specific behaviors. This finding, combined with research suggesting that children find it difficult to extract themes or moral lessons, suggests that children may be most positively affected if the lesson or desired behavior is made very clear. To the extent that there is a prosocial lesson to be learned from some content, stating it explicitly at the start of the program (rather than leaving it to be inferred) and demonstrating what concrete behaviors are covered by that lesson seem more likely to be successful. What is obvious and intuitive to adults may not be as obvious for young viewers.

Modeling only the desired behaviors

Attempts to promote prosocial interactions can be based on characters consistently behaving in prosocial ways, or on characters who initially engage in conflict and then learn to behave more appropriately. Which approach is more effective? On the one hand, social learning theory would predict that showing that conflict gets punished and virtue prevails should be an effective way of encouraging imitation of virtue and inhibiting imitation of conflict. Moreover, it is easier to write a plot and entertain audiences if there can be an arc of personal development from early errors to realization of the values of behaving prosocially. On the other hand, there are several developmental trends that suggest that although modeling conflict resolution may be effective for older children and adults, it may backfire for younger children.

First, conflict is often concrete and arousing, and thus memorable. If younger children tend to remember relatively little content (due to processing constraints), then it is important that a significant portion of what little they remember not be conflict. Second, we noted that young children have greater difficulty extracting moral themes. It takes the ability to reinterpret the conflict as negative and to focus on the prosocial outcome as the lesson to grasp that the program is not about how to fight, but rather how to get along.

Unfortunately, there is little research on this issue, even though it seems important given how prevalent conflict-followed-by-brief-prosocial-resolution is as a plot. In one exception, Silverman and Sprafkin (1980) had children aged 3 to 7 watch approximately 16 minutes of *Sesame Street* featuring either prosocial, conflict-free interactions among child actors, or conflicts between the child actors that were resolved peacefully. Control children saw content with no social lessons. Pairs of children then played a marble game designed to measure cooperation: they could maximize the number of marbles they both got by taking turns, or they could ruin each other's chances by working against each other. Silverman and Sprafkin found that the prosocial-only condition had virtually no effects on cooperation in the marble game relative to the control group. However, those who saw the conflict-plus-peaceful-resolution actually cooperated less than did the control group.

In their meta-analysis, Mares and Woodard (2005) reported that the combination of conflict with prosocial resolution was associated with more negative behaviors than just seeing purely antisocial content. This finding was based on very few studies so it remains tentative, but it suggests the importance of further experimental examinations of possible developmental changes in responses to conflict plus prosocial outcomes. For now, the recommendation would be to focus on portraying only those behaviors that would be appropriate or desirable for young viewers to imitate.

Encourage participation

Another strategy is to encourage viewer participation as a way to increase rehearsal and foster learning of the content. Programs such as *Blue's Clues* and *Dora the Explorer* have characters ask questions of the viewers, followed by a pause in which the viewer can respond. Calvert, Strong, Jacobs, and Conger (2007) studied the extent to which watching *Dora the Explorer* promoted story comprehension among preschoolers. They found that those children who actively responded to the character prompts understood more of the content. The same strategies, presumably, could be used to enhance the effects of prosocial messages.

Parenting style

One study, by Abelman (1985), suggests that prosocial television content may resonate best in families where parents use inductive disciplinary techniques such as reasoning, explanations, and appeals to the child's pride. In contrast, prosocial messages may not be particularly effective in families where parents use sensitizing techniques such as physical punishment and deprivation of privileges or objects. Abelman surveyed mothers of fourth- and fifth-grade children about their disciplinary strategies and asked the children how often they watched 29 prime-time programs (content analyzed for frequency of prosocial and antisocial acts). The children also answered questions about their probable behavior in social situations (e.g., how they would cope with bullies). Their answers were coded to form a "prosocial disposition" score. Abelman found a moderate overall correlation (without controls for background variables) between children's prosocial exposure and their prosocial predispositions of r = .42. However, this relationship was strongly dependent on parenting style: Children whose parents used inductive techniques showed a stronger relationship (r = .48) than did those whose parents used sensitizing techniques (r = .14). Although further research would be needed to confirm and expand these findings, they make intuitive sense – inductive disciplinary techniques such as reasoning are more consistent with prosocial themes and goals in media content than punitive disciplinary techniques are.

Mediating messages/critical viewing

Abelman also suggested that children could be taught to notice prosocial behaviors as they appeared in programs. Abelman (1991) had 208 gifted and 125 learning-disabled fourth graders participate in a three-week, in-school television viewing curriculum designed to increase awareness of their own viewing and of prosocial and antisocial activities contained within their favorite programs. Both groups showed significant increases in their ability to recognize and label prosocial activities, though it is unclear whether they were affected by those depictions beyond noticing them. In a parallel line of research, Nathanson and her colleagues have explored the effects of active mediation as a way of reducing the negative impact of violent media messages (see for example, Nathanson & Cantor, 2000; Nathanson et al., 2002). Mediating messages were often effective in reducing negative outcomes of viewing. It seems at least plausible that mediating messages could be used to enhance the positive outcomes of exposure to prosocial content, by clarifying and reinforcing the lessons presented.

How Much Prosocial Content is Available?

Given the considerable potential of prosocial television to improve children's learning and performance of socially desirable behaviors, how much of that content is available? Unfortunately, very few systematic content analyses have looked at the frequency and context of prosocial behavior on television, and those that exist are dated.

Television content

Early content analyses found that modeling of prosocial behavior often occurred within the context of modeling negative behaviors. In one study, for example, the favorite programs of a sample of fourth, sixth, and eighth graders contained an average of 42.2 acts of antisocial behavior and 44.2 acts of prosocial behavior (such as altruism, empathy, and discussing feelings) an hour (Greenberg et al., 1980). Liss and Reinhardt (1980) compared standard cartoons with prosocial cartoons (those with moral messages apparent to the adult researchers) and reported that both types contained equal amounts of aggression. Thus, to the extent that one would expect any learning or imitation to take place, it seems probable that children would take away rather mixed messages about how to "live with oneself or others." In addition, Liebert and Poulos (1975) reported that television during the 1970s tended to show a rather restricted range of prosocial behaviors, with very few examples of characters resisting temptation or controlling aggressive impulses (see also Poulos, Harvey, & Liebert, 1976).

Children's programming generally contained high levels of aggression and relatively low levels of educational or prosocial content throughout the 1980s until grassroots pressure helped secure the passage of the Children's Television Act in 1990 (Kunkel & Wilcox, 2001). Even after that, commercial broadcasters rarely presented more educational and informational content than required by law, and even that content was of dubious quality (Kunkel & Wilcox, 2001). As is detailed by Calvert (this volume, Chapter 20), the 3-hour rule was then implemented, requiring a minimum of 3 hours of educational/informative (E/I) programs per week during times when children are likely to be awake and in the viewing audience.

The Annenberg Public Policy Center conducted a series of content analyses of E/I programming in the late 1990s and reported that E/I programming was primarily targeted at elementary school children and teens (Woodard, 1999; Jordan, 2000) and that preschool children were the most underserved. Moreover, Jordan (2000) noted that 16 percent of E/I programming still contained multiple acts of physical aggression.

Smith and colleagues (2006) examined the frequency and context of altruistic acts on television during the 2003 season. Even with a very stringent definition of altruism (that excluded, for example, helping by someone whose job it was to help others), they found that child-oriented, basic cable (Nickelodeon, Disney, and the Cartoon Network) had the highest rate of altruistic acts (compared to other channel types such as broadcast channels or PBS), with roughly four instances of helping/sharing per hour. Moreover, these channels were more likely to feature child actors as initiators and targets of altruistic behavior.

Videogames and computer games

There do not appear to be any systematic content analyses of prosocial versus antisocial themes in games available to children of different ages. A few commercial games (e.g., *Kingdom Hearts 2*) have plotlines affirming friendship, loyalty, and kindness. However, even these games embed such prosocial qualities in the context of action-packed fighting scenes and the forces of good against evil (Walsh et al., 2005). While some home education games may encourage prosocial behavior by rewarding player-cooperation, most commercial games focus on aggression and violence as their game objectives (Dietz, 1998). A 2001 content analysis by the children's advocacy group, Children Now, found that 89 percent of the top-selling video games contained violence, with approximately 50 percent of all games featuring serious violence. Examination of the relatively few games recommended by parenting websites and media watchdogs (e.g., Walsh et al., 2005) found no games promoting positive social interactions in a nonviolent context.

Prosocial content in songs

In the music domain, cursory examination reveals a number of prosocially themed titles for young children, with artists such as Raffi singing about love and tolerance. As with videogames and computer games, there are no systematic analyses of prosocial or socio-emotional content in music popular with children of different ages.

Children's and Adolescents' Exposure to Prosocial Content in the Media

It is difficult to determine how much positive content children of different ages are exposed to because of the lack of good data about how much positive content there actually is and where it can be found in the media landscape. We do know more generally that certain types of youth are more likely than others to encounter prosocial content because of their media habits and preferences.

Television program choices

Children's actual exposure to prosocial television content probably changes with age, though conclusions about how much each age group watches prosocial programs vary by how narrowly the age groups are defined. In the most general report, Woodard (1999) found that of the top 20 shows with the highest Nielsen ratings among children aged 2 to 17, only four contained social lessons in the episodes analyzed: *Boy Meets World, Disney's One Saturday Morning* (a block of children's E/I programs), *Hey Arnold*, and *7th Heaven* (a general audience program that is not created for children). Thus, averaging across the entire span of childhood, exposure to prosocial television content may not very high.

However, other research suggests that younger children may be relatively likely to see prosocial content compared to teens, particularly teen males. The results of two Kaiser Family Foundation reports indicate that parents of young children report monitoring the content of their children's viewing quite closely, whereas parents of teens generally do not have rules about what their children can watch. Consistent with this finding, Crane and Chen (2003) reported that among 2–5-year-olds, the most watched programs were *Clifford, Arthur, Dragon Tales, Barney and Friends, Caillou, Dora the Explorer, Sesame Street, Bob the Builder*, and *Teletubbies*. All of these programs have prosocial themes. Crane and Chen also reported that when the age range was expanded (2–11-year-olds), the most watched programs were still largely prosocial (e.g., *Arthur* and *Dragon Tales*) though some were more likely to contain verbal conflict and aggression (e.g., *SpongeBob*

SquarePants and *Rugrats*). This is consistent with Calvert and Kotler's (2003) finding that second- through sixth-grade children often chose a prosocial program mandated by the Children's Television Act as one of their favorites.

In contrast, Nielsen ratings for adolescents indicate that none of the top-rated network and cable television programs in 2001 were educational and informational in nature, and two of the top six were *World Wrestling Federation Smackdown!* and *World Wrestling Federation Heat* (Federal Trade Commission, 2001). Taken together the ratings suggest that as children grow older, prosocial content forms a smaller part of their television diet.

Videogame use

Roberts, Foehr and Rideout (2005) reported that videogame use peaked at around ages 8–10, that males were three times as likely to play videogames as girls, and that African American youth spent more time playing these games than other racial or ethnic groups did. The groups that were relatively unlikely to watch educational programming with prosocial themes were among those most likely to be playing violent videogames.

Musical selections

National surveys have documented the importance of music both in the lives of young children (Rideout & Hamel, 2006) and in the lives of preadolescents and teens (Roberts, Foehr, & Rideout, 2005). The most popular music forms for adolescent boys include heavy metal, hard rock, punk, grunge, and psychedelic rock; adolescent girls prefer forms such as pop, disco, soft rock, and Top 40 (Roberts, Foehr, & Rideout, 2005). None of these musical forms are noted for their pro-social content.

Summary

Overall, the research suggests that media content targeted toward and consumed by young children is more likely to contain prosocial content than media content consumed by older children. Moreover, male and minority teens appear the most avid consumers of antisocial content and the probable lowest consumers of pro-social content. However, this conclusion is a frustrating litany of how little is known about the amount or type or quality of prosocial media content used by children of different ages.

Directions for Future Research

There are numerous glaring holes in this literature that have been noted elsewhere (Mares & Woodard, 2001, 2005). The simple way to summarize many of these holes is to point out that most of the predictions afforded by theories of learning and child development have not been directly tested in relation to prosocial content. The theories suggest that certain aspects of the content may be important and, additionally, that what is effective will vary with age. Relevant aspects include the presence or absence of rewards, attractive models, appeals to different moral schemas, abstract concepts, emotional content, and information about characters' goals and motives.

Overall, we know relatively little about the qualities of viewers that are relevant to prosocial effects. Calvert and her colleagues' (2006) study of adolescents suggests that there are individual differences in empathic responding to characters' emotions, but there is no work linking empathic responding and prosocial effects. No work has tried to link personality variables to prosocial outcomes. Abelman's (1985, 1991) work suggests that the effects of viewing prosocial content at home are strongest among those with parents who use inductive disciplinary techniques but does not indicate if these children tend to be most prosocial anyway. Work by Friedrich, Stein, and their colleagues (Friedrich & Stein, 1973, 1975; Friedrich-Cofer et al., 1979) suggests that viewing prosocial content at preschool was most effective among those who were least prosocial to begin with. We also need direct comparisons of the effects of home versus school viewing among different types of families or children from different levels of socioeconomic status.

Finally, there is no research on any media other than television (or, in the early days of prosocial research, film). This is clearly an area crying out for theory-driven, developmental research, comparing the effects of prosocial messages presented in various media. To focus solely on television ignores the complexity of today's media world, misses an intriguing avenue for exploring medium effects, and disregards some of the communicative features that differentiate adolescents from other age groups (e.g., frequent use of the Internet for information and companionship). As a related point, the focus only on media rather than also considering interpersonal sources of prosocial learning is a limitation. In fact, the field would benefit from turning the central question on its head and asking what media and interpersonal communication patterns are characteristic of the most prosocial youth.

Conclusion

Ever since the early days of *Mister Rogers' Neighborhood* it has been apparent that television had the power to foster children's prosocial development. The 3-hour rule, despite producers' early gloomy prognostications, has not led to plummeting ratings. Rather, as Calvert and Kotler (2003) found, children often report enjoying prosocial programming and learning from it. Given the opportunity afforded by the 3-hour rule, it seems a tremendous waste not to investigate ways to maximize the potential of such programming. We also need to investigate the presence and the effects of prosocial content designed for children and youth in other media. As a community, our intellectual resources have been over-utilized in documenting the harmful effects of media use rather than in considering ways to promote more positive outcomes.

References

Abelman, R. (1985). Styles of parental disciplinary practices as a mediator of children's learning from prosocial television portrayals. *Child Study Journal*, 15, 131–45.

Abelman, R. (1991). TV literacy III – Gifted and learning disabled children: Amplifying prosocial learning through curriculum intervention. *Journal of Research and Development in Education*, 24(4), 51–60.

Bandura, A. (1977). *Social learning theory*. Englewood Cliffs, NJ: Prentice-Hall.

Bandura, A. (1986). *Social foundations of thought and action: A social cognitive theory*. Englewood Cliffs, NJ: Prentice-Hall.

Batson, C. D. (1994). Why act for the public good? Four answers. *Personality and Social Psychology Bulletin*, 20, 603–10.

Calvert, S. L., & Kotler, J. A. (2003). Lessons from children's television: The impact of the Children's Television Act on children's learning. *Journal of Applied Developmental Psychology*, 24, 275–335.

Calvert, S., Strong, B. L., Jacobs, E. L., & Conger, E. E. (2007). Interaction and participation for young Hispanic and Caucasian children's learning of media content. *Media Psychology*, 9, 431–45.

Calvert, S. L., Strouse, G., & Murray, K. (2006). The role of empathy in adolescents' role model selection and learning of DVD content. *Journal of Applied Developmental Psychology*, 27, 444–55.

Crane, V., & Chen, M. (2003). Content development of children's media. In E. L. Palmer & B. M. Young (Eds.), *The faces of televisual media: Teaching, violence, selling to children* (2nd edn.). Mahwah, NJ: Lawrence Erlbaum.

Dietz, T. L. (1998). An examination of violence and gender role portrayals in video games: Implications for gender socialization and aggressive behavior. *Sex Roles*, 38, 425–42.

Donaldson, M. L., & Elliott, A. (1990). Children's explanations. In R. Grieve & M. Hughes (Eds.), *Understanding Children: Essays in honour of Margaret Donaldson* (pp. 26–50). Cambridge, MA: Blackwell.

Eisenberg, N., & Strayer, J. (Eds.). (1990). *Empathy and its development*. Cambridge, MA: Cambridge University Press.

Elliott, R., & Vasta, R. (1970). The modeling of sharing: Effects associated with vicarious reinforcement, symbolization, age, and generalization. *Journal of Experimental Child Psychology*, 10, 8–15.

Federal Trade Commission. (2001). *Marketing violent entertainment to children. A one-year follow-up review of industry practices in the motion picture, music recording, and electronic game industry. A Report to Congress*. Retrieved December 8, 2006, from http://www.ftc.gov/os/2001/12/violencereport1.pdf .

Friedrich, L., & Stein, A. H. (1973). Aggressive and prosocial television programs and the natural behavior of preschool children. *Monographs of the Society for Research in Child Development*, 38(4, Serial No. 151).

Friedrich, L., & Stein, A. H. (1975). Prosocial television and young children: The effects of verbal labeling and role playing on learning and behavior. *Child Development*, 46, 27–38.

Friedrich-Cofer, L. K., Huston-Stein, A., Kipnis, D. M., Susman, E. J., & Clewett, A. S. (1979). Environmental enhancement of prosocial television content: Effect on interpersonal behavior, imaginative play, and self-regulation in a natural setting. *Developmental Psychology*, 15, 637–46.

Ginsberg, H., & Opper, S. (1979). *Piaget's Theory of Intellectual Development* (2nd edn.). Englewood Cliffs, NJ: Prentice-Hall.

Greenberg, B., Edison, N., Korzenny, F., Fernandez-Collado, C., & Atkin, C. (1980). Antisocial and prosocial behaviors on television. In B. Greenberg (Ed.), *Life on television: Content analyses of U.S. TV drama* (pp. 99–128). Norwood, NJ: Ablex.

Hayes, D. S., & Casey, D. M. (1992). Young children and television: The retention of emotional reactions. *Child Development*, 63, 1423–37.

Hearold, S. (1986). A synthesis of 1043 effects of television on social behavior. In G. Comstock (Ed.), *Public communication and behavior*, vol. 1 (pp. 65–133). New York: Academic Press.

Hoffner, C., & Cantor, J. (1985). Developmental differences in responses to a television character's appearance and behavior. *Developmental Psychology*, 21, 1065–74.

Huber, C. H. (2004). Prosocial behavior. In W. E. Craighead & C. B. Nemeroff (Eds.), *The concise Corsini encyclopedia of psychology and behavioral science* (3rd edn., p. 737). Hoboken, NJ: Wiley.

Jordan, A. B. (2000). *Is the three hour rule living up to its potential?* Philadelphia: Annenberg Public Policy Center.

Kohlberg, L. (1971). Stages of moral development as a basis for moral education. In C. M. Beck, B. S. Crittenden, & E. V. Sullivan (Eds.), *Moral education: Interdisciplinary approaches* (pp. 23–92). Toronto: University of Toronto Press.

Kunkel, D., & Wilcox, B. (2001). Children and media policy. In D. G. Singer & J. L. Singer (Eds.), *Handbook of children and the media* (pp. 589–604). Thousand Oaks, CA: Sage.

Liebert, R. M., & Poulos, R. W. (1975). Television and personality development: The socializing effects of an entertainment medium. In A. Davids (Ed.), *Child personality and psychopathology*, vol. 2 (pp. 61–97). New York: Wiley.

Liss, M. B., & Rinehardt, L. C. (1980). Aggression on prosocial television programs. *Psychological Reports*, 46(3), 1065–66.

Lowe, P. J., & Durkin, K. (1999). The effect of flashback on children's understanding of television crime content. *Journal of Broadcasting and Electronic Media*, 43, 83–97.

Mares, M. (2006). Repetition increases children's comprehension of television content – up to a point. *Communication Monographs*, 73(2), 216–41.

Mares, M., & Woodard, E. H. (2001). Prosocial effects on children's social interactions. In D. G. Singer & J. L. Singer (Eds.), *Handbook of children and the media* (pp. 183–205). Thousand Oaks, CA: Sage.

Mares, M., & Woodard, E. H. (2005). Positive effects of television on children's social interactions: A meta-analysis. *Media Psychology*, 7, 301–22.

McKenna, M. W., & Ossoff, E. P. (1998). Age differences in children's comprehension of a popular television program. *Child Study Journal*, 28(1), 53–68.

Narvaez, D. (2001). Moral text comprehension: Implications for education and research. *Journal of Moral Education*, 30, 43–54.

Narvaez, D. (2002). Does reading moral stories build character? *Educational Psychology Review*, 14, 155–71.

Nathanson, A., & Cantor, J. (2000). Reducing the aggression-promoting effect of violent cartoons by increasing children's fictional involvement with the victim: A study of active mediation. *Journal of Broadcasting and Electronic Media*, 44(1), 125–42.

Nathanson, A., Wilson, B., McGee, J., & Sebastian, M. (2002). Counteracting the effects of female stereotypes on television via active mediation. *Journal of Communication*, 52(4), 922–37.

Piaget, J. (1926). *The language and thought of the child*. New York: Harcourt, Brace, & World.

Poulos, R. W., Harvey, S. E., & Liebert, R. M. (1976). Saturday morning television: A profile of the 1974–1975 children's season. *Psychological Reports*, 39(3), 1047–57.

Poulos, R. W., Rubinstein, E. A., & Liebert, R. M. (1975). Positive social learning. *Journal of Communication*, 25, 90–97.

Radke-Yarrow, M. R., Scott, P. M., & Zahn-Waxler, C. (1973). Learning concern for others. *Developmental Psychology*, 8, 240–60.

Rideout, V., & Hamel, E. (2006). *The media family: Electronic media in the lives of infants, toddlers, preschoolers and their parents*. Menlo Park, CA: Kaiser Family Foundation.

Roberts, D. F., Foehr, U. G., & Rideout, V. J. (2005). *Generation M: Media in the lives of 8–18-year-olds*. Menlo Park, CA: Kaiser Family Foundation.

Rosenkoetter, L. I. (1999). The television situation comedy and children's prosocial behavior. *Journal of Applied Social Psychology*, 29, 979–93.

Rust, L. (2001). *Summative evaluation of "Dragon Tales:" Final report*. Children's Television Workshop.

Sheppard, A. (1994). Children's understanding of television programs: Three exploratory studies. *Current Psychology: Developmental, Learning, Personality*, 13, 124–37.

Silverman, L., & Sprafkin, J. (1980). The effects of *"Sesame Street's"* prosocial spots on cooperative play between young children. *Journal of Broadcasting*, 24, 135–47.

Singer, J. L., & Singer, D. G. (1998). *Barney and Friends* as entertainment and education. In J. K. Asamen & G. Berry (Eds.), *Research paradigms, television, and social behavior* (pp. 305–67). Thousand Oaks, CA: Sage.

Smith, S. W., Smith, S. L., Pieper, K. M., Yoo, J. H., Ferris, A. L., Downs, E., et al. (2006). Altruism on American television: Examining the amount of and context surrounding acts of helping and sharing. *Journal of Communication*, 56, 707–27.

Sprafkin, J. N., & Rubinstein, E. A. (1979). Children's television viewing habits and prosocial behavior: A field correlational study. *Journal of Broadcasting*, 23, 265–76.

Thomas, R. M. (2000). *Comparing theories of child development* (5th edn.). Belmont, CA: Wadsworth.

Trabasso, T., Secco, T., & van den Broek, P. (1984). Causal cohesion and story coherence. In H. Mandl, N. L. Stein, & T. Trabasso (Eds.), *Learning and comprehension of text* (pp. 83–111). Hillsdale, NJ: Lawrence Erlbaum.

Van den Broek, P. (1989). Causal reasoning and inference making in judging the importance of story statements. *Child Development*, 60, 286–97.

Van den Broek, P., Lorch, E. P., & Thurlow, R. (1996). Children's and adults' memory for television stories: The role of causal factors, story-grammar categories, and hierarchical level. *Child Development*, 67, 3010–28.

Walsh, D., Gentile, D., Walsh, E., Bennett, N., Robideau, B., Walsh, W., et al. (2005). *Tenth annual MediaWise video game report*. Retrieved December 8, 2006, from http://www.mediafamily.org/research/report_vgrc_2005.shtml.

Wartella, E., & Reeves, B. (1985). Historical trends in research on children and the media: 1900–1960. *Journal of Communication*, 35(2), 118–32.

Wiegman, O., Kuttschreuter, M., & Baarda, B. (1992). A longitudinal study of the effects of television viewing on aggressive and prosocial behaviors. *British Journal of Social Psychology*, 31, 147–64.

Williams, J. P. (1993). Comprehension of students with and without learning disabilities: Identification of narrative themes and idiosyncratic text representations. *Journal of Educational Psychology*, 85, 631–41.

Woodard, E. H. (1999). *The 1999 state of children's television report: Programming for children over broadcast and cable television* (Report No. 28). Philadelphia: Annenberg Public Policy Center.

Zielinska, I. E., & Chambers, B. (1995). Using group viewing of television to teach preschool children social skills. *Journal of Educational Television*, 21, 85–95.

13

Make-Believe Play, Imagination, and Creativity: Links to Children's Media Exposure

Dorothy G. Singer and Jerome L. Singer

After nearly 60 years of research on consciousness and the forms of mentation, we continue to be in awe of how the human brain generates the capacity for imagery and narrative processing as well as for the less frequent and more subtle form of mentation, logical, analytic, or scientific thought. As far as we can tell, our species has evolved alone with the ability to reproduce our perceptual and motor experiences and to sustain them mentally to form a dimension of private reality. In this realm, we can play and replay memories, link memories, shape and reshape organized mental structures such as schemas and scripts, anticipate future encounters or adventures, and, in general, privately inhabit a self-constructed world of life narratives. As Spinoza proposed, "The uses of imagination are also paths to freedom, alongside the uses of reason" (Hampshire, 2005, p. viii).

In this chapter we examine the childhood origins of imaginative thought, and relate its emergence and development not only to children's direct experiences in family and social milieus but also to their exposure to the electronic media of television, videos, and videogames and computer games. We refer specifically to that facet of human consciousness that involves the active re-examination of one's ongoing memories or anticipations. Such a directed effort can reshape and create new mental organizations such as schemas, scripts, prototypes, or life narratives, and then apply these structures for play, self-entertainment, and, often, escapist diversion. Such active guidance serves creative artistic, scientific, or business purposes; it contributes to planning social interactions and achievement of long-standing goals (Baars, 1998; Bruner, 1986; Epstein, 1999; Honeycutt, 2003–4; McAdams, 1993; D. Singer & Singer, 1990, 2005; J. Singer & Singer, 2005–6).

Forms of Imagination in Childhood

Imagination is multifaceted, and hence conceptualized and defined in many different ways (D. Singer & Singer, 2005). One way of considering imaginative processing using a cognitive, computer science model, is to regard it as a form of human information-processing that occurs *offline*, that is, relatively independently of immediate environmental perceptual stimulation (Antrobus, 1999). Such partially stimulus-independent activity initially occurs in those early precursors of overt symbolic play in children such as their involvement with transitional objects like soft toys, stuffed animals, or dolls, and in the occurrence for some children of unseen imaginary companions (D. Singer & Singer, 1990; Taylor, 1999, 2003). Evidence of the offline or stimulus-independent quality of children's play can be observed when they transform or re-label concrete objects and also introduce shifts in space, time, and simulated activities as part of playful storytelling (J. Singer & Singer, 1981). Such pretend play emerges in the late second year and flourishes in the third through fifth or sixth years (D. Singer & Singer, 1990, 2005; Valkenburg, 2001). Make-believe play is often also termed "symbolic," "pretend," or in its more elaborated form in older children, "socio-dramatic" (D. Singer & Singer, 2005).

The prototype of such self-generated consciousness is the 4-year-old child's assertion, "Let's make believe this box is a magic space ship and we can fly up!" The imaginative process is broader than simply the mental reproduction or imaging of a recently experienced concrete stimulus. Imagination may involve elaborated verbal sequences conducted privately in consciousness, or it may take on story-like forms such as reminiscences or wished-for future sequences of events.

By ages 5 or 6, children's spontaneous reports demonstrate that they are showing increasing signs of private imagery and of internalized thought sequences. This internalization of pretend play is apparent in the early school years as classroom discipline combined with the acquisition of reading skills reduce the talking out loud during play and promote the shift to private conscious thought sequences. To the extent that such internalized processes take the form of story-like or playful associations, they may be considered expressions of "imagination," or in their more bizarre or unrealistic forms, as "fantasies."

In Piaget's theoretical structure, symbolic play and its internalized form reflect a pure assimilation process towards eventual operational or logical thinking (Piaget, 1962). The extensions of Piaget's view in work in the 1930s by Vygotsky (1978) and Luria (1932) indicated the influence of adults, and paid more attention to the potentially adaptive role of later, silent information-processing built around storytelling. Bruner's (1986) conception of two adaptive modes of thought, the rational-logical or "paradigmatic," and the play-derived "narrative," carried these distinctions further. The research and theorizing of Bruner, and more recently of Epstein (1999), as well as that of Sutton-Smith (1966) and ourselves (D. Singer & Singer, 1990, 2005), suggest that Piaget capped his developmental analysis with the emergence of the human capacity of rationality. He neglected to consider the importance of imagination and self-narrative as another significant mode of thought.

Daydreaming may be viewed as the special form of offline processing in which imagination, fantasy, reminiscence, and divergent thinking may be detected.

Daydreams have been studied as shifts of attention away from mental or physical concentration on an immediate task into a region of increasingly distantly associated thought drawn from long-term memory (D. Singer & Singer, 2005). These associations may range from mundane recollections of recent events to elaborated emotional memories, short-term plans, more speculative anticipations, or playful as well as frightening fantasies of often quite improbable events (Antrobus, 1999; Klinger, 1971; Singer, 1966, 2006).

Make-believe play, private imagination, and fantasy are often regarded as precursors of the divergent processes and creative thinking that may eventually lead to significant novel productions in the arts, sciences, law, and business. Truly creative products like testable scientific theories or greatly acclaimed works of art can be shown to be combinations of both the narrative and the paradigmatic forms of thought (Bruner, 1986; R. Root-Bernstein & Root-Bernstein, 1999; Sternberg, Grigorenko, & Singer, 2004).

Adaptive play and imagination

There is an increasing body of research evidence suggesting that imaginative play is linked to important developmental processes including reality-fantasy distinctions, the development of a theory of mind, and the ability to defer gratification in the interests of effective adaptive responses (Harris, 2000; Kavanaugh & Harris, 1999; Lillard, 2001; Rosengren, Johnson, & Harris, 2000; Russ, 2004; Schwebel, Rosen, & Singer, 1999; Singer, 1961, 1973; D. Singer & Singer, 2005).

A recent study by Cemore and Herwig (2005) using home observations reported that greater amounts of make-believe play at home were correlated with measures of delay of gratification (Mischel & Baker, 1975). Make-believe play was the only variable significantly related to such self-regulation even when age, sex, family structure, ethnicity, childcare setting, and mother's education were considered. The accumulating research evidence on self-regulation, emotional control, autonomy, and individuality also indicates that the emotional intensity found in play is linked to creative thought as well as to the practice of alternative solutions and evaluative processing that produce effective delay of gratification (Berk, Mann, & Ogan, 2006; Russ, 1993).

Correlates of pretend play in preschoolers and of a broad range of imaginative processes in older children attest further to many constructive possibilities of a varied and active inner consciousness. Children and adolescents who have shown evidence of involvement in or elaboration of pretend play or of positive daydreaming and playful thought have been found to demonstrate greater verbal fluency and vocabulary strength, more use of future or subjunctive grammatical forms, more perseverance, more initiation of activities, and more upbeat moods, as well as less hostility, overt aggression, and uncooperative behavior (Johnson, Christie, & Wardle, 2005; Russ, 2004; Singer, Golinkoff, & Hirsh-Pasek, 2006; D. Singer & Singer, 1990; Singer, 1973; J. Singer & Singer, 1981).

Through interviews with winners of Nobel Prizes, MacArthur Foundation awards, or other creative honors, the Root-Bernsteins have demonstrated that the early development of make-believe playmates or imaginary worlds are anticipations of the adult thinking of a broader group of creative persons, scientists, and inventors (M. Root-Bernstein & Root-Bernstein, 2004; R. Root-Bernstein & Root-Bernstein, 1999; D. Singer & Singer, 1990; Taylor, 1999). These studies also point to the value of early imagination not only for the major forms of creative accomplishment, but also for day-to-day creativity and problem solving as prefigured in such childhood exercises.

There is also a body of research that demonstrates that training encourages play in preschoolers and early school-age children (Bellin & Singer, 2006; Johnson, Christie, & Wardle, 2005; D. Singer & Singer, 1990, 2005; Singer & Lythcott, 2002). The pioneering studies directed by Eli Saltz also revealed that imaginative play provides basic opportunities for children to develop verbal fluency and more complex divergent thought by fostering preschoolers' ability to connect separate events and to form new meaning structures (Johnson, Christie, & Wardle, 2005). We turn now to how the more narrative imaginative or playful features of creativity may be influenced early on in childhood by exposure to the electronic media.

Effects of Media Exposure on Imagination

The development of imagination depends on children addressing the real physical world around them and then recreating that in a pretend form with the support of mediating adults (D. Singer & Singer, 2005). But in the last third of the twentieth century and now early in our new millennium, many children are spending much of their time embedded in an electronically generated world of images in the form of television, videos, and computers. Recent research indicates that by 6 months of age, children are already watching videos and DVDs; by 9 months of age, they also are watching television programs (Weber & Singer, 2004).

The benefits of imaginative play in youngsters and of positive-constructive daydreaming in older children pose a challenge to media researchers. To what extent do play and imaginative processes reflect the useful influence of our electronic milieu? Are there any indications that extensive involvements with such media may be harmful, or are video exposures perhaps simply irrelevant to the emergence of a rich consciousness? This chapter will focus on whether such forms of play may be fostered or enhanced by children's exposure to television and other electronic media, or whether excessive exposure may actually interfere with naturally occurring pretend play. It may even be the case that excessive viewing of violent programs leads to narrowing of subsequent play, or that heavy involvement with violent videogames focuses the content of play or associated thought on angry or aggressive themes.

Television

Forty-five years ago we began our research examining the influences of television on children's imaginative play after our studies of naturally occurring pretend activities in preschoolers showed that such play often incorporated characters or settings from current television shows. We believed that it might be the case that television viewing by children actually could be stimulating or enhancing pretend play as well as suggesting story-content for such play. After all, wasn't it possible that viewing the stories presented on televised cartoons or adventure programming might be serving some of the same stimulating effects as bedtime parental reading or family storytelling (J. Singer & Singer, 1981; Valkenburg, 2001)?

With respect to frequency or complexity of make-believe play, an accumulating body of research does not support this Stimulation Hypothesis. If anything, the indications are that children who are more frequent watchers of television in their preschool years are much less likely to engage in pretend games (J. Singer & Singer, 1981; J. Singer, Singer, & Rapaczynski, 1984a; Valkenburg, 2001). They are also less likely to show evidence of divergent mentation or creativity (Childs, 1979; Furu, 1971; Petterson, Peterson, & Caroll, 1987; D. Singer & Singer, 2005; J. Singer & Singer, 1981; Valkenburg & van der Voort, 1994; van der Voort & Valkenburg, 1994).

Valkenburg's (2001) view as well as our own specific studies of television (J. Singer & Singer, 1981; D. Singer & Singer, 1990, 2005) point to the "stifling" of creativity or the Reduction Hypothesis (Valkenburg, 2001, p. 124). Why might heavy television viewing be associated with less imaginative play or with less evidence of creative thought and, necessarily, less of the constructive behavior associated with these forms of imagination? Valkenburg, (2001) outlined six reasons for a possible stifling effect of heavy television viewing. These involve:

1   the *displacement effect* in which spending time with the easily accessible medium of television reduces time spent "practicing" imaginative play or engaging in the more active exploration of concrete playthings, art objects, musical instruments, or other physically or mentally demanding features of one's environment;

2   the "couch potato" *passivity* premise where viewers consume others' fantasies rather than creating their own;

3   *rapid pacing* in which the scene-changes and frequent interruptions that characterize most commercial television may disrupt thought and preclude opportunities for reflection, a necessary ingredient for imaginative activities;

4   the *arousal* effects of watching television, especially fast-paced violent shows, which may disrupt more contemplative activities involving imagination;

5   the *anxiety effects* that suggest fearfulness brought about by watching violent or scary content may interfere with one's play or attempts at exploration in action or thought; and

6   the *visualization effect*, a more purely cognitive concept in which the ease of drawing on the pictures provided by watching television interferes with the

child's more effortful actions of creating images of scenery, action, and characters that are required when listening to a parent's story, a radio story, or
reading a book oneself.

Valkenburg's (2001) review of the literature pertaining to the effects of television
exposure offers support for the Reduction Hypothesis, with varying levels of evidence that displacement, heightened arousal and anxiety, and decreased visualization
underscore this dampening effect.

The visualization effect has strong support: television viewing disrupts creativity.
An impressive body of studies with similar outcomes support the view that the
"readymade pictures" provided by the television screen preempt opportunities for
children to develop their own imagery skills (Greenfield & Beagles-Roos, 1988;
Kerns, 1981; Meline, 1976; Valkenburg & Beentjes, 1997; Vibbert & Meringoff,
1981). These studies generally indicate that listening to an audio-presented story
yields more novel and interesting responses later on from children than does watching comparable material on television. Valkenburg and Beentjes (1997) tested
an alternative hypothesis, *faulty memory*, to explain why audio story listeners
provided more subsequent novelty in their responses than video viewers did. The
data from this experiment failed to counteract the idea that the personal effort at
visualizing an overheard story would yield more original and creative productions
of the material.

There is also reasonably good support that displacement reduces both imaginative play and more creative responses in children (Valkenburg, 2001). For example,
when television was introduced into a new community, decreases occurred in
children's imagination (Harrison & Williams, 1986).

The anxiety and arousal effects pertain mainly to children's experiences with
violent content (Valkenburg, 2001). Research indicates that frequent viewings of
violent television programs and cartoons are associated with less imaginative play
and with less creative behavior in children (Anderson & McGuire, 1978; Cantor,
1998; D. Singer and Singer, 2005; J. Singer, Singer, & Rapaczynski, 1984b; van
der Voort & Valkenburg, 1994). The causal mechanisms for this disruption are
consistent with the idea that such content can elicit both anxiety and arousal in
children (Valkenburg, 2001).

In a review of the literature, Valkenburg and van der Voort (1994) found that
the weight of the evidence on daydreaming, on the other hand, is consistent with
the Stimulation Hypothesis. That is, television viewing stimulates daydreaming.
In particular, studies show that daydreams are associated with the kind of content viewed; viewing positive content over time is associated with positive-
intensive daydreaming, and viewing violent content over time is associated with
aggressive and heroic daydreams. A study by McIlwraith and Schallow (1982–3)
of daydreaming styles in 6-year-olds found that heavy television viewing was
associated with anxious, hostile, and dysphoric daydreaming patterns. These
results are quite comparable with those obtained from an earlier study of adults
(McIlwraith, 1981).

Summary

In summary, heavy viewing of typical commercial programming, especially of the violent and fear-invoking action-adventure variety, is associated with reductions in make-believe play, with reductions in novel and creative responses, and with increases in heroic, aggressive daydreams. Since practically all children watch a good deal of television, we will turn next to some ways in which viewing more educationally relevant and socially constructive programs can have useful effects. We will also consider some of the influences of other widely used electronic media such as videogames and computers. Although there is not yet research that evaluates possible influences of new devices such as instant messaging, Blackberries, iPods, and the burgeoning applications of cell phones, all of these sources must certainly be affecting forms of play and ways in which children experience their ongoing inner consciousness.

The Importance of Content

Very young children in the preschool age group tend to watch cartoons, cable channels that feature children's programming such as Cartoon Network, Nickelodeon, and Disney, and especially Public Broadcasting Service (PBS) for their educational programs. Infants and toddlers, for example, are watching such programs as *Barney*, *Teletubbies*, *Blue's Clues*, *Sesame Street*, and *Dora the Explorer* (Weber & Singer, 2004).

By the age of 12, children's choices are very much like adults' choices. Situation comedies begin to surpass cartoons as favorites by the time children are in sixth grade (Comstock & Scharrer, 2001). Soaps and reality television are also among the favorites of older children in the United States and in other Western countries (von Feilitzen, 2004). MTV (a music channel), and WB and Fox (channels that deal with dramas involving young people) are watched by teenagers and even by tweens (Strasburger & Wilson, 2002). Girls in fifth through ninth grade tend to prefer drama and music and eleventh graders prefer music, while younger boys prefer adventure shows and sports. Program choices are often defined by time and location rather than by particular preference. Thus, many children watch adult programs together with their families (Paik, 2001). A crucial question, then, concerns the extent to which the nature of the content viewed – action-oriented cartoons versus educational programs – makes a difference in the impact of media on children's imaginations.

Television

Early research revealed that children who were heavy television viewers (watched television more than 3 hours per day) were *less* imaginative than were those who only watched 1 hour a day. Moreover, highly imaginative children had parents who also valued imagination and had some control over their children's television viewing habits. The highly imaginative children's favorite programs were educational in nature and were typically featured on the PBS. The less imaginative children viewed action/adventure television programs and cartoons that contained high levels of violence (D. Singer & Singer, 1981; J. Singer & Singer, 1981, 1986; J. Singer, Singer, & Rapaczynski, 1984a, 1984b; Tower et al., 1979).

Educational programs such as *Barney and Friends* and *Mister Rogers' Neighborhood* include fantasy elements, offer solutions to problems, and foster imagination and creativity. For example, toddlers who viewed *Barney and Friends* for two weeks were more imaginative, less aggressive, less angry, and more socially appropriate than were those in a control group (J. Singer & Singer, 1998). During viewing, children danced along with the characters, sang songs with them, and repeated phrases from the soundtrack. This series makes a point of emphasizing the value of pretend play.

Valkenburg and her collaborators describe three fantasy styles that appear regularly on violent and nonviolent television: positive-intense, aggressive-heroic, and dysphoric (Valkenburg et al., 1992). In one of their studies, a group of 354 children were surveyed three times at one-year intervals beginning when they were in grades 2 or 4. Children's fantasy styles in year one did not predict their television viewing in year three. Children's television viewing in year one, however, did predict their fantasy styles in year three. Exposure to nonviolent programs was related to an increase in the children's positive-intense fantasy style, while exposure to violent programs was positively related to children's aggressive-heroic fantasy style. Television viewing was unrelated to dysphoric fantasy. Similarly, in a review of the literature, Valkenburg and van der Voort (1994) found that the weight of evidence supports the hypothesis that television viewing stimulates daydreaming, with the content of the daydream reflecting the type of viewing diet.

Gotz, Lemish, Aidman, and Moon (2003) studied the daydreams of 177 8- to 10-year-old boys and girls from four countries (Germany, Israel, United States, and South Korea). After children had been exposed to a read-aloud text and music, they were asked to draw their daydreams and write some sentences about them. Gender differences were found in all countries. Girls were less likely to include media content in their make-believe worlds, while boys referred to media and many of their pictures portrayed conflicts. Girls stressed harmony, while boys stressed action, danger, and fighting for a good cause. In confronting dangerous situations, girls tended to make them disappear, while boys fought against the threat or dangers. Boys' renditions reflected prototypical action/adventure films, computer games, documentary programs, and mythical stories where men are heroes. In contrast, media figures were rare for the girls, who preferred androgynous figures like Pokemon or CatDog (half cat, half dog).

Content also plays a key role in long-term effects of media on imagination. For example, a longitudinal study that followed preschoolers into high school demonstrated the importance of *content* rather than just viewing television as fostering cognitive skills and creativity over time (Anderson et al., 2001). In effect, this research supported the value of child-oriented educational programming, specifically *Mister Rogers' Neighborhood*, a program that focuses on pretense and imaginative activity.

Commercials that feature program-based toys inhibit creative imagination, but stimulate *imitative* imagination (Greenfield et al., 1993). Imitative imagination refers to play representations when the children use the toy or animated figure mostly in the exact manner as portrayed in the television story. Thus, children who are viewing commercials and playing with toys based on programs tend to copy what they have seen rather than to create novel play activities that are the hallmark of creativity.

Videogames and computer games

One may reasonably assume that playing videogames on consoles or on computers inherently yields a more interactive experience than what occurs by just viewing television stories. In this sense, especially for violent "shoot em up" videogames, one gains considerable practice in eye-hand coordination with, however, a limited range of cognitive content. Sports videogames are more complex than aggressive videogames, and, while unlikely to produce the skills to be a professional baseball shortstop, football quarterback, or racing-car driver, they may yield richer fantasies and "aesthetic" appreciation in imagery of what good sport play demands. Computer games and their Internet extensions to cyberspace would seem to offer far more opportunity for enhancing imaginative thought than television programs do. Consider the possibilities of games like *Myst*, adventurous variations of *Dungeons and Dragons*, or the diverse forms of *Sim*.

Fishman (2004) raised the question of why videogames or computer-assisted techniques have not become more significant in training children to learn and to be creative. The author argued that, "most designed-based research does not explicitly address systemic issues of usability, scalability, and sustainability" (p. 43). In effect, Fishman proposed that more careful attention be paid to the principles of childhood learning in the design of videogames and computer games. An empirical study with 10- and 11-year-olds using information and communication technologies for concept mapping exemplifies this approach. The data indicate that these techniques not only improve nonverbal reasoning compared with a control group but also are linked to improved writing achievement with possible creativity (Riley, 2004). A qualitative study reflecting comparable principles suggested by Fishman (2004) demonstrated that well-constructed software programs can help motivate seventh-grade students to generate more innovative productions, particularly when there is adult mediation (Garthwait, 2004).

From the standpoint of imagination and its breadth and scope, the violent videogames link is chiefly to direct aggression. There is an extensive literature on the negative effects of playing videogames on children's behaviors: very frequent playing of violent videogames leads to aggressive behavior and to less helpfulness and empathy (Anderson & Bushman, 2001; Anderson et al., 2004; Bartholow, Sestir, & Davis, 2005).

In violent videogames, the limited storylines, and the focus almost exclusively on a player's quick recognition of "bad guys" or "enemies," are followed by practice in simulated shooting or other destructive behavior. In effect, those children's imaginative activities are being narrowed to "aggressive thoughts, feelings and behaviors" (Anderson & Bushman, 2002; Viemeroe & Paajanen, 1992). Carnagey and Anderson (2005) further demonstrate that violent games can directly influence children's angry thoughts. Based on such studies, we concluded that "habitual playing of violent video games may therefore serve to inhibit the scope of a child's imagination and increase the risk of developing an aggressive lifestyle" (D. Singer & Singer, 2005, p. 105).

Some observers propose that the susceptibility to suggestion, the ability to separate thoughts and feelings that are associated with intensive videogame and computer game play, may suspend rational thought and reality (Preston, 1998; Qian, Preston, & House, 1999). These reports are especially intriguing in terms of fantasy/reality distinctions. When a child plays an electronic game, how is later behavior affected and influenced by the game? Young children do play educational games such as *LeapFrog* and other games produced by Children's Television Workshop, Nickelodeon, and Disney, but we have little information on how these games affect the imaginations of children. *Sim*, for example, is a popular computer game series that allows children to construct their own cities or houses, or assemble their own characters. Even with the many icons offered to a child, the games are still limited by the structure of the program. Perhaps such a software-determined format affords less scope for divergent thinking compared to when a child is actively engaged in self-generated make-believe play with unstructured toys or when a child is trying to write a poem or story using his or her own memories or fantasies. Justine Cassell, influenced by her work at the Massachusetts Institute of Technology, has developed a virtual playmate, Sam, that children can interact with during play. Cassell found that in the short term, there was an increase in expressive and in receptive language between pretest and posttest when face-to-face with Sam on the screen (Cassell, 2005). Cassell, so far, has not studied long-term effects of such computer interaction.

With the availability of free software on such Internet sites such as Little-Clikers.com, one can download website content and games for children aged 3 to 12. Some of the sites appeal to the imagination, with features such as games and puzzles, music, drawing, creative cooking ideas, and even one that helps children learn how to juggle, braid, talk like a duck, or ride a unicycle. We do not know of any research studies that have evaluated the effects of these games on young children, but the thrust seems more educational and free of the violence that is prevalent in many of the commercial videogames.

MUDs

Sherry Turkle (1995), a sociologist and psychoanalyst, proposed that computer interactions allow users to explore their identity, and indeed to create multiple identities or selves, that they present to others in online communities. Based on observational and interview data collected from adolescent and adult computer game players, Turkle theorized that one's view of society and one's sense of identity might well be changed by Internet interactions. She focused her study on players in multi-user domains or multi-user dungeons (MUDs).

In MUDs, players assume various personae, including adventurous or romantic identities. The use of computer-specific identities may lead to a de-centered self that exists in many worlds and plays many roles at the same time. According to Turkle, "MUDs . . . offer parallel identities, parallel lives . . . this parallelism encourages treating on-screen and off-screen lives with a surprising degree of equality" (Turkle, 1995, p. 14). There has been a vast increase in the quantitative expansion of such multi-user games and in their qualitative features. There are more than 300 MUDs involving more than 13 different kinds of software (Turkle, 2002).

Multi-user domain studies have been conducted with preadolescent youth. In a study by Calvert, Mahler, Zehnder, Jenkins, and Lee (2003), 84 fifth and sixth graders constructed an avatar, complete with name, gender, and costume, that represented them in a MUD created by the researchers. Pairs of boys, pairs of girls, and mixed-gender pairs interacted with one another. The dependent variables included the name, gender, and costume children gave to their avatars, how active their characters were in their screen movements, and their language (which appeared as overhead bubbles). The researchers also examined the emotional expressions employed, scene changes, role play that involved pretending, and the creation of games such as peek-a-boo or hide-and-seek.

Gender differences were pronounced. Boys expressed more mythological or pure fantasy tendencies, choosing names like *Lord of the Rings*, while names that reflected an interest in popular music culture such as *Britney* or *Shania* were characteristic of girls' choices. Children generally chose to make their avatar congruent with their own biological sex. Boys typically represented themselves with punk identities, wearing "leather jackets," while girls most often chose soccer costumes. Consistent with prior research on sex differences, boys moved more often and girls talked more. When boy players were paired with girl players, they talked more and were less active than when paired with a boy. Similarly, girls in mixed-gender play accommodated their preferred play style, moving their characters more and talking less.

The emergence of Internet applications of avatars and various trial selves has been so extensive in the first years of our new century that we can scarcely grasp all of the implications for effects of computer usage on the imagination. New forms of *Sim* and related games have been extended to cyberspace so that children can create pictorial selves who then encounter other persons in disguised identities in places like hotels or airports. Players may be children or adults, may come from far-off countries in reality, and may be pure "fun" participants as well as even sexual predators. The potential exploitation of children by sexual predators who take advantage of youthful fantasies in chat rooms has been widely documented and is a subject for new legislation (Dowd, Singer, & Wilson, 2006). We need much more research on the consequences of such play for children. We can speculate that with respect to fantasy we are entering a new era of pretense and the reaches of the human imagination.

Helping Children Understand the Fantasy/Reality Distinction in Electronic Media

Young children face the daunting task of figuring out what is real and what is pretend (D. Singer & Singer, 2005). What children see on television and in many videos conveys a sense of reality that may be misleading. For instance, the presence of live actors in a television program can confuse young children, leading them to believe that fantasy episodes can really occur (Skeen, Brown, & Osborn, 1982).

Imaginative play can help children figure out the difference between fantasy and reality (D. Singer & Singer, 2005). When children say, "Let's pretend . . ." or "Let's make-believe . . ." during their self-generated play, they convey their awareness of the difference between fantasy and reality. Programs that encourage such distinctions are emphasized in PBS series such as *Mister Rogers' Neighborhood* and *Barney and Friends* (D. Singer & Singer, 1990, 2005; J. Singer & Singer, 1998). When pretense involves a fantasy character, 4-year-olds are more able to understand that they are involved in pretense (Lillard & Sobel, 1999).

In general, 5-year-olds have a more mature perception of both cartoon and human fantasy television episodes than 4-year-olds do. On many children's television programs, adult characters talk to the fantasy characters (*Mister Rogers' Neighborhood, Sesame Street, Blue's Clues, Barney and Friends*), and this adds to the seeming realism of the puppets or animated characters on the program. Hosts can help children understand distinctions between what is real and what is pretend, such as when Fred Rogers consistently uses the trolley to transit to the Land of Make Believe, thereby separating the live from the puppet pretend segments of the program.

Parental *guidance* through rules about time spent with electronic media and choices of programs, as well as *mediation* involving explanation and discussion of content, may well be the most useful methods for helping children distinguish reality from fantasy. Adult guidance can determine how effectively children overcome the reality/fantasy confusions associated with formal features, which are the audiovisual features that structure, mark, and represent media content (Bickham, Wright, & Huston, 2001). In particular, the active role of parents or other adults in storytelling, in reading, or in responding to children's queries during television viewing may help minimize misunderstandings. Often, however, parents or other adult caregivers may not be readily available, especially for older children and adolescents who often sit alone in front of televisions or computer screens.

Media literacy programs available in school or after-school settings can help children understand what is real and not real on television, videos, DVDs, and the

Internet. Media literacy curricula can teach students how media messages are constructed and how they may differ from reality. They can train children to analyze the content and special properties or conventions of media communications. For example, training elementary-school aged children in a television literacy program helped them to differentiate between reality and fantasy on programs as well as understand formal features such as camera effects (D. Singer & Singer, 1998).

During the 1980s and 1990s many curricula were developed and targeted to create critical viewers of television programs and advertisements (Brown, 2001). Comparable programs oriented to the special properties of videogames, computer usage, and the newest electronic devices such as iPods, cell phones, or Blackberries have not yet appeared or are scarce. The current curricula are aimed at teaching children about the different genres of program content on television, how the news is presented, how stereotypes are fostered on television, how commercials are made, and how violence and sexuality are depicted. Some curricula include parent and teacher training components (Brown, 2001).

At Yale, we developed curricula for kindergartners, for third- to fifth-grade children, and for junior high and high-school students (D. Singer & Singer, 1998). "Reality and Fantasy on Television" was the theme of one of the lessons presented at schools in special sessions for the kindergartners, and in social studies and English classes for older children. Children who received the lessons scored significantly higher on a test of media literacy than did those who did not receive the lessons (Rapaczynski, Singer, & Singer, 1982; D. Singer, Zuckerman, & Singer, 1980). A creative curriculum also has been used successfully with first and third graders in Oregon (Rosenkoetter & Rosenkoetter, 2003). It includes songs, poetry, and guest visitors who are both real and pretend (e.g., a visitor from another planet who needs to learn about television), and it focuses on violence and how to understand what is real and not real on television.

Conclusion

Those of us who grew up in the years before the era of television or computers are always impressed with how quickly children today orient themselves to videogames and computer usage. What we do not know, however, is to what degree this early exposure is extending and enriching their imaginative capacities or, perhaps, narrowing productive direction of consciousness and leading to considerable confusion of reality and fantasy. Consider the intriguing finding from a Kaiser Family Foundation report on multitasking. Foehr (2006) conducted a study based on week-long diaries kept by 694 children and adolescents between ages 8 and 18. She found striking differences in the extent to which these young people limit their attention to a particular medium. Actually, they spend more focused time watching television (55 percent) in contrast to their time spent reading (where they limit their activity to this task only 38 percent of the time), and playing computer games (where they spend almost two thirds of their time in at least one other activity such as instant messaging or listening to music). What impact may these rapid shifts of attention have not only on effective learning but on sustained reflective thought and imaginative and creative processing?

In response to some of these concerns, Senator Joseph Lieberman praised the Senate's passage of bipartisan legislation that he co-sponsored called the Children and Media Research Advancement (CAMRA) Act. The legislation authorizes new research into the effects of viewing and using electronic media, including television, computers, videogames and the Internet on children's cognitive, social, physical, and psychological development. (Lieberman, 2006).

We began this chapter by discussing the origin of adult self-directed consciousness in the imaginative play of children. With the immersion of children today in the extensive make-believe of television as well as their explorations of a new type of "community" in cyberspace (Rheingold, 1995), we may be witnessing the beginnings, for better or worse, of a new source for human imagination. Ongoing research is needed to unravel how imagination is being affected by the various technological changes that characterize the information age.

References

Anderson, C., & McGuire, T. (1978). The effect of TV viewing on the educational performance of elementary school children. *Alberta Journal of Educational Research*, 34, 156–63.

Anderson, C. A., & Bushman, B. J. (2001). Effects of video games on aggressive behavior, cognition, aggressive affect, physiological arousal, and prosocial behavior: A meta-analytic review of the scientific literature. *Psychological Science: American Psychological Society*, 12(5), 353–9.

Anderson, C. A., & Bushman, B. J. (2002). Media violence and the American public revisited. *American Psychologist*, 57, 448–50.

Anderson, C. A., Carnagey, N. L., Flanagan, M., Benjamin, A. J., Eubanks, J., & Valentine, J. C. (2004). Violent video games: Specific effects of violent content on aggressive thoughts and behavior. *Advances in Experimental Social Psychology*, 36, 199–249.

Anderson, D. R., Huston, A. C., Schmitt, K. L., Linebarger, D. L., & Wright, J. C. (2001). Early childhood television viewing and adolescent behavior: The recontact study. *Monographs of the Society for Research in Child Development*, 66(1).

Antrobus, J. S. (1999). Toward a neurocognitive processing model of imaginative thought In J. A. Singer & P. Salovey (Eds.), *At play in the fields of consciousness* (pp. 3–28). Mahwah, NJ: Lawrence Erlbaum.

Baars, B. (1998). *A cognitive theory of consciousness*. Cambridge: Cambridge University Press.

Bartholow, B. D., Sestir, M. A., & Davis, E. B. (2005). Correlates and consequences of exposure to video game violence: Hostile personality, empathy, and aggressive behavior. *Personality and Social Psychology Bulletin*, 31(11), 1573–86.

Bellin, H., & Singer, D. G. (2006). My magic story car: Video based play intervention to strengthen emergent literacy of at-risk preschoolers. In D. G. Singer, R. M. Golinkoff, & K. Hirsh-Pasek (Eds.), *Play = learning: How play motivates and enhances cognitive and social-emotional growth* (pp. 101–23). New York: Oxford University Press.

Berk, L. E., Mann, T. D., & Ogan, A. T. (2006). Make-believe play: Wellspring for development of self-regulation. In D. G. Singer, R. M. Golinkoff, & K. Hirsh-Pasek (Eds.), *Play = learning: How play motivates and enhances cognitive and social-emotional growth* (pp. 74–100). New York: Oxford University Press.

Bickham, D. S., Wright, J. C., & Huston, A. C. (2001). Attention, comprehension, and the educational influences of television. In D. G. Singer & J. L. Singer (Eds.), *Handbook of children and the media* (pp. 101–19). Thousand Oaks, CA: Sage.

Brown, J. A. (2001). Media literacy and critical television viewing in education. In D. G. Singer & J. L. Singer (Eds.), *Handbook of children and the media* (pp. 681–97). Thousand Oaks: Sage.

Bruner, J. (1986). *Actual minds, possible worlds.* Cambridge, MA: Harvard University Press.

Calvert, S. L., Mahler, B., Zehnder, S., Jenkins, A., & Lee, M. (2003). Gender differences in pre-adolescent children's interactions: Symbolic modes of self-presentation and self-expression. *Applied Developmental Psychology*, 24, 627–44.

Cantor, J. (1998). *"Mommy, I'm scared:" How TV and movies frighten children and what we can do to protect them.* San Diego, CA: Harcourt Brace.

Carnagey, N. L., & Anderson, C. A. (2005). The effects of reward and punishment in violent video games on aggressive affect, cognition, and behavior. *Psychological Science*, 16(11), 882–9.

Cassell, J. (2005). *The power of peers: Virtual peers for children's imaginative play and storytelling.* Paper presented at the Jean Piaget Society 35th Annual Meeting, June, Vancouver, BC, Canada.

Cemore, J. J., & Herwig, J. S. (2005). Delay of gratification and make-believe play of children. *Journal of Research in Childhood Education*, 19(3), 251–66.

Childs, J. H. (1979). Television viewing, achievement, IQ, and creativity. *Dissertation Abstracts International*, 39, 6531A.

Comstock, G., & Scharrer, E. (2001). The use of television and other film-related media. In D. G. Singer & J. L. Singer (Eds.), *Handbook of children and the media* (pp. 47–72). Thousand Oaks, CA: Sage.

Dowd, N. E., Singer, D. G., & Wilson, R. F. (Eds.). (2006). *Handbook of children, culture and violence.* Thousand Oaks, CA: Sage.

Epstein, S. (1999). The interpretation of dreams from the perspective of cognitive-experiential self-theory. In J. A. Singer & P. Salovey (Eds.), *At play in the fields of consciousness* (pp. 51–82). Mahwah, NJ: Lawrence Erlbaum.

Fishman, B. (2004). Creating a framework for research on systematic technology innovations. *Journal of the Learning Sciences*, 13(1), 43–76.

Foehr, U. G. (2006). Media multitasking among American youth: Prevalence, predictors and pairings. Menlo Park, CA: Kaiser Family Foundation.

Furu, T. (1971). *The function of television for children and adolescents.* Tokyo: Monumenta Nipponica, Sophia University.

Garthwait, A. (2004). Use of hypermedia in one middle school: A qualitative field study. *Journal of Educational Multimedia and Hypermedia*, 13(3), 219–43.

Gotz, M., Lemish, D., Aidman, A., & Moon, H. (2003). The role of media in children's make-believe worlds. *Televizion*, 16(1), 28–39.

Greenfield, P. M., & Beagles-Roos, J. (1988). Radio versus television: Their cognitive impact on children of different socioeconomic and ethnic groups. *Journal of Communication*, 38(2), 71–92.

Greenfield, P. M., Yut, E., Chung, M., Land, D., Kreider, H., Pantoja, M., & Horsley, K. (1993). The program-length commercial: A study of the effects of television/toy tie-ins on imaginative play. In G. L. Berry & J. K. Asamen (Eds.), *Children and television: Images in a changing sociocultural world* (pp. 53–72). Newbury Park, CA: Sage.

Hampshire, S. (2005). *Spinoza and Spinozism*. New York: Oxford University Press.

Harris, P. (2000). *The work of the imagination*. Oxford: Blackwell.

Harrison, L., & Williams, T. (1986). Television and cognitive development. In T. M. Williams (Ed.), *The impact of television: A natural experiment in three communities* (pp. 87–142). San Diego, CA: Academic Press.

Honeycutt, J. M. (2003–4). Imagined interaction conflict-linkage theory: Explaining the persistence and resolution of interpersonal conflict in everyday life. *Imagination, Cognition and Personality*, 23(1), 3–26.

Johnson, J. E., Christie, J. F., & Wardle, F. (2005). *Play, development and early education*. Boston, MA: Pearson Education, Allyn & Bacon.

Kavanaugh, R., & Harris, P. (1999). Pretense and counterfactual thought in young children. In L. Balter & C. S. Tamis-Lemonda (Eds.), *Child psychology: A handbook of contemporary issues* (pp. 159–76). Philadelphia, PA: Psychology Press.

Kerns, T. Y. (1981). Television: A bisensory bombardment that stifles children's creativity. *Phi Delta Kappa*, 62, 456–7.

Klinger, E. (1971). *Structure and functions of fantasy*. New York: Wiley.

Lieberman, J. (2006). Senate approves Lieberman "Children and Media Research Advancement Act". News release. Retrieved September 14, 2006, from http://lieberman.senate.gov/newsroom/release.cfm?id=262993.

Lillard, A. S. (2001). Pretend play as twin earth: A social-cognitive analysis. *Developmental Reviews*, 21, 495–531.

Lillard, A. S., & Sobel, D. (1999). Lion kings or puppies: The influence of fantasy on children's understanding of pretense. *Developmental Science*, 2(1), 75–80.

Luria, A. R. (1932). *The nature of human conflicts*. New York: Liveright.

McAdams, D. P. (1993). *The stories we live by: Personal myths and the making of the self*. New York: William Morrow.

McIlwraith, R. D. (1981). Fantasy life and media use patterns of adults and children. Unpublished PhD dissertation, University of Manitoba, Canada.

McIlwraith, R. D., & Schallow, J. R. (1982–83). Television viewing and styles of children's fantasy. *Imagination, Cognition, and Personality*, 2(4), 323–32.

Meline, C. W. (1976). Does the medium matter? *Journal of Communication*, 26(3), 81–9.

Mischel, W., & Baker, N. (1975). Cognitive appraisals and transformations in delay behavior. *Journal of Personality and Social Psychology*, 31, 254–61.

Paik, H. (2001). The history of children's use of electronic media. In D. G. Singer & J. L. Singer (Eds.), *Handbook of children and the media* (pp. 7–28). Thousand Oaks, CA: Sage.

Petterson, C. C., Peterson, J. L., & Caroll, J. (1987). Television viewing and imaginative problem solving during preadolescence. *Journal of Genetic Psychology*, 147, 61–7.

Piaget, J. (1962). *Play, dreams and imitation in childhood*. New York: Norton.

Preston, J. (1998). From mediated environments to the development of consciousness. In J. Gackenbach (Ed.), *Psychology and the Internet* (pp. 225–91). San Diego, CA: Academic Press.

Qian, J., Preston, J., & House, M. (1999). *Personality trait absorption and reality status evaluations of narrative mediated messages.* Paper presented at the annual meeting of the American Psychological Association, August, Boston, MA.

Rapaczynski, W., Singer, D. G., & Singer, J. L. (1982). Teaching televisions: A curriculum for young children. *Journal of Communication*, 32(2), 46–55.

Rheingold H. (1995). The virtual community. *Utne Reader*, 68, 60–64.

Riley, N. R. (2004). Investigating the use of ICT-based concept mapping techniques on creativity in literacy tasks. *Journal of Computer Assisted Learning*, 20(4), 244–56.

Root-Bernstein, M., & Root-Bernstein, R. (2004). *Paracosms and imaginary friends in the childhoods of creative adults.* Paper presented at the Annual Convention of the American Psychological Association, Honolulu, Hawaii.

Root-Bernstein, R., & Root-Bernstein, M. (1999). *Sparks of genius: The thirteen thinking tools of the world's most creative people.* New York: Houghton-Mifflin.

Rosengren, K. S., Johnson, C., & Harris, P. L. (2000). *Imagining the impossible: Magical, scientific and religious thinking in children.* Cambridge: Cambridge University Press.

Rosenkoetter, S. F., & Rosenkoetter, L. I. (2003). *The review project curriculum. Reducing early violence: Education works!* Oregon State University, Corvallis, Oregon.

Russ, S. W. (1993). *Affect and creativity: The role of affect and play in the creative process.* Hillsdale, NJ: Lawrence Erlbaum.

Russ, S. W. (2004). *Play in child development and psychotherapy: Toward empirically supported practice.* Mahwah, NJ: Lawrence Erlbaum.

Schwebel, D., Rosen, C., & Singer, J. L. (1999). Preschoolers' pretend play and theory of mind: The role of jointly conducted pretense. *British Journal of Developmental Psychology*, 17, 333–48.

Singer, D. G., Golinkoff, R. M., & Hirsh-Pasek, K. (Eds.). (2006). *Play = learning: How play motivates and enhances children's cognitive and social-emotional growth.* New York: Oxford University Press.

Singer, D. G., & Singer, J. L. (1981). Television and reading in the development of imagination. *Children's Literature*, 9, 126–36.

Singer, D. G., & Singer, J. L. (1990). *The house of make-believe: Children's play and the developing imagination.* Cambridge, MA: Harvard University Press.

Singer, D. G., & Singer, J. L. (1998). Developing critical viewing skills and media literacy in children. In K. H. Jamison and A. B. Jordan (Eds.), *The Annals* (pp. 164–79). Philadelphia, PA: The American Academy of Political and Social Science.

Singer, D. G., & Singer, J. L. (2005). *Imagination and play in the electronic age.* Cambridge, MA: Harvard University Press.

Singer, D. G., Zuckerman, D. M., & Singer, J. L. (1980). Helping elementary school children learn about TV. *Journal of Communication*, 30(3), 84–93.

Singer, J. A. (2006). *Memories that matter.* Oakland, CA: New Harbinger Publications.

Singer, J. L. (1961). Imagination and waiting ability in young children. *Journal of Personality*, 29(4), 396–413.

Singer, J. L. (1966). *Daydreaming.* New York: Random House.

Singer, J. L. (1973). *The child's world of make-believe.* New York: Academic Press.

Singer, J. L. (2006). *Imagery in Psychotherapy.* Washington, DC: American Psychological Association.

Singer, J. L., & Lythcott, M. (2002). Fostering school achievement and creativity through sociodramatic play in the classroom. *Research in the schools*, 9(2), 43–52.

Singer, J. L., & Singer, D. G. (1981). *Television, imagination and aggression: A study of preschoolers.* Hillsdale, NJ: Lawrence Erlbaum.

Singer, J. L., & Singer, D. G. (1986). Family experiences and television viewing as predictors of children's imagination, restlessness, and aggression. *Journal of Social Issues*, 42(3), 107–24.

Singer, J. L., & Singer, D. G. (1998). *Barney and Friends* as entertainment and education: Evaluating the quality and effectiveness of a television series for preschool children. In J. K. Asamen & G. Berry (Eds.), *Research paradigms, television, and social behavior* (pp. 305–67). Beverly Hills, CA: Sage.

Singer, J. L., & Singer, D. G. (2005–2006). Preschooler's imaginative play as precursor of narrative consciousness. *Imagination, Cognition and Personality*, 25(2), 97–117.

Singer, J. L., Singer, D. G., & Rapaczynski, W. (1984a). Children's imagination as predicted by family patterns and television viewing: A longitudinal study. *Genetic Psychology Monographs*, 110, 43–69.

Singer, J. L., Singer, D. G., & Rapaczynski, W. (1984b). Family patterns and television viewing as predictors of children's beliefs and aggression. *Journal of Communication*, 34(2), 73–89.

Skeen, P., Brown, M. H., & Osborn, D. K. (1982). Young children's perception of "real" and "pretend" on television. *Perceptual and Motor Skills*, 54(3), 883–7.

Sternberg, R. J., Grigorenko, E., & Singer, J. L. (Eds.). (2004). *Creativity: From potential to realization.* Washington, DC: American Psychological Association.

Strasburger, V. C., & Wilson. B. J. (2002). *Children, adolescence, and the media.* Thousand Oaks, CA: Sage.

Sutton-Smith, B. (1966). Piaget on play: A critique. *Psychological Review*, 73, 104–10.

Taylor, M. (1999). *Imaginary companions and the children who create them.* New York: Oxford University Press.

Taylor, M. Children's imaginary companions. *Televizion*, 16(1), 11–14.

Tower, R. B., Singer, D. G., Singer, J. L., & Biggs, A. (1979). Differential effects of television programming on preschoolers cognition, imagination and social play. *American Journal of Orthopsychiatry*, 42(2), 265–81.

Turkle, S. (1995). *Life on the screen: Identity in the age of the internet.* New York: Simon & Schuster.

Turkle, S. (2002). E-futures and e-personae. In Leach, N. (Ed.), *Designing for a digital world.* London: Wiley.

Valkenburg, P. M. (2001). Television and the child's developing imagination. In D. G. Singer & J. L. Singer (Eds.), *Handbook of children and the media* (pp. 121–34). Thousand Oaks, CA: Sage.

Valkenburg, P. M., & Beentjes, J. W. (1997). Children's creative imagination in response to radio and television stories. *Journal of Communication*, 47(2), 21–38.

Valkenburg, P. M., & van der Voort, T. H. A. (1994). Influence of TV on daydreaming and creative imagination: A review of research. *Psychological Bulletin*, 116(2), 316–39.

Valkenburg, P. M., Vooijs, M. W., van der Voort, T. H., & Wiegman, O. (1992). The influence of television on children's fantasy styles: A secondary analysis. *Imagination, Cognition, and Personality*, 12(1), 55–67.

Van der Voort, T. H. A., & Valkenburg, P. M. (1994). Television's impact on fantasy play: A review of research. *Developmental Review*, 14(1), 227–51.

Vibbert, M. M., & Meringoff, L. K. (1981). *Children's production and application of story imagery: A cross-medium investigation.* (Technical Report No. 231). Cambridge, MA: Harvard University. ERIC Document Reproduction Service No. ED 2106827.

Viemeroe, V., & Paajanen, S. (1992). The role of fantasies and dreams in the TV viewing aggression relationship. *Aggressive Behavior,* 18(2), 109–16.

Von Feilitzen, C. (2004). Young people, soap operas and reality TV: Introduction. In C. von Feilitzen (Ed.), *Young people, soap operas and reality TV* (pp. 9–45). Goteborg, Sweden: Nordicom.

Vygotsky, L. S. (1978). *Mind in society: The development of higher mental processing.* Cambridge, MA: Harvard University Press.

Weber, D. S., & Singer, D. G. (2004). The media habits of infants and toddlers: Findings from a parent survey. *Zero to Three,* 25(1), 330–36.

14

Parasocial and Online Social Relationships

Cynthia Hoffner

Scholars have argued that humans have a fundamental need to form interpersonal attachments, and thus relationships develop in all contexts in which people encounter other individuals (Baumeister & Leary, 1995; Cohen & Metzger, 1998). According to Hinde (1979), "a relationship implies first some sort of intermittent interaction between two people, involving interchanges over an extended period of time. The interchanges have some degree of mutuality, in the sense that the behaviour of each takes some account of the behaviour of the other" (p. 14).

Children form some of their first and most important relationships with family members. Eventually, friends and teachers become crucial interactants in the child's world. But children also spend a great deal of time with media, especially as they move into elementary school (Strasburger & Wilson, 2002). According to Caughey (1984), nearly all media exposure draws us into "social worlds" and involves some form of social interaction. The Internet is a primary forum for young people to meet and interact with others, and television and other forms of media offer children and adolescents access to a wide range of other human beings. Scholars have debated whether online relationships can be as deep and significant as those formed face-to-face (Walther & Parks, 2002), and have questioned whether a "relationship" can occur at all in contexts that do not involve interaction and true mutuality (Giles, 2002). Certainly mediated channels make available a different set of information about others than is available face-to-face, and the information is acquired in different ways. Yet, as this chapter will show, young people are able to form impressions of and develop affective bonds to individuals known only (or primarily) through symbolic media interfaces. Specifically, the chapter will explore the nature and development of social relationships that occur online and in relation to media personalities, as well as the needs these relationships fulfill for social interaction and identity development. Future research directions in need of empirical inquiry will also be identified.

Types of Relationships

A key developmental task for children and youth involves relationship formation with others (Bowlby, 1969). From these social experiences, a sense of self emerges and develops over time and individual needs are fulfilled, such as companionship and being part of a group (Baumeister & Leary, 1995; Harter, 1999). Both parasocial and online social relationships involve the use of media, but they vary in terms of their degree of reciprocity as well as in the existence of or potential for interaction outside of the media environment.

Parasocial relationships

In their seminal paper, Horton and Wohl (1956) coined the term "parasocial interaction" (p. 215) to describe the development of a "seeming face-to-face relationship" between a viewer and a media personality. Many scholars have used the term "parasocial relationship" to describe the affective bond that develops between an audience member and a media figure encountered primarily through essentially non-interactive media, including television, movies, books, and music (e.g., Brown, Basil, & Bocarnea, 2003b; Caughey, 1984; Giles, 2002; Meyrowitz, in press; Rubin, Perse, & Powell, 1985). Giles (2002) argued that "once we have made a person judgment about a media figure, or attributed person characteristics to that figure (e.g., an anthropomorphized cartoon animal), then we will subsequently respond to that figure 'as if' it occupies our physical space, thereby becoming incorporated into our social network" (pp. 283–4). Of course, parasocial relationships are characterized by minimal or no actual interactivity or mutuality. Thus, the term "parasocial interaction" implies that some form of pseudo-interaction occurs within the mind of the audience member (cf. Honeycutt, 2003).

A distinction has been drawn between parasocial interaction and other ways of relating to media figures, including attraction, similarity, identification, and imitation (e.g., Cohen, 2001; Hoffner & Cantor, 1991; Rosengren et al., 1976). But there are multiple aspects to any relationship, and it is reasonable to assume that they are interrelated. For example, it has been argued that a parasocial relationship with a media figure motivates identification and behavior change (Boon & Lomore, 2001; Brown, Basil, & Bocarnea, 2003a). Moreover, most research has not used clear and consistent labels for the different types of responses (Cohen, 2001), and very little research with young people has explicitly examined parasocial interaction (Giles, 2002). For the purpose of this paper, the concept of a "parasocial" relationship will be used as a parallel to a "social" relationship, to refer to an affective bond that is formed with a media figure.

Online social relationships

The Internet offers young people alternative ways to interact with individuals who are already part of their face-to-face social networks, as well as opportunities to develop new relationships with unknown people from virtually any background and geographical area (e.g., Calvert, 2002; Gross, Juvonen, & Gable, 2002; Wolak, Mitchell, & Finkelhor, 2002). There are many kinds of online forums available for interacting and for assuming imaginary identities, including instant messaging (IM) and emailing, playing online games, participating in chat rooms, and creating or reading blogs. The many communication options available online offer youth a broad array of venues for social interaction and relationship development. Online interaction can deepen existing face-to-face bonds and can also lead to the formation of new relationships that are often close and rewarding (e.g., Gross, Juvonen, & Gable, 2002; Wolak, Mitchell, & Finkelhor, 2002).

Development of Parasocial and Online Social Relationships

Both online and parasocial relationships are a common experience of youth (Hoffner & Cantor, 1991; Wolak, Mitchell, & Finkelhor, 2002). The reasons for socially interacting with others are varied, but are based in the need to create social bonds with others. According to Baumeister and Leary (1995), "a need to belong, that is, a need to form and maintain at least a minimum quantity of interpersonal relationships, is innately prepared (and hence nearly universal) among human beings" (p. 499). This section reviews research on the formation of affective bonds with media figures and with others in online contexts. Before reviewing this literature, a brief overview is provided of theories relevant to the motivations for relationship formation and the processes by which relationships develop.

Theories of relationship development

Within the field of communication, researchers have long recognized the importance of needs and motives in the formation of interpersonal relationships. Uses and gratifications is a functional approach to media use that assumes people are active consumers who make media choices to satisfy their needs, including the need to feel connected to others. Individuals' social and psychological circumstances are considered important determinants of their uses of the media to fulfill their needs (Rubin, 2002). Scholars working within this framework have argued that parasocial relationships are sought in part to fulfill affective needs, including affiliation and companionship (Giles, 2002; McGuire, 1974). The uses and gratifications paradigm has been extended to examine the motivations underlying interpersonal communication, which are quite similar to those that motivate use of the media (Cohen & Metzger, 1998; Rubin & Rubin, 1985). Clearly, the Internet has opened an entirely new domain for interpersonal communication, and it seems likely that young people are turning to online interactions and relationships in part to satisfy their social/interpersonal needs (Papacharissi & Rubin, 2000). Indeed, Cohen and Metzger (1998) argued that "both mass and interpersonal communication are motivated by many needs, all related to social affiliation" (p. 56).

Once an interpersonal connection is made with a media figure or online partner, the process of coming to know that individual has begun. Uncertainty reduction theory states that initial interactions with others are characterized by high levels of uncertainty, and that individuals are motivated to reduce uncertainty (Berger, 1988). According to this theory, uncertainty can be reduced in three ways: interactive strategies (e.g., reciprocal self-disclosure), active strategies (e.g., asking others about an individual), and passive strategies (e.g., observation of the other person in various situations). The theory also contends that greater communication is associated with higher levels of intimacy and increased attributional confidence.

Social penetration theory explains how relational closeness develops. Altman and Taylor (1973) posited that closeness develops as communication proceeds from superficial to more intimate exchanges. Through reciprocal self-disclosure (Dindia, 2000) and other forms of communication (e.g., nonverbal behavior, shared physical space), people come to know more about each other over time. If they find the developing relationship rewarding, they continue to interact and reveal increasingly deeper and more private aspects of themselves. Although reciprocity is generally not possible with parasocial relationships, media offerings are often structured in ways designed to reveal personal information about and intimate secrets of media figures, thereby simulating the process of self-disclosure.

The Internet is a unique context for interpersonal interaction and relationship development. Early work in this area suggested that the lack of nonverbal and social context cues reduced the likelihood that online relationships would develop, and those that did were believed to be shallow and impersonal. More recent evidence shows that individuals are indeed capable of forming and maintaining close, rewarding relationships without face-to-face contact (see Walther & Parks, 2002, for a review). In his social information processing theory, Walther (1992) argued that online communicators use alternative cues (e.g., content, linguistic style) to compensate for the lack of nonverbal cues, and that although online relationships develop more slowly, they are eventually comparable to those formed face-to-face. Moreover, Walther's (1996) hyperpersonal perspective holds that online communication sometimes leads to the rapid development of close, intimate relationships because partners engage in selective self-presentation (which is easier online than face-to-face), leading to idealized perceptions and more personal and intimate self-disclosures.

Parasocial relationship development

Companionship has been identified as an important motivation for media use among children and adolescents (e.g., Rubin, 1979), and one way that need can be satisfied is by forming affective bonds with media figures. Parasocial interactions reflect a sense of real social bonds in that these relationships are deeply felt and have many of the characteristics of "real" relationships (e.g., Giles, 2002; Hoffner & Cantor, 1991; Meyrowitz, in press). Children and adolescents, like adults, often feel as though they are involved in events portrayed in the media, and they respond in some ways as if they were witnessing or participating in real interactions with people they know (e.g., Murray, 1999; Rosengren et al., 1976). The process of impression formation is similar for real people and media figures (Hoffner & Cantor, 1991), and many of the characteristics that affect the development of social relationships, such as appearance, personality, and social behaviors, have been shown to impact the bonds that children and adolescents form with media figures (e.g., Cohen, 1999; Hoffner, 1996; McDonald & Kim, 2001; Reeves, 1979). Also similar to social relationships, young people form different types of attachments to media figures, regarding them as friends with whom they share fundamental similarities, as romantic partners, or as admired idols whom they aspire to be like (e.g., Adams-Price & Greene, 1990; Cohen, 1999; Hoffner, 1996). In videogames, young people can even take on the identity of a fictional character. However, Murphy (2004) argued that, in most game environments, "one must switch between embodying and controlling a character as an avatar and then passively watching the same character in a cinematic" (p. 227).

In research with adults, Rebecca Rubin and her colleagues applied uncertainty reduction theory to the process of parasocial relationship development (see Rubin & Rubin, 2001). They contended that initial attraction to media figures motivates further efforts to "get to know" them, leading to increased confidence in predicting and understanding their behaviors, and greater intimacy or parasocial attachment. Whereas the deepening of social relationships occurs primarily through interactive strategies, such as reciprocal self-disclosure (Dindia, 2000), uncertainty in parasocial relationships is reduced primarily through passive strategies, such as observing media figures in a variety of situations, and active strategies, such as talking with others or searching for information. In television series, for example, viewers can observe characters' interactions in many contexts, their solitary activities, and sometimes even their innermost thoughts and feelings (e.g., via fantasy sequences or voiceovers). In addition, information about fictional characters and public figures is available from a variety of sources, including television interviews, magazines, and the Internet. These sources may serve the same function as self-disclosure in a social relationship (Dindia, 2000), leading audience members to feel as though they know more about some media figures than they know about many of the people with whom they have interpersonal relationships.

No studies with children or adolescents have explicitly examined the process of parasocial relationship development, but much evidence shows that young people often feel as though they know media figures on intimate terms (e.g., Caughey, 1984; Maltby et al., 2005; Murray, 1999). Even very young children talk to and interact with television characters like Dora the Explorer and Steve, the host of *Blue's Clues* (Anderson et al., 2000; Calvert, Strong, Jacobs, & Conger, 2007). With the Internet, opportunities for deepening the parasocial connections formed with media figures have greatly increased, including access to games about television characters as well as materials on fan sites, celebrity websites, and fan fiction (e.g., Bird, 2003; Murray, 1999; Valkenburg & Soeters, 2001). Some young people develop a sense that media figures with whom they feel a parasocial bond know and understand them personally, and sometimes they even make efforts to contact and interact with those individuals (Murray, 1999; Pasquier, 1996; Raviv et al., 1996).

Personal characteristics, such as personality or life experiences, also influence young people's formation of parasocial bonds, through perceived similarity between the self and media figures (e.g., Kivel & Kleiber, 2000; McDonald & Kim, 2001; Murray, 1999). Research with adults has explored the association between social environment and parasocial relationship development, but evidence on this topic among young people is almost nonexistent. Contrary to the deficiency model, there is little evidence that lonely or isolated adults are more likely to form parasocial bonds (Rubin, Perse, & Powell, 1985; Tsao, 1996). However, attachment styles that adults form in childhood are related to their development of parasocial relationships. For example, parasocial bonds tend to be most intense for individuals who crave closeness and intimacy with others but fear loss and rejection (anxious-ambivalent attachment style), and least intense for those who have difficulty with intimacy and trust (avoidant attachment style) (Cohen, 2004; Cole & Leets, 1999). In what appears to be the only relevant study with young people (aged 10–15), Rosengren and colleagues (1976) found that less family integration was associated with greater wishful identification with television characters (mediated by viewing involvement) but not with the tendency to regard characters as friends. Future research should explore the role of family configuration, social connections, and attachment style in the development and consequences of young people's parasocial relationships.

The depth of parasocial bonds is reflected in the emotional reactions of audience members to the loss of favorite characters and the deaths of celebrities. Sturm (1975) argued that children become so emotionally tied to characters in television series that the disappearance of these characters – through the plot or because the series ends – may be emotionally upsetting. Consistent with this view, a study of online fans of the series *My So-Called Life* found that many teen-aged girls were distraught when the show was cancelled, due to their parasocial attachment to the lead character, 15-year-old Angela (Murray, 1999). Recent work on "parasocial break-ups" documents this phenomenon with adolescents and adults (Cohen, 2003, 2004). In addition, deaths of beloved public figures, such as Diana, Princess of Wales, and Fred Rogers, of the children's series *Mister Rogers' Neighborhood*, have had a deep emotional effect on audience members who knew them only through the media (Brown, Basil, & Bocarnea, 2003b; Meyrowitz, in press).

Online social interaction and relationship development

Social interaction is a primary motivator for online social relationships. Young people report that a major aspect of their Internet use involves keeping in contact with people whom they already know offline, primarily through IM (Gross,

Juvonen, & Gable, 2002; Lenhart, Madden, & Hitlin, 2005). They also use the Internet, such as chat rooms, bulletin boards, and fan sites, to meet and interact with people whom they have never encountered face-to-face (e.g., Bird, 2003; Mesch & Talmud, 2006; Subrahmanyam et al., 2001). Chat rooms are based on social interaction among the participants, although many people "lurk" and simply read the postings of others (Subrahmanyam, Greenfield, & Tynes, 2004). Conversations in chat rooms are often public, but they can also occur in "private" chat rooms or move to IM.

Social networking web sites such as MySpace and Facebook have risen rapidly in popularity. These sites allow young people to communicate with friends as well as meet new people. Users post a range of personal information, including profiles, photos, and blog entries, and visitors can post messages. The personal details and the opportunity to interact have made MySpace and similar sites popular hangouts for young people. Although there does not yet appear to be any scholarly research on these networking sites, there is growing concern about the personal information that young people reveal, the sexually explicit nature of the some of the posts, and the safety risks from online predators (Hansell, 2006; Hewitt et al., 2006).

Online game participants interact with other players, many of whom may be in geographically distant locations. Online games vary in terms of their focus, with some more oriented to competition, and others involving more prosocial interaction (Calvert, 2002). The largest multi-user games are known as "massively multiplayer online role-playing games," which involve hundreds of thousands of players participating in ongoing, fantasy-based adventures. Players who collaborate are more likely to succeed, and many of the interactions are social (involving strategy planning, cooperation, and teamwork), as well as personal in nature (Yee, 2006). In one study, social interaction was named most often by adolescents as their favorite aspect of playing a multi-user game (Griffiths, Davies, & Chappell, 2004).

When young people interact with strangers online (e.g., in chat rooms or while playing online games), ongoing relationships sometimes develop. For example, in a recent national sample of American youths (aged 10–17), 17 percent of respondents had formed a close online relationship in the past year, including 2 percent whose relationship was romantic (Wolak, Mitchell, & Finkelhor, 2002). There is currently limited research on young people's relationships with others whom they met online, despite a growing body of research on this topic among adults.

Two studies compared the qualities of online and face-to-face friendships among young people. In one study, children and teens (aged 10–19) felt less close to online friends than they did to friends in their face-to-face network (Subrahmanyam et al., 2001). In the other study, teens (aged 13–18) perceived online friends as less intimate and supportive than face-to-face friends, perhaps because their online relationships were of shorter duration and involved less diverse shared activities (Mesch & Talmud, 2006). It also may be that young people's extensive peer social networks (compared to that of adults) provide greater opportunity to form face-to-face friendships, thus reducing their motivation to form close online friendships. Scholars need to explore further why these results differ from recent research with adults, which generally shows that online relationships are often as close and rewarding as face-to-face friendships (Walther & Parks, 2002).

A study by Cassell and Tversky (2005), however, presented a somewhat different picture of the development of online friendships among young people. The authors examined an online forum designed to connect and empower youths from around the world. A total of 1044 young people (aged 10–16) from 44 different countries participated in the forum, which met online for five years. The authors analyzed messages posted to the forum, and did in-depth interviews with a small subset of participants. They found that 62 percent of those interviewed formed close, supportive online friendships with other participants. This study differs from the other two studies (Mesch & Talmud, 2006; Subrahmanyam et al., 2001) in that the participants were explicitly brought together for a common purpose, and the online interactions lasted for a long period of time.

Wolak, Mitchell, and Finkelhor (2003) reported evidence that the Internet may serve a social compensation function for some adolescents. Using a national sample, the researchers found that young people who had difficulties with parents or were highly troubled were more likely than their peers to have close online relationships. Although the findings are correlational, the authors argued that these young people may have sought online relationships as a way of obtaining companionship or support that they were lacking in other contexts. Similarly, Gross and her colleagues (2002) found that adolescents (aged 11–13) who were lonely and anxious turned to IM for social interaction mostly with people they did not know well, whereas those who were more socially integrated communicated primarily with friends from their face-to-face networks. Thus, adolescents who already had social difficulties did not use online interactions to enhance social connections and intimacy with others. This outcome is consistent with the "rich-get-richer" hypothesis, which contends that extraverts and those with more social support are better able to utilize online opportunities for social involvement (Kraut et al., 2002). The Internet also provides a unique opportunity for young people with stigmatized identities or who are dealing with difficult life issues to find similar others with whom to communicate and form friendships (McKenna & Bargh, 2000; Tichon & Shapiro, 2003).

Peter, Valkenburg, and Schouten (2005) suggested that neither the rich-get-richer hypothesis (Kraut et al., 2002) nor the social compensation hypothesis alone can adequately explain the process of online relationship formation. In a study of young people aged 9 to 18, they found that both introversion/extraversion and motivation for online communication influenced online self-disclosure and friendship formation. Specifically, extending the rich-get-richer hypothesis, extraverted adolescents self-disclosed and communicated more online, which facilitated the formation of friendships. However, introverted adolescents who were motivated to communicate online to compensate for limited social skills also self-disclosed more and formed online friendships, consistent with the compensation hypothesis.

Identity Development through Parasocial and Online Social Interactions

Identity development, a lifelong process, is another theoretical area that sheds light on how and why children use media. Research shows that media can play an important role in the formation of a personal and social identity, and interactions and affective bonds with others facilitate this process (e.g., Arnett, 1995; Calvert, 2002). Before presenting this literature, some key theories of identity development are summarized.

Theories of identity development

Theoretical approaches to identity development are concerned with how children and adolescents form a conceptualization of the self, typically focusing on either personal identity (a sense of "I" as different from others) or social identity (a sense of "we" in which the self is part of a collective). Both are considered fundamental components of identity, and are, to some extent, interdependent. A sense of personal identity (e.g., I am a girl) is a necessary prerequisite for identifying with a social collective, and social identity can have consequences for personal identity, for example by affecting self-esteem (Harter, 1999; Ruble et al., 2004).

Describing the differentiation of self from other, Erikson (1963, 1968) defined ego identity as a sense of individual uniqueness, a feeling of comfort with oneself, and confidence that one is accepted by those whose opinions matter (Kroger, 2003). According to Erikson, children explore a variety of roles and identifications through imitation and play. As young people move into adolescence, and experience changes associated with puberty, the expectations and responses of others and society change as well. This stimulates the process of identity formation, which Erikson identified as the central task of adolescence. A "moratorium" period during adolescence allows young people the freedom to experiment with different identities and adult roles. Ultimately, they must make a series of choices that lead to commitments in a variety of domains, including personal, sexual/romantic, ideological, and occupational. Erikson (1968) stated that the identity formed in adolescence "includes all significant [past] identifications, but it also alters them in order to make a unique and reasonably coherent whole of them" (p. 161). However, the process by which people achieve a unified personal identity (or even whether they do so) is individual, and identity development continues throughout the lifespan (Erikson, 1968).

Other theoretical approaches focus on the relational basis of personal identity (e.g., Harter, 1999; Mead, 1934; Stryker & Burke, 2000). These perspectives define identity in terms of the meanings people attach to their social roles and relationships, and posit the existence of multiple identities within different contexts. Mead (1934) argued that identity is constructed through interactions with others, and that people tend to see themselves as they believe significant others see them. Building on this view, Stryker and Burke (2000) argued that "persons have as many identities as distinct networks of relationships in which they occupy positions and play roles" (p. 286.) According to Harter (1999), children's self-conceptions gradually become more differentiated, with an increasing awareness that they are not the same in all situations. By adolescence they more fully recognize that they have multiple selves that differ based on social context and role relationships. For example, a teen may enact a different "self" with her mother than she does with her friends. Harter (1999) argued that a critical task of adolescence is integrating self-concepts from multiple domains into a coherent, multifaceted sense of self.

Social identity perspectives focus on the conceptualization of the self in terms of membership in social groups or categories (e.g., gender, ethnicity, religion), and the evaluations or affect attached to those memberships (Tajfel, 1978; Turner, 1999). Moreover, once the self is perceived in terms of a collective, characteristics associated with that group/category, such as status, norms, and traits, become part of the self-concept (Turner, 1999). Even young children have an awareness of themselves in terms of basic social categories (especially gender), but during middle childhood they begin to understand the deeper meanings associated with these categories (Ruble et al., 2004). As they move into adolescence, young people develop a more complex understanding of their collective identities, and these identities typically form a significant part of their self-concept. Nonetheless, there are individual and group differences (e.g., ethnic minority/majority status) in the salience, importance, and meaning young people associate with their social identities (Ruble et al., 2004).

Exploring personal identity

Developmental perspectives contend that individual identity formation is of greater concern in early adolescence, leading to more frequent identity experiments; older adolescents are more concerned with relational identity and sexuality (Erikson, 1968; Harter, 1999). Youth use parasocial relationships as a way to express themselves and try out alternate identities. Being a fan of a media character or celebrity, and expressing that attachment through conversation, clothing, or bedroom décor, can communicate something about oneself to others (e.g., Arnett, 1995; Boden, 2006; Murray, 1999; Steele & Brown, 1995). Adolescents' affective bonds with media figures also lead to a desire to become more similar to them, to incorporate characteristics of those figures into their own personality and behavioral repertoire (e.g., Maltby et al., 2005; Murray, 1999; Pasquier, 1996). For example, Caughey (1984) reported that young people made changes in their appearance, attitudes, values, activities and other characteristics, in order to become more like admired celebrities. These types of attachments allow young people to experiment with various identities, yet the nature and range of role models available can also restrict the extent to which parasocial attachments contribute to identity development. Moreover, an intense fascination with one or a few media figures may limit adolescents' development of a complex sense of personal identity, perhaps because it limits their activities in other life domains (Cheung & Yue, 2003; Harrison, 2006).

Erikson (1968) regarded occupational identity as one of the most important aspects of identity formation in adolescence. Involvement with television characters has been associated with young people's occupational aspirations (e.g., Hoffner et al., 2006; King & Multon, 1996), and videogames provide an opportunity to actually try out particular occupations, such as fighter pilot or soldier, via role play (Jansz, 2005). However, media images of the world of work are often inaccurate and stereotypical, potentially restricting the range of occupations to which young people might aspire and leading to an inaccurate understanding of what various occupations involve (Signorielli & Kahlenberg, 2001).

The Internet has several characteristics that should facilitate identity exploration and development among young people (McKenna & Bargh, 2000; Turkle, 1995). In particular, interactivity permits social interactions with peers and others, which are crucial to the development of a mature identity (Harter, 1999). The option of anonymity (or use of a pseudonym) permits participation in relationships and communities that require less commitment than do those in offline contexts, and run less risk of social disapproval (McKenna & Bargh, 2000). The ability to transcend the physical body allows people to interact with others without (or with reduced) assumptions associated with gender, ethnicity, physical abilities, or appearance.

Research examining how young people present their identities online – on home pages, blogs, and social networking sites – found that these forums serve as a form of self-disclosure, allowing the creators to feel as though they are known and understood by others (Huffaker & Calvert, 2005; Moinian, 2006; Stern, 2004). Nearly all the sites in these studies included ways for visitors to post responses, thus encouraging social interaction. Feedback permits young people to obtain confirmation or approval from peers, which can enhance self-worth, especially when the feedback is public (Harter, 1999). Public expression and feedback also provide an opportunity for young people to express who they are, exchange ideas, and further refine values and beliefs, in the process of forming ideological commitments, another important facet of a mature identity (Erikson, 1968).

The opportunity to try out different identities anonymously permits people a great deal of freedom in identity construction online (McKenna & Bargh, 2000). Using Erikson's theory (1963), Turkle (1995) argued that "if our culture no longer offers an adolescent moratorium, virtual communities do. They offer permission to play, to try things out" (pp. 203–4). Lenhart, Rainie, and Lewis (2001) reported that one quarter of adolescents who use email, chat, or IM had pretended to be someone else. Similarly, Valkenburg, Schouten, and Peter (2005) found that fully half of their sample of young people had done so. As predicted, pretending to be someone else was more common among younger (aged 9–12) than older participants (aged 13–18). If people use the Internet as a way to make friends whom they hope may become integrated into their offline social networks, they have less freedom to experiment with identities. Yet they still can withhold details about their physical selves that would be apparent in face-to-face contexts (e.g., obesity, wheelchair use), and choose the time in a developing relationship to make such self-disclosures (McKenna & Bargh, 2000).

Online games provide a rich environment for identity exploration, allowing young people to experiment through role playing in interaction with others (e.g., Calvert, 2002; Talamo & Ligorio, 2001). Online game players typically create their own characters, by developing a character description and selecting or designing a visual icon or avatar to represent the character onscreen. Players can present themselves as humans, animals, or cartoon characters; they can reflect or idealize their own personality or physical appearance or choose something completely different. The range of choices is constrained only by the options offered within the virtual environment (Calvert et al., 2003; Griffiths, Davies, & Chappell, 2004; Talamo & Ligorio, 2001). By playing a character and interacting with other participants within the game environment, young people can take on characteristics that they may wish to explore or develop in themselves (e.g., violent, powerful, outgoing), and can try out possible future roles, such as leader or romantic partner (Calvert, 2002; Turkle, 1995; Yee, 2006).

Exploring sexuality

Whereas younger adolescents are more focused on individual identity, older adolescents are more concerned with relationships and the struggle between isolation and intimacy (Erikson, 1968). Parasocial bonds enable young people to participate vicariously in relationships through imaginary interactions with their favorite characters. Children and pre-teens form stronger attachments to same-gender media figures, but this changes in adolescence, with teens (especially girls) more likely to form cross-gender, romantic attachments (Adams-Price & Greene, 1990; Cohen, 1999, 2003; Hoffner, 1996). Scholars have argued that attachments to media figures in adolescence play a transitional role in identity formation, as young people shift from identification with parents toward an autonomous identity and interest in romantic attachments (Adams-Price & Greene, 1990; Giles & Maltby, 2004; Steele & Brown, 1995). In other words, parasocial relationships help facilitate the transition into adult romance and sexuality.

In a study with young people aged 10 to 16, Adams-Price and Greene (1990) found two primary types of attachments to celebrities. Some adolescents, especially boys, formed identificatory attachments in which they desired to be, or be like, the celebrity. Others, especially girls, formed romantic attachments, which allowed them the opportunity to try out the role of romantic partner in a safe context. Brown, Dykers, Steele, and White (1994) found that adolescents used sexual media images – such as pictures of movie stars and models – in the process of constructing their sexual identity. Numerous other studies have reported that young people use media portrayals and images as a way of role playing romantic relationships and learning about sexual and romantic scripts (e.g., Caughey, 1984; Karniol, 2001; Pasquier, 1996).

Opportunities to explore sexual identity through televised parasocial relationships are relatively rare for youth who are gay or lesbian because characters who are gay or lesbian are infrequently portrayed in television programs (Fouts & Inch, 2005; Meyer, 2003). Yet for gay or lesbian teens, the media are often a key source of information about homosexuality (Kielwasser & Wolf, 1992; Meyer, 2003). According to Meyer (2003), media portrayals of youth who are gays or lesbians, although limited, allow gay and lesbian teens "to access information on how to 'be' gay in the absence of other sources of information on sexual identity" (p. 274).

In contrast to television, the Internet provides many opportunities for young people who are gay or lesbian to express themselves and form social connections. The online context is especially important for teens who are gay, lesbian, bisexual, or transgendered because fears of rejection or ostracism lead many of them to refrain from discussing their sexual orientation with others in their face-to-face networks (Kivel & Kleiber, 2000). In a study of 70 teen bloggers, Huffaker and Calvert (2005) found that 17 percent (mostly males) discussed their homosexuality in their blogs. The authors argued that "male bloggers may have been using blogs as a safe and comfortable environment to be honest, or even candid, about their sexual identity and feelings."

Indeed, the online environment presents many opportunities for all young people to develop their sexual identity. Studies of teen chat rooms revealed that many participants, especially older teens, posted messages with sexual content (Subrahmanyam, Greenfield, & Tynes, 2004; Subrahmanyam, Smahel, & Greenfield, 2006). Teens use chat rooms to "pair off," for example by asking a potential romantic interest to participate in a private conversation via IM (Subrahmanyam, Greenfield, & Tynes, 2004). This can serve as a way of "practicing" for real-life intimate relationships and dating in an environment with less pressure and risk. Both by observing and by participating in sexual interactions (e.g., flirting) in chat rooms, young people can learn sexual norms and scripts, but they also encounter sexual harassment (Subrahmanyam, Greenfield, & Tynes, 2004; Subrahmanyam, Smahel, & Greenfield, 2006; Turkle, 1995). Online games also provide young people with an opportunity to explore intimate relationships (Calvert, 2002). However, online deception – for example, by a partner who misrepresents his/her gender – can be disturbing for young people who are just developing their sexual identities and their trust in intimate relationships (Calvert, 2002; Turkle, 1995).

Social identity development

Parasocial relationships can play an important role in the development of social identity, but the Internet greatly expands the opportunity for developing a sense of self as a group member. Young people can interact online with members of a variety of social groups, thereby refining their understanding of the groups to which they do and do not belong, and their understanding of the characteristics and stereotypes associated with their own groups (Ruble et al., 2004). Gender and ethnicity are two social categories that children become aware of at a young age, and that have a key influence on social interactions and identity (Ruble et al., 2004). The role of the media in the development of gender and ethnic identity are reviewed below, and the development of other social identities is addressed briefly.

Gender identity   Gender is a key component of identity (Ruble et al., 2004), and parasocial bonds have the potential to affect young people's conceptions of their own gender, as well as the other gender. For example, Hoffner (1996) examined children's parasocial relationships with favorite television characters. For male characters, perceived intelligence, attractiveness, and strength were associated with stronger parasocial attachments. For female characters (chosen only by girls), attractiveness was the *only* factor that contributed to parasocial attachment. Cohen (1999) found similar gender differences in the characteristics that teens reportedly used to select favorite characters in a teen serial, with personality more important for male characters and appearance more important for female characters. These findings suggest that television reinforces the societal norm that for females (but not males), appearance is of primary importance. According to Ruble et al. (2004), "collective identity . . . should affect [individuals'] desires to look and act in identity consistent ways" (p. 57). For girls and young women, gender identity may enhance their desire to look like the "ideal" women portrayed in the media, which can lead to lower body satisfaction and an increased risk for eating disorders (Harrison, 1997; Maltby et al., 2005). However, young women can resist messages about female gender roles in popular culture, as African American teens tend to do with regard to the thin ideal body image in the media (Arnett, 1995; Duke, 2002).

Many forms of media portray males in problematic ways as well, most notably as excessively aggressive and violent (e.g., Messner, Dunbar, & Hunt, 2000; Smith, Nathanson, & Wilson, 2002). If boys and young men perceive violent figures on television or in videogames as idols or role models, they may incorporate violence and aggressiveness into their developing sense of what it means to be male (e.g., Hoffner & Buchanan, 2005; Huesmann et al., 2003). However, young men can also use their identification with media characters, especially in videogames, to confront their anger and develop ways of coping effectively (Jansz, 2005).

Gender continues to exert a critical influence in online interactions, with gender often self-identified or implied by the use of gendered screen names

(Subrahmanyam, Greenfield, & Tynes, 2004; Subrahmanyam, Smahel, & Greenfield, 2006). In an analysis of 38 chat sessions, Subrahmanyam and colleagues (2006) found that the interaction dynamics often conformed to traditional gender roles. Males were more active, mentioning explicit sexual topics more often, whereas females were more passive, referencing sexuality implicitly. Moreover, younger chat room participants can observe the gendered behaviors of older teens, which may affect their understanding of what it means to be male and female and serve to reinforce traditional gender roles (Subrahmanyam, Smahel, & Greenfield, 2006). Yet with no visible cues to gender online, young people are free to present themselves as either gender (Calvert, 2002; Turkle, 1995). A study of online gamers found that adolescents (aged 12–19) "gender-swapped" less than adults, but nearly half of the adolescents reported playing characters of the other gender (Griffiths, Davies, & Chappell, 2004). Gender-swapping can allow game participants to play roles that are different from themselves and to explore other aspects of their personality. Some findings indicate that males are more likely to try out female identities online than vice versa (Calvert, 2002; Griffiths, Davies, & Chappell, 2004; Turkle, 1995), perhaps because there are more offline social sanctions for males who behave in feminine ways than there are for females who behave in masculine ways (Deaux & Lafrance, 1998).

Online computer games allow young people to experiment with adult gender roles and learn about their own reactions in different situations, such as danger, confrontation, or intimate relationships (Calvert, 2002; Yee, 2006). Whereas many popular games contain high levels of violence and are played primarily by males (Griffiths, Davies, & Chappell, 2004; Yee, 2006), new games are being designed with features that appeal more to females, such as community building and non-violent narratives (Xiong, 2003). Through early socialization, young people already know a great deal about what it means to be male or female, and they may seek online content that helps them understand and conform with norms and expectations of their own gender group (Arnett, 1995; Deaux & Lafrance, 1998).

Ethnic identity In developing a sense of ethnic identity, young people may seek parasocial relationships with characters of their own ethnicity. However, media portrayals of people of color remain limited and stereotyped, despite substantial improvements in the depictions of African Americans on American television (Greenberg, Mastro, & Brand, 2002). When young people see members of an ethnic group with which they identify portrayed negatively in the media, this may adversely affect their sense of self-worth (Ruble et al., 2004). In addition, some groups rarely see characters of their own ethnicity portrayed – in the United States this is the case for those of Asian and Native American heritage, and to a lesser extent those of Latino heritage – which suggests that those groups are unimportant and powerless (Greenberg, Mastro, & Brand, 2002; Ward, 2004).

Despite limited or negative portrayals, there is little evidence that media exposure is associated with lower self-esteem among youths of color. A few studies have shown either no association or a positive link between overall television use and self-esteem (e.g., Stroman, 1986; Subervi-Vélez & Necochea, 1990). Other research indicates that young people's viewing selectivity and interpretations may play a key role. For example, McDermott and Greenberg (1984) found that black children's exposure to television programs featuring black characters was associated with higher self-esteem and higher racial esteem, but only when they evaluated the characters positively. In a study with African American adolescents, Ward (2004) found that identification with popular black male characters was associated with higher self-esteem, whereas identification with popular white characters was associated with lower self-esteem. These findings are consistent with evidence that there are many ways that members of socially devalued groups can maintain self-esteem (Ruble et al., 2004). In addition, the family and community may serve a buffering effect for children and adolescents of color (McDermott & Greenberg, 1984; Ward, 2004).

The Internet has the potential to provide a color-blind space in which to interact with others, but race and ethnicity information is often revealed online through self-identification, language, or in response to queries. In an analysis of 19 hours of transcripts from general-topic teen chat rooms, for example, Tynes, Reynolds, and Greenfield (2004) found that race was mentioned frequently, with positive and neutral references most frequent but negative references also common, especially in unmonitored chat rooms. In monitored rooms, young people had a 19 percent chance of encountering a negative racial remark during a 30-minute chat session; in unmonitored rooms that chance rose to 59 percent. It is not clear to what extent such prejudice adversely affects teens' ethnic identity, because members of groups devalued by society have strategies to resist such effects (Ruble et al., 2004). One way to bolster ethnic self-esteem is to derogate other ethnic groups, and in fact Tynes and colleagues (2004) found that teens of all racial/ethnic backgrounds, including whites, were targets of attacks. Similarly, McKee (2002) analyzed posts to an online forum on affirmative action by high-school and college students, and found that the exchanges frequently involved aggressive language and misunderstandings between participants of different racial/ethnic backgrounds.

The Internet also can connect young people to a variety of forums oriented toward particular ethnic groups, which allows them to explore their ethnic identity and build a sense of community with others (e.g., Batheja, 2005). Online communities have the potential to aid in the development of national or cultural identities among members of diaspora groups (Thompson, 2002). Yet online forums can pose risks as well, for example when teens (predominantly Caucasian) are drawn to ethnic hate sites, which explicitly target young people who are seeking a sense of community and identity (e.g., Lee & Leets, 2002).

Other social identities Young people can use the media to develop a sense of themselves as group members based on age, religion, political ideology, or a variety of other social categories. Perhaps more importantly, mediated communication can enable young people with identities that are stigmatized by society (e.g., individuals who are gay or lesbian, individuals with chronic illnesses or disabilities) to connect with similar others, which could facilitate the development of a positive social identity. For example, parasocial relationships that youth who are gay or lesbian form with media figures who are gay, lesbian, bisexual, or transgendered may contribute to a sense of themselves as part of a collective identity ("we") based on sexual orientation (e.g., Kivel & Kleiber, 2000). Media portrayals of physical and intellectual disabilities are very limited; people who face these challenges want to see characters like themselves living ordinary lives, which they contend would allow them to feel a part of a social group that is respected and valued by society (Ross, 1997).

Through the Internet, young people with stigmatized social identities can meet and interact with others like themselves. According to McKenna and Bargh (1998), participation in online groups can help "demarginalize" those identities, leading to reduced isolation and greater self-acceptance. They argued that this type of outlet is most important for people whose identity is concealable (as it is for individuals who are gay or lesbian), in part because these individuals have difficulty recognizing others who share their identity. No scholarly research could be located on online group involvement by teens' who are gay or lesbian. However, citing anecdotal evidence, Russell (2002) stated that, for many teens who identify themselves as being gay, lesbian, bisexual, or transgendered, "virtual communities provide spaces to test out identities, find a voice, and develop a sense of solidarity with others who are also excluded from the mainstream" (p. 261).

Future Research Directions

Although parasocial and online social relationships are important venues in which children's and youths' social development is taking place, there are still significant gaps in the literature. Scholars are only beginning to explore parasocial relationships and online social interactions among young people in depth (e.g., Calvert et al., 2003; Maltby et al., 2005; Mesch & Talmud, 2006; Peter, Valkenburg, & Schouten, 2005; Subrahmanyam, Smahel, & Greenfield, 2006). Very little research with children or adolescents has explicitly examined parasocial relationships as distinct from other ways of connecting to media figures, such as attraction or identification (cf. Hoffner, 1996). Although there is a growing body of research with adults (Giles, 2002), there is almost no work that examines how young people form parasocial relationships or whether there are age differences in this process. More importantly, given the significance of media figures in the lives of young people, more evidence is needed regarding the emotional, social, and behavioral consequences of their parasocial bonds (cf. Boon & Lomore, 2001; Brown, Basil, & Bocarnea, 2003a).

Regarding online social interactions, we need to know much more about the role of IM, as well as text messaging, in young people's friendship development and maintenance. How have the features of these technologies changed the way youths communicate with each other? For example, are the nature and depth of self-disclosures different via IM, text message, telephone, and face-to-face communication? Despite a growing body of theoretically grounded research with adults (McKenna & Bargh, 2000; Walther & Parks, 2002), little is known about online relationship development among young people, or about the functions that such relationships serve (but see Peter, Valkenburg, & Schouten, 2005). Research also needs to examine blogs and social networking sites such as MySpace and Facebook, including the functions they serve for young people (e.g., expressing oneself publicly as a form of self-disclosure) and the role of interactions with others through the feedback functions (e.g., Huffaker & Calvert, 2005; Moinian, 2006).

There is much to be learned about the ways that media figures and online social interactions contribute to the development of personal and social identity. What role do peers play in the formation of parasocial bonds and in the consequences that such bonds may have for identity development? Do different types of relations to media figures (e.g., parasocial relationships, attraction, identification) have different consequences for identity formation? Online videogames are blurring the distinctions between social and parasocial relationships. Research should explore how young people use these unique environments in the process of identity construction (cf. Jansz, 2005). Studies have begun to explore the role that online interactions play in identity formation, particularly identities related to sexuality and gender roles (e.g., Subrahmanyam, Smahel, & Greenfield, 2006). However, more research is needed on the ways in which identity is developed online in these domains, as well as in other areas (e.g., ideological identity). More evidence is also needed regarding how young people's online identities relate to their offline identities and social relationships (e.g., McKenna & Bargh, 1998).

Further research on mediated relationships also can help develop the conceptual linkages between mass communication and interpersonal communication (Cohen & Metzger, 1998; Hawkins, Wiemann, & Pingree, 1988; Rubin & Rubin, 2001). Early work on parasocial interaction was grounded in mass communication, most notably the uses and gratifications approach, but a growing body of research suggests that the concept of "relationship" accurately captures the depth and emotion of parasocial bonds, despite the lack of actual interaction and mutuality. Moreover, the Internet has provided an entirely new mediated environment in which to form interpersonal relationships. Clearly relationships form in all contexts in which people encounter others. This chapter has shown that parasocial and online social relationships are based on principles similar to those that govern face-to-face relationships, and that interpersonal communication theories provide insight into the process by which such relationships develop, deepen, and dissolve. Further research on the similarities and differences in relationships formed in various mediated contexts, and the ways these relationships contribute to identity development, could be one way to bridge the areas of mass and interpersonal communication and integrate theory.

Finally, relatively few studies on the topics reviewed in this chapter have explicitly taken a developmental perspective, although some report age differences in specific outcomes. There is a rich tradition of scholarship that has addressed the developmental processes involved in the formation of personal and social identity (Harter, 1999; Kroger, 2003; Ruble et al., 2004). This literature needs to be extended to the role that media experiences play in the development of young people's relationships and identity construction.

Conclusion

The media environment is a social world that offers young people an opportunity to interact with and form attachments to a wide range of people. Research reviewed in this chapter shows that they form deep bonds with media figures, and that they use the Internet to keep in touch with friends, develop new friendships, and interact with others. Parasocial attachments and online social interactions allow young people to extend their social networks, to fulfill needs for affiliation and companionship, and to experiment with roles and identities in many ways – through fantasy, by adopting characteristics of admired figures, or by assuming various roles online. Young people use media figures and online interactions to explore their developing sexuality and intimate relationships, particularly in adolescence, and to construct a self-concept that includes their social identities (Erikson, 1968; Ruble et al., 2004). Thus, it appears that relationships with media figures and social aspects of Internet use fulfill (in part) a deep human need for social affiliation, and also play an important role in identity development. However, the literature also revealed potential negative consequences for identity development, such as reinforcing stereotypes and limiting the complexity of the self-concept. Given the importance of traditional and online media in the lives of young people, scholars need to examine the role that media play in identity construction in more depth and within an explicitly developmental framework.

References

Adams-Price, C., & Greene, A. L. (1990). Secondary attachments and adolescent self-concept. *Sex Roles*, 22, 187–98.

Altman, I., & Taylor, D. (1973). *Social penetration: The development of interpersonal relationships*. New York: Holt.

Anderson, D. R., Bryant, J., Wilder, A., Santomero, A., Williams, M., & Crawley, A. M. (2000). Researching *Blues' Clues*: Viewing behavior and impact. *Media Psychology*, 2, 179–94.

Arnett, J. J. (1995). Adolescents' uses of the media for self-socialization. *Journal of Youth and Adolescence*, 24, 519–33.

Batheja, A. (2005). Strengthening the community online. *Fort Worth Star-Telegram (TX)*, February 15. Retrieved July 22, 2006, from Newspaper Source database.

Baumeister, R., & Leary, M. R. (1995). The need to belong: Desire for interpersonal attachments as a fundamental human motivation. *Psychological Bulletin*, 117, 497–529.

Berger, C. R. (1988). Uncertainty and information exchange in developing relationships. In S. Duck (Ed.), *Handbook of personal relationships: Theory, research, and interventions* (pp. 239–55). New York: Wiley.

Bird, S. E. (2003). *The audience in everyday life: Living in a media world*. New York: Routledge.

Boden, S. (2006). Dedicated followers of fashion? The influence of popular culture on children's social identities. *Media, Culture, and Society*, 28, 289–98.

Boon, S. D., & Lomore, C. D. (2001). Admirer–celebrity relationships among young adults: Explaining perceptions of celebrity influence on identity. *Human Communication Research*, 27, 432–65.

Bowlby, J. (1969). *Attachment and loss*. Vol. 1, *Attachment*. New York: Basic Books.

Brown, J. D., Dykers, C. R., Steele, J. R., & White, A. B. (1994). Teenage room culture: Where media and identities intersect. *Communication Research*, 21, 813–27.

Brown, W. J., Basil, M. D., & Bocarnea, M. C. (2003a). The influence of famous athletes on health beliefs and practices: Mark McGwire, child abuse prevention, and Androstenedione. *Journal of Health Communication*, 8, 41–57.

Brown, W. J., Basil, M. D., & Bocarnea, M. C. (2003b). Social influence of an international celebrity: Responses to the death of Princess Diana. *Journal of Communication*, 53, 587–605.

Calvert, S. L. (2002). Identity construction on the Internet. In S. L. Calvert, A. B. Jordan, & R. R. Cocking (Eds.), *Children in the digital age: influences of electronic media on development* (pp. 57–70). Westport, CT: Praeger.

Calvert, S. L., Mahler, B. A., Zehnder, S. M., Jenkins, A., & Lee, M. S. (2003). Gender differences in preadolescent children's online interactions: Symbolic modes of self-presentation and self-expression. *Journal of Applied Developmental Psychology*, 24, 627–44.

Calvert, S. L., Strong, B. L., Jacobs, E. L., & Conger, E. E. (2007). Interaction and participation for young Hispanic and Caucasian children's learning of media content. *Media Psychology*, 9, 431–45.

Cassell, J., & Tversky, D. (2005). The language of online intercultural community formation. *Journal of Computer-Mediated Communication*, 10(2), article 2. Retrieved July 1, 2006, from http://jcmc.indiana.edu/vol10/issue2/cassell.html.

Caughey, J. L. (1984). *Imaginary social worlds: A cultural approach*. Lincoln, NE: University of Lincoln Press.

Cheung, C.-K., & Yue, X. D. (2003). Identity achievement and idol worship among teenagers in Hong Kong. *International Journal of Adolescence and Youth*, 11, 1–26.

Cohen, J. (1999). Favorite characters of teenage viewers of Israeli serials. *Journal of Broadcasting and Electronic Media*, 43, 327–45.

Cohen, J. (2001). Defining identification: A theoretical look at the identification of audiences with media characters. *Mass Communication and Society*, 4, 245–64.

Cohen, J. (2003). Parasocial breakups: Measuring individual differences in responses to the dissolution of parasocial relationships. *Mass Communication and Society*, 6, 191–202.

Cohen, J. (2004). Parasocial break-up from favorite television characters: The role of attachment styles and relationship intensity. *Journal of Social and Personal Relationships*, 21, 187–202.

Cohen, J., & Metzger, M. (1998). Social affiliation and the achievement of ontological security through interpersonal and mass communication. *Critical Studies in Mass Communication*, 15, 41–60.

Cole, T., & Leets, L. (1999). Attachment styles and intimate television viewing: Insecurely forming relationships in a parasocial way. *Journal of Social and Personal Relationships*, 16, 495–512.

Deaux, K., & Lafrance, M. (1998). Gender. In D. T. Gilbert, S. T. Fiske, & G. Lindzey (Eds.), *The handbook of social psychology* (4th edn., vol. 2, pp. 788–827). New York: McGraw-Hill.

Dindia, K. (2000). Self-disclosure, identity, and relationship development: A dialectical perspective. In K. Dindia & S. Duck (Eds.), *Communication and personal relationships* (pp. 147–62). New York: Wiley.

Duke, L. (2002). Get real!: Cultural relevance and resistance to the mediated feminine ideal. *Psychology and Marketing*, 19, 211–33.

Erikson, E. H. (1963). *Childhood and society*. (2nd edn.). New York: Norton.

Erikson, E. H. (1968). *Identity: Youth and crisis*. New York: Norton.

Fouts, G., & Inch, R. (2005). Homosexuality in TV situation comedies: Characters and verbal comments. *Journal of Homosexuality*, 49, 35–45.

Giles, D. G. (2002). Parasocial interaction: A review of the literature and a model for future research. *Media Psychology*, 4, 279–305.

Giles, D. C., & Maltby, J. (2004). The role of media figures in adolescent development: Relations between autonomy, attachment, and interest in celebrities. *Personality and Individual Differences*, 36, 813–22.

Greenberg, B. S., Mastro, D., & Brand, J. E. (2002). Minorities and the mass media: Television into the twenty-first century. In J. Bryant & D. Zillmann (Eds.), *Media effects: Advances in theory and research* (2nd edn., pp. 333–51). Mahwah, NJ: Lawrence Erlbaum.

Griffiths, M. D., Davies, M. N. O., & Chappell, D. (2004). Online computer gaming: A comparison of adolescent and adult gamers. *Journal of Adolescence*, 27, 87–96.

Gross, E. F., Juvonen, J., & Gable, S. L. (2002). Internet use and well-being in adolescence. *Journal of Social Issues*, 58, 75–90.

Hansell, S. (2006). MySpace to add restrictions to protect younger teenagers. *New York Times*, June 21, C2.

Harrison, K. (1997). Does interpersonal attraction to thin media personalities promote eating disorders? *Journal of Broadcasting and Electronic Media*, 41, 478–500.

Harrison, K. (2006). Scope of self: Toward a model of television's effects on self-complexity in adolescence. *Communication Theory*, 16, 251–79.

Harter, S. (1999). *The construction of the self: A developmental perspective*. New York: Guilford Press.

Hawkins, R. P., Wiemann, J. M., & Pingree, S. (Eds.). (1988). *Advancing communication science: Merging mass and interpersonal processes*. Newbury Park, CA: Sage.

Hewitt, B., Dodd, J., York, M., Finan, E., Nelson, M., Fleming, A. R., & Searls, D. (2006). MySpace nation: The controversy. *People*, 65 (June 5), 113–21.

Hinde, R. A. (1979). *Toward understanding relationships*. New York: Academic Press.

Hoffner, C. (1996). Children's wishful identification and parasocial interaction with favorite television characters. *Journal of Broadcasting and Electronic Media*, 40, 389–402.

Hoffner, C., & Buchanan, M. (2005). Young adults' wishful identification with television characters: The role of perceived similarity and character attributes. *Media Psychology*, 7, 325–52.

Hoffner, C., & Cantor, J. (1991). Perceiving and responding to mass media characters. In J. Bryant & D. Zillmann (Eds.), *Responding to the screen: Reception and reaction processes* (pp. 63–101). Hillsdale, NJ: Lawrence Erlbaum.

Hoffner, C., Levine, K. J., Sullivan, Q., Crowell, D., Pedrick, L., & Berndt, P. (2006). TV characters at work: Television's role in the occupational aspirations of economically disadvantaged youths. *Journal of Career Development*, 33, 3–18.

Honeycutt, J. M. (2003). *Imagined interactions: Daydreaming about communication.* Cresskill, NJ: Hampton Press.

Horton, D., & Wohl, R. R. (1956). Mass communication and para-social interaction. *Psychiatry*, 19, 215–29.

Huesmann, L. R., Moise-Titus, J., Podolski, C.-L., & Eron, L. D. (2003). Longitudinal relations between children's exposure to TV violence and their aggressive and violent behavior in young adulthood: 1977–1992. *Developmental Psychology*, 39, 201–21.

Huffaker, D. A., & Calvert, S. L. (2005). Gender, identity, and language use in teenage blogs. *Journal of Computer-Mediated Communication*, 10(2), article 1. Retrieved July 1, 2006, from http://jcmc.indiana.edu/vol10/issue2/huffaker.html.

Jansz, J. (2005). The emotional appeal of violent video games for adolescent males. *Communication Theory*, 15, 219–41.

Karniol, R. (2001). Adolescent females' idolization of male media stars as a transition into sexuality. *Sex Roles*, 44, 61–77.

Kielwasser, A. P., & Wolf, M. A. (1992). Mainstream television, adolescent sexuality, and the significant silence. *Critical Studies in Mass Communication*, 9, 350–73.

King, M. M., & Multon, K. D. (1996). The effects of television role models on the career aspirations of African American junior high school students. *Journal of Career Development*, 23, 111–25.

Kivel, B. D., & Kleiber, D. A. (2000). Leisure in the identity formation of lesbian/gay youth: Personal, but not social. *Leisure Sciences*, 22, 215–32.

Kraut, R., Kiesler, S., Boneva, B., Cummings, J., Helgeson, V., & Crawford, A. (2002). Internet paradox revisited. *Journal of Social Issues*, 58, 49–74.

Kroger, J. (2003). Identity development during adolescence. In G. R. Adams & M. D. Berzonsky (Eds.), *Blackwell handbook of adolescence* (pp. 205–26). Malden, MA: Blackwell.

Lee, E., & Leets, L. (2002). Persuasive storytelling by hate groups online: Examining its effects on adolescents. *American Behavioral Scientist*, 45, 927–57.

Lenhart, A., Madden, M., & Hitlin, P. (2005). *Teens and technology.* Washington, DC: Pew Internet and American Life Project. Retrieved July 12, 2006, from www.pewinternet.org.

Lenhart, A., Rainie, L., & Lewis, O. (2001). *Teenage life online.* Washington, DC: Pew Internet and American Life Project. Retrieved June 30, 2006, from www.pewinternet.org.

Maltby, J., Giles, D. C., Barber, L., & McCutcheon, L. E. (2005). Intense-personal celebrity worship and body image: Evidence of a link among female adolescents. *British Journal of Health Psychology*, 10, 17–32.

McDermott, S. T., & Greenberg, B. S. (1984). Black children's esteem: Parents, peers, and television. In R. B. Bostrom (Ed.), *Communication yearbook*, vol. 8 (pp. 164–77). Beverly Hills, CA: Sage.

McDonald, D. G., & Kim, H. (2001). When I die, I feel small: Electronic game characters and the social self. *Journal of Broadcasting and Electronic Media*, 45, 241–58.

McGuire, W. (1974). Psychological motives and communication gratification. In J. G. Blumler & E. Katz (Eds.), *The uses of mass communications: Current perspectives on gratifications research* (pp. 167–96). Beverly Hills, CA: Sage.

McKee, H. (2002). "Your views showed true ignorance!!!": (Mis)Communication in an online interracial discussion forum. *Computers and Composition*, 19, 411–34.

McKenna, K. Y. A., & Bargh, J. A. (1998). Coming out in the age of the Internet: Identity "demarginalization" through virtual group participation. *Journal of Personality and Social Psychology*, 75, 681–94.

McKenna, K. Y. A., & Bargh, J. A. (2000). Plan 9 from cyberspace: The implications of the Internet for personality and social psychology. *Personality and Social Psychology Review*, 4, 57–75.

Mead, G. H. (1934). *Mind, self, and society*. Chicago: University of Chicago Press.

Mesch, G., & Talmud, I. (2006). The quality of online and offline relationships: The role of multiplexity and duration of social relationships. *The Information Society*, 22, 137–48.

Messner, M. A., Dunbar, M., & Hunt, D. (2000). The televised sports manhood formula. *Journal of Sport and Social Issues*, 24, 380–94.

Meyer, M. D. E. (2003). "It's me. I'm it.": Defining adolescent sexual identity through relational dialectics in *Dawson's Creek. Communication Quarterly*, 51, 262–76.

Meyrowitz, J. (in press). From distant heroes to intimate friends: Media and the metamorphosis of affection for public figures. In S. Drucker & G. Gumpert (Eds.), *Heroes in a global world* (pp. 95–124). Cresskill, NJ: Hampton Press.

Moinian, F. (2006). The construction of identity on the Internet: Oops! I've left my diary open to the whole world! *Childhood*, 13, 49–68.

Murphy, S. C. (2004). 'Live in your world, play in ours': The spaces of video game identity. *Journal of Visual Culture*, 3, 223–38.

Murray, S. (1999). Saving our so-called lives: Girls fandom, adolescent subjectivity, and *My so-called life*. In M. Kinder (Ed.), *Kids' media culture* (pp. 221–35). Durham, NC: Duke University Press.

Papacharissi, Z., & Rubin, A. M. (2000). Predictors of Internet use. *Journal of Broadcasting and Electronic Media*, 44, 175–96.

Pasquier, D. (1996). Teen series' reception: Television, adolescence and culture of feelings. *Childhood: A Global Journal of Child Research*, 3, 351–73.

Peter, J., Valkenburg, P. M., & Schouten, A. P. (2005). Developing a model of adolescent friendship formation on the Internet. *CyberPsychology and Behavior*, 8, 423–30.

Raviv, A., Bar-Tal, D., Raviv, A., & Ben-Horin, A. (1996). Adolescent idolization of pop singers: Causes, expressions, and reliance. *Journal of Youth and Adolescence*, 25, 631–50.

Reeves, B. (1979). Children's understanding of television people. In E. Wartella (Ed.), *Children communicating: Media and development of thought, speech, understanding* (pp. 115–55). Beverly Hills, CA: Sage.

Rosengren, K. K., Windahl, S., Hakansson, P.-A., & Johnsson-Smaragdi, U. (1976). Adolescents' TV relations: Three scales. *Communication Research*, 3, 347–66.

Ross, K. (1997). Where's me in it? *Media Culture and Society*, 19, 669–77.

Rubin, A. M. (1979). Television use by children and adolescents. *Human Communication Research*, 5, 109–20.

Rubin, A. M. (2002). The uses-and-gratifications perspective of media effects. In J. Bryant & D. Zillmann (Eds.), *Media effects: Advances in theory and research* (pp. 525–48). Mahwah, NJ: Lawrence Erlbaum.

Rubin, A. M., Perse, E. M., & Powell, R. A. (1985). Loneliness, parasocial interaction, and local television news viewing. *Human Communication Research*, 12, 155–80.

Rubin, A. M., & Rubin, R. B. (1985). Interface of personal and mediated communication: A research agenda. *Critical Studies in Mass Communication*, 2, 36–53.

Rubin, R. B., & Rubin, A. M. (2001). Attribution in social and parasocial relationships. In V. Manusov & J. H. Harvey (Eds.), *Attribution, communication behavior, and close relationships* (pp. 320–37). New York: Cambridge University Press.

Ruble, D. N., Alvarez, J., Bachman, M., Cameron, J., Fuligni, A., Coll, C. G., & Rhee, E. (2004). The development of a sense of "we": The emergence and implications of children's collective identity. In M. Bennett & F. Sani (Eds.), *The development of the social self* (pp. 29–76). New York: Psychology Press.

Russell, S. T. (2002). Queer in America: Citizenship for sexual minority youth. *Applied Developmental Science*, 6, 258–63.

Signorielli, N., & Kahlenberg, S. (2001). Television's world of work in the nineties. *Journal of Broadcasting and Electronic Media*, 45, 4–22.

Smith, S. L., Nathanson, A. I., & Wilson, B. J. (2002). Prime time television: Assessing violence during the most popular viewing hours. *Journal of Communication*, 52, 84–111.

Steele, J. R., & Brown, J. D. (1995). Adolescent room culture: Studying media in the context of everyday life. *Journal of Youth and Adolescence*, 24, 551–76.

Stern, S. R. (2004). Expressions of identity online: Prominent features and gender differences in adolescents' World Wide Web home pages. *Journal of Broadcasting and Electronic Media*, 48, 218–43.

Strasburger, V. C., & Wilson, B. J. (2002). *Children, adolescents, and the media*. Thousand Oaks, CA: Sage.

Stroman, C. (1986). Television viewing and self-concept among black children. *Journal of Broadcasting and Electronic Media*, 30, 87–93.

Stryker, S., & Burke, P. J. (2000). The past, present, and future of an identity theory. *Social Psychology Quarterly*, 63, 284–97.

Sturm, H. (1975). The research activities of the Internationales Zentralinstitut fur das Jugend und Bildungsfernsehen. Special English issue of *Fernsehen und Bildung*, 9, 158–62.

Subervi-Vélez, F. A., & Necochea, J. (1990). Television viewing and self-concept among Hispanic children – A pilot study. *Howard Journal of Communications*, 2, 315–29.

Subrahmanyam, K., Greenfield, P. M., Kraut, R., & Gross, E. (2001). The impact of computer use on children's and adolescents' development. *Journal of Applied Developmental Psychology*, 22, 7–30.

Subrahmanyam, K., Greenfield, P. M., & Tynes, B. (2004). Constructing sexuality and identity in an online teen chat room. *Journal of Applied Developmental Psychology*, 25, 651–66.

Subrahmanyam, K., Smahel, D., & Greenfield, P. (2006). Connecting developmental constructions to the Internet: Identity presentation and sexual exploration in online teen chat rooms. *Developmental Psychology*, 42, 395–406.

Tajfel, H. (1978). Social categorization, social identity, and social comparison. In H. Tajfel (Ed.), *Differentiation between social groups: Studies in the social psychology of group relations* (pp. 61–76). New York: Academic Press.

Talamo, A., & Ligorio, B. (2001). Strategic identities in cyberspace. *CyberPsychology and Behavior*, 4, 109–22.

Thompson, K. (2002). Border crossings and diasporic identities: Media use and leisure practices of an ethnic minority. *Qualitative Sociology*, 25, 409–18.

Tichon, J. G., & Shapiro, M. (2003). With a little help from my friends: Children, the Internet and social support. *Journal of Technology in Human Services*, 21, 73–92.

Tsao, J. (1996). Compensatory media use: An explanation of two paradigms. *Communication Studies*, 47, 89–109.

Turkle, S. (1995). *Life on the screen: Identity in the age of the Internet.* New York: Simon and Schuster.

Turner, J. C. (1999). Some current issues in research on social identity and self categorization theories. In N. Ellemers, R. Spears, & B. Doosje (Eds.), *Social identity: Context, commitment, content* (pp. 6–34). Oxford: Blackwell.

Tynes, B., Reynolds, L., & Greenfield, P. M. (2004). Adolescence, race, and ethnicity on the Internet: A comparison of discourse in monitored and unmonitored chat rooms. *Applied Developmental Psychology*, 25, 667–84.

Valkenburg, P. M., Schouten, A. P., & Peter, J. (2005). Adolescents' identity experiments on the Internet. *New Media and Society*, 7, 383–402.

Valkenburg, P. M., & Soeters, K. E. (2001). Children's positive and negative experiences with the Internet: An exploratory survey. *Communication Research*, 28, 652–75.

Walther, J. B. (1992). Interpersonal effects in computer-mediated interaction: A relational perspective. *Communication Research*, 19, 52–90.

Walther, J. B. (1996). Computer-mediated communication: Impersonal, interpersonal, and hyperpersonal interaction. *Communication Research*, 23, 3–43.

Walther, J. B., & Parks, M. R. (2002). Cues filtered out, cues filtered in: Computer-mediated communication and relationships. In M. L. Knapp & J. A. Daly (Eds.), *Handbook of interpersonal communication* (pp. 529–63). Thousand Oaks, CA: Sage.

Ward, L. M. (2004). Wading through the stereotypes: Positive and negative associations between media use and black adolescents' conceptions of self. *Developmental Psychology*, 40, 284–94.

Wolak, J., Mitchell, K. J., & Finkelhor, D. (2002). Close online relationships in a national sample of adolescents. *Adolescence*, 37, 441–55.

Wolak, J., Mitchell, K. J., & Finkelhor, D. (2003). Escaping or connecting? Characteristics of youth who form close online relationships. *Journal of Adolescence*, 26, 105–19.

Xiong, C. (2003). Where the girls are: They're online, solving puzzles and making up characters in narrative-driven games. *Wall Street Journal – Eastern Edition*, October 28, 242, B1–B4. Retrieved July 21, 2006, from Academic Search Premier database.

Yee, N. (2006). The psychology of massively multi-user online role-playing games: Motivations, emotional investment, relationships, and problematic use. In R. Schroeder & A. Axelsson (Eds.), *Avatars at work and play: Collaboration and interaction in shared virtual environments* (pp. 187–207). London: Springer-Verlag.

15

Fear Responses to Media Entertainment

Patti M. Valkenburg and Moniek Buijzen

Most experts on childhood fears agree that some fears are necessary for the healthy cognitive and emotional development of children (e.g., Fraiberg, 1959; Sarafino, 1986). But they also agree that being confronted with shocking events that go beyond a child's processing ability can have a negative effect on children's development (Cantor, 1998). In this chapter, we will examine the role of fictional entertainment media, particularly film and television portrayals, in the development of fear responses (see Smith, Pieper, & Moyer-Guse, this volume, Chapter 10, for children's fear responses to news and non-fictional portrayals). We focus on fear as an outcome of media exposure, not on the underlying reasons that explain why some children seek scary content.

Fictional Entertainment Media

Fictional entertainment involves books, movies, DVDs, television, and computer games. Most research on children's media-induced fears has to date focused only on film and television entertainment. To our knowledge, there is no research on the prevalence of fear reactions to books and computer games. There is also no media-comparison research investigating whether books or computer games are more or less fear inducing than film or television entertainment. Therefore, the insights in this chapter are primarily based on research into the emotional consequences of film and television entertainment.

Some authors believe that audiovisual entertainment has more emotional impact than verbal entertainment, such as print. According to Frijda (1988), "symbolic information generally has weak impact, as compared to the impact of pictures and of events actually seen – 'the vividness effect' discussed in social psychology" (p. 352). However, several other authors believe that verbal stories can be just as fear inducing as audiovisual stories. Although there is no systematic research on fear reactions to books, anecdotal observations clearly indicate that books, such as the *Harry Potter* series, can lead to extreme fright reactions in children (e.g., Needlman, 2004). The underlying processes of emotional reactions to books and verbal stories are imagination and empathy (Valkenburg & Peter, 2006). In particular, people with high imaginative capacities can be intensely emotionally aroused by verbal stories (e.g., Gollnisch & Averill, 1993).

There is also no empirical research on children's fear responses to computer games. On the one hand, it is possible that computer games elicit less fear than film and television entertainment because they offer children the possibility of active control. The game player can choose for him or herself elements such as character, blood, or no blood. This possibility for active control may give the game player the opportunity to regulate the fearfulness of the game. On the other hand, it is possible that computer games elicit more fear than film and television entertainment, because computer games offer more opportunities for identification than film and television entertainment. After all, many games make use of the first-person perspective, whereby the player experiences the game environment from the perspective of the hero (O'Keefe & Zehnder, 2005). This may help to increase identification with the protagonist, and, thereby, the opportunity to experience vicariously his or her emotions.

Although it is unknown whether computer games lead to more or less fear than film and television entertainment, they certainly can cause intense physiological and emotional arousal in viewers (see Anderson & Bushman, 2001, for a meta-analysis). There are currently many horror-themed computer games on the market. The graphics of these games are of the same quality as horror movies. It is conceivable that such games can lead to intensive fright reactions, not only among children but also among adults. The following excerpt from a qualitative study by Ankersmit and Veen (1995) illustrates how frightening a computer game can be for a 14-year-old boy:

> sometimes during *Doom* I'm so frightened . . . my heart goes boom, boom, boom . . . that I just want to stop playing. In *Doom* there was this room . . . you had to play in the dark, the only thing you could see was the machine gun fire coming from the other gun, only then could you shoot back, and then you heard a scream if you hit him. I thought: I'm not playing this anymore, and so I got a code to switch on the lights.

Given the extant literature, our focus will be the development of fears as a function of exposure to scary fictional film and television entertainment. However, there is a clear need for additional research that investigates the role of books and digital games on children's fears.

History of frightening film and television entertainment

During the past decades, audiovisual entertainment has progressively become realistic and gruesome (Tamborini & Weaver, 1996). In addition, children and adolescents are increasingly regarded as a target group for this kind of entertainment (Sapolsky & Molitor, 1996). This trend began in the 1950s when comics, which were extremely popular in those days, started to add horror pictures in a way that was appealing to male adolescents. This change turned out to be very lucrative. Initially even the black-and-white images on television could not compete with the macabre pictures and bright colors of the gory horror comic strips (Tamborini & Weaver, 1996).

The movie industry soon discovered that there was a target group out there that had enough time and money: the youngsters who read those horror comic strips. *The Curse of Frankenstein* from 1957 led to a series of low-budget films with similar themes, in which the camera, unlike in the past, did not shy away from showing any atrocities and horror. After several years, the limited success of these films got the attention of renowned filmmakers such as Alfred Hitchcock. This resulted in *Psycho* in 1960. *Psycho* is considered by historically oriented media researchers as the turning point in the production of horror movies. Due to its overwhelming success, not only did the film lead to a flood of imitations, but the prestige of Hitchcock also legitimized the arrival of a new kind of horror movie: movies with macabre murders and realistically filmed mutilations (Sapolsky & Molitor, 1996; Tamborini & Weaver, 1996).

Young children often watch programs that adults consider intensely terrifying. A study by Sparks (1986) revealed that half of the 4- to 10-year-old children he studied had seen the movies *Poltergeist* and *Jaws*. In a Dutch study of 7- to 12-year-olds by Valkenburg, Cantor, and Peeters (2000), 31 percent of the children indicated that they had been so scared from watching a movie or a television program in the last year that it still bothered them. Almost all children who had had a long-term fear named a film targeted to adults as the source of their fear. Similarly, in a survey conducted by Hoekstra, Harris, and Helmick (1999) among American introductory psychology students, 61 percent said that they had experienced intense and lengthy fear responses from the media during their youth. Of these students, 29 percent stated that they had a specific fear left from film or television entertainment, for example fear of sharks or spiders, and 20 percent reported that they suffered from a variety of sleeping disorders, such as a fear of sleeping alone, nightmares, insomnia, or the need to leave a light on at night.

Harrison and Cantor (1999) asked 153 undergraduate students whether they had seen a television program or movie that frightened them so much that the emotional effects endured after the program was over. About 90 percent of the undergraduates reported having had such an experience. Of these respondents, 26 percent reported that the effects of the media presentation had lasted at least one year and were still persisting at the time of measurement. Over half of the respondents reported disturbances in normal behavior such as sleeping or eating, 36 percent avoided or dreaded the depicted situation, and 18 percent avoided or dreaded other situations related to the depicted situation (such as avoiding swimming in the sea after viewing *Jaws*; Harrison & Cantor, 1999).

Following the procedure by Harrison and Cantor (1999), Valkenburg (2004) asked a group of university students to write down an especially frightening media experience they had had while watching television or a film. Some of the students' descriptions are included in this chapter, using fictitious names. Although our study found somewhat lower percentages than those reported by Harrison and Cantor, there are many similarities in the results.

Of the 75 students who took part in the study, more than 70 percent could remember a specific movie or television program that frightened them intensely. The age at which this fear surfaced varied greatly, as well as the kind of programs that caused the fear. The type of movie was closely related to the age of the viewer (as was the case in Harrison & Cantor, 1999). The scariest program for children younger than 7 was the television series *The Incredible Hulk*. Reality programs and horror movies such as *Jaws* and *Child's Play* especially caused fear in older children and adolescents (Valkenburg, 2004). For example, one female, now age 22, made the following comment about the movie *Child's Play*, which she saw when she was age 9:

> That little doll Chucky. It was a scary, ugly doll in any case. But it got even scarier when it showed its teeth and rolled its eyes, and started to bite . . . It said: "Hi, I'm Chucky, I'm your friend till the end of time." I'll never forget those words. Afterwards I got scared of my own dolls. For months I slept badly, had scary dreams. And still, when I see an ugly doll, I think about Chucky.

With most students, the fear caused by the movie or the program was gone after a few days or weeks. But with some students there were more serious effects: 12 percent turned out to have been troubled by fears for years due to a specific movie and more than half of these students regretted, in retrospect, having seen the program concerned. One female student, now age 25, said that after 20 years she still sometimes wakes up drenched in sweat because of a movie she had seen as a 5-year-old:

> I don't remember the title of the movie, but there was a plague of ants in a town. Everything, people and animals, even elephants were being attacked and eaten. First the arms. Then the head and finally the body. Running was futile . . . I was five when I saw the movie. Afterwards I often dreamt that I was being crushed by something that grew ever larger, just like the group of ants that got bigger and bigger. My aversion to insects may well be because of this film. Even a single ant on the kitchen worktop will start my heart pounding.

The Origins of General Childhood Fears: Three Pathways

Children come into the world with a number of specific fears. Typical fear responses of newborns are reactions to loud noises, bright and flashing lights, and loss of support (Gullone, 2000). However, although some fear responses are inborn, most fears develop after infancy. This happens via three different pathways (Rachman, 1991). A first pathway involves direct, negative experience. If a child, for example, is stung by a jellyfish while paddling in the sea, it is possible that later she or he will be afraid to go into the sea. Fears of animals and insects often originate from a direct negative experience (King, Gullone, & Ollendick, 1998; Rachman, 1991).

A second pathway to fear is observational learning (Rachman, 1991). Children often acquire fears by observing the reactions of other people to potential dangers (Bandura, 1996). Suppose a young child is helping her mother clearing the cellar. As they move a large chest, they see a mouse scurry away. The mother cries out, picks up the child, runs up the stairs, and tells her daughter never to go downstairs again. The young child can do little else but believe that mice are terrifying creatures (Sarafino, 1986). The underlying mechanism of this pathway to fear is empathy, the ability to feel the emotional reactions of others. From birth, children take on the emotions of the people around them. By means of empathy, children are able to feel fear or sadness when their parents are frightened or sad (Hoffman, 2000). It is therefore not surprising that children acquire the phobias of their parents about, for example, mice, dogs, heights, and insects (King, Gullone, & Ollendick, 1998; Sarafino, 1986).

The third pathway to fear is negative information transfer (Rachman, 1991). When a child hears a conversation in which his parents recount an unpleasant experience they had during a visit to a dentist, it is possible that the child may develop a fear of the dentist. The underlying processes of this pathway are imagination and empathy (Hoffman, 2000; Valkenburg & Peter, 2006). On hearing verbal information from other persons, children have to form mental images and feel through empathy the fear that the victims have experienced (Hoffman, 2000).

In short, general childhood fears can develop through three different pathways, via direct negative experience, observational learning, and negative information transfer. Ollendick and King (1991) have investigated which of the three pathways to fear are most common among children. In this study, children were asked to report their worst fears. They were then asked to describe how their fear started: by direct experience, observational learning, and/or negative information transfer. The study showed that observational learning had the strongest impact on children: 56 percent of the children named observational learning most frequently as the cause of their fear. Next came negative information transfer (39 percent), and then personal experience (37 percent).

The Origins of Media-Induced Fears: (Again) Three Pathways

The three pathways to the development of fears are not only useful to understand general childhood fears, they are also helpful to understand fear responses to media content. Media-induced fears can also occur (1) via a direct experience with a mediated danger, (2) via observational learning of fears from media characters, and (3) through negative information transfer via media characters.

Direct experience with mediated dangers

Imagine you are going for a walk in a beautiful tropical wood somewhere in Indonesia. Suddenly, a few feet away you see an enormous snake slithering towards you. You are scared stiff and that is a normal human response, caused by a direct, negative experience. But now, imagine you are watching a movie on television and you see a similar situation. You are safe in your living room where there are no snakes, and yet these kinds of mediated scenes can evoke an intense fear reaction.

Direct experiences with mediated dangers can evoke fear in the same way as direct experience with dangers in reality. According to Joanne Cantor (1991), there are certain situations that have been frightening people from the beginning of time. These are natural disasters, earthquakes, and epidemics; attacks by dangerous animals or people; physical mutilation; and people or animals that look unnatural, such as people who have been mutilated, people with a hunchback, and monsters (Jersild & Holmes, 1935; Yerkes & Yerkes, 1936).

According to Cantor, the stimuli that have been evoking fear since our early human history bring about the same reactions when we are faced with them in the media. Cantor argues that this occurs through stimulus generalization, a concept derived from classic conditioning theory. The stimulus generalization theory assumes that when a stimulus evokes an emotional reaction, other closely related stimuli evoke similar, but less intense emotional reactions. A media stimulus that is similar to a real-life stimulus brings about a similar, but less intense reaction than the real-life stimulus. In short, the process of stimulus generalization is the media variant of fears acquired through direct real-life experiences.

Observational learning of fears from media characters

Media-induced fear responses can also arise through observational learning: by observing the emotional reactions to dangers of main characters or victims in media productions (Bandura, 1996). In audiovisual media productions, it is very common to depict fear through the fear experienced by the main characters or victims. The danger itself is often not even shown; the emotional reactions of main characters are enough to bring about an intense fear response in the viewer. According to Bandura (1994, 1996) these kinds of emotional reactions of media characters can cause short-term as well as permanent fear in viewers.

An experiment conducted by Venn and Short (1973) confirms that observational learning of fear through television characters occurs in young children. The researchers showed a number of 3- and 4-year-olds a short film in which a mother shows a plastic Mickey Mouse doll to her 5-year-old son. Each time the boy in the film sees the doll, he screams with fear. When his mother shows him a plastic Donald Duck doll, he is not frightened at all. He is perfectly relaxed and even smiles a little at the doll. After the children had seen the film the researchers played a game in which both the Mickey Mouse and the Donald Duck dolls were used. The film had had a clear effect on the children: they did not mind playing with Donald Duck, but stayed well away from Mickey Mouse.

Empathy plays a major role in the observational learning of fear from media characters. The emotional response that the viewer experiences with empathy is related to the emotion of the observed character (Borke, 1971; Hoffman, 2000). Viewers feel sad when a main character in a movie is sad, and experience fear when he or she is scared. A main character or victim does not even have to show fear to frighten viewers. Viewers can also become scared when the main characters are unaware of the impending danger. This instrument of the "naive main character" is fairly common in fiction. Take, for example, a movie scenario in which a female walks in the woods. The camera shows the viewer a dangerous monster lurking in the shadows, waiting for the moment to attack the unsuspecting woman. In these cases, viewers are often on the edge of their seats with fear. This sort of scene lacks the emotion of the movie character, and yet empathy plays a part (Tamborini, 1996). In the literature, this phenomenon whereby empathy is felt without actually seeing the emotions of the character is called anticipatory empathy (Stotland, 1969). It refers to the emotions that a viewer feels when he or she realizes that another person's emotional reactions are imminent.

Negative information transfer

The third and final pathway to media-induced fears is through negative inform-ation transfer. Negative information transfer overlaps in certain respects with obser-vational learning. For example, in both pathways imagination and empathy play an important role. However, the two pathways are different in some respects. During observational learning viewers directly experience the emotional ups and downs of a media character. During negative information transfer, viewers hear informa-tion about a danger or a potential danger, but they do not vicariously observe the results of these dangers or potential dangers via a mediated character.

No one will deny that audiovisual media are packed with negative information. A large part of the news deals with crime, wars, and other dangers. Television news is given to us through direct observation of those involved in the danger, but also for a large part through information transfer via the newsreader, news correspondents, or eyewitness accounts of victims. This verbal information from the newsreader or the reports and eyewitness accounts qualify as mediated neg-ative information transfer.

Fears Caused by Fictional Entertainment: The Law of Apparent Reality

The fact that people become frightened because of the news through the above three processes is understandable. News, after all, concerns reality, and one takes that seriously. However, a sizeable number of people, children as well as adults, also experience intense fright reactions in response to fictitious media content (e.g., Johnson, 1980; Sparks, Spirek, & Hodgson, 1993). Why are viewers sometimes as receptive to frightening scenes in fictitious stories as in the reality-based news? In order to understand this process, we will turn to some principles from general emotion theories.

Emotion researchers assume that the intensity of an emotional reaction depends on the reality status of the stimulus that evokes the emotional reaction. Harris (2000) gives a clear example: when we hear a fire alarm, we feel fear. If the alarm turns out to be a false alarm, the fear disappears. This means that the intensity of the emotions experienced is related to the perceived realism of the threat. Nico Frijda (1988) has tried to incorporate this characteristic of emotions into a psychological law: the law of apparent reality. This law states that emotions are triggered by events that the individual regards as realistic, and that the intensity of these emotions corresponds to the degree to which the events are perceived as realistic.

The law of apparent reality is plausible, but does rule out that one can experience emotions while watching fiction. Take, for example, a science fiction movie such as *Alien*, in which a man in excruciating pain has a baby monster burst out of his stomach. Such a scene is far removed from reality, but still has the capacity to evoke strong fear responses. Why don't viewers respond to such fiction as they would when hearing a false fire alarm? This shortcoming in Frijda's law of apparent reality was observed by Walters (1989) and was then acknowledged by Frijda. In a follow-up article Frijda (1989) states that viewers regard movies as true events in a fantasy world. Viewers do not perceive occurrences in fiction as unreal; they just ignore any proof in the movie that points to it being unreal. They voluntarily suspend, as it were, their disbelief. According to Frijda this can only occur when a movie is realistic enough to allow for this suspension of disbelief.

Harris (2000) gives another explanation for the occurrence of aesthetic emotions – emotions in response to fictitious media content. Harris agrees with Frijda that perceived reality is a precondition for feeling emotions, also aesthetic emotions. However, he feels that Frijda's law of apparent reality is not comprehensive enough. Harris believes that fiction can be consumed by viewers in two ways. Firstly, in default mode viewers do not employ their knowledge of the reality status of the movie in order to suppress their emotions. In this default mode viewers are emotionally touched by movies, not because they constantly think that the movie is real, but because they do not include their knowledge of the reality status of the movie in their evaluation.

In the second way in which viewers consume fiction, they do use this knowledge of the reality status of the movie. Sometimes they do this resolutely, for example, when they see a shocking scene such as a mutilation. The viewers then try not to be open to the image and say to themselves that the mutilation is "only pretend." Using the knowledge about the reality value of fiction can also occur unconsciously, for example, when the characters act unconvincingly. In both cases the reality of the production is doubted, and the corresponding emotional responses are immediately decreased.

Although the assumptions of Harris (2000) and Frijda (1989) are plausible, they have never been tested in empirical research. It has also never been investigated why viewers usually process fictitious dangers in default mode, that is, with corresponding emotions. Harris (2000) offers an explanation of why users often process entertainment in the default mode, using an evolutionary theory. According to Harris, at some point in our evolution, humans acquired the capacity to use language. Initially language was probably used for communication about the here and now, for example to show someone the location of edible plants or herbs in the surrounding area, or to coordinate a hunt. At some point, language was used for other purposes. Humans transferred information that was received in other places at other times: They started to rely on eyewitness accounts. Of course, these eyewitness accounts sometimes contained emotionally charged events, for example someone describing how her son had died in excruciating pain after eating a particular fruit. In order to understand these kinds of verbal accounts, the listeners had to form a mental image of the fruit and the serious implications should it be eaten. And with that mental image, the listeners felt emotions.

According to Harris, if this kind of information had left our ancestors cold, they would not be able to respond effectively to other people's warnings. Nor would they be able to anticipate the dangers that the eyewitnesses pointed out to them. The aim of the warnings of eyewitnesses, after all, was to frighten other people, to prevent mistakes being repeated. According to Harris, our emotional involvement with fiction is an inheritance of human beings who use language and who can form mental reenactments from eyewitness accounts. He believes that people's negative emotional responses to drama and fiction is a small "evolutionary price" that they have to pay for their interest in and emotional openness to accounts of eyewitnesses (Harris, 2000, p. 90).

Developmental Trends in General and Media-Induced Fears

The development of both real-life and media-induced fears are related to the cognitive developmental level of the child. A few fears, such as fear of abandonment, start in infancy (Gullone, 2000). Up to 18 months old, children's fears are still very limited. They are usually only afraid of concrete experiences, such as strangers, loud noises, sudden movements, and their mother disappearing from view (Gullone, 2000). However, most other fears develop later on in life. An important explanation for these developmental changes is that children's imagination develops strongly during the early childhood years.

Ages two to seven: crocodiles under the bed

From the ages of 2 to 7 the cognitive development of children makes great advances. Children increasingly use their memory and begin to make causal predictions such as "if this happens, that will happen." This is why in addition to fears of concrete things, fears of *ideas* develop. Children become afraid of things that *could* happen. Children's imagination often causes a significant increase in fears, especially because in the fantasy world of young children virtually anything is possible. There may be a crocodile lurking underneath the bed or a ghost in the bathroom that will grab you when you run down the hallway.

The most common fears of preschoolers involve large animals (that can eat you) and insects (that can crawl over you). Eighty percent of 5- and 6-year-olds say that they are afraid of some sort of animal (Maurer, 1965). In addition, almost three quarters of preschoolers say that they are scared of some type of monsters (Bauer, 1976). Finally, children in this age group are often afraid of the dark, of doctors and dentists, deep water, great heights, and of everything that looks strange or makes sudden movements (Bauer, 1976; Cantor, 2002; Muris et al., 2000).

Audiovisual media can evoke intense fright reactions in this age group. Children up until the age of 7 are mainly scared of fantastic dangers in the media, of events that cannot happen in reality (e.g., Cantor, 2002). They can also get upset by transformations, that is, persons or things that suddenly disappear or acquire another form. At about 7 years of age, the fear of fantastic dangers declines. Although children from that moment on can be frightened by certain fictitious media contents, these contents have to be plausible. A young woman, now age 21, said:

> When I was 5, I was terrified of *The Incredible Hulk*. That man changing into the Hulk has left a long-lasting impression on me. When in bed at night, I would insist on leaving the door open. I was petrified that the Hulk would come into my room with those white eyes of his. This fear lasted several months. But when I see the Incredible Hulk on television now, it just cracks me up.

Children up to 7 also tend to become more easily frightened of movies with clearly visible dangers, such as *The Wizard of Oz*, whereas older children are more scared of movies that have implied dangers, such as some scenes in *Poltergeist*. In the movie *Poltergeist* the inhabitants of a haunted house are being terrorized by ghosts. Many dangers in this movie are implied by suggested dangers; scary music and shifting furniture suggest to the viewer that the poltergeist is lurking somewhere. Young children often may not understand these kinds of dangers. They see a table move around, but do not associate this with the poltergeist. Children need to develop a knowledge of these kinds of implied dangers in order for these fears to form (Cantor, 2002).

Ages seven to twelve: earthquakes and burglars

When children are 7 they are reasonably able to make a distinction between fantasy and reality when processing information (Harris, 2000). The fear of monsters then quickly decreases. Compared with 5- and 6-year-olds, the fear of monsters in 7- and 8-year-olds has already been reduced by a third to a half (Bauer,

1976; Muris et al., 2000). The typical infant and toddler fears are replaced by other fears. A fear often seen in children between 7 and 10 is the fear of illnesses or physical harm and the fear of losing people whom they love. They also become afraid of realistic threats, such as accidents, abductions, burglars, bombardments, and natural disasters.

The media-induced fears of 8- to 12-year-olds often entail plausible themes. In this period, most fantasy characters have been demystified and children seek to discover reality in media productions (Mielke, 1983). Typical media-induced fears in this age group are realistic dangers that can happen to the child, realistic violence or the threat of realistic violence, and stories involving child victims (Cantor, 1998, 2002).

From 12 up to late adolescence: exams, wars, and global warming

The emotional life during adolescence is still characterized by fear of physical harm. But a concern for social relationships is also quite prominent. Teenagers in this age group become afraid of rejection by parents, teachers, and their peers (Schaffer, 1996). They also start to compare themselves with their peers, which may make them feel inferior in certain respects (Schaffer, 1996). When teenagers feel that they are not doing as well in comparison to others, they may become shy and afraid of public attention. Finally, children at this age develop fears of abstract things, such as politics, the economy, wars, and global warming (Cantor, Wilson, & Hoffner, 1986; Gullone, 2000).

Audiovisual entertainment with abstract dangers is particularly scary for this age group. A good example of this is the movie *The Day After* about a nuclear attack on an American community. When this movie was shown on television in the United States, many parents worried about the reactions of their children. Research conducted by Cantor and colleagues (1986) showed, however, that children up to 12 were less upset by this television movie than teenagers were. In fact, the parents were shocked the most. The reason for this is that the emotional effects of this movie are particularly evoked by the speculation regarding the possible destruction of the earth. This is an abstract concept that young children – and even pre-teens – do not grasp. Sensing danger depends on knowledge and experience. An attack by an animal evokes fear in everybody, as it calls upon instinctive reactions to fast-approaching objects, sudden or strange movements, and loud noises. But for other threats, such as nuclear weapons, a certain knowledge is required which is lacking in young children (Cantor, 2002; Cantor, Wilson, & Hoffner, 1986).

Factors that Increase Fear of Media Content

Although fictional media content can evoke intense fear in viewers, there are a number of factors that can increase or decrease those fears. These factors have to do with characteristics of the viewer, the media content, and the context in which it is viewed.

Cognitive developmental level of the viewer

The cognitive developmental level of a viewer is an important determining factor for the intensity of the fear of media dangers. Children up to approximately 7 years old cannot adequately apply their knowledge as to what is and is not fantasy while watching fictional portrayals. Nor can they effectively reassure themselves by thinking that what they see is only "make-believe" (Harris, 2000). Only from the age of 7 are children able to employ this knowledge without help (Harris, 2000). Therefore, children up to 7 can be especially vulnerable for the effects of fantasy media entertainment (Valkenburg, Cantor, & Peeters, 2000).

Developmental level of empathy

Children often acquire fears by observing the fears of media characters. The underlying mechanism of this pathway to media-induced fear is empathy. However, studies of empathy in children have shown significant developmental increases in the tendency to empathize with other persons (Hoffman, 2000). Although 4-year-old children are able to recognize simple emotions of happiness, sadness, anger, and fear in other persons, it is not until the age of 8 that children report putting themselves in a media character's place (Hoffman, 2000).

Developmental differences in empathy may significantly affect the pathways through which media content can frighten children. A study by Wilson and Cantor (1985), for example, showed that younger (3–5) and older (9–11) children differ significantly in the way in which they acquire fear from media. Children were shown one of two versions of a videotape, one in which the viewing children experienced the danger (a large close-up buzzing honey bee) directly, and one in which they experienced it by observational learning through viewing the fear of a boy for the honey bee. Although the older children reported similar levels of fear to both experimental conditions, for the younger children, direct experience with the honey bee resulted in significantly higher levels of fear than did their observational learning of fear from the boy.

Gender of the viewer

A meta-analysis of gender differences in fright responses to mass media (Peck, 1999) demonstrated that the overwhelming majority of studies showed females reporting more fear than males. Harrison and Cantor (1999), for example, found that of the small number of students who reported never having had an enduring fear response to film or television entertainment, 80 percent were men. Other researchers have also found that girls report more and more intense media-induced fear than boys do (e.g., Sparks, 1989; Valkenburg, Cantor, & Peeters, 2000).

However, although girls consistently report more media-induced fears, the degree to which the two genders differ in media-induced fears may be overestimated because of gender-role stereotyping (Peck, 1999). Boys are generally more reluctant to show their emotions than girls are. They are expected to behave in a masculine or stoic fashion. Girls, on the other hand, are allowed or even encouraged to show their emotions and vulnerabilities, with the result that girls may feel fewer constraints on admitting their fears (Valkenburg, Cantor, & Peeters, 2000).

Motivation to be open to fear

Viewers can apply a cognitive viewing strategy to reduce or to increase their fear responses. If viewers want to limit the emotional impact of entertainment they can concentrate on the thought that the events are taking place within the confines of the media production, so that they do not take them seriously (Zillmann, 1982). Conversely, if viewers want to increase the emotional impact of the movie on themselves, they can choose to believe in the events of the movie. Zillmann (1982) calls this process the willing suspension of disbelief. If viewers choose to believe in the events of fictitious entertainment, they may experience stronger fears in response to this entertainment.

Resemblance of media content to reality

Both the stimulus generalization theory and the law of apparent reality suggest that the closer a danger in the media is to reality, the greater the fear experienced by the viewer. These presumptions are confirmed by research. It has been shown that viewers become more scared of violence used by people of flesh and blood than of violence by cartoon or animation characters (Gunter & Furnham, 1984). In a study conducted by Osborn and Endsley (1971), children said that they found a program with human violence more frightening than one in which the same violence was perpetrated by puppets.

Connection of media content with existing fears   Media portrayals that are related to an individual's existing fears have a higher emotional impact. Experiments have shown that people who are afraid of dying are relatively more scared when they watch a movie about a fatal disease than people who fear death to a lesser degree or not all (Weiss, Katkin, & Rubin, 1968). It has also been shown that women who have just had a baby have a higher heart rate when watching a movie about a birth than women who have not just had a baby (Sapolsky & Zillmann, 1978).

The geographical proximity of the danger   Incidents that occur geographically close to the viewer have in general a higher impact than incidents that happen far away. In an experiment conducted by Heath (1984), groups of students were assigned to one of two conditions in which a movie showed a crime being committed. Half the participants were told that the crime had been committed in the area, the other half that it had been in a city far away. The students who thought that the crime had been committed in the area were more afraid than the other students were. An experiment conducted by Smith and Wilson (2000) shows that 10- and 11-year-old children are more afraid of news about a crime that had been committed in their city than of news about a crime far away.

Music and sound effects

Film producers use a number of formal features to increase the effect of fear in fiction. Himmelweit, Oppenheim, and Vince (1958) found that children felt that certain sound effects and certain kinds of music were frightening elements in movies. Thayer and Levinson (1983) showed that adding different kinds of music to a movie can increase or decrease fear responses. Specifically, they found that adding so-called horror music to a documentary about industrial accidents led to more fear than when the usual standard "documentary music" was used.

Factors that Decrease Fear of Media Content

During childhood, children progressively learn to cope with media-induced fears. Children generally use two types of coping strategies: cognitive and non-cognitive strategies. Cognitive strategies are strategies whereby children try to reason their fear away, for instance by telling themselves that what they see is only make-believe, or that blood on television is "only ketchup." Non-cognitive strategies are physical avoidance strategies, like closing one's eyes, hiding behind the couch, or switching off the television, as well as social comfort strategies, for example going to sit on a parent's lap or get a doll or cuddly toy (Cantor, 2002; Valkenburg, Cantor, & Peeters, 2000).

Adult mediation of children's fear responses

As they develop, children learn a number of coping strategies to help them overcome their fears. Whether they successfully learn how to use these strategies may depend on the mediation strategies that their parents use. Parents generally use two types of mediation strategies to help their children cope with their fears: cognitive and non-cognitive strategies (Wilson & Cantor, 1987). Cognitive mediation strategies involve verbal explanation, for instance telling the child that a frightening stimulus or program is not real, emphasizing the positive motivations of a frightening character; or, in the case of more realistic threats, minimizing the perceived severity of the danger (Cantor, Sparks, & Hoffner, 1984; Wilson & Cantor, 1987; Wilson & Weiss, 1991). Non-cognitive mediation strategies include visual desensitization (i.e., gradually exposing children to threatening cues), physical comfort (e.g., sitting with or holding the child), and restriction (e.g., turning off the television) (Cantor, 2002; Wilson, 1989; Wilson & Cantor, 1987).

Developmental differences in coping and mediation strategies

The use and effectiveness of both coping and mediation strategies differ for younger and older children. Preschoolers primarily find reassurance in non-cognitive strategies, whereas above the age of 7 children increasingly find comfort in verbal cognitive strategies (Wilson, Hoffner, & Cantor, 1987). Mediation research has rather convincingly demonstrated that cognitive strategies are only effective in reducing media-induced fears of children from 7 onwards (Cantor, 2002). Nonetheless, most parents report using cognitive mediation strategies to deal with their children's media-induced fears, regardless of the child's age (Wilson & Cantor, 1987).

A study by Wilson and colleagues (1987) suggests that when young children do not understand the statements being presented, the explanation might not only be ineffective, but may even inadvertently enhance children's fear responses. In an experiment by Wilson and Cantor (1987), for example, a pre-exposure reassuring verbal explanation by an adult about a snake decreased older children's post-exposure responses to televised scenes of a snake, but it *increased* such responses among younger children. These findings indicate the importance of considering the child's age when selecting effective mediation strategies.

Three developmental processes may account for the relative difficulty that younger children experience with cognitive mediation strategies (Wilson & Cantor, 1987; Wilson, Hoffner, & Cantor, 1987). First, in order to benefit from a verbal explanation, the child must be able to understand the information being presented. Second, the child must store the information derived from the explanation in memory. At 7 years of age, children start to develop sophisticated information storage strategies, including rehearsal, categorization, visualization, and mnemonics (Siegler, 1998). Third, the child must be able to retrieve the stored information from memory and apply it to subsequent frightening situations. Such information storage and retrieval tasks are too difficult for young children, but continually improve during the elementary school years (Cantor, 2002; Siegler, 1998).

Conclusion

This chapter has shown that most children are at times so scared of something they have seen in the media that they remain afraid afterwards. It has also shown that, for most children, this fear disappears after several hours or days. However, for about 12 percent (Valkenburg, 2004) to 26 percent (Harrison & Cantor, 1999) of the viewers, the media-induced fear is much more serious. These viewers remain frightened for years because of one terrifying scene. Lack of sleep, not wanting to use the shower, and no longer daring to swim are examples revealed by the different studies.

Not only does entertainment designed for adults contain frightening elements for children, but so does children's entertainment programming, such as Disney movies. Although this kind of entertainment is often marketed as "family movies," it is important for adults to realize that such movies can still intensely frighten young children, particularly those under age 7. Media-induced fears of children are age-dependent, and certain adult mediation strategies can moderate fear effects. Overall, the findings from this research base can help parents, educators, and policy makers to select audiovisual entertainment that satisfactorily fits the developmental needs of children.

References

Anderson, C. G., & Bushman, B. J. (2001). Effects of violent video games on aggressive behavior, aggressive cognition, aggressive affect, physiological arousal, and prosocial behavior: A meta-analytic review of the scientific literature. *Psychological Science, 12*, 353–9.

Ankersmit, L., & Veen, J. (1995). Special moves: Gebruik en betekenis van videospellen [Special moves: use and meaning of videogames]. Unpublished master's dissertation, Department of Communication, Universiteit van Amsterdam.

Bandura, A. (1994). Social cognitive theory of mass communication. In J. Bryant & D. Zillmann (Eds.), *Media effects* (pp. 61–90). Hillsdale, NJ: Lawrence Erlbaum.

Bandura, A. (1996). *Social foundations of thought and action: A social cognitive theory.* Upper Saddle River, NJ: Prentice Hall.

Bauer, D. H. (1976). An exploratory study of developmental changes in children's fears. *Journal of Child Psychology and Psychiatry, 17*, 69–74.

Borke, H. (1971). Interpersonal perception of young children: Egocentrism or empathy? *Developmental Psychology, 5*, 263–9.

Cantor, J. (1991). Fright responses to mass media productions. In J. Bryant & D. Zillmann (Eds.), *Responding to the screen* (pp. 169–97). Hillsdale, NJ: Lawrence Erlbaum.

Cantor, J. (1998). *"Mommy I'm scared:" How TV and movies frighten children and what we can do to protect them.* San Diego, CA: Harcourt Brace.

Cantor, J. (2002). Fright reactions to mass media. In J. Bryant & D. Zillmann (Eds.), *Media effects* (pp. 287–306). Hillsdale, NJ: Lawrence Erlbaum.

Cantor, J., Sparks, G. G., & Hoffner, C. (1984). Calming children's television fears: Mr Rogers vs. The Incredible Hulk. *Journal of Broadcasting and Electronic Media, 32*, 271–88.

Cantor, J., Wilson, B. J., & Hoffner, C. (1986). Emotional responses to a televised nuclear holocaust film. *Communication Research, 13*, 257–77.

Fiske, S. T., & Taylor, S. E. (1984). *Social cognition.* New York: Random House.

Fraiberg, S. H. (1959). *The magic years: Understanding and handling the problems of early childhood.* New York: Charles Scriber's Sons.

Frijda, N. H. (1988). The laws of emotion. *American Psychologist, 43*, 349–58.

Frijda, N. H. (1989). Aesthetic emotions and reality. *American Psychologist, 44*, 1546–7.

Gollnisch, G., & Averill, J. R. (1993). Emotional imagery: Strategies and correlates. *Cognition and Emotion, 7*, 407–29.

Gullone, E. (2000). The development of normal fear: A century of research. *Clinical Psychology Review, 20*, 429–51.

Gunter, B., & Furnham, A. (1984). Perceptions of television violence: Effects of programme genre and type of violence on viewers' judgments of violent portrayals. *British Journal of Social Psychology*, 23, 155–64.

Harris, P. L. (2000). *Understanding children's worlds: The work of the imagination.* Oxford: Blackwell.

Harrison, K., & Cantor, J. (1999). Tales from the screen: Enduring fright reactions to scary media. *Media Psychology*, 1, 97–164.

Heath, L. (1984). Impact of newspaper crime reports on fear of crime: Multimethodological investigation. *Journal of Personality and Social Psychology*, 47, 263–76.

Himmelweit, H. T., Oppenheim, A. N., & Vince, P. (1958). *Television and the child: An empirical study of the effect of television on the young.* London: Oxford University Press.

Hoekstra, S. J., Harris, R. J., & Helmick, A. L. (1999). Autobiographical memories about the experience of seeing frightening movies in childhood. *Media Psychology*, 1, 117–40.

Hoffman, M. L. (2000). *Empathy and moral development: Implications for caring and justice.* Cambridge: Cambridge University Press.

Jersild, A. T., & Holmes, F. B. (1935). Methods of overcoming children's fears. *Journal of Psychology*, 1, 75–104.

Johnson, B. R. (1980). General occurrence of stressful reactions to commercial motion pictures and elements in films subjectively identified as stressors. *Psychological Reports*, 47, 775–86.

King, N. J., Gullone, E., & Ollendick, T. H. (1998). Etiology of childhood phobias: Current status of Rachman's three pathways theory. *Behaviour Research and Therapy*, 36, 297–309.

Maurer, A. (1965). What children fear. *Journal of Genetic Psychology*, 106, 265–77.

Mielke, K. W. (1983). Formative research on appeal and comprehension in *3-2-1 Contact*. In J. Bryant & D. Anderson (Eds.), Children's understanding of television: Research on attention and comprehension (pp. 241–63). Hillsdale, NJ: Lawrence Erlbaum.

Muris, P., Merckelbach, H., Gadet, B., & Moulaert, V. (2000). Fears, worries, and scary dreams in 4- to 12-year-old children: Their content, developmental pattern, and origins. *Journal of Clinical Child Psychology*, 29, 43–52.

Needlman, R. (2004). *Why parents should read "Harry Potter."* Doctor Spock Company. Retrieved July 20, 2006, from http://www.drspock.com/article/0,1510,5960,00.html.

O'Keefe, B. J., & Zehnder, S. M. (2005). Understanding media development: A framework and a case study. *Journal of Applied Developmental Psychology*, 25, 729–40.

Ollendick, T. H., & King, N. J. (1991). Origins of childhood fears: An evaluation of Rachman's theory of fear acquisition. *Behaviour Research and Therapy*, 29, 117–23.

Osborn, D. K., & Endsley, R. C. (1971). Emotional reactions of young children to TV violence. *Child Development*, 42, 321–31.

Peck, E. (1999). Gender differences in film-induced fear as a function of type of emotion measure and stimulus content: A meta analysis and laboratory study. Unpublished PhD dissertation, University of Wisconsin, Madison.

Rachman, S. J. (1991). Neoconditioning and the classical theory of fear acquisition. *Clinical Psychology Review*, 11, 155–73.

Sapolsky, B. S., & Molitor, F. (1996). Content trends in contemporary horror films. In J. B. Weaver & R. Tamborini (Eds.), *Horror films: Current research on audience preferences and reactions* (pp. 33–48). Hillsdale, NJ: Lawrence Erlbaum.

Sapolsky, B. S., & Zillmann, D. (1978). Experience and empathy: Affective reactions to witnessing child-birth. *Journal of Social Psychology*, 105, 131–44.

Sarafino, E. P. (1986). *The fears of childhood*. New York: Human Science Press.

Schaffer, H. R. (1996). *Social development*. Oxford: Blackwell.

Siegler, R. S. (1998). *Children's thinking* (3rd edn.). Englewood Cliffs, NJ: Prentice Hall.

Smith, S., & Wilson, B. J. (2000). Children's reactions to a television news story: The impact of video footage and proximity of the crime. *Communication Research*, 27, 641–73.

Sparks, G. G. (1986). Developmental differences in children's reports of fear induced by the mass media. *Child Study Journal*, 16, 55–66.

Sparks, G. G. (1989). The prevalence and intensity of fright reactions to mass media: Implications of the activation-arousal view. *Communication Quarterly*, 37, 108–17.

Sparks, G. G., Spirek, M. M., & Hodgson, K. (1993). Individual differences in arousability: Implications for understanding immediate and lingering emotional reactions to frightening mass media. *Communication Quarterly*, 4, 465–76.

Stotland, E. (1969). Exploratory investigations of empathy. In L. Berkowitz (Ed.), *Advances in experimental social psychology* (pp. 271–314). New York: Academic Press.

Tamborini, R. (1996). A model of empathy and emotional reactions to horror. In J. B. Weaver & R. Tamborini (Eds.), *Horror films: Current research on audience preferences and reactions* (pp. 103–24). Hillsdale, NJ: Lawrence Erlbaum.

Tamborini, R., & Weaver, J. (1996). Frightening entertainment: A historical perspective of fictional horror. In J. B. Weaver & R. Tamborini (Eds.), *Horror films: Current research on audience preferences and reactions* (pp. 1–14). Hillsdale, NJ: Lawrence Erlbaum.

Thayer, J. F., & Levinson, R. W. (1983). Effects of music on psychophysiological responses to a stressful film. *Psychomusicology*, 3, 44–52.

Valkenburg, P. M. (2004). *Children's responses to the screen: A media psychological approach*. Mahwah, NJ: Lawrence Erlbaum.

Valkenburg, P. M., Cantor, J., & Peeters, A. L. (2000). Fright reactions to television: A child survey. *Communication Research*, 27, 82–99.

Valkenburg, P. M., & Peter, J. (2006). Fantasy and imagination. In J. Bryant & P. Vorderer (Eds.), *The psychology of entertainment* (pp. 105–17). Mahwah, NJ: Lawrence Erlbaum.

Venn, J. R., & Short, J. G. (1973). Vicarious classical conditioning of emotional responses in nursery school children. *Journal of Personality and Social Psychology*, 28, 249–55.

Walters, K. S. (1989). The law of apparent reality and aesthetic emotions. *American Psychologist*, 44, 1545–6.

Weiss, B. W., Katkin, E. S., & Rubin, B. M. (1968). Relationship between a factor analytically derived measure of a specific fear and performance after related fear induction. *Journal of Abnormal Psychology*, 73, 461–3.

Wilson, B. J. (1989). The effects of two control strategies on children's emotional reactions to a frightening movie scene. *Journal of Broadcasting and Electronic Media*, 33, 397–418.

Wilson, B. J., & Cantor, J. (1985). Developmental differences in empathy with a television protagonist's fear. *Journal of Experimental Child Psychology*, 39, 284–99.

Wilson B. J., & Cantor, J. (1987). Reducing children's emotional reactions to mass media through rehearsed explanation and exposure to a replica of the fear object. *Human Communication Research*, 14, 3–26.

Wilson, B. J., Hoffner, C., & Cantor, J. (1987). Children's perceptions of the effectiveness of techniques to reduce fear from mass media. *Journal of Applied Developmental Psychology*, 8, 39–52.

Wilson, B. J., & Weiss, A. J. (1991). The effects of two reality explanations on children's reactions to a frightening movie scene. *Communication Monographs*, 58, 307–26.

Yerkes, R. M., & Yerkes, A. W. (1936). Nature and conditions of avoidance (fear) responses in chimpanzees. *Journal of Comparative Psychology*, 21, 53–66.

Zillmann, D. (1982). Television viewing and arousal. In D. Pearl, L. Bouthilet, & J. Lazar (Eds.), *Television and behavior: Ten years of scientific progress and implications for the eighties* (pp. 53–67). Washington, DC: US Government Printing Office.

Part V

Health Effects of Media

16

Media Use and Childhood Obesity

Elizabeth A. Vandewater and Hope M. Cummings

The prevalence of obesity in American youth has reached alarming levels. The proportion of overweight children and adolescents, defined as a body mass index (BMI) exceeding the ninety-fifth percentile for age and sex based norms, has tripled in the past three decades (Troiano & Flegal, 1998). Current estimates indicate that approximately 10 percent of 2–5-year-olds and 15 percent of 6–19-year-olds are overweight (Ogden et al., 2006). The definition of obese and overweight among children is a statistical definition based on the 2000 Centers for Disease Control and Prevention (CDC) growth reference for the United States (Kuczmarski et al., 2002). Obese is defined as at or above the ninety-fifth percentile of BMI-for-age. Overweight is defined as at or above the eighty-fifth percentile, but less than the ninety-fifth percentile, of BMI-for-age. The BMI-for-age growth charts were developed from five national data sets of the National Household Education Survey (NHES) and the National Health and Nutrition Examination Study (NHANES) (NHES 2, NHES 3, NHANES I, NHANES II, and NHANES III for children less than 6 years). It may be worth noting that for children up to 18 years of age, the CDC does not, in fact, use the labels obese or overweight (as they do at the same BMI cut-offs described above for adults). Rather, they refer to children reaching the eighty-fifth percentile as "at-risk for overweight," and to those reaching the ninety-fifth percentile as "overweight." However, we refer to these cut-offs as overweight (eighty-fifth percentile) and obese (ninety-fifth percentile) for ease of discussion.

The increased prevalence of overweight and obese youth has placed an unprecedented burden on children's health. Obesity is strongly related to several chronic diseases, such as cardiovascular disease and diabetes (Must et al., 1999). Overweight and obese children are at an increased risk of suffering co-morbidities including type 2 diabetes, hypertension, dyslipidemia and hyperinsulinemia, fatty liver disease and orthopedic disorders (Lobstein, Baur, & Uauy, 2005). Almost two thirds (60 percent) of overweight children have at least one cardiovascular risk factor (e.g., hypertension, hyperlipidemia; Freedman et al., 1999). Moreover, though overall prevalence rates are still low, the number of youth with some degree of glycemic abnormalities (precursors to type 2 diabetes mellitus) is on the rise and closely parallels the trend in increasing weight status of youth globally (Bloomgarden, 2004).

Finally, obesity in childhood tends to persist in adulthood (Must, 1996; Must et al., 1992). Overweight youth enter adulthood with an increased risk of obesity up to 17 times that of their normal-weight peers (Hauner, 2004). It has been estimated that obesity-related morbidity accounts for approximately 6 percent of national health expenditure in the United States (Wolf & Colditz, 1998). Thus, the striking increase in the prevalence of childhood obesity in the last three decades will dramatically affect public health expenses, programs, and priorities well into the twenty-first century.

The recent spike in childhood obesity rates has accelerated scholarly activity aimed at understanding the causes and contributors to this dramatic increase. A portion of this activity has focused on the relationship between electronic media use (particularly television use) and childhood obesity. There are three major hypothesized mechanisms for the relationship between electronic media use and obesity (Robinson, 2001). These mechanisms include: (1) decreased metabolic rates during television viewing specifically; (2) displacement of physical activity (sedentary behavior); and (3) increased caloric intake (either through eating while watching, or in response to electronically delivered food advertisements and food marketing). Our goals in this chapter are twofold: (1) to present each of these hypotheses, and review existing empirical evidence for each; and (2) to discuss limitations of existing research, and suggest directions for future research in this area.

Children's Media Landscape in the Millennium

Youth of all ages spend a fair proportion of their time using electronic media (3–5 hours a day watching television, for example), more time than in any other single free-time activity except for sleep (Huston & Wright, 1997; Roberts, Foehr, & Rideout, 2005). It is for this reason that television viewing has been linked with sedentary behavior in the minds of many. The Kaiser Foundation has surveyed the media use of youth between 8 and 18 years old in 1999 and 2004 (Rideout et al., 1999; Roberts, Foehr, & Rideout, 2005), as well as very young children between 6 months and 6 years of age in 2002 and 2005 (Rideout & Hamel, 2006; Rideout, Vandewater, & Wartella, 2003). These surveys confirm the general perception that children are growing up in media and technologically saturated environments. Ninety-nine percent of American households report television ownership, 97 percent VCR/DVD player ownership, 83 percent video-game player ownership, and 86 percent computer ownership. Most families (roughly 75 percent) report multiple televisions in the household, with these televisions increasingly located in children's bedrooms. Roughly 70 percent of

8–18-year-olds and 36 percent of very young children (6 months to 6 years old) have televisions in their bedrooms.

Computer and videogame use among children is also growing, with roughly 40 percent of youth ages 8–18 reporting that they use computers or play video-games on a daily basis (Rideout et al., 1999; Roberts, Foehr, & Rideout, 2005). It is often assumed that computer and videogame use is virtually ubiquitous among American youth and consumes much of their media time (e.g., Anderson & Butcher, 2006). In Figure 16.1, we have charted the amount of time American children spent watching television in 2002, playing electronic games, and using com-puters (excluding games). We draw upon time-diary data drawn from the second wave of the Child Development Supplement (CDS-II) to the Panel Study of Income Dynamics (PSID) – a representative sample of US children ages 6–18 (publicly available at http://psidonline.isr.umich.edu/CDS/). The Child Development Supplement is virtually the only existing public-use data set that collects infor-mation regarding children and adolescents' activities (including media use) via 24-hour time-use diaries. Time-use diaries have been shown to be a highly valid and reliable method of documenting time spent in various activities for both children and adults (Juster & Stafford, 1985, 1991). As shown in this figure, the majority of the time children spend with electronic media is still predominantly

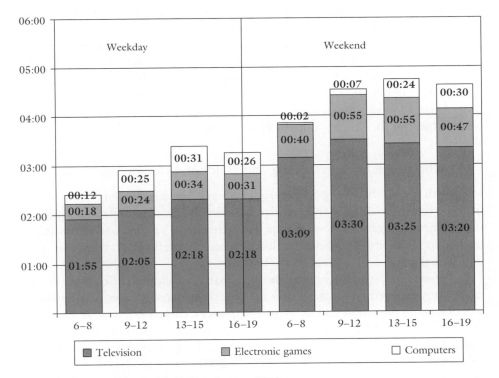

Figure 16.1   Children's Media Landscape: 2002
Source: PSID, Child Development Supplement (CDS-II).

with television (about 3 hours), while youth spend about a half hour with electronic games on each weekday and an hour on weekend days. Computer use averages just under a half hour on each weekday and only 15 minutes each weekend day. The findings from these data are quite similar to those of the Kaiser surveys. Thus, survey data reveal that neither videogame nor computer use is nearly as ubiquitous or time-consuming as is generally assumed.

Linking Media Use and Childhood Obesity

Partly because children spend so much of their time with it, electronic media have been charged with contributing to the rising obesity rates among US children. The conviction that television viewing and video/computer game use, in particular, bear much of the responsibility for the increased prevalence of obesity in American youth is held by the lay public and scholars alike (Chen & Kennedy, 2001; Dietz, 2001; Dietz & Gortmaker, 1985; Gortmaker et al., 1993). An expert panel convened by the American College of Sports Medicine stated unequivocally that "obesity is directly related to the number of hours spent watching television" (Bar-Or et al., 1998, p. 4).

Moreover, this conviction has shaped prominent public health policies. Noting that high levels of viewing time and television in the bedroom have been linked (at least by correlational measures) with childhood weight status, the American Academy of Pediatrics (AAP) policy statement on prevention of pediatric obesity recommends that viewing time and videogame play be limited to no more than 2 hours per day (AAP, 2003). In its continuing series of *Healthy People* mission statements, the US Department of Health and Human Services listed the reduction of television viewing as a means of promoting physical activity as a national health objective for the first time in *Healthy People 2010*.

Charting television viewing and childhood obesity over time

It is worth noting that many believe that children's television viewing has increased over the years. In scholarly and popular literature, it is generally taken for granted that children's television viewing time has increased in proportion with increases in childhood obesity. This belief has led to statements such as "As television viewing has increased, so has childhood obesity."

In Figure 16.2, we present data showing that US children's television viewing has in fact remained fairly steady over the past three decades or so. Taking estimates of viewing time from various sources (Comstock et al., 1978; Lyle & Hoffman, 1972; Nielsen Media Research, 1976; Timmer, Eccles, & O'Brien, 1985; Vandewater & Lee, in press; Wright et al., 2001), we have charted the time children spend with television from the 1970s through 2002 against the prevalence of childhood obesity based upon NHANES estimates in the same time periods (Flegal et al., 2002; National Center for Health Statistics, 2004; Ogden et al., 1997).

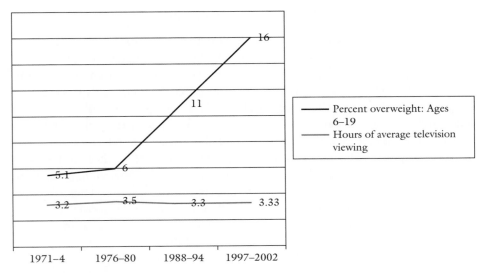

Figure 16.2   Prevalence of Child Overweight and Television Viewing: Past 30 years

The figure clearly shows that children have been watching roughly 3 to 3.5 hours of television per day, and this has remained fairly steady since the mid-1970s. This is not the case for childhood obesity rates, which began to rise precipitously after 1980. Though 3.5 hours is still a sizable amount of time, it is not true that children's television viewing has been increasing in proportion to the increased prevalence rates of childhood obesity. Carter (2005) examined the media use of Australian children in 1960 and 2003 and came to the same conclusion.

In contrast, using Nielsen estimates from 1970 to 1998, Anderson and Butcher (2006) found that average daily minutes of television viewing have been steadily increasing from 1970 to 2000. There are notable problems with these estimates however, including that they are estimates based on all viewers, not children alone, and that Nielsen estimates can only account for the time the television is on, not time spent actually *viewing*.

Mechanisms Linking Electronic Media and Obesity

Fundamentally, being overweight and obese arise due to an imbalance of energy – the individual does not expend as much energy as he or she takes in. The reasons for this imbalance are complex and varied. However, electronic media use has been hypothesized to play a major role in this imbalance. In this section, we review the three major hypothesized mechanisms linking electronic media and obesity: (1) decreased metabolic rates, (2) displacement of physical activity, and (3) increased caloric intake (Robinson, 1999).

Decreased metabolic rates

This hypothesis reflects the intriguing notion that television viewing decreases resting metabolic rates (RMR) to levels actually below that of RMR in other sedentary activities. If this premise is true, this would mean that energy expenditure during television viewing is lower than in other sedentary activities (such as sleeping or reading) and therefore should be discouraged – even in lieu of other sedentary activities. In some sense, at the most fundamental level this hypothesis puts forth the notion that there is something about watching television itself that increases adiposity. This idea was first suggested by Klesges, Shelton and Klesges (1993) who found evidence that 8–12-year-old children's metabolic rates were lower during television viewing than during resting or sleeping. These findings received much attention in the press, but they have generally proven unreplicable (Buchowski & Sun, 1996; Dietz et al., 1994). Current consensus in the field is that this is not a viable hypothesis (Robinson, 2001).

Decreased activity levels

Electronic media use is thought to be related to increased weight in children because time spent viewing or playing displaces physical activity. This is essentially the "couch potato" hypothesis, whereby time spent using electronic media is thought to interfere with time spent in more energy-expending activities and positively relate to time spent in sedentary activities (including media use itself). This is by far the most popular hypothesis connecting television use and obesity in children. Although this hypothesis was first thought to apply equally well to interactive media (videogames, computers), new evidence suggests that this may not be the case. First, there is emerging evidence that energy expended during videogame play (even while sitting) is higher than when watching television or engaged in other sedentary activities (Wang & Perry, 2006). Additionally, newly developed videogames which require participants to be active in the game (such as *Dance Dance Revolution*) clearly have the potential to encourage activity, rather than discourage it (Bulik, 2004). In general however, screen-related activities are assumed to displace more active activities (e.g., playing outside) and facilitate sedentary lifestyles in children and adolescents.

If time spent in activities is zero-sum, then the assumption that time spent watching television impinges upon the total time available for physically active activities makes some intuitive sense. This idea that television might replace other activities has been referred to as the "displacement effect" (Mutz, Roberts, & van Vuuren, 1993). However, it is worth noting that empirical examination of displacement or time "trade-offs" requires a full accounting of all activities children engage in over a 24-hour period. Otherwise, it is impossible to accurately assess the extent of the relationships among activities in which children engage (Vandewater, Bickham, & Lee, 2006). This realization is far from recent. In 1977, Robinson remarked "A major weakness of the available literature has been its failure to employ an adequate sampling framework of daily life with which to assess television's full impact" (Robinson, 1977, p. 412). Surprisingly, however, few existing studies utilize an appropriate time-sampling method. Most studies utilize global questions regarding media and other activities, asking respondents to indicate how much, on average, they watch television or read in a typical day, for example. Yet it is impossible to assess displacement by simply examining the relationship between the average amount of television and reading. Again, a full accounting of how time is used over an entire day is required for this examination. Given that concern about the displacement of healthier activities by television has loomed large in both popular and academic consciousness for decades, the relative dearth of empirical research utilizing 24-hour time diaries is surprising.

Early evidence for the displacement of physical activity by television came from studies documenting decreases in participation in physical activities following the introduction of television into small, mainly rural, communities (Brown, Cramond, & Wilde, 1974; Williams, 1986). In particular, Williams (1986) found a lower level of participation in sports activities for both children and adults in rural communities with access to either a single television channel or multiple (four) television channels, compared to a community with no television.

However, results from ensuing epidemiologic studies have consistently found either small or nonexistent relationships between television viewing or videogame/ computer use and physical activity among children and adolescents. Robinson and colleagues (1993), Durant and colleagues (1994), and Vilhjalmsson and Thorlindsson (1998) report negative but weak associations between media use and physical activity. Biddle and colleagues (2004), Katzmarzyk and colleagues (1998), Robinson and Killen (1995) and Zarkarian and colleagues (1994) all report no relationship. In our study utilizing time diaries to assess the relationship between television viewing and various activities (the one study we are aware of that utilizes an appropriate time-sample method for examining displacement), we found no relationship between television viewing and physical activity (Vandewater, Bickham, & Lee, 2006). In one of the few studies to explicitly examine computer use, Ho and Lee (2001) found a correlation of −.03 between adolescent computer use and exercise.

In a recent meta-analysis, Marshall and colleagues (2004) examine findings from 52 independent samples and report an average effect size (Pearson r) of −.12 for the relationship between television viewing and physical activity, and an effect size of −.10 for the relationship between video/computer game use and physical activity. Although these are in the predicted direction, their sizes are extremely small. Effects of this size would lead one to conclude that the relationship between media use and physical activity is not particularly meaningful. Indeed, the authors conclude that "media-based inactivity may be unfairly implicated in recent epidemiologic trends of overweight and obesity among children and youth" (Marshall et al., 2004, p. 1238).

These findings have important implications for the notion that electronic media use has contributed to the obesity epidemic in US youth via its impact on physical activity. Given the dire problem of overweight children in this country, it seems reasonable to assume that American children are not active enough. The question at hand is whether youths' electronic media use plays an important role in this relation or not. Generally, the assumption seems to be that if children were not watching television, playing videogames, or using the computer, they would be outside running up and down a soccer field. However, existing evidence simply does not support this assumption. In fact, it seems that the main thing electronic media use may be displacing is other kinds of sedentary activities. In our research, we found that television viewing was significantly related to decreased time spent in indoor play (board games, pretend play, card games, etc.) (Vandewater, Bickham, & Lee, 2006). Others have also found that television viewing is negatively related to indoor leisure activities (Huston et al., 1999). Taken as a whole, the current body of empirical evidence suggests that the reduction of strenuous physical activity is not one of the major mechanisms by which electronic media are contributing to childhood obesity.

If neither decreased metabolic rates, nor decreased physical activity are the mechanism by which electronic media affects childhood obesity – what is left? Examining Figure 16.2 again, if television is indeed implicated in the increased prevalence of obesity, then the diverging plots of obesity rates and television viewing suggest that there is something else happening during viewing that is related to obesity (besides the inactivity inherent in watching television). This brings us to the other major hypothesized mechanism – the notion that television viewing is linked to children's eating behaviors.

Increased caloric intake

The third major hypothesis links electronic media use to increased caloric intake either from eating during viewing (particularly television viewing), or as a result of electronic media based food advertising, which tends to emphasize high-calorie, high-fat foods with poor nutritional content (IOM, 2006).

Eating while viewing   Although it is often assumed that both children and adults "mindlessly" eat while using media, empirical efforts aimed at directly assessing this notion are scarce, and the few existing studies focus only on television. Coon and colleagues (2001) examined the foods consumed by a sample of fourth- to sixth-grade children ($N = 91$) in families who also reported whether or not the television was on during the three main meals of the day. Overall, they found that children in families that ate meals in front of the television two or more times per day derived 6 percent more of their total daily energy from meat, 5 percent more from pizza, salty snacks and sodas combined, and nearly 5 percent less from fruits, vegetables, and juices combined. Interestingly, they also found that added fats were consumed *less* often by children from families with the television on during two or more meals. This finding may be because these children are eating fattier foods to begin with – one rarely adds butter to pizza.

In a similar study utilizing a sample of ethnically diverse third- and fifth-grade children ($N = 60$), Matheson and colleagues (2004) found that food was consumed more often during television viewing than any other activity, and that on average, 75 percent of children ate while viewing on weekdays, and 60 percent ate while watching on weekend days. Both of these studies are based on small, community-based samples, with limited generalizability. We examined eating while viewing based on time diary data from the 2002 Child Development Supplement referred to previously. Overall, we found that 35 percent of children (out of a total of 2569) ate meals in front of the television at least once on a weekday, and 37 percent did so on a weekend. These numbers are considerably lower than those reported by Matheson and colleagues (2004). This incongruency may be due to sample differences, cohort differences, or a combination of both. Though intriguing, the findings of these studies are far from definitively answering whether television increases caloric consumption. The notion of "mindless" eating implies either that individuals eat more during meals consumed in front of the television than they normally would, or that television viewing provides additional opportunities to eat aside from meals. To date however, these subtleties have not been put to any empirical test. With respect to other media, given that children's hands are occupied when playing videogames, the notion that children eat more when playing games seems less likely. This is true of computer games as well, although perhaps Internet use and other kinds of use might allow eating during the activity. Again, these questions remain to be examined. Clearly, much more empirical work utilizing a variety of designs and methods (experimental, epidemiological, longitudinal) is needed.

Televised food advertising   After the automotive industry, the US food industry is the second largest advertiser in the American economy (McCall, 2003). The food industry spent $7 billion on food advertising in 1997 (Harris et al., 2002). Of this total, advertising expenditures for confectionary and snacks, breakfast cereals, and soft drinks together totaled $2.3 billion. By contrast, the US Department of Agriculture spent $333 million on nutrition education, evaluation, and demonstrations (Gallo, 1999).

Children have been viewed as an increasingly important market by advertisers. In the past decade in particular, US children and adolescents have been targeted with intensive and aggressive forms of food advertising (Story & French, 2004). For industry, the stakes are huge. It is estimated that children ages 14 and younger directly purchase $14 billion in goods annually, and influence another $190 billion in family purchases (McNeal, 1998).

Advertisers spend approximately $1 billion annually on messages aimed at the youth market, and television is the preferred mode of reaching them (IOM, 2006; Janz, Dawson, & Mahoney, 2000; Kunkel et al., 2004; Lauro, 1999; Rice, 2001). Over 75 percent of US food manufacturers advertising budgets, and 95 percent of US fast-food restaurant advertising budgets are allocated to television (Gallo, 1999). The proliferation of television channels due to the diffusion of cable television and direct broadcast satellite technologies has brought with it numerous channels with programming aimed at children such as Nickelodeon, Disney Channel, and Cartoon Network (Kunkel et al., 2004). The concentration of demographic collections of viewers, brought about by such "niche" channels, has made it easier for advertisers to target specific markets, including children.

Evidence suggests that food is one of the most frequently advertised products on television, accounting for approximately 50 percent of all commercials (Byrd-Bredbenner, 2002; Story, Neumark-Sztainer, & French, 2002; Taras & Gage, 1995). The average child watches more than 40,000 television commercials per year and commercial advertising has been found to account for as much as 16 percent of children's total viewing time (Kunkel, 2001; Taras & Gage, 1995). It has been estimated that children are exposed to an average of one food commercial for every five minutes of television viewing, and may see as many as three hours of food commercials every week (Gamble & Cotunga, 1999).

The heavy food marketing directed at children, especially young children, seems to be driven largely by the desire to develop and build brand awareness, preference, and loyalty (Story & French, 2004). Hite and Hite (1994) demonstrated that preschoolers rely heavily on "branding" for food preferences. The researchers found that young children evaluated product samples presented with nationally advertised brand names/labels as tasting significantly better than products presented with store names/labels. This brand reliance was in fact most prominent among very young children. Children ages 2 to 3 chose brand names/labels 10 to 1 over store names/labels, while children ages 4 to 5 chose brand names 2 to 1 over store names/labels.

These findings have not gone unnoticed by marketers, who have been intensifying efforts to develop brand relationships with young consumers, particularly toddlers (Zollo, 1999). Eighty percent of food items are branded (Harris et al., 2002), and marketers know young children can affect parental purchases through what is known in the business as the "nag factor" or "pester power" (McNeal, 1998; Story & French, 2004). Marketers also know that a child's first request for a product occurs at around 2 years of age, that 75 percent of the time this request occurs in a grocery store or supermarket, and that the most requested product is breakfast cereal (47 percent), followed by snacks and beverages (30 percent) and toys (21 percent) (McNeal, 1998; Story & French, 2004).

Most televised food advertising to children falls into one of five categories. These are known as the "big 5" of food advertising and they include: (1) pre-sugared breakfast cereals, (2) soft-drinks, (3) candy, (4) salty snack-products and (5) fast-food and/or highly processed foods (Kotz & Story, 1994). Not surprisingly, these foods also account for almost 50 percent of the US food market share (Kuribayashi, Roberts, & Johnson, 2001; Taras & Gage, 1995). Kotz and Story (1994) constructed a "Saturday morning food pyramid," based on food advertising to children in 1994. They found that 50 percent of advertised foods during children's television programs fell into the fats, oils, and sweets food group;

5 percent into dairy; 2 percent into meat, poultry, fish, eggs, nuts, and legumes; and 43 percent into bread, cereal, rice, and pasta. Thus, sweets comprised the majority of the "Saturday morning pyramid," and vegetables and fruits were completely absent – the antithesis of the US Department of Agriculture's food guide pyramid at the time. A recent analysis of food advertising during child-audience programming in 2003 revealed that convenience foods, fast foods, and sweets (including candy and soft-drinks) comprised 83 percent of advertised foods (Harrison & Marske, 2005). There is little doubt that food advertising is a major form of advertising to children, and that the vast majority of food advertising to children is for foods of poor or questionable nutritional content.

Food advertising in other forms of media   Although there is no sign that televised food advertising is decreasing, marketers concerned about the use of TiVo and other recording devices that can limit exposure to commercials have been expanding efforts to capture market share in other ways. Food marketers have also sought to capitalize on the popularity of videogames and the Internet among youth. Product placement is a marketing strategy whereby products are placed in a setting outside of a typical advertisement (IOM, 2006). Typically, popular actors, programs and characters are seen using the product in the context of the storyline. Product placement in movies has become commonplace since the character ET ate Reese's Pieces candy and short-term national candy sales increased 66 percent (IOM, 2006). Though product placement is illegal in programs aimed at children, it is common in prime-time programming as well as in movies aimed at children and adolescents (IOM, 2006; Linn, 2005).

Product placement has been more difficult to implement effectively in traditional console videogames, because the placement must be part of the original programming and cannot be changed once the game is released (IOM, 2006) – though the industry is actively working to "fix" this problem (see, for example, Webster & Bulik, 2004). However, product placement on Internet-based games is easily incorporated and can be changed with product popularity. This has given rise to what are known as "advergames" or "advertainment" (Kretchmer, 2004). Advergames are Internet-based games with a commercial message, either subtle or overt. Advergames can be found on product or brand websites. Most (if not all) websites for popular children's channels (Nick.com, Cartoonnetwork.com) or toy products (Lego.com, Hasbro.com) feature games incorporating characters and products, in order to build and extend brand loyalty (Calvert, 2003; Kretchmer, 2004). Increasingly, advergames can be found on websites for foods marketed almost exclusively to children and adolescents. The McDonalds, Kelloggs, General Mills, and Hostess Websites all have games for children featuring their products. Though games on food and restaurant websites currently account for an extremely small percentage (less than 1 percent) of the combined Internet and television commercials for these companies (IOM, 2006), it seems likely that this share will increase in the next five to ten years.

Children's understanding of advertising

Part of the problem with all of this advertising is the plethora of evidence indicating that young children have difficulty making sense of commercials and commercial content. Under the age of 4, children have difficulty differentiating between programs and commercials (Kunkel et al., 2004). Children under the age of 7 do not understand the persuasive intent of advertising – they are more likely to perceive advertisements simply as "information" provided by someone with their best interests at heart (Blosser & Roberts, 1985; Ward, Wackman, & Wartella, 1977). Even children between the ages of 7 and 11 have difficulty questioning commercial claims (John, 1999). The matter is complicated by the fact that language providing important information about the product is often presented in ways children cannot understand. For example, evidence shows that children under 7 do not understand the meaning of "part of a balanced breakfast" which is commonly (almost ubiquitously) used in sugared cereal advertisements (Palmer & McDowell, 1981). As noted by Kunkel and colleagues, "Rather than informing young viewers about the importance of a nutritious breakfast, this common disclaimer actually leaves many children with the misimpression that cereal alone is sufficient for a meal" (2004, p. 5).

Features of advertising to children

Market researchers and advertisers have spent a great deal of time and effort understanding how to best appeal to child audiences (John, 1999). Formal features of advertising to children include music, quick-cut editing, sound effects and animation – all used because they capture children's attention (Huston & Wright, 1989). Utilizing findings from educational research indicating that repetition is an effective educational strategy (especially for young children), television advertisers repeat advertisements more during children's programming than during adult programming (Kuribayashi, Roberts, & Johnson, 2001). Marketers have also learned that products are most appealing when framed in terms of "fun" (Cantor, 1981; IOM, 2006). The most common persuasive strategy employed in advertising to children is to associate the product with fun and happiness (Barcus, 1980; Kunkel & Gantz, 1992). Popular and well-liked branded cartoon characters are frequently used in advertising directed to children because they aid children's recall and enhance children's product preference (Atkin & Block, 1983; Lieber, 1998).

Effects of food advertising on children

There is little doubt that the diets of American children and adolescents are poor and do not meet national dietary goals (Cavadini, Siega-Riz, & Popkin, 2000; Neumark-Sztainer et al., 2002; Nicklas et al., 2001). Moreover, US food consumption data show a shift over the past few decades. Children and adolescents are eating more food away from home, drinking more soft-drinks, and snacking more frequently (Gleason & Suitor, 2001a; Jahns, Siega-Riz, & Popkin, 2001). In combination, American children now obtain over 50 percent of their calories from fat (32 percent) or added sugar (20 percent) (Gleason & Suitor, 2001b). But does this shift have anything to do with the heavy marketing of such foods to children?

There exist a fair number of studies examining the impact of advertising on children's food preferences, requests to parents for food products, and parental purchase of such products (Borzekowski & Robinson, 2001; Isler, Popper, & Ward, 1987; McNeal, 1998; Taras et al., 2000; Taras & Gage, 1995; Taras et al., 1989). Coon and Tucker (2002) recently reviewed this literature and came to the following conclusions: (1) evidence from experimental studies consistently shows that exposure to advertised food products increases children's choice of and preference for such products; (2) exposure to televised food advertising increases children's requests to parents for the purchase of advertised items; (3) purchase requests for specific brands or categories of food products reflect product advertising frequencies. Thus, there is a plethora of evidence that, from the perspective of marketers at least, food advertising works and it works well.

However, because our concern here is the mechanism by which television may lead to childhood obesity, the critical question is whether televised food advertising actually increases children's *consumption* of advertised foods. The answer to this question is somewhat harder to come by. Only a few studies have been conducted on the effects of food advertising on actual food intake, in part due to inherent difficulties in controlling children's exposure to advertising or foods outside experimental settings (Coon & Tucker, 2002).

Gorn and Goldberg (1982) conducted the now classic study examining the effect of exposure to televised snack food commercials on children's actual food consumption. Children ages 5–8 years old attending a summer camp viewed a 30-minute cartoon with roughly 5 minutes of embedded food advertising daily for 2 weeks. The kinds of advertising were varied to create four experimental conditions: (1) candy and Kool-Aid advertisements; (2) fruit and fruit juice advertisements; (3) public service advertisements for healthy foods; and (4) no advertisements (control). Each day after the television exposure, the children were offered a selection of fruits, juices, candy, or Kool-Aid to choose from for their snack. Children in the candy/Kool-Aid advertisements condition chose candy as their snack more than children in the fruit advertisements conditions did, and also chose fruit and juice less than children in any other condition did.

Hitchings and Moynihan (1998) found that 9–11 year old children's recall of food advertisements was related to consumption of the advertised food as assessed by three-day food diaries. The researchers report correlations between children's knowledge of specific food advertisements and food consumption on the order of between .50 and .60. A more recent study (Halford et al., 2004) of recognition of food advertising and consumption of specific foods in response to advertising found that overweight and obese children recognized more advertisements and ate more of the food advertised following experimental exposures to food advertising compared to normal weight children. However, all children in this study, regardless of weight, ate more of the advertised food following exposure to televised advertising compared to controls.

Thus, in contrast to the evidence linking media use with either physical activity or childhood weight status, evidence does suggest that media-based marketing of high fat and sugared foods is one probable mechanism linking electronic media with childhood obesity. Yet, important gaps in this literature remain. There is a dearth of studies examining the impact of advertising other than televised advertising, and many that exist were conducted in the late 1970s and early 1980s, when marketing approaches and children's media use were different than today (IOM, 2006). Thus, new studies examining both the impact of televised food advertising as well as product placement and advergaming are sorely needed.

To date, no meta-analysis examining the size of the relationship between food advertising and children's food preferences, food choices, food intake, or purchase requests has been undertaken, and prospective longitudinal studies are similarly absent (see however, IOM, 2006, for the most comprehensive and recent review available at this time). Finally, there is a particular need for research focusing on questions of the relationship between advertising and caloric intake, as well as questions pertaining to the marketing and exposure of ethnic minority children to food advertising.

Despite these limitations, however, the evidence as a whole implicates food advertising as a main mechanism linking television viewing with childhood obesity. There is little doubt that the diets of American children and adolescents do not meet national dietary goals (Cavadini, Siega-Riz, & Popkin, 2000; Neumark-Sztainer et al., 2002; Nicklas et al., 2001). The question at hand is whether this is due in large part to food marketing. A recent World Health Organization/Food and Agriculture Organization (WHO/FAO) report concluded that sufficient (albeit indirect) evidence exists that advertising of fast-food restaurants and high caloric, nutrient-poor food and beverages to children promotes obesity and suggests advertising as a "probable" causal factor in youth obesity (World Health Organization, 2003). The even more recently released Institute of Medicine (IOM) report, *Food Marketing to Children and Youth: Threat or Opportunity?*, came to a similar conclusion: Although evidence linking food advertising to childhood obesity is insufficient to support a call for a ban on all such advertising, enough evidence exists to support recommending approaches similar to those used to control cigarette and alcohol advertising to children (IOM, 2006). Despite the conclusions of both the WHO and the IOM, it is important to note that the data connecting marketing to adiposity remains correlational. The IOM (2006) notes that though the data are consistent with the interpretation that marketing to children is at least partly causing weight problems, it is not possible to rule out every alternative explanation at this time. Even so, they argue that even a small causal relation translates into a very large health problem (IOM, 2006).

Promoting healthy food choices: the potential of public service announcements

Overall, then, the existing literature indicates that children are susceptible to advertising, and that their food preferences, food choices, and food intake are shaped by their exposure to food advertising. In some sense, this should be no surprise since it is tantamount to saying that children learn the things they are taught. If this is so, then we should be able to shape children's food behaviors in more desirable ways through advertising of healthy foods and food behaviors.

Various studies have demonstrated that children who were shown advertisements for healthy products or pro-nutritional public service announcements chose more fruit and juice than those seeing advertisements for sugared products (Gorn & Goldberg, 1982), ate fewer sugared foods in a post-viewing test (Galst & White, 1976), and scored higher on nutritional knowledge tests (Sylvester, Achterberg, & Williams, 1995). Recently, *Sesame Workshop* has been exploring the issue of whether the appeal of well-known *Sesame Street* characters would increase children's preferences for fruits and vegetables. They found that placing a favorite Muppet character sticker on foods increased children's preferences for those foods, and that placing a character sticker on a healthier food (broccoli) could increase children's preference for that food over a less healthy choice (a chocolate bar). Though the children were choosing pictures of the foods rather than the foods themselves, these findings suggest that the simple placement of stickers depicting popular and well-known characters on healthier foods could play an important role in increasing the appeal of healthy foods (Cohen & Kotler, 2005). Given evidence that it is easier to reinforce children's preferences for sweet and/or high-fat foods than for healthier foods (Birch, 1992, 1999), these findings are promising.

Linking media use and children's weight status

Regardless of the specific mechanism involved, confirmation of any or all of the hypotheses above would require a positive relationship between television and/or videogame use and increased weight or obesity in youth. However, this link appears to be somewhat elusive. Dietz and Gortmaker (1985) found a small but significant relationship between television viewing and obesity. They reported that the prevalence of obesity in a large epidemiological sample of adolescents aged 12–17 increased 2 percent for each additional hour of television watched per week. They did not examine videogame use. It is this study that is widely cited as evidence that television, and by extension, videogame use, causes obesity in children and adolescents.

Yet results of ensuing epidemiologic studies have been mixed. Robinson and Killen (1995) found that while television viewing was associated with increased dietary intake in a large ($N = 1,912$) sample of ninth graders, it was only weakly associated with BMI, and the relation held true only among white boys. Robinson and colleagues (1993) found that baseline hours of television view-ing were not associated with either baseline or longitudinal change in BMI in a large ($N = 971$) sample of sixth- and seventh-grade girls. Durant and colleagues (1994) also found no relationship between BMI and television watching in a longitudinal sample of young children (ages 3–4). McMurray and colleagues (2000) found that there was no relationship between television or videogame use and BMI in a sample of 2,389 adolescents ages 10–17 once the influence of socio-economic status (SES) and ethnicity were controlled. Similarly, Wake, Hesketh and Waters (2003) found no relationship between BMI and videogame use in a sample of children ages 5–13, and no relationship between BMI and television viewing when SES was controlled.

Yet other researchers continue to find small but significant associations between electronic media use and BMI. Jago and colleagues (2005) found positive rela-tionships between BMI and television viewing among 3–6-year-olds. Davison, Marshall, and Birch (2006), found significant associations between television view-ing and BMI, but only for girls ages 7–10. Vandewater, Shim, and Caplovitz (2004) found that videogame use (but not television viewing) was related to elevated weight status – but only for girls ages 9–12 who played moderate amounts of games.

Experimental intervention studies, while promising, have yet to yield consistent findings. Epstein and his colleagues, based on a family intervention aimed at increasing physical activity and reducing sedentary behavior (specifically television viewing), have shown long-term success in obesity remission for children and adolescents (Epstein et al., 1994; Epstein et al., 2004). However, they have also noted differences in responses to treatment by gender, with boys responding to treatment but girls showing no treatment effects (Epstein, Paluch & Raynor, 2001). Gortmaker and his colleagues designed "Planet Health", a school-based intervention designed to reduce obesity in middle-school youth (grades 6–8) by altering key physical activity and dietary risk factors, including reductions in television viewing. They found reductions in the prevalence of obesity were related to reduced television viewing for girls, but not for boys, in the intervention group (Gort-maker et al., 1999). Robinson (1999) found that compared to a control group, elementary-school children who received a classroom curriculum designed to reduce television use over one school year showed significant relative decreases in BMI and eating meals in front of the television, but no differences in high-fat food intake or moderate-to-vigorous physical activity. Despite the promise of these inter-vention studies, it remains unclear why some interventions seem to work for some groups of children but not others.

Implications for research

In sum, the data available to date do not support the simple notion that turning off the television or unplugging the videogame console amounts to a "magic bullet" that will reduce the prevalence of childhood obesity. Overall, this "mixed bag" of findings seems to suggest that *some* relationship between children's media use and weight status exists – the problem is we cannot tell exactly what that relationship is or for whom it is strongest.

Overall, the relationship between electronic media use and childhood obesity, though perhaps not as strong as has been assumed, is evident in enough studies to warrant concern. The difficulty has been uncovering the *reason* for this relationship. Thus far, there is no evidence that television use is related to metabolic rate, little to no evidence that electronic media use is related to children's activity levels, and good evidence that food advertising is related to children's food preferences and nutritional knowledge. However, there are serious limitations to existing research. These are discussed below.

Limitations of Existing Research

So what are we to make of the equivocal findings linking childhood obesity and media use to date? We believe that the inconsistent results of research thus far are the result of at least four factors: (1) general reliance on poor measures of children's media use; (2) a dearth of examinations of key moderating influences; (3) a lack of longitudinal data crucial for understanding growth and change over time; and (4) little examination of electronic media use other than television (e.g., videogames, computers). These are discussed in turn below.

Reliance on poor measures of media use

This shortcoming, as far as we can tell, is characteristic of virtually every existing study (including randomized controlled trials, see, e.g., Robinson, 1999) examining the links between media use and obesity. Existing studies rely almost exclusively on global estimates of use by parents or children in which they are asked to estimate how much media they use on a typical day, an average day, or an average week.

Unfortunately, evidence suggests that this is one of the least valid methods available for assessing media use. In the sole existing experiment assessing the validity of various estimates of media use, Anderson and colleagues (1985) compared both global estimates and time diary estimates to videotaped documentation of the actual time children spent *watching* television (not simply the time the television was turned on). They found that parental time diary estimates were highly correlated (mean $r = .85$) with observed estimates, and that the two procedures differed only slightly in the total amount of viewing estimated (with diaries estimating a little less than an hour more of weekly viewing than taped observations). However, global estimates were only moderately correlated with observed estimates (mean $r = .54$), and global estimates overestimated the total amount of time spent viewing by as much as 8 hours (6 hours, on average). These findings suggest that relying on global estimates of media use is extremely problematic and a source of considerable error (see also Vandewater & Lee, in press). In fact, it has been argued that measurement issues are the single most important reason for the lack of evidence linking television viewing and obesity to date (Jago et al., 2005).

Failure to examine moderating factors affecting the nature of the relationship between media use and childhood obesity

It seems likely that the connections between electronic media use and childhood obesity may hold only for certain groups (for example, post-menarchal girls, or children at risk for obesity), thus diluting the linear relationships in more heterogeneous samples. Studies finding relationships between electronic media and BMI only among children of a certain age and gender certainly seem to suggest that moderating factors may be at work (e.g., Davison, Marshall, & Birch, 2006; Gortmaker et al., 1999; Vandewater, Shim, & Caplovitz, 2004). In our research, we examined the moderating effect of familial risk of obesity on the relationship between television viewing and weight status. We found that among girls ages 10–13 with familial risk of obesity, the risk of being overweight and obese increased dramatically for every additional hour of television viewed. For girls this age with no risk of familial obesity, television viewing and BMI were virtually unrelated (Vandewater & Huang, 2006). Such findings suggest that moderating factors may be an important key to developing a deeper understanding of the relationship between electronic media use and childhood obesity. Yet, despite this evidence, moderators of the relationship between media use and childhood obesity have rarely been examined.

Lack of longitudinal data

Research thus far has overwhelmingly relied on cross-sectional rather than longitudinal data, making it difficult to identify developmental patterns and to distinguish normative from non-normative change. Although it is certainly plausible that media use is related to childhood obesity because it encourages inactivity, increased food consumption, or both, it is equally plausible that obesity may lead to more sedentary activity, including increased media use. For example, because overweight children are more socially isolated (Strauss & Pollack, 2003), they may watch more television. Though the majority of existing findings depend on cross-sectional data (IOM, 2006), hypotheses such as these can only be examined with prospective longitudinal data.

Little examination of videogame and computer use and current media environments

The spectrum of available electronic interactive media is expanding and changing rapidly. Videogame platforms have exploded and there is a proliferation of hand-held videogames for very young children. CD-Rom computer programs for children now range from interactive reading and storytelling to elaborate and extended games of adventure and strategy that can be played at many levels. There is also a proliferation of websites aimed at children and youth. It is imperative that researchers examine the impact of these newer forms of media on childhood obesity.

Summary and Conclusions

It may be that electronic media use is implicated in the childhood obesity epidemic in this country. If this is true, then it behooves public health scholars to understand the ways (and for whom) it is implicated – as well as the ways (and for whom) it is not. In this paper, we have reviewed evidence for the possible major mechanisms linking electronic media and childhood obesity. Given the depth of both popular and scholarly conviction that television, videogame, and Internet use is implicated in the increased prevalence of childhood obesity, the supporting evidence is surprisingly equivocal. There are many possible explanations for this outcome. Moderating factors may be at work, which would mean that these relationships are strong for some children and nonexistent for others. Inexact measurement of media use, caloric intake, activity level, or all three, may be hampering our ability to detect relationships. Perhaps the relationships unfold over longer periods of time (years rather than months), which would require longitudinal data. Or perhaps electronic media use (television viewing, videogame play, Internet use, etc.) is simply a marker of other factors – such as the social isolation of obese adolescents, or poor parenting in general (including providing nutritionally poor – but easy to provide – food for children).

Whatever the case, it behooves us to understand the true nature of the role that media use plays in the development of obesity. As a very real threat to public health, it is crucial to identify central contributing factors to the development of obesity, so that we may appropriately target prevention and intervention efforts. It seems safe to say that technology is here to stay, and is virtually guaranteed to play an ever increasing role in young people's daily lives. Thus, a thorough understanding of the nature of its impact on health and well-being is a vital component of the public health agenda in the United States.

Corresponding Author Address: Population Research Center, University of Texas at Austin, 1 University Station, G1800, Austin, TX 78712-1097 Tel 512-475-6886 evandewater@ mail.utexas.edu. Funding for this research was provided by grant R01-HD40851-01 from the National Institute of Child Health and Human Development, and population center grant 5-R24-HD42849 from the National Institute of Child Health and Human Development. Funding was also provided by the Children's Digital Media Center at the University of Texas at Austin (funded by grant BCS-0126127 from the National Science Foundation). The Panel Study of Income Dynamics Child Development Supplement (CDS) is funded by grants R01-HD33474 and R01-HD044027 from the National Institute of Child Health and Human Development.

References

American Academy of Pediatrics (AAP). (2003). Prevention of pediatric overweight and obesity. *Pediatrics*, 112, 424–30.

Anderson, D. R., Field, D. E., Collins, P. A., Lorch, E. P., & Nathan, J. G. (1985). Estimates of young children's time with television: A methodological comparison of parent reports with time-lapse video home observation. *Child Development*, 56, 1345–57.

Anderson, P. M., & Butcher, K. F. (2006). Childhood obesity: Trends and potential causes. *The Future of Children*, 16, 19–45.

Atkin, C., & Block, M. (1983). Effectiveness of celebrity endorsers. *Journal of Advertising Research*, 23, 57–61.

Bar-Or, O., Foreyt, J., Bouchard, C., Brownell, K. D., Dietz, W. H., Ravussin, E., et al. (1998). Physical activity, genetic and nutritional considerations in childhood weight management. *Medicine and Science in Sports and Exercise*, 30, 2–10.

Barcus, F. E. (1980). The nature of television advertising to children. In E. Palmer & A. Dorr (Eds.), *Children and the faces of television* (pp. 273–85). New York: Academic Press.

Biddle, S. J., Gorely, T., Marshall, S. J., Murdey, I., & Cameron, N. (2004). Physical activity and sedentary behaviors in youth: Issues and controversies. *Journal of the Royal Society of Health*, 124, 29–33.

Birch, L. L. (1992). Children's preferences for high-fat foods. *Nutrition Review*, 50, 249–55.

Birch, L. L. (1999). Development of food preferences. *Annual Review of Nutrition*, 1999, 41–62.

Bloomgarden, Z. T. (2004). Type 2 diabetes in the young: The evolving epidemic. *Diabetes Care*, 27, 998–1010.

Blosser, B. J., & Roberts, D. F. (1985). Age differences in children's perceptions of message intent. Responses to TV news, commercials, educational sports, and public service announcements. *Communication Research*, 12, 455–84.

Borzekowski, D. L. G., & Robinson, T. N. (2001). The 30 second effect: An experiment revealing the impact of television commercials on food preferences of preschoolers. *Journal of The American Dietetic Association*, 101(1), 42–6.

Brown, J. R., Cramond, J. K., & Wilde, R. J. (1974). Displacement effects of television and the child's functional orientation to media. In J. Blumler & E. Katz (Eds.), *The uses of mass communications: Current perspectives on gratifications research* (pp. 93–112). Beverly Hills, CA: Sage.

Buchowski, M. S., & Sun, M. (1996). Energy expenditure, television viewing and obesity. *International Journal of Obesity and Related Metabolic Disorders*, 20, 236–44.

Bulik, B. S. (2004). Arcade craze swings into living room. *Advertising Age*, 75, 3–52.

Byrd-Bredbenner, C. (2002). Saturday morning children's television advertising: A longitudinal content analysis. *Family and Consumer Science Research*, 30, 382–403.

Calvert, S. (2003). Future faces of selling to children. In E. L. Palmer & B. M. Young (Eds.), *The faces of televisual media* (pp. 347–57). Mahwah, NJ: Lawrence Earlbaum.

Cantor, J. (1981). Modifying children's eating habits through television ads: Effects of humorous appeals in a field setting. *Journal of Broadcasting*, 25, 37–47.

Carter, O. (2005). Changes in obesity, sedentary behaviours, and Perth children's television viewing from 1960 to 2003. *Australian and New Zealand Journal of Public Health*, 29, 235.

Cavadini, C., Siega-Riz, A. M., & Popkin, B. M. (2000). US adolescent food intake trends from 1965 to 1996. *The Western Journal of Medicine*, 173, 378–83.

Chen, J. L., & Kennedy, C. M. (2001). Television viewing and children's health. *Journal of Science and Pediatric Nursing*, 6, 35–8.

Cohen, D. I., & Kotler, J. A. (2005). *Preschoolers' perceptions of healthy food*. Paper presented at the biennial meeting of the Society for Research in Child Development, Atlanta, GA.

Comstock, G., Chaffee, S., Katzman, N., Maxwell, M., & Roberts, D. (1978). *Television and Human Behavior*. New York: Rand Corporation.

Coon, K. A., Goldberg, J., Rogers, B. L., & Tucker, K. (2001). Relationships between use of television during meals and children's food consumption patterns [Electronic Version]. *Pediatrics*, 107, e1.

Coon, K. A., & Tucker, K. (2002). Television and children's consumption patterns: A review of the literature. *Minerva Pediatrica*, 54, 423–36.

Davison, K. K., Marshall, S. J., & Birch, L. L. (2006). Cross-sectional and longitudinal associations between TV viewing and girls' body mass index, overweight status, and percentage of body fat. *Journal of Pediatrics*, 149, 32–7.

Dietz, W. H. (2001). The obesity epidemic in young children: Reduce television viewing and promote playing. *British Medical Journal*, 322, 313–14.

Dietz, W. H., Bandini, L. G., Morelli, J. A., Peers, K. F., & Ching, P. (1994). Effect of sedentary activities on resting metabolic rate. *Pediatrics*, 59, 556–9.

Dietz, W. H., & Gortmaker, S. L. (1985). Do we fatten our children at the television set? Obesity and television viewing in children and adolescents. *Pediatrics*, 75, 807–12.

Durant, R. H., Baranowski, T., Johnson, M., & Thompson, W. O. (1994). The relationship among television watching, physical activity, and body composition of young children. *Pediatrics*, 94(4), 449–55.

Epstein, L. H., Paluch, R. A., Kilanowski, C. K., & Raynor, H. A. (2004). The effects of reinforcement or stimulus control to reduce sedentary behavior in the treatment of pediatric obesity. *Health Psychology*, 23(4), 371–80.

Epstein, L. H., Paluch, R. A., & Raynor, H. A. (2001). Sex differences in obese children and siblings in family-based obesity treatment. *Obesity Research*, 9, 746–53.

Epstein, L. H., Valoski, A., Wing, R. R., & McCurley, J. (1994). Ten-year outcomes of behavioral family based treatment for childhood obesity. *Health Psychology*, 13(5), 373–83.

Flegal, K. M., Carrol, M. D., Ogden, C. L., & Johnson, C. L. (2002). Prevalence and trends in obesity among US adults, 1999–2000. *Journal of the American Medical Association*, 288, 1723–7.

Freedman, D. S., Dietz, W. H., Srinivasan, S. R., & Berenson, G. S. (1999). The relation of overweight to cardiovascular risk factors among children and adolescents: The Bogalusa heart study. *Pediatrics*, 103, 1175–82.

Gallo, A. E. (1999). *Food advertising in the United States. America's eating habits: Changes and consequences* (No. 811). Washington, DC: US Department of Agriculture Economic Research Service.

Galst, J., & White, M. (1976). The unhealthy persuader: The reinforcing value of television and children's purchase influence attempts at the supermarket. *Child Development*, 47, 1089–96.

Gamble, M., & Cotunga, N. (1999). A quarter century of TV food advertising targeted at children. *American Journal of Health Behavior*, 23, 261–7.

Gleason, P., & Suitor, C. (2001a). *Children's diets in the mid 1990s: Dietary intake and its relationship with school meal preparation* (No. CN-01-CD1). Alexandria, MD: US Department of Agriculture, Food, and Nutrition Service.

Gleason, P., & Suitor, C. (2001b). *Food for thought: Children's diets in the 1990s.* Princeton, NJ: Mathematica Policy Research Inc.

Gorn, G. J., & Goldberg, M. E. (1982). Behavioral evidence for the effects of televised food messages to children. *Journal of Consumer Research, 9,* 200–205.

Gortmaker, S. L., Must, A., Perrin, J. M., Sobol, A. M., & Dietz, W. H. (1993). Social and economic consequences of overweight in adolescence and young adulthood. *The New England Journal of Medicine, 329*(14), 1008–12.

Gortmaker, S. L., Peterson, K., Wiecha, J., Sobol, A. M., Dixit, S., Fox, M. K., et al. (1999). Reducing obesity via a school-based interdisciplinary intervention among youth: Planet Health. *Archives of Pediatric and Adolescent Medicine, 153,* 409–18.

Halford, J. C. G., Gillespie, J., Brown, V., Pontin, E. E., & Dowling, H. (2004). Effect of television advertisements for foods on food consumption in children. *Appetite, 42,* 221–5.

Harris, J. M., Kaufman, P., Martinez, S., & Price, C. (2002). *The US food marketing system, 2002* (No. 811). Washington, DC: US Department of Agriculture Economic Research Service.

Harrison, K., & Marske, A. L. (2005). Nutritional content of foods advertised during the television programs children watch most. *American Journal of Public Health, 95,* 1568–74.

Hauner, H. (2004). Transfer into adulthood. In W. Kiess, C. Marcus, & M. Wabitsch (Eds.), *Obesity in childhood and adolescence,* vol. 9 (pp. 219–28). Basel, Switzerland: Karger.

Hitchings, E., & Moynihan, P. J. (1998). The relationship between television food advertisements recalled and actual foods consumed by children. *Journal of Human Nutrition and Dietetics, 11,* 511–17.

Hite, C. F., & Hite, R. E. (1994). Reliance on brand by young children. *Journal of the Market Research Society, 37*(2), 185–93.

Ho, S. M. Y., & Lee, T. M. C. (2001). Computer usage and its relationship with adolescent lifestyle in Hong Kong. *Journal of Adolescent Health, 29,* 258–66.

Huston, A. C., & Wright, J. A. (1989). Television forms and children. In G. Comstock (Ed.), *Public communication and behavior,* vol. 2 (pp. 103–59). New York: Academic Press.

Huston, A. C., & Wright, J. C. (1997). Mass media and children's development. In I. E. Sigel & K. A. Renninger (Eds.), *Handbook of child psychology,* vol. 5 (pp. 999–1058). New York: Wiley.

Huston, A. C., Wright, J. C., Marquis, J., & Green, S. B. (1999). How young children spend their time: Television and other activities. *Developmental Psychology, 35,* 912.

Institute of Medicine (IOM). (2006). *Food marketing to children and youth: Threat or opportunity?* Washington, DC: National Academies Press.

Isler, L., Popper, H. T., & Ward, S. (1987). Children's purchase requests and parental responses: Results from a diary study. *Journal of Advertising Research, 27,* 28–39.

Jago, R., Baranowski, T., Baranowski, J. C., Thompson, D., & Greaves, K. A. (2005). BMI for 3–6 years of age is predicted by TV viewing and physical activity, not diet. *International Journal of Obesity, 29,* 557–65.

Jahns, L., Siega-Riz, A. M., & Popkin, B. M. (2001). The increasing prevalence of snacking among US children from 1977 to 1996. *Journal of Pediatrics*, 138, 493–8.

Janz, K. F., Dawson, J. D., & Mahoney, L. T. (2000). Tracking physical fitness and physical activity from childhood to adolescence: The Muscatine study. *Medicine and Science in Sports and Exercise*, 32, 1250–57.

John, D. R. (1999). Consumer socialization of children: A retrospective look at twenty-five years of research. *Journal of Consumer Research*, 26, 183–213.

Juster, F. T., & Stafford, F. P. (Eds.). (1985). *Time, goods, and well-being*. Ann Arbor: University of Michigan, Institute for Social Research.

Juster, F. T., & Stafford, F. P. (1991). The allocation of time: Empirical findings, behavioral models, and problems of measurements. *Journal of Economic Literature*, 29, 471–522.

Katzmarzyk, P. T., Malina, R. M., Song, T. M. K., & Bouchard, C. (1998). Television viewing, physical activity, and health related fitness of youth in the Quebec Family Study. *Journal of Adolescent Health*, 23, 318–25.

Klesges, R. C., Shelton, M. L., & Klesges, L. M. (1993). Effects of television on metabolic rate: Potential implications for childhood obesity. *Pediatrics*, 91(2), 281–6.

Kotz, K., & Story, M. (1994). Food advertisements during children's Saturday morning television programming: Are they consistent with dietary recommendations? *Journal of The American Dietetic Association*, 94(11), 1296–301.

Kretchmer, S. B. (2004). Advertainment: The evolution of product placement as a mass media marketing strategy. *Journal of Promotion Management*, 10, 37–54.

Kuczmarski, R. J., Ogden, C. L., Guo, S. S., Grummer-Strawn, L. M., Flegal, K. M., Mei, Z., et al. (2002). 2000 CDC growth charts for the United States: Methods and development. *Vital and Health Statistics*, 246, 1–190.

Kunkel, D. (1988). Children and host-selling television commercials. *Communication Research*, 15, 71–92.

Kunkel, D. (2001). Children and television advertising. In D. G. Singer & J. L. Singer (Eds.), *The handbook of children and the media* (pp. 375–94). Thousand Oaks, CA: Sage.

Kunkel, D., & Gantz, W. (1992). Children's television advertising in the multi-channel environment. *Journal of Communication*, 42(3), 134–52.

Kunkel, D., & Gantz, W. (1993). Assessing compliance with industry self-regulation of television advertising to children. *Journal of Applied Communication Research*, 21, 148–62.

Kunkel, D., Wilcox, B. L., Cantor, J., Palmer, E., Linn, S., & Dowrick, P. (2004). *Report of the APA task force on advertising and children*. Washington, DC: American Psychological Association.

Kuribayashi, A., Roberts, M. C., & Johnson, R. J. (2001). Actual nutritional information of products advertised to children and adults on Saturday. *Children's Health Care*, 30, 309–22.

Lauro, P. W. (1999). Coaxing the smile that sells: Baby wranglers in demand in marketing for children. *The New York Times*, November 1, p. C1.

Lieber, L. (1998). *Commercial and character slogan recall by children aged 9 to 11 years: Budweiser frogs versus Bugs Bunny*. Berkeley, CA: Center on Alcohol Advertising.

Linn, S. (2005). Food marketing to children in the context of a marketing maelstrom. *Journal of Public Health Policy*, 25, 24–35.

Lobstein, T., Baur, L., Uauy, R. (2005). Obesity in children and young people: A crisis in public health. Report to the World Health Organization by the International Obesity Task Force. *Obesity Reviews*, 5 (Supplement 1), 5–104.

Lyle, J., & Hoffman, H. R. (1972). Children's use of television and other media. In E. A. Rubinstein, G. A. Comstock, & J. P. Murray (Eds.), *Television and social behavior*. Vol. 4, *Television in day-to-day life: Patterns of use*. Washington, DC: US Government Printing Office.

Marshall, S. J., Biddle, S. J. H., Gorley, T., Cameron, N., & Murdey, I. (2004). Relationships between media use, body fatness and physical activity in children and youth: A meta-analysis. *International Journal of Obesity*, 28, 1238–46.

Matheson, D. M., Dillen, J. D., Wang, Y., Varady, A., & Robinson, T. N. (2004). Children's food consumption during television viewing. *American Society for Clinical Nutrition*, 79, 1088–94.

McCall, K. L. (2003). What's the big dif?: Differences between marketing and advertising. Retrieved October 3, 2005, from http://www.marketingprofs.com/preview.asp?file=/2/mccall5.asp.

McMurray, R. G., Harrel, J. S., Deng, S., Bradley, C. B., Cox, L. M., & Bangdiwala, S. I. (2000). The influence of physical activity, socioeconomic status, and ethnicity on the weight status of adolescents. *Obesity Research*, 8, 130–39.

McNeal, J. (1998). Tapping the three kids' markets. *American Demographics*, 20(4), 37–41.

Must, A. (1996). Morbidity and mortality associated with elevated body weight in children and adolescents. *American Journal for Clinical Nutrition*, 63(Supplement 3), 445S–447S.

Must, A., Jacques, P. F., Dallal, G. E., Bajema, C. J., & Dietz, W. H. (1992). Long-term morbidity and mortality of overweight adolescents: A follow-up of the Harvard growth study 1922 to 1935. *The New England Journal of Medicine*, 327, 1350.

Must, A., Spadano, J., Coakley, E. H., Field, A. E., Colditz, G., & Dietz, W. H. (1999). The disease burden associated with overweight and obesity. *Journal of the American Medical Association*, 282, 1523–9.

Mutz, D. C., Roberts, D. F., & van Vuuren, D. P. (1993). Reconsidering the displacement hypothesis: Television's influence on children's time use. *Communication Research*, 20, 51–75.

National Center for Health Statistics. (2004). *Chartbook on trends in the health of Americans*. Retrieved from http://www.cdc.gov/nchs/hus.htm.

Neumark-Sztainer, D., Story, M., Hannan, P. J., & Croll, J. (2002). Overweight status and eating patterns among adolescents: Where do youths stand in comparison with the healthy people 2010 objectives? *American Journal of Public Health*, 92, 844–51.

Nicklas, T. A., Elkasabany, A., Srinivasan, S. R., & Berenson, G. (2001). Trends in nutrient intake of 10-year-old children over two decades (1973–1994): The Bogalusa Heart Study. *American Journal of Epidemiology*, 153, 969–77.

Nielsen Media Research. (1976). *National audience demographics report*. New York: Nielsen Media Research.

Ogden, C. L., Carroll, M. D., Curtin, L. R., McDowell, M. A., Tabak, C. J., & Flegal, K. M. (2006). Prevalence of overweight and obesity in the United States, 1999–2004. *Journal of the American Medical Association*, 295, 1549–55.

Ogden, C. L., Troiano, R. P., Briefel, R. R., Kuczmarski, R. J., Flegal, K. M., & Johnson, C. L. (1997). Prevalence of overweight among preschool children in the United States, 1971 through 1994. *Pediatrics*, 99, 1–7.

Palmer, E., & McDowell, C. (1981). Children's understanding of nutritional information presented in breakfast cereal commercials. *Journal of Broadcasting*, 25, 295–301.

Rice, F. (2001). Superstars of spending: Marketers clamor for kids. *Advertising Age*, February 12, p. S1.

Rideout, V. J., Foehr, U. G., Roberts, D. F., & Brodie, M. (1999). *Kids and media @ the new millennium*. Menlo Park, CA: Kaiser Family Foundation.

Rideout, V. J., & Hamel, E. (2006). *The media family: Electronic media in the lives of infants, toddlers, preschoolers and their parents*. Menlo Park, CA: Kaiser Family Foundation.

Rideout, V. J., Vandewater, E. A., & Wartella, E. A. (2003). *Zero to six: Media use in the lives of infants, toddlers, and preschoolers*. Menlo Park, CA: Kaiser Family Foundation.

Roberts, D. F., Foehr, U. G., & Rideout, V. J. (2005). *Generation M: Media in the lives of 8–18-year-olds*. Menlo Park, CA: Kaiser Family Foundation.

Robinson, J. P. (1977). *How Americans use time: A social-psychological analysis of everyday behavior*. New York: Praeger.

Robinson, T. N. (1999). Reducing children's television viewing to prevent obesity: A randomized controlled trial. *Journal of the American Medical Association*, 282, 1561–7.

Robinson, T. N. (2001). Television viewing and childhood obesity. *Childhood and adolescent obesity*, 48(4), 1017–25.

Robinson, T. N., Hammer, L. D., Wilson, D. M., Killen, J. D., Kraemer, H. C., Hayward, C., & Barr Taylor, C. (1993). Does television viewing increase obesity and reduce physical activity? Cross-sectional and longitudinal analyses among adolescent girls. *Pediatrics*, 91(2), 273–80.

Robinson, T. N., & Killen, J. D. (1995). Ethnic and gender differences in the relationships between television viewing and obesity, physical activity, and dietary fat intake. *Journal of Health Education*, 26, S91–S98.

Story, M., & French, S. (2004). Food advertising and marketing directed at children and adolescents in the US. *International Journal of Behavioral Nutrition and Physical Activity*, 1. Retrieved from http://www.ijbnapa.org/content/1/1/3.

Story, M., Neumark-Sztainer, D., & French, S. (2002). Individual and environmental influences on adolescent eating behaviors. *Journal of The American Dietetic Association*, 102, S40–S51.

Strauss, R. S., & Pollack, H. A. (2003). Social marginalization of overweight children. *Archives of Pediatrics and Adolescent Medicine*, 157, 746–52.

Sylvester, G. P., Achterberg, C., & Williams, J. (1995). Children's television and nutrition: Friends or foes? *Nutrition Today*, 30, 6–14.

Taras, H., Zive, M., Nader, P., Berry, C. C., Hoy, T., & Boyd, C. (2000). Television advertising and classes of food products consumed in a pediatric population. *International Journal of Advertising*, 19, 487–93.

Taras, H. L., & Gage, M. (1995). Advertised foods on children's television. *Archives of Pediatric and Adolescent Medicine*, 149, 649–52.

Taras, H. L., Sallis, J. F., Patterson, T. L., Nader, P. R., & Nelson, J. A. (1989). Television's influence on children's diet and physical inactivity. *Journal of Development and Behavioral Pediatrics*, 10, 176–80.

Timmer, S. G., Eccles, J., & O'Brien, K. (1985). How children use time. In F. T. Juster & F. P. Stafford (Eds.), *Time, goods, and well being* (pp. 353–69). Ann Arbor: The University of Michigan, Institute for Social Research.

Troiano, R. P., & Flegal, K. M. (1998). Overweight children and adolescents: Description, epidemiology, and demographics. *Pediatrics*, 101, 497–504.

Vandewater, E. A., Bickham, D. S., & Lee, J. H. (2006). Time well spent? Relating media use to children's free-time activities. *Pediatrics*, 117, e181–e185.

Vandewater, E. A., & Huang, X. (2006). Parental weight status as a moderator of the relationship between television viewing and childhood overweight. *Archives of Pediatric and Adolescent Medicine*, 160, 425–31.

Vandewater, E. A., & Lee, S. J. (in press). Measuring children's media use in the digital age: Issues and challenges. *American Behavioral Scientist*.

Vandewater, E. A., Shim, M., & Caplovitz, A. G. (2004). Linking obesity and activity level with children's television and video game use. *Journal of Adolescence*, 27, 71–85.

Vilhjalmsson, R., & Thorlindsson, T. (1998). Factors related to physical activity: A study of adolescents. *Social Science Medical*, 47(5), 665–75.

Wake, M., Hesketh, K., & Waters, E. (2003). Television, computer use, and body mass index in Australian primary school children. *Journal of Pediatrics and Child Health*, 39, 130–34.

Wang, X., & Perry, A. C. (2006). Metabolic and physiologic responses to video game play in 7- to 10-year-old boys. *Archives of Pediatric and Adolescent Medicine*, 160, 411–15.

Ward, S., Wackman, D., & Wartella, E. (1977). *How children learn to buy: The development of consumer information processing skills*. Beverly Hills, CA: Sage.

Webster, N. C., & Bulik, B. S. (2004). Now down to business: Counting gamer thumbs. *Advertising Age*, 75, S6–S7.

Williams, T. M. (Ed.). (1986). *The impact of television: A natural experiment in three communities*. Orlando, FL: Academic Press.

Wolf, A., & Colditz, G. A. (1998). Current estimates of the economic cost of obesity in the United States. *Obesity Research*, 6, 97–106.

World Health Organization. (2003). *Joint WHO/FAO expert consultation on diet, nutrition and the prevention of chronic disease*. Geneva, Switzerland: World Health Organization.

Wright, J. C., Huston, A. C., Vandewater, E. A., Bickham, D. S., Scantlin, R. M., Kotler, J. A., et al. (2001). American children's use of electronic media in 1997: A national survey. *Journal of Applied Developmental Psychology*, 22, 31–47.

Zakarian, J. M., Melbourne, F. H., Hofstetter, C. R., Sallis, J. F., & Keating, K. J. (1994). Correlates of vigorous exercise in a predominantly low SES minority school population. *Preventative Medicine*, 23, 314–21.

Zollo, P. (1999). *Wise up to teens: Insight into marketing and advertising to teenagers* (2nd edn.). Ithaca, NY: New Strategist Publications, Inc.

17

Media, Body Image, and Eating Disorders

Kristen Harrison and Veronica Hefner

As Americans become increasingly concerned about the growing rate of obesity in this country, it may seem misguided to continue studying the pursuit of excessive thinness as a public health issue. Yet it is erroneous to regard obesity and eating disorders as contradictory conditions, when they both signal disturbed eating (American Psychiatric Association: APA, 2000). Overeating and undereating are both departures from a healthy, balanced medium. Moreover, longitudinal research shows that undereating leads to overeating. Unhealthful weight control behaviors in childhood and adolescence increase the risk of overeating and obesity years later, even for youngsters who were thin when they started dieting (Neumark-Sztainer et al., 2006).

It should not be surprising, then, that as the rate of obesity among children in the United States has increased, so have the rates of anorexia nervosa, bulimia nervosa, and related eating disorders associated with the fear of becoming fat (APA, 2000). Young Americans' relationships with food and their bodies are becoming increasingly complicated. Another chapter in this volume addresses obesity as one outcome of this complication (Vandewater & Cummings, Chapter 16); the current chapter addresses body image disturbance and thinness-favoring eating disorders (chiefly anorexia nervosa and bulimia nervosa) as the others.

One contributing factor to body image disturbance and eating disorders is the mass media, particularly what Harrison and Cantor (1997) called "thinness depicting and promoting" media. We use the term *thin-ideal media* to describe media that glamorize the lean body ideal. Both slender female bodies and muscular, "cut" male bodies represent this ideal because they are both relatively free of body fat. Although we summarize research focusing on the role of media exposure in the development and maintenance of eating disorders, by no means do we intend to imply that media exposure is the only causal factor, or even the most important causal factor, in the development of disordered eating. The theme of this chapter is not that media exposure causes eating disorders where no potential otherwise existed, but that thin-ideal media exposure may coax body image disturbance and disordered eating into expression by activating related cognitions and emotions. We argue that the media's chief role is helping to create a social environment that (1) normalizes dieting and excessive thinness, and (2) encourages young people to repeatedly evaluate their bodies, to find them wanting, and to engage in extreme dieting, overexercising, and other health-compromising behaviors in an effort to relieve perceptions of inadequacy.

Definitions, Significance, Prevalence, and Risk Factors

Conceptual distinctions between body image and eating disorders

In this chapter we distinguish research on eating disorders from research on body image because eating disorders and body image are distinct phenomena. Eating disorders such as anorexia and bulimia are patterns of behavior that unfold over time (APA, 2000). It is normal to occasionally wish for a thinner body, fear becoming fat, skip a meal, or exercise until exhaustion. The quotidian and compulsive repetition of these cognitions, emotions, and behaviors is what defines them as disordered. Therefore, experimental manipulations cannot be said to cause or even to influence eating disorders *per se*; they can only be said to influence cognitions (e.g., body dissatisfaction, see Hargreaves & Tiggemann, 2003), emotions (e.g., dejection, see Harrison, 2001), or behaviors (e.g., food avoidance, see Harrison, Taylor, & Marske, 2006) that increase the risk for and eventually become part of the pattern of disordered eating. Body image and especially body dissatisfaction, on the other hand, may be immediately influenced in a significant and measurable way by stimuli in the environment such as comments from a critical parent or images of models in a fashion magazine. Thus, most of the research on the *effects* of ideal-body media concerns body image, not eating disorders. Although body image problems are not considered health- or life-threatening in and of themselves, they are well worth studying because they constitute risk factors for the development of much more serious problems, including but not limited to anorexia and bulimia (Thompson, 2004).

Eating disorders

Definitions Anorexia nervosa is defined as a routine refusal to maintain the minimum normal body weight for a given age and height along with a loss of 15 percent, or failure to gain more than 85 percent, of expected weight (APA, 2000). Weight is typically controlled by undereating and overexercising. Like anorexia, bulimia is characterized by a drive for thinness, but the technique for the attainment thereof involves recurrent binges in which the amount of food consumed is significantly larger than what the average person would eat under similar circumstances, followed by compensatory behavior (purging) via techniques such as vomiting or the abuse of diuretics and laxatives. Clinical-level bulimia involves binge-purge episodes that occur more than twice a week for more than six months (APA, 2000).

Significance   Disordered eating is a cause for concern because it can be deadly. Anorexia has the highest mortality rate of any psychiatric disorder; one study spanning 21 years reported a death rate of 15.6 percent (Zipfel et al., 2000). The complications of eating disorders include depression, anxiety disorders, attempted suicide, chronic pain, infectious diseases, insomnia, and cardiovascular and neurological problems (Johnson et al., 2002). Protracted restrained eating in childhood also raises the risk for obesity in young adulthood, regardless of starting weight (Neumark-Sztainer et al., 2006). Eating disorders are a problem for children and adolescents in particular because the vast majority of cases (86 percent, according to a report by the National Association of Anorexia Nervosa and Associated Disorders, 2000) begin before the age of 20. Indeed, clinical-level disordered eating has been identified in children as young as 7 (Nicholls, 2004). Prepubertal disordered eating carries with it all of the harmful effects faced by adults, plus the additional complications of delayed menarche and depleted bone density prior to full skeletal development (Nicholls, 2004).

Prevalence   For girls and women in the United States, prevalence estimates for anorexia range from 0.5 percent to 3.7 percent, whereas rates for bulimia range from 1.1 percent to 4.2 percent (APA, 2000). Since one defining feature of anorexia is a loss of 15 percent of expected weight, these prevalence estimates reflect only those individuals who have succeeded in losing or failing to gain this weight. Young people who plateau at 14 percent may have all of the cognitive, emotional, and behavioral hallmarks of anorexia but are not technically defined as such; thus, the percentage of young people with anorexic-like symptoms that stop short of full-blown clinical anorexia is likely to be significantly higher. The same is true for bulimia and bulimic-like symptoms. Indeed, the classification "eating disorder not otherwise specified" (EDNOS) is reserved for cases of disordered eating that are missing one or more clinical criteria, such as anorexia without the loss of 15 percent body weight or bulimia with fewer than two binge/purge episodes per week. The inclusion of such cases in prevalence statistics could increase the number of individuals with eating disorders worthy of clinical intervention by some 50 percent (Nicholls, Chater, & Lask, 2000). One of the more comprehensive prevalence studies of disordered eating among adolescent girls reported rates of 1.4 percent for anorexia, 2.8 percent for bulimia, and 4.4 percent for EDNOS (Lewinsohn, 2001). Thus disordered eating that is extreme enough to be worthy of clinical attention may occur among nearly 10 percent of girls and young women in the United States. Anorexia and bulimia are about 10 times more common among girls and women than boys and men (Thompson & Kinder, 2003), but contrary to the popular belief that people of color are immune to disordered eating, researchers report prevalence rates for African American women that fall within the range reported for Whites (albeit at the low end; Mulholland & Mintz, 2001). These rates are certainly large enough to merit concern, but still small enough to constitute a minority; therefore, most of the research linking media exposure with disordered eating measures eating-disorder *symptomatology* in normal populations rather than diagnosed eating disorders in clinical populations.

Body image

Body image is generally defined as an individual's collective evaluative perceptions of his or her body, particularly its appearance. Body image disturbance is conceptualized as either demonstrably inaccurate perceptions (such as the perception of an underweight anorexic that she is fat) or discontent with one or more of the body's observable features, such as overall size or weight (Botta, 2000). Body image disturbance is much more prevalent than disordered eating. The chief body image disturbance identified in research is body dissatisfaction, in particular the perception of having too much body fat. Over 20 years ago, Rodin, Silberstein, and Striegel-Moore (1985) reported that women's discontent with their body weight was so common that it could be called normative. Recent research suggests that this is still the case: 40 to 60 percent of adolescent girls and women are dissatisfied with some aspect of their appearance (Thompson, 2004), and boys and men are becoming increasingly dissatisfied with theirs (Cafri, Strauss, & Thompson, 2002). The drives for thinness and, among males, for muscularity are frequently construed as extensions of body dissatisfaction. Body image disturbance may not affect life expectancy the way eating disorders do, but it can erode quality of life, prevent optimal functioning, disrupt relationships, increase the risk for steroid use (Brower, Blow, & Hill, 1994), and lead to vanity-driven spending among young people on goods and services to improve their bodies (Morris et al., 1995). Given how many young people deal with poor body image and its consequences, then, it is important to understand its causes.

Risk factors

Several broad classes of risk factors for disordered eating and body image disturbance have been identified; these include biological, psychological, familial, and sociocultural factors (White, 1992). Studies of monozygotic and dizygotic twins show greater concordance of both anorexia and bulimia among monozygotics, suggesting a moderate degree of genetic susceptibility (Bulic, 2004). This biological propensity may interact with the other risk factors, making it difficult to disentangle the independent influence of each. To paraphrase an example offered by Bulic (2004), a father with a genetic predisposition toward disordered eating may pass this predisposition to his daughter. He also creates a perfectionistic family environment in which the importance of appearance is stressed and dieting is normative; perhaps he brings ideal-body media into the home. His daughter inherits his genotype and then grows up in an environment that encourages the expression of that genotype. Thus, it makes little sense to argue that eating disorders are caused purely by biology *or* by environmental factors like media use, because these factors most likely interact.

Thin-ideal media exposure, then, may be viewed as an environmental risk factor for the development and maintenance of body image disturbance and disordered eating, perhaps most potently for young people with a genetic predisposition toward disordered eating, as these individuals may be particularly sensitive to environmental cues that encourage excessive dieting or purging. Regardless of their genotype, young people are surrounded by thin-ideal media images and messages waiting to coax into expression whatever biological vulnerabilities they may have. The next section of this chapter describes just how common this ideal is in American mass media.

The Thin Body Ideal in American Mass Media

A truly comprehensive media content analysis should report not only the presence of some phenomenon (e.g., the proportion of television characters who are conspicuously thin) but also features of the context in which that phenomenon appears (e.g., whether thin characters are portrayed more positively than fat characters). Ample presence and a positive context both contribute to the "ideal" aspect of thin-ideal media. Content analyses of the presence and/or context of the thin body ideal in mass media have tended to focus either on print media (mainly magazines) or electronic media (mainly television).

Print media

Girls and women The best-known analyses of the body sizes of female beauty icons concern *Playboy* magazine centerfold subjects, also known as Playmates. Playmates' weights and body measurements are printed within the centerfold of the magazine, so they can be recorded and analyzed with ease. An analysis of Playmates from the 1950s through the 1970s showed that their bodies shrank significantly over time (Garner et al., 1980). A replication and extension (Wiseman et al., 1992) revealed a continuing decline through the 1980s. A more comprehensive analysis from 1977 to 1996 (Spitzer, Henderson, & Zivian, 1999) translated Playmates' heights and weights to their body mass index (BMI), a ratio representing weight for height. The Centers for Disease Control and Prevention (2006) maintain that a BMI of 18.5–24.9 is optimal for health; people with BMIs below 18.5 are considered underweight. The study by Spitzer and colleagues showed that the average BMIs of Playmates, which ranged from 17.91 to 18.40, did not decline over the period studied, perhaps because they were already as low as they could realistically be. Interestingly, a recent replication of this research by Sypeck and colleagues (2006) showed that the measurements of Playmates increased slightly since the 1980s, although their body mass was still less than 90 percent of what is considered normal for their height. The authors argued that perhaps this increase represents a response to the public's increasing awareness of the perils of disordered eating. (It might also reflect a subtle shift in editorial priorities occurring after Christie Hefner succeeded Hugh Hefner as *Playboy* chief executive in 1988.) Studies of female bodies in other magazines, especially the fitness, fashion, and entertainment genres, also document portrayals of thinness. Content analyses of adult-audience magazines (e.g., Byrd-Bredbenner, 2003), for instance, show a steady trend toward increasing thinness.

Boys and men   Like female bodies, male bodies in magazines have changed over time. Spitzer and colleagues (1999) analyzed the BMIs of *Playgirl* magazine centerfold subjects from 1986 to 1997 and found that their BMIs increased significantly (presumably due to hypermuscularity). Some of the centerfold subjects had BMIs above 32, which would translate to more than 235 pounds of muscle on a 6-foot frame. Other content analyses of advertisements in male-audience magazines like *Business Week, Rolling Stone,* and *Sports Illustrated* (Kolbe & Albanese, 1996) show that the mesomorphic, or v-tapered, muscular body is depicted as the male ideal.

Children's print media   Analyses of the lean body ideal in magazines directed specifically toward prepubescent audiences have not been published as of this writing, but because children and adolescents frequently read magazines meant for older audiences (Garfield, Chung, & Rathouz, 2003), they are routinely exposed to the grown-up genres (e.g., fitness, fashion, and entertainment magazines) that have been analyzed and shown to glamorize thinness.

Electronic media

Portrayals of thinness as desirable   Television is the electronic medium studied most frequently in the context of body ideals. Spitzer and colleagues (1999) reported that the BMIs of Miss America Pageant winners declined significantly from an average of 19.35 for the years 1953 to 1958, to an average of 18.06 for the years 1983 to 1988. Although many regard Miss America Pageant winners as important role models for girls and young women, the potential impact of exposure to a once-a-year pageant is probably minimal. Content analyses of television genres to which young people are routinely exposed offer a better view of the media body ideals children and adolescents see on a regular basis. To that end, Greenberg and colleagues (2003) analyzed the body sizes of characters in a sample comprised of 275 episodes of 56 different prime-time fictional television programs. Results showed that whereas about 5 percent of US women are underweight, over 30 percent of female television characters were underweight. Greenberg and colleagues (2003) also coded male characters and reported that whereas 2 percent of US men are underweight, 12 percent of male television characters were underweight.

Portrayals of fatness as deplorable   The term "thin-ideal television" suggests that thinness in the media is cast in a positive light via associations with beauty and success, but there is another way to convey the message that thin is normal and good, and that is to portray fat as abnormal and bad. Greenberg and colleagues (2003) showed that fatness, which has become normative in the general population, is a rarity on prime-time television: compared to 51 percent of US women and 59 percent of US men, only 13 percent of female television characters and 24 percent of male television characters were overweight or obese. Further, Fouts and Burggraf (2000) reported that fat female characters were more likely than their thin counterparts to be insulted by male characters. Because analyses showed that insults were almost always followed by audience laughter, Fouts and Burggraf (2000) argued that television reinforces the idea that it is acceptable to be rude to fat women. In a follow-up study, Fouts and Vaughan (2002) showed that fat male characters were more likely than thin male characters to make fun of themselves, with similar audience approval. The resulting message, that fatness is worthy of ridicule, reinforces the thin ideal.

Children's electronic media   Positive portrayals of thinness and negative portrayals of fatness are also present in electronic media aimed at child audiences. An analysis of animated cartoons by Klein and Shiffman (2005) showed that thinner characters were more likely than fatter characters to display positive characteristics such as intelligence, physical attractiveness, prosocial behavior, and positive affect. A content analysis of 25 popular children's videos and 20 popular children's books by Herbozo and colleagues (2004) revealed that thinness was portrayed as a positive female trait in 60 percent of the videos, and muscularity was depicted as a positive male trait in 32 percent of the videos. In 64 percent of the videos and 20 percent of the books, obesity was associated with negative traits such as being evil, unattractive, and cruel.

Ideal-body portrayals on the Internet   Content analyses of body types on the Internet are practically nonexistent, and none investigates children specifically. In the only published content analysis we were able to locate, Owen and Laurel-Seller (2000) compared the bodies of female models in Internet advertisements with those of *Playboy* centerfold subjects and reported that a curvaceously thin body ideal (large breasts on a skinny body) was the norm for both Internet models and centerfold subjects. Analyses of the Internet at large are challenging due to the seemingly insurmountable task of assembling a truly representative sample from a universe of millions of webpages, but efforts to do so should be encouraged, given the popularity of the Internet among children and adolescents.

Pro-anorexia Internet websites   Pro-anorexia or pro-ana (and pro-bulimia or pro-mia) sites offer information, resources, and support for people who view disordered eating as a lifestyle choice and wish to maintain rather than overcome their disorders. A textual analysis of 12 pro-ana sites by Norris and colleagues

(2006) revealed common themes such as success (i.e., only the strongest individuals can succeed at losing weight); sacrifice (i.e., one must give up cherished pursuits and relationships to maintain one's disorder); and transformation (i.e., weight loss can transform a "fat and ugly" person into a "thin and beautiful" one). These themes were transmitted through religious icons, metaphors, and terminology such as "psalm" and "creed," as well as "thinspirational" content such as photographs of extremely thin models intended to motivate viewers to lose more weight. Some sites even offered merchandise designed to foster a sense of community, such as red "ana bracelets" that signal affiliation and remind wearers to maintain anorexic practices whenever they are tempted to indulge their appetites.

In summary, both general-audience and child-audience electronic and print media convey messages in favor of a lean body. In the case of pro-ana sites on the Internet, this content can be extreme in its promotion of dietary restraint. The question of how and to what extent exposure to these messages affects young people is addressed in the following section of this chapter.

Effects of Exposure to Thin-Ideal Media

Research approaches

Researchers have used a variety of approaches to study the relationship between media exposure, body image, and eating disorders. The method that is most useful for documenting actual effects rather than just correlates of exposure is experimentation with random assignment to condition. However, experimentation is inappropriate for gauging media effects on eating disorders because eating disorders are patterns of behavior that unfold over time rather than discrete acts that can be observed and identified as "disordered" immediately following exposure to some stimulus. Furthermore, even if it were possible to create or increase the severity of an eating disorder with an experimental manipulation, it would be ethically questionable to do so. Experiments on the effects of thin-ideal media are therefore confined chiefly to variables related to body image and body satisfaction. Cross-sectional surveys and longitudinal panel studies, in contrast, have been used to assess both body image and eating disorders as correlates of ideal-body media exposure. All three types of studies are reviewed below.

Media exposure and body image

Experimental research   The most common type of study is experimental research testing the effects of exposure to ideal-body media imagery on various indices of body image. A meta-analysis of 25 such experiments by Groesz, Levine, and Murnen (2002) yielded 43 d values (i.e., effect sizes) representing the standardized difference between control and experimental conditions on subsequently measured body satisfaction. Thirty-five of these d values were negative, indicating a modest but significant drop in body satisfaction after exposure to thin-ideal images compared to controls. The overall d value was $-.31$. Notably, the average effect size was greater for participants who were under the age of 19 ($d = -.36$), suggesting some degree of heightened sensitivity to thin-ideal images among adolescents. However, subsequently published research suggests that this may be true only for girls. Hargreaves and Tiggemann (2004) exposed adolescents aged 13–15 to 20 television commercials depicting either idealized images or non-appearance products and services, and found that girls (but not boys) who viewed the idealized images reported significantly greater body dissatisfaction than did those who viewed the control commercials. Research with older boys and men (ages 17–27), in contrast, reports increases in depression and muscle dissatisfaction following exposure to television advertisements featuring the muscular male body ideal (Agliata & Tantleff-Dunn, 2004).

Only one published study to date has employed an experimental design to test the effects of exposure to a pro-anorexia (i.e., pro-ana) website. In a small pilot study, Bardone-Cone and Cass (2006) randomly assigned 24 female college undergraduates to view one of three websites: a typical pro-ana website complete with a "thinspirations" photo gallery; a women's fashion website featuring attractive images of average-sized women; and a home décor website without human images. Only the women who viewed the pro-ana site experienced increases in negative affect and perceived weight status, along with decreases in self-esteem, confidence in their ability to improve their appearance, and perceived attractiveness to the opposite sex. Unfortunately, the sample size was so small ($n = 9$ in the pro-ana condition) that the authors could not generalize their conclusions with confidence. Larger, more comprehensive studies of the effects of pro-anorexia sites are clearly needed.

Cross-sectional survey research   Cross-sectional research generally reveals a small-to-moderate positive correlation between exposure to both thin-ideal television and magazines such as the fitness and fashion genres, and variables such as the drive for thinness, body dissatisfaction, and body shame (Levine & Harrison, 2003). Those studies (e.g., Harrison & Cantor, 1997) comparing multiple media frequently point to larger correlations for magazine exposure than television viewing, particularly if television viewing is measured in terms of overall hours viewed rather than exposure to specific thin-ideal content. Botta (1999) reported that actual television exposure was not a significant predictor of adolescent girls' body dissatisfaction and endorsement of the thin ideal, but body image processing while viewing (as indicated by agreement with items like "I think about how my body compares to television characters' bodies") predicted 33 percent of the variance in endorsement of the thin ideal and 14 percent of the variance in both body dissatisfaction and drive for thinness. The studies that report gender differences reveal larger correlations for females than males (Harrison, 2000a) and for European Americans than African Americans (Botta, 2000). Although the majority of surveys on media exposure and body image focus on overall body thinness, at least one study has shown that television exposure is linked with the idealization of a very thin waist and hips paired with an average-size bust (Harrison, 2003). Television viewing is also associated among college women with approval of surgical body-change tactics – such as breast augmentation and liposuction – used to help dieters attain the skinny-yet-busty look (Harrison, 2003).

Longitudinal research   Longitudinal research linking media exposure with body image is sparse, but the few published studies suggest that early exposure to thin-ideal television predicts a subsequent increase in body image problems. For girls aged 5–8, viewing of appearance-focused television programs (but not magazines) predicted a decrease in appearance satisfaction one year later (Dohnt & Tiggemann, 2006). For girls aged 7–12, overall television exposure predicted the choice of a thinner ideal adult body shape one year later (Harrison & Hefner, 2006). For boys, the patterns are somewhat different. One study showed that the only predictor over time of body dissatisfaction among boys aged 8–11 was their actual body mass; however, boys who perceived pressure from the media to gain muscle and control their weight were more likely to report adopting body-change strategies to do so (Ricciardelli et al., 2006).

Media exposure and disordered eating

Experimental research   Experimental research has not, for the most part, incorporated measures of disordered eating *per se* because immediate changes in eating disorders are impossible to measure. Longer-term changes, however, can be measured, as achieved in an experiment by Stice and colleagues (2001). These researchers assigned some adolescent girls to receive a subscription to *Seventeen Magazine* while others received no subscription. The girls were then tracked over 15 months. There was no main effect of the subscription on body image or disordered eating, but bulimic symptoms increased for girls who received the subscription and who had initially reported relatively low levels of peer/parent support.

Additional experimental research has tested the effects of media exposure on temporary affective states and eating behaviors that have been identified as antecedents to disordered eating. Harrison (2001) showed varying depictions to adolescents with pre-existing discrepancies between what they believed they looked like and what they thought others expected them to look like. Those who were exposed to a televised portrayal of thinness being rewarded felt more dejected, whereas those who were exposed to a portrayal of fatness being punished felt more agitated. Because bingeing and avoiding food have been identified as mechanisms for coping with dejection and agitation, respectively, Harrison (2001) argued that the emotional effects of consistent exposure to such portrayals could lead to bulimic and anorexic patterns of eating. In a similar vein, Harrison, Taylor, and Marske (2006) found that college students who had the same type of discrepancies and were exposed to same-sex ideal-body print images (thin women or muscular men) altered the way they ate in front of same-sex peers – women ate less in the presence of other women and men ate more in the presence of other men. The authors argued that these temporary and subtle changes in eating could, if repeated daily for an extended period of time, become part of a pathological pattern of eating.

Cross-sectional survey research   Using a sample of female college undergraduates, Stice and colleagues (1994) tested a path model investigating possible mediators of the relationship between media exposure (a composite measure of exposure to various magazine and television genres) and eating disorder symptoms. The data were consistent with a model in which media exposure predicts disordered eating both directly (β = .30) and indirectly through a chain of variables including gender-role endorsement, ideal-body stereotype internalization, and body dissatisfaction.

Further cross-sectional survey research on college women by Harrison and Cantor (1997) and Botta (1999) measured television and magazine exposure separately. Harrison and Cantor (1997) found that overall magazine exposure predicted increased disordered eating (β = .25), but overall television viewing did not. Likewise, Botta (1999) found that overall television exposure did not predict bulimic behavior; however, the tendency to compare one's body to television characters did (β = .29). Additional research underscores the importance of such self-to-character comparisons by revealing that, beyond mere media exposure, interpersonal attraction (defined as a composite of liking, wanting to be like, and feeling similar) to thin media personalities predicted disordered eating among college women (Harrison, 1997).

Cross-sectional studies that include male samples, however, point to different patterns as a function of gender. Harrison (2000a) reported that for adolescent girls, television viewing predicted an increase in bulimic symptoms (β = .20) independent of interest in fitness and dieting as media topics. For boys, however, television exposure failed to predict disordered eating; instead, boys who reported greater interest in viewing fitness and dieting television content scored higher on measures of anorexia and drive for thinness. These gender differences may not emerge until puberty, though: a cross-sectional survey on prepubescent boys and girls by Harrison (2000b) demonstrated that television viewing predicted eating disorder symptomatology equally well for girls and boys (both βs = .20).

Longitudinal research   Longitudinal panel studies linking media exposure with disordered eating corroborate and extend the findings of cross-sectional reports. A longitudinal panel study of 257 European American and African American girls aged 7–12 showed that, independent of initial perceived body size and disordered eating, girls who viewed more television at the start of the study scored higher (β = .21) on a measure of disordered eating one year later, with no race or age differences (Harrison & Hefner, 2006). Prospective research outside the United States points to similar trends. The research program of Anne Becker has focused on the effects of the introduction of television to the Polynesian island of Fiji. The citizens of Fiji have historically embraced a robust female body ideal, and by the mid-1990s there was only one reported case of anorexia nervosa on the island (Becker et al., 2002). Television was introduced in 1995, with broadcast content consisting chiefly of Western commercial programming. Becker and her colleagues were able to compare secondary school girls' levels of disordered eating one month after the introduction of television with the scores of a similar sample of girls three years later. Comparisons showed that the proportion of girls with high scores on a scale of disordered eating was significantly greater three years after television's introduction than one month after (19 percent versus 8 percent), and vomiting as a means of controlling weight had increased from an incidence of 0 to 7 percent. These increases parallel an increase of household television ownership from 26 percent one month after television's introduction to 46 percent three years later. In-depth interviews revealed that 77 percent of participants felt pressure to lose weight from viewing television programs, with a primary motivation being to emulate a Western television personality.

In summary, research assessing the impact of media exposure on body image and disordered eating is fairly consistent, such that increased exposure is associated with increased body dissatisfaction, a greater drive for thinness, and the adoption of increasingly disordered eating behavior. These effects and correlations are small to moderate, and mere exposure does not appear to be as powerful a predictor as engagement with the body-relevant content of the media. The precise nature of this engagement is explored in the next section of this chapter.

Theoretical Mechanisms Underlying Observed Correlations and Effects

The question of *whether* media exposure harms body image and increases the risk of disordered eating has been addressed in research. The question of *how* this occurs is still under investigation. The underlying assumption is that the viewer or reader engages with the body-relevant content in a way that involves observations about characters' and models' bodies and, subsequently, about the viewer's or reader's own body, resulting in changes in his or her body image or eating/exercise habits or both. The effects of this critical evaluation may be cognitive, behavioral, or emotional, or some combination thereof. Accordingly, we divide our discussion of theoretical approaches into cognitive, behavioral, and emotional categories; however, it is probably most accurate to regard them as cognitive, cognitive-behavioral, and cognitive-emotional, because the theoretical approaches that identify behavioral and emotional processes also incorporate cognitions such as evaluative judgments of the self in relation to others.

Cognitive processes

Cultivation For the purposes of this chapter we define cognitive processes as those revolving primarily around conscious thought, such as the creation or rehearsal of attitudes and beliefs about the world and the self in relation to the world. The first such process is cultivation, which holds that exposure to television influences viewers' normative beliefs about the world (Gerbner et al., 1994). Cultivation theory offers an explanation for how the thin body ideal portrayed so prominently in the mass media may come to be perceived as ubiquitous, normal, and achievable, and fatness, by contrast, as aberrant and grotesque. In support of the cultivation model, Harrison (2000b) found that television exposure among boys predicted an increased tendency to believe that a fat girl they have never met will be lazy, greedy, stupid, and have no friends.

Social comparison The second major cognitive process commonly invoked in research is social comparison. Social comparison theory (Festinger, 1954) holds that people are driven to evaluate themselves by way of comparison with others, especially others who are perceived as reasonably similar to the self. Comparisons that cast the self in an unfavorable light motivate behavior change to meet the standards embodied by the target of comparison. Several scholars have applied social comparison theory to the ongoing discussion of media and body image (Botta, 1999; Tiggemann, 2005). Their research reveals a consistent pattern such that media exposure predicts body image disturbance, disordered eating symptomatology, and endorsement of the thin ideal, particularly among individuals who report a general propensity to engage in social comparisons with media images. Their findings have led these scholars to conclude that mere exposure is a weak predictor of body image problems compared to the viewer's tendency to make comparisons while viewing.

Thin-ideal internalization Internalization of a thin body ideal has long been implicated as a major risk factor in the development of disordered eating (Thompson & Stice, 2001). Thin-ideal internalization refers to the degree to which an individual consciously accepts the slim societal standard of attractiveness as his or her own personal standard and engages in behaviors designed to meet that standard (Thompson & Stice, 2001). Research demonstrating positive correlations between media exposure, disordered eating, and a drive for thinness (e.g., Hargreaves & Tiggemann, 2003) supports the idea that media exposure fosters internalization of the thin ideal, and that this internalization can lead over time to disordered eating.

In spite of the fact that even young children embrace the thin body ideal (Sands & Wardle, 2003), research calls into question the notion that, among prepubescent children at least, disordered eating in response to media exposure occurs *due to* thin-ideal internalization. Harrison's (2000b) cross-sectional survey of 6–8-year-old children revealed that television viewing predicted increases in disordered eating but did not predict internalization of the thin ideal. Sands and Wardle (2003) also found that media exposure did not predict internalization of the thin ideal in a sample of 9–12-year-old girls; perceived pressure from friends and family was a more significant factor. Further, a longitudinal study of prepubescent girls reported no evidence that media exposure predicted thin-ideal internalization conceptualized as the desire for a thinner current (prepubescent) body, although television exposure did predict the desire for a thinner future (post-pubescent) body (Harrison & Hefner, 2006). The importance of thin-ideal internalization as a mediator may thus depend on the developmental stage of the audience under study. Based on her finding that hours of television viewed per week predicted an increase in disordered eating without predicting the idealization of a slim body, Harrison (2000b) argued that exposure to a multitude of advertisements for diet- and weight-related products might lead young children to glamorize dieting as a grown-up practice before exposure to thin-ideal entertainment leads them to internalize a thin body ideal. The question of when in the developmental process thin-ideal internalization begins to play a key role in the media-disorder relationship awaits further investigation.

Behavioral processes

Social learning/modeling   The process of modeling outlined in social cognitive theory (Bandura, 2002) has been invoked to explain why people change their eating and exercise behaviors in response to media messages. Two components of the social cognitive model, prevalence and incentives, explain more precisely how media exposure may foster the acquisition of dieting behaviors. Prevalence refers to how frequently an event is depicted; greater prevalence increases opportunities for behavioral modeling. Incentives, in turn, increase motivation to execute modeled behaviors. As demonstrated in the content analyses, the thin body ideal is highly prevalent in American media, and audience members are given scores of incentives to attain the thin bodies they see displayed on television and in magazines.

Experimental research testing the modeling effects of exposure to a picture book featuring the popular Mattel doll Barbie showed that, compared to girls who viewed a picture book of a plus-size doll or one featuring no dolls, 5–7-year-old girls exposed to the Barbie book reported decreased body esteem and the desire for a thinner body (Dittmar, Halliwell, & Ive, 2006). The same effect did not emerge, however, for 7–8-year-old girls. The authors reasoned that the older girls no longer used Barbie as an aspirational role model. Of course, other developmental processes such as an improved appreciation of the distinction between reality (human models) and fantasy (dolls) may have contributed to the absence of an effect for the oldest girls. More research on children's responses to ideal-body fantasy portrayals, such as those contained in videogames, is needed to address this question.

Emotional processes

Self-discrepancy activation　Social cognitive theory is useful for understanding how dieting behaviors may be adopted in response to ideal-body media, but the approach becomes problematic as an explanation for the development of eating *disorders*. Clinical-level disordered eating is much more than dieting with the intention of losing weight to secure social approval. Eating disorders have a pronounced affective or emotional component (APA, 2000) that likens them to addiction. This component is not adequately addressed by the cultivation, social cognitive, and social comparison perspectives, all of which take a relatively rational approach to behavior adoption and modification. Both anorexia and bulimia have been conceptualized as methods of coping with noxious emotions, in particular agitation and dejection (Strauman et al., 1991). Food avoidance appears to calm feelings of agitation or anxiety, whereas bingeing appears to relieve feelings of dejection or depression. Thus, environmental stimuli that activate feelings of agitation or dejection could be contributing to disordered eating as a method of coping with those emotions.

Some researchers (e.g., Harrison, 2001) have argued that ideal-body media activate self-discrepancies (Strauman & Higgins, 1988), thereby increasing feelings of emotional distress that are relieved through food avoidance (anorexic behavior) or overindulgence (bulimic behavior). Experimental and survey data with adolescent girls and boys suggest that self-discrepancies and their attendant emotions at least partly mediate the relationship between media exposure and disordered eating symptomatology (Harrison, 2001). Moreover, self-discrepancies appear to amplify the effects of exposure to ideal-body media on college women's and men's actual eating behavior (Harrison, Taylor, & Marske, 2006). Thus, in addition to teaching young people how to diet in pursuit of a thin body, the messages contained in thin-ideal media may remind vulnerable children and adolescents of their self-discrepancies, thereby temporarily increasing noxious emotions that are then managed with food avoidance or overindulgence. The presence of self-discrepancies, then, might be conceptualized as a vulnerability predisposing some young people to react more strongly than others to ideal-body media.

Moderators of the Effects of Thin-Ideal Media

Beyond self-discrepancies, what personal or media characteristics make one youngster more vulnerable to ideal-body media effects than another? The research has revealed six notable moderators thus far: genre, gender, age, race, body image disturbance, and social support.

Genre

Many researchers have identified and measured exposure to thin-ideal media based on the reasonable assumption that media glamorizing thinness and muscularity will have the most pronounced effects on body image and disordered eating. However, even measures of overall media exposure, such as the number of television hours viewed per week, undoubtedly capture a good deal of exposure to thin-ideal content in the forms of diet- and appearance-related advertising and entertainment featuring attractive actors. Experiments that contrast the effects of exposure to thin models with exposure to average-weight or heavy models show that exposure to thin models generally hurts body image, whereas exposure to average-weight or heavy models does nothing or even improves it (Groesz, Levine, & Murnen, 2002). Further, children whose favorite television characters are average-weight have a more positive body image than do children whose favorite characters are either conspicuously thin or conspicuously fat (Harrison, 2000b). It appears that assessments of one's own body are encouraged by exposure to material that makes salient the shape and size of others' bodies.

Gender

Because eating disorders affect so many more females than males (APA, 2000), the vast majority of media-disorder studies have been conducted with all-female samples. For this reason, the most comprehensive meta-analysis to date on media effects on body satisfaction (Groesz, Levine, & Murnen, 2002) includes only studies of female samples. Numerous studies have compared females and males, however, and these generally speak to greater vulnerability among females. Although research on 6–8-year-olds showed no gender difference in the correlation between television viewing and disordered eating (Harrison, 2000b), research with adolescents reveals a different pattern. Harrison (2000a), for instance, found that overall television exposure predicted bulimic symptomatology, and exposure to thin-ideal magazines predicted anorexic symptomatology, in adolescent girls but not boys. The research that reveals notable effects on boys tends to focus on the drive for muscularity as an outcome (e.g., Agliata & Tantleff-Dunn, 2004; Botta, 2003). Thus, while girls appear to be more vulnerable to the effects of exposure to thin-ideal media, media that focus on a muscular male body ideal may activate uniquely male insecurities.

Age

Most studies employ college-age samples because such students are conveniently accessed for research, and they tend to exhibit more body image problems and disordered eating than older adults do (APA, 2000). However, media exposure has a negative effect on the body image of younger adolescents as well (McCabe & Ricciardelli, 2001). A study of 13–15-year-olds by Hargreaves and Tiggemann

(2003) suggested that high schoolers are as vulnerable as college students to the effects of ideal-body media exposure on body dissatisfaction and drive for thinness. The meta-analysis by Groesz and colleagues (2002) reported that the average experimental effect size for college students and older was $d = .34$, whereas for high schoolers and younger it was $d = .36$. Research on the media-body link for younger children is comparatively scarce, but studies have shown that media exposure predicts disordered eating and/or the idealization of thinness for girls and boys as young as 5 (Dohnt & Tiggemann, 2006; Harrison, 2000b; Harrison & Hefner, 2006). More research is needed on prepubescent samples to better understand the role of media exposure in young children's developing perceptions of self and body.

Race

Research comparing racial groups points to a stronger effect for white, Anglo, or European-American individuals than for African American and Latina individuals (Botta, 2000; Milkie, 1999; Schooler et al., 2004). In a combination quantitative/qualitative investigation by Milkie (1999), African American girls reported that they resisted identifying with thin-ideal media images of white women. The result was a smaller correlation between exposure to ideal-body media messages and body image disturbance for black girls than for white girls. Black and Latina girls may certainly be affected by media messages, but it appears that effects are largely contingent upon their ability to identify with the depictions (Schooler et al., 2004). Because the media-depicted thin body ideal is still mostly a white female phenomenon (Baker, 2005), individuals from other gender and racial groups have fewer opportunities to be affected in a self-relevant way. However, research is pointing to increasing similarities in effects among white and black girls (Botta, 2000), especially prior to puberty. In their longitudinal study of black and white elementary school girls, Harrison and Hefner (2006) found no race differences in the relationship between television viewing, disordered eating, and the idealization of a thin adult body. Perhaps because depictions of bodies of color are becoming increasingly thinner in mainstream media (Baker, 2005), the ethnic gap in effect is closing.

Body image disturbance

Individuals who are dissatisfied with their bodies prior to a thin-ideal media encounter tend to be more negatively affected by images of the thin ideal (Harrison, 2001); conversely, people who are satisfied with their current physique appear to be less affected (Posavac, Posavac, & Posavac, 1998). The meta-analysis of media effects on body satisfaction by Groesz and colleagues (2002) reported an average effect size of $d = -.50$ for individuals with significant pre-existing body issues, but only $d = -.10$ for those without significant body issues. Thus, there appears to be the potential for something of a vicious cycle for child and adolescent media users such that early exposure predicts the development of body image disturbance, which in turn increases vulnerability to thin-ideal media images. This is especially problematic given that young people with body and eating issues may actively seek out thin-ideal media (Thomsen et al., 2002).

Social support

One promising direction in research on moderators that *decrease* the adverse effects of exposure to ideal-body media points to the role of perceived social support from parents and peers. Stice and colleagues (2001) found that adolescent girls who received a subscription to a teen fashion magazine known for depicting the thin body ideal were subsequently unaffected by the subscription *only* if they reported receiving a relatively high level of social support from parents and peers. These findings underscore the importance of conceptualizing the mass media as part of a broader environment composed of multiple influences including family, friends, and community. Such influences may work to reinforce *or* dilute the effects of media exposure. Increased attention to these factors, and the way in which they interact with the media, is needed.

Outstanding Theoretical Questions and Problems

We currently know a great deal about how thin ideals in the media exert their influence; the nature and magnitude of this influence; and the characteristics that make certain individuals more susceptible than others to this influence. Yet many of these processes and characteristics remain poorly understood, especially in a developmental context. Research on prepubescent children (e.g., Harrison & Hefner, 2006) points to different relationships and processes than those that are playing out among older adolescents and adults. With an eye toward solving these developmental mysteries, we now turn to three outstanding theoretical questions or problems, namely, the social, maturational, and technological factors that merit further investigation.

Social factors

It is important that media effects be considered within a social context. Virtually all of the research concerning media effects on body image and eating disorders relies upon the assumption of direct effects. Yet adolescents interviewed by Milkie (1999) reported that they were not directly influenced by media ideals but felt pressured to meet them nonetheless because they believed their friends "bought into" these ideals. This finding describes a model of indirect effects such that presumptions about the media's influence on others exert their own influence on the person doing the presuming (Gunther & Storey, 2003). Recent research supports the notion that this presumed media influence may play as important a role as exposure itself in the development of body dissatisfaction and disordered eating (Park, 2005).

Maturational factors

Research on mass media and body ideals almost always considers youngsters' desire for a thinner *current* body to be the most important indicator of body dissatisfaction and a drive for thinness. Yet prepubescent children actually have two body ideals: their current (child) body and their future (adult) body. A child on the verge of puberty may be content with her current body shape but be motivated to diet in anticipation of the thin adult body she desires. Research on elementary school girls has shown television viewing to predict the subsequent idealization of a thin adult body but not a thin child body (Harrison & Hefner, 2006). Since television viewing among the same age group also predicts disordered eating, media-induced dieting may be done in the service of the body type the child wishes to have as an adult even if it does not influence the type of body she idealizes in the present. This research speaks to the importance of using developmentally sensitive methods and measures to study the way media exposure affects children before and after sexual maturation.

Technological factors

Some research suggests that age protects children from the effects of exposure to body ideals conveyed by dolls (Dittmar, Halliwell, & Ive, 2006), perhaps because older children can distinguish fantasy from reality. But even if children and adolescents are aware that the stimuli they are viewing are not real, will that knowledge fail to matter if the images *look* real? This question will increase in importance as animated media become increasingly sophisticated. We were unable to find published research on the body-related effects of children's exposure to such media. Research on this topic is clearly needed, especially as figure-rendering technologies become more advanced and are used to create bodies with impossible proportions that still look perfectly real.

Mitigating Adverse Effects

The idea that encouraging children to dismiss thin-ideal media stimuli as unrealistic and personally irrelevant will protect them from adverse effects holds great appeal, but unfortunately it is somewhat naïve. The ability to distinguish fantasy from reality alone cannot offer adequate protection in a society in which body-focused imagery, both fantastic and realistic, is so ubiquitous. Multiple protective strategies are needed.

What the media can do

Efforts to discourage media outlets from portraying idealized bodies and faces are unlikely to meet with success because attractive models sell products by fostering more favorable consumer evaluations (Reichert & Lambiase, 2003). Furthermore, consumer insecurity is the stuff of profits. People who are happy with their bodies buy few body-altering products and services. Thus, although we would like to recommend that producers, editors, and advertisers cut back on the number of thin, attractive models and actors featured in their offerings, a more feasible approach may be to use exposure to healthy-body media to offset the influence of thin-ideal media. Several studies suggest that such an approach could be useful.

Sports are one genre that has been associated with a healthier body image (Bissell & Zhou, 2004). Harrison and Fredrickson (2003) conducted an experiment testing the effects of exposure to women's sports television on adolescent girls' tendency to define themselves in an objectified manner. For white girls (but not black girls), exposure to sports whose athletes typically have bulky, muscular bodies was associated with a decrease in self-objectification compared to no exposure. For white girls at least, viewing larger-than-usual yet attractive bodies had a beneficial effect.

Research also suggests that the Internet might be of value in combating the negative effects of other media. In particular, it could be used to provide psychological interventions designed to prevent, treat, and help guard against relapses associated with body dissatisfaction and disordered eating (Luce et al., 2003). In one longitudinal experiment with a sample of female undergraduate students, Internet-delivered psycho-educational interventions designed to reduce body dissatisfaction and disordered eating symptoms significantly reduced those attitudes and behaviors over the course of four months (Celio et al., 2000).

What educators can do

Media literacy programs are intended to help individuals make sense of messages transmitted in media by teaching audience members to critically analyze those messages (Hobbs, 1998). Research has substantiated the value of media literacy programs that encourage a healthy skepticism of media portrayals of idealized images (e.g., Irving, DuPen, & Berel, 1998). For instance, high-school sophomores enrolled in a media literacy program designed to help teen girls think critically about media and body satisfaction reported lower perceived realism of thin-ideal media images and less internalization of the thin beauty standard than did their peers who were not enrolled in the program (Irving, DuPen, & Berel, 1998). Furthermore, media literacy programs focusing on societal standards and those focusing on internal attributes of program participants were equally successful at increasing college women's skepticism of the similarity, realism, and desirability of media images of the thin ideal (Irving & Berel, 2001). Thus, media literacy programs may be effective regardless of their specific approach.

What audience members can do

What can audience members themselves do to minimize the effects of exposure? The research summarized above suggests that they can start by choosing to view "healthy body" media such as non-lean sports (Bissell & Zhou, 2004; Harrison & Fredrickson, 2003) or playing with normal-weight to full-figured dolls like Emme, who is modeled after a plus-size celebrity (Dittmar, Halliwell, & Ive, 2006). Another option is to use media that take the focus off the body entirely. Research suggests that identifying with characters who are not defined visually or textually by their body weight may serve a protective function (Harrison, 2000b). The final option is to cut back on media exposure altogether. Harrison (2006) reported a pattern that emerged across several studies, such that teens who viewed more television defined themselves and their bodies more unidimensionally. Thus, television may encourage a narrow-minded view of self, while the time demands of a heavy television diet limit teens' opportunities to take part in the real-world experiences that would otherwise broaden and add complexity to their self-definition.

Conclusion

Our goal in this chapter was to review research demonstrating the prevalence of a thin body ideal in electronic and print media, and to present and evaluate the evidence relating exposure to this ideal with body image and disordered eating. We can conclude that (1) demonstrations of the thin body ideal are ubiquitous in American media, even media aimed at children, and the idealization of thinness is communicated through depictions of thinness as a good attribute and fatness as a bad one; (2) exposure to thin-ideal media produces deficits in body satisfaction and other measures of body image disturbance both immediately and over time; and (3) direct media exposure predicts a modest but significant increase in disordered eating symptomatology for both genders, but for girls especially through puberty and beyond. What is still unknown is how much additional body image disturbance and disordered eating can be explained by *indirect* media exposure, such as the acquisition of body ideals and eating behaviors from peers who learned them directly from television and magazines.

We need to recognize that disordered eating and obesity are not opposing conditions. The fact that childhood obesity is on the rise does nothing to negate the fact that excessive dieting and disordered eating are critical health problems affecting an increasing proportion of America's youth. Indeed, since excessive dieting in childhood actually increases the risk of obesity later on, those who profess concern about the obesity epidemic should be just as concerned about early and overzealous adherence to the thin body ideal. We will not be able to solve the obesity problem until we are willing to acknowledge its linkages to all types of eating pathology, whether they lead to underweight or overweight.

Recent reports of children as young as 7 engaging in extreme dieting and exercise to stay skinny (CBS, 2006) suggest that it is time for action. A society free of media extolling the virtues of beauty may be impossible, but a society full of young people who value a balanced physique and eat for vitality and strength is within reach. Parental encouragement to avoid excessive exposure to appearance-focused content, family and peer commitment to support and value young people as they are, the adoption of media literacy programs encouraging skepticism of the media's narrow definition of beauty, and continued efforts on the part of media professionals to transmit a more balanced picture of beauty will all be needed to create an environment in which all children and adolescents feel free to eat a balanced diet and maintain a normal, healthy weight.

References

Agliata, D., & Tantleff-Dunn, S. (2004). The impact of media exposure on males' body image. *Journal of Social and Clinical Psychology*, 23(1), 7–22.

American Psychiatric Association (APA). (2000). *Diagnostic and statistical manual of mental disorders* (4th edn., text revision). Washington, DC: American Psychiatric Association.

Baker, C. N. (2005). Images of women's sexuality in advertisements: A content analysis of black- and white-oriented women's and men's magazines. *Sex Roles*, 52(1–2), 13–27.

Bandura, A. (2002). Social cognitive theory of mass communication. In J. Bryant & D. Zillmann (Eds.), *Media effects: Advances in theory and research* (pp. 121–54). Mahwah, NJ: Lawrence Erlbaum.

Bardone-Cone, A. M., & Cass, K. M. (2006). Investigating the impact of pro-anorexia websites: A pilot study. *European Eating Disorders Review*, 14, 256–62.

Becker, A. E., Burwell, R. A., Gilman, S. E., Herzog, D. B., & Hamburg, P. (2002). Eating behaviors and attitudes following prolonged exposure to television among ethnic Fijian adolescent girls. *British Journal of Psychiatry*, 180(6), 509–14.

Bissell, K., & Zhou, P. (2004). Must-See TV or ESPN: Entertainment and sports media exposure and body-image distortion in college women. *Journal of Communication*, 54(1), 5–21.

Botta, R. A. (1999). Television images and adolescent girls' body image disturbance. *Journal of Communication*, 49(2), 22–41.

Botta, R. A. (2000). The mirror of television: A comparison of black and white adolescents' body image. *Journal of Communication*, 50(3), 144–59.

Botta, R. A. (2003). For your health? The relationship between magazine reading and adolescents' body image and eating disturbances. *Sex Roles*, 48(9–10), 389–99.

Brower, K. J., Blow, F. C., & Hill, E. M. (1994). Risk factors for anabolic-androgenic steroid use in men. *Journal of Psychiatric Research*, 28(4), 369–80.

Bulic, C. M. (2004). Genetic and biological risk factors. In J. K. Thompson (Ed.), *Handbook of eating disorders and obesity* (pp. 3–16). Hoboken, NJ: Wiley.

Byrd-Bredbenner, C. (2003). A comparison of the anthropometric measurements of idealized female body images in media directed to men, women, and mixed gender audiences. *Topics in Clinical Nutrition*, 18(2), 117–29.

Cafri, G., Strauss, J., & Thompson, J. K. (2002). Male body image: Satisfaction and its relationship to psychological functioning using the somatomorphic matrix. *International Journal of Men's Health*, 1, 215–31.

CBS. (2006). Genetic link to anorexia? CBS Broadcasting, Inc, February 3. Retrieved June 2, 2006, from http://www.cbsnews.com/stories/2006/02/03/earlyshow/contributors/melindamurphy/main1277855.shtml.

Celio, A. A., Winzelberg, A. J., Wilfley, D. E., Eppstein-Herald, D., Springer, E. A., Dev, P., & Taylor, C. B. (2000). Reducing risk factors for eating disorders: Comparison of an Internet- and a classroom-delivered psychoeducational program. *Journal of Consulting and Clinical Psychology*, 68(4), 650–57.

Centers for Disease Control and Prevention. (2006). *BMI – body mass index: About BMI for adults*. Retrieved October 16, 2006, from http://www.cdc.gov/nccdphp/dnpa/bmi/adult_BMI/about_adult_BMI.htm.

Dittmar, H., Halliwell, E., & Ive, S. (2006). Does Barbie make girls want to be thin? The effect of experimental exposure to images of dolls on the body image of 5–8-year-old girls. *Developmental Psychology*, 42(2), 283–92.

Dohnt, H., & Tiggemann, M. (2006). The contribution of peer and media influences to the development of body satisfaction and self-esteem in young girls: A prospective study. *Developmental Psychology*, 42(5), 929–36.

Festinger, L. (1954). A theory of social comparison processes. *Human Relations*, 7, 117–40.

Fouts, G., & Burggraf, K. (2000). Television situation comedies: Female weight, male negative comments, and audience reactions. *Sex Roles*, 42(9–10), 925–32.

Fouts, G., & Vaughan, K. (2002). Television situation comedies: Male weight, negative references, and audience reactions. *Sex Roles*, 46(11–12), 439–42.

Garfield, C. F., Chung, P. J., & Rathouz, P. J. (2003). Alcohol advertising in magazines and adolescent readership. *Journal of the American Medical Association*, 289(18), 2424–9.

Garner, D. M., Garfinkel, P. E., Schwartz, D., & Thompson, M. (1980). Cultural expectations of thinness in women. *Psychological Reports*, 47(2), 483–91.

Gerbner, G., Gross, L., Morgan, M., & Signorielli, N. (1994). Growing up with television: The cultivation perspective. In J. Bryant & D. Zillmann (Eds.), *Media effects: Advances in theory and research* (pp. 17–41). Hillsdale, NJ: Lawrence Erlbaum.

Greenberg, B. S., Eastin, M., Hofschire, L., Lachlan, K., & Brownell, K. D. (2003). Portrayals of overweight and obese individuals on commercial television. *American Journal of Public Health*, 93(8), 1342–8.

Groesz, L. M., Levine, M. P., & Murnen, S. K. (2002). The effect of experimental presentation of thin media images on body satisfaction: A meta-analytic review. *International Journal of Eating Disorders*, 31, 1–16.

Gunther, A. C., & Storey, J. D. (2003). The influence of presumed influence. *Journal of Communication*, 53(2), 199–215.

Hargreaves, D., & Tiggemann, M. (2003). Longer-term implications of responsiveness to "thin ideal" television: Support for a cumulative hypothesis of body image disturbance? *European Eating Disorders Review*, 11, 465–77.

Hargreaves, D., & Tiggemann, M. (2004). Idealized media images and adolescent body image: "Comparing" boys and girls. *Body Image*, 1(4), 351–61.

Harrison, K. (1997). Does interpersonal attraction to thin media personalities promote eating disorders? *Journal of Broadcasting and Electronic Media*, 41, 478–500.

Harrison, K. (2000a). The body electric: Thin-ideal media and eating disorders in adolescents. *Journal of Communication*, 50, 119–43.

Harrison, K. (2000b). Television viewing, fat stereotyping, body shape standards, and eating disorder symptomatology in grade school children. *Communication Research*, 27(5), 617–40.

Harrison, K. (2001). Ourselves, our bodies: Thin-ideal media, self-discrepancies, and eating disorder symptomatology in adolescents. *Journal of Social and Clinical Psychology*, 20(3), 289–323.

Harrison, K. (2003). Television viewers' ideal body proportions: The case of the curvaceously thin woman. *Sex Roles*, 48, 255–64.

Harrison, K. (2006). Scope of self: Toward a model of television's effects on self-complexity in adolescence. *Communication Theory*, 16(2), 251–79.

Harrison, K., & Cantor, J. (1997). The relationship between media consumption and eating disorders. *Journal of Communication*, 47(1), 40–66.

Harrison, K., & Fredrickson, B. L. (2003). Women's sports media, self-objectification, and mental health in black and white adolescent females. *Journal of Communication*, 53, 216–32.

Harrison, K., & Hefner, V. (2006). Media exposure, current and future body ideals, and disordered eating among preadolescent girls: A longitudinal panel study. *Journal of Youth and Adolescence*, 35(2), 146–56.

Harrison, K., Taylor, L. D., & Marske, A. L. (2006). Women's and men's eating behavior in response to exposure to thin-ideal media images and text. *Communication Research*, 33(6), 507–29.

Herbozo, S., Tantleff-Dunn, S., Gokee-Larose, J., & Thompson, J. K. (2004). Beauty and thinness messages in children's media: A content analysis. *Eating Disorders: The Journal of Treatment and Prevention*, 12(1), 21–34.

Hobbs, R. (1998). The seven great debates in the media literacy movement. *Journal of Communication*, 48(1), 16–32.

Irving, L. M., & Berel, S. R. (2001). Comparison of media-literacy programs to strengthen college women's resistance to media images. *Psychology of Women Quarterly*, 25(2), 103–22.

Irving, L. M., DuPen, J., & Berel, S. (1998). A media literacy program for high school females. *Eating Disorders: Journal of Treatment and Prevention*, 6, 119–31.

Johnson, J. G., Cohen, P., Kasen, S., & Brook, J. S. (2002). Eating disorders during adolescence and the risk for physical and mental disorders during early adulthood. *Archives of General Psychiatry*, 59, 545–52.

Klein, H., & Shiffman, K. S. (2005). Thin is "in" and stout is "out:" What animated cartoons tell viewers about body weight. *Eating and Weight Disorders*, 10(2), 107–16.

Kolbe, R. H., & Albanese, P. J. (1996). Man to man: A content analysis of sole-male images in male-audience magazines. *Journal of Advertising*, 25(4), 1–20.

Levine, M. P., & Harrison, K. (2003). Media's role in the perpetuation and prevention of negative body image and disordered eating. In J. K. Thompson (Ed.), *Handbook of eating disorders and obesity* (pp. 695–717). New York: Wiley.

Lewinsohn, P. M. (2001). *The role of epidemiology in prevention science.* Paper presented at the annual meeting of the Eating Disorders Research Society, December, Bernalillo, NM.

Luce, K. H., Winzelberg, A. J., Zabinski, M. F., & Osborne, M. I. (2003). Internet-delivered psychological interventions for body image dissatisfaction and disordered eating. *Psychotherapy: Theory, Research, Practice, Training*, 40(1–2), 148–54.

McCabe, M. P., & Ricciardelli, L. A. (2001). Parent, peer, and media influences on body image and strategies to both increase and decrease body size among adolescent boys and girls. *Adolescence*, 36(142), 225–41.

Milkie, M. (1999). Social comparisons, reflected appraisals, and mass media: The impact of pervasive beauty images on black and white girls' self-concepts. *Social Psychology Quarterly*, 62(2), 190–210.

Morris, S. B., McDaniel, M. A., Worst, G. J., & Timm, H. (1995). Vanity-motivated over-spending: Personnel screening for positions of trust. *Educational and Psychological Measurement*, 55(1), 95–104.

Mulholland, A. M., & Mintz, L. B. (2001). Prevalence of eating disorders among African American women. *Journal of Counseling Psychology*, 48(1), 111–16.

National Association of Anorexia Nervosa and Associated Disorders. (2000). Summary of ANAD 10-year-study. Retrieved November 1, 2006, from http://anad.org/site/anadweb/content.php?type=1&id=6982.

Neumark-Sztainer, D., Wall, M., Guo, J., Story, M., Haines, J., & Eisenberg, M. (2006). Obesity, disordered eating, and eating disorders in a longitudinal study of adolescents: How do dieters fare 5 years later? *Journal of the American Dietetic Association*, 106(4), 568.

Nicholls, D. (2004). Eating problems in childhood and adolescence. In J. K. Thompson (Ed.), *Handbook of eating disorders and obesity* (pp. 635–55). Hoboken, NJ: Wiley.

Nicholls, D., Chater, R., & Lask, B. (2000). Children into DSM don't go: A comparison of classification systems for eating disorders in childhood and early adolescence. *International Journal of Eating Disorders*, 28, 317–24.

Norris, M. L., Boydell, K. M., Pinhas, L., & Katzman, D. K. (2006). Ana and the Internet: A review of pro-anorexia websites. *International Journal of Eating Disorders*, 39(6), 443–7.

Owen, P. R., & Laurel-Seller, E. (2000). Weight and shape ideals: Thin is dangerously in. *Journal of Applied Social Psychology*, 30, 979–90.

Park, S. Y. (2005). The influence of presumed media influence on women's desire to be thin. *Communication Research*, 32(5), 594–614.

Posavac, H. D., Posavac, S. S., & Posavac, E. J. (1998). Exposure to media images of female attractiveness and concern with body weight among young women. *Sex Roles*, 38(3–4), 187–201.

Reichert, T., & Lambiase, J. (2003). How to get "kissably close:" Examining how advertisers appeal to consumers' sexual needs and desires. *Sexuality and Culture*, 7(3), 120–36.

Ricciardelli, L. A., McCabe, M. P., Lillis, J., & Thomas, K. (2006). A longitudinal invest-igation of the development of weight and muscle concerns among preadolescent boys. *Journal of Youth and Adolescence*, 35(2), 177–87.

Rodin, J., Silberstein, L. R., & Striegel-Moore, R. (1985). Women and weight: A norm-ative discontent. In T. B. Sonderegger (Ed.), *Nebraska Symposium on Motivation, 1984: Psychology and gender* (pp. 267–307). Lincoln, NE: University of Nebraska Press.

Sands, E. R., & Wardle, J. (2003). Internalization of ideal body shapes in 9–12-year-old girls. *International Journal of Eating Disorders*, 33, 193–204.

Schooler, D., Ward, L. M., Merriwether, A., & Caruthers, A. (2004). Who's that girl: Television's role in the body image development of young white and black women. *Psychology of Women Quarterly*, 28, 38–47.

Spitzer, B. L., Henderson, K. A., & Zivian, M. T. (1999). Gender differences in population versus media body sizes: A comparison over four decades. *Sex Roles*, 40(7–8), 545–65.

Stice, E., Schupak-Neuberg, E., Shaw, H. E., & Stein, R. I. (1994). Relation of media exposure to eating disorder symptomatology: An examination of mediating mechanisms. *Journal of Abnormal Psychology*, 103(4), 836–40.

Stice, E., Spangler, D., & Agras, W. S. (2001). Exposure to media-portrayed thin-ideal images adversely affects vulnerable girls: A longitudinal experiment. *Journal of Social and Clinical Psychology*, 20(3), 270–88.

Strauman, T. J., & Higgins, E. T. (1988). Self-discrepancies as predictors of vulnerability to distinct syndromes of chronic emotional distress. *Journal of Personality*, 4, 685–7.

Strauman, T. J., Vookles, J., Berenstein, V., Chaiken, S., & Higgins, E. T. (1991). Self-discrepancies and vulnerability to body dissatisfaction and disordered eating. *Journal of Personality and Social Psychology*, 61, 946–56.

Sypeck, M. F., Gray, J. J., Etu, S. F., Ahrens, A. H., Mosimann, J. E., & Wiseman, C. V. (2006). Cultural representations of thinness in women, redux: Playboy magazine's depiction of beauty from 1979 to 1999. *Body Image*, 3, 229–35.

Thompson, J. K. (2004). Eating disorders and obesity: Definitions, prevalence, and associated features. In J. K. Thompson (Ed.), *Handbook of eating disorders and obesity* (pp. xiii–xix). Hoboken, NJ: Wiley.

Thompson, J., K., & Kinder, B. (2003). Eating disorders. In M. Hersen & S. Turner (Eds.), *Handbook of adult psychopathology* (4th edn., pp. 555–82). New York: Plenum Press.

Thompson, J. K., & Stice, E. (2001). Thin-ideal internalization: Mounting evidence for a new risk factor for body-image disturbance and eating pathology. *Current Directions in Psychological Science*, 10(5), 181–3.

Thomsen, S. R., McCoy, J. K., Gustafson, R. L., & Williams, M. (2002). Motivations for reading beauty and fashion magazines and anorexic risk in college-age women. *Media Psychology*, 4(2), 113–35.

Tiggemann, M. (2005). Television and adolescent body image: The role of program content and viewing motivation. *Journal of Social and Clinical Psychology*, 24(3), 361–81.

White, J. H. (1992). Women and eating disorders, Part I: Significance and sociocultural risk factors. *Health Care for Women International*, 13, 351–62.

Wiseman, C. V., Gray, J. J., Mosimann, J. E., & Ahrens, A. H. (1992). Cultural expectations of thinness in women: An update. *International Journal of Eating Disorders*, 11(1), 85–9.

Zipfel, S., Lowe, B., Deter, H. C., & Herzog, W. (2000). Long-term prognosis in anorexia nervosa: Lessons from a 21-year follow-up study. *Lancet*, 355, 721–2.

18

Media and Advertising Effects

Brian Young

Advertising is an essential component of a thriving economy (Chiplin & Sturgess, 1981). Indeed, it can be argued that advertising is beneficial to the economy by encouraging informed consumers and by accelerating consumption and consequently production of goods to satisfy increased demand (Chiplin & Sturgess, 1981). However, advertising is often seen as harmful; when paired with "the child," the two put together evoke strong responses by both media and public, in part because of age-based limitations in how children understand persuasive messages.

The purpose of this chapter is to provide a description and an analysis of the literature on advertising of goods and services to children and how children respond to and are influenced by it. I begin by defining some of the key concepts of this field, the first one being advertising. I then turn to where children are exposed to advertising as well as the kinds of products that are targeted at them. Next I discuss the effects of advertising on children, focusing on their attention, knowledge of persuasive intent, and attitudinal and behavioral effects. Family and peer moderators are examined. Finally, I examine policy issues in the advertising and marketing area.

What Is Advertising?

There is no shortage of definitions of advertising so rather than present these as a litany, I have extracted the main themes that occur regularly in these definitions. This approach permits us to see what children have to learn in order to understand advertising and other associated marketing activities.

Advertising is paid for and, as such, is part of the economic arrangements that characterize most free market, capitalist societies in the world where goods and services are exchanged and consumption is encouraged. This first aspect of advertising is recognizable as economic or consumer socialization (Furnham, 1996; Gunter & Furnham, 1998; Webley et al., 2001), or how children grow up to understand and behave in economic and political worlds. Secondly, advertising has traditionally been broadcast to many rather than few and is in the tradition of mass communication (although recent advances in integrated communications would suggest that customized one-to-one commercial communications is a feasible goal). This aspect of advertising would locate the study of children and advertising as part of the research agenda subsumed under children and media. Finally, advertising and other forms of promotional activity comprise a rather ill-defined category of persuasive or promotional communication where the source is attempting to change or influence the receiver using carefully designed messages that are attractive or seductive and maybe not completely truthful. This final issue deals with the communicative genre called advertising and raises intriguing theoretical, developmental, and policy-related issues. All three of these aspects of advertising could constitute areas of research with children.

Another way to define advertising is to describe it as an accumulation of family resemblances (Wittgenstein, 1969). That is, advertising shares some but not all of the attributes of other kinds of communication. So advertising imparts information and, in this sense, is similar to encyclopedias or instructions on how to install and program a digital television. Advertising is designed to attract attention and engage the audience. There are many communicative forms that have this quality such as telling ghost stories or listening to a good teacher. Advertising, however, differs from other communication forms in that it provides information about goods and services where the area of discourse is commercial. Put simply, advertising has the intent to sell, to persuade consumers to purchase some brands rather than others. Because of this promotional purpose, advertising only tells consumers about the positive aspects of the brand that is advertised, never the negative qualities. To do so, advertising uses visual and verbal rhetoric in order to communicate propositions and positive feelings about their brands. Brands consist of identifiable symbols that refer to the particular good or service being promoted and are, according to Kumatoridani (1982), the topic of the advertisement; all the rest of the advertisement is considered comment. These concepts of topic and comment are used in the analysis of any discourse (Brown & Yule, 1983).

Our Uneasy Alliance with Advertising Economics

Advertising and marketing fuel the economies of many cultures (Chiplin & Sturgess, 1981). That is, when consumers buy products, economies prosper. Moreover, the economics of television, especially in countries with no established tradition of a national public broadcasting service, necessitate the presence of advertising in programs in order to fund them (Cahn, Kalagian, & Lyon, this volume, Chapter 2).

While advertising is essential to the economies of many countries, the extent to which brands have a ubiquitous presence in the child's life in most countries of the world varies. Some brands appear in contexts such as sports sponsorship where they can be seen as part of deliberate promotional activity. The "branded environment," such as the McDonald's large yellow "M," is all around us and is part of the consumer ecology in many countries throughout the world. Other brands are more localized and specific to a culture. For example, in Spain a sherry manufacturer (Osborne) uses large silhouettes in the shape of a black bull on hilltops and hillsides to advertise its brand.

Young (1990) has argued that advertising to children is often seen as a malevolent influence because of its ambiguous relationship with "the truth" and because of the combination of reason and emotion that it employs. In particular, advertising uses legitimate exaggeration called "puffery" and uses rhetoric as a device to persuade potential consumers. If children are the audience, then there is of course an *a priori* case that the immaturity of children at different stages in development must be considered when legislating or regulating advertising to children. However there is a deeper concern that is evoked when advertising and the child are put together. The child is perceived as innocent – in need of protection – and the advertiser is viewed as seducer, subverting reason and seducing with rhetoric. This argument is firmly rooted within the sociological tradition of critical analysis and would suggest that public concern can erupt at regular intervals and that these waves of "moral panic" (Goode & Ben-Yehuda, 1994) are driven by the cultural anxieties that are endemic within the child-advertiser relationship.

The moral panic argument would suggest that there are particular sites or places where advertising has no place. In a sense these are "sacred" places as opposed to "profane," and this distinction, originally proposed by Durkheim, has been reworked by consumer researchers (e.g., Belk, Wallendorf, & Sherry, 1989). One sacred space is the home; the other is the school. Although homes and schools are considered as taboo for advertising to children, both homes and schools are places where advertising occurs on a regular basis.

There are two faces of television that appear in people's homes. One is as a window on the world where the television set occupies a pivotal place in the living room, and the nuclear family watches, learns, and is entertained together (Alexander, this volume, Chapter 6). The other is the darker face, where television lets the murkier and more sinister side of the world into the home via inappropriate program content or via advertisements that attempt to sell products to youth who are considered to be "innocent" or at least "naïve" by adult standards. Similar arguments are made for the Internet as a potentially intrusive agent into children's homes; however, Internet interactions are two way, allowing the child to respond directly to outside influences (Turow, 2000). Television and the Internet, then, are perceived at times as intruders that transmit information from the marketplace into the home, as well as agents that are expected to alter the behavior of consumers, including children. Advertising in the latter instance is perceived as the culprit as it carries with it the unmistakable smell of wheeling and dealing, of buying and selling in smoke-filled rooms. These evocations are worlds away from home and the security of motherhood and apple pie.

Schools are also sacred as they are places where reason is paramount and rhetoric is presumably under the control of the teacher. The advocatory nature of advertising, where the merits of the brand and the product are the only position offered, can never do justice to the academic nature of learning both sides of the question. Moreover, advertising has become an integral part of the financial arrangements of many US schools as it provides television sets for classrooms, classroom textbooks that feature products, and fund-raising mechanisms for expensive school activities (Institute of Medicine: IOM, 2006). For example, Channel One is a television channel that provides schools with the equipment needed to show a 12-minute daily program, which includes two minutes of advertising. Schools sign a contract guaranteeing that they will show Channel One to most students almost every school day. Although school students can see advertising directed at them in other places, there is public concern that such invasive practices are being permitted and encouraged (for financial returns) in a place of education with a captive audience of peers (see for example http://www.obligation.org/). If not a welcome "intruder," advertising and marketing practices are nonetheless an essential component of financial viability in the US school system.

Reaching the Child Audience

Although much advertising and marketing can be found in small advertisements in newspapers and billboards and print, most of the research over the last 30 years or so has been devoted to the content of television advertising (Gackenbach, 2007; Joinson, 2003). The dominant interest has been in ascertaining how much food advertising is found on television, and the earliest work in this area was done in the 1970s (Barcus & McLaughlin, 1978; Cuozzo, 1971). However, the criteria for specifying how to identify the "child audience" as the target of advertising have varied across this research (Young, 1990). One approach is to look specifically at programming designed for child viewers.

In the 1970s the phrase "kid-vid ghetto" was used to describe the preponderance of advertisements targeted at children at a particular time – on Saturday mornings. Many of the studies in that decade focused on the after-school hours and Saturday mornings when much of the programming was for children. However, more children in absolute terms were watching advertising in prime time or early evening (Melody, 1973), yet these prime-time slots were relatively neglected in the research because even more adults were watching and most of the programming was designed for the adult rather than the child audience (Melody, 1973). Although Saturday morning audiences *in toto* were relatively small in absolute terms, the proportion of that audience (the "demographic purity" of the child sector of the market) was high.

Television advertising is still the major delivery system for marketing to children and youth in the early twenty-first century (IOM, 2006). Households with children in the developed world now have more than one television set, often with one set in the child's bedroom (Rideout & Hamel, 2006; Roberts, Foehr, & Rideout, 2005). For example, a recent UK survey (BBC News, 2006) claimed that in a poll of 1300 families, 7 in 10 children have their own television. The prevalence of television sets in children's bedrooms means that advertisements are being viewed by children without a parent present who can explain or moderate persuasive messages.

Changes in the media landscape and children's media-use patterns have altered the reliance on television spot advertising that characterized much of the promotional activities in the 1970s, the 1980s, and even much of the 1990s to include new venues such as the Internet, videogames, and cell phones (IOM, 2006). There are now telephones with a landline and possibly a dedicated line for Internet use, usually broadband (http://internetworldstats.com/articles/art047.htm). Advertising using spare band width on cell phones is growing (Mobiledia, 2005). Many urban households in Europe and many more in the United States have cable feeds for hundreds of television channels or have installed satellite dishes that can receive various bundles of television transmissions at different subscription rates. A computer with Internet capabilities and storage devices that include CD-ROM and DVD is available in many homes. There are other forms of storage like TiVo, a solid state store that affords instant playback and smart memory to prompt the user to record frequently viewed program categories at the touch of a button (Tarpley, 2003).

Children are early adopters of new technologies. Consequently, these changes in media access provide new avenues for reaching children with advertisements and marketing techniques. For example, a six-year study on Internet use by children (79 percent from the United States) showed that a quarter of children in 2001 can be classified as "heavy users" "spending ten hours or more online each week – up from an average of just 19 percent for the previous four years" (Clarke, 2002, p. 45). Cell phone use by children is increasing; although only 22 percent of UK children aged 9–10 years use mobile phones, this figure has increased to over 60 percent for 11–12 year olds (Jones, 2002). Thus, the venues in which advertisers and marketers can approach children are rapidly expanding.

What kind of products are being marketed and advertised to children? What are the messages being sent to children about these products? We turn next to the content of the advertisements and marketed messages.

Content Analyses

Content analyses involving large samples of television content document that the advertisements during children's programs have been primarily for foods and toys (Kunkel & McIlrath, 2003). The picture that emerges is consistent. Overall, studies have found that advertising to children primarily consists of food goods and services, and none of it is particularly healthy (Barcus & McLaughlin, 1978; Kunkel & McIlrath, 2003). About half the advertisements are for some form of food and about two thirds of these food advertisements are for products with added sugar (Young, 1990). In these advertisements, food is portrayed as fun, in a fantasy realm, and as sensuous where taste, texture, and shape are desirable qualities (Young, 1990).

In one review, Gamble and Cotugna (1999) compared their findings with other studies that have been conducted in the United States since 1972. The authors concluded that "the types of products advertised [to children] have remained constant over 25 years" (p. 264). Breakfast cereals are the most commonly advertised food, comprising slightly over a third of all television food commercials to children; this pattern has remained relatively unchanged since 1972 (Gamble & Cotugna, 1999). The next most advertised product is convenience foods (canned dessert, frozen dinner, "drive-ins"), a change from 1994 when the second most advertised products were cookies, candy, gum, popcorn, and snacks. Gamble and Cotugna note that there have been a negligible number of television commercials for fruit and vegetables over these years. In a more recent review of the television advertising literature, Kunkel and McIlrath (2003) found that one third of all advertisements directed at children were for toys. Cereals (22 percent), candy/snacks (18 percent) and restaurants/fast foods (6 percent) were the next three highest frequency categories; overall, these three food categories plus toys accounted for 80 percent of the total number of advertisements directed at children.

Similarly, recent content analyses of online marketing practices demonstrate that the foods advertised to children are low in nutritional value. Specifically, products marketed on food websites are high in calories and low in nutrients (Alvy & Calvert, 2007; Moore, 2006; Weber, Story, & Harnack, 2006). Advergames, in which children play with products, appear frequently on children's food websites and focus on foods that are low in nutritional value (Moore, 2006).

It can be said with confidence, then, that much of the advertising on television and the Internet directed at children consists of foods that would constitute an unhealthy diet (e.g., IOM, 2006). How advertising exposure translates into children's product preferences and behavioral choices is the topic of the next section.

Effects of Advertisements on Children

I turn now to how advertising impacts children. One view focuses on how children learn to cope with the communicative arm of economic and commercial reality, and the other view focuses on the effects of exposure on children. These constitute two ways of talking about advertising to children – the child as active participant acquiring a literacy or understanding with this communicative genre, or the child as passive recipient of a constant stream of audiovisual media. The first approach suggests a growing literacy with advertising, while the second implies that children learn norms and values and extract meaning from stimuli largely as a function of what they see and hear and how that has an effect on them. For some time, the former was seen as characteristic of much writing in Europe on media and children, and the latter was characterized as the "effects" approach with a long tradition of empirical research. However, the two are not incompatible or contradictory and should be seen rather as having different emphases. Nevertheless, there are contrasting images of childhood inherent in the two models, just as there are images of children and childhood implied in the debates over advertising to children.

The first approach places the child firmly at the center, immersed in an audio-visual culture of which promotional activity is a part. From infancy, he or she will actively learn the rules of that culture and will gradually acquire an ability to decode, understand, and collectively utilize the symbolic meanings in these experiences and share them with others. An effects approach, by contrast, suggests a gradual cultivation of habits and schemata that are based on past experience informing future predictions and behaviors. The flow is not necessarily one way and certainly not "straight through," as mediational variables such as parents and peers are important in determining outcomes.

Much of the empirical work used to inform the argument about the role that advertising plays in the child's life is implicitly based on an effects model. This research is often conducted using large-sample cross-sectional methodologies with multivariate analyses. In order to review this research in a theoretical context that does justice to this evidence, an effects model, with a reliance on mediating variables and their role, will be used.

Children's attention to, and interest in, advertisements

Advertising is emotionally involving and attracts the child's attention. Children under the age of 5 years like to watch moving objects with primary colors and sharp contrasts (Jaglom & Gardner, 1981). By 3 years of age they can become involved in television personalities and recognize them (McNeal, 2007; Valkenburg, 2004). Of course, these would include the celebrity endorsers or character endorsers that accompany advertisements – people like Ronald McDonald or cartoon characters like Bart Simpson.

Kid features, such as the use of branded icons and characters, also influence children's interest in specific products. For example, brand logos such as the McDonald's yellow "M" are recognized immediately by most preschool children (Weller, 2002), and older children attribute considerable added value to owning branded clothing (Elliott, 2004). Younger children, by contrast, identify with the characters associated with brands, rather than the brand itself (Derscheid, Kwon, & Fang, 1996; Haynes, Burts, & Dukes, 1993).

Children's understanding of commercial intent

Ever since advertising to children became a matter of public concern in the early 1970s, the question of how much children understand about advertising has been central to the debate. If children do not comprehend advertising and perhaps do not see it as being persuasive, then there is a good case that advertising to children is inherently unfair. So legislators and those in charge of regulating advertising want to know at what age we can regard children as having a mature understanding of commercial intent. Developmental psychologists are often hard pressed to find a simple answer as there are several components that constitute a full understanding of advertising, and each of these might have its own developmental trajectory.

Some years ago I coined the phrase "advertising literacy" which I hoped would do justice to this complex achievement (Young, 1986), and since that time it has been developed by others (Ritson & Elliott, 1995). Although young children from infancy onwards are aware of brands and will recognize them in contexts such as television advertising, they think that television advertising is just there for fun and entertainment. Studies have asked children as young as 4 years of age what advertising is for and their replies are consistently the same: "To make us laugh" or "It's there for fun" (Young, 1990).

However, there were some early claims made that very young children do actually understand the purpose or intent of advertising, depending on how their abilities are measured. For example, Donohue, Henke, and Donohue (1980) designed a nonverbal procedure for use with very young children. An old commercial that used a fantasy spokesman called Toucan Sam to sell a cereal called Froot Loops was examined. The product was shown to 97 children ranging from 2 to 6 years of age. It was highly unlikely that the children had seen this commercial before. Each child was then shown two pictures. One was of a mother and a child in a supermarket aisle with the mother holding a box of Froot Loops in her hand as if she had just picked the box off the shelf. The other picture showed a child watching a television screen. The child was asked to point to the picture that best indicated, "what Toucan Sam wants you to do." Seventy five percent of the two- to three-year-olds chose the supermarket picture, the "correct" response, and 25 percent selected the television viewing picture. The authors concluded that "the first major implication of this study is that children understand the intent of television commercials at a younger age than has been reported in the literature" (Donohue, Henke, & Donohue, 1980, p. 56).

This choice-paradigm has a design problem. First, using only one distracter item means the child has a 50 percent chance of getting it right by chance alone. Second, the processes that a child uses in making the "correct" choice need not involve an understanding that television commercials exist to persuade people to buy products. Because there is no cereal box in the television viewing picture, the child could choose the correct answer for the wrong reasons – it is the only one showing the product. Gunter, Oates, and Blades (2005) have discussed this problem and provided evidence from other more recent nonverbal studies showing that preschool children are unable to provide a mature response to such queries.

From about 6 to 7 years of age, the beginnings of an understanding of the purpose of advertising emerge. Although there had been various research studies published in the 1970s using interviews that asked direct questions such as "What is a television commercial?" and "Why are commercials shown on television?" (e.g., Ward, Wackman, & Wartella, 1977), in most of this early work there were few attempts to explore the processes that mediated the child's understanding of advertising. Results were limited to findings about the age when children did or did not understand different functions of advertising. For example, according to Ward and colleagues (1977) only a quarter of 11- to 12-year-olds were able to provide an explanation of why commercials were shown on television that demonstrated a full understanding of selling and profit motives.

Research conducted by Robertson and Rossiter (1974) used multivariate analysis on interview data with children to establish that there were two attributions of intent by children. One was assistive (commercials "tell you about things") and the other was persuasive (commercials "try to make you buy things"). Although both types of attribution of intent can co-exist in the individual child, there is a trend towards persuasive intent attribution, as compared with assistive intent attribution, becoming more frequent as the child gets older. By 10 to 11 years of age, practically all children are able to attribute persuasive intent to advertisements. Children of parents with higher educational levels tend to attribute persuasive intent to commercial advertisements at an earlier age than do children of parents with lower educational levels. The difference in age norms between Ward and colleagues (1977) and Robertson and Rossiter (1974) is a result of different definitions of competence. For example, to be eligible for "full understanding" in Ward's categories the child would have to demonstrate that the source behind the advertisement had a selling motive such as "to get you to buy stuff so they can make money." Robertson and Rossiter (1974) used a cluster of variables (such as an awareness of the symbolic nature of commercials and perceiving an intended audience for the commercials) to diagnose children's understanding of persuasive intent. Robertson and Rossiter approached the research problem of understanding advertising intent from communication theory, and the measures taken to assess intent were not the same as those used by Ward and colleagues (1977).

This body of research, then, demonstrates that children gradually come to understand that television commercials have more than one function and, most importantly, that there is a difference between the essential aspects of advertising (that it is persuasive and that the ultimate goal is to sell) and the instrumental aspects of advertising (that commercials are there in order to "inform" children about the product and thereby help achieve the ultimate goal of product purchases). These latter features, that it is fun to watch for example, are probably accurate perceptions of the world inasmuch as a lot of television advertising is designed to please the viewer. Therefore, children are not "wrong." Nonetheless, the attention-grabbing or mood-enhancing qualities of the message are there to encourage the viewer to watch and to create a favorable attitude about the product.

Robertson and Rossiter (1974) also found that an understanding of symbolic perception was the main determinant of persuasive intent recognition. The "symbolic" nature of commercials means that advertisements use devices such as idealized settings or dramatized character emotions and these devices symbolize or represent "real" situations or "real" emotions. Robertson and Rossiter considered this skill as key to an understanding of advertising intent. An understanding of the "symbolic nature of product, character and contextual representation in commercials" (Robertson & Rossiter, 1974, p. 13) would be reflected in being able to discriminate between products as advertised and products as experienced. For example, in the genre called advertising, products are presented in idealized settings or the emotions of characters are dramatized. Real-life experience with products occurs in more mundane settings such as store cupboards. An understanding of the difference is important when understanding the intent behind advertising.

What other skills are necessary to understand advertising? Selman (1980) has argued that "self-reflective role taking," which is characterized by awareness that others might have different opinions or motives just because they have different information, is beginning to emerge among 6–8-year-olds whereas 8–10-year-olds are usually quite capable of understanding that others have different opinions or motives even when sharing similar information. This approach would suggest that children's understanding of advertising and commercial communications in general, where the interests of the seller are often not the same as the interests of the buyer, will not materialize until later childhood.

Although the emergence of an understanding of aspects of the nature of human communication (such as knowing that others have different beliefs from oneself) shares several similarities with the emergence of an understanding of advertising, it also differs from it. Advertising and marketing are social arrangements in a free economy and knowing about that is part of the process of economic and consumer socialization. There is a developmental lag between the child's folk psychology of other people, which is quite sophisticated by 5 years of age, and his or her understanding of advertising intent which emerges in middle to late childhood. This lag could be accounted for by hypothesizing that children need to know about the human intentions behind the communication to understand advertisements. In other words, advertising is not just there; someone or some agency is behind it and has deliberate intentions.

Although the age at which children understand advertising has always been important in policy debates about regulating such content, the extent to which children actually utilize or benefit from knowledge they have about advertising's purpose has been less frequently addressed. John (1999) framed this issue in information processing terms. Children under 7 years of age have limited processing ability. They have difficulties storing and retrieving information even when they are prompted and cued to do so. Children over 12 years of age are able to use various strategies for storing, retrieving, and utilizing information, and these mental operations can occur even in the absence of prompting and cueing. Between the ages of 7 and 11, children might be able to deploy strategies to enhance information storage and retrieval that are similar to those used by older children, but they need to be aided by explicit prompts and cues.

In summary, children below 5 years of age think that advertising is there to entertain. From 5–6 years, an understanding of advertising begins to emerge slowly. Most of the evidence would suggest that by age 8, children recognize the commercial and persuasive intent behind advertising. Although children might know a lot about advertising by 8 years of age, they could still have a problem with accessing and utilizing that knowledge when watching television or surfing the Web until roughly 12 years of age.

Preferences and desires

Do advertisements increase children's preference or desire for various products? Although the answer to this question is difficult to ascertain, it can be inferred using proxies such as behavioral measures (change in choice between various alternatives after watching advertising) or by asking questions using a self-report inventory.

In a study by Goldberg and Gorn (1978), a treatment group was shown an advertisement for a new toy, and the control group saw no such advertisement. In the short term, significantly more 4–5-year-olds in the treatment group were prepared to play alone with the new toy than play with a friend that had no toy when compared to the control group. The treatment group also was more likely to choose the toy over playing in the sandbox, which was the favorite activity in the preschool. The results demonstrate that even at this early stage of development, exposure to advertisements results in a strong desire for possession of particular material goods.

Likewise, a review of the literature on the effects of food promotion on children (Hastings et al., 2003) concludes that there is "reasonably robust evidence that food promotion influences food preferences" (Hastings et al., 2003, p. 14). Similar conclusions were found by a National Academies panel: food advertising increases children's desire and interest for specific foods (IOM, 2006). Taken together, the studies find that exposure to advertisements does influence children's interest in certain products.

Attitudinal and behavioral outcomes

Does advertising have an effect on children's attitudes and behaviors? Two particular areas will be examined: (1) does advertising influence materialistic values in children; and (2) does junk food advertising encourage poor dietary habits and contribute to current alarming obesity levels.

Advertising and materialism Material goods are embedded and contextualized in consumption, and happiness is identified in many cultures as intimately associated with success and self-fulfillment (Chan, 2003; Easterlin & Crimmins, 1991). Therefore, it is not surprising that materialism is now seen as a core value for many children and that commercial culture, including advertisements, is perceived as the cause (Seiter, 1993). If part of "being materialistic" is a belief that material goods can bring personal happiness, then the message in the rhetoric of much advertising is that the particular good or service advertised is the way of achieving it.

A 14-item scale for measuring children's materialism was used with children in Beijing and Hong Kong (Chan, 2003, 2005). It was based extensively on the Goldberg, Gorn, Peracchio, and Bamossy (2003) scale that used items such as "when you grow up, the more money you have, the happier you are." Although Beijing has an emerging consumer economy, Hong Kong has had a tradition for over 40 years of encouraging production and consumption. Chan discovered that 6–13-year-old children in Hong Kong scored more highly on materialism than those in Beijing did, which suggests that the level of economic development and consumer activity in the culture played a role in the level of reported materialism by children. In another study that involves media more directly, a positive correlation was reported between heavy television viewing and materialism, presumably because more exposure to television advertisements leads to more materialistic values of children (Moschis & Moore, 1982).

Characteristics of children may also influence materialistic attitudes. Males report higher levels of materialism than females do (Achenreiner, 1997; Churchill & Moschis, 1979). Age, socioeconomic status, and birth order have been included as factors in several studies but they have not produced consistent results. Baker and Gentry (1996) did find that the youngest children were more likely to compare themselves with friends to see who got more toys. Kapferer (1986) surveyed 362 children aged 8 to 15 years, as well as their parents, and found high mother-child correlations on materialism.

Buijzen and Valkenburg (2003) used structural equation modeling to test a proposed set of relationships between exposure to advertising and various consequences such as unhappiness and general life-dissatisfaction, purchase requests leading to parent-child conflict, materialism, and unhappiness as a result of not getting the desired product. They used a survey technique with 360 parent-child pairs and various self-report measures to operationalize these variables. This comprehensive analysis supported the hypothesis that advertising enhances materialism. Specifically, children who frequently watched television commercials held stronger materialistic values than did their peers who watched television commercials less often. When families discussed consumer and advertising matters, there was a weaker advertising-materialism link. The authors suggest that the role of the parent in explaining advertising and consumer issues is vital in counteracting these effects on children.

Advertising and children's food consumption   Food advertisements dominate television advertising directed to children. The question of how food advertisements influence children's diets is an important one, as there is now an "epidemic" of childhood obesity in many Western countries (IOM, 2006). Reviews of the literature have led to the general conclusion that advertising is one of many factors that are linked to adiposity, i.e., body fatness (Hastings et al., 2003; IOM, 2006; Kaiser Family Foundation, 2004; Ofcom, 2004). In one review of 123 empirical studies, for example, television food advertisements influenced children's food preferences and requests as well as their short-term food consumption (IOM, 2006). Although there was also a positive correlation between exposure to food advertisements and obesity, all other potential causal factors could not be ruled out because the data are correlational (IOM, 2006). Put another way, the data that would establish a clear causal relationship between advertising and obesity is still lacking. The topic of media's role in obesity is covered in a separate chapter in this volume (Vandewater & Cummings, Chapter 16). In this chapter, I will discuss one of the intermediary steps in this relation: the influences of food advertising on children's short-term dietary intake.

There are several key studies about food marketing and dietary selection that are cited by most reviews. One study by Gorn and Goldberg (1982) examined 72 children aged 5 to 8 at a summer camp where it was possible, with the cooperation of the camp supervisors, to offer no fresh fruit or candy to the children other than that offered experimentally as part of the afternoon snack. Children did not watch television apart from the half-hour per day that was the critical part of the experimental treatment. Experimental groups watched videos with commercials for either fruit or candy products. Control groups either watched a video with no commercials or one with health messages concerned with a balanced diet and limited sugar intake. Afterwards the child was asked to select a drink and a snack. The drink choice was between orange juice and Kool Aid. The snack choice was to pick two items, from a collection of two candy bars and two fruits.

Under these well-controlled conditions, children who were exposed to orange juice commercials selected the most orange juice. Children who were exposed to candy commercials chose the most candy. Children in all conditions indicated that they knew the camp doctor wanted them to eat fruit as opposed to candy. Whether they acted upon this awareness and actually chose fruit depended on whether or not they had been exposed to candy commercials (Gorn & Goldberg, 1982).

The procedures used in these experiments, which we can call "watch then choose" studies, are cited in all the major reviews as evidence that advertising to children has a direct behavioral effect. The experimental format with different treatment manipulations has a distinct advantage over correlational, cross-sectional studies in establishing causality. However it is questionable whether this research answers questions of long-term effects of advertising.

Correlational approaches are typically used to study the naturally occurring relations among variables, such as food advertising and obesity. Using multiple self-report measures, Bolton (1983), for example, identified the key constructs underlying children's dietary behavior and their relationships. By using parent questionnaires and diaries about their children's diet and television viewing, the extent to which the child had been exposed to food commercials, the kind of supervision and behavior of the parents, and the prevailing patterns of diet and other characteristics of the child were assessed. The sample consisted of 262 children who were aged 2–11. Using multivariate statistical analysis and structural equation modeling, Bolton found that children's exposure to television food advertising significantly increased the number of their snacks. Moreover, viewing television advertisements had a subsequent and independent effect on the child's dietary efficiency and caloric intake. The effect was small, however, with about 2 percent of the variance accounted for. Bolton concluded that "it is unlikely that effects of this magnitude could seriously affect their nutritional and physical well-being" (p. 194). However, these findings are from correlational data.

Overall, children's diet is influenced by multiple factors beyond advertising. First, children's food habits are acquired early in life (Birch, 1990), and the structure of what children watch in advertising is not written onto a blank slate in terms of reception by the child; rather it is assimilated into an already established set of preferences and choices. Second, there is no simple mapping of how much the child views onto how much the child wants to eat or actually consumes. Even a basic communication theory like cultivation would predict no simple linear relationship between advertising and effects, as parents, peers, and developmental level have to be considered. Finally, television and Internet advertising of foods to children is only part of the media information children receive about nutrition.

A final caveat is that many of the foods advertised are not ones that young children will purchase directly. Even so, the rhetoric of cereal boxes and cereal advertisements with cartoon figures like Tony the Tiger and the Sugar Puffs Honey Monster would suggest that sugar-coated cereals are attractive to the younger child as the consumer. The parents are the providers, and children will pester or nag them to purchase these products for them (Valkenburg & Cantor, 2002). Food promotion to children can also be accompanied with toys as free gifts, known as premiums. Mothers report that premiums influence children's cereal selections; effects are particularly strong for those children who are heavy viewers of Saturday morning cartoons where cereals are frequently advertised (Atkin, 1980). The recent tie-in between Disney and McDonald's could lead children to use the nag factor, not necessarily to eat a Happy Meal *per se*, but to get the free gift that goes with it. Empirical research is needed to investigate this relation.

Reviews of the extant literature, then, provide clear evidence that food advertising has a direct causal effect on children's food preferences and short-term food consumption, but links between food advertising and obesity are only correlational at present (e.g., IOM, 2006). Currently, there is also a major gap in the literature about how marketing and advertising practices in the newer technologies, such as the Internet, videogames, and cell phones, influence children's diet.

Potential Moderators

Two important moderators of advertising effects on children will be considered in this section. These are family and peers influences.

The family nexus

The effects of advertising on children cannot be understood without considering the family. Although the influence of the family might conflict with the input of peers, the family is the first influence in the child's life and can still be there into the child's early twenties. In addition, parents are a major source of income in the form of regular allowances, although the power of the child as a quasi-autonomous consumer should not be underestimated (Webley et al., 2001). So the family does have some influence on all aspects of the child's behavior, values, and plans as well as how children respond to advertising and become consumers and economic agents.

Any approach to intra-familial influence should be comprehensive and cover all the members' communication patterns, lines of influence, and individual perceptions of "what's going on." Nonetheless, the dominant relationship in the context of consumer socialization has been on the parent and child, and how commercial sources like advertising result in disruption of the normal flow of influence from parent to child. Occasionally how children influence the consumption patterns, tastes, and preferences of their parents are discussed under the heading of "reverse" socialization. This phenomenon is known as "pester power" or the "nag factor" in commercial spheres or as purchase influence attempts (i.e., PIAs) in the academic literature (Galst and White, 1976). What does the child know and do to get his or her own way?

Weiss and Sachs (1991) identified "positive sanctions" as the most frequent tactic 4–6-year-old children use when faced with scenarios such as persuading their mother to buy them a toy in a shop. Children, for example, said that they would offer to reciprocate in some way if the purchase were made. "Negative sanctions" like nagging, begging, and crying were also common, but psychological sanctions based on persuasion or trying to change mother's mind were rare. Clark and Delia (1976) sampled older children aged 7 to 14 years, and there was little indication that children under 8 years would use counter-argumentative, persuasive strategies. Maybe young children nag because they cannot do much else to get what they want.

In a review of the literature, John (1999) identified three age-based stages in children's negotiation styles with their parents. In the first stage, preschool children exert their influence directly on parents by using behavioral strategies such as pointing, grabbing, begging, screaming, and whining. In the second stage, older children (7–11-year-olds) interact with parents by bargaining, compromising, and persuading. In the third stage, adolescents use complex influence strategies that appeal to reason and compromise in negotiating with their parents.

So where does that leave "pester power"? The most recent review of the literature on pester power (McDermott et al., 2006) has identified five studies that are methodologically sound and that provide evidence for a causal relationship between watching television commercials and pestering parents in supermarkets. For example, a study by Stoneman and Brody (1982) looked at behavior by mothers and children in the supermarket after watching specially designed television programs. The families were not aware of the real purpose behind the experiment. Eighteen children watched a television program of cartoons with children's food commercials, and 18 children watched the same television program with no commercials. In both conditions, the mother was in a separate room where she watched the same program as her child did, but without commercials. Children who were exposed to commercials made significantly more purchase requests to their mother overall and made significantly more purchase requests for advertised products. Mothers whose children had watched television commercials used power assertion techniques, defined as saying "no" to requests, telling the child to put the item back, and offered more alternatives in response to children's purchase requests than did mothers whose children had not seen commercials. In Stoneman and Brody's apt phrase "the food advertisements served to increase the vigor with which the child approached grocery shopping" (p. 374). Consequently, the mother employs control and power strategies. Stoneman and Brody concluded that "the experience of grocery shopping with their mothers was characterized by increased strife and conflict for those children who viewed food commercials prior to shopping" (p. 374).

How do parents cope with children's purchase requests? Parental mediation styles with specific reference to television have been identified as social co-viewing, instructive guidance (sometimes called active mediation), and restrictive guidance (Valkenburg et al., 1999). Social co-viewing is when parents just watch television with their child without discussing its content; instructive guidance involves parents talking about the content of television with their child in order to help him or her understand the meaning of television programs or the commercial intent of advertising. Restrictive mediation refers to regulating the amount and content of what a child sees. Research suggests that restrictive guidance can reduce the amount of time children spend watching television and diminish purchase requests (Van den Bulck & Van den Bergh, 2000). Similarly, classroom instruction can reduce children's body mass index as well as eating when viewing television (Robinson, 1999).

Peer influence

There are several ways that friends and classmates can influence children's consumer behaviors. One is by providing a source of norms which are established and maintained by the group and against which the child will compare herself or himself. Such social comparison can be upward, where the child aspires to be "cool" or have "street cred." It can also be downward, where self-esteem is protected or enhanced by comparison with others who are perceived in derogatory terms such as being a "geek." The dynamics of such social identity maintenance are complex. Because social identity can be constructed by self-categorization (Turner, 1987), it can shift and change depending on how children label themselves and their relationships between in- and out-groups.

Material culture and in particular possessions such as clothes and brands, and preferences such as music and hair have acted as symbols – originally for status (Veblen, 1899) – but nowadays also as a resource for constructing aspects of social identity (Dittmar, 1992). Consumer researchers have used the language of innovation and adoption to discuss how trends and fashions emerge. There is a clear relevance here for children and adolescents but, with the occasional exception (Hansen & Hansen, 2005), how new products diffuse through social networks has been relatively unexplored. Word of mouth, known as viral marketing, is an effective pathway for peer communications and more research is needed in this area (IOM, 2006).

Children become aware of the symbolic meaning of brands at about 7–8 years of age (Belk, Mayer, & Driscoll, 1984). That is, they can attribute social characteristics to the users of these brands and, to that extent, begin to understand how brands can add value to goods and services. More importantly, from this age children begin to craft their own social identities using aspects of material culture. It is no coincidence that consumer researchers working with children and companies who market to children have coined the phrase "tweenies" to describe the period from 8–9 to 13–14 years when kids are accused of "growing older younger."

Belk, Bahn, and Mayer (1982) examined the child's ability to recognize consumption symbolism. Pairs of photographs of houses and cars were shown to children ranging in age from 5 to 14 years, who were asked to choose the one that was most likely to be owned by a particular type of person such as a doctor or someone with a lot of money. The youngest preschool group was unable to do this task and their choices were at about the chance level. By 7 or 8 years of age, there was definite agreement on certain kinds of people owning certain kinds of things and this tendency was almost fully developed by adolescence. Belk and colleagues (1984) then presented photographs of products familiar to children in the United States, such as different kinds of jeans and bicycles. Each child checked a list of attributes that described the kind of child who owned that product. This study confirmed the premise that consumption symbolism grew stronger from 9 to 11 years of age, was stronger in girls than boys, and was stronger in higher-social-class children than in lower-social-class children. There was also a "brand name bias." Some of the photographs (e.g., Levi jeans) were identifiable from markings or names as particular brands whereas others, for example, were simply a style of shoe. The mere presence of a brand was enough to cause a more positive stereotype of the owner to emerge. In older children, the presence of brand names may be enough to enhance the image of the user of that brand.

Overall, then, peer influence in terms of normative pressure on consumption, style, and trends is well documented. This influence emerges during the school years and becomes stronger throughout adolescence. Less is known about interpersonal strategies of influence with peers on consumption patterns in children (but see Wooten, 2006).

Policy Implications

Although concern about advertising to children has been expressed at regular intervals since the 1970s, there has been an ebbing and flowing of regulatory mechanisms worldwide. Therefore, the conclusions of experts may or may not be listened to. I have always adhered to the view that regulation of advertising to children has been a bit of a political football depending on which party is or is not in power (also see Calvert, 1999). Nevertheless it is important to draw together the findings reported in this chapter and interpret them in the context of policy, as academics can and should examine the policy implications of their research.

There are a couple of sources where country-by-country details of regulation of advertising to children can be found. The *International Journal of Advertising and Marketing to Children*, now resurrected as *Young Consumers*, carries a regular feature on such regulation in different countries. In addition, the Advertising Education Forum (www.aeforum.org) has detailed links to other sites within countries that provide information on regulatory frameworks. Both of these sources are of interests to lawyers, marketers, and others who are primarily concerned about the parameters within which they are trading.

Regulation of advertising to children can be considered under two main categories. One concerns restricting advertising to children below a certain age, and the other concerns controlling or banning the use of certain promotional techniques to children.

Restricting advertisements directed at young children

Restricting advertisements to young audiences historically has focused on when children have a "good enough" understanding of advertising (see for example Young, 1990). Sweden, for example, has banned advertising to children below the age of 12 years as children below this age are not capable of fully understanding advertising (Bjurstrom, 1994). The research of John (1999) would appear to support this age-related ban on advertising to young children. Although there is evidence that children have an understanding of the commercial and persuasive intent behind advertising by about 8–9 years of age, they are unable to utilize this knowledge in the absence of cues when faced with advertising until at least 12 years of age.

It would be difficult, however, to gain the political cooperation of all the major stakeholders, including industry and commerce, to implement this kind of measure in other countries. In the United States, for example, the Federal Trade Commission recommended a ban on advertisements during television programs directed at children under the age of 8 because is was unfair to advertise to children who did not understand the persuasive intent of commercial advertisements. This policy was deemed unacceptable by Congress, partly because the financial underpinnings of US television are commercially based (Calvert, 1999).

Calls for bans on advertisements in programs directed at young children continue in the United States (e.g., Kunkel et al., 2004). Without advertisements, however, there would be no revenue source to create children's programs in countries such as the United States and Japan (Cahn, Kalagian, & Lyon, this volume, Chapter 2).

Setting the bar a bit lower, there is a much better case for restricting advertising to children below the age of 5 years: there is almost complete consensus in the literature that very young children do not understand the purpose of advertising and think that it is there as entertainment. Some research suggests that such an understanding is not clear until age 8 (e.g., Kunkel et al., 2004). However, the economic realities of creating children's television programs in the absence of a revenue stream remain a challenge if a ban on advertising occurs.

Banning certain advertising techniques

There is a good case for regulation of techniques used by advertisers such as celebrity or character endorsement or tie-ins between two child-oriented companies where free gifts or discounted offers are made. Children are susceptible to these techniques. Wilson and Weiss (1992) demonstrated how the use of popular characters (whether real or fictional) from children's programs may make it difficult for children to distinguish between advertisements and programs, even when they are not being used in time slots adjacent to their programs.

In the United States, advertisers once had the hosts of children's television programs sell products to young children in commercial messages adjacent to their program. Because children could not distinguish between the commercial and the program content, and because of the unique trusting relationship that children built with television characters, the Federal Communications Commission (1974) banned this host selling practice.

There is also ample evidence that television advertising, including celebrity endorsements, plays a dominant role in shaping children's product preference. Ross and colleagues (1984), for instance, showed how using celebrities to endorse a product could increase children's preference for that product and their belief that the celebrity was an expert on its subject. Similarly, a study by Atkin (1980) examined 5–7 year olds' perceptions of trade characters from food advertisements. He found that children, particularly heavy television viewers, actually believed that cartoon characters like Fred Flintstone and Barney Rubble knew a great deal about breakfast cereals, accepting them as credible sources of nutritional information. Likewise, Bandyopadhyay, Kindra, and Sharp (2001) showed how children feel validated in their choice of product when a celebrity endorses it.

In the online environment, less regulatory action has taken place than in the world of television. One piece of legislation in the United States, the Children's Online Privacy Protection Act, banned the use of certain techniques on children's websites that violated children's privacy (Montgomery, 2001). For instance, marketers cannot have media characters like Batman ask children to respond to a Gotham City census to collect personal information from them for marketing purposes without obtaining parental consent (Montgomery & Pasnik, 1996).

Summary

Despite children's problems in understanding commercial intent, advertising on children's television programs is a normative practice in most cultures. Restricting certain kinds of practices, such as host selling, is a more viable option for controlling children's exposure to unfair advertising and marketing practices than is a complete ban on advertisements targeted to younger ages.

Conclusion

This chapter has focused on the main issues and research evidence concerning media advertising and youth. I have spent some time looking at definitions of advertising and asking the basic question "why does advertising to children cause such concern?" Answers to these points serve two purposes. One is to locate the child's literacy with advertising in a theoretical context because theory in this field has been lacking. The other is to question whether the advertising debate is based on sound evidence. An examination of the evidence does establish a case that advertising to children is prevalent and that children constitute an important market for advertisers. Most of the advertising is for food products that are not healthy or for toys.

An examination of the effects of advertising on children demonstrates that a major mediating variable is the extent to which children understand the intent behind advertising. The evidence shows that preschool children think that advertising is there to entertain. Between about 6–7 and 8–9 years, children gradually understand the functions of advertising beginning with its informative function. The fact that this information is persuasive and is designed to sell the brand only emerges later, about 8–9 years. There is evidence that exposure to advertising influences desire for the brand and hence preferences. There is also evidence that behaviors such as short-term food consumption are affected by exposure to advertising.

Some of the policy implications of this well-established body of research were explored – largely in the context of regulating exposure to the content altogether or to particular techniques employed. Two categories of potential moderators, the family and peers, can work to attenuate the influence of advertising or to reinforce it. Evidence points especially to the positive role of parental discussion in ameliorating the effect of advertising on children (Buijzen & Valkenburg, 2003). Given the challenges associated with banning or even heavily regulating advertisements during children's television programs and on the Internet, the importance of parental "buffering" of media content is essential for children to come to understand and to cope with the ever-present commercial world of goods and services.

References

Achenreiner, G. B. (1997). Materialistic values and susceptibility to influence in children. In M. Brucks & D. J. MacInnis (Eds.), *Advances in consumer research*, vol. 24 (pp. 82–8). Provo, UT: Association for Consumer Research.

Alvy, L., & Calvert, S. L. (2007). *Food marketing on popular children's websites: A content analysis.* Paper presented at the International Communication Association, May, San Francisco, CA.

Atkin, C. K. (1980). Effects of television advertising on children. In E. L. Palmer & A. Dorr (Eds.), *Children and the faces of television: Teaching, violence, selling* (pp. 287–306). New York: Academic Press.

Baker, S. M., & Gentry, J. W. (1996). Kids as collectors: A phenomenological study of first and fifth graders. *Advances in Consumer Research*, 23, 132–7.

Bandyopadhyay, S., Kindra, G., & Sharp, L. (2001). Is television advertising good for children? Areas of concern and policy implications. *International Journal of Advertising*, 20(1), 89–116.

Barcus, F. E., & McLaughlin, L. (1978). *Food advertising on children's television: An analysis of appeals and nutritional content.* Newtonville, MA: Action on Children's Television.

BBC News. (2006). *Most children have TV in bedroom,* February 1. Retrieved March 5, 2007, from http://news.bbc.co.uk/1/hi/education/4669378.stm.

Belk, R. W., Bahn, K. D., & Mayer, R. (1982). Developmental recognition of consumption symbolism. *Journal of Consumer Research*, 9, 4–17.

Belk, R., Mayer, R., & Driscoll, A. (1984). Children's recognition of consumption symbolism in children's products. *Journal of Consumer Research*, 10, 386–97.

Belk, R. W., Wallendorf, M., & Sherry, J. F. (1989). The sacred and the profane in consumer behavior: Theodicy on the odyssey. *Journal of Consumer Research*, 16, 1–38.

Birch, L. (1990). Development of food acceptance patterns. *Developmental Psychology*, 26, 515–19.

Bjurstrom, E. (1994). *Children and television advertising: A critical study of international research concerning the effects of TV-commercials on children.* Konsument Verket, Stockholm: National Swedish Board for Consumer Policies.

Bolton, R. N. (1983). Modeling the impact of television food advertising on children's diets. In J. H. Leigh & C. R. Martin Jr. (Eds.), *Current issues and research in advertising.* Ann Arbor, MI: Graduate School of Business Administration.

Brown, G., & Yule, G. (1983). *Discourse analysis.* Cambridge, MA: Cambridge University Press.

Buijzen, M., & Valkenburg, P. M. (2003). The unintended effects of television advertising; a parent-child survey. *Communication Research*, 30(5), 483–503.

Calvert, S. L. (1999). *Children's journeys through the information age.* Boston: McGraw Hill.

Chan, K. (2003). Materialism among Chinese children in Hong Kong. *International Journal of Marketing and Advertising to Children*, 4(4), 47–61.

Chan, K. (2005). Materialism among children in urban China. *Proceedings of the 2005 Asia-Pacific Conference of the American Academy of Advertising* (pp. 22–33). Ohio: American Academy of Advertising.

Chiplin, B., & Sturgess, B. (1981). *Economics of advertising* (2nd edn.). London: Holt, Rinehart & Winston.

Churchill, G. A., Jr., & Moschis, G. P. (1979). Television and interpersonal influences on adolescent consumer learning. *Journal of Consumer Research*, 6, 23–35.

Clark, R. A., & Delia, J. G. (1976). The development of functional persuasive skills in childhood and early adolescence. *Child Development*, 47, 1008–14.

Clarke, J. (2002). The Internet according to kids. *International Journal of Advertising and Marketing to Children*, 3(2), 45–52.

Cuozzo, P. F. (1971). An inquiry into the image of food and food habits as presented by television food commercials. Unpublished master's dissertation, University of Pennsylvania.

Derscheid, L. E., Kwon, Y.-H., & Fang, S. R. (1996). Preschoolers' socialization as consumers of clothing and recognition of symbolism. *Perceptual and Motor Skills*, 82, 1171–81.

Dittmar, H. (1992). *The social psychology of material possessions: To have is to be*. New York: St Martin's.

Donohue, T. R., Henke, L. L., & Donohue, W. A. (1980). Do kids know what TV commercials intend? *Journal of Advertising Research*, 20(5), 51–7.

Easterlin, R., & Crimmins, E. (1991). Private materialism, personal self-fulfilment, family life, and public interest: The nature, effects, and causes of recent changes in the values of American youth. *Public Opinion Quarterly*, 55, 499–533.

Elliott, R. (2004). Peer pressure and poverty: Exploring fashion brands and consumption symbolism among children of the "British poor." *Journal of Consumer Behaviour*, 3(4), 347–59.

Federal Communications Commission. (1974). Children's television programs: Report and policy statement. *Federal Register*, 39, 39396–409.

Furnham, A. (1996). The economic socialization of children. In P. Lunt & A. Furnham (Eds.), *Economic socialization: The economic beliefs and behaviours of young people* (pp. 11–34). Cheltenham: Edward Elgar.

Gackenbach, J. (Ed.). (2007). *Psychology and the Internet* (2nd edn.). Burlington, MA: Academic Press.

Galst, J. P., & White, M. A. (1976). The unhealthy persuader: The reinforcing value of television and children's purchase influencing attempts at the supermarket. *Child Development*, 47, 1089–96.

Gamble, M., & Cotugna, N. (1999). A quarter century of TV food advertising targeted at children. *American Journal of Health Behavior*, 23(4), 261–7.

Goldberg, M. E., & Gorn, G. J. (1978). Some unintended consequences of TV advertising to children: *Journal of Consumer Research*, 5, 22–9.

Goldberg, M. E., Gorn, G. J., Peracchio, L. A., & Bamossy, G. (2003). Understanding materialism among youth. *Journal of Consumer Psychology*, 13, 178–288.

Goode, E., & Ben-Yehuda, N. (1994). *Moral panics: The social construction of deviance*. Oxford: Blackwell.

Gorn, G. J., & Goldberg, M. E. (1982). Behavioral evidence of the effects of televised food messages on children. *Journal of Consumer Research*, 9, 200–205.

Gunter, B., & Furnham, A. (1998). *Children as consumers: A psychological analysis of the young people's market* (pp. 9–34). London: Routledge.

Gunter, B., Oates, C., & Blades, M. (2005). *Advertising to children on TV*. Mahwah, NJ: Lawrence Erlbaum.

Hansen, F., & Hansen, H. (2005). Children as innovators and opinion leaders. *Young Consumers*, 6(2), 44–59.

Hastings, G., Stead, M., McDermott, L., Forsyth, A., & MacKintosh, A. M. (2003). *Review of research on the effects of food promotion to children: Final report.* London: Food Standards Agency.

Haynes, J. L., Burts, D. C., & Dukes, A. (1993). Consumer socialization of preschoolers and kindergarteners as related to clothing consumption. *Psychology and Marketing*, 10(2), 151–66.

Institute of Medicine. (2006). *Food marketing to children and youth: Threat or opportunity?* Washington, DC: National Academies Press.

Jaglom, L. M., & Gardner, H. (Eds.). (1981). The preschool television viewer as anthropologist. In H. Kelly & H. Gardner (Eds.), *Viewing children through television* (pp. 9–30). San Francisco: Jossey-Bass.

John, D. R. (1999). Consumer socialization of children: A retrospective look at twenty-five years of research. *Journal of Consumer Research*, 26(3), 183–213.

Joinson, A. N. (2003). *Understanding the psychology of Internet behaviour.* London: Palgrave Macmillan.

Jones, A. (2002). Wireless marketing: The linking value of text messaging. *International Journal of Advertising and Marketing to Children*, 3(2), 39–44.

Kaiser Family Foundation. (2004). *The role of media in childhood obesity.* Menlo Park, CA: Kaiser Family Foundation.

Kapferer, J. N. (1986). A comparison of TV advertising and mothers' influence on children's attitudes and values. In S. Ward, T. Robertson, & R. Brown (Eds.), *Commercial television and European children* (pp. 125–42). Hants, England: Gower.

Kumatoridani, T. (1982). The structure of persuasive discourse: A cross-cultural analysis of the language in American and Japanese television commercials. Unpublished PhD dissertation, Georgetown University, Washington, DC.

Kunkel, D., & McIlrath, M. (2003). Message content in advertising to children. In E. L. Palmer & B. M. Young (Eds.), *The faces of televisual media: Teaching, violence, selling to children* (2nd edn., pp. 287–300). Mahwah NJ: Lawrence Erlbaum.

Kunkel, D., Wilcox, B. L., Cantor, J., Palmer, E., Linn, S., & Dowrick, P. (2004). *Report of the APA task force on advertising to children.* Retrieved July 25, 2005, from http://www.apa.org/releases/childrenads.pdf.

McDermott, L., O'Sullivan, T., Stead, M., & Hastings, G. (2006). International food advertising, pester power and its effects. *International Journal of Advertising*, 25(4), 513–39.

McNeal, J. U. (2007). *On becoming a consumer: Development of consumer behaviour patterns in childhood.* Oxford: Butterworth-Heinemann.

Melody, W. H. (1973). *Children's television: The economics of exploitation.* New Haven, CT: Yale University Press.

Mobiledia. (2005, September 15). *Cell phone advertising has promise.* Retrieved April 16, 2007, from http://www.mobiledia.com/news/36373.html.

Moore, E. (2006). *It's child's play: Advergaming and the online marketing of food to children.* Menlo Park, CA: The Kaiser Family Foundation.

Montgomery, K. (2001). Digital kids: The new on-line children's consumer culture. In D. Singer & J. Singer (Eds.), *Handbook of children and the media* (pp. 635–50). Thousand Oaks, CA: Sage.

Montgomery, K., & Pasnik, S. (1996). *Web of deception: Threats to children from online marketing.* Washington, DC: Center for Media Education.

Moschis, G. P., & Moore, R. L. (1982). A longitudinal study of television advertising effects. *Journal of Consumer Research*, 9, 279–86.

Ofcom. (2004). *Child obesity – food advertising in context*. Retrieved January 13, 2005, from http://www.ofcom.org.uk/research/tv/reports/food_ads/.

Rideout, V. J., & Hamel, E. (2006). *The media family: Electronic media in the lives of infants, toddlers, preschoolers and their parents*. Menlo Park, CA: Kaiser Family Foundation.

Ritson, M., & Elliott, R. (1995). Advertising literacy and the social signification of cultural meaning. *European Advances in Consumer Research*, 2, 113–17.

Roberts, D. F., Foehr, U. G., & Rideout, V. (2005). *Generation M: Media in the lives of 8–18-year-olds*. Menlo Park, CA: Kaiser Family Foundation.

Robertson, T. S., & Rossiter, J. (1974). Children and commercial persuasion: An attributional theory analysis. *Journal of Consumer Research*, 1, 13–20.

Robinson, T. N. (1999). Reducing children's television viewing to prevent obesity: A randomized controlled trial. *Journal of the American Medical Association*, 282, 1561–7.

Ross, R. P., Campbell, T., Wright, J. C., Huston, A. C., Rice, M. L., & Turk, P. (1984). When celebrities talk, children listen: An experimental analysis of children's responses to TV ads with celebrity endorsement. *Journal of Applied Developmental Psychology*, 5, 185–202.

Seiter, E. (1993). *Sold separately: Children and parents in consumer culture*. Brunswick, NJ: Rutgers University Press.

Selman, R. L. (1980). *The growth of interpersonal understanding*. New York: Academic Press.

Stoneman, Z., & Brody, G. H. (1982). The indirect impact of child-oriented advertisements on mother-child interactions. *Journal of Applied Developmental Psychology*, 2, 369–76.

Tarpley, T. (2003). The future of televisual media. In E. L. Palmer & B. M. Young (Eds.), *The faces of televisual media: Teaching, violence, selling to children* (2nd edn., pp. 27–40). Mahwah NJ: Lawrence Erlbaum.

Turner, J. C. (1987). *Rediscovering the social group: Self-categorization theory*. Oxford: Blackwell.

Turow, J., & Nir, L. (2000). *The Internet and the family 2000: The view from parents, the view from kids*. Philadelphia, PA: Annenberg Public Policy Center of the University of Pennsylvania.

Valkenburg, P. M. (2004). *Children's responses to the screen: A media psychological approach*. Mahwah NJ: Lawrence Erlbaum.

Valkenburg, P., & Cantor, J. (2002). The development of a child into a consumer. In S. L. Calvert, A. B. Jordan, & R. R. Cocking (Eds.), *Children in the digital age: Influences of electronic media on development* (pp. 201–14). Westport, CT: Praeger.

Valkenburg, P. M., Krcmar, M., Peeters, A. L., & Marseille, N. M. (1999). Developing a scale to assess three styles of television mediation: "Instructive mediation," "restrictive mediation," and "social coviewing," *Journal of Broadcasting and Electronic Media*, 43(1), 52–66.

Van den Bulck, J., & Van den Bergh, B. (2000). The influence of perceived parental guidance patterns on children's media use: Gender differences and media displacement. *Journal of Broadcasting and Electronic Media*, 44(3), 329–48.

Veblen, T. (1899). *The theory of the leisure class: An economic theory of institutions*. New York: Macmillan.

Ward, S., Wackman, D., & Wartella, E. (1977). *How children learn to buy.* Beverly Hills, CA: Sage.

Weber, K., Story, M., & Harnack, L. (2006). Internet food marketing strategies aimed at children and adolescents: a content analysis of food and beverage brand web sites. *Journal of the American Dietetic Association,* 106(9), 1463–6.

Webley, P., Burgoyne, C. B., Lea, S. E. G., & Young, B. M. (2001). *The economic psychology of everyday life.* Hove, East Sussex: Psychology Press.

Weiss, D. M., & Sachs, J. (1991). Persuasive strategies used by pre-school children. *Discourse Processes,* 14, 55–72.

Weller, D. C. (2002). When is a brand not a brand? *International Journal of Advertising and Marketing to Children,* 3(3), 13–18.

Wilson, B. J., & Weiss, A. J. (1992). Developmental differences in children's reactions to a toy advertisement linked to a toy-based cartoon. *Journal of Broadcasting and Electronic Media,* 36, 371–94.

Wittgenstein, L. (1969). *Preliminary Studies for the "Philosophical Investigations:" Generally known as the Blue and Brown Books.* Oxford: Blackwell.

Wooten, D. B. (2006). From labeling possessions to possessing labels: Ridicule and socialization among adolescents. *Journal of Consumer Research,* 33, 188–98.

Young, B. M. (1986). New approaches to old problems: The growth of advertising literacy. In S. Ward & R. Brown (Eds.), *Commercial television and European children: An international research digest* (pp. 67–77). Aldershot, Hants: Gower.

Young, B. M. (1990). *Television advertising and children.* Oxford: Oxford University Press.

19

Adolescents and Media Messages about Tobacco, Alcohol, and Drugs

Dina L. G. Borzekowski and Victor C. Strasburger

Despite recent declines in adolescent rates of smoking, drinking, and drug use, these risky behaviors continue to be major public health concerns. Numerous ecological and personal factors impact an adolescent's decision to experiment with and use these different substances, including the media. In particular, specific and general media messages shape young people's perceptions about tobacco, alcohol, and drug use and exposure to these messages affects children's knowledge, attitudes, and behaviors. In this chapter, we provide information on the patterns of and determinants of tobacco, alcohol, and drug use among youth, theories relevant to the impact of media portrayals, the existing media messages about smoking, drinking, and drug use, and studies describing youth awareness and the potential effect of these messages. The chapter concludes with recommended solutions and policies that could lessen the negative and increase the positive effects of media on adolescents' use of tobacco, alcohol, and drugs.

Patterns of Tobacco, Alcohol, and Drug Use among Youth

Experimentation with and the use of tobacco, alcohol, and various narcotics have been and remain commonplace among adolescents. In countries like England and Australia, adolescent drug use has become so widespread and accepted that some no longer consider it to be deviant (Parker, Aldridge, & Measham, 1998). Annual data from the Monitoring the Future Study, a national school-based survey of eighth-, tenth-, and twelfth-grade students in the United States, offers prevalence and trend data for tobacco, alcohol, and drug use (Johnston et al., 2005). The 2005 data shows that half of all high-school seniors have tried cigarette smoking and around 14 percent are daily smokers. It should be noted, however, that there has been a steady decline in adolescents' tobacco use; the highest prevalence rates in the last few decades was observed in 1977 when 76 percent of high-school seniors had tried cigarette smoking. In terms of drinking, 75 percent of recently surveyed high-school seniors have tried alcohol, and 28 percent report that they have engaged in binge drinking (having five or more drinks in a row) in the last two weeks (Johnston et al., 2005). But even adolescent alcohol use has decreased somewhat; in 1985, the prevalence of a teenager's lifetime alcohol use was 92 percent and in 1995, it was 81 percent. By contrast, similar rates of illicit drug use have been observed in the past few decades. Roughly half of the twelfth graders surveyed in a 2005 study indicated that they had used an illicit drug, 45 percent reported that they had tried marijuana or hashish (Johnston et al., 2005). In 1985, 46 percent of twelfth graders had used any type of illicit drug and 41 percent had used marijuana or hashish in the past 12 months (Johnston et al., 2005).

Adolescents who use tobacco, alcohol, and drugs are likely to experience short- and long-term negative health consequences, more so than their abstaining peers. At the turn of the century, tobacco accounted for over 435,000 annual deaths in the United States (Mokdad et al., 2004). The epidemiological literature reveals that the top causes of death among adult Americans (heart disease, cancer, stroke, lung disease) are strongly associated with tobacco use (Mokdad et al., 2004). Although these studies refer to adults, practically all adult smokers become regular smokers by age 18 (US Department of Health and Human Services, 1994). As another negative consequence, tobacco use is highly associated with future use of alcohol, marijuana, and other illicit drugs – serving as a "gateway drug" (Golub & Johnson, 2001).

In the United States, approximately 85,000 annual deaths are associated with alcohol use (Mokdad et al., 2004). Sometimes the association is strong and immediate, other times it is weak and suggested; but it is accepted that alcohol significantly contributes to the top three leading causes of death among young people – accidents, homicide, and suicide (Windle, Miller-Tutzauer, & Domenico, 1992). Adolescents who are heavy alcohol users or had an early onset drinking age are more likely than non-drinking teens to engage in behaviors that pose a risk to themselves or others (Hingson, Heeren, & Winter, 2006). These risky behaviors include driving after drinking, riding with drinking drivers, getting injured in fights, having unplanned and unprotected sex, and using tobacco, marijuana, and other illicit drugs. Controlling for family and personal characteristics, young people who drink at an earlier age are more likely than their non-drinking peers to experience a lifetime of alcohol dependence (Hingson, Heeren, & Winter, 2006).

The use of one illicit drug is strongly associated with the use of other illicit drugs. A child who uses marijuana is 100 times more likely to use cocaine compared with abstaining peers (NIDA, 1995). The younger a child begins to use drugs, the higher the risk of serious health problems and abuse carrying into adulthood (Belcher & Shinitzky, 1998). While marijuana and other illicit drugs contribute to a small percentage of adolescent deaths in the United States, their use is significantly associated with a range of medical and behavioral problems. Adolescent substance use is linked to immediate dangers (i.e., car accidents, fighting, truancy), as well as long-term developmental disruptions (i.e., risky sexual behavior, dropping out of school) (Weinberg et al., 1998). Drug use is also one of many risky behaviors that cluster; teenagers reporting that at least half of their friends are sexually active are 31 times more likely to drink alcohol, 5 times more likely to smoke, and 22 times more likely to try marijuana (National Center on Addiction and Substance Abuse, 2004).

Determinants of Adolescent Use of Tobacco, Alcohol, and Drugs

Using an ecological framework, the risk and protective factors associated with adolescents' use of tobacco, alcohol, and other illicit substances include individual, family, peer, school, community, and sociocultural influences (Bronfenbrenner, 1989; Kulig & the Committee on Substance Abuse, 2005). On an individual level, sensation-seeking and impulsivity are risk factors while a resilient temperament is a protective factor (Palmgreen et al., 2001). Sensation-seekers are those individuals who are attracted to novel, exciting, and stimulating life experiences (Palmgreen et al., 2001) and impulsive individuals often perform behaviors without planning or contemplating the impact of the behavior (Colder & Chassin, 1997). Resilient adolescents often exhibit successful coping strategies in dealing with negative and/or stressful events; these youth are less likely to use substances (Vakalahi, 2001).

An adolescent is more likely to use various substances if his or her peers and microenvironment support substance use – primarily from increased opportunity and access to the substances (Allison et al., 1999). Rather than peers pressuring individual group members to engage in these behaviors, many adolescents selectively associate with a particular peer clique because of the clique's known status of using or abstaining from substance use (Engels et al., 1997). Additionally, an adolescent is more likely to engage in these risky behaviors if he or she overestimates tobacco, alcohol, and drug use rates among peers and acquaintances (Prinstein & Wang, 2005).

Media can contribute to adolescents' perceptions and behaviors by functioning as a "super-peer" (Strasburger, 2004). Similar to a group of friends, the media may encourage substance use by portraying tobacco, alcohol, and drug use as a normative behavior (Signorielli, 1993). Media can also promote use by delivering creative alcohol advertisements or informative stories about where and how to obtain illicit substances (Botvin, 1990). The media, like friends, might also dissuade use. Comprehensive, theory-based anti-substance use campaigns and programs can be communicated through print, radio, television, and Internet sources (Borzekowski & Rickert, 2001; Kurtz et al., 2001). The media are a pervasive source of health information for youth, and, as such, media can offer pro- and anti-substance use messages that affect adolescent behavior. Although tobacco, alcohol, and drug use (or lack of use) among adolescents emerges from multiple and concurrent influences, it is the impact of media that we will focus on for the remainder of this chapter.

Theories Relevant to the Influence of Media Portrayals

Several communication and public health theories offer insight into how and why the media affect adolescents' tobacco, alcohol, and drug use. While there are other explanatory theories, this chapter focuses on two: social cognitive theory and cultivation theory.

The social cognitive theory, as developed by Albert Bandura, provides a useful explanation of how young people can learn about smoking, drinking, and drug use from the media. This theory asserts that behaviors develop and are maintained through a context and interplay of personal, behavioral, and environmental factors (Bandura, 1986). Exposure to media messages can facilitate the learning and adoption of behaviors through the processes of attention, retention, production, and motivation (Bandura, 1986; Robinson & Borzekowski, 2006). *Attention* has to do with one's exploration and perception of messages; attention is highly influenced by factors such as salience, conspicuousness, functional value, affective valence, and attractiveness. *Retention* concerns processes of symbolic coding, organization of information, cognitive or imagined rehearsal, and enactive rehearsal. *Production* is the conversion of conceptual representations into actions and is influenced by immediate intrinsic and extrinsic feedback. This process is closely linked to efficacy expectancies, that is, the belief that one can successfully engage in a particular behavior. *Motivation* is most directly linked to outcome expectancies and is strongly influenced by external, vicarious, and internal incentives (Bandura, 1986; Robinson & Borzekowski, 2006). To illustrate this process, the observation of modeled behaviors that are linked to desirable outcomes might motivate individuals to take up that behavior. For example, adolescents can form expectations concerning the positive rewards of smoking and drinking from watching a favorite movie character capture the attention of attractive suitors, while sitting in a tavern smoking a cigar and drinking a beer (Wallack et al., 1990).

The second theory, cultivation theory, provides an additional perspective on how media can influence adolescents' beliefs and behaviors regarding smoking, drinking, and drug use. Cultivation theory, as developed by George Gerbner, proposes that one's perceptions of the real world are shaped or "cultivated" from one's media exposure (Shanahan & Morgan, 1999). People who are heavier consumers of media are more likely than those who consume less media to believe that the world resembles that which they see on screens. For example, people who watch a great deal of television are more suspicious of others and more likely to believe that the real world is more crime-ridden and dangerous than are people who watch less television (Gerbner et al., 1980). Recent research has shown that heavier television viewers start smoking at an earlier age (Gutschoven & Van den Bulck, 2005), providing some evidence that messages in the media may portray drug use as normative. Given the pervasive presence of alcohol on television, heavier viewers may overestimate the percentage of drinkers among real-world peers and acquaintances and be more likely to be drinkers themselves (Wallack et al., 1990). Cultivation theory suggests that media's influence is more likely to occur when an individual's prior experience aligns with the messages delivered through media exposure (Shanahan & Morgan, 1999).

Social cognitive and cultivation theory differ in their specificity and scope. Cultivation theory considers an individual's overall exposure and immersion in media messages. This theory does not attempt to link one's beliefs and behaviors to specific programming or content; rather, it focuses on broad beliefs and value systems shaped by overall and mainstream messages. In contrast, social cognitive theory might be used to explain how one's actions are attributable to a given advertisement, television show, or movie. Social cognitive theory might focus on how one learns an action or task while cultivation theory concerns an individual's beliefs about norms and value systems.

Regardless of which explanatory theory is employed, researchers assert that there is likely a causal relationship between viewing tobacco, alcohol, and drug media messages and the use of these substances by adolescents (Flay & Sobel, 1983; Wallack et al., 1990). To better understand the relationship between media messages and adolescents' use of tobacco, alcohol, and drugs, a variety of methodological approaches have been used. We describe the available research in the following pages.

Media Messages about Smoking, Drinking, and Drug Use

Because cultivation theory focuses on the prevalence and nature of media messages, content analyses – that is, the systematic assessments that count and describe the messages viewers might see when they are exposed to print, audio, video, and interactive media – are often used to assess the kinds of messages that people may encounter (Krippendorf, 2004). Through content analyses, information is made available on the frequency and nature of tobacco and alcohol messages in diverse venues, from magazine spreads to televised sporting events to web-based advertisements. A benefit of this methodology is that it allows comparisons across sources reaching different audiences. It also offers data on if and how these messages vary in their quantity and quality over time. We turn next to how tobacco, alcohol, and illegal drugs are presented in various media.

Tobacco

Since their inception, print, radio, and television media have been supported by the tobacco industry and have promoted tobacco products. In the 1920s and 1930s, tobacco companies, including R. J. Reynolds, American Tobacco Company, and

Lorrilard, were the primary sponsors of radio programs. One long-running radio music show, *The Lucky Strike Hit Parade*, offered a free carton of "Luckies" for correctly answering each week's three most popular tunes (Hettinger & Neff, 1938). In a count of the *Raleigh Review* radio show, a single hour featured 70 promotional references to Raleigh cigarettes (Fox, 1984). By the 1960s, the tobacco industry switched its focus and advertising budget from radio to television. In 1963, cigarette companies sponsored 55 different shows, representing a total of 125 hours a week. Based on these numbers, it was estimated that the average adolescent was exposed to around 1,350 cigarette commercials that year (Pollay & Compton, 1992).

As evidence mounted that smoking tobacco caused serious health problems such as lung cancer and heart disease, the use of television to advertise cigarettes and other tobacco products began to change. In a ruling known as the Fairness Doctrine, the Federal Communications Commission (FCC) decided in 1967 that television stations needed to offset the possible negative effects of tobacco advertising (Aufderheide, 1990). To implement this policy, the FCC required that stations broadcast one anti-smoking public service announcement (PSA) for every three cigarette advertisements that were aired. Three years later, a bill was proposed and passed into law banning radio and television commercials that advertised tobacco products (Aufderheide, 1990).

Despite the lack of tobacco advertisements, tobacco has remained a mainstay on broadcast television because of its presence in programming. In a study of prime-time television in the early 1980s, tobacco was shown at a rate of 1.3 times per hour and the typical smoker was a 41-year-old white working- or middle-class male (MacDonald & Estep, 1985). During this decade, only a small percentage of television characters smoked, but these characters were usually important and portrayed in a positive manner (Breed & DeFoe, 1983; Hazan & Glantz, 1995). Social cognitive theory would suggest that these characters could be "teaching" viewers the benefits of smoking. Content analyses of prime-time programs appearing in the late 1990s have found a substantial increase in the portrayal of smoking. In one study, tobacco use was found in 22 percent of all episodes (Christenson, Henriksen, & Roberts, 2000) and in another, tobacco appeared an average of four times per hour on television, an increase from 2.7 times per hour in 1999 (Armstrong, 2002). Cultivation theory would offer that this frequency may impact viewers' normative perceptions of smoking.

Tobacco use is frequently depicted in televised music videos. Among a sample of over 500 music videos airing in the mid 1990s, smoking-related behaviors appeared in 27 percent of the videos, with rap music videos featuring the highest percentage (DuRant et al., 1997). A more recent content analysis of 300 videos on all three major music television networks (MTV, VH-1, and BET) found that tobacco appeared visually in 21 percent and verbally in 5 percent of the videos (Roberts et al., 2002)

More so than on television, feature films show and promote cigarette smoking. It seems that Hollywood writers and directors use cigarette smoking as a short-cut for depicting characters who are troubled, conflicted, or rebellious. From 1988 to 1997, 85 percent of the 250 highest-grossing movies depicted characters who were smoking tobacco (Sargent et al., 2001). While smoking rates have been and continue to be highest in R-rated films (i.e., restricted films, with viewers under age 17 requiring an accompanying parent or guardian), more than half of all G-rated animated films (i.e., those suitable for a general audience) between 1937 and 1997 contained smoking scenes (Mekemson et al., 2004; Omidvari et al., 2005). In contemporary movies released after 1990, 8 percent of the characters in PG-rated movies (i.e., movies for which parental guidance is suggested) smoked compared to 16 percent and 37 percent of the characters in PG-13 (parental guidance strongly cautioned) and R-rated movies, respectively (Omidvari et al., 2005). Paid product placements, in which products are integrated into program content for a fee, were voluntarily banned by the Cigarette Advertising and Promotion Code in 1991; even so, researchers report that the four most heavily advertised cigarette brands (Marlboro, Winston, Lucky Stripe, and Camel) are the ones that most frequently appeared in movies released between 1988 and 1997 (Sargent et al., 2001).

The Internet offers both positive and negative messages about substance use. Websites sell a host of different types of tobacco products and practically none of these sites use effective age verification procedures at sale or delivery (Ribisl, 2003). Besides e-commerce, many websites encourage a pro-tobacco culture. Similar to what has been observed with print messages about smoking, male models on these websites are usually muscular and rugged and female models are thin, glamorous, and sexy (Hong & Cody, 2002). The Internet also offers anti-smoking messages and websites; there are even legitimate online smoking cessation programs designed specifically for teenagers who no longer want to smoke (Edwards et al., 2003).

Alcohol

Alcohol use has always been popular on television. A content analysis of prime-time broadcast television in the fall of 1998 found that a full 77 percent of programs depicted alcohol use (Christenson, Henriksen, & Roberts, 2000). Looking at individual characters, 29 percent of main characters and 11 percent of all characters are shown drinking alcohol in prime-time television (Long et al., 2002). Drinking is usually portrayed as a positive behavior, with negative consequences rarely mentioned (Signorielli, 1993). When alcohol-related problems are shown, programs and characters offer unrealistic and simple solutions (Christenson, Henriksen, & Roberts, 2000). Quite simply, alcohol-abusing characters need only to admit that they have a problem and the issue is resolved by the end of the program (Wallack et al., 1990). In addition, drinking alcohol is frequently joked about and intoxicated characters act in a humorous manner (Signorielli, 1993). Underage drinking in television programs is rare, however (Christenson, Henriksen, & Roberts, 2000; Long et al., 2002). In situation comedies and dramas, young characters that drink alcohol are often depicted as troubled youth who will learn, usually within the episode, that alcohol does not solve one's problems (DeFoe & Breed, 1988).

In televised music videos, alcohol is the most popular substance used, with 37 percent of videos portraying visual images of drinking and 19 percent of videos containing verbal references to alcohol consumption (Roberts et al., 2002). In these videos, alcohol use is often glamorized by having lead singers, as opposed to other characters, drink alcohol (DuRant et al., 1997; Roberts et al., 2002). In addition, music videos that have higher levels of sex and eroticism also show higher levels of alcohol use. In contrast, researchers have not seen higher rates of alcohol depictions in music videos showing hostile or violent behaviors (Roberts et al., 2002).

In practically all contemporary films, viewers will see alcohol consumed. One content analysis of top-grossing movies from 1985 to 1995 found that 80 percent of the films showed at least one major character drinking (Everett, Schnuth, & Tribble, 1998). These drinking characters, compared to their non-drinking screen-mates, were likely to be older, wealthier, more attractive, and involved in romantic and sexual relationships. Similarly, an analysis of 100 films from 1940 to 1989 found that drinkers were usually shown in a more positive light than non-drinkers were and the negative consequences of alcohol use were seldom shown (McIntosh et al., 1999). Roberts, Henriksen, and Christenson (1999) found that only 10 percent of contemporary films contained an anti-alcohol message. Of the 200 most popular movie rentals for 1996–7, 93 percent contained drinking, though only 9 percent of the films showed underage drinking (Roberts, Henriksen, & Christenson, 1999). Underage drinking, however, appears to be on the rise. For example, in a study of 1999 to 2001 films popular with and featuring teenaged characters, around 40 percent of the major teen characters were shown drinking and just 11 percent of these characters exhibited any regret about their alcohol consumption (Stern, 2005).

Illegal drugs

Content analyses of television programs find that marijuana and other illicit drug use appears less often than tobacco or alcohol use does. Of the substances featured on prime-time television between 1982 and 1985, illegal drugs were visually portrayed or verbally mentioned in just 22 percent of the shows (MacDonald & Estep, 1985). In contrast to smoking and drinking, drug use is commonly depicted as a negative behavior, done by abusers and unscrupulous characters (MacDonald & Estep, 1985). Data from the mid-1990s revealed that only 1.5 percent of main and 0.8 percent of all prime-time characters used illicit drugs (Long et al., 2002). Analyses of television music videos have found that very few (3 percent) music videos feature a visual depiction of illicit drug use; however, a greater number (20 percent) do contain verbal references to drugs (Roberts et al., 2002).

The positive depiction of illicit drug use has been discouraged; in fact, Hollywood refused to give a seal of approval for its Production Code to one of the earliest depictions of drug use – *The Man with the Golden Arm* – a 1955 film which starred Frank Sinatra and dealt with heroin use (Shapiro, 2002). In more recent times, illicit drugs do appear in about one fifth of all movies, with marijuana depicted more than half of the time drug and illicit substances are shown (Roberts & Christenson, 2000). Harmful consequences are rarely featured, but 21 percent of movies with drug use do include a character that refuses to use drugs (Roberts & Christenson, 2000). Although critics have charged that teenage movies glamorize adolescent marijuana use (Williams, 2000), a recent content analysis of teen-centered films found that only 15 percent of major teenage characters were shown using drugs (Stern, 2005). These characters were less virtuous than non-drug using characters were and 41 percent experienced negative consequences as a result of their drug use (Stern, 2005).

The Internet now appears to be another media outlet communicating both positive and negative messages about substance use. Not only do numerous websites offer information about recreational drug use, but also there are a host of websites that provide information on how to quit using these substances (Borzekowski, 2006). Consider one of the most extensive websites – the Vaults of Erowid (www.erowid.org). This website, founded in 1995, has the mission to offer accurate, specific, and responsible information about how alcohol and drugs are used; it considers itself a harm-reduction service (Borzekowski, 2006).

The Impact of Media Messages about Tobacco, Alcohol, and Drugs

Awareness of media messages and substance use

Even among very young children, there is very high awareness of media messages about tobacco, alcohol, and other drugs (Fox, 1996; Strasburger & Wilson, 2002). A study in the early 1990s found that around 80 percent of US 6-year-olds were familiar with the Joe Camel cartoon character and could identify this logo as frequently as the Disney Channel's Mickey Mouse logo (Fischer et al., 1991). Even at age 3, 30 percent of children could make the association between Old Joe and Camel cigarettes (DiFranza et al., 1991). In response to Anheuser-Busch's 1995 claim that that there was no feasible way to determine the degree to which children noticed its advertising, Leiber (1996) found that over 80 percent of a random sample of elementary school students could identify that beer was the product being promoted by the Budweiser frogs, named "Bud," "Weis," and "Er." A recent study found that 75 percent of fourth graders could recognize the characters featured in the current Budweiser campaign that showed claymation lizards and an animated ferret (Collins et al., 2005). Given such high levels of awareness, it is not surprising that children age 8 to 12 years can name more beer brands than American Presidents (CSPI, 1988). Interestingly, in one study of seventh through twelfth graders, there was a strong and positive correlation ($r = .73$) between teens' unaided awareness of various alcohol brands and the advertising budgets for the different brands (Gentile et al., 2001). In this same study, there also was a positive ($r = .66$) correlation between the adolescents' brand preference and the amount of money spent to advertise each brand (Gentile et al., 2001).

Besides frequently seeing advertisements, young people are familiar with and own promotional material distributed by the tobacco and alcohol industries. Among a sample of seventh graders, researchers found that 27 percent of these youth reported that they had acquired tobacco promotional items. The most commonly owned products were lighters and t-shirts, and these items were most likely promoting either Marlboro or Camel (Schooler, Feighery, & Flora, 1996). Similarly, a 2001 study found that a quarter of the sampled seventh through twelfth graders owned an alcohol-related product, such as a t-shirt, cup, or baseball cap (Gentile et al., 2001). More than half the products were advertising either Budweiser or Bud Lite, two alcohol brands that have the highest annual advertising budgets (Gentile et al., 2001).

Numerous studies show that children and adolescents who are aware of and like tobacco and alcohol advertisements and promotions are also more likely to use these substances, compared to their less aware and more disapproving peers (Botvin et al., 1991). In a 1998 study, Feighery and colleagues found that adolescents who had experimented with smoking and lacked a firm commitment not to smoke in the future also had high levels of receptivity, that is, they were aware of and liked the tobacco advertisements and promotions (Feighery et al., 1998). Those who only saw advertisements, but did not want or own tobacco promotional material, were less likely to be susceptible to current or future cigarette smoking (Feighery et al., 1998). In a study of seventh through twelfth graders, exposure to pro-alcohol advertisements and ownership of promotional materials accounted for 21 percent of the variance in frequency of drinking. This marketing factor accounted for less than peer influence (30 percent of the variance), but more than the parent-related (4 percent) and demographic (4 percent) variables that were controlled for in the regression analyses (Gentile et al., 2001).

Effects of exposure to media messages about smoking, drinking, and drug use

Exposure to cigarette advertising in the media may actually pose more risk to youth than having family members and peers who smoke (Evans et al., 1995). Furthermore, media exposure can even undermine the impact of strong parenting practices (Pierce et al., 2002). More than 20 correlational studies have found that children exposed to cigarette advertisements or promotions are more likely to be susceptible to smoking (Pierce, Gilpin, & Burns, 1991; Sargent, 2005). In several studies, there is a strong correlation between the most heavily advertised brands of cigarettes – Marlboro and Camel – and the brands that teenage smokers take up when they begin to smoke (CDC, 1992).

Two unique, large longitudinal studies have found that approximately one third of all adolescent smoking can be attributed to tobacco advertising and promotions (Biener & Siegel, 2000; Pierce et al., 1998). One study by Biener and Siegel was based on a random probability sample using random-digit dialing of Massachusetts households and included just over 1,600 youth. The researchers surveyed the youth at two points in time, once in 1993 and once in 1997. They found that adolescents who were aware of and liked tobacco marketing at time one were more than twice as likely to become an established smoker four years later, compared to those with low receptivity (Biener & Siegel, 2000). Among the sub-sample who had not engaged in any smoking experimentation at baseline, 29 percent of the youth with high receptivity compared to 11 percent with low receptivity took up smoking by the follow-up data collection (Biener & Siegel, 2000). In the Pierce and colleagues 1998 study, a cohort of 1,752 adolescents who had never smoked were interviewed twice, first in 1993 and then in 1996. For these adolescents, owning, or even wanting to own, a tobacco company promotional item was significantly and strongly associated with later experimentation and use of tobacco products (Pierce et al., 1998).

Significant associations are observed between exposure to certain types of media and alcohol and illicit drug use. For example, research has found that adolescent drinkers are more likely to be exposed to various types of messages about alcohol than non-drinkers are (Austin & Knaus, 2000; Austin & Meili, 1994; Grube, 1999; Robinson, Chen, & Killen, 1998; Strasburger, 2002). Furthermore, exposure to pro-alcohol messages represents a significant risk factor for later adolescent drinking (Grube & Waiters, 2005). What remains uncertain is the direction of the relationship. Do young people who are susceptible to substance use pay more attention to alcohol messages and seek them out, or do the messages actually get young people to begin drinking?

One way to explore this issue is to assess the onset of a behavior. In one study, the onset of drinking was significantly associated with greater television viewing, especially previous high exposure to music videos where drinking alcohol often occurs (Robinson, Chen, & Killen, 1998). In a recent longitudinal study of over 3,000 teenagers, seventh graders' exposure to in-store beer displays, magazines with alcohol advertisements, and beer concession stands at sporting and music events significantly predicted drinking onset by ninth grade (Ellickson et al., 2005). A more simplistic analysis of the data shows a relationship between seeing televised beer advertisements and later drinking; however, when the researchers did a more sophisticated analysis and controlled for more person and environmental variables, this effect did not remain significant (Ellickson et al., 2005).

In addition to longitudinal studies investigating behavior onset, experimental research should be conducted to better understand the relationship between media exposure and substance use. Work is now being done where youth are randomly assigned to groups where media exposure and use is reduced. In these studies, those youth with less exposure and use have better health outcomes than do those whose media use stays the same or increases (Robinson & Borzekowski, 2006). Such approaches allow researchers an ethical and viable way to examine if altering media use results in lower rates of substance use.

Potential Public Policy and Other Solutions

Bans and restrictions

Over a decade ago, the American Academy of Pediatrics (AAP) called for a complete media ban on tobacco advertising, and a limitation of alcohol advertising to "tombstone" advertisements (AAP, 1995). Tombstone advertisements are typically advertisements that feature unadorned black-and-white text, enclosed in a simple box. Several countries have instituted these types of bans or severe restrictions on cigarette advertisements (Strasburger, 2004). While some studies have found advertising bans and restrictions to reduce alcohol sales and consumption, others have found no or reverse, unintended effects (Saffer & Dave, 2006).

Industry supporters suggest that bans and restrictions would challenge First Amendment rights of free speech; however, commercial speech does not operate under the same full-out protections that non-commercial speech has under the First Amendment (Central Hudson Gas & Electric Company v. Public Service Commission, 1980). Most restrictions and limitations of alcohol advertising involve self-regulation codes created by the alcohol industry (Jernigan, Ostroff, & Ross, 2005). These codes currently prohibit blatant appeals to young audiences and advertising in venues where most of the audience is under the legal drinking age (FTC, 1999). In addition, the Federal Trade Commission (FTC), an independent agency of the US government, is already empowered by Congress to restrict or ban "unfair and deceptive" advertising. Given the increasing ease of access to media messages across international borders, it is not clear that isolated bans and restrictions will limit adolescents' exposure to pro-substance use messages.

Ratings

A number of critics (www.smokefreemovies.com) argue that movies that contain smoking should be rated R (Restricted), which would deny children and young adolescents access to them in theater venues (Polansky & Glantz, 2004). Currently, the Motion Picture Association of America (MPAA) ratings system does not routinely assess movies for the depiction of legal drugs, only illegal ones (Vaughn, 2006). It is unlikely that the MPAA will ever acquiesce to such a change as there is great resistance to monitoring content on this level. To improve the effect and influence of ratings, it would be useful to educate parents about what the ratings system actually screens for and what is associated with exposure to these types of messages (Sargent et al., 2004). Several online parent resources, such as www.screenit.com, www.kids-in-mind.com, and www.familystyle.com, provide very detailed information on whether and how smoking, drinking, and drug use appear in current and previously released films. It is not yet known the extent to which parents use these resources or if these resources are effective.

Anti-drug messages and campaigns

Counter advertising has been recommended as a way to limit the potential influence of pro-smoking and pro-drinking messages. In the past, counter messages have yielded mixed results; that is, various aspects of the individual and the message, like a person's level of sensation-seeking or a message's delivery tone, appear to affect whether counter messages influence attitudes and behaviors (Strasburger & Wilson, 2002). Following the Master Settlement Agreement between tobacco companies and 46 states, greater efforts have been made to disseminate creative and hard-hitting anti-smoking messages. The literature is just now emerging on the influence of these messages and campaigns.

In the late 1990s, for instance, Florida embarked on an effort to target 12- to 17-year-olds with an intense counter-advertising campaign. This "Truth" campaign, which later became a national effort, was designed to empower youth to refrain from smoking tobacco. Campaign messages characterized the industry as being "predatory, profit hungry, and manipulative" (Sly et al., 2001). One longitudinal assessment of Florida's "Truth" campaign found that youth who were more aware of the television advertisements were significantly less likely to smoke than were youths who could not confirm exposure to the campaign (Sly et al., 2001). This effect was observed among non-smoking youth as well as established smokers. With a more recent national sample, Farrelly and colleagues (2005) reported that US students who had more exposure experiences with the "Truth" campaign were less likely to smoke.

Currently, teenagers are 400 times more likely to see alcohol advertisements than to see public service announcements (PSAs) discouraging underage drinking (MADD, 2004). Given the high appeal of pro-alcohol media messages, there is a call to create well-produced public service messages that effectively gain the attention and resonate with adolescent audiences (Andsager, Austin, & Pinkleton, 2001; Wallack et al., 1990). There is the hope that the successes observed with anti-smoking campaigns can be replicated with anti-alcohol campaigns. Researchers have found that perceived realism, desirability, and similarity are important constructs in creating higher-quality and more effective alcohol PSAs for young people (Andsager, Austin, & Pinkleton, 2001).

Federal efforts to create anti-substance use campaigns have focused on illegal substances, rather than on tobacco and alcohol. The National Institute of Drug Abuse (NIDA) allocates nearly $200 million a year for PSAs targeting illegal drugs. In Kentucky, for example, one public service campaign, supported by NIDA, resulted in a 27 percent decline in marijuana use among adolescents defined as sensation-seekers (Palmgreen et al., 2001). Although criticized in the public press, the "fried egg" PSA aired by the Partnership for a Drug Free America (PDFA) proved effective (Reis et al., 1994). Not only has the PDFA published data about the effectiveness of its campaigns (PDFA, 2003), but independent researchers have confirmed the efficacy of these messages (Strasburger & Wilson, 2002).

Changes in mainstream programming

An ideal venue to alter adolescents' perceptions about tobacco, alcohol, and drug use could be mainstream and popular media, including broadcast television, cable television, film, and the Internet. Messages about smoking, drinking, and illegal drug use could simply be incorporated into plotlines, as was done with the "designated driver" campaign, without altering the entertainment value of a program. The designated driver initiative involved working with and encouraging television producers, writers, and top network executives to insert messages about the dangers of drinking and driving into more than 25 program storylines (Signorielli, 1993). Public health organizations and coalitions, such as the Hollywood, Health, and Society project out of the USC Annenberg Norman Lear Center as well as the Entertainment Industries Council, continue to help influence scripts by including accurate and realistic messages about the problems involved with substance use. These efforts can have a positive impact, as exposure to "edutainment" approaches has been positively associated with engaging in healthy sexual behaviors in the United States and abroad (Singhal et al., 2004; Whittier et al., 2005). Hollywood movies also represent an ideal place to intervene, especially when practically all contemporary movies contain tobacco use (Sargent et al., 2001). Media messages about smoking need to be "denormalized;" that is, depictions of smoking should suggest that tobacco use is infrequent and not a normative behavior for youth (Males, 1999).

Another approach to affect media messages is to commend and reward those who offer high-quality and accurate messages about the effects of substance abuse. Established in 1997, the Entertainment Industries Council has been presenting the PRISM award to honor media productions that are not only entertaining but also realistic in their presentation of substance abuse and addiction. Widely released films, such as *Blow, Ray,* and *Walk the Line,* and popular television programs like *Without a Trace* and *My Wife and Kids* have received PRISM awards in recent years (Entertainment Industries Council, 2007). While considering broader health topics, the Centers for Disease Control and Prevention (CDC) offers the Sentinel for Health Awards for outstanding television productions. Recognized programs have high entertainment value and great potential benefits for the viewing audience (Norman Lear Center, 2007).

Media education

There is some evidence that media literacy education for children and teenagers can be protective against early drug use, particularly alcohol and tobacco (AAP,

2001; Austin & Johnson, 1997; McCannon, 2005). Media literacy involves teaching young people how to decode media and media messages (Rich & Bar-on, 2001). To promote media literacy, the CDC has developed MediaSharp, a creative unit to be incorporated into existing smoking and drinking prevention curricula. This unit teaches young people to deconstruct actual advertisements and television and film excerpts, and to analyze how media can influence their health and spending behaviors (Parvanta & Freimuth, 2000). In one study, researchers found that a media literacy training intervention had both immediate and delayed effects in preventing 250 third-grade students from developing alcohol-related behaviors (Austin & Johnson, 1997).

Despite the fact that the majority of US public school districts use standard drug prevention programs like DARE (Drug Abuse Resistance Education), studies are showing that they are not effective (Perry et al., 2003; West & O'Neal, 2004). In contrast, programs that incorporate lessons about the media's influence and strategies to resist peer pressure, such as Life Skills Training, appear to be successful in decreasing adolescents' levels of substance use. Seventh-grade students who participated in the ALERT Plus, a comprehensive drug prevention curriculum that includes lessons on identifying and resisting pro-drinking and pro-drug media messages, were less likely in ninth grade to drink and be susceptible to advertising appeals (Ellickson et al., 2005). Although more expensive and time-consuming than DARE-like programs, programs like ALERT Plus have been shown repeatedly to cut projected rates and levels of youngsters' tobacco, alcohol, and illicit drug use (Botvin & Griffin, 2005; Ellickson et al., 2005).

Conclusion

"Just Say No" has become "Just Say Yes" with the aid of $21 billion worth of tobacco, alcohol, and drug advertising as well as a Hollywood industry that has not enthusiastically embraced its public health responsibilities. Pro-tobacco, pro-alcohol, and even pro-drug messages abound in media venues. Public health campaigns do exist but they do not have the same finances and organization behind them that alcohol and tobacco companies have. Considerable research confirms the power of positive and negative media messages as influences on children's and adolescents' attitudes about and actual decisions regarding whether to use drugs, be they legal or illegal. At the same time, most drug prevention programs in schools use little or none of this new information, instead relying on programs which have been found to be ineffective. To decrease rates of smoking, drinking, and drug use among adolescents, policy makers, producers, parents, and educators will have to be considerably savvier about pro-substance use messages and their influence on young people.

References

Allison, K. W., Crawford, I., Leone, P. E., Trickett, E., Perez-Febles, A., Burton, L. M., et al. (1999). Adolescent substance use: Preliminary examinations of school and neighborhood context. *American Journal of Community Psychology*, 27, 111–41.

American Academy of Pediatrics (AAP). (1995). Children, adolescents, and advertising. *Pediatrics*, 95, 295–7.

American Academy of Pediatrics (AAP). (2001). Tobacco's toll: Implications for the pediatrician. *Pediatrics*, 107, 794–8.

Andsager J. L., Austin, E. W., & Pinkleton, B. E. (2001). Questioning the value of realism: Young adults' processing of messages in alcohol-related public service announcements and advertising. *Journal of Communication*, 51, 121–42.

Armstrong, J. (2002). Smoke signals. *Entertainment Weekly*, June 7, 2002, p. 9.

Aufderheide, P. (1990). After the Fairness Doctrine: Controversial broadcast programming and the public interest. *Journal of Health Communication*, 40, 47–72.

Austin, E. W., & Johnson, K. K. (1997). Effects of general and alcohol-specific media literacy training on children's decision making about alcohol. *Journal of Health Communication*, 2, 17–42.

Austin, E. W., & Knaus, C. S. (2000). Predicting the potential for risky behavior among those "too young" to drink, as the result of appealing advertising. *Journal of Health Communication*, 5, 13–27.

Austin, E. W., & Meili, H. K. (1994). Effects of interpretations of televised alcohol portrayals on children's alcohol beliefs. *Journal of Broadcasting and Electronic Media*, 38, 417–35.

Bandura, A. (1986). *Social foundations of thought and action: A social cognitive theory*. Englewood Cliffs, NJ: Prentice Hall.

Belcher, H. M. E., & Shinitzky, H. E. (1998). Substance abuse in children: Prediction, protection, and prevention. *Archives of Pediatric and Adolescent Medicine*, 152, 952–60.

Biener, L., & Siegel, M. (2000). Tobacco marketing and adolescent smoking: more support for a causal inference. *American Journal of Public Health*, 90, 407–11.

Borzekowski, D. L. G. (2006). Adolescents' use of the Internet: A controversial, coming-of-age resource. *Adolescent Medicine Clinics*, 17, 205–16.

Borzekowski, D. L. G., & Rickert, V. I. (2001). Adolescent cybersurfing for health information: A new resource that crosses barriers. *Archives of Pediatrics and Adolescent Medicine*, 155(7), 813–17.

Botvin, G. J. (1990). Substance abuse prevention: Theory, practice, and effectiveness. *Crime and Justice*, 13, 461–519.

Botvin, E. M., Botvin, G. J., Michela, J. L., Baker, E., & Filazzola, A. D. (1991). Adolescent smoking behavior and the recognition of cigarette advertisements. *Journal of Applied Social Psychology*, 21, 919–32.

Botvin, G. J., & Griffin, K. W. (2005). Models of prevention: School-based programs. In J. H. Lowinson, P. Ruiz, R. B. Millman, & J. G. Langrod (Eds.), *Substance abuse: A comprehensive textbook* (4th edn.) (pp. 1211–29). Baltimore: Lippincott, Williams, & Wilkins.

Breed, W., & DeFoe, J. R. (1983). Cigarette smoking on television: 1950–1982. *New England Journal of Medicine*, 309, 617 (letter).

Bronfenbrenner, U. (1989). Ecological systems theory. In R. Vasta (Ed.), *Six theories of child development* (pp. 187–250). Greenwich, CT: JAI Press.

Centers for Disease Control and Prevention (CDC). (1992). Comparison of the cigarette brand preferences of adult and teenage smokers – United States, 1989, and 10 U.S. communities, 1988 and 1990. *Morbidity and Mortality Weekly Report*, 41, 169–81.

Center for Science in the Public Interest (CSPI). (1988). *Kids are aware of booze as presidents, survey finds.* News release, September 4. Washington, DC: CSPI.

Central Hudson Gas and Electric Company v. Public Service Commission. (1980). 447 US 557, 566.

Christenson, P. G., Henriksen, L., & Roberts, D. F. (2000). *Substance use in popular prime-time television.* Washington, DC: Office of National Drug Control Policy.

Colder, C. R., & Chassin, L. (1997). Affectivity and impulsivity: Temperament risk for adolescent alcohol involvement. *Psychology of Addictive Behaviors*, 11(2), 83–97.

Collins, R. L., Ellickson, P. L., McCaffrey, D. F., & Hambarsoomians, K. (2005). Saturated in beer: Awareness of beer advertising in late childhood and adolescence. *Journal of Adolescent Health*, 37(1), 29–36.

DeFoe, J. R., & Breed, W. (1988). Youth and alcohol in television stories, with suggestions to the industry for alternative portrayals. *Adolescence*, 23, 533–50.

DiFranza, J. R., Richards, J. W., Jr., Paulman, P. M., Wolf-Gillespie, N., Fletcher, C., Jaffe, R. D., et al. (1991). RJR Nabisco's cartoon camel promotes Camel cigarettes to children. *Journal of the American Medical Association*, 266, 3149–53.

DuRant, R. H., Rome, E. S., Rich, M., Allred, E., Emans, S. J., & Woods, E. R. (1997). Tobacco and alcohol use behaviors portrayed in music videos: a content analysis. *American Journal of Public Health*, 87, 1131–5.

Edwards, C. C., Elliott, S. P., Conway, T. L., & Woodruff, S. I. (2003). Teen smoking cessation help via the Internet: A survey of search engines. *Health Promotion Practice*, 4, 262–5.

Ellickson, P. H., Collins, R. L., Hambarsoomians, K., & McCaffrey, D. F. (2005). Does alcohol advertising promote adolescent drinking? Results from a longitudinal assessment. *Addiction*, 100, 235–46.

Engels, R., Knibbe, R. A., Drop, M. J., & de Haan, Y. T. (1997). Homogeneity of cigarette smoking within peer groups: influence or selection? *Health Education and Behavior*, 24, 801–11.

Entertainment Industries Council. (2007). *About the Prism Awards, Los Angeles, CA, the Entertainment Industries Council, Inc., Norman Lear Center.* Retrieved May 22, 2007, from http://www.prismawards.com/about/.

Evans, N., Farkas, A., Gilpin, E., Berry, C., & Pierce, J. P. (1995). Influence of tobacco marketing and exposure to smokers on adolescent susceptibility to smoking. *Journal of the National Cancer Institute*, 87, 1538–45.

Everett, S. A., Schnuth, R. L., & Tribble, J. L. (1998). Tobacco and alcohol use in top-grossing American films. *Journal of Communication Health*, 23, 317–24.

Farrelly, M. C., Davis, K. C., Haviland, M. L., Messeri, P., & Healton, C. G. (2005). Evidence of a dose-response relationship between "truth" antismoking ads and youth smoking prevalence. *American Journal of Public Health*, 95, 425–31.

Federal Trade Commission (FTC). (1999). *Self-Regulation in the alcohol industry: A review of industry efforts to avoid promoting alcohol to underage consumers.* Washington, DC: FTC.

Feighery, E., Borzekowski, D. L. G., Schooler, C., & Flora, J. (1998). Seeing, wanting, owning: The relationship between receptivity to tobacco marketing and smoking susceptibility in young people. *Tobacco Control*, 7, 123–8.

Fischer, P. M., Schwartz, M. P., Richards, J. W., Jr., Goldstein, A. O., & Rojas, T. H. (1991). Brand logo recognition by children aged 3 to 6 years: Mickey Mouse and Old Joe the Camel. *Journal of the American Medical Association*, 266, 3145–8.

Flay, B. R., & Sobel, J. L. (1983). The role of mass media in preventing adolescent substance abuse. In T. J. Glynn et al. (Eds.), Preventing adolescent drug abuse: Intervention strategies. *NIDA Research Monograph*, 47, 5–35.

Fox, R. F. (1996). *Harvesting minds: How TV commercials control kids.* Westport, CT: Praeger.

Fox, S. (1984). *The mirror makers: A history of American advertising and its creators.* New York: William Morrow.

Gentile, D. A., Walsh, D. A., Bloomgren, B. W., Atti, J. A., & Norman, J. A. (2001). *Frogs sell beer: The effects of beer advertisements on adolescent drinking knowledge, attitudes, and behavior.* Paper presented at the biennial conference of the Society for Research in Child Development, April, Minneapolis, MN.

Gerbner, G., Gross, L., Signorielli, N., & Morgan, M. (1980). Aging with television: images on television drama and conceptions of social reality. *Journal of Communication*, 30, 37–47.

Golub, A., & Johnson, B. D. (2001). Variation in youthful risks of progression from alcohol and tobacco to marijuana and to hard drugs across generations. *American Journal of Public Health*, 91, 225–32.

Grube, J. W. (1999). *Alcohol advertising and alcohol consumption: A review of recent research. NIAA tenth special report to Congress on alcohol and health.* Bethesda, MD: National Institute on Alcohol Abuse and Alcoholism.

Grube, J. W., & Waiters, E. (2005). Alcohol in the media: content and effects on drinking beliefs and behaviors among youth. *Adolescent Medicine Clinics*, 16, 327–43.

Gutschoven, K., & Van den Bulck, J. (2005). Television viewing and age at smoking initiation: Does a relationship exist between higher levels of television viewing and earlier onset of smoking? *Nicotine and Tobacco Research*, 7, 381–5.

Hazan, A. R., & Glantz, S. A. (1995). Current trends in tobacco use on prime-time fictional television. *American Journal of Public Health*, 85, 116–17 (letter).

Hettinger, H. S., & Neff, W. J. (1938). *Practical radio advertising.* New York: Prentice Hall.

Hingson, R. W., Heeren, T., & Winter, M. R. (2006). Age at drinking onset and alcohol dependence: Age at onset, duration, and severity. *Archives of Pediatric and Adolescent Medicine*, 160, 739–46.

Hong, T., & Cody, M. J. (2002). Presence of pro-tobacco message on the Web. *Journal of Health Communication*, 7, 273–307.

Jernigan, D. H., Ostroff, J., & Ross, C. (2005). Alcohol advertising and youth: A measured approach. *Journal of Public Health Policy*, 26, 312–25.

Johnston, L. D., O'Malley, P. M., Bachman, J. G., & Schulenberg, J. E. (2005). *Monitoring the future national survey results on drug use, 1975–2004.* Vol. 1, *Secondary school students* (NIH Publication No. 05-5727). Bethesda, MD: National Institute on Drug Abuse.

Krippendorf, K. (2004). *Content analysis: An introduction to its methodology* (2nd edn.). Thousand Oaks, CA: Sage.

Kulig, J. W., & the Committee on Substance Abuse. (2005). Tobacco, alcohol, and other drugs: The role of the pediatrician in prevention, identification, and management of substance abuse. *Pediatrics*, 115, 816–21.

Kurtz, M. E., Kurtz, J. C., Johnson, S. M., & Cooper, W. (2001). Sources of information on the health effects of environmental tobacco smoke among African-American children and adolescents. *Journal of Adolescent Health*, 28, 458–64.

Leiber, L. (1996). *Commercial and character slogan recall by children aged 9 to 11 years: Budweiser frogs versus Bugs Bunny.* Berkeley: Center on Alcohol Advertising.

Long, J. A., O'Connor, P. G., Gerbner, G., & Concato, J. (2002). Use of alcohol, illicit drugs, and tobacco among characters on prime-time television. *Substance Abuse*, 23(2), 95–103.

MacDonald, P. T., & Estep, R. (1985). Prime Time Drug Depictions, *Contemporary Drug Problems*, 12(3), 419–38.

Males, M. (1999). *Smoked: Why big tobacco is still smiling.* Monroe, ME: Common Courage Press.

McCannon, R. (2005). Adolescents and media literacy. *Adolescent Medicine Clinics*, 16, 463–80.

McIntosh, W. D., Smith, S. M., Bazzini, D. G., & Mills, P. S. (1999). Alcohol in the movies: characteristics of drinkers and nondrinkers in films from 1940 to 1989. *Journal of Applied Social Psychology*, 29, 1191–9.

Mekemson, C., Glik, D., Titus, K., Myerson, A., Shaivitz, A., Ang, A., et al. (2004). Tobacco use in popular movies during the past decade. *Tobacco Control*, 13, 400–402.

Mokdad, A. H., Marks, J. S., Stroup, D. F., & Gerberding, J. L. (2004). Actual causes of death in the United States, 2000. *Journal of the American Medical Association*, 291, 1238–45.

Mothers Against Drunk Driving (MADD). (2004). *Latest CAMY study shows TV alcohol ads outnumber responsibility ads 226 to 1* (News release, May 26). Retrieved September 30, 2005, from http://madd.org/news/0,1056,8239,00.html.

National Center on Addiction and Substance Abuse. (2004). *National survey of American attitudes on substance abuse IX: Teen dating practices and sexual activity.* New York: NCASA.

National Institute on Drug Abuse (NIDA). (1995). *Drug use among racial/ethnic minorities 1995* (NIH Publication No. 95-3888). Rockville, MD: NIDA.

Norman Lear Center. (2007). *Sentinel for Health Awards.* Retrieved May 22, 2007, from http://www.learcenter.org/html/projects/index.php?cm=hhs/sentinel.

Omidvari, K., Lessnau, K., Kim, J., Mercante, D., Weinacker, A., & Mason, C. (2005). Smoking in contemporary American cinema. *Chest*, 128, 746–54.

Palmgreen, P., Donohew, L., Lorch, E. P., Hoyle, R. H., & Stephenson, M. T. (2001). Television campaigns and adolescent marijuana use: Tests of sensation seeking targeting. *American Journal of Public Health*, 91, 292–6.

Parker, F., Aldridge, H., & Measham, J. (1998). The teenage transition: From adolescent recreational drug use to the young adult dance culture in Britain in the mid-1990s. *Journal of Drug Issues*, 28, 9–32.

Partnership for a Drug-Free America (PDFA). (2003). *Partnership attitude tracking study, teens 2003.* New York: PDFA.

Parvanta, C. F., & Freimuth, V. (2000). Health communication at the Centers for Disease Control and Prevention. *American Journal of Health Behavior*, 24, 18–25.

Perry, C. L., Komro, K. A., Veblen-Mortenson, S., Bosma, L. M., Farbakhsh, K., Munson, K. A., et al. (2003). A randomized controlled trial of the middle and junior high school DARE and DARE plus programs. *Archives of Pediatrics and Adolescent Medicine*, 157, 178–84.

Pierce, J. P., Choi, W. S., Gilpin, E. A., Farkas, A. J., & Berry, C. C. (1998). Tobacco industry promotion of cigarettes and adolescent smoking. *Journal of the American Medical Association*, 279, 511–15.

Pierce, J. P., Distefan, J. M., Jackson, C., White, M. M., & Gilpin, E. A. (2002). Does tobacco marketing undermine the influence of recommended parenting in discouraging adolescents from smoking? *American Journal of Preventive Medicine*, 23, 73–81.

Pierce, J. P., Gilpin, E., & Burns, D. M. (1991). Does tobacco advertising target young people to start smoking? *Journal of the American Medical Association*, 266, 3154–8.

Polansky, J. R., & Glantz, S. A. (2004). First-run smoking presentations in US movies 1999–2003. San Francisco, CA: Center for Tobacco Control Research and Education. Retrieved September 29, 2005, from http://repositories.cdlib.org/ctcre/tcpmus/Movies2004/.

Pollay, R. W., & Compton, D. J. (1992). *Cigarette ad exposure to youth: TV use under self-regulation*. Vancouver: Faculty of Commerce, University of British Columbia, History of Advertising Archives, Working Paper, June 1992.

Prinstein, M. J., & Wang, S. S. (2005). False consensus and adolescent peer contagion: Examining discrepancies between perceptions and actual reported levels of friends' deviant and health risk behaviors. *Journal of Abnormal Child Psychology*, 33, 294–306.

Reis, E. C., Duggan, A. K., Adger, H., Jr., & DeAngelis, C. (1994). The impact of anti-drug advertising. *Archives of Pediatrics and Adolescent Medicine*, 148, 1262–8.

Ribisl, K. M. (2003). The potential of the Internet as a medium to encourage and discourage youth tobacco use. *Tobacco Control*, 12, i48–i59.

Rich, M., & Bar-on, M. (2001). Child health in the information age: media education of pediatricians. *Pediatrics*, 107, 156–62.

Roberts, D. F., & Christenson, P. G. (2000). *Here's looking at you, kid: Alcohol, drugs, and tobacco in entertainment media*. Menlo Park, CA: Kaiser Family Foundation.

Roberts, D. F., Christenson, P. G., Henriksen, L., & Bandy, E. (2002). *Substance use in popular music videos*. Washington, DC: Office of National Drug Control Policy.

Roberts, D. F., Henriksen, L., & Christenson, P. G. (1999). *Substance use in popular movies and music*. Washington, DC: Office of National Drug Control Policy.

Robinson, T. N., & Borzekowski, D. L. G. (2006). Effects of the SMART classroom curriculum to reduce child and family screen time. *Journal of Communication*, 56(1), 1–26.

Robinson, T. N., Chen, H. L., & Killen, J. D. (1998). Television and music video exposure and risk of adolescent alcohol use. *Pediatrics*, 102, e54.

Saffer, H., & Dave, D. (2006). Alcohol advertising and alcohol consumption by adolescents. *Health Economics*, 15, 617–37.

Sargent, J. D. (2005). Smoking in movies: impact on adolescent smoking. *Adolescent Medicine Clinics*, 16, 345–70.

Sargent, J. D., Beach, M. L., Dalton, M. A., Ernstoff, L. T., Gibson, J. J., Tickle, J. J., et al. (2004). Effect of parental R-rated movie restriction on adolescent smoking initiation. *Pediatrics*, 114, 149–56.

Sargent, J. D., Tickle, J. J., Beach, M. L., Ahrens, M., & Heatherton, T. (2001). Brand appearances in contemporary cinema films and contribution to global marketing of cigarettes. *Lancet*, 357, 29–32.

Schooler, C., Feighery E., & Flora, J. (1996). Seventh graders' self-reported exposure to cigarette marketing and its relationship to their smoking behavior. *American Journal of Public Health*, 86, 1216–21.

Shanahan, J., & Morgan, M. (1999). *Television and its viewers: Cultivation theory and research.* Cambridge: Cambridge University Press.

Shapiro, H. (2002). From Chaplin to Charlie – cocaine, Hollywood and the movies. *Drugs: Education, Prevention and Policy*, 9, 133–41.

Signorielli, N. (1993). *Mass media images and impact on health.* Westport, CT: Greenwood Press.

Singhal, A., Cody, M. J., Rogers, E. M., & Sabido, M. (2004). *Entertainment-education and social change: History, research and practice.* Mahwah, NJ: Lawrence Erlbaum.

Sly, D. F., Hopkins, R. S., Trapido, E., & Ray, S. (2001). Influence of a counteradvertising media campaign on initiation of smoking: The Florida "truth" campaign. *American Journal of Public Health*, 91(2), 233–8.

Stern, S. (2005). Messages from teens on the big screen: Smoking, drinking, and drug use in teen-centered films. *Journal of Health Communication*, 110(4), 331–46.

Strasburger, V. C. (2002). Alcohol advertising and adolescents. *Pediatric Clinics of North America*, 49, 1–24.

Strasburger, V. C. (2004). Children, adolescents, and the media. *Current Problems in Pediatric and Adolescent Health Care*, 34, 51–113.

Strasburger, V. C., & Wilson, B. J. (2002). *Children, Adolescents, and the Media.* Thousand Oaks, CA: Sage.

US Department of Health and Human Services. (1994). *Preventing tobacco use among young people: A report of the Surgeon General.* Atlanta, GA: US Department of Health and Human Services, Public Health Service, CDC National Center for Chronic Disease Prevention and Health Promotion, Office on Smoking and Health.

Vakalahi, H. F. (2001). Adolescent substance use and family-based risk and protective factor: A literature review. *Journal of Drug Education*, 31(1), 29–46.

Vaughn, S. (2006). *Freedom and entertainment: Rating the movies in an age of new media.* New York: Cambridge University Press.

Wallack, L., Grube, J. W., Madden, P. A., & Breed, W. (1990). Portrayals of alcohol on prime-time television. *Journal of Studies on Alcohol*, 51(5), 428–37.

Weinberg, N. Z., Rahdert, E., Colliver, J. D., & Glantz, M. D. (1998). Adolescent substance abuse: A review of the past 10 years. *Journal of the American Academy of Child and Adolescent Psychiatry*, 37, 252–61.

West, S. L., & O'Neal, K. K. (2004). Project DARE outcome effectiveness revisited. *American Journal of Public Health*, 94, 1027–9.

Whittier, D. K., Kennedy, M. G., St Lawrence, J. S., Seeley, S., & Beck, V. (2005). Embedding health messages into entertainment television: Effect on gay men's response to a syphilis outbreak. *Journal of Health Communication*, 10, 251–9.

Williams, J. (2000). Movies about marijuana are sprouting like weeds. *St Louis Post-Dispatch*, August 20. Retrieved May 22, 2007, from http://www.stltoday.com/archives.

Windle, M., Miller-Tutzauer, C., & Domenico, D. (1992). Alcohol use, suicidal behavior, and risky activities among adolescents. *Journal of Research on Adolescence*, 2, 317–30.

Part VI

Media Policy and Interventions

20

The Children's Television Act

Sandra L. Calvert

Since the beginnings of television, the promise of well-designed programming for advancing children's cognitive and social development has been apparent though rarely realized. On the one hand, television programs have always had considerable power to deliver an educational message to a mass audience. On the other hand, economic and legislative realities limit that possibility. The challenges for creating quality children's television programs, then and now, include: (1) getting a child audience to view educational television voluntarily during their free time in a competitive marketplace where programs are available solely for entertainment purposes (Mitroff, 2003; Stipp, 2003); (2) providing a viewing experience that is not dominated by commercial material (Kunkel, 2003); and (3) regulating televised content in an environment where the First Amendment, which guarantees freedom of speech, is a centerpiece of American liberty (Kunkel, 2003; Wilcox, 2003).

After decades of controversy about the kinds of content being created for and consumed by children (e.g., violent cartoons), Congress passed the Children's Television Act in 1990. The Children's Television Act (CTA) was groundbreaking legislation that consisted of two parts. First, the CTA required broadcasters to provide educational and informational television programs as a condition for license renewal. Second, the CTA limited the amount of commercial material that could be shown during children's television programs to 10.5 minutes per hour during weekend programs and 12 minutes per hour during weekday programs.

In this chapter, I describe how the Children's Television Act became a law. Then I describe early implementation and subsequent changes in the implementation of the law. One key issue involves the definition of an educational television program, a controversy that has led to court challenges when certain broadcasters have attempted to renew their licenses with programs of dubious educational value. Next, I review content analyses of educational and informational (E/I) television programs and research on what children learn after viewing

E/I programs, including why certain segments of the child audience are less interested in E/I programs. I discuss the challenges in creating quality programs for the child audience. I end with a discussion of what the CTA will mean in the digital age when convergence allows new online opportunities for children to interact with educational content, and whether that interactive promise will be a legal CTA requirement in the future. My overall focus in this chapter is on the requirement for E/I television programs, but I include a brief discussion about the CTA's limits on the amount of commercial material as well.

The Children's Television Act

Children's programming is the key policy area in which efforts have taken place to alter television content (Huston, Watkins, & Kunkel, 1989). Although much of the controversy has centered around the negative impact of violent content on children, it also involves the lack of quality programming developed and distributed to child audiences as well as advertisements directed at young viewers (Calvert, 1999).

The Federal Communications Commission (FCC) regulates all television programming on the airwaves. Because these airwaves are public domain and belong to the people, broadcasters are required to "serve the public interest, convenience, and necessity" (Communications Act of 1934, p. 51). Licenses are held by local broadcasters, including local affiliates of national parent companies (e.g., ABC, CBS) as well as independent stations (Calvert, 1999). Every eight years commercial broadcasters are required by law to apply to the FCC for license renewal. The FCC establishes rules and guidelines to determine if each commercial broadcast station is fulfilling its public interest obligations (Kunkel, 2003).

The First Amendment, which guarantees freedom of speech, creates a tension between the FCC's role of regulating content and the freedom of broadcasters to show the content that they choose (Huston & Wright, 1998). These two conflicting roles – to regulate content while ensuring freedom of speech – have made it difficult for the FCC to enforce media policies (Liebert & Sprafkin, 1988). The outcome of this tension has consistently favored the broadcasters' right for freedom of speech. For instance, no television station has ever lost its license for the kind of programming it broadcasts.

Years of debate and efforts to implement voluntary compliance procedures, by which broadcasters were expected to regulate themselves, resulted in little change in the quality of children's television programs (Kunkel, 2003). This failure by broadcasters to implement voluntary changes, coupled with concerns about the violence and commercialization pervading the airwaves, led Congress to take action and pass the Children's Television Act of 1990 (Kunkel, 1991).

When the Children's Television Act became a law, the license renewals of commercial broadcasters were linked to the inclusion of E/I programming in their schedules as part of their public obligation requirement (Kunkel, 2003). The

E/I guideline does not apply to cable stations because they do not use the public airways (Kunkel, 2003), a source of concern for many commercial broadcasters who believe that the CTA puts them at a competitive disadvantage with the cable industry.

Because of the link to license renewal, the FCC was essentially charged with implementing rules for commercial broadcasters to follow to fulfill their E/I obligations to viewers. However, the statutory obligations of the commercial broadcasters were not clear (Wilcox, 2003). For instance, the word "children" was not explicitly defined in terms of relevant ages, and there was no clarity on what must be done to meet the E/I programming requirements (Kunkel & Wilcox, 2001; Wilcox, 2003).

The FCC commissioners defined educational and informational programs as those that "further the positive development of the child in any respect, including the child's cognitive/intellectual or social/emotional needs" (FCC, 1991, p. 2114). The FCC interpreted the law to include programs designed for children ages 16 and under. Because broadcasters could decide if programs met those criteria, no firm guidelines were made about the number of hours or the time of day when programs had to be broadcast. As a consequence, short-form programs that were less than 5 minutes in length could be counted as meeting the guidelines, and there were no uniform rules about how broadcasters should document their compliance with the law in their license renewal filings (Kunkel & Canepa, 1994). Issues quickly arose about which programs met the guidelines of the Children's Television Act.

Broadcaster Compliance with the Children's Television Act

Because the definition of educational content was so broad and because there were minimal guidelines provided by the FCC, broadcasters had considerable latitude in what they presented as an E/I television program. As license renewal procedures began to occur, some broadcasters submitted highly questionable television programs which they claimed were meeting the requirements of the CTA. Content analyses of the broadcaster reports on file at the FCC and content analyses of the actual television programs were the initial ways that researchers challenged broadcaster compliance with the Children's Television Act.

Content analyses of license renewal claims

Researchers who examined broadcaster reports to the FCC often found distorted and inaccurate classifications of E/I programs (Calvert, 1999). For example, the license renewal form of WGNO, New Orleans, LA, claimed many animated programs, such as *Ducktales, GI Joe, Tiny Toon Adventures*, and *Bucky O'Hare*, as E/I offerings by redefining these cartoons to make them sound educational.

The station described one episode of *Bucky O'Hare* as follows: "Good-doer Bucky fights off the evil toads from aboard his ship. Issues of social consciousness and responsibility are central themes of the programs" (Center for Media Education and Institute for Public Representation, 1992, p. 5).

Similarly, Kunkel and Canepa (1994) found widespread distortions in the meaning of the term "educational and informational." In their examination of 48 stations applying for license renewal, broadcasters aired an average of only 3.5 hours of E/I programs per week. Averaging only about 30 minutes per day, this amount of programming is but a fraction of the time that television programs are broadcast on public airwaves. Moreover, many of the programs identified as E/I offerings were suspect, including *The Jetsons, Bettlejuice,* and *Goof Troop. The Jetsons,* for instance, was described as an E/I program because it taught children about the future. Some broadcasters also labeled short-form programs, such as 3-minute vignettes of *School House Rock,* which were designed to teach English, math, science, and history, as educational programs that fit the short attention spans of child viewers (Kunkel, 1998). Rather than improving the quality of children's programs, the Children's Television Act seemed to be a hurdle that broadcasters often passed with little intent to go beyond the minimal requirements of the law.

Content analyses of E/I television programs

From the 1995–2000 broadcast seasons, Jordan and her colleagues (e.g., Jordan, Schmitt, & Woodard, 2002) from the Annenberg Public Policy Center (APPC) conducted annual content analyses of the programs that broadcasters in the Philadelphia, Pennsylvania, area claimed to be E/I. Major parent companies such as ABC, CBS, and NBC often provide programming, including E/I programming, to local stations that are affiliated with them (i.e., local affiliates). Thus, the Annenberg sample provided a representative look at the kinds of programs children could view throughout the United States. These content analyses revealed a lack of consensus between the broadcasters' claims of educational and informational value and the researchers' evaluations of these programs.

Over this five-year period, Jordan examined the kind of lesson portrayed as well as the educational and informational value of programming classified as E/I. The primary lesson of the program was classified as one that focused on knowledge/information, cognitive skills, social-emotional skills, or physical well-being. One score, an index of the educational value of these lessons, was created by assessing four program criteria: (1) lesson clarity (explicitly presented message that can readily be understood by the target audience); (2) lesson integration (lesson is consistently presented in program and culminates in final lesson); (3) lesson involvement (age-appropriate content, use of child characters, and interesting production techniques); and (4) lesson applicability (lesson that can easily be translated into children's own lives). A second score assessed the program's overall educational value on a 3-point scale, ranging from 0–2. A composite score was created by summing and weighting these two scores about the specific educational lessons

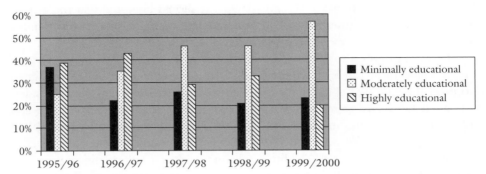

Figure 20.1   Ratings of Educational and Informational Television Programs 1995–2000

and the overall educational value of programs, yielding an overall rating of high, moderate, and low educational value (Jordan, Schmitt, & Woodard, 2002).

As seen in Figure 20.1, Jordan's team found that highly educational television programs declined over the five broadcast seasons. Moderately educational television programs, by contrast, increased over time, accounting for more than half of the E/I programs by the 1999/2000 broadcast season. Minimally educational television programs dropped after the first season in their sample (i.e., 1996), but then have remained steady over several years, accounting for 20 to 25 percent of E/I offerings (Jordan, 1996, 2000; Jordan & Woodard, 1998; Jordan, Schmitt, & Woodard, 2002; Jordan & Woodard, 1997; Schmitt, 1999). The majority of the programs had social emotional themes with lower frequencies of informational, cognitive, or physical well-being themes. Programs with informational and cognitive lessons were rated as having greater educational strength than were those with prosocial themes. With low-quality programming consistently representing roughly a fifth to a quarter of the E/I programs over a five-year period, questions persist about which programs should qualify as meeting the requirements of the Children's Television Act.

Changes in FCC Broadcaster Guidelines

Because researchers consistently documented problems with broadcaster compliance in meeting the E/I programming requirements of the Children's Television Act, the FCC moved to strengthen the law. In 1997, the FCC introduced several new guidelines.

The *3-hour rule*, which requires broadcasters to provide a minimum of 3 hours of E/I programs each week, was implemented by the FCC in September of 1997. This rule addresses the concern that financial liabilities occur if some commercial stations broadcast more educational television programs than others do (Jordan, 1997). Because all stations have to provide the same amount of programming, Reed Hundt, then the FCC Chair, argued that no commercial station would be at an economic disadvantage (Hundt, 1995). It should be noted that the 3-hour rule is actually 30 minutes less of E/I programming than the broadcasters claimed they were airing on a weekly basis (Kunkel & Canepa, 1994).

The FCC (1996) also mandated that only *core educational television programming* would meet the E/I requirement. Core programs must be: (1) designed to meet the educational and informational needs of children ages 16 and under; (2) aired between 7 a.m. and 10 p.m.; (3) scheduled on a weekly basis; and (4) at least 30 minutes in length (FCC, 1996). When programs were preempted, E/I programs were to be broadcast in a predictable alternate time-slot. Effective January 2, 1997, stations also had to label educational and informational programs with an E/I logo so that parents and children could find them (FCC, 1996). These new FCC rules addressed practices such as broadcasting E/I programs at 5 a.m. when children were not in the audience, preempting educational programs for more lucrative adult programs, and failing to identify the programs so that viewers could find them (Jordan, Schmitt, & Woodard, 2002).

Those broadcasters who complied with the new guidelines were rewarded with an expedited license renewal. Those who did not had to follow a lengthier license renewal process (Calvert, 1999).

Children's Learning from E/I Television Programs

Even when high-quality educational programs are broadcast, it does not ensure that children will watch them or learn any lessons of value. In a study assessing the effects of the CTA programs on children's learning, Calvert and Kotler (2003) analyzed five different sets of data to address this issue.

In the first data set, longitudinal information was collected from approximately 500 second- to sixth-grade children who lived in numerous locations throughout the United States. These children reported their viewing patterns over a nine-month period. Naturalistic data were obtained on the different E/I programs that children viewed, their favorite programs, and the lessons that they learned from their favorite programs. The lessons learned were assessed by scoring a written report about their favorite program. In the second set of data, Nielsen Media Research ratings were collected and used to validate children's self-reports about their naturalistic viewing habits. A third data set involved a laboratory study in which a subset of the overall naturalistic sample was examined, assessing children's comprehension of popular and unpopular E/I programs, as determined by the naturalistic data. In a fourth prong of the study, the educational strength of children's reports from the laboratory study was linked to the educational strength of these programs, using the Annenberg Public Policy ratings of the E/I programs. In the fifth data set, a follow-up comparison of favorite programs, educational lessons, and educational strength was conducted for a subset of children who could select any program as their favorite rather than choosing from our earlier fixed menu of educational programs.

The naturalistic study

To collect the naturalistic data, children were invited to come online as a Georgetown Hoya television reporter from different areas of the country, primarily by visiting our specially designed website from their schools. All the E/I programs from ABC, CBS, NBC, and Fox were available on our webpage as visual icons with program names. For comparison purposes, educational programs were selected from PBS and Nickelodeon; even though these broadcasters were not required to meet the E/I requirements of the Children's Television Act, they often create high-quality programs for the child audience.

After logging in under a pretend name, each child clicked on icons of all the educational programs that had been viewed the preceding week. Then the child selected his or her favorite educational program. Finally each child wrote a report about this favorite educational program. Because some program series aired multiple episodes each week, we could not determine the total amount of time spent viewing educational programs. However, our methodology did allow us to determine the number of different educational programs viewed as well as children's overall favorite educational programs.

On average, each child viewed about three different educational programs per week. Younger children and girls viewed the most educational programs. Favorite programs generally had a social-emotional focus, partially reflecting the fact that programs with prosocial, social-emotional themes were what broadcasters were making available for children to view. The most frequently viewed educational programs were also children's favorite programs. These programs were *Hey Arnold!* (Nickelodeon), *The Wild Thornberrys* (Nickelodeon), *Doug* (Nickelodeon and ABC), *Recess* (ABC), *Cousin Skeeter* (Nickelodeon), and *Sabrina the Animated Series* (ABC). It is noteworthy that all of children's favorite programs featured social-emotional themes even though programs with a more traditional academic focus (e.g., *The Magic School Bus*, *Bill Nye, the Science Guy*) were also available for selection. Thus, broadcasters may have been airing programs with social-emotional themes, in part, because children like them the most.

The lessons in children's reports were scored on a system that was adapted from the APPC scoring system for the programs. In particular, children's reports were scored for lesson clarity (child describes the point or main message of the program in his or her report), lesson consistency (child discusses content relevant to the lesson throughout the report), lesson engagement (child reports lesson in an excited and interested style), and lesson generalizability (child describes lesson as applicable to his or her life).

Girls wrote stronger reports than boys did. However, the strength of children's reports were no different if they chose a commercial or a PBS/Nickelodeon favorite educational program, suggesting comparability in what children were taking away across varying broadcaster offerings. Even so, most of children's favorite programs were from PBS and Nickelodeon rather than the four commercial broadcast networks, in large measure due to the popularity of the Nickelodeon programs.

A sample of a third-grade girl's report in which she conveys a social-emotional lesson about her favorite program, *Doug* (broadcast both on ABC and Nickelodeon during our nine-month study), follows. This report was scored highly on lesson applicability, clarity, and integration:

> I watched Doug. It was about when Patty spent a week with Doug. Doug tried to make Patty like him more by doing wierd things. Then Patty said that she liked him just the way he is. I thought this was a good cartoon because it shows that you should just be yourself.

For comparison purposes, here is a report from a sixth-grade girl who also described a social-emotional lesson from her favorite program, *Hey Arnold!* (broadcast on Nickelodeon during our study, but which became part of the CBS educational schedule after this study ended). This report was scored highly on lesson involvement, applicability, clarity, and integration. Note that we did not delete points for spelling errors because writing involved the use of a keyboard, which is challenging for children. Here is what she said:

> Dear Friend,
> "Hey Arnold" was about Granpa entering a chinese checkers tournament. This event was a big deal for Grandpa because he used to be the champion until he was beat 40 years ago. Grandpa douted himself, but Arnold convinsed him to enter. After a week of training Grandpa was nervous but did very well in the tournament anyway. Finally, there were only two people left – Grandpa and the man he had lost to forty years ago! They played and played until it got to only one move left – the same one that made Grandpa lose last time! Grandpa learns from his mistakes though, and made a move to tie the game! They shared the trophy!
> From watching this show, I learned to beleave in yourself and to never give up even when the chances are slim.
>
> Your Friend,
> VollyGrrl88

Programs with academic lessons were also selected as favorites by children. The following report about *The Magic School Bus* (broadcast on Fox during our study but originally a part of the PBS program schedule) was scored highly on lesson clarity and integration.

> I watched The Magic School Bus. The episode that I watched was the episode where all of the class except for Arnold go into Arnold's body. By watching The Magic School Bus I learned that the villi is what sucks up the food in the small intestine. And I learned that all of the water is sucked out of the food in the large intestine. I also learned that not all food can be completely broken down. The episode also told me that the food that can not be completely broken down remains in a solid form when you eliminate it. And the food that is completely broken down comes out as a liquid.

Nielsen ratings

As the year progressed, our naturalistic data revealed that educational television programs increasingly lost their audience. Older children, particularly older boys, were most likely to view fewer educational television programs. Moreover, the strength of children's reports began to diminish. Nielsen ratings were examined to validate the decline in E/I program viewing over the course of the academic year. Consistent with children's self-reports of their natural viewing patterns, Nielsen ratings confirmed that E/I programs were indeed losing their national audience over time. *Pokemon*, a very popular television program that was strictly entertainment-based, was associated with the drop in children's E/I viewing at home. The findings suggest that broadcasters were not providing educational programs that were sufficiently engaging to retain the older child audience.

The laboratory study

The laboratory study was designed to provide a more in-depth look at what children learned from educational programs that were most and least popular, as determined by our naturalistic data. Programs were selected by popularity (high versus low) and by the kind of content involved (academic or prosocial message). Second- to sixth-grade children viewed two programs (one academic, one prosocial) in small groups at their school. They then answered questions about how much they liked the programs as well as verbal multiple-choice, picture sequencing, and free recall questions that assessed their understanding of program lessons. The free recall measure involved writing a report about each program episode, as was done in the naturalistic study.

Just as was found in the naturalistic study, girls and younger children liked the educational programs best. Children also liked and understood the prosocial programs better than the academic ones; even the unpopular prosocial programs were well understood by most children. Those programs with an academic focus were best understood by the older children. The results suggest that comprehension was not the reason that older children left the viewing audience in our naturalistic study. Rather, children of all ages, particularly the older ones, understood the central content of the educational programs well.

Educational strength of children's reports and of program offerings

The strength of children's reports about educational programs (i.e., lesson clarity, integration, involvement, and applicability) was scored at Georgetown University. Program ratings of educational strength (i.e., lesson clarity, integration, engagement, and applicability) were scored at the Annenberg Public Policy Center. These two sets of scores were then correlated. There was no relationship between the strength of children's reports and the adult ratings of the strength of those programs, nor was there a relationship between children's comprehension of the programs and adult ratings of those programs.

Two potential limitations of the current research could have hindered our ability to find a relationship between adult program ratings and child reports. One is that there was a small sample size of programs in the experimental study ($N = 16$), and that number may have been insufficient to yield enough power to produce significant effects. Another is that the educational programs with social-emotional messages were easier to understand than those with an academic focus, thereby inflating the learning scores of the social-emotional lessons (see Jordan, 2003). Even so, it remains noteworthy that what adults think is good for children may not be what they like and learn from the most.

Educational versus strictly entertainment programs

We continued to collect online data for a subset of our sample during the next academic year. This time, however, the site was modified so that children could choose any program that they desired as their favorite. To see if the effects of viewing educational television programs were different from strictly entertainment-based programs, only children who chose both a non-educational and an educational program as their favorite during the follow-up phase of the study were examined.

Children's reports about their favorite educational programs contained more lessons, particularly social-emotional lessons, than their reports about their favorite non-educational programs did. Girls wrote stronger reports, whether they were writing about educational or non-educational programs, than boys did. Engagement with the educational program content was the most pronounced difference in reports, favoring girls over boys. Because girls were more interested in viewing educational programs than boys were, girls may have been more motivated to view E/I programs, and hence to learn from them.

Summary

Taken together, the findings of this study indicate that motivational variables played a central role in children's learning from educational television programs. Program popularity was a key to children's learning from educational programs. Specifically, programs that were better liked were understood the best.

The audience that liked educational programs best was the younger grade school-aged children and girls. Older children, particularly boys, left the audience by the time they were in the fifth and sixth grades. Therefore, even though older children understood the academic programs best in the laboratory study, they were rarely viewing them at home.

In a naturalistic environment, children decide if they are going to watch a program or not. If they choose not to watch educational programming, they cannot possibly benefit from such content. Put another way, the programs have to be popular enough to pull in an audience over time (Stipp, 2003). With that said, it was clear that most children in the study reported viewing a favorite educational program during the course of the year. Many children selected educational programs as favorites, even when they could choose any program, and children's reports about educational programs contained significantly more social and emotional lessons than their favorite entertainment-based programs. Overall, then, there was an audience for educational television programs and children learned prosocial and/or academic lessons after viewing those programs.

Gender Differences in E/I Programs

The loss of boys as viewers of the E/I programs over time limits the potential impact of the CTA, particularly when longitudinal research reveals that boys benefit more than girls do from exposure to educational television content (Anderson et al., 2001). At least three possible explanations could account for boys' diminished interest in educational programs: (1) males prefer programs that feature male characters and traditional male interests; (2) E/I programs are designed for a girl audience; and/or (3) boys avoid programs that are supposed to be educational. I examine evidence related to each of the three explanations below.

Boys' and girls' interest in educational programs

Because the gender differences in children's naturalistic viewing of, and learning from, E/I programs were pronounced (Calvert & Kotler, 2003), we pursued a more in-depth analysis for part of our sample. Using naturalistic online data, second- to sixth-grade boys' and girls' reports of what they liked and learned from E/I television programs were examined.

For these analyses, Calvert, Kotler, Zehnder and Shockey (2003) found that the favorite educational programs were similar for both girls and boys, and these selections were consistent over time. *Hey Arnold!* and *Brand Spanking New Doug*, which both feature male lead characters, the *Wild Thornberrys*, which features an adventurous female lead character, and *Disney's Recess*, which features a mixed-gender cast, were popular with all children. Boys preferred *Cousin Skeeter*, which is a predominantly male cast, whereas girls preferred *Sabrina the Animated Series* and *Disney's Pepper Ann*, which feature female characters. Over time, older fifth- to sixth-grade girls increasingly preferred programs with female lead characters.

For each report, the dependent variables analyzed included the number of male and female characters, the number of male and female pronouns, gender-stereotyped behaviors and traits, and the use of specific emotions in children's reports. Children wrote more often about male characters and about traditionally masculine behaviors, such as aggression, independence, heroism, and competition, than they wrote about female characters and traditionally feminine behaviors, such as dependence, gentleness, and being body-conscious. Traditionally masculine characteristics were attributed to male characters, but traditionally masculine and feminine behaviors were attributed to female characters. The pattern of attributing more masculine characteristics to male characters was more pronounced in the reports of boys than of girls, reflecting the tight adherence that boys follow to fit the cultural constraints of the traditional male gender role (Ruble, Martin, & Berenbaum, 2006).

For educational programs, male characters were no more likely to be reported as being heroic than were female characters. This outcome occurred in large part because of the character Eliza Thornberry who was the single character written about most often as a hero. Although girls were significantly more likely to identify Eliza as a hero than were boys, the reports of boys who did choose her as a hero contained just as many female as male characters and just as many feminine as masculine pronouns. These effects were present for older boys, the same group who watched fewer educational programs in their homes over time.

Taken together, the findings suggest that while boys do prefer male characters, providing nontraditional roles for girl characters appears to pull even the older boys into the viewing audience. Contrary to broadcaster beliefs, older girls really prefer and learn from female characters. The implication is that broadcasters can get both boys and girls into the audience to watch female characters if the girl characters act in fun and exciting ways that are in keeping with the male role. This approach has long been rejected by broadcasters who believe that boys will only watch programs that feature male leads (Jordan & Woodard, 1998).

Are E/I programs designed for girls?

Although girls like educational television programs more than boys do (Calvert & Kotler, 2003), content analyses reveal gendered presentations in children's educational programs that favor boys. Barner (1999), for example, found that male and female characters in educational television programs often engaged in gender-stereotypical behavior. In particular, male characters were depicted as more dominant, aggressive, active, and constructive. By contrast, female characters were portrayed as being dependent, nurturant, and deferent.

Similarly, Calvert, Stolkin, and Lee (1997) found that there were three times as many male as female characters in children's educational television programs, a pattern that is consistent with typical broadcast television. The duration of time that on-screen male characters spoke was actually higher than the duration of time that female characters were on-screen. These patterns reveal the dominance of male characters in children's educational television programs, just as is the case in all children's programs. Thus, it does not appear that educational programs are catering to girls.

Do boys avoid programs with E/I labels?

One FCC rule concerning the Children's Television Act required broadcasters to label E/I television programs so that parents and children could find them (FCC,

1996). Broadcasters, however, believed that such labels would have a dampening effect on children's interest in, and viewing of, educational programs (Jordan, 1996, 1997). Do children, particularly boys, avoid programs branded as E/I?

To test the effects of E/I ratings, Krcmar and Albada (2000) showed children an educational television program with an E/I rating or without an E/I rating (control). There were also two additional treatment conditions where an adult either pointed out the E/I rating (E/I rating with mediation), or where the adult explained that the E/I rating meant that children could learn something from viewing the program (E/I rating with instruction). Children who were ages 5–7 were compared to children who were ages 8–11. The dependent variables were how much the program was liked, visual attention to the program, and recall of the content.

Consistent with broadcaster beliefs (Jordan, 1996, 1997), older boys liked the program less when it had an E/I rating than older girls did. Older boys who had adult mediation or adult instruction with the E/I labels liked the program better than did the boys who just got a rating or who did not have any E/I rating. Girls liked the programs better when they had the E/I rating or when the E/I rating occurred with mediation than when there was no label at all or when there was a label with adult instruction. It was not clear why girls did not like the E/I rating with instruction. The authors pointed out, however, that there was considerable variance within the E/I instruction condition: children either liked that approach or they did not. Younger children's interest in the educational program was not affected by the presence or absence of the E/I rating or by what the adults did.

Children's visual attention to the program was comparable regardless of the presence or absence of an E/I rating. However, having the adult instruction of the E/I label prior to viewing the program led to less attentional interest by older children. Younger children's visual attention to the program dropped when they viewed the E/I rating with adult mediation, perhaps because attention was pulled off the screen and to the adult; this group also showed less recall of the program content, presumably because they were less attentive. There were no other differences in recall.

The authors suggested that E/I labels *per se* may attract some children (primarily older girls), but repel others (primarily older boys). Thus, E/I labels appear to undermine efforts to create an audience for educational television programs by making it clear to older children that there is something to be learned. These results dovetail nicely with the finding that older children discontinue their viewing of educational television programs over time, an effect that occurs primarily because boys drop out of the audience (Calvert & Kotler, 2003).

Broadcasters, then, may be correct: appeal and attentional interest is sometimes the cost when older children learn that a program is educational in nature. Even so, adults can potentially moderate this negative "spinach" effect for older boys, perhaps because adults provide an implicit endorsement of educational television programs when they talk about them (see Krcmar & Albada, 2000).

Summary

In summary, the characters in children's E/I programs are often male and these male characters generally have more powerful roles than the female characters. Thus, E/I programs are not catering to females in terms of character roles. Boys and girls also select many of the same E/I programs as their favorites. When differences emerge in favorite programs, they feature same-gendered casts for both boys and girls. Moreover, boys like programs with female lead characters who are engaged in nontraditional activities. Even so, the Nielsen data discussed earlier indicate that girls view educational programs more than boys do which was consistent with our viewing patterns and reported preferences of E/I programs favoring girls over boys (see Calvert & Kotler, 2003). Based on the available data, the older boys appear to be leaving the E/I audience because of the on-screen rating that programs are educational and informational. In addition, boys seem to prefer other genres of programming, such as action-adventure stories, over the social-emotional educational programs that tend to be more popular with girls.

Court Challenges about E/I Programs

In addition to research that challenged the educational value of certain broadcaster's E/I offerings, legal challenges have also taken place. In particular, as local broadcasters renewed their licenses, disputes about whether some of the broadcasters' E/I programs met the guidelines of the CTA ended up in court. In 2004, for example, the Office of Communication of the United Church of Christ, Inc., and the Center for Digital Democracy, represented by the Institute for Public Representation at Georgetown University, challenged the application for renewal of broadcast station licenses of Paxson Washington License, Inc. (WPXW in Manassas, Virginia) and Fox Television Stations, Inc. (WDCA in Washington, DC) for failing to air a minimum of three hours of educational programs per week (Campbell & Bachtell, 2004).

The challenge to WPXW involved *Miracle Pets*, a program that the petitioners argued was not a core educational program because it was not specifically designed for children, nor did it have education as a central purpose. In addition, the program was not identified with an educational icon. Even though WPXW relied almost exclusively on this program to meet its E/I requirement, the show did not even appear on a regular schedule because it was often preempted.

For WDCA, the allegations involved the use of *Ace Lightning* and *Stargate Infinity* to meet their E/I requirements. *Ace Lightning* and *Stargate Infinity*, the petitioners argued, lacked any educational purpose and in fact were action-adventure programs that conveyed antisocial, violent messages. In addition, there were concerns raised that the E/I logo for *Ace Lightning* was not readily identifiable as it appeared very briefly and blended in with a busy background. Nor did WDCA even identify *Ace Lightning* as educational on its own website. Thus, parents and children would have difficulty finding this purported E/I program, an FCC requirement. The E/I programs that stations broadcast to meet their E/I require-ment are submitted to the FCC on a quarterly basis. In 10 previous quarters, WDCA had broadcast only one single show – *Disney's Recess* – as fulfilling its E/I requirement. Because only one program was broadcast, the petitioners argued, the diverse needs of children were not being met even if the program could be rated as core programming.

Because of these alleged failures to meet the public interest requirement, the petitioners requested that the license renewal requests of WPXW and of WDCA be designated for formal hearing and that their license renewal requests be denied. In addition, they requested that the FCC clarify how many times a program could be repeated and still count as meeting the CTA processing guidelines. They also requested that the FCC create rules that would help parents easily find E/I programs by the station's use of E/I icons. Professor Dale Kunkel, then a Professor at the University of California at Santa Barbara, reviewed several episodes from these program series and provided expert testimony to support the petitioners' claims.

In reply, DIC Entertainment, who created the Fox programs, opposed the petition to deny license renewal to WDCA, the Fox affiliate. DIC argued that its programs were designed to be educational and informational through plot, character development, and program outcomes. DIC argued that it hired educational experts, in this instance Professor Donald Roberts from Stanford University, to assist in the creation of E/I programs (DIC Entertainment Corp., 2004). While DIC conceded that *Ace Lightning* and *Stargate Infinity* were action-adventure programs that contained violent content, they argued that such content was not banned by the CTA and that such content could also con-tain prosocial and educational elements. For example, Professor Roberts, the educational consultant, testified that the themes of *Stargate Infinity* included accepting consequences for one's actions, accepting diversity, being independent, respecting others, and being willing to make mistakes. At the time of going to press, a ruling on this petition was still pending before the FCC.

Court challenges to other programs being broadcast as meeting the E/I requirement have continued. In 2005, the Institute for Public Representation at Georgetown University represented petitioners in additional cases brought against two television stations in Cleveland, Ohio. A petition against the Raycom-owned UPN affiliate station, WUAB, challenged the claim that *Sabrina the Animated Series*, a DIC animated creation about a child witch, was an educational program. A petition brought against the Univision station WQHS-TV challenged its claim than an imported telenovela *Complices al Rescate* was an educational children's program. Kevin Martin, the current Chair of the FCC, has indicated that the FCC will impose a major fine on Univision for failing to meet the E/I programming requirements of the Children's Television Act (Labaton, 2007). The expected $24 million fine will send a strong message to broadcasters about their responsibilities to provide quality E/I programming for young audiences (Labaton, 2007). The other petitions are still awaiting a ruling by the FCC.

Challenges for Creating Quality Children's Television Programs

In interviews conducted by Jordan and Sullivan (1997), commercial broadcasters voiced their belief that there is really no audience for children's E/I programs. By the time children get home from school, commercial broadcasters believe that children are ready to be entertained, not engaged in more learning activities during their leisure time. While younger children below age 6 might watch educational shows, older children will not (Jordan & Woodard, 1998). This belief is supported by our research (Calvert & Kotler, 2003), but partly because of a self-fulfilling prophecy: broadcasters make E/I programs that are targeted at the younger audience, and children know it. For instance, our laboratory sample thought that the educational programs they viewed were made for a younger age group (Calvert & Kotler, 2003).

Broadcasters also believe that the public truly does not care much about educational television programs (Jordan & Sullivan, 1997). However, parents report that they are interested in having their very young children view educational television programs and videos (Rideout, Vandewater, & Wartella, 2003); there are few data to support or refute this belief for parents of older children.

Another issue that broadcasters have with E/I programs is that academic programs, by their very nature, have to be targeted at a narrow age range (Jordan & Sullivan, 1997). Indeed, this perspective partly explains the overabundance of prosocial television programs to meet E/I programming requirements. So too, though, does the link between storytelling and the arts: scriptwriters come out of a tradition of writing stories, and hence they do what they know how to do – write stories (Mitroff, 2003). The prosocial programs that these writers create can deliver a bigger audience than academic programs because the writers know how to write about social and emotional themes and because prosocial themes are less age specific, and hence pull in larger audiences (Calvert & Kotler, 2003). Moreover, businesses like Nickelodeon make money by producing prosocial programs (Friend, 1997). Overall, then, prosocial stories work for the commercial and cable media companies.

Even so, creating high-quality children's programs is an expensive enterprise. The lack of financial business models in the US to support educational television programs creates a negative perception about E/I programs among broadcasters because such content is expensive to produce (Jordan & Sullivan, 1997). In Canada and France, for instance, the government subsidizes the creation of educational television programs (Cahn, Kalagian, & Lyon, this volume, Chapter 2). By contrast, the US provides little financing of children's programs; even PBS struggles to find sufficient government funding to produce educational programs (Cahn, Kalagian, & Lyon, this volume, Chapter 2).

Amount of Commercial Time Allowed

Although the focus of this chapter has been on the E/I programming require-ment, the overabundance of commercials on children's television is another reason that the CTA came into being. Furthermore, commercialization makes it hard to create and sustain quality programs for children. Scholars have not investigated broadcaster compliance with commercial time limits, but violations are a matter of public record.

Although the rules about commercial time limits are very straightforward – 10.5 minutes per hour during weekend programs and 12 minutes per hour during the weekdays (CTA, 1990) – numerous broadcaster violations have occurred. For instance, from 1992 to 1994, approximately one in four of the nation's 900 television stations violated the CTA advertising limit (Farhi, 1995a). Among these, 44 stations received fines of over $1 million, 98 stations were reprimanded, and 100 stations received written warnings (Farhi, 1995b). In 2004, the FCC fined Viacom $1 million and fined Disney $500,000 for violating the CTA commercial advertising limits (de Moraes, 2004). In the digital age, the issues of commercial content in children's programs will become more complicated.

What Will the CTA Rules Mean when Digital Television (DTV) Becomes the Norm?

Digital television (DTV) will soon become the standard format, completely replacing the former analog system on February 17, 2009. By transmitting the picture and sound in data bits like a computer does, DTV will allow broadcasters to carry more content than the traditional analog format, which has used mag-netic waves to transmit content (http://www.dtv.gov/consumercorner.html# whatisdtv). DTV allows high-definition images, multi-casting 4–6 channels simultaneously in standard-definition format, and ancillary or supplemental ser-vices such as Video on Demand, computer software distribution, and interactive services (FCC, 2000).

The emerging digital environment provides unique opportunities and challenges for how media is experienced. Because DTV allows Internet capabilities to be merged with the broadcasting of children's programs, children will be able to use their television screen much like they use a computer (Calvert, 1999). For example, children will be able to click on images on the screen that will take them to web-sites. If those websites emphasize the content of an E/I program, there is a clear opportunity for interactivity to facilitate a more in-depth educational experience with the content (FCC, 2000). However, if those websites focus on commercial content, children will potentially be exposed to much more commercialization than they receive in current television broadcasts. Exposure to marketing messages is a major issue because children under age 8 have difficulty in distinguishing commercial intent, i.e., in understanding that commercials are intended to persuade people to buy certain products (see Wartella & Robb, this volume, Chapter 1).

FCC rules

In serving as a steward in this transition to digital technology, the FCC (2000) decided to put out a notice for comment on the public service obligations of commercial broadcasters, which include their obligations to children. In 2004, the FCC ruled that the CTA also applied to the new digital format and that broadcasters had responsibilities to protect and serve the child audience. Key facets of these new DTV rules deal with the amount of E/I programming that will be required when multiple programming streams are available for each broadcaster, how to help parents find the E/I programs, and limits on the amount and nature of children's advertisements.

For E/I programming, the FCC (2004) ruled that broadcasters will have to provide additional educational programming that is in keeping with the total amount of time they will have available to broadcast programs. More specifically, broadcasters will have as much as six times the programming capacity with digital television as they currently have with analog television (Children Now, 2004). Thus, if a digital broadcaster has 6 stations that are broadcasting 24 hours of programming per day, that broadcaster will be required to provide 18 hours of E/I programming (i.e., 6 stations times 3 hours of E/I programming; Children Now, 2004). To be counted as core programming, not more than 50 percent of episodes can have aired within the same week (FCC, 2004). To qualify as a core program, the FCC initially ruled that preemption can occur for only 10 percent of that series (FCC, 2004).

A second requirement addressed concerns that consumers are unable to find E/I programming. The FCC (2004) ruled that one uniform E/I label must be adopted by all commercial DTV broadcasters. In addition, that standard E/I icon must stay on the screen throughout the program. Previously, different E/I icons were adopted by each broadcaster and often shown very briefly, making it difficult for parents to understand what they even meant (Schmitt, 1999).

The third requirement concerned particular facets of commercialization: host selling and interactive advertising (FCC, 2004). In 1974, the FCC had ruled that children's program content had to be separate from the commercial content, often termed the "separation principle." Thus, host selling, in which the host of a children's television program had sold products to children during the program or in commercial slots adjacent to that program, was banned. Such host selling was thought to take advantage of the special relationship that children form with the main characters, i.e., the hosts of their programs. In addition, young children cannot discriminate between the commercial and the program content, and hence, host selling was inherently unfair (FCC, 1974). But what will the program boundaries be in the digital age when there is synergy between the characters in a television program and children's websites featuring those characters? The FCC (2004) ruled that in the digital age, television characters that appear on the broadcast airwaves were prohibited from selling products on commercial websites if the website addresses were displayed on the television screen.

Interactive advertising, the other commercial practice addressed by the FCC (2004), involves the website links that can be embedded in children's television programs. By simply clicking on a link within a children's television program, children will be able to go directly to an associated website in the near future. Building on the separation principle, the FCC (2004) tentatively concluded that there could be no interactive advertising embedded within children's television programs that would take children to a commercial website unless parents also had the technology to opt out of click-through advertising (Children Now, 2004).

The joint industry-advocacy proposal on FCC rule changes

Legal challenges to the FCC (2004) order came from both industry and child advocacy groups (Joint Proposal of Industry and Advocates on Reconsideration of Children's Television Rules, 2006). Industry thought the new FCC rules were too restrictive and advocacy groups thought the new rules did not go far enough (Patti Miller, Vice President and Director of the Children and the Media Program at Children Now, personal communication). To ensure a smooth transition to DTV for the child audience, industry and advocacy groups forged a compromise on rules about E/I programming and commercial content. The industry group consisted of various counsels representing Viacom Inc., CBS Corporation, The Walt Disney Company, Fox Entertainment Group, Inc., NBC Universal, Inc., NBC Telemundo License Co., 4Kids Entertainment, Inc., The Association of National Advertisers, Inc., Time Warner, Inc., and Discovery Communications, Inc. The advocacy groups were represented by Angela Campbell from the Institute for Public Representation, who served as counsel for the United Church of Christ, Inc., Children Now, the National Parent Teacher Association, the American Academy of Pediatrics, Action Coalition for Media Education, and the American Psychological Association (Joint Proposal of Industry and Advocates on Reconsideration of Children's Television Rules, 2006). The groups together developed a joint proposal that specifically addressed the new FCC (2004) rules (Joint Proposal of Industry and Advocates on Reconsideration of Children's Television Rules, 2006). Key components of the compromise relevant to the Children's Television Act are as follows.

In the joint proposal, the FCC (2004) rule requiring three hours of E/I television programming on every digital channel outlet remained the same. The joint proposal asked the FCC to delete the percentage of time (10 percent) in which E/I programs could be preempted. Instead, the joint proposal requested that the FCC look at broadcasters on a case-by-case basis to ensure that excessive violations were not occurring in preempting children's E/I programming. This compromise was vital to the industry because of its desire to air sporting events to viewers on the West Coast; Saturday morning children's programs are the ones that are typically preempted to air these sports programs (Mohammed, 2005).

The FCC (2004) rule to help parents find E/I programs remained unchanged in the joint proposal. That is, a constant logo has to be used by all stations for E/I programs and the logo must remain on the television screen throughout the entire program (Joint Proposal of Industry and Advocates on Reconsideration of Children's Television Rules, 2006).

Issues about the amount of commercial exposure in children's programs were addressed in the host selling and interactive advertising components of the joint proposal. For host selling, the joint proposal asked the FCC to amend the rule as follows: a character that is shown on a television program cannot sell products on an associated website *during that television program* if a web address to that website is on the television screen (Mohammed, 2005). For instance, when Sponge Bob is on television and the Nickelodeon website address is on the television screen, Sponge Bob cannot sell products on a webpage primarily devoted to his character.

However, Sponge Bob can sell products on webpages primarily devoted to his show, when his television show is not being aired (Miller, personal communication). This compromise keeps Sponge Bob the program character separate from Sponge Bob as a spokesperson for a product, at least during that block of time when Sponge Bob is on the televsion. This compromise by the joint proposal addressed the DTV host selling issue.

Broadcasters and cable operators voluntarily agreed to implement these rules, effective March 1, 2006. In September of 2006, the FCC formally adopted rules consistent with the joint proposal of advocates and media industry representatives, and the rules officially went into effect in January of 2007. However, concerns about interactive advertising were not resolved by the joint proposal; this issue remains on the FCC docket for future consideration (Miller, personal communication).

Conclusion

The Children's Television Act was passed to provide E/I programming for children in a format that can entertain as it informs. The E/I programs have been of mixed quality over time, with prosocial programs dominating the schedule. E/I programs generally pull in a younger audience that is predominantly female. The male audience, often favored by broadcasters in programming decisions, generally leaves the viewing audience by the tween years. The loss of boys coupled with the lack of government subsides to create children's educational programs make the financial models difficult for broadcasters. Court challenges have been brought against broadcasters who claim that programs of questionable quality fulfill their E/I obligations, and fines have been levied for violating rules about the amount of time commercials can be shown. However, no broadcaster has ever lost a license for CTA violations.

Quality programs can make a difference in what children take away after viewing television. As the US transits into DTV, new options will become available for improving the effectiveness of educational programs as well as for increasing the reach of marketing techniques. Although it is clear that media will continue to play an integral role in children's daily lives, the question remaining is whether children's media will ever live up to its educational promise. Policies like the Children's Television Act are one way to move that educational promise a step closer to reality.

Special thanks go to Patti Miller, Barbara Wilson, and the Children's Digital Media Center team for their helpful comments in writing this chapter. Funding was provided by a grant from the Smith Richardson Foundation to Sandra Calvert to study the impact of the Children's Television Act on children's learning.

References

Anderson, D. R., Huston, A. C., Schmitt, K. L., Linebarger, D. L., & Wright, J. C. (2001). Early childhood television viewing and adolescent behavior. *Monographs of the Society for Research in Child Development*, 66, vii–156.

Barner, M. (1999). Sex-role stereotyping in FCC-mandated children's educational television programs. *Journal of Broadcasting and Electronic Media*, 43, 551–64.

Calvert, S. L. (1999). *Children's journeys through the information age*. Boston: McGraw Hill.

Calvert, S. L., & Kotler, J. A. (2003). Lessons from children's television: Impact of the Children's Television Act on children's learning. Special issue of the *Journal of Applied Developmental Psychology*, 24, 275–335.

Calvert, S. L., Kotler, J. A., Zehnder, S., & Shockey, E. (2003). Gender-stereotyping in children's reports about educational and informational television programs. *Media Psychology*, 5, 139–62.

Calvert, S. L., Stolkin, A., & Lee, J. (1997). *Gender and ethnic portrayals in Saturday morning television programs*. Poster presented at the annual meeting of the Society for Research in Child Development, April, Washington, DC.

Campbell, A., & Bachtell, J. (2004). *Application for renewal of broadcast station licenses of Paxson Washington License, Inc.; and Fox Television Stations, Inc. for renewal of station licenses WPXW, Manassas, VA; and WDCA, Washington, DC. Petition to Deny*. Before the FCC (File Nos. BRCT-20040527AGS; BRCT-20040527AKL).

Center for Media Education, & Institute for Public Representation, Georgetown University Law School. (1992). *A report on broadcaster compliance with the Children's Television Act*, September. Washington, DC: Center for Media Education.

Children Now. (2004). *Digital Television: Sharpening the focus on children*. Retrieved December 18, 2006, from http://publications.childrennow.org/publications/media/dtvconvening_2004.cfm.

Children's Television Act of 1990 (CTA). (1990). Publ. L. No. 101-437, 104 Stat. 996–1000), codified at 47 USC Sections 303a, 303b, 394.

Communications Act of 1934. (1934). 47, USC Section 307a. Washington, DC; Federal Communications Commission.

De Moraes, L. (2004). FCC Fines 2 Networks For Violating Limits On Kids' Show Ads. *Washington Post*, October 22, p. C01.

DIC Entertainment Corp. (2004). *Submission of DIC Entertainment Corp. in support of opposition of Fox Television to United Church of Christ and Center for Digital Democracy petition to deny application for renewal of WDCA-TV, Washington, DC.* In the matter of application for renewal of broadcast station licenses of Fox Television Stations, Inc., WDCA, Washington, DC. Before the FCC (File No. BRCT-20040527AKL).

Digital television. (2006). Retrieved December 15, 2006, from http://www.dtv.gov/consumercorner.html#whatisdtv.

Farhi, P. (1995a). FCC's Hundt pushing for tougher TV station license renewal standards. *Washington Post*, October 13, p. A33.

Farhi, P. (1995b). Children's advertising: The rules not followed. FCC finds violations of commercial time limits are widespread. *Washington Post*, October 13, p. A33.

Federal Communications Commission (FCC). (1974). Children's television programs: Report and policy statement. *Federal Register*, 39, 39396–409.

Federal Communications Commission (FCC). (1991). Policies and rules concerning children's television programming. *Federal Communications Commission Record*, 6, 2111–27.

Federal Communications Commission (FCC). (1996). In the matter of policies and rules concerning children's television programming: Revision of programming policies for television broadcasters. (FCC MM Docket No. 93-48).

Federal Communications Commission (FCC). (2000). In the matter of children's television obligations of digital television broadcasters: Notice of proposed rule making. (FCC MM Docket No. 00-167).

Federal Communications Commission (FCC). (2004). In the matter of children's television obligations of digital television broadcasters: Report and order and further notice of proposed rule making. (FCC MM Docket No. 00-167).

Friend, B. (1997). *Roundtable discussion comments about the measurement of children's television viewing*, September. New York: Annenberg Public Policy Center.

Hundt, R. (1995). Reading the First Amendment in favor of children. Speech presented at the Brooklyn Law School, December, Brooklyn, NY.

Huston, A. C., Watkins, B. A., & Kunkel, D. (1989). Public policy and children's television. *American Psychologist*, 44, 424–33.

Huston, A. C., & Wright, J. C. (1998). Television and the informational and educational needs of children. *The Annals of American Academy of Political and Social Science*, 557, 9–23.

Joint proposal of industry and advocates on reconsideration of children's television rules. (2006). In the matter of children's television obligations of digital television broadcasters. (FCC MM Docket No. 00-167).

Jordan, A. B. (1996). *The state of children's television: An examination of quantity, quality, and broadcaster beliefs* (Report No. 2). Philadelphia: University of Pennsylvania, Annenberg Public policy Center.

Jordan, A. B. (1997). *Industry perspectives on the challenges of educational television.* Paper presented at the International Communication Association, May, Montreal, Canada.

Jordan, A. B. (2000). *Is the Three-Hour Rule living up to its potential: An analysis of educational television for children in the 1999/2000 broadcast season.* Retrieved December 19, 2006, from University of Pennsylvania, Annenberg Public Policy Center website: http://www.annenbergpublicpolicycenter.org/05_media_developing_child/childrensprogramming/3hour-rule.pdf.

Jordan, A. B. (2003). Children remember prosocial lessons but how much are they learning? *Journal of Applied Developmental Psychology,* 24, 341–5.

Jordan, A. B., Schmitt, K., & Woodard, E. (2002). Developmental implications of commercial broadcasters' educational offerings. In S. L. Calvert, A. B. Jordan, & R. R. Cocking (Eds.), *Children in the digital age: Influences of electronic media on development* (pp. 145–64). Westport, CT: Praeger.

Jordan, A. B., & Sullivan, J. (1997). *Children's educational television regulations and the local broadcaster: Impact and implementation.* Philadelphia: University of Pennsylvania, Annenberg Public Policy Center.

Jordan, A. B., & Woodard, E. (1997). *The 1997 state of children's television report: Programming for children over broadcast and cable television,* June. Philadelphia: University of Pennsylvania, Annenberg Public Policy Center.

Jordan, A. B., & Woodard, E. (1998). Growing pains: children's television in the new regulatory environment. *The Annals of the American Academy of Political and Social Science,* 557, 83–95.

Krcmar, M., & Albada, K. (2000). The effect of an educational/informational rating on children's attraction to and learning from an educational program. *Journal of Broadcasting and Electronic Media,* 44, 674–89.

Kunkel, D. (1991). Television, children, and social policy: Issues and resources for child advocates. *Journal of Clinical Child Psychology,* 20, 88–93.

Kunkel, D. (1998). Policy battles over defining children's educational television. *The Annals of the American Academy of Political and Social Science,* 557, 39–53.

Kunkel, D. (2003). The truest metric for evaluating the Children's Television Act. *Journal of Applied Developmental Psychology,* 24, 347–53.

Kunkel, D., & Canepa, J. (1994). Broadcasters' license renewal claims regarding children's educational programming. *Journal of Broadcasting and Electronic Media,* 38, 397–416.

Kunkel, D., & Wilcox, B. (2001). Children and media policy. In D. Singer & J. Singer (Eds.), *Handbook of children and media* (pp. 589–604). Thousand Oaks, CA: Sage.

Labaton, S. (2007). Record fine expected for Univision. *New York Times,* February 24, p. C1.

Liebert, R. M., & Sprafkin, J. (1988). *The early window: Effects of television on children and youth* (3rd edn.). Elmsford, NY: Pergamon Press.

Mitroff, D. (2003). On the horns of a dilemma. *Journal of Applied Developmental Psychology,* 24, 355–61.

Mohammed, A. (2005). Child advocates, TV come to terms. *Washington Post,* December 16.

Rideout, V. J., Vandewater, E. A., & Wartella, A. (2003). *Zero to six: Electronic media in the lives of infants, toddlers, and preschoolers.* Menlo Park, CA: Kaiser Family Foundation.

Ruble, D. N., Martin, C. L., & Berenbaum, S. A. (2006). Gender development. In N. Eisenberg (Vol. Ed.), *Handbook of child psychology*. Vol. 3, *Social, Emotional, and Personality Development* (6th edn., pp. 858–932). Hoboken, NJ: Wiley.

Schmitt, K. L. (1999). *The Three-Hour Rule: Is it living up to expectation?* (Report No. 30). Philadelphia: University of Pennsylvania, Annenberg Public Policy Center.

Stipp, H. (2003). How children can learn from television. *Journal of Applied Developmental Psychology*, 24, 363–5.

Wilcox, B. (2003). The research/policy nexus: The Children's Television Act as a case in point. *Journal of Applied Developmental Psychology*, 24, 367–73.

21

Regulating the Media: Sexually Explicit Content

Joah G. Iannotta

Since entertainment media became an integral part of children's lives in the 1930s, concerns have been repeatedly raised about children's exposure to content, particularly sexually explicit content, that may not be appropriate for them (Peters, 1933; Sprafkin, Silverman, & Rubinstein, 1980; Thornburgh & Lin, 2002). The Federal Communications Commission (FCC) and the Federal Trade Commission (FTC) were charged with regulating media content and advertising, respectively, and can take actions such as levying fines, initiating legal action against parties, and revoking broadcasting licenses (FCC, n.d.; Thornburgh & Lin, 2002). Despite these resources, regulating content in a manner that effectively meets the changing developmental needs of youth as well as the legal requirements of our judiciary system is a complicated matter.

This chapter begins by briefly discussing some key issues in children's development. It then reviews the parameters that guide the circumstances under which the government is permitted to regulate media content. Next I discuss when and how policy meant to regulate content is implemented given different types of media technologies, emphasizing that different technologies pose different challenges (e.g., regulating content on the Internet is a very different prospect from regulating content broadcast over the radio). I also review some of the different regulatory approaches that have been applied to different types of media as well as options that may or may not require public policy to be implemented (e.g., media rating standards developed and implemented by the industry and media literacy programs).

Media and the Developmental Needs of Children and Youth

When parents and policy makers talk about protecting "children," "youth," or "minors" from sexually inappropriate material, they are referring to a wide range of ages (Thornburgh & Lin, 2002). This is not necessarily unintentional, as many families are interested in exerting some level of control over what media their very young children are exposed to as well as what their adolescents view. At the same time, most families would consider a more narrow range of media content as appropriate for young children and a broader range acceptable for adolescents, all of which is in keeping with what we know about children's developmental needs (Thornburgh & Lin, 2002).

Media content is a pervasive presence in young people's lives (Escobar-Chaves et al., 2005). One recent study found that 99 percent of our youngest children (i.e., those under age 6) live in a home with a television, 78 percent live in a home with a computer, 69 percent have Internet access from home, and one third of these children have a television in their bedroom (Rideout & Hamel, 2006). Adolescents spend about 6.5 hours per day consuming some type of media, be it television, movies, radio, print media, the Internet, or videogames (Roberts, Foehr, & Rideout, 2005).[1] Both violent and sexually explicit content is readily available in the media, and although some research suggests that the amount of sexual content on television may have peaked in the late 1990s (Escobar-Chaves et al., 2005), the proliferation of new types of media and new niche audiences (e.g., adult consumers of videogames, cable television programs targeting gay, lesbian, bisexual, and transgender communities, satellite radio programming) may have created additional avenues for sexual content more recently.

Mass media have been shown to influence the behaviors and attitudes of young people in a number of areas, including violence, tobacco and alcohol use, and eating disorders (Escobar-Chaves et al., 2005). There have been fewer empirical studies assessing the effect of media consumption on the sexual behaviors and attitudes of youth, and legal issues have limited experimental designs to college-aged youth only. However, techniques for assessing media content and tracking young people's use patterns as well as statistical modeling to control for other factors have become more sophisticated, and several recent studies have shown strong relationships between youth exposure to media diets heavy in sexual content and earlier initiation of sexual activity (Brown et al., 2006; Brown & Newcomer, 1991; Collins et al., 2004). For example, 12-year-olds who watched the highest levels of sexual content compared to their peers were as likely to engage in sexual activity as youths 2 to 3 years older who watched the lowest levels of sexual content (Collins et al., 2004). Also, 12- to 14-year-olds who watched high levels of sexual media content were more likely to engage in sexual activity within the next 2 years than were young people of the same age who had more limited exposure (Brown et al., 2006). Although it is not possible to fully account for the effect of adolescents' growing interest in sexual activity on later sexual behavior, both of these studies controlled for previous sexual experience. In addition, these studies controlled for a number of other factors, such as age, socioeconomic status, parent education, and puberty status, that could contribute to sexual behavior. Thus, the studies strongly support the idea that exposure to high levels of sexual media content can influence young people's sexual behaviors.

The findings of these studies were applicable to boys and girls, but other studies have found that gender can affect how young people relate to media, especially with respect to sexual content (LaTour & Henthorne, 1993; Rouner, Slater, & Domenech-Rodriguez, 2003). Adolescent female responses to sexualized media content – at least that depict women – is somewhat complicated. Compared to boys, who generally view female nudity favorably, adolescent girls and college-aged women can be critical of nude and erotic images of women, yet, in certain media contexts, they seem to identify with sexualized depictions of females. For example, while some studies have found girls and women to be critical of sexualized images of females in advertising, research on teenaged girls' reactions to music videos suggests that they internalize negative gender roles and develop permissive attitudes toward sexual activity (Kalof, 1999; LaTour & Henthorne, 1993; Rouner, Slater, & Domenech-Rodriguez, 2003).

Age also affects how young people use and interpret media content. Researchers at a National Academy of Sciences workshop in 2000 (Iannotta, 2001) noted that children under age 9 are less likely to seek out sexual media content and may be more easily upset by graphic – especially sexually violent – images. However, even young children ages 3–11 years may rely on the media as a source for sexual learning (Sprafkin, Silverman, & Rubinstein, 1980). Children over age 9 begin to experience a growing interest in sexuality, and they are more likely to intentionally seek out sexual content for a number of reasons, including a desire for information on normative sexual behavior, sexual health, and contraception as well as for the sake of arousal (Iannotta, 2001). More complicated still is that adolescents are not just passive consumers of media, but rather, through tools like Internet chat rooms, youth actually construct their own media cultures, which are often sexualized (Subrahmanyam, Greenfield, & Tynes, 2004).

What all of this implies for strategies to reduce young people's exposure to sexually explicit material is that different approaches are necessary for different age groups and potentially for boys and girls. Because children under 9 years may find explicit sexual content upsetting and this group is less likely to seek out such content, strategies to reduce accidental exposure – such as enforcing the ban on sexually explicit content over radio and television broadcasts during the day, television parental controls, and Internet filters – may be best suited to their developmental needs. Because adolescents may use sexual content in the media as a guide for their own behavior, and because it may be difficult to prevent older youth from accessing sexual content when they are intent on doing so, strategies that emphasize good decision-making, accurate interpretation of content, and open communication between parents and their teenagers (even if that means talking about sex) may be more important for older youth (Collins et al., 2004; Iannotta, 2001). These are vastly different strategies, which makes finding solutions in public policy somewhat challenging. In the next section, I will begin to discuss what options are available through public policy.

The First Amendment's Role in Setting the Parameters for Regulating Media Content

Although a number of legal issues factor into the policy options available to regulate sexually explicit content, the First Amendment creates the context in which these options can be implemented. The First Amendment holds that the government may not pass any law that would abridge the freedom of speech or expression even when the speech in question advocates ideas that are considered to be wrong or improper, or that might result in behavior that would be unlawful or socially undesirable.[2] At the heart of the First Amendment is the recognition that individuals should make choices about their lives through exposure to a broad range of ideas and discourses that have not been edited or filtered by the government. There is also an implicit recognition that societies change and different ideas as well as forms of communication may develop over time (Thornburgh & Lin, 2002).

Perhaps on the surface, sexually explicit media content (broadly defined) would seem to have little relevance to these issues – for example, can we really argue that pornography contributes to making informed choices about the government? Perhaps pornography *per se* does not, but public policy concerning the regulation of sexuality represents some of the most contentious and socially divisive issues in our culture: Consider how deeply held are beliefs about abortion, gay marriage, welfare benefits for women with children born out of wedlock, and most recently the debate over whether pharmacists and healthcare workers have the right to decline to provide clients birth control pills and fertility treatments. Drawing a line between information, political exchanges of ideas about sexuality, artistic representation, and sexually explicit content lacking in social value is difficult. If it were easy, our judicial system would have already provided a clear and simple definition by which to regulate media content.

Defining obscenity

Although the First Amendment protects a very wide range of expression, the government can take steps to stop the distribution of *obscene* material whether that material is distributed in magazines, through broadcast or cable television, or over the Internet (FCC, n.d.a).[3] The Supreme Court has narrowly defined obscenity[4] as material that "taken as a whole, and judged by *contemporary community standards*, must appeal to the prurient interest in sex, must depict sexual conduct in a patently offensive manner, and must lack serious literary, artistic, political, and scientific value"[5] (Thornburgh & Lin, 2002, p. 88). However, in addition to providing this definition, the Court has carefully noted that not all material dealing with sexuality is obscene, but material that is deemed obscene is *not* protected by the First Amendment (Thornburgh & Lin, 2002).

Despite its effort to provide clear guidance regarding what does and does not constitute obscene material, the Court itself has recognized that whether or not material is obscene or sexual in a manner that has some social value is highly subjective and does not lend itself well to legal definitions (Thornburgh & Lin, 2002). In addition, the use of contemporary community standards allows for changing cultural attitudes about the depiction of sex.[6] Arguably this is a great strength of the definition, but it does preclude more specific characterizations about what kinds of images or speech are obscene. For example, it may have been considered obscene to show images of a naked woman in a movie 50 years ago, but now such images would have to be very lewd to be considered obscene. Furthermore, technologies like the Internet allow a rapid global exchange of media content, and identifying the community by whose standard that material should be judged is more complicated (Thornburgh & Lin, 2002).

Variable obscenity

The subjectivity involved in making decisions about whether or not material is obscene creates challenges in regulating media content as does the fact that media audiences frequently include youth and adults. The Court has recognized that there are developmental differences between children and adults and has found it constitutional for the government to regulate the distribution of sexually explicit material to minors even if contemporary community standards would not find the material obscene for an adult.[7] Importantly, distribution of this material cannot also be restricted for adults, and this has significant implications for developing actual strategies to limit young people's access to sexually explicit content. For instance, it may be permissible for state or local government agencies to insist that vendors do not sell or rent sexually explicit material to minors,[8] but these agencies cannot restrict the sale of sexually explicit material to adults, nor can agencies ban such material altogether (Thornburgh & Lin, 2002).

The complexity of implementing obscenity bans

Given that a wider range of sexually explicit material can be restricted with respect to distribution to minors but this same material cannot be restricted for adults,[9] how can such a policy be implemented? To answer this question, we must consider two different regulatory contexts: In the first, it is possible to differentiate adults and minors and in the second it is not.

When adults and minors can be differentiated, a gatekeeper is usually present to screen the audience and prevent minors from obtaining sexually explicit material. For instance, in book, video, DVD, and game stores as well as movie theaters, a salesperson can identify minors and decline to sell sexually explicit material to them. Likewise, sexually explicit adult websites that make use of some type of age verification technique implement a mechanism that serves as a gatekeeper to differentiate the audience and to prevent minors from accidentally or intentionally accessing content that might be considered obscene for them. Arguably, there are ways around online age verification, but this is true for most other contexts as well (e.g., youth under 17 find ways to sneak into R-rated movies and sometimes use older friends or other means to buy DVDs or magazines that a cashier might not otherwise sell directly to them). Age verification systems will always be imperfect against youth determined to view such material. However, in terms of what is feasible from a public policy perspective, when minor and adult audiences can be differentiated, it is possible to implement policies that regulate distribution practices to minors.

In the second case, in which it is not possible to separate minors and adults and grant access accordingly, the Court has generally found unconstitutional strategies that would deny both minors and adults access to the material. Put simply, the Court has been unwilling to allow regulation of media content in a manner that would limit adults only to that content which is appropriate for minors (Thornburgh & Lin, 2002). For example, the Communications Decency Act of 1996 would have made illegal any "indecent" communication over the Internet if the person originating the communication knew that a recipient might be a minor.[10] The Court found this approach far too restrictive, stating that it would unduly interfere with the rights of adults to view and obtain Internet content.[11] Instead the Court suggested that the government explore strategies that would facilitate parental control over Internet material entering their homes.[12]

The Court has ruled on the side of freedom of expression in cases such as the Communications Decency Act, and it has put down approaches that would significantly limit media content for adult audiences as a way to reduce distribution to minors. That said, in certain circumstances the Court has been amenable to strategies that would place some limits on adult access to sexually explicit content. For example, the Court has supported the longstanding FCC ban on sexually explicit material on public airwaves (i.e., non-cable radio and television broadcasts) between the hours of 6:00 a.m. and 10:00 p.m. This restriction prevents adults from viewing or listening to material that could be obscene for minors during these hours, but the restriction is not absolute because later at night when it is reasonable to expect that young children are in bed, broadcasters are free to air adult content. In short, the FCC's time-bound ban over broadcast media makes it less convenient for adults to access sexual media content without denying them the material completely (Holohan, 2005; Thornburgh & Lin, 2002).

The government's ability through the FCC to ban sexually indecent material on broadcast media during certain hours is an interesting case in that it calls attention to yet another level of complexity to regulating the media – namely, the special treatment that the Court has given broadcast media. Originally, the Court justified this restriction on the basis that because broadcast frequencies were a scarce *public* resource, the government was justified in exerting more regulatory power over the content.[13] In a later case, the Court upheld this ban and made a specific reference to the role of broadcast media in children's lives, noting their omnipresence in American homes and their easy accessibility for children.[14] Broadcast radio and television are perhaps uniquely accessible – to view programming one must simply have a television or radio and possess the faculty to hit the power button.

The programming that is on is what you are able to view or listen to, making it particularly easy for children to access material that could be obscene for them (Holohan, 2005; Thornburgh & Lin, 2002).

Although at the time of the ruling the Courts did not have alternative media examples in mind, we might consider how this type of accessibility is somewhat different from other media technologies such as cable television or the Internet. Unlike broadcast media, which are free and available to anyone owning a television or radio, cable and satellite television requires a consumer to choose a specific package of programming and voluntarily elect to pay for access to that programming. Because the viewer must "opt in" (and pay) to access programming, these media do not fall under the same content-based broadcast restrictions (FCC, 2000). Likewise, the Internet requires a series of choices by the user – first to pay for some sort of home access, next to log onto the Internet, and finally to choose which webpages to view.

The distinction in context between broadcast media on the one hand and other media technologies such as cable television and the Internet creates different challenges and opportunities for regulation. With respect to the Court's decisions about how to balance free speech and preventing minors from accessing inappropriate sexually explicit material, the Court has permitted regulation focused on distribution when the media context provides the opportunity to differentiate minors and adults and grant access accordingly. The Court has also permitted regulation in cases like broadcast media when the media is pervasive, easily accessed, and is carried over a public resource (i.e., public airwaves). Under these circumstances, the Court has supported regulation that infringes somewhat on adult access to sexually explicit material as long as the regulation does not completely reduce the media landscape to that which is appropriate for children (i.e., in this case adult content can be shown later at night; Holohan, 2005; Thornburgh & Lin, 2002). In contrast, the Court has not supported policy that would completely prevent adult access to sexually explicit content through certain media technologies. This is particularly true for media sources like the Internet, cable, and others in which the user must make a series of choices to access content (including paying for programming) and in which there are alternative strategies to reduce children's exposure (FCC, 2000; Holohan, 2005; Thornburgh & Lin, 2002).

Regulating child pornography and commercial advertising to children

Two final concepts for regulating sexually explicit media content are worth highlighting, namely prohibitions on child pornography and the government's ability to regulate commercial advertising. The Court has interpreted bans on child pornography in a very different light than it has prohibitions against obscenity (Thornburgh & Lin, 2002). Because the production of child pornography involves clear harm to a minor in the form of sexual abuse, which has been shown to have lasting negative effects into adulthood (Mullen & Fleming, 1998), the

Court has upheld penalties for possessing, distributing, or producing this type of content.[15] In contrast, the Court has been less inclined to regulate sexually explicit material depicting adults because adults can consent to participate in the production of such material, and the Court has not been convinced that viewing sexually explicit media content is inherently harmful to adults or youth.[16]

That questions remain about whether and to what extent harm is done to young people by exposure to sexually explicit material has likely factored into the Court's resistance to support more sweeping regulation of such material. Federal courts may be placing a greater emphasis on the demonstration of actual harm to young people when content restrictions are implemented. For example, a 2003 Circuit Court decision struck down a county ordinance prohibiting the sale of violent videogames to minors on the grounds that the county needed to demonstrate that real harm is done to minors by playing these games and that regulating such games will actually alleviate the harm (Holohan, 2005). This is perhaps ironic for researchers of the media and child development – research on the effects of violent media content on children is fairly robust in showing specific negative outcomes (Bushman & Anderson, 2001; Centerwall, 1992; Escobar-Chaves et al., 2005; Singer, Singer, & Rapaczynski, 1984). In short, questions about the nature and extent of harm done to children exposed to sexually explicit material have likely factored into court decisions, encouraging courts to show restraint about regulating sexually explicit content; this is in contrast to court decisions to ban child pornography, where there is consensus regarding harm.

With respect to commercial advertising, the Court has also allowed greater levels of regulation than for other types of speech. In particular, advertising that is false or deceptive and therefore likely to affect a consumer's decision about a product can be banned. The FTC regulates advertisements (http://www.ftc.gov/bcp/conline/pubs/general/guidetoftc.htm), and the agency has helped to end several practices on the Internet that contribute to exposure of minors to sexually explicit material. For example, the FTC has taken formal action against unsolicited commercial emails that use deceptive means to encourage a user to go to a website with sexually explicit material. It has also worked against "mousetrapping," a technique that lures users to adult websites under false pretenses and then makes it difficult to exit the website even by closing your web browser. The FTC has also taken informal steps to pressure companies publishing adult websites not to use web addresses that are similar to innocuous websites – for example, www.whitehouse.gov was very different than the infamous www.whitehouse.com (Thornburgh & Lin, 2002).

The Court's support of regulating commercial advertising has also created an environment in which the Children's Online Privacy Protection Act of 1998 (COPPA) could be implemented and enforced. This act prohibits commercial websites from collecting, using, or disclosing personal information from children under age 13 unless parental consent has been obtained to do so, and the FTC has established methods it considers to be valid techniques to obtain parental consent (Thornburgh & Lin, 2002).

COPPA is a noteworthy example of how public policy can sometimes be designed to target children's developmental needs: By targeting websites aimed at children under the age of 13, COPPA is very much in keeping with the developmental tendencies of this age group to be vulnerable to manipulation and less equipped to make sound decisions such as when it is appropriate to give out personal information (Montgomery, 2001). COPPA offers one policy venue through which some of the aggressive strategies to mislead and capitalize on children's vulnerability can be controlled.

Summary of regulatory options for media content

Given the previous discussion of the types of regulatory options the Court has been inclined to support, what principles might we use to guide future efforts to develop policy options meant to reduce young people's exposure to sexually explicit media content? Table 21.1 summarizes some key aspects that are related to Court decisions, but several principles should be kept in mind. First, obscenity and child pornography are prohibited and are illegal to distribute. However, sexually explicit material featuring adult actors that is not obscene and commercial advertising about adult sexuality are allowed but can face some regulatory restrictions. Second, if the media technology makes it possible to differentiate minors from adults in the audience, then distribution to minors can be restricted. Third, media that are pervasive and very easily accessed (e.g., broadcast media) can face regulatory restrictions on content, particularly regarding when certain content can be aired. Media that force users to make a series of decisions to access content, including paying fees for access, has generally escaped content restrictions.

As noted earlier, public policy focused on restricting content may be most viable with respect to meeting the developmental needs of younger children. For example, the restrictions on sexually explicit content over public airwaves during certain hours leverage the fact that young children tend to have earlier bed times and therefore reduce the likelihood that they will be accidentally exposed to inappropriate content. In addition, the limitations that COPPA places on the type of content and marketing strategies employed on websites targeting children under age 13 are congruent with younger children's developmental needs, because younger children require the help of their parents to obtain parental consent. Internet filters and parental controls on television programming are also likely to be effective in preventing younger children from accidentally viewing content not appropriate for them, perhaps even in cases in which a younger child was trying to find sexually explicit content. For instance, younger children *might* not know enough about their Internet service to be able to get past the filter.

In contrast, older children have many more resources at their disposal to obtain media content that they wish to view, including better cognitive skills, increased skill with media technologies, and a social network of other teens that may also have an interest in developing strategies to "beat the system" and obtain material many if not most adults would find inappropriate for them. Older teens

Table 21.1 Regulating Sexually Explicit Media Content

Obscene Content

Type of accessibility	*Examples of media technology*	*Options supported*	*Options not supported*
Applies to all media regardless of type of accessibility	Any – television, Internet, DVD, etc.	Restriction on *content*: Obscene material is prohibited	N/A

Sexually Explicit Content

Type of accessibility	*Examples of media technology*	*Options supported*	*Options not supported*
Media that permit differentiation of minors from adults in terms of access	DVD, videogame, book, or other stores; movie theaters; websites with age verification strategy	Restrictions on *distribution* to minors permitted	Restrictions on distribution to adults not permitted
Media that allow easy and open access	Broadcast television and radio	Limited restrictions on *content* (e.g., during certain times of the day) and therefore some infringement on availability of content to adults	Restrictions that would entirely prevent adults from accessing sexually explicit content and would limit adults to only that content suitable for children not permitted
Media that are restricted to users who pay and/or have special technology	Cable television or radio, Internet, email and other online communication or file-sharing technology	Court prefers non-public policy options such as voluntary industry adherence to best practices and technology facilitating user choice	Restrictions on content or other requirements that would subject adults to content only suitable for minors not permitted (e.g., mandatory filtering of the Internet at public libraries)

who are not interested in finding sexually explicit material may have fewer accidental exposures if parents use some of the strategies noted above for younger children such as Internet filters and television parental controls. However, teens interested in obtaining sexually explicit material are likely to get it with a little effort given the current media environment (Thornburgh & Lin, 2002). Policy options that would further restrict content would be needed to deter determined teens, but such approaches would likely infringe on adult access and therefore would not likely withstand judicial scrutiny.

Beyond Stringent Content Restriction

In this section, I will review some of the strategies currently being implemented to reduce young people's exposure to sexually explicit media content, focusing on strategies that do not seek to restrict content beyond the terms already set by the Court. Such strategies include public policy to leverage distribution, an administrative tone that exerts pressure on the media, industry standards and self-regulation, and facilitating user control. In reviewing these strategies, I draw on examples from many media types to show some of the current concerns about television, videogames, the Internet, and other media technologies. Not all of these strategies are the direct result of public policy, but in many cases the threat of greater government involvement inspired media industries to take action on their own.

Leveraging age differentiation to restrict distribution to minors

In the fall of 2005, *Grand Theft Auto: San Andreas*, a videogame for the Play Station 2 system, created significant controversy when a sexually explicit mini-game was discovered that involves the main character taking a girlfriend on a series of dates. If the main character succeeds in charming the girlfriend, she invites him home for "coffee," and the player can watch the girlfriend and main character have sex. In addition, the player can use the controller to cycle through several different sexual positions (Sex controversy over GTA game, 2005; Gamespot, n.d.).

In December 2005, Senators Hillary Clinton, Joe Lieberman, and Evan Bayh introduced the Family Entertainment Protection Act (S. 2126) in the Senate. The bill proposes to capitalize on the Entertainment Software Ratings Board system, which rates videogames in a similar fashion to movies, by requiring stores that sell or rent videogames to restrict sales to adults over age 17. The bill does not attempt to limit the type of content in videogames, but rather focuses on regulating distribution only to minors. The focus on retailers also capitalizes on a venue that allows for age differentiation (e.g., the store can have a policy of checking identification during the purchase to ensure that the buyer is old enough to buy the game). At the time of going to press, the legislation was still pending, and it will be very interesting to track the outcome. Some of the lower courts have been less inclined to support strategies like these, viewing them as inappropriately restricting content without clearly showing a benefit for teens, and courts have struck down such legislation at the state and county level (Holohan, 2005). For example, Illinois with the support of its governor introduced similar legislation in 2005, but the legislation was not upheld by the state courts. The judge ruling on the matter cited concerns that supporting the legislation would create a chilling effect on the creation and distribution of videogames and that there was no evidence to support the view that playing violent videogames has a lasting effect on aggressive thoughts and behavior (ZDNet, 2005). This case suggests that regulation at the point of distribution may be losing viability as a policy option to pursue in future efforts to reduce young people's exposure to sexually explicit content.

Administrative tone

Each presidential administration has its own position regarding what constitutes inappropriate sexual material for children as well as the extent to which government regulation should be the tool through which to control the media landscape. Although administrations do not always choose to push for changes in public policy, other kinds of actions on the part of government agencies like the FCC or cabinet-level staff, who are appointed by the President, can exert social control over the media by creating a certain tone about what media content will and will not be tolerated. Public statements, suggesting the potential for greater regulation, reduced funding, or the enforcement of regulations for high-profile cases of inappropriate content making the airwaves (but not necessarily greater regulation consistently across all programming), can have a powerful effect on media industries (Holohan, 2005). Simply put, administrations often decide to influence the media landscape through the threat of greater government involvement but often fall short of seeking greater agency authority through new legislation.

A number of recent examples fall into this category of an administration exerting social power over the media, and the FCC has been the conduit in several cases. In 2004, the Superbowl halftime show created considerable controversy when, after a somewhat provocative performance, Janet Jackson experienced her infamous "wardrobe malfunction," which exposed one of her breasts on national television. This occurred during the hours that sexually explicit material is banned from broadcast television, and there was a barrage of public complaints filed with the FCC. The agency responded through several means. Michael Powell, then Chairman of the FCC and appointed by President George W. Bush, publicly made a number of statements condemning the network and characterized it as one of a growing list of inappropriate incidents that were happening more frequently on the airwaves (First Amendment Center, 2004). He also told lawmakers and broadcasters that the FCC would start doing more to discourage such incidents, including fining broadcasters for each incident rather than each program and revoking licenses of repeat offenders (First Amendment Center, 2004). Moreover, Powell sent letters not just to CBS, the network airing the Superbowl, but to all the major networks as well as the National Cable Television Association (NCTA), informing them of the growing discontent the FCC has heard from citizens about what they see and hear on television (http://www.fcc.gov/commissioners/letters/indecency/).

Importantly, the FCC has very little jurisdiction over cable television – remember that the Court has not supported content restrictions on cable because these airwaves are essentially private, not public, and individuals must choose to obtain and pay for this service (FCC, 2000). People must "opt in" to the content offered on cable and cannot accidentally be exposed to those offerings that they did not choose when they signed up for service. Although the FCC threat to cable was largely that – a threat – NCTA president Robert Sachs responded publicly by taking the FCC concerns seriously (First Amendment Center, 2004). His letter in response to the FCC noted the money and programs that cable has developed to educate consumers about family-friendly programs as well as the tools to help parents block children's access to adult programming. Although Sachs indicated that cable would do more in the future, the strategies he noted that are currently in place focus on improving user choice and not limiting content (First Amendment Center, 2004).

Powell's letters warned the industry that there was a change in the administration's approach to these issues, and that the industry should be careful to do more self-policing lest the government enact more restrictive policies. Following the Superbowl incident, the FCC did not pursue any legislative changes that would give the agency greater latitude to go after a broader range of content or a broader range of media outlets (e.g., broader jurisdiction over regulating content on cable television), although the agency did request an increase in the amount of the maximum fine it could levy (First Amendment Center, 2004). The FCC also pursued another very high-profile case about a month after the Superbowl incident – namely, it levied record-setting fines against Clear Channel Radio for sexually explicit material broadcast on the Howard Stern show during the hours that such material is banned from public airwaves (CNNMoney.com, 2004; Fox News, 2004).

One additional aspect of how the FCC carries out its mission is worth noting: unlike many other regulatory agencies, which fulfill their mission by conducting regular audits to determine if the programs falling under their jurisdiction are adhering to standards (e.g., are commuter rail agencies adhering to national rail safety standards?), the FCC performs its mission by responding to complaints (FCC, n.d.a). When a complaint is filed by a consumer or organization, the agency reviews the complaint and makes judgments regarding whether a specific complaint is serious enough to warrant action. If the FCC finds that a complaint is valid, the agency may or may not elect to impose fines (FCC, n.d.a).

One might argue that designing the FCC's enforcement procedures in this manner is very much in keeping with the intentions of the Court to use contemporary community standards to make determinations about whether material is sexually inappropriate. If the community does not voice objections through complaints filed with the FCC, then the community must not find the material indecent or obscene. However, the FCC process is guided not only by complaints, but also by an administration's response to incidents that could cause problematic political fallout. Note, for example, that the Howard Stern Show, infamous for its racy content, had been on broadcast radio for years before the FCC levied its record-setting fines against Clear Channel in 2004 (CNNMoney.com, 2004; Fox News, 2004). In addition, the FCC process is potentially vulnerable to special interest groups rather than an inclusive set of community standards. For example, the FCC estimated that about 99.8 percent of complaints in 2003 and 99.9 percent of complaints through October 2004 that were unrelated to the Superbowl incident were filed by the Parents Television Council, a conservative media watchdog group (Holohan, 2005, p. 10).

Although the FCC is the most commonly used conduit for administrations to communicate their tolerance (or lack thereof) toward media content, one other recent example is worth discussing. In January 2005, PBS received a letter from the newly appointed Secretary of Education, Margaret Spellings, warning the network not to air an upcoming episode of the children's show *Postcards from Buster*. The show depicts a cartoon rabbit, Buster, who travels around the country visiting with families of different backgrounds and introducing the audience to the families' way of life. For example, Buster has been monoskiing in Park City, Utah, has danced the Arapaho Grass Dance at the Wind River Reservation in Wyoming, and, in the episode to which Spellings objected, Buster was to farm maple syrup in Vermont and have dinner with a family headed by a lesbian couple. Although Spellings did not threaten this directly, her letter indicated that airing the episode might call some of PBS's program funding into question (de Moraes, 2005).

The controversial episode of *Postcards From Buster* did not in any way violate policy about sexually inappropriate material being aired on broadcast television. However, recognition of gay and lesbian families is a highly contentious issue in our culture that relates to ongoing public policy discourses about legal recognition of gay families and partnerships as well as the regulation of sexuality. That the Bush administration would wish to exert influence over the media's portrayal of a lesbian family in a show receiving federal funds is in keeping with the Republican party's position of not providing legal recognition to gay and lesbian partnerships. With the exception of a few stations (e.g., Boston reported they would air the episode; de Moraes, 2005), this example also shows that political pressure to regulate the media is not limited to obscene or indecent material, nor is the FCC the only agency through which this power is exerted.

Industry standards and facilitating user choice

Often in order to avoid greater government regulation, the media have developed standards to guide what type of content is available to certain types of audiences. Two examples – one relating to cable television and a second regarding a controversial book for teens – are helpful in understanding both the conditions under which the media will self-regulate and what types of programs are likely to be implemented. The Telecommunications Act of 1996 motivated cable networks to develop a rating system for programs containing sexually explicit, violent, and other material that parents might find inappropriate for their children. Specifically, the act established an advisory committee of parents, television broadcasters, public interest groups, and others to develop a rating system if the industry had not developed an acceptable system on its own within one year from the passage of the Act (FCC, n.d.b). The message to the industry was clear – do it yourself, or the federal government will do it for you (and you might be less happy with the results).

The industry complied, and the National Association of Broadcasters, the National Cable Television Association, and the Motion Picture Association of America developed a system known as "TV Parental Guidelines." The system is similar to that developed by the Motion Picture Association of America for movies,[17] but the television version has finer gradations with respect to younger children as well as additional symbols for the particular type of content the parent may find inappropriate (see Table 21.2; Cable Puts You in Control, n.d.); Motion Picture Association of America, n.d.).

Table 21.2 Movie and Television Rating Systems

Movie Rating	*Television Rating*
G: All ages admitted	TV-Y: All children even those 2–6 years
	TV-Y7: Children age 7 and above
	TV-G: Suitable for most ages, including younger children
PG: Parental guidance suggested	TV-PG: Includes material that may be unsuitable for younger children
PG-13: Parental guidance for children under 13	TV-14: Includes material that may be unsuitable for youth under age 14
R: Children under 17 not admitted	TV-MA: Includes material that may be unsuitable for youth under age 17
NC-17: No one under 17 admitted (replaced the X rating for sexually explicit adult content)	No television equivalent
No movie equivalent	Additional television content indicators
	V: Violence
	FV: Fantasy violence
	S: Sexually explicit or suggestive content
	L: Coarse language
	D: Sexually suggestive dialogue

Note: Prior to a television program, one rating and as many indicators as appropriate are displayed (Cable Puts You in Control, n.d.).

To complement the ratings system, the act also required that new televisions larger than 13 inches be equipped with the V-Chip, a new technology at the time that allowed parents to block programming based on the ratings and content indicators. A password allows the parent to turn the blocking on and off and prevents children from doing the same – that is as long as the parent has kept the password a secret (FCC, n.d.b). More recently, digital cable systems come with their own parental controls that also allow parents to block programming based on the rating. The parental controls accomplish the same objective as the V-Chip, just with slightly different technology. Although the V-Chip and parental controls are widely available, it is not clear that parents make use of these tools. Amy Jordan's research on the V-Chip found that only 8 percent of parents in her study used it, and many commented that setting the V-Chip was awkward and confusing (Jordan, 2003). Although I could not find data on the level of use of cable and satellite parental controls, it is possible that the recent media campaigns by cable companies are designed to make parents more aware of these tools and increase utilization.[18]

While the pressure of potential government regulation was the basis for new television ratings standards, an administrative tone is not always necessary to encourage the media – or at least media retailers – to take action to reduce youth exposure to sexually explicit content. In 2005, Simon & Schuster published *Rainbow Party*, a novel in which teens plan an oral sex party and each of the girls wears a different color lipstick (hence the name of the book). The author and editors state that the book deals with a current issue affecting teenagers, and their hope was that the book would scare young readers out of the idea of such activity. Nonetheless, the book contains sexually explicit content and not all readers will interpret the material in the manner intended by the author. The book was highly controversial when it was published, making it a slightly risky item for bookstores to distribute – recall that sexually explicit material deemed obscene for young people can face regulation at the point of distribution (Memmott, 2005). To be clear, this book was not deemed to be obscene for young people, and there was no requirement for booksellers to make identification checks on youth attempting to buy it.

Rather than face an onslaught of public outrage (or potentially a lawsuit), Borders and Barnes & Noble, two of the largest book store chains in the country, decided to sell the book online but not stock the book in their stores (Memmott, 2005). In doing so, the companies balanced supporting freedom of expression while also reducing the potential for parents to become outraged that the booksellers allowed their child to purchase the book. By making the book available online, the booksellers increased the likelihood that children would have to consult with an adult to obtain the book – for example, payment online generally comes by credit card, which for many kids means using (and asking for) a parent's card. There are, of course, ways around this for the determined teen, and selling the book online does not guarantee that young people would not be able to obtain it without parental involvement.

Strategies for the Internet

Ratings systems in conjunction with parental controls allow families to make informed decisions about the programs they watch and the programs they choose to block. Many parents have a desire for similar options for Internet content, but the task is somewhat more challenging compared to broadcast and cable television. For example, the content of television programming, movies, videogames, and music CDs can easily be rated as a part of its production, and the content is static (i.e., an episode of a sitcom does not change every time it is aired). In contrast, anyone can create and publish a webpage, and the content can change as often as the publisher wishes. Furthermore, the Internet offers opportunities for communication such as chat rooms and message boards, which are conversations that can be read by anyone logging onto the page. Rating this content is very difficult because it is highly dynamic, changing as often as someone elects to participate in the conversation. These conditions as well as the unrestricted nature of the Internet, which is a global resource, make developing and implementing a rating system that Internet filters could use very challenging.

Instead, Internet filters rely on more sophisticated technology, which is always being refined and improved. That said, the limitation of Internet filters is that they will always have some level of error, either allowing some inappropriate content to be viewed or restricting content the parent would think is perfectly acceptable (Thornburgh & Lin, 2002). AOL's parental controls, a popular item many households are familiar with, offers restricted access to the Web in three different manners, depending entirely on which side of caution the parent wishes to err on. These include totally unrestricted access, unrestricted access except for websites deemed inappropriate (the likely error here is that some inappropriate content will slip through), and access limited to websites explicitly deemed appropriate for children (the likely error here is that content that could be enjoyed by young people might be screened out). AOL's parental controls can also restrict email, instant messaging, restrictions on participating in chat rooms, and restricted access to news groups like message boards (America Online, n.d.; Thornburgh & Lin, 2002). More recently, AOL began offering a monitoring service that sends a report card updating parents on their children's online activities, including time spent on email, Web surfing, and instant messaging (America Online, n.d.).

Each of these tools helps to put a greater level of control in parents' hands when they are not available to supervise their children's Internet activity directly, but as with most strategies they are not foolproof against a young person determined to obtain objectionable content. There are more restrictive tactics parent's can take – for example, subscribing to an Internet service provider that only allows access to a subset of pre-screened Internet content, blocking all the rest, but these services are not widely used. Parents can also monitor their children's Internet use either by checking Internet caches to see what websites have been accessed (provided the young person has not emptied the cache) or through commercial monitoring devices. In monitoring, young people can access inappropriate content, and it is up to the parent to punish this action later if they choose to do so. Like Internet filters, there are always ways to circumvent the software – for instance, by using another Internet source – and developmental psychologists have questioned whether monitoring effectively develops good decision-making in young adults (Thornburgh & Lin, 2002).

Although Internet filters are imperfect, they may be particularly helpful in reducing accidental exposure, which is important for younger children, and they certainly offer parents some level of control especially when they are unavailable to supervise their children's activities. Furthermore, these types of technologies, which do not infringe upon adults' access, have had full support from the Courts at least with respect to the availability of these tools for the home, private institutions, and to a large extent public elementary and high schools. Given that content restrictions on the Internet are very difficult to enforce, technologies that help facilitate user control are an important option for many parents (Thornburgh & Lin, 2002).

Media literacy and improving decision-making skills

Potentially, some of the most viable and possibly most effective strategies to reduce adolescent's exposure to inappropriate media content are those that are responsive to their developmental needs by fostering skills such as decision-making, especially as they pertain to content choices and how to manage online communication with strangers (Collins et al., 2004). Policy that supports programs such as media literacy may be particularly helpful in this area.

Media literacy is the development of skills to critically analyze images and information represented in the media and has the potential to help young people deal with a wide range of problematic content, including sexually explicit content, misleading commercial solicitations, differentiating between good sources of information and poor ones, and effective search techniques (Chakroff & Nathanson, this volume, Chapter 24). For example, young people can be vulnerable to commercial advertising, and developing young people's skepticism toward such content can be important to maintaining privacy. In addition, improving a young person's search techniques and their ability to recognize hits that are likely to lead to inappropriate content can help young people get to information that interests them more efficiently and also can reduce unintentional exposure. Not only are these important skills for any young person to learn, but media literacy programs can be tailored to the developmental level of the young person, teaching them skills appropriate for their age and type of media use (Iannotta, 2001; Thornburgh & Lin, 2002).

Learning to think critically about media content can also help protect young people from sexually explicit content by teaching them to be critical of media messages and to judge them against their own beliefs (Iannotta, 2001; Keller, 2000). One media literacy project described by researcher Sarah Keller at a National Academy of Sciences workshop taught teenage girls to examine the underlying messages they found in media content. At the end of the project, girls were much more critical about media messages suggesting that young women should focus on trying to attract boyfriends and become sexually active early (Keller, 2000; Iannotta, 2001). Not only may this new analytic skill encourage these girls to avoid content their parents might find objectionable, but it may also help them to make better decisions about their own sexual activity. In addition, research by Subrahmanyam and colleagues (2004) on teens and the Internet shows that young people are not passive recipients of media but construct their own media environments through places like chat rooms and message boards. Teaching young people to make good decisions may also help them to create better virtual environments in which to interact.

For older teens, strategies that focus less on further restricting media content and more on helping teens improve cognitive and decision-making skills are a more viable public policy option. Policies can be designed to support educational resources for parents and teachers that leverage teens' growing developmental skills to make good decisions about content. Media literacy programs, in particular, can teach children about Internet safety and strategies about media use (Iannotta, 2001). In conjunction with these educational strategies, tools such as thorough media ratings systems tailored closely to young people's developmental needs can be encouraged through public policy (and often just the threat of formal policy) to support the latter strategy of improving decision-making skills about what content to access. None of these options would face the kinds of constitutional challenges that restrictions on content do.

Media literacy can be a helpful tool in teaching young people these decision-making skills, but parental involvement and communication are also very important (Blum, McNeely, & Nonnemaker, 2001; Nightingale & Fischoff, 2001). Parental involvement, specifically a close, open relationship in which young people and parents can communicate about their online experiences, can help young people deal with media content that is disturbing or raises difficult questions for them (Collins et al., 2004; Greenfield, 2004). Research on adolescent vulnerability and risk-taking has shown that parental involvement can exert a protective effect, helping teens to make decisions that are safer and involve less risk-taking behavior (Blum, McNeely, & Nonnemaker, 2001; Greenfield, 2004; Nightingale & Fischoff, 2001). Families that convey to their children a strong set of values by which to base their choices – particularly as those values pertain to media content – can put their offspring in a better position to handle disturbing material; if those conversations include discussions about online communications with strangers, these strategies may also help to keep youth safe (Collins et al., 2004; Greenfield, 2004).

Teaching young people how to handle communication on the Internet is also vitally important. Inadvertent exposure to sexually explicit activity is certainly a concern, but it pales in comparison to the potential for young people to be drawn into the prospect of meeting an adult "friend" from the Internet (Thornburgh & Lin, 2002). There are some new supports to help protect young people – the non-profit organization Perverted Justice, which has been featured on *Dateline* and other television shows, works with law enforcement agents to identify online predators soliciting sex from minors (http://www.perverted-justice.com/).

Arguably, the best defense against online predators is a young person already armed with the skills to recognize when communication with another user could be problematic and the confidence to shut it down.

Conclusion

Determining how best to capitalize on the positive aspects of new advances in media while also limiting children's exposure to sexually explicit and other kinds of inappropriate media content can be very challenging for parents, especially when most teens are more savvy than their parents at using these technologies. There also is no single solution available through public policy that would address the diverse developmental needs of minors from young children through older teenagers almost of legal age. Policy options that regulate content are effective and supported by our judicial system under some circumstances but generally not when they infringe on adults' rights to obtain content. Other approaches that involve technology such as parental controls and Internet filters can help reduce young people's exposure to sexually explicit content but fall short when older youth are interested in finding such material. Industry ratings systems can help inform parents and youth of the content so that they can make good decisions, but without efforts to develop young people's cognitive and decision-making skills, the information cannot be fully leveraged. With respect to new media, including the Internet, file sharing, and newer forms of communication such as chat rooms, educational strategies might be the best approach because they directly arm young people to make good decisions about technologies that are not very amenable to filtering or other outside controls.

The National Academy of Sciences committee that examined how to prevent children from being exposed to sexually explicit content on the Internet recommended a three-tiered approach including public policy, technology, and educational strategies (Thornburgh & Lin, 2002). This approach is appropriate for media beyond the Internet – for example, broadcast television is subject to federal regulations regarding content, V-Chip technology can be used to reduce accidental exposure, and media literacy can help young people interpret television content. Programs that are the result of either public policy or simply parents' interest in improving their children's decision-making skills can make a difference in how young people will interact with and react to their media environment.

Notes

Special thanks to Farah B. Angersola.

1   Note that total time of media exposure was 8.5 hours, but this is reduced by 2 hours per day (to 6.5 hours) when multitasking is considered, i.e., youth use multiple media simultaneously.

2   See US Const. Amend I.
3   See Chaplinksy v. New Hampshire, 315 US 568 (1942); Ashcroft v. ACLU, 217
    F. 3d 162 (3d Cir. 2000), cert granted, 121 S. Ct. 1997 (2001); Roth, 354 US 476,
    482–5 (1957); Paris Adult Theater I v. Slaton, 413 US 49, 54 (1973); Miller v.
    California, 413 US 15, 23 (1972); Ginsberg v. State of New York, 390 US 629, 635
    (1968); Ashcroft v. ACLU, 535 US 564, 574 (2002).
4   See Roth v. United States, 354 US 482–5 (1957); and Miller v. California, 413 US
    15 (1973).
5   See Roth, 354 US at 489; 47 USC §231 (e)(6).
6   See Roth, 354 US 482–5 (1957).
7   See Ginsberg, 390 US at 634, n. 4 (1968).
8   Policy banning retailers from selling or renting sexually explicit material to young
    people has both come under fire recently and been turned to as a solution to problems
    with media content such as videogames. This is an issue worth watching in the near
    future as it may or may not remain as a viable public policy option for limiting young
    people's access to sexually explicit and violent content. This topic is also discussed in
    greater detail later in the chapter. For case law, see Paris Adult Theater I, 413 US at
    57 citing, *inter alia*, Miller 413 US at 18–20; Ginsberg 390 US at 633.
9   United States v. Playboy Entertainment Group, Inc., 529 US 803, 816 (2000).
10 The Communications Decency Act of 1996, which constitutes Title V of the
    Telecommunications Act of 1996, is codified at 47 USC §223(a) to (h) ("CDA").
11 See Reno v. ACLU, 521 US 844 (1997).
12 The Court's decision in Reno v. ACLU left intact the remainder of the CDA, includ-
    ing the "On-line Family Empowerment," provision. Section 509 of the 1996 Act,
    "Online Family Empowerment," amended Title II of the Communications Act of 1934
    by adding §230, "Protection for Private Blocking and Screening of Offensive
    Material."
13 See Red Lion Broadcasting Co. v. FCC, 395 US 367 (1969).
14 FCC v. Pacifica Foundation, 438 US 726 (1978)
15 See New York v. Ferber, 458 US 747 (1982).
16 Ginsberg, 390 US at 641–3; Miller, 413 US at 18–19; Paris, 413 US at 57.
17 The movie rating system was developed under similar public pressure in the 1960s as
    the social pressures of an evolving culture created changes in the types of films pro-
    duced. In response to pubic outcry over some movie content, the industry developed
    a ratings system to "balance pressure between preserving creative freedoms" and warn-
    ing viewers of content they may find objectionable. The ratings system underwent
    a few revisions, most notably adding the PG-13 category in 1984. (Motion Picture
    Association of America, n.d.).
18 I was not able to find information about cable television parental controls, but it would
    be very interesting to learn, especially given some of the industry's recent efforts to
    educate parents, whether parents found this system more accessible.

References

America Online. (n.d.). *Parental controls.* Retrieved August 31, 2006, from http://site.
    aol.com/product/parcon.adp.

Blum, R. W., McNeely, C., & Nonnemaker, J. (2001). Vulnerability, risk, and protection. In B. Fischoff, E. O. Nightingale, & J. G. Iannotta (Eds.), *Adolescent risk and vulnerability: Concepts and measurement*. Washington, DC: National Academy Press.

Brown, J., L'Engle, K., Pardun, C., Guo, G., Kenneavy, K., & Jackson, C. (2006). Sexy media matter: Exposure to sexual content in music, movies, television and magazines predicts black and white adolescents' sexual behavior. *Pediatrics*, 117, 1018–27.

Brown, J., & Newcomer, S. (1991). Television viewing and adolescents' sexual behavior. *Journal of Homosexuality*, 21, 77–89.

Bushman, B. J., & Anderson, C. A. (2001). Media violence and the American public. Scientific facts versus media misinformation. *American Psychology*, 56, 477–89.

Cable Puts You in Control. (n.d.). *Defining the Ratings System*. Retrieved August 31, 2006, from http://www.controlyourtv.org/DetailPage.php?PageID=23.

Centerwall, B. S. (1992). Television and violence. The scale of the problem and where to go from here. *Journal of the American Medical Association*, 267, 3059–63.

CNNMoney.com. (2004). *FCC fine prompts Clear Channel to drop Stern*, April 8. Retrieved August 31, 2006, from http://money.cnn.com/2004/04/08/news/fortune500/stern_fines/.

Collins, R., Elliott, M., Berry, S., Kanouse, D., Kunkel, D., Hunter, S., et al. (2004). Watching sex on television predicts adolescent initiation of sexual behavior. *Pediatrics*, 114(3), e280–e289.

De Moraes, L. (2005). PBS's "Buster" gets an education. *Washington Post*, January 27. Retrieved December 6, 2005, from http://www.washtingontpost.com/wp-dyn/articles/A41088-2005Jan26.html.

Escobar-Chaves, S., Tortolero, S., Markham, C., Low, B., Eitel, P., & Thickstun, P. (2005). Impact of the media on adolescent sexual attitudes and behaviors. *Pediatrics*, 116(1), 303–26.

Federal Communications Commission (FCC). (n.d.a). *Obscene, profane and indecent broadcasts: FCC consumer facts*. Retrieved December 9, 2005, from www.fcc.gov/cgb/consumerfacts/obscene.html.

Federal Communications Commission (FCC). (n.d.b). *Excerpts from V-Chip legislation*. Retrieved December 6, 2005, from http://www.fcc.gov/vchip/legislation.html.

Federal Communications Commission (FCC). (2000). *Fact sheet: Program content regulations*. Retrieved December 6, 2005, from www.fcc.gov/mb/facts/program.html.

First Amendment Center. (2004). *FCC Chairman to Congress: TV, radio must clean up act*, February 11. Retrieved December 6, 2005, from http://www.firstamendmentcenter.org/news.aspx?id=12661&printer–friendly=y.

Fox News. (2004). *Clear Channel nixes Howard Stern*, April 9. Retrieved December 6, 2005, from http://www.foxnews.com/story/0,2933,116594,00.html.

Gamespot. (n.d.). *Confirmed: Sex minigame in PS2 San Andreas*. Retrieved December 8, 2005, from www.gamespot.com/news/2005/07/15/news_6129301.html.

Greenfield, P. M. (2004). Inadvertent exposure to pornography on the Internet: Implications of peer-to-peer file-sharing networks for child development and families. *Applied Developmental Psychology*, 25, 741–50.

Holohan, M. C. (2005). Political, technology, and indecency: Rethinking broadcast regulation in the 21st century. *Berkeley Technology Law Journal*, 20, 341–71.

Iannotta, J. G. (2001). *Nontechnical strategies to reduce children's exposure to inappropriate material on the Internet: Summary of a workshop*. Washington, DC: National Academy Press.

Jordan, A. (2003). *Television and children's media policy: Where do we go from here?* Retrieved August 31, 2006, from http://www.annenbergpublicpolicycenter.org/05_media_developing_child/childrensprogramming/2003ChildrensMediaPolicyConference_tr.pdf#search=%22annenberg%20public%20policy%20center%20philadelphia%20experiment%22.

Kalof, L. (1999). The effects of gender and music video imagery on sexual attitudes. *The Journal of Social Psychology*, 139(3), 378–85.

Keller, S. (2000). How do early adolescent girls use media to shape their romantic identities? Unpublished PhD dissertation, University of North Carolina, Chapel Hill.

LaTour, M. S., & Henthorne, T. L. (1993). Female nudity: Attitudes toward the ad and the brand, and implications for advertising strategy. *The Journal of Consumer Marketing*, 10(3), 25–32.

Memmott, C. (2005). Controversy colors teen book. *USA Today*, May 23. Retrieved August 31, 2006, from http://www.usatoday.com/life/books/news/2005-05-22-rainbow-usat_x.htm.

Montgomery, K. A. (2001). Digital kids – The new on-line children's consumer culture. In D. G. Singer & S. L. Singer (Eds.), *Handbook of children and the media* (pp. 635–50). Thousand Oaks, CA: Sage.

Motion Picture Association of America. (n.d.). *Ratings History*. Retrieved January 30, 2006, from http://www.mpaa.org/Ratings_history1.asp.

Mullen, P. E., & Fleming, J. (1998). Long-term effects of child sexual abuse. *Issues in Child Abuse Prevention*. Retrieved January 7, 2006, from http://www.aifs.gov.au/nch/issues9.html#lon.

National Research Council. (2002). *Technical, business, and legal dimensions of protecting children from pornography on the Internet: Proceedings of a workshop*. Washington, DC: National Academy Press.

Nightingale, E. O., & Fischoff, B. (2001). Adolescent risk and vulnerability: Overview. In B. Fischoff, E. O. Nightingale, & J. G. Iannotta (Eds.), *Adolescent risk and vulnerability: Concepts and measurement*. Washington, DC: National Academy Press.

Peters, C. C. (1933). *Motion pictures and standards of morality*. New York: Macmillan.

Rideout, V. J., & Hamel, E. (2006). *The media family: Electronic media in the lives of infants, toddlers, preschoolers and their parents*. Menlo Park, CA: Kaiser Family Foundation.

Roberts, D. F., Foehr, U. G., & Rideout, V. (2005). *Generation M: Media in the lives of 8–18-year-olds*. Menlo Park, CA: Kaiser Family Foundation.

Rouner, D., Slater, M. D., & Domenech-Rodriguez, M. (2003). Adolescent evaluation of gender role and sexual imagery in television advertisements. *Journal of Broadcasting and Electronic Media*, 47(3), 435–54.

Ruditis, P. (2005). *Rainbow Party*. New York: Simon & Schuster.

Sex controversy over GTA game. (2005). *BBC News*, July 11. Retrieved December 8, 2005, from http://news.bbc.co.uk/1/hi/technology/4671429.stm.

Singer, J. L., Singer, D. G., & Rapaczynski, W. S. (1984). Family patterns and television viewing as predictors of children's beliefs and aggression. *Journal of Communication*, 34, 73–89.

Sprafkin, J. N., Silverman, T., & Rubinstein, E. A. (1980). Reactions to sex on television: An exploratory study. *The Public Opinion Quarterly*, 44(3), 303–15.

Subrahmanyam, K., Greenfield, P. M., & Tynes, B. (2004). Constructing sexuality and identity in an online teen chat room. *Applied Developmental Psychology*, 25, 651–66.

Thornburgh, D., & Lin, H. S. (Eds.). (2002). *Youth, pornography, and the Internet*. Washington, DC: National Academy Press.

ZDNet. (2005). *Court blocks Illinois video game laws*, December 5. Retrieved November 1, 2006, from http://news.zdnet.com/2100-1040_22-5983061.html.

22

Media-Related Policies of Professional Health Organizations

Marie Evans Schmidt, David S. Bickham, Amy Branner, and Michael Rich

From the time that technological advances and increasing affluence made entertainment media widely accessible, healthcare professionals have been concerned about the influences of those media on physical, mental, and social health. Although concerns were first voiced in the *Journal of the American Medical Association* (*JAMA*) shortly after television became widely available (Smith, 1952), organized responses by associations of health professionals did not materialize until the mid-1970s. Health professional organizations began to examine the health implications of media exposure and to establish policies for their member professionals and those whom they serve after three important events: (1) the United States Surgeon General's 1972 report on television and social behavior (Murray et al., 1972); (2) T. Berry Brazelton's 1974 advice to the American Academy of Pediatrics (AAP) (Brazelton, 1974); and (3) a 1975 *JAMA* review of the research on media violence (Rothenberg, 1975).

At their 1976 annual meetings, both the AAP and the American Medical Association (AMA) passed resolutions that opposed violence on television, urged producers to create more positive programming, and encouraged their memberships to educate themselves about the effects of television on health (AAP, 1977; AMA, 1976). In 1977, the AMA passed a resolution expanding their concern to pornographic or sexually suggestive programming, authorizing grants to research and monitor violence and sex on television, and convening a symposium on the positive and negative effects of television for their membership (AMA, 1977a, 1977b). That same year, the AAP president appointed a task force charged with evaluating and making recommendations on television commercials and their effects on children (AAP, 1978).

Over the ensuing decades, as media evolved and a variety of health concerns arose, the AAP and AMA were joined by the American Psychological Association (APA) and the American Academy of Child and Adolescent Psychiatry (AACAP) in making practice recommendations and policy statements with the intent to limit or eliminate negative health effects and to promote positive applications of media.

Organizations of health professionals developed policies that addressed broad media effects, the use of specific media, specific health outcomes of concern, and techniques for using media in healthy ways.

The Creation and Intent of Health Professional Associations' Media Policies

To establish consistent, evidence-based care on a rapidly expanding information base, health professional organizations develop policies by conducting reviews of the research literature, translating the data into the context of clinical practice, and making recommendations to their memberships. In the following sections, we review media policies put forth by various professional health organizations, focusing on the data to support these policies. We also highlight the successes and failures encountered by these groups in obtaining compliance from members of their professional organizations, from industry, from the government, and from the public (see Figure 22.1 for a timeline of the policies addressed in this chapter).

Media Health Policies Addressing Particular Types of Media Content

Violence

The AAP, AMA, AACAP, and APA all advise against consumption of violent media. This position is based on a large and diverse body of evidence on the effects of exposure to media violence (Wilson, this volume, Chapter 11). Exposure to violence in media has been found to contribute to fear and anxiety (e.g., Cantor, 2001), desensitization (e.g., Thomas et al., 1977), and aggressive behavior (e.g., Bushman & Anderson, 2001). These findings compelled the AAP, AMA, AACAP, and APA, later joined by the American Academy of Family Physicians and the American Psychiatric Association, to release a first-ever "Joint Statement on the Impact of Entertainment Violence on Children" in 2000. The statement concluded that "well over 1000 studies . . . point overwhelmingly to a causal connection between media violence and aggressive behavior in some children" (AAP et al., 2000, p. 1).

The APA, AAP, and AMA also support voluntary industry efforts to reduce children's exposure to media violence. The APA "requests industry representatives to take a responsible attitude in reducing direct imitatable violence on "real-life" fictional children's programming or violent incidents on cartoons . . . consistent with the guarantees of the First Amendment" (APA, 1996, para 15). The AAP specifically discourages weapon carrying and unrealistic portrayals of violence, and requests that the industry "demonstrate sensitivity to the issue of media violence," recommending such "voluntary remedies" as "parental advisories,

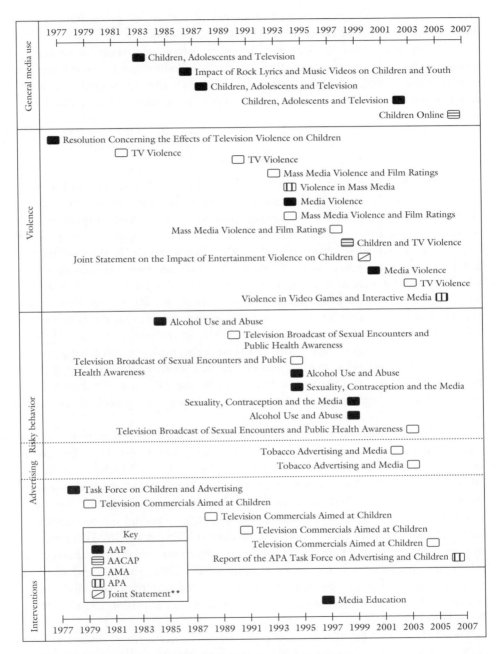

Figure 22.1 Timeline of Media-Related Policy Statements*
Source: Created by the Center on Media and Child Health, 2006. *This timeline is intended as a reference point for policy statement mentioned in this chapter, not as a comprehensive overview of all policy statements in existence. **Joint Statement by AAP, AACAP, APA, AMA, American Academy of Family Physicians, American Psychistic Association.

ratings systems, and careful (i.e., late night) placement of programming and promotions with violent content" (AAP, 1995b, p. 950).

Voluntary regulation by industry, however, often falls short of sweeping changes. The APA, therefore, has also specifically called for government intervention to reduce media violence, adopting the policy that "reasoned regulatory action should be pursued, consistent with constitutional guarantees" (APA, 1996, para 1).

Sexual content

The AAP and AMA call on the entertainment industry, pediatricians, and parents to limit children's exposure to unhealthy media messages about sex. Teens' viewing of television programs with heavy amounts of sexual content predicts their sexual attitudes and behaviors, including age of first intercourse and positive attitudes about casual sex (Brown et al., 2006; Brown, Steele, & Walsh-Childers, 2002). In one prospective study, 12-year-olds who were heavy viewers of sexual television content were as likely to initiate intercourse as were 14- or 15-year-olds who were light viewers of sexual content (Collins et al., 2004). Another recent study found that youth who listen to popular music with sexually degrading lyrics are nearly twice as likely to initiate sexual activity in the next two years as those who do not (Martino et al., 2006). Although the evidence associating media use with sexual behavior is both newer and less developed than that linking media and violence, the negative effects of early and risky sexual behavior have motivated health organizations to recommend reducing young people's exposure to sexual content in media.

A 2001 AAP policy statement, supported by the AACAP and APA, recommends that pediatricians "encourage discussions between patients and their families on the effect of media on sexual attitudes, beliefs, and behavior" (AAP, AACAP, & APA, 2001, p. 192). The limited research evidence available supports this policy. Adolescents who watched an episode of *Friends* about condom failure and discussed it with an adult were twice as likely as those who did not to remember that condoms are more than 95 percent effective (Collins et al., 2003). Television may, in some cases, stimulate important discussions about sexual topics that a child might find uncomfortable to initiate (Collins et al., 2004). In fact, one third of teens in a Kaiser Family Foundation survey indicated that they have discussed a sexual issue with their parents because of something on television (Kaiser Family Foundation, 2002).

The AMA and AAP also recommend that the entertainment industry offer public service announcements (PSAs) to promote healthy and responsible sexual behaviors. Although little is known about the effectiveness of PSAs in promoting safe sexual practices, the AMA proposes broadcast rules that allow advertising and PSAs promoting contraception and safe sex (AMA, 1991–2005). The AAP, endorsed by the AACAP and APA, urges television networks to "use PSAs that promote abstinence from sexual intercourse for adolescents" as well as to promote condom use (AAP, AACAP, & APA, 2001, p. 193). More research is necessary to determine how best to influence young people with positive media information about sex.

Advertising

The AAP, AMA, and APA have all supported reducing or eliminating children's exposure to advertisements. In 2004, the APA Task Force on Advertising and Children prepared an extensive report detailing the effects of advertising on children (Kunkel et al., 2004). Summarizing numerous studies on children's understanding of advertising, the APA Task Force concluded that advertising to young children is inherently unfair, because most children cannot differentiate commercials from television programs until the age of 4 or 5, and children rarely understand the persuasive intent of advertisements until age 7 or 8 (Young, this volume, Chapter 18). On this basis, the APA has specifically called on the government to ban all advertising to children under 7 or 8 years of age (Kunkel et al., 2004).

The AMA "opposes TV advertising and programming aimed specifically at exploiting children" (AMA, 2001, para 1), and the AAP proposes that food, specifically, should not be advertised to children. However, neither the AAP nor the AMA has called for legislation to ban all advertising to children.

Because of the adverse health implications of alcohol and tobacco use, the AAP and the AMA advise their members to help reduce children's exposure to advertisements for these products. Exposure to alcohol advertisements promotes positive attitudes about drinking and is associated with drinking and driving (Grube & Wallack, 1994). Children with more exposure to tobacco marketing are more likely to have positive attitudes about tobacco use and to initiate smoking (Schooler, Feighery, & Flora, 1996). Alcohol companies continue to aggressively market their products to children and adolescents, despite the fact that the number one cause of death in teenagers is alcohol-related motor vehicle crashes, and alcohol often contributes to homicides, suicides, and unintended injuries (Johnston, O'Malley, & Bachman, 1996).

The AMA has specifically called for a ban on all tobacco advertising (AMA, 2005, para 6). In addition, the AMA supports petitioning appropriate government agencies "to prohibit advertising that falsely promotes the alleged benefits and pleasures of smoking as well worth the risks to health" (AMA, 2005). While cigarette advertisements are not shown on television, they continue to appear in magazines, billboards, and other media formats that are accessible and attractive to children and youth.

Over the last 20 years, in numerous policy statements, the AAP has called for a government ban on alcohol advertising on television, largely because alcoholic beverage producers were unresponsive to the requests of health professionals (AAP, 1987, 1995a, 2001a). Unlike cigarettes, alcohol is advertised on television, especially during sports programs. Much sports programming, such as football and stock car racing, is inextricably associated with sponsorship by alcoholic beverages. Although these commercials are largely for beer or wine, a voluntary moratorium by the alcohol industry on television commercials for distilled liquors was broken by NBC and Smirnoff in 2001. Under heavy public pressure, this strategy was abandoned six months later, but many distillers now promote "alcopops," or soft drink-like, flavored malt liquor beverages specifically intended to attract young people and establish brand loyalty to hard liquor (Rich, 2003). Alcohol is now advertised on the Internet, using techniques such as interactive "advergames" to attract young people to the websites of brewers and distillers (Center for Media Education, 1997).

Health Policies Addressing Media Use in General

In addition to policies addressing specific areas of health concern, professional health organizations have developed policies that have the broad goal of providing healthy media environments for children. These policies direct member clinicians to work for the production and consumption of healthier media through parents, community groups, policy makers, and media producers. They range from general strategies, such as teaching critical viewing and reducing media use, to specific recommendations, such as not using media as an "electronic babysitter" and discouraging screen use by children under age 2. Various policies encourage clinicians to work with parents, policy makers, and the media industry.

Encourage media education programs

The APA and AAP have made a series of recommendations regarding the development of media literacy programs to help children become informed, critical, and responsible consumers of media. In its 1996 policy statement on violence in media, the APA urged industry, government, and private foundations to develop and implement programs to enhance the media literacy skills of teachers, parents, and children (APA, 1996).

In 1999, the AAP released its first policy statement supporting media literacy as an intervention, recommending that pediatricians advise parents to teach critical viewing skills to their children. Maintaining that a media-literate public is better able to decipher media messages, to recognize media's potential effects, and to make healthier choices about their exposure, the AAP urged pediatricians to encourage state and federal governments to explore mandating and funding universal media education programs in American schools (AAP, 1999). Their statement was supported with psychological research demonstrating that media literacy programs can teach children critical viewing skills, reduce the effects of violent television, change beliefs about body image, and change attitudes about substance use (Austin & Johnson, 1997; Dorr, Graves, & Phelps, 1980; Huesmann et al., 1983; Rabak-Wagener, Eickhoff-Shemek, & Kelly-Vance,

1998). The AAP also suggested that pediatricians encourage government and foundations to increase available funding for media education research.

Recently, the APA has made policy statements encouraging media literacy as a technique for educating children about advertising, videogames, and interactive media. Relying on research that has investigated media literacy as an intervention on television effects, the organization encourages psychologists to teach media literacy skills to children, teachers, and parents, so that children and their caregivers are better equipped to make critical evaluations and informed choices about interactive media (APA, 2005). The APA also supports development of curricula to help children understand advertising and recommends continuing education programs on advertising and marketing to children (Kunkel et al., 2004).

Schools in all 50 states in the US have standards for media literacy in their English, Language, and Communication Arts programs; 92 percent have media literacy standards in their Health or Consumer Skills programs and 68 percent have media literacy standards in their Social Studies, History, or Civics programs (Kubey & Baker, 1999). Implementing these standards into full-scale media literacy programs would require mandated curricula, identification of effective educational techniques, and evaluations to improve program effectiveness.

Learn about media effects and educate parents

The AMA and AAP recommend that physicians educate themselves about the research on media effects and counsel families about the influence of media on children (AAP, 1984; AMA, 1982–2003). For more than two decades, the AAP has made specific recommendations for pediatricians as they advise children and their families regarding television use, providing information, assessment tools, and support (AAP, 1984, 1999, 2001b). In response to the changing media landscape and the growing body of research investigating media effects on health, the AAP has regularly updated key media policies, including limiting children's television viewing, encouraging alternative activities such as reading, parents watching with and interpreting television content for children, and selecting quality programming for viewing on video (AAP, 1990).

In 1997, the AAP launched Media Matters, a national initiative to: (1) educate pediatricians about media effects; (2) encourage them to ask patients about media use as part of the medical history taken during health maintenance visits; and (3) train them to use media literacy tools for intervention. With funding from the White House Office of National Drug Control Policy and the Center for Substance Abuse Prevention, the AAP developed training courses, media education guides for parents and pediatricians, and a media history form to assess a child's media exposure. AAP policies recommend that pediatricians become involved in the Media Matters campaign to remain informed about media effects and incorporate the AAP media history form as part of their health evaluation and anticipatory guidance (AAP, 1999, 2001b). Although Media Matters has received positive reviews from participants, a 2001 survey of US pediatric residency program directors revealed that fewer than 30 percent were aware of the Media Matters initiative and only 3 percent had received Media Matters training. Those program directors who had completed Media Matters training were significantly more likely to make media education a part of the residency curriculum (Rich & Bar-on, 2001).

Limit the amount of time children spend using media

Despite the fact that many parents express concern about children's media use, over half of 8- to 18-year-olds report their parents have no rules about watching television. Among children who do have rules, only 20 percent indicate that those rules are enforced most of the time (Roberts, Foehr, & Rideout, 2005). Furthermore, few 12- to 18-year-old children have rules limiting the amount (13 percent) or content (14 percent) of television they watch or the amount of time they spend playing videogames (17 percent) each day. While these results are the most recent and representative, studies over the last 40 years have consistently reported that less than one half of parents surveyed enforce television viewing limits or regularly discuss television content with their school-age children (Abelman, 2001; Desmond, Singer, & Singer, 1990; Warren, 2001).

Parents of younger children, however, are more likely to have and enforce rules limiting their children's media use. Approximately 85 percent of parents of children under age 6 report having rules about the content of television they watch (63 percent enforce these rules "all the time"), whereas 60 percent report limiting the amount of time their children watch television (Rideout & Hamel, 2006).

Most AAP policy statements urge pediatricians to encourage parents to limit children's media use. Specific recommendations have been made to limit children older than 2 to no more than 2 hours of screen media (including television, videogames, and computer use) a day. This recommendation is well below the national averages of screen time for children 8 to 18 years old (4 hours and 15 minutes; Roberts, Foehr, & Rideout, 2005), but it is consistent with the average screen exposure for children under 7 years old (1 hour and 58 minutes) (Rideout, Vandewater, & Wartella, 2003).

Research indicates that rules are an effective way to reduce children's media use. Children whose parents set rules for television viewing watch 40 minutes less television and read for 16 more minutes per day than children without television rules (Roberts, Foehr, & Rideout, 2005). Having family media use rules may have other positive outcomes as well, such as reduced aggression (Desmond, Singer, & Singer, 1990; Nathanson, 1999).

One reason for recommending a limitation on children's screen time is the link between children's television use and obesity. Several studies have shown a dose-response relationship between average hours of television children watched and the amount they were overweight (Dietz & Gortmaker, 1993, 2001). The evidence suggests that this link is due to a reduction in children's exposure to food advertisements rather than to a reduction of sedentary viewing behaviors

(Vandewater & Cummings, this volume, Chapter 16). Children who watch more television are exposed to advertisements for foods high in sugar, fat, and calories and have diets containing larger proportions of unhealthy foods (Kuribayashi, Roberts, & Johnson, 2001). In experimental studies, children who saw this type of advertisement were more likely to make poorer food choices (Gorn & Goldberg, 1982). Programs that limit children's media use have been successful in reducing their overall level of obesity, even when children's general level of activity did not increase (Robinson, 1999). In fact, the notion that turning off the television will result in more physical activity may not always be true; children appear able to balance media use with sports, physical activities, and other hobbies (Roberts, Foehr, & Rideout, 2005; Robinson, 1999).

Allow only educational television

AAP policy not only encourages parents to limit children's television viewing, but it also suggests allowing only educational television. Well-designed educational television programs have been shown to have both short- and long-term positive effects on children's cognitive abilities and school achievement (Anderson et al., 2001; Linebarger et al., 2004). Children between the ages of 2 and 3 are especially receptive to educational television messages (Wright et al., 2001). Preschool children who view only high-quality, age-appropriate educational programs will avoid many of the potential harms of television while benefiting from educational and prosocial information.

Co-view and discuss

Since 1996, the AAP has officially recommended that pediatricians encourage parents to watch television with their children and to discuss the content viewed. Policy statements specifically addressing violence (AAP, 2001c) and sex (AAP, AACAP, & APA, 2001) in media have highlighted the need for parents to discuss these types of media content in particular, to "use controversial programming as a stepping-off point to initiate discussions about family values, violence, sex and sexuality, drugs" (AAP, 2001b, p. 424).

When parents talk with their children about television, children demonstrate improved understanding of the content, plots, and production techniques (Collins, Sobol, & Westby, 1981; Corder-Bolz, 1980; Desmond et al., 1985; Wright, St Peters, & Huston, 1990). Co-viewing with discussion has been associated with reduced acceptance of aggression (Corder-Bolz, 1980; Nathanson & Cantor, 2000). It also helps children to distinguish fantasy and reality (Desmond et al., 1985; Messaris, 1983), to develop skepticism regarding the news (Austin, 1993), and to decrease fear reactions (Cantor, 2001). Parents must comment specifically about content that is unacceptable, however; if parents simply co-view, without discussion, children may interpret parents' silence as endorsement of the content (Nathanson, 1999; Valkenburg et al., 1999). Co-viewing of antisocial programming may, in fact, actually enhance attention to that content (Valkenburg et al., 1999) and has been associated with increased acceptance of violence (Nathanson, 1999).

Use available technology to monitor media use

The advent of new forms of entertainment technology has brought tools that parents can use to help monitor and reduce their children's media use. The AAP has suggested that parents record educational programs for later viewing by their children.

While parents recognize the increased control that videocassette recorders (VCRs) have given them, there has been little difference in the way families function around recorded versus broadcast television viewing (Kim, Baran, & Massey, 1988). Co-viewing and conflict around recorded video viewing does not differ from that observed in the context of broadcast television viewing (Morgan et al., 1990). In general, the content of recorded programming watched closely matches what children and adolescents watch on broadcast television (Wachter & Kelly, 1998). Although VCRs provided an unprecedented level of control over televised content, it is not certain if the majority of parents utilize the device to its fullest potential as a tool for mediating children's viewing in the manner recommended by the AAP.

More recently, the introduction of the digital video recorder (DVR) (e.g., TiVo, ReplayTV) has revolutionized television viewing. Already these devices are found in about one out of every three homes with children aged 8 to 18 (Roberts, Foehr, & Rideout, 2005). A much simpler tool than the VCR for recording television programs, a DVR can be programmed to capture every episode of a given program. It is also allows viewers to fast-forward through commercials. These abilities could allow a young child to grow up only seeing educational programming with limited exposure to commercial content. While such a powerful device certainly has the potential to enhance parental involvement in children's television use, no scientific research has yet explored how the DVR is being used in American households.

The APA took the official stance that it supported "the development of technologies that empower viewers to prevent the broadcast of violent material in the home" (APA, 1996). While the VCR, DVD player, and DVR can be used to this end, the V-chip was designed specifically to block certain types of content from being viewed on a specific television. The V-Chip was launched with great expectations, but does not appear to be meeting its full potential. Parents rarely use the device (Kaiser Family Foundation, 2001). They may be unaware of its presence, they may not fully understand the procedures necessary to program the chip, or they may not completely accept or understand the television rating system on which this filtering device is based (Gentile, this volume, Chapter 23).

Compared to television, the Internet provides even greater access to a variety of information and content that is inappropriate for children and teenagers.

Exposure to Internet content can be both intentional and unintentional. Among 10- to 17-year-old Internet users, 42 percent have seen unwanted sexual content online (Wolak, Mitchell, & Finkelhor, 2007). The AACAP suggests that parents "make use of the parental control features offered with . . . online service or . . . commercially available software programs to restrict access to 'chat lines,' news groups, and inappropriate websites" (AACAP, 2001). Parents appear to be utilizing Internet filtering software as suggested by the AACAP – more than half of all households with teenagers use this type of software (Lenhart, 2005). However, parents and teenagers both believe that teenagers are going to websites that parents would not approve of (Lenhart, 2005). An early concern about these filtering programs was that they would block children from doing research on medical topics for school projects. This does not necessarily seem to be true, but certain health related searches such as "condom use," "condom," and "gay" are blocked by some programs (Richardson et al., 2002).

The policies concerning the use of VCRs, the V-Chip, and Internet filtering software show a consensus among these health organizations in recommending technological tools that allow parents control over the media messages that enter their homes. More education and outreach initiatives are necessary so that parents can fully benefit from the available electronic tools designed to help them provide a safe media environment for their children.

Bedrooms free of electronic media

Since 1999, the AAP has recommended that children's bedrooms be "electronic media-free." The AACAP suggested that parents "consider removing the TV set from the child's bedroom" in order to protect children from "excessive TV violence" (AACAP, 2002). In 2001, the AAP encouraged pediatricians, in two separate policy statements, to advise parents to "remove television sets from children's bedrooms" and keep "children's bedrooms media free" (AAP, 2001b).

Despite these recommendations, recent surveys have shown that approximately two thirds (68%) of 8–18-year-old American children have televisions in their bedrooms. Other electronic devices are also common, including VCR/DVD players (54%), videogame players (49%), and computers (31%; Roberts, Foehr, & Rideout, 2005). Among children aged 6 and under, one third (33%) have televisions in their bedrooms; fewer still have VCR/DVD players (23%), videogame players (10%), or computers (5%) in their bedrooms (Rideout & Hamel, 2006).

Research on the impact of media in a child's bedroom supports the AAP and AACAP guidelines for television, but not entirely for computers. Children who have television sets in their bedrooms watch 5 to 8 more hours of television per week and are at increased risk for overweight (BMI above ninety-fifth percentile) compared to children without televisions in their bedrooms (Dennison, Erb, & Jenkins, 2002). Several studies have found that having a television in the bedroom is associated with reduced academic achievement. In one study, third-grade children who had television in their bedrooms scored approximately 7 to

9 points lower on standardized tests than did their peers without television in their bedrooms; having access to a computer, and computer use, however, were associated with higher standardized test scores (Borzekowski & Robinson, 2005). Furthermore, children *without* television in their bedrooms read, on average, an additional 16 minutes per day (Roberts, Foehr, & Rideout, 2005).

Television in the bedroom has also been associated with sleep disturbances. Children (10 years old or younger) with television in their bedrooms go to bed later at night, take fewer naps, and sleep less overall, compared to children without television in their bedrooms. Children with television in their bedrooms are also more likely to have night-time fears (National Sleep Foundation, 2004).

As of yet, no research has specifically examined how having other electronic media in the bedroom affects children's health. While there is certainly mounting evidence that having a television in the bedroom may be harmful to children, research has yet to demonstrate that removing the television from the bedroom has beneficial or protective effects.

No screen media for children under 2

In its 1999 "Media Education" policy statement (AAP, 1999), the AAP recommended that pediatricians advise parents to discourage television viewing by children under the age of 2. The first AAP policy to receive front-page attention in the *New York Times*, it has been, arguably, the most controversial AAP media policy to date. The controversy has centered primarily on whether the recommendation is firmly supported by evidence and whether it is appropriate for pediatricians to make recommendations about issues that some perceive as not directly "medical" (Mifflin, 1999). Since the time the statement was issued, however, research has been conducted and the current evidence supports the AAP recommendation for exposure to television programs made for adults (Anderson & Pempek, 2005; Zimmerman & Christakis, 2005). Less is known about programs designed specifically for very young children (Barr, this volume, Chapter 7).

The 1999 policy statement reads: "Research on early brain development shows that babies and toddlers have a critical need for direct interactions with parents and other significant caregivers (e.g., child care providers) for healthy brain growth and the development of appropriate social, emotional, and cognitive skills. Therefore, exposing such young children to television programs should be discouraged" (AAP, 1999, p. 342). In 2001, this recommendation appeared again, in the "Children, Adolescents, and Television" statement (AAP, 2001b, p. 424), followed by the recommendation that parents "encourage more interactive activities that will promote proper brain development, such as talking, playing, singing, and reading together."

This AAP policy is based on the assumptions that infants need to interact directly with their caregivers for optimal brain development, and that activities such as talking, playing, singing, and reading together are more interactive than television viewing. While there is as of yet no specific evidence that direct inter-action with caregivers is more beneficial for brain development than television viewing, a few recent studies suggest that television viewing rarely involves inter-action with caregivers (Weber & Singer, 2004).

While not directly supporting the premises of the recommendation, several stud-ies have shown that viewing adult programs before age 2 is associated with adverse developmental outcomes. Evans and colleagues (2003) found that the average length of 1-, 2-, and 3-year-old children's play and episodes of focused attention were reduced when an adult television program was playing in the background (Evans, 2003). A related study found that parent-child interactions were significantly less frequent for 1-, 2-, and 3-year-old children when an adult television program was on in the background (Kirkorian, 2004). These results suggest that television programs designed for adults that play in the background may have deleterious effects on children's attention and possibly their cognitive development.

A few field studies have measured how home environments, including measures of television viewing, influence the development of children under 2 years old. Although these studies were conducted in the 1970s and 1980s (before programs for very young children were developed), the general finding was that the amount of television viewed in the home was negatively correlated with children's subse-quent cognitive and language development. In one study, television watching at 18–21 months significantly predicted lower IQ scores (Carew, 1980). In another study, the mean number of hours that 2-year-olds watched television negatively correlated with rate of language acquisition (Nelson, 1973). None of these studies distinguished exposure to educational television from exposure to other types of programs, however, which remains a major weakness of this research.

In older children, educational programming has proven beneficial for the develop-ment and practice of some learning skills, while violent content has been linked to aggression, impulsivity, and reduced academic achievement (Anderson et al., 2001; Huesmann et al., 2003; Wright et al., 2001). A recent study found that total television viewing (adult and child programming) between 6 and 30 months of age was negatively correlated with vocabulary size at 30 months, whereas view-ing of programs like *Dora the Explorer*, *Arthur*, and *Blue's Clues* was positively correlated with language development (Linebarger & Walker, 2005). Thus, the kind of program viewed is a key to assessing positive or negative effects of early media exposure.

No research has specifically evaluated the effects of the AAP policy on infants' use of screen media. However, a recent survey of Minnesota pediatricians concluded that almost 40 percent of pediatricians "rarely or never" communicate to parents the AAP recommendation of no screen media for children under 2, while only 12 percent "almost always" convey it. Over 90 percent of pediatricians are aware of the recommendation, and while only 4 percent disagree with it, 25 percent consider it unrealistic for families. This may explain why only 6 percent of surveyed parents are aware of the "no television under 2" recommendation, despite the publicity it has received (Gentile et al., 2004).

What is clear, however, is that infants continue to watch television and videos, despite the AAP recommendation. A 2003 randomized national survey found that children under 2 years of age average 2 hours of screen time each day and that 25 percent of zero- to 2-year-olds have a television in their bedroom (Rideout, Vandewater, & Wartella, 2003). In 2004, television viewing diaries kept by parents also indicated that, on average, 2.5- to 24-month-olds were exposed to 2 hours of television each day; 50 percent of the exposure was to programs for infants and toddlers, 40 percent to programs for adults, and 9 percent to programs for pre-teens (Pierroutsakos et al., 2004). A study of highly educated parents found that, on average, their infants began watching baby videos at 6 months of age and television at 10 months (Weber & Singer, 2004). In a recent nationwide survey, 32 percent of parents who watched adult programming for an average of one hour and 43 minutes each day stated that their child under the age of 2 years was present in the room with them for most or all of the time (Rideout & Hamel, 2006). While there is little information available about very young children's use of interactive media, a recent national survey indicated that 5 percent of children under the age of 2 used the computer in a typical day, and 3 percent played videogames (Rideout, Vandewater, & Wartella, 2003).

Encouraging the Entertainment Industry to Promote Responsible Programming

In its first policy statement about media, released in 1984, the AAP's Task Force on Children and Television called on its members to "establish liaisons with networks, producers, writers, and other professional organizations to improve the quality of programming and advertising" (AAP, 1984, p. 8). In 2001, the AAP continued to encourage its members to "challenge the entertainment industry" to accomplish several goals: (1) "take responsibility" for its programming; (2) comply with the ratings system; (3) hold seminars with producers to collaborate on improving programming for children; and (4) increase the amount of educational programming, while reducing the amount of violence, unhealthy sexual behaviors, and drug use on television (AAP, 2001b). The AAP also specifically urged pediatricians to encourage the industry to air public service announcements that promote both abstinence from sexual intercourse and condom use (AAP, AACAP, & APA, 2001).

The APA has similarly recommended that its members work to improve programming for children. As its first recommendation in its 1996 "Violence in Mass Media" statement, the APA "urges psychologists to inform the television and film industry personnel . . . that viewing violence in the media produces aggressive and violent behavior in children who are susceptible to such effects" (APA, 1996).

Over the last several decades, many individual psychologists and pediatricians have taken it upon themselves to better the media environment for children by speaking out about its harms and benefits to the press and to government officials. Consulting by individual health professionals has also significantly improved the quality of programming for children, especially with regards to educational content (Anderson et al., 2000; Fisch & Truglio, 2001; Gladwell, 2000).

The AAP, as an organization, has also made significant efforts to advise the industry. The AAP Media Resource Team (MRT) was formed in 1994 as a resource office and physicians' hotline for the entertainment industry. Although the MRT was unable to convince Fox not to distribute *Power Rangers*, it did have some successes with ABC, CBS, and PBS. For example, the MRT influenced the program *America's Funniest Home Videos* not to show scenes potentially dangerous to children, such as one child using another's body as a sled. Despite these successes, the AAP Board of Directors closed the office for financial reasons in 1997. Since that time, members of the MRT have continued, on a volunteer basis, to maintain the hotline and offer free advice to the television industry.

Overall, health professionals have perhaps been most effective when working directly as consultants with content producers, in an effort to improve programming for children. While professional calls for increased industry responsibility have raised public awareness, the industry's standard response has been to dispute the research evidence and to claim that it is making efforts to protect children. Given this pattern, the extent to which the efforts of health professional organizations have influenced industry change is unclear.

Encouraging the Government and Industry to Promote a Healthy Media Environment

Introduce legislation that influences the media environment

Several policies of the AAP, AMA, and APA have called for government control to ensure that the entertainment landscape is as safe as possible for children. While all of the health organizations explicitly reject censorship, they have advocated for legislation to improve the quality of media for children. Because of the entertainment industry's lack of response to the recommendations of health professionals, the AAP has specifically urged its members to encourage governmental action by supporting "legislative activity to increase quality programming and reduce advertising directed at children" (AAP, 1984, p. 8). The APA and AMA have taken a slightly different approach from the AAP (whose policy addresses its members) by directly addressing the government in their statements recommending legislative action.

The Children's Television Act (CTA), passed in 1990 and revised in 1996, represents governmental legislation that is in line with the policies made by health organizations. The act strongly encouraged television stations to air at least 3 hours a week of educational television for children and to limit the amount of commercial advertising in order to qualify for broadcasting license renewal (Calvert, this volume, Chapter 20). This policy was implemented with the goal of improving the overall television landscape for children. Governmental action that supports media-related health policy is quite rare, but when it occurs it has the potential to make broad, progressive changes for the betterment of children's health.

Develop and implement effective ratings systems

The AMA, APA, and AAP urge the development and implementation of effective and accurate media ratings to protect and guide parents and children. All call for an objective, independent, accurate, easy-to-use, content-based, universal ratings system. While this ideal has not been reached, pressure from health professionals and the public at large has resulted in media ratings systems for each major entertainment industry sector (Gentile, this volume, Chapter 23).

Speaking directly to those who produce and distribute media, the AMA, the APA, and the AAP have all urged that the media rating systems include precise information about the presence of violent and sexual content (AAP, AACAP, & APA, 2001; AMA, 1994–8; APA, 1996). Media ratings that provide information about a product's content rather than recommend ages of users have consistently been shown to be desired by parents (Cantor, Stutman, & Duran, 1996). Additionally, there is empirical evidence that content labels are less likely than age restrictions to attract children to inappropriate content via the forbidden fruit effect (Cantor, Harrison, & Nathanson, 1997).

Violent content is central to the APA's ratings related policies. The organization supports "revising the ratings system to take into account violent content that is harmful to children and youth" (APA, 1996). Labeling programs as violent can potentially encourage parents to protect their children from these effects and give useful information to children who choose to avoid it on their own.

Health organization policies support media ratings that are clear, precise, and as easy to understand and use as possible. Currently, each medium (television, film, or videogames) has its own rating system which uses different standards, different (or no) content labels, and different age recommendations. Parents must learn each system. The AMA has explicitly suggested developing one ratings system that can be applied universally across all types of entertainment media (AMA, 1994–8).

A number of ratings-related health policy statements and health professionals contributed to the creation of the 1996 Telecommunications Act, which required a V-Chip in every television set over 13 inches by the year 2000. The V-Chip, a filtering technology, is linked directly to the government-encouraged but industry-applied and industry-regulated television rating system. Individual psychologists, pediatricians, and other health professionals testified in favor of this legislation, wrote comments to the Federal Communications Commission (FCC) supporting it, performed research to determine the most effective rating system, and sat on the board that created the ratings. While the resulting system may have flaws, the process that led to its creation reflects the potential impact of media-related health policy statements and policy-targeted research.

Encourage research

The AAP, AMA, and APA have all officially encouraged health professionals to conduct and support research on the effects of media on children. The AAP first specifically called for media effects research in its 1989 statement on the "Impact of Rock Lyrics and Music Videos on Children and Youth" (AAP, 1989). Since that time, virtually every media-related AAP policy statement has called for further research, as well as increased government funding for such research.

Recently, a bipartisan effort has been made in the US Senate to authorize federal funding for research on media effects. The Children and Media Research Advancement (CAMRA) bill, sponsored by Senators Joseph Lieberman, Sam Brownback, and Hillary Clinton, is designed to provide this direct funding. Academics and health professionals were vitally involved in the authorship and introduction of this bill and have been working hand-in-hand with policy makers as it progresses through the legislative process. This potential funding source represents another governmental action that is directly in line with media-related policy statements made by the AMA, AAP, and APA.

The Effectiveness of Health Policies

Health organizations have been extremely active in providing media-based policy statements to their membership. What is still unknown, however, is whether these policies are affecting the ways young people are using media. Apart from policies directed toward government and the entertainment industry, these statements must filter through healthcare professionals to parents who can then directly influence children's media use.

The AAP and AMA policies are based on the assumption that physicians can intervene on unhealthy media use through anticipatory guidance and health education of patients and their families. Although no studies have directly tested the impact of media counseling on children's media use, a recent review of the effectiveness of pediatric counseling found mixed results for other types of health recommendations (Moyer & Butler, 2004). In particular, office-based pediatric health supervision has successfully increased use of car seats, home smoke alarms, and bicycle helmets, but it has been ineffective at preventing violence, adolescent alcohol use, sexually transmitted infections, or dental cavities (Moyer & Butler, 2004). Since the professional policies of both the AAP and the AMA are built on the reasoned assumption that counseling can change behavior, research testing the effectiveness of media counseling by clinicians is warranted.

For health organization recommendations to be effective, physicians must inform patients and families of them. The recent survey of Minnesota pediatricians revealed that while 90 percent of US pediatricians were aware of the AAP recommendations of no screen exposure before age 2, they varied greatly in whether or not they usually made this recommendation to patients and their families (Gentile et al., 2004). Though most pediatricians (76 percent) reported that they "almost always" encouraged parents to provide alternative activities for their children, just over half (51 percent) "almost always" recommended media use time limits, and even fewer (33 percent) recommended no television viewing for children under 2 years of age. The survey also found that 88 percent of pediatricians *never* asked parents to complete the AAP's media history form, in part because 72 percent reported being "not at all familiar" with it (Gentile et al., 2004). In another national survey, only 15 percent of parents said their pediatricians mentioned media at their child's health maintenance visits and just 6 percent were even aware that the AAP discouraged screen media for children under 2 years old (Rideout & Hamel, 2006). It is clear that the AAP and other professional organizations have not been effective at communicating their media-related practice policies to their membership. It is unlikely that such policies will significantly influence children's health as long as doctors remain uninformed or unconvinced about media effects and fail to counsel families about them. More effective dissemination of the policies and evaluation of their implementation are necessary to realize the potential of physician education programs and pediatric anticipatory guidance.

Conclusion

Health policy statements are dynamic, evolving strategies. Clinical decisions are made on the basis of patient information of variable quality and constantly evolving scientific data. The best strategy for moving one patient toward health may be ineffective or counterproductive for another. As a result, most practice policies serve as advisory guidelines, using the language of persuasion, rather than absolutism. They recommend, rather than order, "best practices." Recommendations will invariably focus on doing least harm, a position that may not reflect an even-handed review of the data, but is driven by commitment to the patient's well-being. It is expected that clinicians will use their judgment and experience in developing and communicating plans for patients, and that ongoing discussion, disagreement, and the provision of contradictory evidence will be welcomed. It is through this dialogue among researchers, clinicians, and those they serve that the best strategies for living with media will be determined and implemented.

With growing evidence of a variety of positive and negative health effects from media exposure, health professionals have increasingly incorporated recommendations on media use as part of patient care. Pediatricians and physicians, as well as psychologists and psychiatrists, supported by varying amounts of evidence, have concluded that media represent a significant influence on physical, mental, and social health. As health professionals operate in a clinical community that is increasingly focused on prevention, the current, admittedly incomplete, state of knowledge is enough to warrant moderation and directedness in media use. Just as a good nutritional plan focuses on both quantity and quality to promote healthy bodies, children's media use should be moderated and directed toward healthy content.

Yet the media use policies of health professional organizations have had limited effect on member clinicians' practice styles and even less influence on the media choices of patients and their families. It is clear that for physicians and their media-consuming patients, much more definitive research on specific media effects is required. Better understanding and evaluation of the process through which clinicians impart health promotion information and strategies to patients will ensure improved communication. Ultimately, however, the goal of any of these policies is a consistent message from health professionals that results in broad changes in behavior and improved public health. Such changes are often glacial in speed, taking as much as a generation to vary, as in the case of smoking. Yet, just like the phenomenal public health success of the anti-smoking initiative in the United States, health-improving changes in media use may occur slowly over time, if clinicians and others who work with children are determined and persistent in developing and implementing rational and effective strategies for healthy media use.

The authors would like to thank Brandy King, MLIS, of the Center on Media and Child Health for coordinating the literature search and creating the timeline.

References

Abelman, R. (2001). Parents' use of content-based TV advisories. *Parenting: Science and Practice*, 1(3), 237–65.

American Academy of Child and Adolescent Psychiatry (AACAP). (2001). *Children online*. Retrieved December 21, 2006, from http://www.aacap.org/page.ww?name=Children+Online&section=Facts+for+Families.

American Academy of Child and Adolescent Psychiatry (AACAP). (2002). *Children and TV violence*. Retrieved December 21, 2006, from http://www.aacap.org/page.ww?name=Children+And+TV+Violence&section=Facts+for+Families.

American Academy of Pediatrics (AAP). (1977). *Resolution concerning the effects of television violence on children*. Elk Grove, IL.

American Academy of Pediatrics (AAP). (1978). *Task Force on Children and Advertising – action memorandum*. Elk Grove, IL.

American Academy of Pediatrics (AAP). (1984). Children, adolescents, and television. *News and Comment*, 35, 8.

American Academy of Pediatrics (AAP). (1987). Alcohol use and abuse: A pediatric concern. *Pediatrics*, 79(3), 450–53.

American Academy of Pediatrics (AAP). (1989). Impact of rock lyrics and music videos on children and youth. *Pediatrics*, 83(2), 314–15.

American Academy of Pediatrics (AAP). (1990). Children, adolescents, and television. *Pediatrics*, 85(6), 1119–20.

American Academy of Pediatrics (AAP). (1995a). Alcohol use and abuse: A pediatric concern. *Pediatrics*, 95(3), 439–42.

American Academy of Pediatrics (AAP). (1995b). Media violence. *Pediatrics*, 95(6), 949–50.

American Academy of Pediatrics (AAP). (1999). Media education. *Pediatrics*, 104(2), 341–3.

American Academy of Pediatrics (AAP). (2001a). Alcohol use and abuse: A pediatric concern. *Pediatrics*, 108(1), 185–9.

American Academy of Pediatrics (AAP). (2001b). Children, adolescents, and television. *Pediatrics*, 107(2), 423–6.

American Academy of Pediatrics (AAP). (2001c). Media violence. *Pediatrics*, 108(5), 1222–6.

American Academy of Pediatrics, American Academy of Child and Adolescent Psychiatry, & American Psychological Association. (2001). Sexuality, contraception, and the media. *Pediatrics*, 107(1), 191–4.

American Academy of Pediatrics, American Academy of Child and Adolescent Psychiatry, American Psychological Association, American Medical Association, American Academy of Family Physicians, & American Psychiatric Association. (2000). *Joint statement on the impact of entertainment violence on children*. Washington, DC: Congressional Public Health Summit.

American Medical Association (AMA). (1976). *Proceedings, House of Delegates*. Dallas, TX.

American Medical Association (AMA). (1977a). *Proceedings, House of Delegates*. Paper presented at the Thirty-first Interim Meeting, December, Chicago, IL.

American Medical Association (AMA). (1977b). *Why the AMA is concerned about the effects of television*. Paper presented at the AMA Annual Meeting, Chicago, IL.

American Medical Association (AMA). (1982–2003). *TV violence*. Retrieved May 26, 2006, from http://www.ama-assn. org/apps/pf_new/pf_online?f_n=browse&doc=policyfiles/ HnE/H-485.995.HTM.

American Medical Association (AMA). (1991–2005). *Television broadcast of sexual encounters and public health awareness*. Retrieved April 18, 2006, from http://www.ama-assn.org/apps/pf_new/pf_online? f_n=browse&doc=policyfiles/HnE/H-485.994.HTM.

American Medical Association (AMA). (1994–8). *Mass media violence and film ratings*. Retrieved May 26, 2006, from http://www.ama-assn.org/apps/pf_new/pf_online?f_ n=browse&doc=policyfiles/HnE/ H-515.974.HTM.

American Medical Association (AMA). (2001). *Television commercials aimed at children*. Retrieved December 21, 2006, from http://www.ama-assn.org/apps/pf_new/pf_ online?f_n=resultLink&doc=policyfiles/HnE/H-485.998. HTM&s_t=485.998.

American Medical Association (AMA). (2005). *Tobacco advertising and media*. Retrieved June 2, 2006, from http://www.ama-assn.org/apps/pf_new/pf_online?f_n=result Link&doc=policyfiles/HnE/H-495.984.HTM.

American Psychological Association (APA). (1996). *Resolution on violence in mass media*. Retrieved April 18, 2006, from http://www.apa.org/pi/cyf/res_media.html.

American Psychological Association (APA). (2005). *Resolution on violence in video games and interactive media*. Retrieved April 18, 2006, from http://www.apa.org/releases/ resolutiononvideoviolence.pdf.

Anderson, D. R., Bryant, J., Wilder, A., Santomero, A., Williams, M., & Crawley, A. M. (2000). Researching *Blue's Clues*: Viewing behavior and impact. *Media Psychology*, 2(2), 179–94.

Anderson, D. R., Huston, A. C., Schmitt, K. L., Linebarger, D. L., & Wright, J. C. (2001). Early childhood television viewing and adolescent behavior. *Monographs of the Society for Research in Child Development*, 66(1), 1–147.

Anderson, D. R., & Pempek, T. A. (2005). Television and very young children. *American Behavioral Scientist*, 48(5), 505–22.

Austin, E. W. (1993). Exploring the effects of active parental mediation of television content. *Journal of Broadcasting and Electronic Media*, 37(2), 147–58.

Austin, E. W., & Johnson, K. (1997). Immediate and delayed effects of media literacy training on third graders' decision making for alcohol. *Health Communication*, 9(4), 323–49.

Borzekowski, D. L. G., & Robinson, T. N. (2005). The remote, the mouse, and the no. 2 pencil: The household media environment and academic achievement among third grade students. *Archives of Pediatrics and Adolescent Medicine*, 159(7), 607–13.

Brazelton, T. B. (1974). TV and children: A pediatrician's advice. *News and Comment*, 25(9), 10–11.

Brown, J. D., L'Engle, K. L., Pardun, C. J., Guo, G., Kenneavy, K., & Jackson, C. (2006). Sexy media matter: Exposure to sexual content in music, movies, television, and magazines predicts black and white adolescents' sexual behavior. *Pediatrics*, 117(4), 1018–27.

Brown, J. D., Steele, J. R., & Walsh-Childers, K. B. (2002). *Sexual teens, sexual media: Investigating media's influence on adolescent sexuality.* Mahwah, NJ: Lawrence Erlbaum.

Bushman, B. J., & Anderson, C. A. (2001). Media violence and the American public: Scientific facts versus media misinformation. *American Psychologist*, 56(6–7), 477–89.

Cantor, J. (2001). The media and children's fears, anxieties, and perceptions of danger. In D. G. Singer & J. L. Singer (Eds.), *Handbook of children and the media*. Thousand Oaks, CA: Sage.

Cantor, J., Harrison, K., & Nathanson, A. (1997). Ratings and advisories for television programming. In Center for Communication and Social Policy (Ed.), *National television violence study*, vol. 2 (pp. 267–322). Thousand Oaks, CA: Sage.

Cantor, J., Stutman, S., & Duran, V. (1996). *What parents want in a television rating system: Results of a national survey.* Chicago, IL: National PTA, Institute for Mental Health Initiatives, and University of Wisconsin-Madison.

Carew, J. V. (1980). Experience and the development of intelligence in young children at home and in day care. *Monographs of the Society for Research in Child Development*, 45(6–7), 1–115.

Center for Media Education. (1997). *Alcohol and tobacco on the web: New threats to youth.* Washington, DC: Center for Media Education.

Collins, R. L., Elliott, M. N., Berry, S. H., Kanouse, D. E., & Hunter, S. B. (2003). Entertainment television as a healthy sex educator: The impact of condom-efficacy information in an episode of *Friends. Pediatrics*, 112(5), 1115–21.

Collins, R. L., Elliott, M. N., Berry, S. H., Kanouse, D. E., Kunkel, D., Hunter, S. B., et al. (2004). Watching sex on television predicts adolescent initiation of sexual behavior. *Pediatrics*, 114(3), 280–89.

Collins, W. A., Sobol, B. L., & Westby, S. (1981). Effects of adult commentary on children's comprehension and inferences about a televised aggressive portrayal. *Child Development*, 52(1), 158–63.

Corder-Bolz, C. R. (1980). Mediation: The role of significant others. *Journal of Communication*, 30, 106–18.

Dennison, B. A., Erb, T. A., & Jenkins, P. L. (2002). Television viewing and television in bedroom associated with overweight risk among low-income preschool children. *Pediatrics*, 109(6), 1028–35.

Desmond, R. J., Singer, J. L., & Singer, D. G. (1990). Family mediation: Parental communication patterns and the influences of television on children. In J. Bryant (Ed.), *Television and the American family* (pp. 293–309). Hillsdale, NJ: Lawrence Erlbaum.

Desmond, R. J., Singer, J. L., Singer, D. G., Calam, R., & Kolimore, K. (1985). Family mediation patterns and television viewing: Young children's use and grasp of the medium. *Human Communication Research*, 11, 461–80.

Dietz, W. H., & Gortmaker, S. L. (1993). TV or not TV: Fat is the question. *Pediatrics*, 91(2), 499.

Dietz, W. H., & Gortmaker, S. L. (2001). Preventing obesity in children and adolescents. *Annual Review of Public Health*, 22, 337–53.

Dorr, A., Graves, S. B., & Phelps, E. (1980). Television literacy for young children. *Journal of Communication*, 30(3), 71–83.

Evans, M. K. (2003). *The impact of background television on very young children's play with toys*. Amherst: University of Massachusetts.

Evans, M. K., Frankenfield, A., Kirkorian, H., Pempek, T., & Anderson D. R. (2003). *The impact of television on very young children's play with toys*. Poster presented at the biennial meeting of the Society for Research in Child Development, April, Tampa, FL.

Fisch, S. M., & Truglio, R. T. (Eds.). (2001). *"G" is for growing: Thirty years of research on children and "Sesame Street."* Mahwah, NJ: Lawrence Erlbaum.

Gentile, D., Oberg, C., Sherwood, N. E., Story, M., Walsh, D. A., & Hogan, M. (2004). Well-child visits in the video age: Pediatricians and the American Academy of Pediatrics' guidelines for children's media use. *Pediatrics*, 114(5), 1235–41.

Gladwell, M. (2000). *The tipping point: How little things can make a big difference*. London: Little Brown.

Gorn, G. J., & Goldberg, M. E. (1982). Behavioral evidence of the effects of televised food messages on children. *Journal of Consumer Research*, 9(2), 200–205.

Grube, J. W., & Wallack, L. (1994). Television beer advertising and drinking knowledge, beliefs, and intentions among schoolchildren. *American Journal of Public Health*, 84(2), 254–9.

Huesmann, L. R., Eron, L. D., Klein, R., Brice, P., & Fischer, P. (1983). Mitigating the imitation of aggressive behaviors by changing children's attitudes about media violence. *Journal of Personality and Social Psychology*, 44(5), 899–910.

Huesmann, L. R., Moise-Titus, J., Podolski, C.-L., & Eron, L. D. (2003). Longitudinal relations between children's exposure to TV violence and their aggressive and violent behavior in young adulthood: 1977–1992. *Developmental Psychology*, 39(2), 201–21.

Johnston, L., O'Malley, P., & Bachman, J. (1996). *National survey results on drug use from the monitoring the future study, 1975–1995*. Vol. 1, *Secondary school students* (NIH Publication No. 97-4139). Rockville, MD: National Institute on Drug Abuse.

Kaiser Family Foundation. (2001). *Parents and the V-Chip 2001*, July (Publication No. 3158). Menlo Park, CA: Kaiser Family Foundation.

Kaiser Family Foundation. (2002, May). *Teens, sex, and TV survey snapshot* (Publication No. 3229). Menlo Park, CA: Kaiser Family Foundation.

Kim, W. Y., Baran, S. J., & Massey, K. K. (1988). Impact of the VCR on control of television viewing. *Journal of Broadcasting and Electronic Media*, 32(3), 351–8.

Kirkorian, H. L. (2004). The impact of background television on parent-child interaction for very young children. Unpublished master's dissertation, University of Massachusetts at Amherst.

Kubey, R. B., & Baker, F. (1999). Has media literacy found a curricular foothold? *Education Week*, 19, 56.

Kunkel, D., Wilcox, B. L., Cantor, J., Palmer, E., Linn, S., & Dowrick, P. (2004). Psychological issues in the increasing commercialization of childhood. In *Report of the APA Task Force on Advertising and Children*. American Psychological Association. Retrieved May 7, 2007, from http://www.apa.org/releases/childrenads.pdf.

Kuribayashi, A., Roberts, M. C., & Johnson, R. J. (2001). Actual nutritional information of products advertised to children and adults on Saturday. *Children's Health Care*, 30(4), 309–22.

Lenhart, A. (2005). *Protecting Teens Online*. Washington, DC: Pew Internet and American Life Project.

Linebarger, D. L., Kosanic, A. Z., Greenwood, C. R., & Doku, N. S. (2004). Effects of viewing the television program *Between the Lions* on the emergent literacy skills of young children. *Journal of Educational Psychology*, 96(2), 297–308.

Linebarger, D. L., & Walker, D. (2005). Infants' and toddlers' television viewing and language outcomes. *American Behavioral Scientist*, 48(5), 624–45.

Martino, S. C., Collins, R. L., Elliott, M. N., Strachman, A., Kanouse, D. E., & Berry, S. H. (2006). Exposure to degrading versus nondegrading music lyrics and sexual behavior among youth. *Pediatrics*, 118(2), pp. e430–e441.

Messaris, P. (1983). Family conversations about television. *Journal of Family Issues*, 4(2), 293–308.

Mifflin, L. (1999). Pediatricians suggest limits on TV viewing by children. *New York Times*, August 4, p. A1.

Morgan, M., Alexander, A., Shanahan, J., & Harris, C. (1990). Adolescents, VCRs, and the family environment. *Communication Research*, 17(1), 83–106.

Moyer, V. A., & Butler, M. (2004). Gaps in the evidence for well-child care: a challenge to our profession. *Pediatrics*, 114(6), 1511–21.

Murray, J. P., Rubinstein, E. A., Comstock, G. A., United States Surgeon General's Scientific Advisory Committee on Television and Social Behavior, & National Institute of Mental Health. (1972). *Television and social behavior: Reports and papers*. Rockville, MD: National Institute of Mental Health.

Nathanson, A. I. (1999). Identifying and explaining the relationship between parental mediation and children's aggression. *Communication Research*, 26(2), 124–43.

Nathanson, A. I., & Cantor, J. (2000). Reducing the aggression-promoting effect of violent cartoons by increasing children's fictional involvement with the victim: A study of active mediation. *Journal of Broadcasting and Electronic Media*, 44(1), 125–42.

National Sleep Foundation. (2004). *2004 Sleep in America Poll*. Washington DC: National Sleep Foundation.

Nelson, K. (1973). Structure and strategy in learning to talk. *Monographs of the Society for Research in Child Development*, 38(1–2).

Pierroutsakos, S. L., Hanna, M. M., Self, J. A., Lewis, E. N., & Brewer, C. J. (2004). *Baby Einsteins everywhere: The amount and nature of television and video viewing of infants birth to 2 years*. Paper presented at the International Conference for Infant Studies, May, Chicago, IL.

Rabak-Wagener, J., Eickhoff-Shemek, J., & Kelly-Vance, L. (1998). The effect of media analysis on attitudes and behaviors regarding body image among college students. *Journal of American College Health*, 47(1), 29–36.

Rich, M. (2003). Boy, mediated: effects of media on adolescent male health. *Adolescent Medicine: State of the Art Reviews: The Adolescent Male*, 14(3), 691–715.

Rich, M., & Bar-on, M. (2001). Child health in the information age: Media education of pediatricians. *Pediatrics*, 107(1), 156–62.

Richardson, C. R., Resnick, P. J., Hansen, D. L., Derry, H. A., & Rideout, V. J. (2002). Does pornography-blocking software block access to health information on the Internet? *Journal of the American Medical Association*, 288(22), 2887–94.

Rideout, V., & Hamel, E. (2006). *The media family: Electronic media in the lives of infants, toddlers, preschoolers, and their parents*. Menlo Park, CA: Kaiser Family Foundation.

Rideout, V. J., Vandewater, E. A., & Wartella, E. A. (2003). *Zero to six: Electronic media in the lives of infants, toddlers, and preschoolers*. Menlo Park, CA: Kaiser Family Foundation.

Roberts, D. F., Foehr, U. G., & Rideout, V. J. (2005). *Generation M: Media in the Lives of 8–18-year-olds*. Menlo Park, CA: Kaiser Family Foundation.

Robinson, T. N. (1999). Reducing children's television viewing to prevent obesity: A randomized controlled trial. *Journal of the American Medical Association*, 282(16), 1561–7.

Rothenberg, M. B. (1975). Effects of television violence on children and youth. *Journal of the American Medical Association*, 234, 1043–6.

Schooler, C., Feighery, E., & Flora, J. A. (1996). Seventh graders' self-reported exposure to cigarette marketing and its relationship to their smoking behavior. *American Journal of Public Health*, 86(9), 1216–21.

Smith, A. (1952). Influence of TV crime programs on children's health. *Journal of the American Medical Association*, 150(1), 37.

Thomas, M. H., Horton, R. W., Lippincott, E. C., & Drabman, R. S. (1977). Desensitization to portrayals of real-life aggression as a function of television violence. *Journal of Personality and Social Psychology*, 35(6), 450–58.

Valkenburg, P. M., Krcmar, M., Peeters, A. L., & Marseille, N. M. (1999). Developing a scale to assess three styles of television mediation: "Instructive mediation," "restrictive mediation," and "social coviewing." *Journal of Broadcasting and Electronic Media*, 43(1), 52–66.

Wachter, C., & Kelly, J. (1998). Exploring VCR use as a leisure activity. *Leisure Sciences*, 20(3), 213–27.

Warren, R. (2001). In words and deeds: Parental involvement and mediation of children's television viewing. *Journal of Family Communication*, 1(4), 211–31.

Weber, D. S., & Singer, D. G. (2004). The media habits of infants and toddlers: Findings from a parent survey. *Zero to Three*, 25(1), 30–36.

Wolak, J., Mitchell, K., & Finkelhor, D. (2007). Unwanted and wanted exposure to online pornography in a national sample of youth Internet users. *Pediatrics*, 119(2), 247–57.

Wright, J. C., Huston, A. C., Murphy, K. C., St Peters, M. F., Pinon, M. F., Scantlin, R. M., et al. (2001). The relations of early television viewing to school readiness and vocabulary of children from low-income families: The early window project. *Child Development*, 72(5), 1347–66.

Wright, J. C., St Peters, M., & Huston, A. C. (1990). Family television use and its relation to children's cognitive skills and social behavior. In J. Bryant (Ed.), *Television and the American family* (pp. 227–52). Hillsdale, NJ: Lawrence Erlbaum.

Zimmerman, F. J., & Christakis, D. A. (2005). Children's television viewing and cognitive outcomes: A longitudinal analysis of national data. *Archives of Pediatric and Adolescent Medicine*, 159(7), 619–25.

23

The Rating Systems for Media Products

Douglas A. Gentile

Parents have raised many concerns about the potential impact of the media on their children. Most of these concerns have pertained to media content that contains violence, sexuality, offensive language, and graphic horror. Today, 95 percent of American parents believe that exposure to media violence contributes to increased aggression in children, and 95 percent believe that sexual content contributes to children becoming involved in sexual situations before they are ready (Rideout, 2004). Parents also believe that it is important to protect their children from exposure to explicitly graphic, violent, or sexual content (Nathanson et al., 2002). Yet it is increasingly difficult to do so in a media world that is filled with multiple technologies in the home, 24-hour television networks, media in children's bedrooms, and websites that are unrestricted and often quite explicit.

In an effort to help parents navigate these terrains, media industries have developed a number of rating systems to label the content of different products. The movie rating system has been in existence for over 30 years. Other systems have developed more recently, in response to newer technologies or to controversies over explicit content that children are exposed to. The purpose of this chapter is to provide an overview of these different rating schemes. The chapter will begin with a brief description of the stated goals for the various rating systems. The next section will describe the different systems that exist, comparing and contrasting the historical factors that lead to their creation as well as their resulting structures. The third section will discuss seven major limitations of the rating systems as they currently exist: inconsistency in the assignment of ratings, ratings creep, lack of content-based information, incongruence with scientific research on harm, lack of agreement with parent ratings, lack of publicity and clarity of the ratings, and the forbidden fruit problem. The final section will offer some suggestions for improving the ratings of media products in the United States.

The Goals of Rating Systems

There are several different rating systems – one for each major medium with which children spend time (i.e., television, movies, videogames, music, Internet). Although each of these media has different characteristics, the rating systems all share the same goals: (1) to provide information to parents and caregivers that will allow them to make informed decisions about which media products are appropriate for their children, which in turn will (2) help parents reduce children's exposure to content that may be inappropriate. For example, the stated goal of the Motion Picture Association of America (MPAA) rating system is to "offer to parents some advance information about movies so that parents can decide what movies they want their children to see or not to see" (MPAA, 2000). The other industries make similar statements, such as the videogame industry's stated goal "to help consumers make informed decisions about which games might be appropriate for their children and family" (ESRB, n.d.a).

In 1996 (prior to the creation of the television rating system), Children Now, a non-profit organization, surveyed 18 of the country's top children's media experts to define what would make an ideal rating system. Almost every expert reported independently that the major goal of a rating system should be to provide as much relevant and correct information as possible, and that it should be in a format that is as simple and understandable as possible. The experts stated clearly that the goals of a rating system should not be to censor material or to dictate taste, but instead to provide information that is descriptive, objective, meaningful, reliable, and valid. Surveys also show that parents and child development experts feel that it is important to know about several areas of media content, such as violent content, sexual content, offensive language, and fear-producing themes/scenes (e.g., Children Now, 1996; Gentile, 1996). Although parents and experts agree on what is desirable, the rating systems are quite variable in how well they provide the desired information.

History and Description of Current Rating Systems

The media rating systems described here have differences among them, but there is one striking similarity. Each of them was created only after political pressure was placed on the industries, including threats of government regulation and restrictions (Cantor, 2003a). As will be illustrated, the rating systems vary considerably in the types of information provided and in the extent to which they emphasize age restrictions and/or content descriptions.

Movies

The film industry was the first to adopt a rating system. The system was created in 1968 by the MPAA, which is the trade association funded by the major

movie studios. The ratings were prompted by public and governmental concern when filmmakers began adding more adult material into movies following
the revision of the "Hays Code," which had censored film content since the 1930s.
The shift from internal censorship to external information is reflected in comments made by Jack Valenti, architect of the film ratings: "The movie industry
would no longer 'approve or disapprove' the content of a film, but we would
now see our primary task as giving advance cautionary warnings to parents so that
parents could make the decision about the movie-going of their young children"
(Valenti, 2005).

Initially, there were four ratings: G for general audiences, M for mature
audiences, R for restricted under 16, requiring a parent or guardian, and X for
no admission under 17. The system has undergone many changes over the years.
Because of parent confusion, the M rating was changed to GP (for General
audiences, Parental guidance suggested), and later changed to PG. In 1984, two
movies were released with a PG rating that upset children and parents because of
their scary images: *Indiana Jones and the Temple of Doom* and *Gremlins*. These
movies caused concerns that the PG rating was too uninformative, given that it
combined all children from toddlers up to age 17 into one group (Breznican,
2004). In response, the PG rating was split into two ratings: PG and PG-13. In
1990, the X category was changed to NC-17, meaning no children 17 or under
admitted, and brief explanations of why films received an R rating began to be
provided. As shown in Figure 23.1, there are currently five ratings that a movie
can receive. Each of the ratings attempts to gauge approximately the "proper"
age a viewer should be in order to watch a particular film.

Movie distributors and producers submit their movies to the Classification
and Ratings Administration (CARA), which is the ratings board created by the
MPAA. Although submission is nominally voluntary, it is in essence mandatory
because the National Association of Theater Owners, which comprises over
29,000 theater screens in the US (NATO, 2006), will not show movies that have
no rating. The CARA rating board is composed of 8 to 13 individuals who are
parents and do not have ties to the movie industry (MPAA, 2006). The ratings
are determined by a majority vote, and raters are required to give feedback on
ways to reduce a rating if the directors, producers, and distributors so desire (e.g.,
if they wish the movie to have a PG-13 rating when it initially received an R
rating). Most raters are considered junior raters, who serve for up to five years
(Waxman, 2001). A minority are senior raters who have unlimited terms and
special responsibilities, such as leading discussions about ratings with movie
directors. The raters are required to sign a secrecy contract, stating that they will
not disclose any information about how the ratings are given.

Music

The music industry was the next to adopt a rating system in 1985, again due
to government pressure. Congressional hearings were prompted by the Parents

Movie rating	
Rating	Explanation
G GENERAL AUDIENCES All Ages Admitted	General audiences. All ages admitted.
PG PARENTAL GUIDANCE SUGGESTED SOME MATERIAL MAY NOT BE SUITABLE FOR CHILDREN	Parental guidance suggested. Some material may not be suitable for children.
PG-13 PARENTS STRONGLY CAUTIONED Some Material May Be Inappropriate for Children Under 13	Parents strongly cautioned. Some material may be inappropriate for children under 13.
R RESTRICTED UNDER 17 REQUIRES ACCOMPANYING PARENT OR ADULT GUARDIAN	Restricted. Under 17 requires accompanying parent or adult guardian.
NC-17 NO ONE 17 AND UNDER ADMITTED	No one under 17 admitted.
Videogame ratings	
EARLY CHILDHOOD **eC** CONTENT RATED BY **ESRB**	Content may be suitable for ages 3 and older. Contains no material that parents would find inappropriate.
EVERYONE **E** CONTENT RATED BY **ESRB**	Content may be suitable for persons ages 6 and older. Titles in this category may contain minimal violence, some comic mischief, and/or mild language.
EVERYONE 10+ **E 10+** CONTENT RATED BY **ESRB**	Content may be suitable for ages 10 and older. Titles in this category may contain more cartoon, fantasy, or mild violence, mild language, and/or minimal suggestive themes.

Figure 23.1 The Major US Rating Systems and their Meanings

TEEN T CONTENT RATED BY ESRB	Content may be suitable for persons ages 13 and older. May contain violent content, mild or strong language, and/or suggestive themes.
MATURE M CONTENT RATED BY ESRB	Content may be suitable for persons ages 17 and older. Titles in this category may contain mature sexual themes, more intense violence, and/or strong language.
ADULTS ONLY AO CONTENT RATED BY ESRB	Content suitable only for adults. Titles in this category may include graphic depictions of sex and/or violence. Adult Only products are not intended for persons under the age of 18.
Television ratings	
TV Y	This program is designed to be appropriate for all children. Whether animated or live-action, the themes and elements in this program are specifically designed for a very young audience, including children from ages 2–6. This program is not expected to frighten younger children.
TV Y7	This program is designed for children age 7 and above. It may be more appropriate for children who have acquired the developmental skills needed to distinguish between make-believe and reality. Themes and elements in this program may include mild fantasy violence or comedic violence, or may frighten children under the age of 7. Therefore, parents may wish to consider the suitability of this program for their very young children.
TV Y7 FV	For those programs where fantasy violence may be more intense or more combative than other programs in this category.
TV G	General audiences.

Figure 23.1 (*Cont'd*)

TV PG	Parental guidance suggested.
TV 14	Parents strongly cautioned.
TV MA	Mature audience only.
V, FV	Includes violence or fantasy violence.
S	Includes sexual situations.
L	Includes coarse language.
D	Includes sexually suggestive dialogue.
Music rating	
PARENTAL ADVISORY EXPLICIT CONTENT	The recording may contain strong language or depictions of violence, sex, or substance abuse. Parental discretion is advised.

Figure 23.1   (*Cont'd*)

Music Resource Center (US Senate, 1985), a group created by Tipper Gore, wife of then Senator Al Gore (later Vice President) and three other Washington wives, who became upset over the blatant sexual and violent lyrics of popular songs, such as Prince's song "Darling Nikki." Although no legislation was ever proposed, there was an implied threat that government regulation could occur if the industry did not respond appropriately. For example, Senator Hollings stated in his opening remarks, "I will be looking from the Senator's standpoint, not just to bring pressures to try to see if there is some constitutional provision to tax, but [for] an approach that can be used by the Congress to limit this [offensive music]" (US Senate, 1985, p. 3). The Recording Industry Association of America (RIAA) agreed to provide a warning label on music releases that contained explicit lyrics, including violent and sexual lyrics. As shown in Figure 23.1, the warning label provides no information regarding the ages for which a given music release is appropriate, nor does it provide any information about the type(s) of explicit content that the album contains. The label simply states: "Parental Advisory Explicit Content." The decision to use or not to use the label is determined solely by each record company and musical artist, and the RIAA states that the number of sound recordings carrying the label is less than one half of one percent of available recordings (RIAA, 2006). This rating has not undergone any particular changes since 1985, other than to standardize the size of the label in 1990.

Videogames and the Internet

In response to congressional hearings led by US Senators Lieberman and Kohl, two competing rating systems were developed for videogames and software in 1994. Both systems were sponsored by the software and videogame industries. One was developed by the Software Publishers Association (SPA) and the other by the Interactive Digital Software Association (IDSA, now renamed the Entertainment Software Association). The SPA created the Recreational Software Advisory Council (RSAC, now renamed the Internet Content Rating Association) to design a rating system that focused mostly on providing content information. Games were rated using a questionnaire with standardized definitions, providing separate information on the level or quantity of nudity/sex, violence, and offensive language in each game (levels 1 through 4 for each type of content, depicted by increasing amounts on a thermometer). This descriptive approach was designed in part by expert media researchers such as Dorothy Singer and Don Roberts. Game developers rated their games on each dimension, using the standardized definitions (a full list of current definitions is available at http://www.icra.org/vocabulary).

At the same time, the IDSA created the Entertainment Software Rating Board (ESRB) to design a system that classified games into age-based categories similar to movie ratings. There were four original categories: K-A (Kid through Adult), T (Teen; ages 13 and older), M (Mature; ages 17 and older), and AO (Adults Only; ages 18 and older). The K-A category was soon split into two categories, EC (Early Childhood; ages 3 and older) and E (Everyone; ages 6 and older). In 2005, a sixth category was introduced – E10+ (Everyone 10 and older). These labels were required on the fronts of game packaging (see Figure 23.1). Content descriptors were added to the backs of the videogame boxes as well. The content descriptors provided some information about the amount of violent, sexual, and other potentially objectionable content in the games, though they were less detailed than the four levels in the RSAC system.

The ESRB rating system soon became the dominant videogame and software rating system, in part because the RSAC labels were criticized for being difficult to decipher on game packaging and for not including age suitability information (http://www.chipriv.com/privacy-policies/recreational-software-advisory-council.html). The ESRB process for rating software and videogames begins by game developers submitting representative game footage to the ESRB. Although getting a rating is voluntary, again most major retail outlets will only sell games that have ratings, so most game developers submit their games to get ratings. Three paid ESRB raters view the material in private and recommend a rating for the game. The raters are not supposed to have any ties to the videogame or computer industries, and their names are kept confidential (ESRB, n.d.a).

Internet

In 1995, the RSAC videogame rating system was modified to become a rating system for Internet websites (called the RSACi system). This system was incorporated into several Internet browsers, such as Internet Explorer and Netscape, as well as into parental blocking software. In 1999, the RSACi was turned into a new corporation, the Internet Content Rating Association (ICRA). The ICRA provides a questionnaire to participating web content providers, in which they note the presence or absence of several types of content, including nudity, sexual content, violence, potentially offensive language, and other potentially harmful behaviors (e.g., drug use, gambling). The burden is on each web designer to choose to rate their own material and add the ratings tags to their webpages. Users (e.g., parents) would need to enable software to look for the ratings tags and filter based on their personal choices. However, this is not the only Internet rating system in existence. There are competing rating systems provided by SafeSurf, the Emmis Austin Radio Broadcasting Company, and the Platform for Internet Content Selection (supported by Microsoft); and the ESRB is rumored to be creating an Internet rating system called ESRBi.

Television

Although television networks had occasionally provided the message that "viewer discretion" was advised for particular shows, it is the most recent medium to "voluntarily" adopt a rating system. The Telecommunications Act of 1996 mandated that all televisions with screens 13 inches or larger include a "V-Chip" starting January 1, 2000. The V-Chip is a computer chip in a television that can filter out content in accordance with parents' wishes. For the V-Chip to work, programs needed to be rated so that parents could block particular content, such as violence (the "V" in V-Chip). Hence, by legislating the V-Chip, Congress had effectively required that a rating system be created for the V-Chip to be able to read. The Telecommunications Act offered the broadcasting industry the first opportunity to create voluntary ratings, and if none had been created within a year, the Federal Communications Commission was to appoint a committee to create one (FCC, 2003; Kunkel et al., 1998).

Jack Valenti, former president of the MPAA, led the development effort, in collaboration with the National Association of Broadcasters and the National Cable Television Association. The system originally created was an age-based approach, similar to the movie rating system. It contained six ratings, two for children's programs (TV-Y and TV-Y7) and four for non-children's programs (TV-G, TV-PG, TV-14, TV-MA). Soon after the system was released, parents, researchers, and child advocacy organizations voiced strong criticism of it, in part because it contained no information about the content of programming (Kunkel, 2003). In response to the criticisms, the ratings were amended to include five content descriptors as a complement to the six age-based categories (Figure 23.1). The five content descriptors are V (violence), FV (fantasy violence), L (offensive language), S (sexual situations), and D (suggestive dialogue). However, not all combinations of age and content ratings are used in the system. For example, none of the main five content ratings is applied to programs rated TV-G, for general audiences. In addition, none of these five descriptors is applied to children's programs, or those rated TV-Y or TV-Y7. Instead, the only content label that is sometimes applied to children's programming is FV (fantasy violence), and then it is only used in conjunction with the TV-Y7 rating. The ratings are displayed on-screen for the first 15 seconds of a program on a broadcast network (FCC, 2003), and some networks also display them at other times. Until 2005, the network NBC had refused to provide the content descriptors.

Each network rates its own programming, which means that two networks can give the same program or movie a different rating. Although this is a rare occurrence, it does happen from time to time, and it is made more likely as shows go into syndication. A network provides a "prerating" for each show before it is delivered to local affiliate stations. The prerating could be changed by local broadcasters if they disagreed with it, but in practice most broadcasters do not review the programs and simply accept the preratings to save time and costs (Kunkel et al., 1998).

To summarize, five different systems exist to inform consumers about media content. Even those that are somewhat similar have distinct differences. For example, a movie that may not be appropriate for a preteen would be rated PG-13 whereas a television program with similar qualities would be rated TV-14 and a videogame would be rated T. In addition to having different symbols, the systems vary in how much information they provide. The videogame ratings are arguably the most informative because they not only contain age recommendations and content information, but the content is sometimes also rated in terms of intensity. At the other end of the continuum, music recordings are not labeled for appropriate age or the nature of the content – they simply get a warning for "explicit content." In the middle are television ratings and movie ratings, which provide age guidelines and some content information, although not for every rating.

Limitations of the Rating Systems

Although several of the rating systems have undergone changes over the years in response to scientific and parent concerns, they still have limitations. In this section, seven weaknesses that pertain to most of the ratings collectively are discussed.

Consistency

Many critics have lamented an apparent lack of consistency within and among the rating systems, questioning the diverse range of content that can fit within a single rating category. For example, after the film *Billy Elliot* received an R rating for multiple uses of a swear word, one critic wrote, "it seems reasonable to wonder why a film like *Billy Elliot* – which doesn't feature any sex, extreme violence, or mature themes – should get the same rating as . . . *8MM* (full of some of the most disturbing imagery this side of hell)" (Tharps, 2000, p. 24). Furthermore, it is confusing to many parents how movies such as *Shrek* and *Star Wars Episode 2* both received a PG rating. *Shrek* includes depictions of alcohol use and some more mature humor. But *Star Wars Episode 2* has massive counts of characters killed, including many beheadings. These do not appear to be the same kind of PG. One former rater broke the MPAA secrecy restrictions to comment that raters are given no clear standards for how the ratings should be determined, such as what distinguishes a PG-13 movie from an R (Waxman, 2001). The confusion appears widespread:

> "I don't understand the system, and I'm a filmmaker," says producer Hawk Koch (*Wayne's World, Primal Fear*). "I want to follow the rules, but I can't figure out what they are, and no one is able to explain them. I see action films with blood and gore rated PG-13. And I have this sweet little comedy, and I'm trying to get the same rating" [but finding it difficult not to get an R]. (Fleming, 2000, p. 36)

Similarly, for music, the same parental advisory label is used for albums that include a small number of potentially objectionable content as for those that include hundreds. There are no uniform standards to be used to determine which albums should carry the label (Funk et al., 1999). For example, the self-titled *American HI FI* CD contains four swear words and some sexual references, whereas *The Marshall Mathers LP* CD by Eminem contains hundreds of swear words and many violent, sexual, and drug references. Both contain the same label with no other distinctive information for consumers.

For videogames, there is empirical research documenting inconsistency in the ratings. In one content analysis of 55 E-rated ("Everyone") games, the researchers found that about two thirds (64 percent) included violence, yet nearly half of these (44 percent) did not receive a violence content descriptor in their ESRB ratings (Thompson & Haninger, 2001). In a separate random sample of 81 T-rated ("Teen") games, again almost half (48 percent) included violent, sexual, and drug-use content that was not listed in their ratings (Haninger & Thompson, 2004). Finally, in a random sample of 36 M-rated ("Mature") games, a majority (81 percent) included violent, sexual, profane, or drug/alcohol/tobacco-related content that was not listed in the ESRB rating information (Thompson, Tepichin, & Haninger, 2006).

Likewise, for television, the content descriptors are not applied consistently to programming. In one large-scale content analysis of 2,757 television programs, 79 percent of shows that contained violence did not include the V (violence) descriptor rating, 91 percent of shows with offensive language did not include the L rating (offensive language), and 92 percent of shows with sexual content did not receive the S rating (sexual scenes; Kunkel et al., 1998). Among children's shows containing violence, 81 percent did not include the FV rating (fantasy violence). These inconsistencies may be due to the fact that there are no industry-wide standards for how shows should be rated, or how the content descriptors should be defined (Kunkel et al., 1998).

Related to this issue of inconsistency, the ratings often treat violence and sex differently as well. In one study, Leone (2002) content analyzed 210 sequences that were removed from NC-17 films in order to secure an R-rating. He found that significantly more sexual sequences were removed from these films than violent sequences were. In a subsequent study, Leone (2004) analyzed the rating descriptions of 52 R-rated and NC-17 rated films. He found that violence was mentioned in 81 percent of the R-rated movie descriptions but in only 31 percent of the supposedly more explicit NC-17 descriptions. In contrast, sexuality was mentioned in 58 percent of the R-rated descriptions and 96 percent of the NC-17 descriptions. Based on these two studies, Leone argued that the MPAA ratings employ a double standard and that violence is treated more liberally than is sex in assigning labels to films.

This double standard appears to be typical across rating systems. Table 23.1 displays an analysis of 12,668 videogame ratings I conducted in November 2006. Violent and sexual content do not appear to be treated similarly. For example, very few (only 23) games have ever received the strictest rating, AO (Adults only), and of these, 87 percent have sexual content whereas only 22 percent have violent content. This pattern is reversed for all the other rating categories (except games with an EC rating, which had no violent or sexual content). For example, 89 percent of M-rated (Mature) games have violent content, but only 19 percent have sexual content. This pattern still holds if we limit the analysis to only the strongest descriptors ("Intense Violence" and "Strong Sexual Content") rather than including any type of violent/sexual content. AO-rated games are much more likely to have strong sexual content (87 percent) but few have intense violence

Table 23.1 Percentages of Videogames with Violent and Sexual Content by Rating

Rating	AO	M	T	E10+	E
Total number of games	23	1034	3059	296	8011
Have any violent content	22% (5)	89% (919)	91% (2781)	91% (269)	31% (2521)
Have "intense violence"	4% (1)	18% (183)	0%	0%	0%
Have any sexual content	87% (20)	19% (196)	18% (559)	17% (50)	1% (46)
Have "strong sexual content"	87% (20)	7% (76)	0%	0%	0%

Note: AO (Adults only); M (Mature); T (Teens ages 13 and older); E10+ (Everyone 10 and older); E (Everyone).

(4 percent), whereas M-rated games are more likely to have intense violence (18 percent) than strong sexual content (7 percent). If we examine the next strongest descriptors ("Violence" and "Sexual Themes"), this pattern is also found in T-rated games, which are more likely to have "violence" (91 percent) than "sexual themes" (18 percent).

Ratings creep

A second problem is that the meaning of ratings seems to change across time. Indeed, there is increasing evidence that ratings are undergoing what has been called "ratings creep." That is, over time, more "adult" or explicit content filters down into less restrictive ratings. In a study of G-rated animated films released between 1937 and 1999, for example, Yokota and Thompson (2000) found that there was a statistically significant increase in the duration of violence across time, even after controlling for film length. In other words, more violence was permitted in G-rated films in the later years. In a more recent study, Thompson and Yokota (2004) assessed nearly 2,000 movies released between 1992 and 2003. They found that the amount of objectionable content had increased significantly over time. In particular, a movie rated PG-13 in 2003 included approximately as much violence, nudity, and offensive language as did an R-rated movie of 10 years before. Acknowledging this time shift in the meaning of the ratings, Fox film executive Tom Sherak stated, "It used to be you could use the F-word once and still get a PG-13. Then it was twice. Now it can be three times, as long as the usage is not sexual. Frontal nudity used to be an X or an NC-17. Now it can be an R. It's always changing" (Fleming, 2000, p. 36).

Although technically not ratings creep, Walsh and his colleagues (2005) found that M-rated games in 2004 contained 46 percent more violence, 800 percent more sexual content, and 3,000 percent more profanity than did M-rated games from the late 1990s. These results should be viewed with some caution because they are based on a small sample, but the findings suggest that ratings creep may be due in part to an overall increase over time in violent and sexual content in media products. It appears that the creators of media entertainment are including more "edgy" adult content in games, music, television programs, and movies. If so, our culture may be becoming acclimatized to increasing amounts of explicit material in the media, and even raters may experience desensitization in their judgments of what constitutes material that parents need to know about.

Parents may be most likely to notice ratings creep in the categories just below the most restrictive rating (i.e., PG-13 for movies, TV-14 shows, and T games), as previously restricted content trickles down. In an analysis comparing movie, television, and videogame ratings with parent-validated ratings, this is exactly the pattern that was observed (Walsh & Gentile, 2001). That is, parents were most likely to disagree with ratings in the PG-13, TV-14, and T categories.

One could argue that the ratings *should* change to reflect changing norms. "I have tried to make sure that [we] keep up with the American ethic," [MPAA president] Valenti says. "We cannot be sterner than television. More than 125 million people a day watch TV. Only three to five million people a day go to the movies. TV sets the tone, and TV, of course, has changed. So we have changed" (Fleming, 2000, p. 38). Researchers have noted that the existing media ratings are generally based more on what is considered offensive than on what is likely to be harmful to children (Kunkel et al., 2001; Wilson, Linz, & Randall, 1990). However, if parents' main goal is to protect their children from harm, then what is culturally unacceptable or offensive is not likely to be very relevant to their decision-making. In other words, the ratings should not change over time if they are truly designed to help shield children from potentially harmful content, unless of course, new evidence is discovered about the types of messages that are detrimental to youth.

Lack of content-based information

When asked what they would like in a rating system, parents overwhelmingly state that they would prefer ratings to be content-based rather than age-based (Bushman & Cantor, 2003; Cantor, 1998a; Cantor, Stutman, & Duran, 1996; Gentile, 1996). Over three quarters of parents say that it is "very important" to have information about the amount of violence, offensive language, and sexual content present in media (Gentile, 1996). Yet at least one of the systems, that for music, provides no information about content at all. And other systems, such as those for television and movies, provide content information only for certain rating categories. For example, the movie system offers no content information for G-rated films, although all of the G-rated films studied by Yokota and Thompson (2000) included at least one act of violence, with the average duration of violence totaling 9.5 minutes. Similarly, the television rating system provides no content descriptors for the TV-Y or TV-G ratings, and only one possible content descriptor for the TV-Y7 rating (i.e., FV). The videogame ratings appear to be the most useful for parents, in that content information accompanies all ratings (although studies have shown that relevant content information is often not documented; Haninger & Thompson, 2004; Thompson & Haninger, 2001; Thompson, Tepichin, & Haninger, 2006).

Even when content is signaled, the information may not be as helpful as it could be. Most of the content descriptors are vague, at best. For example, the movie ratings provide content information on their website (www.mpaa.org), but the phrases used (such as "pervasive language," "intense action," "creature violence," and "thematic material") are not particularly clarifying and are not likely to be of much help to parents. The videogame system gives better indication about the *amount* and the *graphicness* of explicit material. For example, the violence and blood descriptor options are:

Violence content descriptors	Blood content descriptors
Mild cartoon violence	Mild animated blood
Mild fantasy violence	Animated blood
Mild violence	Mild blood
Cartoon violence	Blood
Fantasy violence	Blood and gore
Violence	
Intense violence	
Sexual violence	

Although this approach is clearly better than providing no content information or even vague information, it is unclear how useful it is for parents. For example, can parents really distinguish between what is meant by "animated blood" compared to "blood?" All videogame blood is animated. Cantor (2006) has suggested that the descriptors should be much more explicit and illustrative, such as "first-person shooter," "blood-spurting," "exposed brain matter," "sever heads with sword," "shoot and kill police officers," and "sex with prostitute," rather than broad euphemistic terms like "intense violence." Furthermore, some of the current descriptors may actually suggest to parents that the violence will have no effect, such as calling the violence "mild" or "cartoon" or "fantasy." In one study of 161 elementary school children and 354 college students (Anderson, Gentile, & Buckley, 2007), participants were randomly assigned to play either a violent or a non-violent E-rated game (college students could also play a T-rated game). In this context, violence was defined as demonstrating intentional harm to victims who would be motivated to avoid that harm, and it was not an indication of how graphic the depictions were. After playing, the participants had an opportunity to punish another person with very loud noise blasts. Those who had played one of the violent games punished their opponents with significantly more high noise blasts than did those who played the non-violent videogames. The violent E-rated games had an equally large effect on short-term aggression as the more graphic violent T-rated games. In other words, practicing being aggressive mattered more in terms of harmful outcomes than did how graphic or cartoonish the violence was. Therefore, descriptors that downplay the violence, such as calling it "mild," "fantasy," or "cartoon," actually may be a disservice to parents who are concerned about the effects it may have. To date, however, no research has been published to see how parents interpret the ESRB or MPAA content descriptors.

Other content information is completely absent. None of the rating systems currently labels media for frightening or horrific content, although research indicates that media images can cause both short-term and long-term fear reactions in children (see Cantor, 1998b, 2003b, for reviews). Moreover, parents, especially parents of younger children, are concerned about shielding their offspring from images that can cause nightmares and even phobias (Cantor, 2003b).

It would also be useful if the ratings distinguished between the *amount* of violence and the *explicitness* of the violence, and a similar distinction could be made for the sexual content of media. Furthermore, only some of the rating systems (ESRB and MPAA) provide information about tobacco, alcohol, and drug use. None provides much information on other behaviors that, if copied by children, would be either illegal or dangerous, although the ESRB ratings provide information on gambling. Only the ESRB and television systems include any information on what products may have educational value (while technically not part of the television rating system, television has another symbol "E/I" for shows that have educational or informational content).

It should be noted that across movie, television, and videogame ratings, there is a correlation between the industry ratings and independent content ratings (Walsh & Gentile, 2001). When a media product receives a more restrictive rating, it also tends to receive higher scores for violence, sex, and profanity by independent judges. However, there are also inconsistencies, and they do not appear to be random. When there are disagreements between industry ratings and content analyses or independent rating systems, the disagreements appear to be due to the industry ratings not including sufficient information about the content (Walsh & Gentile, 2001).

Thompson and Yokota (2004) compared the MPAA ratings of 1,269 movies with two independent content-based rating systems, both of which were designed to provide detailed information to parents. The two content-based systems (Screen-It! and Kids-in-Mind) correlated very highly with each other ($r = .83$). However, there was considerably less agreement when comparing these two content-based systems with the MPAA age-based ratings or with the MPAA's content descriptors. Funk and colleagues (1999) found that consumer agreement with the videogame ratings is dependent on the content of the games. There was high agreement with the ratings when the games had an obviously high level of violence or were clearly non-violent, but there was considerable disagreement when the games included cartoon violence or fantasy violence.

The discrepancies between the industry age-based ratings and independent content-based ratings have two important implications. First, the one type of rating that parents can rely on is the most restrictive rating (e.g., R, M, TV-MA, or Parent Advisory labels) – if the industry itself says the product is not for children, parents almost always agree. Second, if the product receives a less restrictive rating, parents will often be surprised to find content that they did not expect.

Incongruence with scientific research about harm

If parents want to protect their children, they need a system of information that signals the degree of risk that a media product poses to youth. The parallel, here, is food labeling. We know a great deal about the risk of ingesting foods with high fat or cholesterol, for example. Food labels provide consumers with accurate descriptions of the amount of these potentially harmful ingredients, regardless of what type of food product it is. Yet media ratings frequently do not correspond to what is known scientifically about the types of messages that can harm children. In fact, one original movie ratings member claimed that "much of the classification was actually done with an eye to what disturbs *adults*" rather than what is likely to be risky or disturbing for children (Farber, 1972).

Kunkel and his colleagues content analyzed 1,332 television shows, focusing on dimensions that pose the greatest likelihood of risk for children and adolescents (Kunkel et al., 2001). Take violent content as an example. Not all portrayals of violence increase the risk of children copying the violence. Violence that is punished or that portrays the consequences to victims can actually reduce the likelihood that children will imitate such materials, whereas violence that is rewarded increases that risk (for review, see Wilson, Linz, & Randall, 1990). Kunkel and his colleagues (2001) found that the ratings had little relationship to whether the programs included high-risk content. Over two thirds (69 percent) of children's shows with high-risk violent content were assigned the rating TV-Y, indicating they were appropriate for even the youngest children, and thus did not include the FV content descriptor when they should have. Among all general audience shows (those not specifically designed for children) that included high-risk violent content, two thirds (65 percent) did not include the V label, and 40 percent of shows with high-risk violent content were given a TV-PG rating. Among shows including high-risk sexual content, most (80 percent) did not include the S content descriptor, and 29 percent of shows with high-risk sexual content were given a TV-PG rating.

Lack of agreement with parent ratings

Do parents rate media in the same way that the industries do? Only one study has clearly addressed this issue. The National Institute on Media and the Family created a combination age-based and content-based rating system designed to be applicable to all media. The system (called KidScore) was designed to use panels of parent raters, who were trained to make scientifically reliable judgments on several dimensions. The parent ratings are reduced to a stoplight-style rating, green-yellow-red. The KidScore ratings were independently assessed by a randomly selected national sample of 600 untrained parents; parents were sent videotapes of television programs and videogame footage and they showed high agreement with the KidScore ratings (Walsh & Gentile, 2001). The KidScore ratings were then compared with the industry ratings for 276 movies, 253 television shows, and 166 videogames. The industry ratings should match up with the KidScore ratings – that is, if a show/film/game is rated as acceptable for children (e.g., given a TV-G, G, or E rating), then ideally it should also receive a "green light" from parent raters. Furthermore, if a show/film/game is rated as not for children (e.g., TV-MA, R, or M rating), then ideally it should not receive a green light from parent raters. This pattern was observed only partially. In general, parents always agreed when a product had an R, M, or TV-MA rating by the industries, but there was far less agreement with the other ratings.

For movies, the trained parent raters considered only half (50 percent) of G-rated movies to be clearly appropriate (that is, given a green light) for children between the ages of 3 and 7. Only 63 percent of PG-rated movies were considered completely appropriate for children aged 8 to 12, and only 60 percent of PG-13-rated movies were clearly appropriate for teenagers.

For videogames, parents considered two thirds (67 percent) of E-rated games to be clearly appropriate for children aged 3 to 7, and 87 percent to be clearly appropriate for children aged 8 to 12. There was much lower agreement for T-rated (Teen) games, with less than half (43 percent) considered completely appropriate for children aged 13 to 17. As before, parents agreed with the most restrictive rating (M) 100 percent of the time.

Television had the lowest agreement of the three media assessed in this study. The most valid ratings were the extremes, TV-Y and TV-MA, with 76 percent of shows with a TV-Y rating considered to be clearly appropriate for children aged 3 to 7, and 100 percent of shows with a TV-MA rating considered inappropriate for children. Only 40 percent of shows rated TV-G were judged to be clearly appropriate for children aged 3 to 7. Over half (57 percent) of shows rated TV-Y7 and fewer than one out of four (23 percent) shows with a TV-PG rating were rated as appropriate for children aged 8 to 12. Only 15 percent of TV-14-rated shows were given green lights for teens aged 13 to 17. In other nationally representative studies of parents, only *two percent* of parents who had used the TV ratings thought that they always reflected the content of the shows accurately (Rideout, 2004), and half stated that they have disagreed with a rating given a show (Kunkel et al., 1998). This lack of agreement may explain why only about half or fewer of parents believe that the ratings are "very useful" in making decisions about media for their children (45 percent for movies, 48 percent for music, 53 percent for videogames, and 38 percent for television; Rideout, 2004).

Lack of publicity and clarity of ratings

Because parents are the intended users of ratings, the ratings should be clearly understandable and easy for parents to use, and should provide information that parents find useful. Almost all parents (90 percent) agree that ratings are a good idea (Kunkel et al., 1998), but they are not as widely used as one might expect. Over three quarters (78 percent) of parents say they use the movie ratings to guide their family's movie choices (Rideout, 2004). However, only about half of parents say they have *ever* used the music advisories (54 percent), the video-game ratings (52 percent), or the television ratings (50 percent). Among parents who own televisions with V-Chips, over half are unaware of that feature (Kaiser Family Foundation, 2001), and few parents actively use it (see Kunkel, 2003, for a review). In a recent review of television policy, the Federal Communications Commission (2007, p. 14) concluded that the "evidence clearly points to one conclusion: the V-Chip is of limited effectiveness in protecting children from violent television content."

Why do so few parents find the ratings useful, given that they reportedly want ratings? One reason may be that parents find the current rating systems to be confusing. For example, Rideout (2004) conducted a phone survey with a nationally representative sample of 1,001 parents of 2- to 17-year-olds regarding their understanding and use of the television ratings. Only 43 percent of parents reported that they understand all of the television rating symbols, and when required to actually name what the various symbols mean, correct responding was even lower for many ratings. For example, only 24 percent of parents of 2- to 6-year-olds could name *any* of the ratings that would be relevant for children that age, with about one in ten (12 percent) knowing that FV stands for "fantasy violence," whereas almost as many (8 percent) thought it stood for "family viewing." At least half of parents could define the age-based ratings (TV-PG, TV-14, and TV-MA) and the V descriptor. However, parents were less successful with the other descriptors, with D (sexual dialogue) being the least understood at 4 percent.

We know much less about parents' understanding of other rating systems. In a national survey of 145 parents, fewer than half (47 percent) reported understanding all of the videogame rating symbols (Walsh et al., 2005). Not only do parents find the symbols within a particular system to be confusing, it is likely that they also are confused about the different systems, although this has yet to be studied carefully. To add to parents' difficulty, the ratings are not always available or well publicized. The television ratings, for example, are generally only presented on screen for the first 15 seconds of a show.

Forbidden fruit problem

Another problem with creating useful ratings is that certain types of labels can actually attract children to content that is not appropriate for them. This effect is known as the "forbidden fruit effect." Research suggests that this type of attraction is most likely to occur with ratings that communicate age restrictions (e.g., Bickham & Wright, 2001; Bushman, 1998; Cantor, 1998a, 2003b). In one experimental study of television ratings, 8- to 13-year-olds were given information about what all the television rating symbols meant, and then given an opportunity to choose a videotape to watch while the experimenter was out of the room. There were three videotape conditions – (1) only age-based ratings on the spines, (2) only content-based ratings, or (3) both age and content ratings. Children were most interested in viewing shows that were rated as highly restrictive (i.e., TV-MA) if they were solely provided with the age-based rating (Bickham & Wright, 2001). This effect was dampened when content descriptors were included with age-based ratings, and was eliminated altogether when only content-based ratings were provided.

In another set of experiments examining the movie ratings (reviewed in Cantor, 1998a), 297 children between 5 and 14 were given information on the MPAA ratings and asked to vote for movies they would like to watch. The MPAA ratings had a significant effect on children over 9 and on boys. Specifically, these groups were more interested in a video when it was given a rating of PG-13 or

R, instead of a G or PG rating. Not a single older boy (10–14) in the sample selected the movie when it was rated G, but at least half wanted to see it when the movie was rated PG-13 or R. If instead of a rating, the video was tagged with the statement, "parental discretion advised," this too made older boys more interested in seeing it, whereas the statement "viewer discretion advised" had no effect on any group, and actually caused some children, specifically younger girls (5–9), to be less interested in the program, a "tainted fruit effect."

An experiment the following year with 374 children between 5 and 15 replicated these results (Cantor, 1998a). Again, MPAA ratings of PG-13 and R increased children's desire to see the movie, and a rating of G decreased this desire. Adding the phrase "contains some violent content" did not increase a child's desire to view a program. This study also included tests of three content-based systems (i.e., the violence rating system that was used by HBO, the RSAC ratings for videogames, and the rating system used in Canada to work with the V-Chip). In contrast to the MPAA ratings, none of these content-based rating systems increased children's desire to see the programs.

A meta-analysis of 70 independent study samples including 5,519 participants demonstrated that age-based ratings consistently increase adolescents' interest in viewing rated material (Bushman & Cantor, 2003). However, there were some moderating effects of sex and age. In general, the forbidden fruit effect was stronger for males than females, and there was a curvilinear relation with age. More restrictive ratings tended to deter media interest for younger children up to about age 8, and then began to increase interest from age 11 until at least age 22. In addition, the meta-analysis revealed a small forbidden fruit effect when violence (but not sex) was labeled.

The music parental warning label is neither clearly age-based nor clearly content-based, but has an element of each. It is directed to parents, but the warning is for "explicit content." In one study, 11- to 15-year-olds listened to song excerpts while looking at a CD cover that either displayed or did not display the warning label (Christenson, 1992). Then they were asked to judge how much they liked the band and how much they would like to own the album. Although the results were not entirely straightforward, they tended to favor the tainted fruit hypothesis in that children liked the unlabelled music better. This pattern is similar to the results with television programs labeled "viewer discretion advised" (Cantor, 1998a), although this study focused on liking *after* listening, rather than selectively choosing to listen, so its applicability to the forbidden fruit issue is unclear.

One psychological theory that helps to explain the forbidden fruit results is called *reactance theory* (e.g., Brehm, 1966). In brief, whenever people perceive that there is an unfair restriction on their freedoms, they tend to react negatively, which motivates them to act against the restriction. In accord with this theory, if a rating suggests that the individual's freedom to engage in a behavior is restricted, the individual is likely to act according to the forbidden fruit hypothesis. In contrast, if the information provided by a rating decreases the attractiveness of the media product by describing what may be upsetting or offensive, the individual is more likely to act according to the tainted fruit hypothesis.

What Happens When Ratings Are Used?

Despite the many documented shortcomings of the existing systems, there is some research to demonstrate that the use of ratings may provide a benefit. For example, in a study of 607 eighth and ninth graders, adolescents who played a high amount of violent videogames were more likely to get into arguments with teachers (antisocial behavior) and to get into physical fights (aggressive behavior; Gentile et al., 2004). Yet, if parents checked the videogame ratings and put limits on the amount of time the adolescents played, this appeared to act as a protective factor, resulting in less antisocial and aggressive behavior. In fact, parental use of the videogame ratings reduced the risk of physical fights even after controlling for respondent sex, hostility, weekly amount of videogame play, and videogame violence exposure. These results have recently been replicated and extended with other samples of children and adolescents (Anderson, Gentile, & Buckley, 2007). It is unclear whether this effect is due to use of the ratings, to parental monitoring and mediation more broadly, or to the effects of more highly involved parents. Yet from a practical side, it may not matter. Even if the core issue is being an involved parent, one cannot simply tell parents to "be more involved." Educating parents about media content and giving them informational tools such as ratings will presumably assist them in being more proactive and involved in their children's media experiences. Nevertheless, many parents appear unmotivated to use ratings. One psychological finding that helps to explain this is called the *third-person effect* (e.g., Hoffner et al., 2001; McLeod, Eveland, & Nathanson, 1997; Paul, Salwen, & Dupagne, 2000; Salwen & Dupagne, 1999). In brief, people tend to believe that others are more influenced by the media than they themselves are. This pattern holds true even when parents consider their own children. In one nationally representative sample, parents were asked whether their children are affected by the media more, less, or about the same as other children are. Only 4 percent say their children are influenced more than other children, whereas 40 percent say their children are affected less (Gentile, 1996). It is likely that the third-person effect limits the effectiveness of rating systems, although more research needs to be conducted to determine the extent to which parents do not use media ratings because of the third-person effect.

Conclusion

Based on the current research, the media ratings could be improved in at least seven domains: (1) Improving the consistency with which they are applied; (2) maintaining consistent definitions and standards across time to guard against ratings creep; (3) increasing and improving the industries' use of content information in ratings; (4) modifying ratings to focus on content features that have been empirically demonstrated to increase the risk of harm to youth; (5) modifying the ratings to provide information in a manner less likely to increase children's interest in seeing age-inappropriate material (i.e., the forbidden fruit problem); (6) increasing the clarity of the ratings; and (7) providing increased education about the rating systems and why it is important that parents use them.

The use of multiple rating systems for different media products is sometimes confusing to parents. One possibility for resolving this situation is to create a single universal rating system. Many industry spokespeople have claimed that a universal rating system is not possible, and that because the various media are different, the ratings must also be different (Baldwin, 2001; Lowenstein, 2001; Rosen, 2001; Valenti, 2001). However, two independent universal rating systems (KidScore and Screen-It!) have been used since 1996 to rate movies, television shows, and videogames, so it can be done. Furthermore, although music, movies, television, videogames, and the Internet have real differences, the concerns that parents have about them are similar. In fact, the various rating systems are already based on essentially the same things – amount of violence, sex, and offensive language. When asked whether they would support the creation of one standard rating system that could be used by all media, 84 percent of parents say they would (Walsh, 2001). If a universal rating system were to be created, two key concerns surface: who would design the system, and who would judge the content? Although these questions are beyond the scope of this chapter, some suggestions may be useful.

There are several categories of people who could appropriately be called "experts" on ratings. At a minimum, these include (1) the current media rating professionals from the television, film, videogame, music, and Internet industries, (2) academic researchers who have studied rating systems and their effects, (3) pediatric and public health professionals, (4) child development researchers, (5) child advocacy organizations, (6) organizations that have developed and utilized universal rating systems, (7) researchers who have conducted content analyses and research on the effects of media, and (8) parents. Since the creation of most of the rating systems, a great deal more is known now about how to rate media products, what types of ratings are most useful and effective, how to define the types of content that are most important to rate, and what the effects of different ratings may be. Therefore, it seems possible to build on the expertise of each of these eight stakeholder groups to create the next generation of rating systems.

Since their inception, the ratings have been conducted on a voluntary basis by the media industries themselves. If one universal rating system were created, it is not necessary that this should change. Each industry could continue to rate its own products, but would use one common system and vocabulary. However, there are economic pressures within each industry to keep products accessible to the widest audience (Goldstein, 2003). Furthermore, producers continue to push the envelope on the types of "edgy" material that is included in media products, partly as a response to the wider competition for the public's eyeballs, ears, and wallets, and partly as a response to the fact that the public becomes desensitized over time. Such issues suggest that a ratings oversight committee that is independent of all media organizations could be useful. Such a committee could regularly conduct research on the ratings, helping to improve and maintain their consistency across media and across time. It might also be involved in training and educating industries' raters. Ultimately, parents want ratings that are clear, consistent, accurate, and useful. The current media ratings have been useful for many parents, but the research reviewed in this chapter demonstrates that improvements could be made (see Gentile, Humphrey, & Walsh, 2005, for additional suggestions). Furthermore, as digital technologies continue to converge, the lines between the different media types will continue to blur. This blending of television/film/ DVD/ videogame/Internet technology will likely make the use of multiple rating systems more unwieldy and confusing for parents, exacerbating any difficulties with the ratings as they currently exist.

References

Anderson, C. A., Gentile, D. A., & Buckley, K. B. (2007). *Violent video game effects on children and adolescents. Theory, research, and public policy.* New York: Oxford University Press.

Baldwin, W. (2001). *Testimony submitted to the Committee on Governmental Affairs, United States Senate*, July 25. Retrieved July 25, 2001, from http://www.senate.gov/ ~gov_affairs/072501_baldwin.htm.

Bickham, D. S., & Wright, J. C. (2001). *Television ratings and the viewing preferences of children: A comparison of three systems.* Poster session presented at biennial meeting of the Society for Research in Child Development, April, Minneapolis, MN.

Brehm, J. (1966). *A theory of psychological reactance.* New York: Academic Press.

Breznican, A. (2004). PG-13 remade Hollywood ratings system. *Seattle Post-Intelligencer*, August 24. Retrieved November 11, 2006, from http://seattlepi.nwsource.com/ movies/187529_pg13rating24.html.

Bushman, B. J. (1998). Effects of warning and information labels on consumption of full-fat, reduced fat, and no-fat products. *Journal of Applied Psychology*, 83, 99–104.

Bushman, B. J., & Cantor, J. R. (2003). Media ratings for violence and sex: Implications for policymakers and parents. *American Psychologist*, 58, 130–41.

Cantor, J. R. (1998a). Ratings for program content: The role of research findings. *Annual of the American Academy of Political Social Science*, 557, 54–69.

Cantor, J. R. (1998b). *"Mommy, I'm scared:" How TV and movies frighten children and what we can do to protect them.* San Diego, CA: Harcourt Brace.

Cantor, J. R. (2003a). Rating systems for media. In D. H. Johnston (Ed.), *Encyclopedia of international media and communications*, vol. 4 (pp. 47–57). San Diego, CA: Academic Press.

Cantor, J. R. (2003b). Media and fear in children and adolescents. In D. A. Gentile (Ed.), *Media violence and children* (pp. 185–204). Westport, CT: Praeger.

Cantor, J. R. (2006). *Desired features of media ratings.* Paper presented at the National Summit on Video Games, Youth, and Public Policy, October, Minneapolis, MN.

Cantor, J. R., Stutman, S., & Duran, V. (1996). *What parents want in a television rating system: Results of a national survey.* Chicago, IL: The National PTA.

Children Now. (1996). *Making television ratings work for children and families: The perspective of children's experts.* Oakland, CA: Children Now.

Christenson, P. (1992). The effects of parental advisory labels on adolescent music preferences. *Journal of Communication*, 42, 106–13.

Entertainment Software Rating Board (ESRB). (n.d.a). *Frequently asked questions page.* Retrieved November 11, 2006, from http://www.esrb.org/ratings/faq.jsp.

Entertainment Software Rating Board (ESRB). (n.d.b). *Game ratings page.* Retrieved December 11, 2004, from http://www.esrb.org/esrbratings.asp.

Farber, S. (1972). *The movie rating game.* Washington, DC: Public Affairs Press.

Federal Communications Commission (FCC). (2003, July 8). *V-Chip: Viewing television responsibly.* Retrieved May 11, 2007, from http://www.fcc.gov/vchip/.

Federal Communications Commission (FCC). (2007). *Violent television programming and its impact on children*, April 25. Retrieved May 11, 2007, from http://hraunfoss.fcc.gov/edocs_public/attachmatch/FCC-07-50A1.pdf.

Fleming, C. (2000). The rules of the ratings game. *Premiere*, 14(3), 35–8.

Funk, J. B., Flores, G., Buchman, D. D., & Germann, J. N. (1999). Rating electronic games: Violence is in the eye of the beholder. *Youth and Society*, 30, 283–312.

Gentile, D. A. (1996). *National survey of parent media attitudes, behaviors, and opinions.* Minneapolis, MN: National Institute on Media and the Family.

Gentile, D. A. (Ed.). (2003). *Media violence and children.* Westport, CT: Praeger.

Gentile, D. A., Humphrey, J., & Walsh, D. A. (2005). Media ratings for movies, music, video games, and television: A review of the research and recommendations for improvements. *Adolescent Medicine Clinics*, 16, 427–46.

Gentile, D. A., Lynch, P. J., Linder, J. R., & Walsh, D. A. (2004). The effects of violent video game habits on adolescent hostility, aggressive behaviors, and school performance. *Journal of Adolescence*, 27, 5–22.

Goldstein, P. (2003, January 28). How *Jack* hopped away with a PG rating. Retrieved January 30, 2003, from www.calendarlive.com/movies/goldstein/cl-et-gold28jan28. story.

Haninger, K., & Thompson, K. M. (2004). Content and ratings of teen-rated video games. *Journal of the American Medical Association*, 291, 856–65.

Hoffner, C., Plotkin, R. S., Buchanan, M., Anderson, J. D., Kamigaki, S. K., Hubbs, L. A., et al. (2001). The third-person effect in perceptions of the influence of television violence. *Journal of Communication*, 51(2), 283–300.

Kaiser Family Foundation. (2001). *Parents and the V-Chip.* Menlo Park, CA: Kaiser Family Foundation.

Kunkel, D. (2003). The road to the V-Chip: Television violence and public policy. In D. A. Gentile (Ed.), *Media violence and children* (pp. 227–46). Westport, CT: Praeger.

Kunkel, D., Biely, E., Eyal, K., Cope-Farrar, K., Donnerstein, E., & Fandrich, R. (2003). *Sex on TV 3.* Menlo Park, CA: Kaiser Family Foundation.

Kunkel, D., Farinola, W. M., Cope, K. M., Donnerstein, E., Biely, E., & Zwarun, L. (1998). *Rating the TV ratings: One year out: An assessment of the television industry's use of the V-Chip ratings.* Menlo Park, CA: Kaiser Family Foundation.

Kunkel, D., Farinola, W. J. M., Cope, K. M., Donnerstein, E., Biely, E., Zwarun, L., & Rollin, E. (2001). Assessing the validity of V-Chip rating judgments: The labeling of high-risk programs. In B. Greenberg (Ed.), *The alphabet soup of television program ratings* (pp. 51–68). Cresskill, NJ: Hampton Press.

Leone, R. (2002). Contemplating ratings: An examination of what the MPAA considers "too far for R" and why. *Journal of Communication*, 52(4), 938–54.

Leone, R. (2004). Rated sex: An analysis of the MPAA's use of R and NC-17 ratings. *Communication Research Reports*, 21, 68–74.

Lowenstein, D. (2001). *Testimony submitted to the Committee on Governmental Affairs, United States Senate*, July 25. Retrieved July 25, 2001, from http://www.senate.gov/~gov_affairs/072501_baldwin.htm.

McLeod, D. M., Eveland, W. P., Jr., & Nathanson, A. I. (1997). Support for censorship of violent and misogynic rap lyrics: An analysis of the third-person effect. *Communication Research*, 24, 153–74.

Motion Picture Association of America (MPAA). (2000). *The purpose of the rating system*. Retrieved March 19, 2001, from http://www.mpaa.org/movieratings/about/content3.htm.

Motion Picture Association of America (MPAA). (2006). *Film ratings*. Retrieved November 11, 2006, from http://www.mpaa.org/FilmRatings.asp.

Nathanson, A. I., Eveland, W. P., Jr., Park, H. S., & Paul, B. (2002). Perceived media influence and efficacy as predictors of caregivers' protective behaviors. *Journal of Broadcasting and Electronic Media*, 46, 385–410.

National Association of Theater Owners (NATO). (2006). *Homepage*. Retrieved November 11, 2006, from http://www.natoonline.org/Default.htm.

Paul, B., Salwen, M. B., & Dupagne, M. (2000). The third-person effect: A meta-analysis of the perceptual hypothesis. *Mass Communication and Society*, 3, 57–85.

Recording Industry Association of America (RIAA). (2006). *Parental advisory*. Retrieved November 12, 2006, from http://www.riaa.com/issues/parents/advisory.asp.

Rideout, V. (2004). *Parents, media and public policy: A Kaiser Family Foundation survey*. Menlo Park, CA: Kaiser Family Foundation.

Rosen, H. (2001). *Testimony submitted to the Committee on Governmental Affairs, United States Senate*, July 25. Retrieved July 25, 2001, from http://www.senate.gov/~gov_affairs/072501_baldwin.htm.

Salwen, M. B., & Dupagne, M. (1999). The third-person effect: Perceptions of the media's influence and immoral consequences. *Communication Research*, 26, 523–49.

Tharps, L. L. (2000). Foul Plié. *Entertainment Weekly*, October 27, 1(565), 24.

Thompson, K. M., & Haninger, K. (2001). Violence in E-rated video games. *Journal of the American Medical Association*, 286, 591–8.

Thompson, K. M., Tepichin, K., & Haninger, K. (2006). Content and ratings of Mature-rated video games. *Archives of Pediatric and Adolescent Medicine*, 160, 402–10.

Thompson, K. M., & Yokota, F. (2004). Violence, sex and profanity in films: Correlation of movie ratings with content. *Medscape General Medicine*, 6, 3.

US Senate, Committee on Commerce, Science, and Transportation. (1985, September 19). *Record Labeling*. Retrieved May 11, 2007, from US Senate Reports Online via GPO Access: http://www.joesapt.net/superlink/shrg99-529/index.html.

Valenti, J. (2001, July 25). *Testimony submitted to the Committee on Governmental Affairs, United States Senate*. Retrieved July 25, 2001, from http://www.senate.gov/~gov_affairs/072501_baldwin.htm.

Valenti, J. (2005). *How it all began*. Retrieved November 11, 2006, from http://www.mpaa.org/Ratings_HowItAllBegan.asp.

Walsh, D. A. (2001, December 13). *6th annual MediaWise video game report card.* Retrieved December 4, 2006, from http://www.mediafamily.org/research/report_vgrc_2001-1.shtml.

Walsh, D. A., & Gentile, D. A. (2001). A validity test of movie, television, and video-game ratings. *Pediatrics, 107*, 1302–8.

Walsh, D. A., Gentile, D. A., Walsh, E., Bennett, N., Robideau, B., Walsh, M., et al. (2005, November 29). *10th annual MediaWise video game report card.* Retrieved November 20, 2006, from http://www.mediafamily.org/research/report_vgrc_2005.shtml.

Waxman, S. (2001, April 8). Rated S, for Secret. *Washington Post*, p. G01.

Wilson, B. J., Linz, D., & Randall, B. (1990). Applying social science research to film ratings: A shift from offensiveness to harmful effects. *Journal of Broadcasting & Electronic Media, 34*, 443–68.

Yokota, F., & Thompson, K. M. (2000). Violence in G-rated animated films. *Journal of the American Medical Association, 283*, 2716–20.

24

Parent and School Interventions: Mediation and Media Literacy

Jennifer L. Chakroff and Amy I. Nathanson

The mass media are not only a significant presence in children's lives (Roberts, Foehr, & Rideout, 2005), but also they can be agents of socialization. The research, which to date has mostly focused on television, suggests that the medium can have a variety of effects on children. This work demonstrates that, compared to light television viewers, children who are heavy viewers are more aggressive, more stereotyped in their attitudes toward women and minorities, less healthy, and less successful in school (Herrett-Skjellum & Allen, 1996; Huesmann et al., 2003; Morgan, 1987; Paik & Comstock, 1994; Sprafkin & Gadow, 1986; Strasburger, 1986; Taras et al., 1989). Research on videogame use among children also shows that heavy use of this medium is associated with increased aggression (Anderson & Dill, 2000; Sherry, 2001). Although work on the effects of the Internet is sparse, we know that at the very least, children who use this medium can encounter a wide variety of inappropriate content, such as pornography, violent messages, and bad language (Wilson, this volume, Chapter 11; Iannotta, this volume, Chapter 21).

At the same time, some media effects are positive. Educational television can expand children's vocabularies and increase school readiness (Linebarger & Walker, 2005; Rice et al., 1990; Wright et al., 2001), prosocial television can promote prosocial behaviors like helping and sharing (Friedrich & Stein, 1973, 1975; Lovelace & Huston, 1983; Silverman & Sprafkin, 1980), and videogame playing can improve visual spatial and coordination skills (Griffith et al., 1983; Subrahmanyam & Greenfield, 1994).

How, then, can we prevent children from experiencing the negative effects of the mass media and help them enjoy the positive outcomes as well? Researchers have discovered two possible mechanisms. The first relies on parents to mediate their children's media use by talking with them about media, enforcing rules regarding media use, and/or watching or using content with them. The second relies on schools to institute media literacy curricula designed to educate children about media and teach them to become more critical consumers.

Mediation and media literacy are related, but separate constructs. Although critical viewing tends to be one of the main focuses of media literacy interventions, it is only *one* of the possible outcomes mediation could influence. Furthermore, media education curricula tend to be intense, long-term projects that are integrated throughout the educational system. Mediation, on the other hand, need not be. Therefore, media literacy curricula should be distinguished from mediation techniques in order to alleviate misconceptions that mediation needs to be a complicated set of lesson plans adults must follow to the letter. Even though both concepts may be a form of media education, referring to mediation and media literacy under the same construct confuses both concepts.

In this chapter, we review the research on both parental mediation and media literacy. We discuss the conceptual and theoretical issues that surround both concepts and the research on the effects of both types of interventions.

Conceptual Issues

Although the definitions of both mediation and media literacy may seem straightforward, both constructs are multidimensional and require care in explication. Particularly in the case of mediation, inattention to the construct's complexity has produced a literature that is difficult to identify and synthesize. In this section, we will describe some of the conceptual issues that surround each construct.

Mediation

In the last few years, more research has begun to see mediation as a higher-order construct that contains a variety of types of interactions, including active mediation, restrictive mediation, and co-viewing (Bybee, Robinson, & Turow, 1982; Nathanson, 2001a; Valkenburg et al., 1999). In doing so, researchers are able to incorporate the multiple ways adults interact with children about television. However, the dimensions themselves also have their own conceptual issues that need to be resolved (Nathanson, 2001a).

Active mediation   Although most researchers agree that active mediation involves discussion, the term they use to label this discussion varies. Early studies (e.g., Bybee, Robinson, & Thurow, 1982) used the term evaluative mediation. Although this term is applicable to some studies and their use of comments like, "It's bad to fight," (Corder-Bolz, 1980) or "That's wrong," (Hicks, 1968), the label is misleading to researchers since not all discussions about television need to include evaluating comments. Similarly, some research has referred to this type of interaction as instructive mediation (Valkenburg et al., 1999). And still other work has used the term active mediation (Austin, 1993; Nathanson, 1999).

Not surprisingly, each label for active mediation seems to carry a unique measurement approach. In some work, active mediation is tapped with questions that assess how frequently parents promote their children's critical viewing (e.g., by encouraging children to discount the reality of programs), whereas other research allows the construct to encompass any form of parent-child communication about television. The diversity in measurement is a serious limitation that prohibits researchers from synthesizing the body of work and drawing strong conclusions about the predictors and effects of active mediation.

In addition, the content or valence (whether statements are positive or negative) of active mediation is of particular importance to the outcome of the mediation. Therefore, researchers should take this into account when measuring mediation behaviors. Given the differential effects of various forms of active mediation (Austin et al., 1999; Hicks, 1968), we recommend that researchers analyze each of these types of interactions separately. This way, researchers are able to further examine the specific form of active mediation they feel is most essential to their interests.

Restrictive mediation   Of the three major types of mediation outlined above, restrictive mediation appears to be the most self-explanatory. In most research, restrictive mediation is said to be the occurrence of rules or restrictions in the home about television. These rules could involve the amount of time a child is allowed to watch television, when a child is able to watch, and/or the content or specific shows a child is restricted from viewing. Although some use the label restrictive guidance (e.g., Bybee, Robinson, & Thurow, 1982), others prefer the term restrictive mediation (Nathanson, 2001a; Valkenburg et al., 1999).

Is restrictive mediation as uncomplicated as it seems? Much like active mediation, restrictive mediation often is assessed by asking the parents or the children if there are rules in their home about television. Even though the occurrence of rules or restrictions is important to know, this simple frequency measure does not help researchers determine the reasons behind some of the interesting findings involving this construct. For example, it is unclear why there appears to be a curvilinear relationship between the amount of restrictive mediation and aggression (Nathanson, 1999) when researchers simply attempt to know the number of rules in a home.

It would be useful to assess if and how rules are negotiated or explained to children. It could be that the adult who sets the rules for watching television has discussed the content with the child to explain why the rules are in place. This could make the rules more understandable and acceptable to the child and might produce different reactions than restrictive mediation that does not include any explanation. Along the same lines, the level of enforcement of these rules may vary. As studies of parenting styles indicate, consistency of parenting in general and rule enforcement specifically help children internalize standards for behavior and increase their social competence (Roopnarine, Church, & Levy, 1990; Warash & Markstrom, 2001). Therefore, how well parents discuss, negotiate, and set rules could be important for how well the child is able to understand and comply with what is expected. However, few studies have attempted to determine how strict parents are at following through with the rules they have set. By discerning the context in which the rules were determined and how the rules are enforced, researchers will have a better understanding of restrictive mediation and could begin to answer some of the questions surrounding this concept.

Co-viewing Of the three dimensions of mediation, co-viewing is the one with the least amount of clarity. Co-viewing is defined as watching television with a child (St Peters et al., 1991; Valkenburg et al., 1999). Although this seems straightforward, it should be noted that watching with a child does not mean that any discussion occurs. Once discussion occurs, it could be said that active meditation is now taking place, if the discussion is about television.

This is an important distinction because there is empirical evidence that co-viewing and active mediation can have very different effects on the children involved. For example, co-viewing a violent program with a child has been shown to be related to children's later aggressive tendencies (Nathanson, 1999). However, several forms of active mediation have been shown to be related to reductions in subsequent aggressive behavior (Nathanson & Cantor, 2000).

And yet, the literature often blurs the distinction between active mediation and co-viewing. For example, a construct called "unfocused guidance," which seems to parallel co-viewing on a conceptual level, is measured with items that tap how often parents talk with their children about television (Bybee, Robinson, & Thurow, 1982; van der Voort, Nikken, & Vooijs, 1992). Because of the difficulty of distinguishing between co-viewing and active mediation, steps should be taken to ensure that measures of co-viewing are not also measuring active mediation. This could be accomplished through careful wording of questions when developing questionnaire items. Or, after data have been gathered, researchers could statistically partial out the shared variance between the two measures by regressing active mediation scores onto co-viewing scores and creating residualized co-viewing scores. This approach would produce a measure of co-viewing that does not include a measure of parent-child discussion.

Another distinction recently made in the literature concerns the intentionality of co-viewing. Yang and Nathanson (2005) explained that although measures of both active and restrictive mediation assume intent to influence children, co-viewing measures only tap the actual frequency without addressing the motivational side of this form of mediation. In fact, in their study, the authors found evidence of both intentional and passive co-viewing. Intentional co-viewing was defined as co-viewing which occurs because the parents are concerned about the effects of the media and want to co-view to protect their child. On the other hand, passive co-viewing occurs as a side-effect of the child being in the room when the parents are viewing programs they have selected. As Yang and Nathanson (2005) explained, intentional co-viewing could be seen as child-oriented whereas passive co-viewing could be seen as parent-oriented. Therefore, in order to gain a more accurate reflection of co-viewing behavior, it is important that future work include both types of co-viewing.

Media literacy

Like mediation research, much of the work in media literacy has stemmed from a desire to protect children from the negative influence of television, particularly the development of stereotypical attitudes and aggressive behavior. In fact, early work on mediation also used media education research as a means of justifying the effectiveness of potential intervention techniques.

Currently, the general consensus is that media literacy is defined as the critical viewing perspective through which one approaches the media (Potter, 1998). Even though there is general agreement as to how media literacy is defined, researchers and educators alike still have differing opinions as to how people should become more active consumers of the media. Within this overarching goal, researchers in particular have tended to further delineate two distinct routes to understanding media (Singer & Singer, 1998). The first goal is to understand the production aspects of the media. This route includes, for example, being aware of the economic structure of the media and comprehending formal features of each medium (e.g., special effects, camera techniques). The second goal focuses more on understanding and interpreting the content of the media. This route can include awareness of stereotyped depictions, understanding of plots, and interpreting the motives and emotions of characters. This second goal centers on critical viewing.

Although most scholars agree that media literacy encompasses the ability to think critically about the formal features of the medium and the content itself, there is some disagreement regarding how much emphasis should be placed on each type of understanding. Therefore, it becomes increasingly important for future research to test the effects of each distinct type of intervention so that educators can begin to understand where the focus of the curricula should be placed.

Potter (1998) explained that media literacy is a multidimensional concept that includes cognitive, emotional, aesthetic, and moral aspects. The cognitive dimension refers to our ability to understand how media content is created and the social structures that help produce it. The emotional aspect explains how well we are able to identify, understand, and relate to emotions displayed in the mass media. Aesthetically, one is media literate when one is able to enjoy the media from an artistic point of view. This dimension, like the cognitive dimension, also requires an understanding of the formal features of the media. Finally, the moral dimension refers to our ability to comprehend the values and the themes within media messages.

In addition to understanding the multidimensional nature of media literacy, it also is helpful to understand how it is distinct from other similar concepts. One debate that appears to surface when discussing media literacy is whether the concept is the same as media activism, or the desire to reform the state of the media (Hobbs, 1998). Therefore, it is especially important for researchers involved with the media to make this distinction rather than treat them as identical concepts.

Theoretical Issues

The majority of work on mediation and media literacy has been atheoretical. In the case of mediation, perhaps this is because researchers have been focused on simply understanding how parents mediate and the typical characteristics of those who do. This work has been very important in helping us clarify the mediation construct and to contemplate its potential in shaping the effects of media on children.

However, it is important to go a step beyond this work and understand exactly how mediation can work. Researchers have documented that adult-child communication can change how children respond to television, but they have not focused much attention on the features of the communication that can make a difference.

It seems that the goal for any mediation message would be to counter the features of the media content that are likely to cause harmful effects. For example, if research on the effects of television violence demonstrates that children are more likely to imitate aggressive behavior when it goes unpunished, then mediation messages should enumerate the many possible punishments that perpetrators may endure. Mediation should work, then, when it is tailored to the features of television content that are most problematic for children.

On the other hand, one could argue that any form of parent-child communication will inhibit negative media effects on children. That is, perhaps the message itself is not the most important element. Rather, it could be that the process of parents talking with their children about television sends a subtle message to the children about the parents' concern for and involvement in their children's lives. Knowing they are loved and watching television in a warm and open environment may make children less vulnerable to negative media effects than watching alone. Perhaps mediation is simply a surrogate measure for the quality of the parent-child relationship. In fact, Warren (2001) found that parents' accessibility was related to the amount of co-viewing and discussion that occurred in the home and he recommended that future research should study parental involvement with children. In addition, it could be that the similarity between the experimenter and the children may be an important, but to date overlooked, variable that may explain the effectiveness of mediation for some children and not others.

In the area of media literacy, the lack of theory is unfortunate as well, as it prevents us from anticipating what curricular messages will be most effective to children of different ages. It seems that media literacy programs are designed under the assumption that increasing children's understanding of media – how programs are produced, how special effects are used, and so on – will prevent children from being negatively affected by the content (Nathanson, 2004). However, even on logical grounds, this assumption is unjustified. That is, we know that adults, who presumably have a more sophisticated understanding of television, still can be influenced by media in undesirable ways (Gerbner et al., 1994; Herrett-Skjellum & Allen, 1996). As with mediation research, it would be helpful to turn to theories of media effects in order to target the variables that produce unwanted outcomes and then to design media literacy programs around those variables.

Studies of media literacy often report that the tested programs worked because they observed significant differences between children who participated and those who did not on posttest measures. However, researchers seldom measure whether children who participate in media literacy programs are less vulnerable to harmful media effects. Instead, they usually measure whether participants learned from the curriculum (e.g., Dorr, Graves, & Phelps, 1980; Watkins, Sprafkin, & Gadow, 1988). Certainly, it is encouraging that children who are exposed to media literacy lessons do learn key concepts from the programs. But, the question remains as to whether understanding those key concepts makes a difference when it comes to experiencing media effects.

In fact, it is theoretically possible for media literacy programs to increase the likelihood that children will absorb and mimic the negative behaviors they observe on television. For example, because media literacy programs encourage children to study content, it is possible that their increased attention to the negative content will lead them to store the acts in their memories and perhaps retrieve them later. Perhaps by explaining the formal features, like special effects or editing techniques, children are better able to comprehend the scenes. Because of this greater comprehension, the children become more susceptible to the negative influence of the program. In fact, intervention research is prone to boomerang effects, in which the exact opposite effect of what was intended occurs. This will be shown later in this chapter. Without theory in place, though, it becomes difficult to understand why such outcomes have been observed.

The possibility that increased attention to violent scenes will lead to harmful media effects does not mean that media literacy curricula should do away with this kind of instruction. However, it does suggest that mere comprehension of media is not enough to reduce children's vulnerability to media. Other messages may be required in conjunction with the traditional media literacy lessons. Perhaps media literacy curricula need to include mediation-like messages, such as ones that address the typicality and desirability of undesirable behaviors seen in the media.

A logical step, then, in designing intervention research is to turn our attention to theories that explain the effects of media on children. These theories can help us design messages to be used at home or in schools that will counteract the features of media that are responsible for the unwanted effects in the first place.

For example, beyond explaining why mediation is effective in general, Bandura's social cognitive theory (1986) can help researchers derive successful intervention strategies. In general, social cognitive theory explains how behaviors are learned and produced (Bandura, 1986). According to this theory, there are four main processes that guide the adoption of new behaviors: attention, retention, production, and motivation.

The motivation component seems particularly relevant to intervention research. Bandura (1986) explained that people have self-regulatory and self-reflective capabilities. Several inhibitors and disinhibitors are part of our self-regulatory capacity. If a mediation strategy invokes an inhibitor, then that inhibitor restrains the individual from performing those behaviors that are socially and individually viewed as unacceptable. The self-reflective capability refers to our personal and social standards that we wish to uphold, and it works in conjunction with the self-regulation process. These mechanisms regulate how one behaves and whether the motivation to behave in a certain manner is present. Therefore, by engaging these processes through mediation, adults have the ability to control whether the motivation is present or not. For example, mediation strategies that encourage children to think about how others would feel may encourage children to consider those social standards and consequences. When a person self-regulates and anticipates negative affect, he or she will be less likely to engage in destructive behavior.

Other media effects theories could be used as a framework for research on mediation and media literacy. Nathanson, Wilson, McGee, and Sebastian (2002) used gender schema theory to design a mediation study. The researchers hoped to curb the negative effects of gender stereotyped programs on children's adoption of gender stereotypes. Gender schema theory helps us understand how the media can affect the development and maintenance of gender stereotypes in the first place – as a result, this theory was used as a framework for developing mediation strategies intended to counteract this effect. The theory suggests that consistent exposure to stereotyped messages leads us to develop schemas of males and females with stereotyped features and behaviors. Accordingly, the researchers repeated counter-stereotypical messages several times during exposure to a stereotyped children's program to reduce the likelihood that stereotyped gender schemas would be activated. The theory not only was useful in developing mediation messages, but also it provided guidelines for the actual timing of administering the messages during the experiment. For example, the theory suggests that gender stereotypes are most malleable after they have been activated. As a result, mediation messages were delivered after stereotyped messages from television were shown. Using this approach, the researchers found that mediation messages that refute the universality of rigid gender roles helped children, especially younger children, reject gender stereotypes.

Gender schema theory also could be used to drive media literacy curricula. For example, lesson plans could teach children that men and women can engage in a wide variety of activities and are not confined to stereotyped roles. We might expect that children who particulate in media literacy programs will be less accepting of gender stereotypes they observe on television than would other children.

Another media effects approach that could be useful in this kind of work is the information processing approach (Shiffrin & Schneider, 1977; Siegler, 1991). This perspective emphasizes our capacity for taking in, interpreting, and remembering information. It is a particularly useful approach to consider when studying the effects of media on children, as it provides a sensible explanation for why younger children, as less efficient and sophisticated processors, are affected by television differently than are older children. For example, because young children can process only a limited amount of information at once, they tend to prioritize information that is presented visually (Pezdek & Stevens, 1984). So, in recalling a television story, young children may remember the color of the clothing that characters wear and the violent actions they perform rather than the dialogue because visual material is more salient to them (Collins, 1983).

Using the information processing approach, then, researchers might design different messages intended for different ages. Knowing that younger children may attend more to violent actions and the circumstances that surround those actions rather than the dialogue, researchers could develop mediation messages that help children process this information differently (e.g., "the people in the TV show are not really fighting"). Moreover, this approach may remind researchers that the mediation messages themselves may be processed differently by children of different ages. Younger children, for example, may be unable to benefit from long or complex mediation messages. Potter (2004) also explained that a media literacy theory would benefit from an information processing perspective. This perspective appears particularly relevant since it discusses how people filter, match, and interpret information. Theoretical explanations of media literacy must take into account what a child does with the curricula messages and the media messages once they are received. For example, how is it that a child filters the information, and how does that child interpret the media messages with respect to curricula messages?

A final theoretical issue that intervention research should consider is the developmental level of the recipients. The cognitive and moral development of younger and older children has implications for their processing abilities (Collins, 1973; Dorr, 1983). For example, younger children are not able to understand abstract reasoning (Collins, 1983). Furthermore, younger children do not have a fully developed conscience because of their lower levels of moral development (Kohlberg, 1969, 1984). These developmental differences can influence how a child would process intervention messages. For example, younger children who are told to think about how victims feel may not be able to process this message because they do not have the cognitive ability to take the perspective of another person (Flavell, 1963). In addition, there has been much research conducted on the differences in children's abilities to process media messages. These include skills such as assessing the realism of media and distinguishing between programs and commercials (Kunkel, 1988, 2001; Potter, 1988). Given the varied responses younger and older children can have both to the content of intervention messages and to the media content itself, it is important that researchers looking to design such interventions take these developmental differences into account.

The Effects of Interventions on Children

Mediation: intended effects

The majority of work on the effects of mediation has focused on active mediation. Both surveys and experiments have been used to assess whether parents who use active mediation in the home and adults who provide mediation in a laboratory setting can alter the way that children respond to television. Overall, this work reveals that active mediation has a desirable effect on children.

When surveys are used to assess effects, a variety of approaches to data collection have been taken. Some work asks children to report how often parents mediate (e.g., Austin, 1993; Lin & Atkin, 1989), whereas other research gathers information from the parents (e.g., Austin & Pinkleton, 2001; Messaris & Kerr, 1984). Outcome measures almost always come from the children and include assessments of children's aggression, skepticism toward television, and other critical viewing skills.

Survey work suggests that parent-child communication about television is related to critical viewing in children. For example, Austin (1993) found that adolescents whose parents talked to them about television were more skeptical of television news. Austin also found that active mediation was a stronger predictor of skepticism than general parental communication styles. Messaris and Kerr (1984) found that active mediation, in the form of telling children that television is fake, was related to lower perceived television reality scores among children, after controlling for the child's age, sex, and television exposure and the family's social class.

Surveys also have shown that active mediation is related to less antisocial behavior among children. For example, Nathanson (1999) found that parents who reported more active mediation had second through sixth graders who were less aggressive, both in general and in response to a violent cartoon. This finding suggests that children internalize the messages their parents provide at home and are more critical viewers when watching television in a different setting.

Experiments testing the effects of active mediation are more plentiful. Here, researchers typically have a trained researcher deliver mediation messages to children who view television in a laboratory. After viewing, children complete a questionnaire that assesses the extent to which they have been affected by the content. These children then are compared to a control group that watched the same programming but did not receive any mediation.

To date, the majority of researchers using experiments to study active mediation have focused on whether messages can curb unwanted responses to violent television. Overall, the results suggest that mediation can inhibit aggressive responses, especially among boys, younger children, and heavy viewers (Corder-Bolz, 1980; Hicks, 1968; Horton & Santogrossi, 1978; Nathanson, 2004; Nathanson & Cantor, 2000; Nathanson & Yang, 2003). For example, early work found that comments such as "That's wrong" and "It is bad to fight. It is better to help" reduced elementary school-aged children's tendency to imitate televised violence (Hicks, 1968; Corder-Bolz, 1980). Nathanson (2004) labeled these type of comments "evaluative mediation" and found that they are superior to "factual mediation," in which only the technical aspects of violent content are explained, in reducing harmful effects of watching television violence.

In some instances, theory has been used to drive mediation research. For example, using ideas drawn from social learning theory, Nathanson and Cantor (2000) found that mediation that encouraged children to think about the consequences of violence to a victim in a cartoon was effective. Specifically, children who heard this type of mediation liked the aggressor less, liked the victim more, and believed that the violence was less justified than did children who did not hear the mediation. Also, boys who heard the mediation were less aggressive after viewing than were boys who did not hear the mediation.

And, drawing on moral development theories, Yang (2006) found that children who heard "moral mediation" had more prosocial attitudes after viewing a violent action adventure program than did children who had not heard moral mediation messages. Moral mediation messages appeal to children's morality and provide judgments about behaviors (e.g., "Fighting like that is wrong. You don't solve a problem that way and it's wrong to hit people"). Sometimes, reasoning that highlights the motives for or consequences of behaviors accompanies the judgments (e.g., "It is wrong to fight because you could get into trouble"). Yang's study found that moral mediation with reasoning was effective both in a laboratory setting and when parents used it at home.

In some studies, though, the effect of mediation may reflect children's interest in appearing socially desirable to the adult experimenters. For instance, Hicks (1968) found that the positive effects of mediation on children's aggressive behavior only held when the experimenter was in the room and observing the children's behavior. Likewise, Horton and Santogrossi's (1978) study involved having children do the experimenter a favor after he had delivered mediation messages to them. This kind of social setting may have subtly exerted some pressure on the children to appear in a socially desirable way. On the other hand, Nathanson and Yang (2003) explicitly tested whether children's responses reflected a social desirability bias. In their study, 5- to 12-year-old children were asked whether they thought the person who had delivered mediation messages liked the program that was viewed. Although the researchers found significant differences in the effects of mediation on children's post-viewing aggressive attitudes, they failed to find differences among the treatments in children's perceptions of the experimenters' feeling about the program. As a result, the researchers concluded that the success of some mediation strategies over others was not due to children's desire to imitate or adopt the experimenter's attitudes.

A handful of studies have explored the possibility that active mediation can prevent the development of other undesirable effects beyond aggression. This work suggests that active mediation can reduce children's desires for advertised products (although only up to a certain point; Prasad, Rao, & Sheikh, 1978) and their tendency to endorse gender stereotypes (Corder-Bolz, 1980; Nathanson, Eveland, et al., 2002). In addition, messages can reduce children's fright responses to scary content (Cantor, 1994).

In addition to curbing unwanted effects, active mediation can enhance positive effects from television. That is, when adults comment on educational programming, children learn more from the content (Corder-Bolz, 1980; Reiser, Tessmer, & Phelps, 1984; Reiser, Williamson, & Suzuki, 1988; Valkenburg, Krcmar, & de Roos, 1998). Usually, these effects are observed when experimenters provide additional information to the children during viewing (Corder-Bolz, 1980; Corder-Bolz & O'Bryant, 1978; Valkenburg, Krcmar, & de Roos, 1998) rather than simply drawing children's attention to important content (Resier, Williamson, & Suzuki, 1988). This work is encouraging because it demonstrates that adults can help television viewing become a positive and educational experience for children.

The effects of mediation of both undesirable and educational content often vary according to the age of the recipients. As a result, it is important for mediation researchers to look for developmental differences. In their attempt to mediate violent content, Nathanson and Yang (2003) found that straightforward, evaluative-type statements worked best for the youngest children, ages 5- to 8-years-old. On the other hand, questions that encouraged children to view the material critically were most effective for older elementary school-aged children. Likewise, research on mediating fright reactions has found that "cognitive strategies" (i.e., those which encourage children to think about scary content differently) work for older children whereas "behavioral strategies" (those which teach children to engage in calming behaviors while viewing scary content, such as covering their eyes) work best for younger children (Cantor, 1994; Cantor & Wilson, 1984).

Active mediation may lose its effectiveness as children mature into adolescents. In her survey, Nathanson (2002) failed to find a significant relationship between parental active mediation and adolescents' attitudes toward violent television. However, given that Nathanson's measures were based on those developed for younger children, it could be that other forms of active mediation, which were not tapped in this survey, can be effective at reaching adolescents. For example, messages that ask questions and encourage critical viewing (e.g., "Do you think people in real life should act this way?") might be more palatable and interesting to adolescents. It is likely that messages will need to adapt to the developmental level of the recipients.

Unlike active mediation, there is virtually no research that assesses the effects of restrictive mediation alone. Instead, restrictive mediation has been researched alongside other communication behaviors, including other forms of mediation and more general parenting styles. This is unfortunate, as it leaves us with a rather weak understanding of this concept and its effects.

However, we do know that restrictive mediation can be effective. Survey research indicates that parents who restrict television viewing have youngsters who are more literate viewers (Desmond et al., 1985; Desmond et al., 1987), less stereotyped in their attitudes toward women (Rothschild & Morgan, 1987), less likely to desire advertised products (Reid, 1979), and less aggressive than are children whose parents do not restrict television viewing (McLeod, Atkin, & Chaffee, 1972a, 1972b; Nathanson, 1999). Some of these findings pertain to adolescents as well as younger children (e.g., McLeod, Atkin, & Chaffee, 1972a, 1972b; Rothschild & Morgan, 1987).

Some argue that the reason why restrictive mediation works is not because children view less television, but because it sends a message to them about the value of television. Reid (1979) found that television rules were related to fewer requests for advertised products among children. He suggested that the rules helped communicate to children that televised information is not especially worthwhile or desirable. Similarly, Nathanson (1999) found that children whose parents used restrictive mediation believed that the mediated content was less important and deserving of less attention than did children whose parents did not use restrictive mediation. As a result, restrictive mediation is more than simply a measure of how much television children view; instead, it embodies messages about the value of television.

The research on co-viewing suggests that this form of mediation generally enhances the effects of media on children. This can sometimes lead to unintended negative outcomes, which will be discussed later in this chapter. However, in the case of educational material, the effects of co-viewing are positive. Perhaps the presence of parents communicates to children that the co-viewed material is worth attending to and important, thereby increasing the likelihood that children will be affected by it (Nathanson, 1999, 2001b).

Salomon (1977) offered this argument to explain the results of his work. He found that kindergarteners whose mothers co-viewed *Sesame Street* learned more from the series and enjoyed it more than kindergarteners who watched without mothers. Although he did not know whether mothers had discussed the material with their children, Salomon suggested that mothers' presence while viewing encouraged children to take the content more seriously. Interestingly, Dorr, Kovaric, and Doubleday (1989) found that parents who co-view do so to enhance their children's ability to learn from the material. In addition, Messaris and Kerr (1984) found that children of co-viewing parents believed that the co-viewed content was more real than children whose parents did not co-view. Nathanson (2001b) also found that children interpret the presence of parents during television viewing as a sign that parents approve of the content. As a result, it is likely that children are able to sense their parents' goals for co-viewing and thereby become more attentive during viewing. Given that parents who co-view usually have positive attitudes toward the material (Nathanson, 2001b), it is not surprising that children are more receptive to content.

It is also likely that co-viewing creates an environment that makes children feel good. Like active mediation, co-viewing may be interpreted by children as an indicator that parents are involved with them and enjoy their company. Wilson and Weiss (1993) found, in a study of sibling co-viewing, that preschoolers who co-viewed a suspenseful movie with an older sibling enjoyed the experience more than did preschoolers who viewed the movie alone.

One major limitation of the research on parental mediation is that scholars have not devoted much effort to understanding how parents mediate newer technologies and whether this type of intervention has any effect on children. Children are using these technologies, such as the Internet and videogames, more and more (Roberts, Foehr, & Rideout, 2005). For example, the percentage of third through twelfth graders that reported going online for more than an hour in a typical day increased from 5 percent in 1999 to 22 percent in 2005 (Roberts, Foehr, & Rideout, 2005). Furthermore, it has been found that even children younger than 6 years old are using all types of media (Rideout & Hamel, 2006). Although television is still the most heavily used medium, media use trends are changing, and children may favor other technologies in the near future.

Eastin, Greenberg, and Hofschire (2006) took a first step in understanding how parents mediate these newer technologies in their survey of mothers' regulation of children's Internet use. They found that parenting styles have an influence on what type of mediation is used. For example, authoritative parents (controlling and warm) used both evaluative and restrictive mediation more than did the authoritarian (controlling) or neglectful (uninvolved, ignoring) parents. When mediating the Internet, evaluative mediation takes the form of discussing the content or specific sites to indicate what is good or realistic. Interestingly, only 2 percent of parents claimed never to use interpretive mediation with the Internet. In addition to this study, Clark, Demont-Heinrich, and Webber (2005) interviewed parents at different income levels to determine if their attitudes toward the Internet were related to their concern for their children using the technology. The authors found that parents in higher-income brackets were more likely to see Internet competence as an important skill that is needed for success than parents in lower-income brackets. Furthermore, these higher-income parents were less concerned with using technology to restrict their child's use of the Internet. Rather, they were confident in their ability to guide their child's use in an educational direction.

As Eastin and colleagues (2006) explained, active mediation that occurs during media use is difficult with the newer technologies because the rate that information is accessed has increased. In particular, it is the speed at which images and information change that makes it difficult for parents to discuss each message. Therefore, active mediation that occurs before or after media use may be the most appropriate time for this type of intervention. In addition, those discussions may be most helpful if they concentrate on how to use the Internet effectively and efficiently. That way, children do not accidentally encounter inappropriate content or divulge too much personal information. However, using restrictive mediation, either by rule enforcement or technological blocking programs, could be beneficial to avoid such content all together (Iannotta, this volume, Chapter 21). As new technologies become more pervasive, researchers should continue to consider the applicability of television mediation to other technologies and study how parents can manage their children's exposure to them.

Media literacy: intended effects

Although many researchers have called for more evaluation of media literacy curricula, there is a noticeable disconnect between those programs which are implemented and those which have been evaluated. That being said, there have been some researchers who have been able to test the effectiveness of different types of curricula.

Typically, researchers provide teachers with the curriculum, complete with any materials they may need. Children usually are pretested on their knowledge of the information provided in the curriculum and any attitudinal measures. Then, either students in certain classrooms or students in certain schools are given the curriculum. At the end of the program, children complete questionnaires that again ask about their knowledge of the material presented, attitudes of interest, and sometimes behavior to determine if the curriculum was successful. In some studies, these children are compared with control groups that do not receive the curriculum.

In terms of learning about television production, the programs have been quite successful. For example, Singer, Zuckerman, and Singer (1980) designed and tested a series of eight lesson plans that sought to teach the children about the formal features of television, differences in program types, the realism of television, and a variety of other topics. Results revealed that those children who received the lessons were better able to understand special effects and assess the realism of the programming than were those not exposed to the lessons. In fact, media literacy curricula focusing on formal features have shown that children exposed to the program also are better able to distinguish camera effects and editing (Rapaczynski, Singer, & Singer, 1982).

Multiple studies have found that children exposed to media literacy curricula are better able to distinguish between reality and fantasy (Doolittle, 1980; Dorr, Graves, & Phelps, 1980). For example, Dorr and colleagues (1980) tested a media literacy intervention that provided children with information about how programs are produced and encouraged discussion about how programs compared to their own life. Results revealed that the children did learn the material and in doing so, were better able to determine what was real on television.

In addition to distinguishing between reality and fantasy, media literacy curricula also have helped children to distinguish between commercials and television programs (Rapaczynski, Singer, & Singer, 1982; Singer, Zuckerman, & Singer, 1980). Rapaczynski and colleagues (1982), for example, provided teachers with six lessons that ranged in topics from introducing special effects to explaining why there are commercials on television. The results indicated that the curriculum did improve children's ability to determine the difference between commercials and television programming and their understanding of commercials in general.

In addition to this factual information, media literacy curricula also have been successful at influencing participants' attitudes. In one of the more stringent tests of a media literacy program, Austin and Johnson (1997) examined how effective media literacy was at influencing third graders' perceptions of alcohol. In an alcohol-related media literacy program, which included strategies drawn from mediation research, Austin and Johnson (1997) found that those students exposed to the program understood the persuasive intent of the commercials more and reported less desire to emulate characters and less positive perceptions of the consequences of drinking than did those students not exposed to the curriculum.

Not only has media literacy been shown to influence the attitudes children have about alcohol, but it also has influenced how much children are aware of stereotypical portrayals of characters. Singer, Zuckerman, and Singer (1980) found that those children exposed to a media literacy curriculum that discussed stereotyped depictions on television were more knowledgeable about stereotypes in general and were better able to recognize and understand these types of portrayals.

Since media literacy research began, in part, from a desire to protect children from the harmful effects of the media, it is not surprising that many of the studies on the effectiveness of such interventions look at ways to curb the negative effects of viewing television violence. For example, Sprafkin, Watkins, and Gadow (1990) tested a curriculum that focused on the lack of reality in television and found that emotionally disturbed children were less likely to identify with aggressive characters after receiving the instruction.

In a similar attempt to discredit the violent actions depicted on television, Vooijs- and van der Voort (1993) used a media literacy curriculum in an effort to make children appreciate the consequences of violence and the lack of justification for violence. The curriculum consisted of nine 45-minute lessons given to 10- to 12-year-olds. Vooijs and van der Voort (1993) found that those children who had participated in the curriculum were less likely to approve of violent acts and were more likely to understand the seriousness of violence than were those children who had not participated in the program.

Although the ability to increase technical knowledge and influence attitudes is important, one question that still remains is how effective media literacy is at influencing actual behaviors. In their study on the effects of treatments designed to reduce aggressive behaviors, Huesmann, and colleagues (1983) did not find any differences in aggressive behavior between those students who heard lessons about the special effects of television and those students who did not receive any instruction. Therefore, both groups were just as likely to imitate the aggressive behavior depicted in the programs. In an effort to determine what would work at reducing aggressive behaviors, the researchers designed a second intervention that focused on how people should not imitate what they see on television in addition to employing activities that required the children to form their own arguments against modeling the behavior, like writing essays directed at younger children. Those students receiving this second intervention were less aggressive than were those not receiving the intervention. These studies seem to indicate the media literacy programs designed to influence factual knowledge are not successful at altering behaviors. However, those programs that focus more directly on the negative behavior are effective.

Taken together, these studies show that media literacy training has the ability to affect the way children view television. However, the content of this training is important. Media literacy programs can work if their goal is to increase knowledge of television production or realism of portrayals. On the other hand, programs that focus on evaluating the depictions are more successful at altering behaviors or attitudes. These results illustrate why it is important for programs to be evaluated prior to implementing them.

Unfortunately, research that evaluates the effectiveness of media literacy curricula is rare. Given the previous discussion of the potential for certain aspects of the curriculum to fail, it is important to be cautious in disseminating a media literacy curriculum without first determining the results one could expect. Furthermore, in order for these programs to be taken seriously by the people who have the power and money to implement them, researchers must provide more concrete answers to what works and what does not. That way, those in charge of curriculum decisions are able to make more informed decisions.

In addition to this lack of evaluation, in those cases where there has been some sort of evaluation process, important outcomes are often ignored. For example, Cantor and Wilson (2003) noted that instead of measuring actual behavior, interpretations or attitudes are more likely to be measured. If media literacy stems from a protectionist point of view, then the behaviors researchers are trying to reduce must be measured in order to determine how successful programs have been.

Finally, media literacy research has a few other limitations. First, despite the public concern about the Internet and videogames, evaluations of media literacy programs that focus on newer technologies are noticeably absent. As discussed in Thornburgh and Lin (2002), by teaching children how to search for information on the Internet and how to evaluate the content they find, children would be less likely to access inappropriate material accidentally. Eastin, Yang, and Nathanson (2006) also argued that researchers need to study "Internet literacy." In their study, they found that elementary school-aged children often become confused by common Internet features, such as advertising and distracting graphics, and fail to recall important site content. To date, scholars have recommended studying the effectiveness of media literacy programs at mitigating the effects of newer technologies (Livingstone, 2004), but only one study has as yet taken on the project (Eastin, Yang, & Nathanson, 2006).

Overall, research on media literacy needs to begin to create theoretically driven curricula which are then systematically implemented in order to allow a thorough evaluation. By evaluating each part of a program individually, researchers would be able to make more informed recommendations to parents and educators. In addition to evaluating the content of the media literacy curricula, it is important that researchers consider the developmental differences that could impact the effectiveness of such programs. Finally, this area of research would benefit from longitudinal studies that can help determine how effective programs are over time.

Unintended effects of interventions

Despite their successes, interventions can not only fail, but backfire and produce undesirable effects. In some cases, the very outcome that researchers had hoped to decrease becomes more likely to occur as a result of mediation or media literacy training.

Active mediation has mostly been found to be effective, but there have been a few cases where messages have produced undesirable outcomes. In the fright reactions literature, for example, Wilson and Cantor (1987) found that a cognitive strategy for reducing fright from a scary movie unexpectedly increased kindergartners' and first graders' fear responses. Nathanson and Yang (2003) found that a mediation technique that consisted of questions designed to prompt critical viewing actually increased 5- to 12-year-old children's positive attitudes toward violent material. Similarly, Doolittle's (1980) media literacy program backfired. In this curriculum, sixth-grade boys received lessons about the reality of entertainment television and production techniques. Although the goal of the lessons was to reduce children's aggression, this program increased the children's aggression relative to children who did not participate in the curriculum.

It is likely that in all of these cases, active mediation or media literacy training created unintended effects because the messages simply drew children's attention to the harmful content and could not successfully prompt critical viewing. For younger children, this could be because of their inability to understand complex messages. As a result, the mediation message leads them to focus on the harmful content without giving them the tools for evaluating and contextualizing it. In the case of older children and media literacy training, it is possible that information about television production alone, without any education about harmful media effects, simply increases children's involvement in the material. As a result, the increased involvement may make them more vulnerable to being affected by harmful content (Perse, 1990; Rubin & Perse, 1987a, 1987b).

This kind of unintended effect has been found among adolescents as well. In their study of active mediation, Nathanson and Botta (2003) found that adolescents whose parents talked with them about characters' bodies were more likely to have a negative body image and symptoms of eating disorders. For this particular outcome, it could be that active mediation, even when negative, leads adolescents to study characters' appearance and increases their desire to look like them. On the other hand, given that this study was a survey, it could be that active mediation was a response to adolescents who already had poor body images. That is, knowing that their adolescents have a body image problem, perhaps parents comment on characters' appearances in an effort to communicate that the media's "thin ideal" is not attractive or realistic.

Likewise, restrictive mediation can have unwanted effects. In a study of elementary school-aged children, Nathanson (1999) found a curvilinear relationship between restrictive mediation and aggression such that very low and very high amounts of restrictions were related to higher aggression levels among children.

It could be that children become very curious about restricted content and frequently seek it out elsewhere, thereby encouraging more aggression. Or, perhaps the strict rules themselves lead children to feel angry and resentful and thus more aggressive.

In fact, some support for the former explanation has been found, at least among adolescents. Nathanson (2002) found that adolescents whose parents restrict viewing of violent and sexual content were more likely to watch the forbidden content with friends. Research on the effects of movie ratings also shows that children become more interested in content that has restricted access (Cantor, Harrison, & Nathanson, 1997).

As a result, restrictive mediation may be effective only when delivered in moderate doses. Or, a good strategy might be to use both restrictive mediation and active mediation. Nathanson (2002) found that restrictive mediation did not backfire among adolescents when used alongside active mediation. The possibility that multiple approaches to television mediation might be ideal is logical, but it has not been studied adequately yet.

Co-viewing also has been linked with unintended effects. Nathanson (1999) found that co-viewing at home was related to more aggressive responses to a violent cartoon shown in a laboratory. This finding again suggests that mediation performed at home encourages children to internalize certain attitudes about content or viewing styles that lead them to respond differently to television they view in other contexts. In addition, Rothschild and Morgan (1987) found that adolescents whose parents co-viewed were more likely to endorse gender stereotypes. As a result, regardless of the content, it seems that co-viewing may lead children to become more attentive to and interested in the co-viewed material, and therefore they are more likely to be affected by it. Also, given that Messaris and Kerr (1984) found that co-viewing increased children's perceptions of the reality of television, it could be that co-viewing affects outcomes via children's perceived reality. That is, if co-viewing communicates to children that the content is real or realistic, then media effects become more likely.

Overall, it is clear that various kinds of interventions may backfire and produce effects that are not intended. Rather than offer post-hoc explanations for these outcomes, researchers should turn their attention toward studying unintended effects and identifying the conditions that produce them. Understanding and anticipating these effects is an essential component of conducting research on interventions.

Conclusion

The research on mediation and media literacy is promising. After decades of research documenting the many possible effects of media exposure on children, it is encouraging to know that interventions performed at home and in school can prevent harmful outcomes and promote positive effects.

There are several avenues for future research that should receive priority. First, researchers should devote more attention to understanding boomerang effects, in which experimental interventions result in the opposite effect of what was intended. Second, research should more thoroughly investigate restrictive mediation. In particular, it would be useful to understand whether the way in which rules are negotiated shapes their effectiveness. Third, researchers should study interventions in the context of newer media. And lastly, scholars in this area should use theory to help them understand the effectiveness of interventions. By turning to theories of media effects, researchers could design better messages and anticipate their effects with more confidence than they could by working without theory.

References

Anderson, C. A., & Dill, K. E. (2000). Video games and aggressive thoughts, feelings, and behavior in the laboratory and in life. *Journal of Personality and Social Psychology*, 78, 772–90.

Austin, E. W. (1993). Exploring the effects of active parental mediation of television content. *Journal of Broadcasting and Electronic Media*, 37, 147–58.

Austin, E. W., Fujioka, Y., Bolls, P., & Engelbertson, J. (1999). How and why parents take on the tube. *Journal of Broadcasting and Electronic Media*, 43, 175–92.

Austin, E. W., & Johnson, K. K. (1997). Effects of general and alcohol-specific media literacy training on children's decision-making about alcohol. *Journal of Health Communication*, 2, 12–42.

Austin, E. W., & Pinkleton, B. E. (2001). The role of parental mediation in the political socialization process. *Journal of Broadcasting and Electronic Media*, 45(2), 221–40.

Bandura, A. (1986). *Social foundations of thought and action: A social cognitive theory.* Englewood Cliffs, NJ: Prentice-Hall.

Bybee, C., Robinson, D., & Turow, J. (1982). Determinants of parental guidance of children's television viewing for a special subgroup: Mass media scholars. *Journal of Broadcasting*, 26, 697–710.

Cantor, J. (1994). Fright reactions to mass media. In J. Bryant & D. Zillmann (Eds.), *Media effects: Advances in theory and research* (pp. 213–45). Hillsdale, NJ: Lawrence Erlbaum.

Cantor, J., Harrison, K., & Nathanson, A. (1997). Ratings and advisories for television programming. In Center for Communication and Social Policy (Ed.), *National television violence study*, vol. 2 (pp. 267–322). Thousand Oaks, CA: Sage.

Cantor, J., & Wilson, B. J. (1984). Modifying fear responses to mass media in preschool and elementary school children. *Journal of Broadcasting*, 28, 431–43.

Cantor, J., & Wilson, B. J. (2003). Media and violence: Intervention strategies for reducing aggression. *Media Psychology*, 5, 363–403.

Clark, L. S., Demont-Heinrich, C., & Webber, S. (2005). Parents, ICTs, and children's prospects for success: Interviews along the digital "Access Rainbow." *Critical Studies in Media Communication*, 22(5), 409–26.

Collins, W. A. (1973). Effect of temporal separation between motivation, aggression, and consequences: A developmental study. *Developmental Psychology*, 8, 215–21.

Collins, W. A. (1983). Interpretation and inference in children's television viewing. In J. Bryant & D. R. Anderson (Eds.), *Children's understanding of television: Research on attention and comprehension* (pp. 125–50). New York: Academic Press.

Corder-Bolz, C. R. (1980). Mediation: The role of significant others. *Journal of Communication*, 30, 106–18.

Corder-Bolz, C. R., & O'Bryant, S. L. (1978). Can people affect television? Teacher vs. program. *Journal of Communication*, 28, 97–103.

Desmond, R. J., Hirsch, B., Singer, D., & Singer, J. (1987). Gender differences, mediation, and disciplinary styles in children's responses to television. *Sex Roles*, 16, 375–89.

Desmond, R. J., Singer, J. L., Singer, D. G., Calam, R., & Colimore, K. (1985). Family mediation patterns and television viewing – young children's use and grasp of the medium. *Human Communication Research*, 11, 461–80.

Doolittle, J. C. (1980). Immunizing children against possible antisocial effects of viewing television violence: A curricular intervention. *Perceptual and Motor Skills*, 51, 498.

Dorr, A. (1983). No shortcuts to judging reality. In J. Bryant & D. R. Anderson (Eds.), *Children's understanding of television* (pp. 199–220). New York: Academic Press.

Dorr, A., Graves, S. B., & Phelps, E. (1980). Television literacy for young children. *Journal of Communication*, 30(30), 71–83.

Dorr, A., Kovaric, P., & Doubleday, C. (1989). Parent-child coviewing of television. *Journal of Broadcasting and Electronic Media*, 33, 35–51.

Eastin, M. S., Greenberg, B. S., & Hofschire, L. (2006). Parenting the Internet: Examining the influence of parenting styles and access. *Journal of Communication*, 56, 486–504.

Eastin, M. S., Yang, M-S., & Nathanson, A. I. (2006). Children on the Net: An empirical explanation of the evaluation of Internet content. *Journal of Broadcasting and Electronic Media*, 50, 211–30.

Flavell, J. (1963). *The developmental psychology of Jean Piaget*. New York: Van Nostrand.

Friedrich, L. K., & Stein, A. H. (1973). Aggressive and prosocial television programs and the natural behavior of preschool children. *Monographs of the Society for Research in Child Development*, 38, 1–64.

Friedrich, L. K., & Stein, A. H. (1975). Prosocial television and young children: The effects of verbal labeling and role playing on learning and behavior. *Child Development*, 46, 27–38.

Gerbner, G., Gross, L., Morgan, M., & Signorelli, N. (1994). Growing up with television: The cultivation perspective. In J. Bryant & D. Zillmann (Eds.), *Media effects: Advances in theory and research* (pp. 17–41). Hillsdale, NJ: Lawrence Erlbaum.

Griffith, J. L., Voloschin, P., Gibb, G. D., & Bailey, J. R. (1983). Differences in eye–hand motor coordination of video-game users and non-users. *Perceptual and Motor Skills*, 57, 155–8.

Herrett-Skjellum, J., & Allen, M. (1996). Television programming and sex stereotyping: A meta-analysis. In B. R. Burelson (Ed.), *Communication yearbook*, vol. 19 (pp. 157–85). Thousand Oaks, CA: Sage.

Hicks, D. (1968). Effects of co-observer's sanctions and adult presence on imitative aggression. *Child Development*, 39, 303–9.

Hobbs, R. (1998). The seven great debates in the media literacy movement. *Journal of Communication*, 48(1), 16–32.

Horton, R. W., & Santogrossi, D. A. (1978). The effect of adult commentary on reducing the influence of televised violence. *Personality and Social Psychology Bulletin*, 4, 337–40.

Huesmann, L. R., Eron, L. D., Klein, R., Brice, P., & Fischer, R. (1983). Mitigating the imitation of aggressive behaviors by changing children's attitudes about media violence. *Journal of Personality and Social Psychology*, 44, 899–910.

Huesmann, L. R., Moise-Titus, J., Podolski, C-L., & Eron, L. D. (2003). Longitudinal relations between children's exposure to TV violence and their aggressive and violent behavior in young adulthood: 1977–1992. *Developmental Psychology*, 39, 189–200.

Kohlberg, L. (1969). Stage and sequence: The cognitive-developmental approach to socialization. In D. A. Goslin (Ed.), *Handbook of socialization theory and research* (pp. 347–480). Chicago: Rand McNally.

Kohlberg, L. (1984). *Essays on moral development*. Vol. 2, *The psychology of moral development*. San Francisco: Harper & Row.

Kunkel, D. (1988). Children and host-selling television commercials. *Communication Research*, 15, 71–92.

Kunkel, D. (2001). Children and television advertising. In D. G. Singer & J. L. Singer (Eds.), *Handbook of children and the media* (pp. 375–93). Thousand Oaks, CA: Sage.

Lin, C. A., & Atkin, D. J. (1989). Parental mediation and rulemaking for adolescent use of television and VCRs. *Journal of Broadcasting and Electronic Media*, 33(1), 53–67.

Linebarger, D., & Walker, D. (2005). Infants' and toddlers' television viewing and language outcomes. *American Behavioral Scientist*, 48, 624–45.

Livingstone, S. (2004). Media literacy and the challenge of new information and communication technologies. *Communication Review*, 7, 3–14.

Lovelace, V. O., & Huston, A. C. (1983). Can television teach prosocial behavior? In J. Sprafkin, C. Swift, & R. Hess (Eds), *Rx television: Enhancing the preventive impact of TV* (pp. 93–106). New York: Haworth Press.

McLeod, J. M., Atkin, C. K., & Chaffee, S. H. (1972a). Adolescents, parents, and television use: Adolescents' self-report measures from Maryland and Wisconsin samples. In G. A. Comstock & E. A. Rubinstein (Eds.), *Television and social behavior*. Vol. 3, *Television and adolescent aggressiveness* (pp. 173–238). Washington, DC: US Government Printing Office.

McLeod, J. M., Atkin, C. K., & Chaffee, S. H. (1972b). Adolescents, parents, and television use: Adolescents' self-report measures from Maryland and Wisconsin samples. In G. A. Comstock & E. A. Rubinstein (Eds.), *Television and social behavior*. Vol. 3, *Television and adolescent aggressiveness* (pp. 239–313). Washington, DC: US Government Printing Office.

Messaris, P., & Kerr, D. (1984). TV-related mother-child interaction and children's perceptions of TV characters. *Journalism Quarterly*, 61, 662–6.

Morgan, M. (1987). Television, sex-role attitudes, and sex-role behavior. *Journal of Early Adolescence*, 7, 269–82.

Nathanson, A. I. (1999). Identifying and explaining the relationship between parental mediation and children's aggression. *Communication Research*, 26, 124–43.

Nathanson, A. I. (2001a). Mediation of children's television viewing: Working toward conceptual clarity and common understanding. In W. B. Gudykunst (Ed.), *Communication yearbook*, vol. 25 (pp. 115–51). Mahwah, NJ: Lawrence Erlbaum.

Nathanson, A. I. (2001b). Parent and child perspectives on the presence and meaning of parental television mediation. *Journal of Broadcasting and Electronic Media*, 45, 201–20.

Nathanson, A. I. (2002). The unintended effects of parental mediation of television on adolescents. *Media Psychology*, 4, 207–30.

Nathanson, A. I. (2004). Factual and evaluative approaches to modifying children's responses to violent television. *Journal of Communication*, 54(2), 321–36.

Nathanson, A. I., & Botta, R. A. (2003). Shaping the effects of television on adolescents' body image disturbance: The role of parental mediation. *Communication Research*, 30, 304–31.

Nathanson, A. I., & Cantor, J. (2000). Reducing the aggression-promoting effect of violent cartoons by increasing children's fictional involvement with the victim: A study of active mediation. *Journal of Broadcasting and Electronic Media*, 44, 125–42.

Nathanson, A. I., Eveland, W. P., Park, H. S., & Paul, B. (2002). Perceived media influence and efficacy as predictors of caregivers' protective behaviors. *Journal of Broadcasting and Electronic Media*, 46, 385–410.

Nathanson, A. I., Wilson, B. J., McGee, J., & Sebastian, M. (2002). Counteracting the effects of female stereotypes on television via active mediation. *Journal of Communication*, 52(4), 922–37.

Nathanson, A. I., & Yang, M. S. (2003). The effects of mediation content and form on children's responses to violent television. *Human Communication Research*, 29, 111–34.

Paik, H., & Comstock, G. (1994). The effects of television violence on antisocial behavior: A meta-analysis. *Communication Research*, 21, 516–46.

Perse, E. M. (1990). Involvement with local television news: Cognitive and emotional dimensions. *Human Communication Research*, 16, 556–81.

Pezdek, K., & Stevens, E. (1984). Children's memory for auditory and visual information on television. *Developmental Psychology*, 20, 212–18.

Potter, W. J. (1988). Perceived reality in television effects research. *Journal of Broadcasting and Electronic Media*, 32, 23–41.

Potter, W. J. (1998). *Media literacy*. Thousand Oaks, CA: Sage.

Potter, W. J. (2004). Argument for the need for a cognitive theory of media literacy. *American Behavioral Scientist*, 48, 266–72.

Prasad, V. K., Rao, T. R., & Sheikh, A. A. (1978). Mother vs. commercial. *Journal of Communication*, 28, 91–6.

Rapaczynski, W., Singer, D. G., & Singer, J. L. (1982). Teaching television: A curriculum for young children. *Journal of Communication*, 32(2), 46–54.

Reid, L. N. (1979). Viewing rules as mediating factors of children's responses to commercials. *Journal of Broadcasting*, 23, 15–26.

Reiser, R. A., Tessmer, M. A., & Phelps, P. C. (1984). Adult-child interaction in children's learning from *Sesame Street. Educational Communication and Technology Journal*, 32, 217–23.

Reiser, R. A., Williamson, N., & Suzuki, K. (1988). Using *Sesame Street* to facilitate children's recognition of letters and numbers. *Educational Communication and Technology Journal*, 36, 15–21.

Rice, M. L., Huston, A. C., Truglio, R. T., & Wright, J. C. (1990). Words from *Sesame Street*: Learning vocabulary while viewing. *Developmental Psychology*, 26, 421–8.

Rideout, V., & Hamel, E. (2006). *The media family: Electronic media in the lives of infants, toddlers, preschoolers, and their parents.* Menlo Park, CA: Kaiser Family Foundation.

Roberts, D. F., Foehr, U. G., & Rideout, V. (2005). *Generation M: Media in the lives of 8–18-year-olds.* Menlo Park, CA: Kaiser Family Foundation.

Roopnarine, J., Church, C., & Levy, G. (1990). Day care children's play behaviors: Relationships to their mothers' and fathers' assessments of their parenting behaviors, marital stress, and marital companionship. *Early Childhood Research Quarterly*, 5, 335–46.

Rothschild, N., & Morgan, M. (1987). Cohesion and control: Adolescents' relationships with parents as mediators of television. *The Journal of Early Adolescence*, 7, 299–314.

Rubin, A. M., & Perse, E. M. (1987a). Audience activity and soap opera involvement: A uses and effects investigation. *Human Communication Research*, 14, 246–68.

Rubin, A. M., & Perse, E. M. (1987b). Audience activity and television news gratifications. *Communication Research*, 14, 58–84.

Salomon, G. (1977). Effects of encouraging Israeli mothers to co-observe *Sesame Street* with their five-year-olds. *Child Development*, 48, 1146–51.

Sherry, J. (2001). The effects of violent video games on aggression: A meta-analysis. *Human Communication Research*, 27, 409–31.

Shiffrin, R. M., & Schneider, W. (1977). Controlled and automatic human information processing: Perceptual learning, automatic attending and a general theory. *Psychological Review*, 84, 127–89.

Siegler, R. S. (1991). *Children's thinking* (2nd edn.). Englewood Cliffs, NJ: Prentice-Hall.

Silverman, L. R., & Sprafkin, J. N. (1980). The effects of *Sesame Street* prosocial spots on cooperative play between young children. *Journal of Broadcasting*, 24, 135–47.

Singer, D. G., & Singer, J. L. (1998). Developing critical viewing skills and media literacy in children. *Annals of the American Academy of Political and Social Science*, 557, 164–79.

Singer, D. G., Zuckerman, D. M., & Singer, J. L. (1980). Helping elementary school children learn about TV. *Journal of Communication*, 30(3), 84–93.

Sprafkin, J., & Gadow, K. D. (1986). Television viewing habits of emotionally disturbed, learning disabled, and mentally retarded children. *Journal of Applied Developmental Psychology*, 7, 45–59.

Sprafkin, J., Watkins, L. T., & Gadow, K. D. (1990). Efficacy of a television literacy curriculum for emotionally disturbed and learning disabled children. *Journal of Applied Developmental Psychology*, 11, 225–44.

St Peters, M., Fitch, M., Huston, A. C., Wright, J. C., & Eakins, D. J. (1991). Television and families: What do young children watch with their parents? *Child Development*, 62(6), 1409–23.

Strasburger, V. C. (1986). Does television affect learning and school performance? *Pediatrician*, 13, 141–7.

Subrahmanyam, K., & Greenfield, P. M. (1994). Effect of video game practice on spatial skills in girls and boys. *Journal of Applied Developmental Psychology*, 15, 13–32.

Taras, H. L., Sallis, J. F., Patterson, T. L., Nader, P. R., & Nelson, J. A. (1989). Television's influence on children's diet and physical activity. *Journal of Developmental and Behavioral Pediatrics*, 10, 176–80.

Thornburgh, D., & Lin, H. S. (Eds.). (2002). *Youth, pornography, and the Internet.* Washington, DC: National Academy Press.

Valkenburg, P. M., Krcmar, M., & de Roos, S. (1998). The impact of a cultural children's program and adult mediation on children's knowledge of and attitudes towards opera. *Journal of Broadcasting and Electronic Media*, 42, 315–26.

Valkenburg, P. M., Krcmar, M., Peeters, A. L., & Marseille, N. M. (1999). Developing a scale to assess three styles of television mediation: "Instructive mediation," "restrictive mediation," and "social coviewing." *Journal of Broadcasting and Electronic Media*, 43, 52–66.

Van der Voort, T. H. A., Nikken, P., & Vooijs, M. W. (1992). Determinants of parental guidance of children's television viewing: A Dutch replication study. *Journal of Broadcasting and Electronic Media*, 36, 61–74.

Vooijs, M. W., & van der Voort, T. H. (1993). Learning about television violence: The impact of a critical viewing curriculum on children's attitudinal judgments of crime series. *Journal of Research and Development in Education*, 26, 133–42.

Warash, B. G., & Markstrom, C. A. (2001). Parental perceptions of parenting styles in relation to academic self-esteem of preschoolers. *Education*, 121, 485–93.

Warren, R. (2001). In words and deeds: Parental involvement and mediation of children's television viewing. *The Journal of Family Communication*, 1, 211–31.

Watkins, L. T., Sprafkin, J., & Gadow, K. D. (1988). Effects of a critical viewing skills curriculum on elementary school children's knowledge and attitudes about television. *Journal of Educational Research*, 81, 165–70.

Wilson, B. J., & Cantor, J. (1987). Reducing children's fear reactions to mass media: Effects of visual exposure and verbal explanation. In M. M. McLaughlin (Ed.), *Communication yearbook*, Vol. 10 (pp. 553–73). Newbury Park, CA: Sage.

Wilson, B. J., & Weiss, A. J. (1993). The effects of sibling coviewing on preschoolers' reactions to a suspenseful movie scene. *Communication Research*, 20, 214–48.

Wright, J. C., Huston, A. C., Murphy, K. C., St Peters, M., Pinon, M., Scantlin, R., & Kotler, J. (2001). The relations of early television viewing to school readiness and vocabulary of children from low-income families: The Early Window Project. *Child Development*, 72, 1347–67.

Yang, M. S. (2006). Understanding the effectiveness of moral mediation through theories of moral reasoning. Unpublished PhD dissertation, Ohio State University.

Yang, M. S., & Nathanson, A. I. (2005, May). *Reconceptualizing coviewing as a kind of mediation*. Paper presented at the International Communication Association Conference, New York, NY.

Author Index

Subject Index